MALT
WHISKY
YEARBOOK
2013

www.maltwhiskyyearbook.com

First published in Great Britain in 2012 by
MagDig Media Limited

© MagDig Media Limited 2012

ISBN 978-0-9552607-9-7

MagDig Media Limited
1 Brassey Road
Old Potts Way, Shrewsbury
Shropshire SY3 7FA
ENGLAND

E-mail: info@maltwhiskyyearbook.com
www.maltwhiskyyearbook.com

Previous editions

Contents

Introduction and acknowledgements..6

Secondary Malts Take Centre Stage...8
by Gavin D Smith

The Creation of an Industry...16
by Charles Maclean

The Scientific Approach to Whisky 24
by Ian Buxton

In Search of New Flavours 32
by Ian Wisniewski

A World in Motion...40
by Dominic Roskrow

The Born (and Bred) Identity..48
by Neil Ridley

Feel the Burn 56
by Jonny McCormick

Working on the Frontline..64

Malt Whisky Distilleries of Scotland and Ireland 76-219

An Introduction to Whisky Cocktails 83

Websites to Watch 99

Whisky Tapas - the Perfect Match..125

Books and Magazines 133

Doing the Whisky Math..151

Whisky Chronology part 1 187

Whisky Chronology part 2 193

Distilleries per Owner 209

Single Malts from Japan 220
by Nicholas Coldicott

Distilleries Around the Globe..228

The Year That Was..260

Independent Bottlers..276

Whisky Shops...282

Tables & Statistics..288

Maps...294

Index 296

Introduction

This is the 8th edition of Malt Whisky Yearbook and never before have I experienced such an optimism in the whisky industry and in particular in Scotland and Ireland. Investment plans totalling more than £1bn have been announced for the next years and the worst fears at the moment seem to be how to keep up with demand. At the same time producers in other than the traditional whisky making countries challenge their rivals by breaking rules and crossing boundaries with completely new types of whisky. We live in interesting times indeed as you will see when you start browsing through the Malt Whisky Yearbook 2013.

My excellent team of whisky writers have excelled themselves again this year and contribute with some fascinating articles;

Time to leave the beaten track and try some new whiskies? *Gavin D Smith* presents a handful of distilleries that have come out of the closet.

Old traditions make way for innovative experiments. *Ian Wisniewski* lets you in on the distillers´ most intimate secrets.

How can you make a cask last longer and will there be enough oak for the whisky industry in the future? *Jonny McCormick* takes a closer look at wood management.

How do you separate your brand from the rest? The key word is identity. *Neil Ridley* met with some of the producers to discuss their strategies.

Charles Maclean looks at some determining factors explaining why Scotch whisky is the world´s most respected spirit.

Everything changes, nothing stays the same. Follow *Dominic Roskrow* around the world of whisky when he proves his theory.

Ian Buxton explains how science has helped the industry in making better and more consistent whisky.

The Japanese whisky industry celebrates its 90th anniversary in 2013. *Nicholas Coldicott* can report on an industry in good shape.

In Malt Whisky Yearbook 2013 you will also find the unique, detailed and much appreciated section on Scottish and Irish malt whisky distilleries. It has been thoroughly revised and updated, not just in text, but also including numerous, new pictures and tasting notes for all the core brands. The chapter on Japanese whisky is completely revised and the presentation of distilleries from the rest of the world is larger than ever. You will also find a list of 130 of the best whisky shops in the world with their full details and suggestions where to find more information on the internet and through books and magazines. The summary of The Whisky Year That Was has been expanded again this year, in order to reflect on the exciting times. Meet the people behind the whiskies - the distillery managers and find out how to make whisky cocktails and how to create exciting whisky and food combinations. Finally, the very latest statistics gives you all the answers to your questions on production and consumption.

Thank you for buying Malt Whisky Yearbook 2013. I hope that you will have many enjoyable moments reading it and I can assure you that I will be back with a new edition in 2014.

Great care has been taken to ensure the accuracy of the information presented in this book. MagDig Media Ltd can, however, not be held liable for inaccuracies.

**Malt Whisky Yearbook 2014 will be published in October 2013.
To make sure you will be able to order it directly, please register at
www.maltwhiskyyearbook.com.**

**If you need any of the previous seven volumes of Malt Whisky Yearbook,
they are available for purchase (in limited numbers) from the website
www.maltwhiskyyearbook.com**

Acknowledgments

First of all I wish to thank the writers who have shared their great specialist knowledge on the subject in a brilliant and entertaining way – Ian Buxton, Nicholas Coldicott, Charles MacLean, Jonny McCormick, Neil Ridley, Dominic Roskrow, Gavin D. Smith and Ian Wisniewski.

A special thanks goes to Gavin and Dominic who put in a lot of effort nosing, tasting and writing notes for more than 100 different whiskies. Thanks also to Dominic for the tasting notes for independent bottlings and to Nicholas for the Japanese notes.

The following persons have also made important photographic or editorial contributions and I am grateful to all of them:

Alistair Abbott, Stewart Adamson, Iain Allan, Rob Allanson, Alasdair Anderson, Russel Anderson, Raymond Armstrong, Patrik Axelsson, David Baker, Duncan Baldwin, Nick Ballard, Keith Batt, Jan Beckers, Kirsteen Beeston, Darek Bell, Barry Bernstein, John Black, Cornelia Bohn, Etienne Bouillon, Stephen Bremner, Katrin Broger, Martin Brosamer, Andrew Brown, Graham Brown, Alex Bruce, Gordon Bruce, Stewart Buchanan, Alexander Buchholz, Trevor Buckley, Simon Buley, Sarah Burgess, Stephen Burnett, Mike Cameron, John Campbell, Peter Campbell, Andy Causey, Ian Chang, Ian Chapman, Yuseff Cherney, Ryan Chetiyawardana, Ashok Chokalingam, Stewart Christine, Gordon Clark, Margaret Mary Clarke, Willie Cochrane, Donald Colville, Francis Conlon, Neal Corbett, Graham Coull, Sandy Coutts, Georgie Crawford, Andrew Crook, Gloria Cummins, Francis Cuthbert, Kirsty Dagnan, Susie Davidson, Stephen Davies, David Doig, Gavin Durnin, Hazel Eadie, Alicia Eason, Ben Ellefsen, Gerald Erdrich, Gable Erenzo, Graham Eunson, Berle Figgins Jr, Douglas Fitchett, Erik Fitchett, Walter Fitzke, Robert Fleming, Tim Forbes, Callum Fraser, Robert Fullarton, Jesse Gallagher, Rosemary Gallagher, Gillian Gibson, Gregg Glass, John Glass, Kenny Grant, Brian Hamilton, Andy Hannah, Wendy Harries Jones, Steve Hawley, Ailsa Hayes, Ralph Haynes, Marcus Hofmeister, Paul Hooper, Robbie Hughes, Jill Inglis, Pat Jones, Jens-Erik Jörgensen, Marko Karakasevic, Jenny Karlsson, Colin Keegan, Davin de Kergommeaux, Cara Laing, Bill Lark, Claudia Liebl, Stephen Light, Karl Locher, Ian Logan, Jim Long, Alistair Longwell, Eddie Ludlow, Horst Lüning, Eddie McAffer, Iain MacAllister, Des McCagherty, Alistair McDonald, Andy Macdonald, Gillian Macdonald, John MacDonald, Polly MacDonald, Willie MacDougall, Frank McHardy, William McHenry, Sandy Macintyre, Doug McIvor, Ian Mackay, Bruce Mackenzie, Ewen Mackintosh, Ian MacMillan, Grant MacPherson, Melissa MacPherson, Patrick Maguire, Dennis Malcolm, Graham Manson, Stephen Marshall, Chris Maybin, Kwanele Mdluli, Lee Medoff, Jean Metzger, Ann Miller, Andrew Millsopp, Jamie Milne, Euan Mitchell, Henric Molin, Carol More, Nick Morgan, Jayne Murphy, Andrew Nairn, Andrew Nelstrop, Johanna Ngoh, Stuart Nickerson, Graham Nicolson, Julia Nourney, Linda Outterson, Casey Overeem, Mahesh Patel, Richard A Pelletier, Chris Pepper, Marion Pepper, John Peterson, Sean Phillips, Phil Prichard, Anssi Pyysing, Rachel Quinn, Jeff Quint, Robert Ransom, Mark Renner, Claire Richards, Patrick Roberts, Jackie Robertson, Stuart Robertson, Duncan Ross, Ronnie Routledge, Hans Rubens, Niels Römer, Torsten Römer, Ian Schmidt, Tyler Schramm, Bryan Schultz, Jacqui Seargeant, Andrew Shand, Rubyna Sheikh, Sam Simmons, Sukhinder Singh, Gigha Smith, Jolanda Stadelmann, Melanie Stanger, Karen Stewart, Pamela Stewart, Billy Stitchell, Katy Stollery, Michael Svendsen, Duncan Tait, Chip Tate, Stephen Teeling, Marcel Telser, Marie Tetzlaff, Joanie Tseng, Laura Vernon, Lasse Vesterby, Clare Vickers, Alistair Walker, Malcolm Waring, Mark Watt, Andy Watts, Stuart Watts, Iain Weir, James Whelan, Nick White, Ronald Whiteford, Robert Whitehead, Cristina Wilkie, Anthony Wills, Anna Wilson, Helen Windle, Gordon Winton, Stephen Woodcock, Patrick van Zuidam.

Finally, to my wife Pernilla and our daughter Alice,
thank you for your patience and your love and to Vilda,
the lab, my faithful companion during long working hours.

Ingvar Ronde
Editor
Malt Whisky Yearbook

Secondary Malts Take Centre Stage

Not so long ago, the number of single malts was pretty limited. The output from a majority of the distilleries went into blends. Today more and more producers recognise the greatness ot their whiskies and are eager to put them on the market. Gavin D Smith has found some true gems that he recommends.

The number of single malt Scotch whiskies available to consumers seems to grow by the week. Many are new expressions from very familiar distilleries, but the past few years have also seen some lower-profile names emerging from below the radar.

A variety of previously hard-to-find brands, often almost entirely confined to a role in blending, have begun to establish themselves alongside their better-known rivals, and the response from consumers suggests that they were hiding impressive lights under their bushels.

In some instances, the emergence of more obscure single malt brands has come about due to changes in ownership and consequent variations in strategy relating to the role of the whisky being produced, while in other cases it is due to an alteration in emphasis relating to brands which are already part of producers' portfolios. In some instances, silent distilleries have been revived, and a new stand-alone role has been assigned to a significant percentage of their 'make.'

Glen Moray at Elgin on Speyside is an example of a distillery which has changed hands with the result that its single malt has achieved a more prominent position. Until 2008, Glen Moray was in the Glenmorangie Company's portfolio, where it was always going to play third fiddle to Glenmorangie itself and the Islay malt of Ardbeg.

As part of Glenmorangie, owned since 2004 by Louis Vuitton Moet Hennessy (LVMH), Glen Moray often occupied the role of a cut-price 'entry level' single malt, frequently to be found on special offer in supermarkets and other multiple outlets. The facts of commercial life decreed that the principal focus of the company was on its two high-profile single malts and Glen Moray was always destined to be the bridesmaid and never the bride.

Then, in 2008, Glen Moray was acquired by the French company La Martiniquaise, and there were initial fears that the bulk of the distillery's output would be directed into the new owner's popular Glen Turner and Label 5 brands. However, as distillery manager Graham Coull says,

"At a brand level there has actually been an increased focus on Glen Moray as a single malt. Whilst Glen Moray Classic [with no age statement] is still very much the mainstay of the Glen Moray range, there is now a much greater emphasis on the older expressions

Graham Coull - Glen Moray's distillery manager.

such as 12 year old and 16 year old. The long term strategy is to develop the sales of Glen Moray in existing markets and also open up new ones."

"To facilitate this, there is now a structured approach to laying down stock and development of new Glen Moray expressions. To support this strategy we are increasing the capacity of the distillery by 50 per cent in 2012, and there are plans to expand beyond that in the next two to three years. Glen Moray has re-launched itself in mature markets like the USA and Australia with instant success. The benefit of having a dedicated sales force working with distributors is reaping rewards. To support the sales team a number of brand ambassadors are being recruited and the first of them will support the USA market."

When it comes to the 'new expressions' mentioned by Graham Coull, 2011 saw a significant addition to the core range in the shape of a 10 year old variant which was fully matured in ex-Chardonnay casks. Coull notes that "A single cask Glen Moray 2003 fully matured in Chenin Blanc has recently been released for sale in the visitor centre and a Glen Moray 25-year-old port wood finish is imminent."

Like Glen Moray, Fettercairn single malt spent several decades in the shadow of two higher-profile stable mates, namely The Dalmore and Isle of Jura, but in the case

Fettercairn Distillery has finally stepped forward with some impressive single malt releases

of Fettercairn it did not take a change of ownership to precipitate a new and more vigorous strategy for the brand.

Fettercairn is located at the foot of the Cairngorm Mountains, some 35 miles northeast of Dundee, and has been owned by Whyte & Mackay Ltd since 1973, with only a 12-year-old bottling generally available until 2009. In that year, a decision was taken to totally reinvent the Fettercairn offerings, and 24, 30 and 40 year old vintages were marketed, followed in 2010 by Fettercairn Fior, a replacement for the existing 12 year old. Fior comprises a significant amount of 14 and 15 year old spirit, along with 15 per cent heavily-peated five-year-old whisky from first-fill Bourbon barrels.

Whyte & Mackay's Rare Whisky Director David Robertson declares that "We always felt that Fettercairn was a hidden gem of a distillery, with terrific heritage, a unique distillation process and some stunning whiskies. It has been much maligned in the recent past and I personally felt that this was unjustified."

Robertson adds that "We knew from our stock profile that we could never build a volume brand and intuitively also felt that a small, artisan and boutique distillery should release small volumes, but at more premium prices. We hypothesised that we would pitch at attracting the malt connoisseur who had tried many other malts and was looking to discover a hidden gem!"

The results of giving Fettercairn such a dramatic makeover have been notably posi-tive, with Robertson saying that "Our business has doubled in the last 12 months – admittedly from a small base. Our aged range has won awards, Fior has done extremely well in specialist outlets, Tesco has requested an exclusive bottling, and many European markets are seeing dynamic interest. We are delighted that the unjust reputation of the past is being put right today."

Once Scotland's largest distillery

Another distillery whose owners have adopted a new strategy towards its output is Tomatin, which stands in rugged, moorland countryside 15 miles south of Inverness. Back in the 1970s, Tomatin enjoyed the distinc-tion of having the largest capacity of any malt Scotch whisky distillery, with no fewer than 23 stills giving a theoretical capacity of 12 million litres per annum, and produc-tion was unapologetically geared towards turning out bulk malt for blending.

Today 11 of those stills have gone, and re-cent years have witnessed a greater empha-sis being placed on the Tomatin single malt brand. Stephen Bremner is Sales Director for The Tomatin Distillery Company Ltd and he explains the change of emphasis by saying that,

"Primarily we did it so that we would have greater control over our own destiny. During the mid-1990s, Tomatin lost a lot of its new-filling business, and as a result we tried to compensate by selling three-year-old blended malt in bulk to third parties.

This type of business is unstable and reliant on the success of those to whom you are selling. You also have to have a core of industry partners who are willing to enter into exchange programmes.

"It seems crazy to adopt this type of strategy when all the while you are producing a high quality single malt which, if marketed properly, can bring you great success and sustained growth. The management felt comfortable moving towards a strategy that placed more focus on selling Tomatin as a brand."

The core range now comprises 12, 15, 18 and 30 year olds, while a number of vintage and limited editions have also been released. Bremner notes that "We have noticed a change in consumers' attitudes towards Tomatin over the last few years, in that many no longer just perceive it as a malt used for blending. This is down to the fact that a great deal of time and effort is spent assessing stock and ensuring that it is matured in the very best casks."

The reward has been brand growth of 65% over the past three years, and looking to the future, Stephen Bremner says that "We have done some experimenting with different casks types, but we don't see ourselves as the type of distillery that would release numerous cask finishes. In that sense we are fairly traditional and tend to stick with ex-Bourbon and different varieties of sherry casks. I think you will see some nice sherry-influenced Tomatin in the near future, and there will also be some older expressions hitting the market over the next couple of years, as we do have a reasonable amount of stock from the 1970s and '80s."

As with Tomatin, Glen Garioch single malt has benefitted from a recent change in direction, but in the case of the Aberdeenshire dram that change has been altogether less gradual and more radical, much like Fettercairn, with the range undergoing a total overhaul during 2009.

Glengarioch distillery – spelled as one word, while the whisky itself is spelled as two – was mothballed by owners Morrison Bowmore Distillers Ltd from 1995 to 1997, and as Morrison Bowmore's Brand Ambassador Gordon Dundas explains,

"From that time there was a clear perception of bringing the single malt brand back to where we thought it should be. We started to lay down good stock. Glen Garioch had first been sold as a single malt in 1979 but had always operated below the radar, as it were. It represents a small part of Morrison Bowmore's business, but it deserves a larger share, due to the sheer quality of the liquid."

Until 2009, most of the Glen Garioch 'make' was allocated for blending, and single malt bottlings were almost a side line, with those that did see the light of day boasting eye-catching, if slightly clichéd, 'tartan-and-stag' style packaging.

In that year, not only was the presentation changed, with the use of the stag motif being left to Glenfiddich and The Dalmore, but the old line-up of 8, 12, 15 and 21 year old expressions was ditched in favour of two core bottlings, one with no age statement, named 1797 Founder's Reserve, and the other a 12 year old.

As Gordon Dundas observes, "The new packaging retained the distinctive tartan element of the previous presentation around the sides of the box and we've gone back to a nice, sturdy bottle. For me, that reflects the sturdy, hardy nature of the spirit itself. The packaging also tells the story of the brand now."

"When it came to the re-launch we looked at our stock situation and made the decision that we wanted to use post-1997 spirit in our core range. That is unpeated, as the old floor maltings which produced a peatier malt, closed in 1995. We also decided to bottle at a strength of 48%abv and not to chill-filter."

Significantly, in addition to the two core bottlings, there is a rolling programme of vintage releases, with the oldest to date having been distilled in 1978. "These give consumers the chance to try older variants which were made with peatier malt," notes Dundas.

"We are re-invigorating the brand, certainly not re-inventing it," he insists, explaining that "We have been seeing double-digit growth each year since. We have turned over 15,000/16,000 cases in 2012 and would hope to be selling 20,000 by 2015." When it comes to marketing Glen Garioch, Dundas and his team have a secret weapon at their disposal, namely cheese.

"Because of the house style of Glen Garioch, with its sweet fruitiness, spice and creamy mouth-feel, we decided that the whisky works really well as an accompaniment to cheese," says Dundas. "We offer

Glen Garioch single malt and cheese - a combination frequently used by the owners at whisky shows all around the world

different cheeses that both complement the whisky and contrast with it. We present Glen Garioch and various cheese pairings on our stand at events all over the world now. Cheese is a big part of our current marketing, and it's certainly not a gimmick."

Key target markets for Glen Garioch tend to be ones where Morrison Bowmore Distillers already has a strong presence with its Bowmore and Auchentoshan single malts, and include the USA and a number of countries in mainland Europe, as well as the UK. Gordon Dundas says that "We are particularly keen to get local people in Aberdeen and the surrounding area involved. The company has Auchentoshan which can be seen as Glasgow's malt whisky and we would like Glen Garioch to be Aberdeen's single malt.

"In 2012 we launched two new vintage expressions, one from 1995 and the other from 1997," notes Dundas. "The 1997 is exclusive to travel retail outlets, and is the first one we have done just for them, which shows our commitment to that particular arena. Glen Garioch is still a relatively unknown brand, and in general, we are targeting people with some whisky knowledge."

"We are looking at sustainable growth with the brand and we know it's never going to go through the roof in terms of sales. In the longer term, we wouldn't rule out adding to our two core bottlings, but for now we are very happy offering those and the various vintages."

New owners means new life

In the case of Tullibardine distillery in Perthshire, a decision to give focus to single malt bottlings came about after the distillery, mothballed by Whyte & Mackay Ltd in 1994, was acquired by a business consortium for £1.1 million in 2003 and subsequently returned to production.

According to International Sales Manager James Robertson, "The original investors saw the opportunity to purchase Tullibardine due to its location, stock profile, and the fact that the plant had not been ripped out for use at other distilleries. I think also the world of whisky was changing rapidly, and although Tullibardine had never been taken seriously in its own right previously, there was an interest out there for new or re-opened distilleries. Whisky tourism was also a key element in the decision process, and with the location of the distillery being so close to Edinburgh and Glasgow it seemed logical that people would want to visit a revamped Tullibardine."

When it came to the actual product itself, rather than offer a 10 year old, the decision was taken to bottle by vintage, thus creating

Tullibardine's road to success has been through single casks and vintages

a point of difference from previous Tullibardine expressions. A range of cask finishes was also marketed, and, as James Robertson explains, "Some single casks were bottled to serve as a reminder that Tullibardine was a serious single malt distillery."

Then, in 2011, Tullibardine was purchased by the third-generation family-owned French company Maison Michel Picard, based in Chassagne Montrachet, Burgundy. Maison Michel Picard was an existing customer for the distillery's new-make spirit, and James Robertson notes that "They see Tullibardine as the jewel in the crown of their whisky portfolio. For some time it has become apparent that Tullibardine needed to take its profile to the next level with re-branding and renewed focus on gaining better awareness with the consumer. In the past, in order to generate cash-flow, a great deal of our new-make was sold, but now we are in a position to mature more for future Tullibardine use, rather than selling it on to other companies."

Like Tullibardine, BenRiach distillery, south of Elgin, had been owned by a major distiller, in this case Chivas Brothers, who considered it surplus to requirements and were prepared to sell it to an independent operator. For BenRiach, which changed hands during 2004, the new owner was a

consortium comprising two South African businessmen and former Burn Stewart Distillers Director Billy Walker, with Walker's son, Alistair, acting as Sales & Marketing Director.

BenRiach had experienced an even lower single malt profile than Tullibardine in the past, but rather than view this as a stumbling block, Billy Walker and his team saw it as an opportunity.

"The strength was that BenRiach was a blank canvas," he says, "We could bring our own 'fingerprint' and strategy to it. The brand wasn't carrying any baggage from a previous owner's strategy. The downside was that there was no existing distribution network, but that really just required energy and effort."

"The distillery was in fantastic condition when we bought it from Chivas, and we got a great stock inventory with it, ranging from spirit distilled in 1966 right up to just 18 months prior to our purchase. Our strategy was to define ourselves as the equivalent of a chateau wine, working with private and independent distributors, and generally ones who did not deal with the multiple retailers."

From the start, BenRiach offered a wide portfolio of bottlings, including a 10 year old peated variant under the Curiositas label.

The owners of BenRiach have managed to build an impressive range of both unpeated and peated whiskies

"Having a heavily-peated Speyside was a great USP for us," says Billy Walker, "and getting peated stock from Chivas was a nice bonus! We were soon offering 12, 16, 20, 25 and 30 year old expressions of BenRiach and have issued single cask bottlings during each year of trading. We wanted to develop a sustained and sustainable presence."

In the early days, BenRiach came to be associated with a wide-ranging and vigorous release policy, but Alistair Walker explains that "The emphasis on new releases from BenRiach has changed a little. We have cut back on any new wood finishes, and most of the new releases over the next couple of years will be either single cask bottlings or limited availability expressions that will disappear from the range once sold out."

"For example, during 2012 we launched the ninth batch of BenRiach Limited Release single cask bottlings, followed by our oldest BenRiach expression to date, namely BenRiach 1966. This is one of just two casks that we have left from 1966, our oldest stock at BenRiach, and it is the most ultra-premium bottling we have ever released."

A significant recent development at Ben-Riach distillery itself was the re-commissioning of the old floor maltings during 2012, with the intention being to produce batches of malt, ranging from unpeated to heavily-peated, which will be ultimately be used to make spirit for 'stand-alone' bottlings.

While Tullibardine and BenRiach had both experienced a period of silence prior to their reinvigoration and more intense focus on single malt bottlings, the Portsoy distillery of Glenglassaugh presented an altogether greater practical, physical challenge to its new owners The Scaent Group, when they acquired it from The Edrington Group in 2008. Glenglassaugh had last made whisky in 1986, necessitating investment in the region of £1 million, before spirit began to flow again in December 2008.

According to Glenglassaugh Distillery Company Ltd's Managing Director Stuart Nickerson, "The short-term plan was to raise our profile through direct contact with the whisky industry media, informing them of our return. This was supported by the release of a range of three whiskies which came from the small amount of maturing stock which we had purchased. The range was 21 year old (subsequently replaced by 26 year old), 'Aged Over 30 Years Single Cask Release' and 'Aged Over 40 Years Single Cask Release.'

"We then began to interact as much as possible with our final customers and this has led to our growing presence on

Facebook and Twitter and has resulted in increased sales of bottled products and very importantly, our small cask (Octave) sales." In the longer term, Nickerson wants to see Glenglassaugh with a presence in as many international markets as possible, noting that the brand is currently on sale in 25 countries, with another five due to be added to the list very soon.

Product releases have been innovative in the extreme, as Nickerson explains. "In 2009 we introduced our 'Spirit Drink' range with 'The Spirit Drink that dare not speak its name,' which was our new spirit straight from the stills, but reduced to 50% abv, and this was quickly followed by 'The Spirit Drink that Blushes to speak its name,' which was spirit matured for six months in ex-red wine casks from California. In 2010 we extended the range to include 'Fledgling XB,' which was the same new-make spirit, but this time matured for 12 months in ex-Bourbon casks, and also 'Peated,' which was our new-make spirit made from peated malt. We have also increased the number of single cask whiskies available.

"Our innovative approach to creating and selling Spirit Drinks and aiming these at non-traditional whisky drinkers and trying to get people to sample them in cocktails has helped us, and so has our continued focus on limited edition single cask bottling rather than larger runs. Indeed, the only whiskies we have released which are not single cask are the 26-year-old and Revival."

Glenglassaugh Revival was the distillery's major 2012 offering, and is described by Stuart Nickerson as "The first whisky from the refurbished distillery. It is a mix of refill casks and first-fill casks which are then finished for six months in first-fill Oloroso sherry casks. We have plans for a second, limited edition young whisky, one that has had a different maturation profile and so will be a contrast to Revival. This will be followed in early 2013 by a peated version of Revival."

2012 also saw the opening of visitor facilities at the distillery, and Stuart Nickerson says that "Over time we hope to extend these facilities, as our brand grows and we become better-known, and we would like to be in a position to offer whisky schools and on-site accommodation for visitors."

As Scotch whisky continues to follow its dynamic global growth trajectory there is surely more room than ever for the single malt brands featured above to take their places at the top table. After all, as the Roman writer Publilius Syrus declared, "No pleasure endures unseasoned by variety."

Gavin D Smith is one of Scotland's leading whisky writers and Contributing Editor to www.whisky-pages.com and www.forwhiskeylovers.com. He regularly undertakes writing commissions for leading drinks companies and produces feature material for a wide range of publications, including Whisky Magazine, Whisky Advocate, Whiskeria, Drinks International and Whisky Etc. He is the author of more than 20 books, including The Whisky Men, Ardbeg: A Peaty Provenance, Discovering Scotland's Distilleries and Goodness Nose (with Richard Paterson). He collaborated with Dominic Roskrow to produce a new edition of the Michael Jackson's Malt Whisky Companion in 2010 and was also a major contributor to the 2012 publication 1001 Whiskies You Must Try Before You Die. His latest book is The Whisky Opus, co-written with Dominic Roskrow. He is a Keeper of the Quaich and lives in the Scottish Borders.

Photo: Glenglassaugh Distillery

Ronnie Routledge gently awakens Glenglassaugh's newest release - Revival

The Creation of an Industry

*The Scotch whisky industry has gone through
a tremendous change since 1945 with boom and bust
succeeding each other. At the moment the mood is buoyant
but Charles Maclean tells a story of whisky companies
having been forced to navigate a stormy sea.*

It is well known that the history of Scotch whisky is punctuated by up-swings and down-turns – periods of dramatic expansion, investment and prosperity, followed by equally dramatic times of contraction, closure and general belt-tightening.

Happily, the current mood is buoyant, but it is well to remember the not-so-distant past, the decades of confidence and expansion after the conclusion of the Second World War, when demand for Scotch whisky was strong – so strong that the industry gave no thought to possible changes in fashion, to fiscal constraints, to down-turns in the global economy and built up stocks which were far greater than the demand turned out to be, leading to radical changes in the way the industry was structured, to distillery closures and contraction, and then to the beginnings of a recovery, through the 'rediscovery' of malt whisky.

For the Malt Whisky Yearbook 2013 the editor asked me to consider individuals who have made important contributions to the history of Scotch in the post-war period. With the help of friends, I began to make a list, but it soon became apparent, first, that individual achievements had to be viewed within the context of the overall history of whisky in this period and, second, that the driving forces were economic and, increasingly, global, rather than being attributable to individuals.

So I have identified three broad themes which provide the background to where we are today, and where possible I have mentioned individuals who have played notable roles in the development of these themes.

Developments in Production

A short background; at the close of the 19th Century the Scotch whisky industry was producing around 30 million proof gallons of spirit per annum (136m litres). This was not surpassed until 1939, so there was little incentive to innovate or renew plant. Between 1940 and 1945 both malt and grain distilling more or less ceased, although bottling continued, so by the conclusion of hostilities, the stocks of mature whisky under bond had fallen from 144m proof gallons to 84m proof gallons.

It was essential to increase stock, but the Labour government elected in 1945 ignored Winston Churchill's famous memo – "On no account reduce the barley for whisky" – and adopted the slogan "Food Before Whisky".

Duty was increased repeatedly and the quantity of cereals made available to distillers was strictly controlled.

Yet demand had never been stronger. Scotch whisky had terrific caché. It epitomized the new post-war/post-fascist world and was widely promoted by Hollywood films. Exports of Scotch became a key component of the drive to pay back the war debt, and whisky companies were required by government to sell at least 75% of their product in hard currency markets – particularly the U.S.A. This quota system remained in force until 1954 (the same year that food rationing finally ceased), but was voluntarily kept in place for older whiskies until around 1962, owing to lack of mature fillings.

When controls were abandoned, overseas demand made it imperative to expand capacity. As early as 1945 the Manufacture of Spirits Regulations allowed concurrent brewing and distilling. This had been prohibited since 1823 – brewing taking place from midnight on Sunday to early Wednesday; distilling from Wednesday morning to Saturday evening – but until 1954 the measure was of academic interest only since there was not enough barley to increase production.

As soon as money and cereals were available whisky companies began to modernize and expand existing sites and to build new distilleries.

New Distilleries

Tullibardine was designed and built by William Delmé Evans in 1949. He went on to design Jura (1963) and Glenallachie (1967), and has been described as 'the greatest distillery designer of the 20th century'.

A key feature of these modern malt whisky distilleries was to make use of gravity flow to move liquids from one stage of the process to another. This is very apparent in the so-called 'Waterloo Street' design of Dr. Charlie Potts, Scottish Malt Distillers' Chief Engineer – named after the company's engineering department in Glasgow – and applied to Balmenach (1962), Brackla (1964), Craigellachie (1965), Glentauchers (1966), Glen Ord (1966), Clynelish (1968), Linkwood (1970), Teaninich (1970), Mannochmore (1971), Glendullan (1972) and Caol Ila (1974). Charlie Potts was much praised by operators for incorporating massive windows, capable of being opened, in his stillhouses.

Several companies built malt distilleries within existing grain distilleries – Kinclaith/ Strathclyde (1957/58), Glen Flagler/Moffat

The expansion during the 1960s and 70s prompted the building of a new type of huge, racked warehouses

(1965), Killyloch/Moffat (1965), Ladyburn/ Girvan (1966) – while Hiram Walker's Chief Chemical Engineer, Alistair Cunningham adapted the neck of a pot still so as to make it capable of producing different styles of spirit. He named it the 'Lomond still'.

Maltings
Increased capacity inevitably led to a need for more malted barley than could be produced by individual distilleries. All but three distilleries (Glen Grant, Speyburn and St. Magdalene) had their own floor maltings – labour intensive, affected by weather conditions and inconsistent in the quality of malt they produced. In 1948 North British Distillery installed Saladin boxes, and during the 1950s and early 1960s their example was followed by ten malt distilleries.

But still they could not meet their requirement, and increasingly turned to independent maltsters, operating large industrial drum maltings, for supplies of malted barley. Hiram Walker's subsidiary, Robert Kilgour Ltd., built a large modern maltings at Kirkaldy. Scottish Malt Distillers built or expanded large-scale maltings at Burghead (1966), Muir of Ord (1966), Montrose (1968), Port Ellen (1973) and Roseisle (1979/80) and

in 1968 ceased floor malting at twenty-nine distilleries. Other distillers followed this example, and by the end of the 1970s only seven distilleries retained their traditional, on-site maltings.

Plant Modification
Many existing distilleries were doubled or tripled in size, and equipped with modern plant and processes. One significant change was the invention of the semi-lauter mash tun by Bill Rankin, Long John International's Production Director, to replace the traditional cast iron 'rake and plough' mash tuns. Such tuns were more efficient, easier to operate and easier to clean, what's more they could comfortably handle eighteen mashes a week, rather than the standard six.

Many distilleries introduced mechanical stoking to fire their stills, and then almost all went over to indirect firing by steam heated pans and coils – cleaner, more easily controlled, less labour intensive, less likely to boil over. The last had always been a problem, and was largely eliminated by the fitting of sight glasses to the necks of wash stills. All but a handful of distilleries also replaced their old worm tubs with shell and tube condensers, which were cheaper to install and more easily replaced, and which produced the lighter style of spirit required at the time by blenders.

Casks and Warehousing

Even more significant for flavour was the use of American oak ex-Bourbon barrels, re-made into hogsheads, rather than traditional European oak ex-sherry butts.

Ex-Bourbon casks were unknown by the Scotch whisky industry prior to 1946. Their availability after this date was owing to a deal struck by American coopers' unions shortly before the outbreak of war, in terms of which 'straight' Bourbon or Rye whiskey had to be matured in new oak barrels. Since the demand for straight Bourbon in the U.S. also increased dramatically during and after the war, large numbers of barrels were available at a fraction of the price of ex-sherry butts to cope with the increased production of spirit.

Many new warehouses were required, and now they were built to hold many more casks in steel frames, racked up to ten high with access for mechanical handing by fork-lift trucks, rather than the traditional, low and labour intensive dunnage warehouses where casks were stored three high and moved by hand.

Amalgamation and Consolidation

The industry continued to expand until the middle of the 1970s, with many distilleries being rebuilt and four brand new distilleries – Braeval (1973), Auchroisk (1972/74), Allt a'Bhainne (1975) and Pittyvaich (1975) – being commissioned on Speyside. Stocks of whisky in bond reached unprecedented levels, rising from 2.2 million litres in 1965 to 4.5 billion litres in 1975.

Then came a severe slump, prompted by the oil crisis and the end of the Vietnam War, which had stimulated the American economy. To make matters worse, whisky was no longer as fashionable as it had been during the past two decades, and many consumers were switching to vodka or white rum, or wine. Orders for fillings and mature whisky began to drop, and malt distillers' traditional customer base – the blenders – began to shrink.

The slump in 1975 encouraged amalgamation – indeed, there were rumours in the Stock Market that all independent whisky companies might be taken over. The impetus towards this came mainly from large U.K. brewing groups.

Under the skillful direction of Ernie Epps, J&B Rare was the first Scotch to top one mil-

Photo: Getty Images

The end of the Vietnam War had a negative impact on the American economy which in turn affected the sales of Scotch - Le Duc Tho and Henry Kissinger at the Paris Peace Conference in 1973

Ernest Saunders (centre) during the Guinness trial in 1990

lion case sales in the U.S., in 1962. The same year Justerini & Brooks merged with W.& A. Gilbey, the gin distillers, to form International Distillers & Vintners. Ten years later IDV was taken over by Watney Mann, brewers, and within months both were acquired by Grand Metropolitan Hotels.

Schenley Industries Inc. of New York had entered the Scotch trade by buying the old-established firm of wine merchants and distillers, Seagar Evans in 1956. The latter changed its name to Long John International in 1969, after its most famous brand, and in 1975 Schenley sold to Whitbread along with Black Bottle and Long John, Laphroaig, Tormore, Strathclyde (grain), Kinclaith and Glenugie distilleries.

In 1976 Allied Breweries bought Wm. Teacher & Sons, with Ardmore Distillery, and in 1987 went on to buy Hiram Walker, owner of Ballantine's, Glenburgie, Miltonduff and Dumbarton (grain) Distilleries.

In order to avoid take-over by a brewery, Whyte & Mackay/Dalmore turned to Sir Hugh Fraser's Scottish & Universal Investment Trust in 1972, but SUITS was swallowed by Tiny Rowland's Lonhro Group seven years later.

The most dramatic take-overs, however, were Guinness' acquisition of first Arthur

Bell & Sons, in 1985, then the Distillers Company Limited in 1986.

Driven by Raymond Miquel, who had joined Bell's in 1956 and risen to managing director in 1968, Bell's was the success story of the 1970s. The company's output increased from 1.8 mpg in 1970 to 4.25 mpg in 1976, while its trading profit rose from £1.5m to £11.5m. By 1980, Bell's was the best selling Scotch in the U.K., commanding 20% of the market. The company's success also made it vulnerable to hostile takeover, however, and Miquel's nemesis was Ernest Saunders, the dynamic CEO of Guinness PLC, who skillfully won over Bell's shareholders during the summer of 1985.

Later the same year, Jimmy Gulliver, CEO of the Argyll (Food) Group, mounted a bid to take over the DCL – "one of the most traditional and conservative companies in Britain – and also among the most badly managed". The company owned most of the leading brands of blended Scotch, including Johnny Walker Red Label – the world's best seller – and over thirty distilleries, but its share of the U.K. market had dropped from 75% in the early 1960s to 16% in 1985.

Initially scornful of Gulliver's raid, the DCL board soon became concerned and turned to Ernest Saunders as a 'white knight' to

Drinking habits during the 1980s changed in favour of wine and white spirits

defend their position. In fact he had already been considering the feasibility of merging Guinness with DCL, and after a very dramatic struggle – which finished with Saunders and four of his closest colleagues being sent to prison for fraud – the deal went through.

The Renaissance of Malt Whisky

As we have seen, by 1980 the production of malt whisky had far outstripped demand from the blenders – between 1960 and 1980 the amount of whisky in bond quadrupled, to well in excess of a billion gallons. To make matters far worse, Scotch was no longer fashionable in the U.S.A. – the leading export market since 1939. Both there and in the U.K. the competition from vodka and white rum was stiff, and there was a large increase in wine consumption, actively encouraged in the U.K. by the British Government.

In 1984 duty on wine was reduced by 20% to comply with an EC ruling on harmonisation, but that on spirits was increased by nearly one third in five consecutive budgets (1979-1985). While consumption of alcohol in the U.K. remained virtually static, wine sales rose by 40% and whisky sales declined by 21%. Inevitably, many blenders cut their filling orders, and distilleries began to close. These hard facts, combined with the amalgamations of the 1970s, made the smaller whisky companies nervous, since it reduced their traditional customer base for new fillings, and by the mid-1980s, their problem was compounded by a steady decline in demand for blended Scotch whisky. Several looked with interest at the success enjoyed by companies which were now promoting their makes as 'single' whiskies: Glenfiddich, The Glenlivet and Glen Grant.

Under the ownership and management of the descendants of its eponymous founder, William Grant & Sons launched Glenfiddich Straight Malt in April 1961. After 1963 they were selling it in over one hundred export markets through existing agents for their popular Standfast blend, and supporting the brand with print advertising. In 1963 Grants sold 11,422 cases (of which 1,800 were export sales); in 1967, 26,577 cases (of which over a 1/3 was for export); in 1970, slightly over 52,000.

In 1963, The Glenlivet Distillery signed a contract with the Barton Distilling Company, to distribute The Glenlivet in the USA and the Caribbean. This year around 3,000 cases were sold in USA. Four years later, The Weekly Scotsman reported that "98.5% of

The Glenlivet goes to blending, but 6,000 cases of single malt are bottled each year, of which 50% goes to the US market".

In 1961 Armando Giovinetti was appointed as Glen Grant's agent in Italy. Extensive and clever promotion, combined with a product which he knew would appeal to the Italian palate – he specified that in Italy Glen Grant should be offered at five years old, and sought to challenge grappa – led to Italy becoming Glen Grant's leading market by 1970, and by 1977 sales were topping 200,000 cases a year.

The growing interest in malt whisky did not go un-noticed by the boards of other distilleries, not least by the Management Committee of the DCL, which noted in 1964 that the previous year's sales of all their single malts amounted to only 819 cases – less even than Haig's Cameron Brig single grain whisky which sold 1,166 cases.

A sub-committee was asked to investigate and report back, and led by Ronnie Cumming (later Sir Ronald, Chairman of the DCL), they recommended that Cardhu, Aultmore and Linkwood be offered as singles at 8 years old, and that Cardhu should have a £15,000 advertising budget.

Next year it was reported that Cardhu was 'doing well in Italy' but in the home market, in the six months to Sept 1967 sales totalled only 462 cases, in spite of advertising. 'The experiment' was put on hold: Cardhu could continue to be sold in the home market, but no more was to be spent on advertising.

As early as 1963, Macallan's chairman, George Harbinson, reported that "the sale of Macallan in bottle is gaining momentum with a steadily increasing demand for the over 15 years old from the south of England," and again in 1965: "the interest in single malts is undoubtedly increasing and larger sales are expected."

During the decade several companies began to release and promote their makes as singles. Balvenie Pure Malt from Grants; Blair Athol, Dufftown and Inchgower from Bells; Dalmore, Old Fettercairn and Tomintoul-Glenlivet from Whyte & Mackay; Knock-

The forerunners - in the early 1960s it was Glenfiddich, Glen Grant and Glenlivet that paved the way for the other single malts

ando from J&B; Highland Park, Tamdhu and Bunnahabhain, with small amounts of Glenrothes, from Highland; Laphroaig and Tormore from Long John; Bruichladdich and Tullibardine from Invergordon.

In 1974 sales of bottled malt moved up by 70% in volume to 700,000 gallons, while value advanced by 52% to £4.24 million. But this was the decade's peak, and still amounted to less than one per cent of the total whisky market.

In his Scotch Whisky Industry Review (1976), Alan Gray notes that:

"The severity of the recession is illustrated by the fall in single malt sales in 1975, in particular with the economic problems of Italy, one of the main markets for this kind of whisky".

However, in the 1980s, single malt bottlings began to proliferate. In 1981 a symposium of malt whisky exporters estimated that sales should rise by between 8% and 10% over the period 1981-86. In fact the increase over this period was 15%, and over the decade to 1990 was 14%.

By 1981 both Macallan and Glenmorangie had built up sufficient stocks of mature malt whisky to begin to advertise in the home market. Around the same time, Campbell Distillers (owned by Pernod Ricard since 1973) began to promote Aberlour vigorously in France, and Long John International did the same for Tormore in the U.S.A.

In 1982 the D.C.L. introduced 'The Ascot Malt Cellar' – Ascot was the company's home trade base - a collection of four single malts and two vatted malts: Rosebank 8yo, Linkwood 12yo, Talisker 8yo, Lagavulin 12yo, Strathconon and Glenleven. It made little impact, owing to the company's continuing reluctance to advertise, but the idea of representing regionally different styles, would become highly significant after the Distillers' Company was taken over by Guinness, and the concept was revived in 1988 as the highly successful 'Classic Malts Selection': Glenkinchie 10yo, Dalwhinnie 15yo, Cragganmore 12yo, Oban 14yo, Talisker 10yo and Lagavulin 16yo.

Conclusion

By the end of the 1980s, the Scotch whisky industry was recovering, albeit slowly (at the rate of around 2% per annum), from the shocks of the mid-decade. Export markets played a crucial role in this, with Japan joining the U.S.A., France, Italy and Spain as the leaders. Production levels were now under control, and this led to higher selling prices and profit margins. Ninety-four malt distilleries were in operation in 1990, compared with eighty-one in 1985. Sales of single malts grew steadily after 1985 and now stood at 10m litres of alcohol, a 3.6% market share – four times the amount sold in 1980, when the market share was less than 1% – and this was down to greater consumer awareness, greater choice, an increase in specialist retailers with expertise in and enthusiasm for the subject, and a substantial increase in advertising budgets, rising from 11% in 1981 to between 25%-30% in 1990.

A report published in 1989 noted that 60% of malt whisky drinkers "have a keen thirst for more information on malts", and this was reflected by the dramatic increase in the number of books on the subject and by the number of distilleries which now opened their doors to visitors.

It is beyond the remit of this article to bring the story of Scotch whisky up to date, but the fact is – moments ago – I received a call from a senior Diageo executive informing me that the company would today announce plans to invest £1 billion in Scotch whisky production over the coming five years. Such confidence in the future demand for Scotch speaks for itself ! Are we done with booms and busts? I hope so.

Charles MacLean has spent the past twenty-five years researching and writing about Scotch whisky and is one of the leading authorities. He spends his time sharing his knowledge around the world, in articles and publications, lectures and tastings, and on TV and radio. His first book (Scotch Whisky) was published in 1993 and since then he has published nine books on the subject, his most recent being Charles MacLean's Whiskypedia, published in 2009. He was elected a Keeper of the Quaich in 1992, in 1997 Malt Whisky won the Glenfiddich Award and in 2003 A Liquid History won 'Best Drinks Book' in the James Beard Awards. In 2012 he also starred in Ken Loach's film The Angel's Share.

The Scientific Approach to Whisky

Is the quality of Scotch whisky a result of keeping the old traditions alive or is there another approach that can help the industry to make better and more consistent whisky? Ian Buxton is convinced that science is the way forward.

The progress of the industries to which science is a hand-maid has become so rapid that, figuratively speaking, the discoveries of today speedily eventuate in the well-proved method or system of tomorrow, and it is hereby borne in upon us that whilst science and scientific research give a true stimulus to the various technologies, these, in their turn – owing to the earnestness of purpose and desire for knowledge of the individuals who guide and control them – stimulate research. This can be very truly affirmed of the industries in which fermentation plays the most important role...

That's the view of Charles G Matthews in his Manual of Alcoholic Fermentation, published in 1901. Now, while Matthews has been consigned to history, it's worth reflecting that he was able to write nearly 300 pages on fermentation chemistry as it applied to beverage alcohol less than 50 years following the discovery of the basic scientific principles.

So let's step back – briefly – into whisky's history. The science of distilling has been keenly studied and, as scientific understanding and analytical techniques developed

from the eighteenth century onwards, so distillers have been keen to understand exactly what was happening at every stage of the distilling process.

But, as we've just learned, it wasn't until 1856 that the French scientist Louis Pasteur conducted the first studies on the production of alcohol (from beet juice as it happened) and thus outlined the basic science of fermentation. His work on yeast chemistry was ground-breaking for the brewing and distilling industry and remains a fundamental building block in the scientific as opposed to the wholly artisanal school of distilling (perhaps we need new vocabulary for today's 'artisanal' distillers, guided as they are by a body of knowledge unavailable to their predecessors).

Until Pasteur's discoveries distillers, brewers and wine-makers knew they needed yeast, but not why it worked or, more importantly, sometimes didn't. A 300 page volume on fermentation less than 50 years after Pasteur's first experiments demonstrates just how far and how fast this vital knowledge progressed.

Today science continues to help the industry in making better and more consistent

WHAT IS WHISKY?

EXPERTS SAMPLING.

whisky. Some readers, perhaps of a romantic or nostalgic turn of mind might take issue with that, especially the "better" but I'm unrepentant. The exceptional 'stand-out' casks that were turning up in the 1980s and early 1990s may have largely disappeared but that's because the average standard of wood management is going steadily up – and that, in turn is because the science is getting better and the average quality of whisky is increasing.

And better science is helping a new generation of small craft distillers, some with little or no industry experience but pursuing their big dream undaunted, get started and begin making interesting and drinkable whisky almost from their first batch.

But, after Pasteur, who were the pioneers? Practical men, not trained scientists, could refer to standardised references, such as the *Tables of Spirit Proofs*, published in 1877 by Duncan McGlashan of Edinburgh's Caledonian Distillery to ensure the consistency of measurement of their new make once it was produced.

More controversially, the Glasgow analytical chemist Dr James St Clair Gray exposed widespread adulteration of whisky in Glasgow's less salubrious drinking dens in the pages of the North British Daily Mail (as recounted in Edward Burns' Bad Whisky). A lively correspondence ensued.

But history records principally the name of J A Nettleton who trained originally in the Inland Revenue Laboratory in London. His early work *Original Gravity* was followed in 1884 by *Every Brewer His Own Analyst*, described as "a plain and brief Summary of Reliable Chemical and other Practical Tests". Though designed principally for the brewing industry, Nettleton's work had applications in distilling and he soon found much to interest him in that field.

Between 1893 and 1897 he published increasingly important and influential works on the manufacture of spirit; flavour in whisky and condensing and cooling and, as we shall see, his influence grew in subsequent years.

Shortly afterwards Sir Walter Gilbey (then the owner of the Glen Spey, Strathmill and Knockando distilleries) published his *Notes on Alcohol* (1904), with a spirited defence of the pot still and direct firing and in 1906 the famous 'What is Whisky?' case occurred. The subsequent Royal Commission heard from a number of distillers and various expert witnesses (some more or less expert it may

LAGAVULIN DISTILLERY.

Lagavulin Distillery from the late 1800s when J A Nettleton wrote several of his groundbreaking books on brewing and distillation

be felt) and there was much public comment and discussion of the issues.

These were followed in 1913 by Nettleton's magisterial *The Manufacture of Whisky and Plain Spirit* which was to remain the standard text on the subject for many years and is still consulted by distillers to this day, especially if seeking to recreate a 'traditional' flavour profile.

Nettleton however, remained a consultant to the industry and, so far as I can determine, the first trained chemist to be permanently employed was S H Hastie, who worked for Sir Peter Mackie in a dedicated laboratory in Campbeltown. Notwithstanding Mackie's reputation (in his obituary he was described as "one third genius, one third megalomaniac, one third eccentric" and he was, of course, responsible for the construction of Malt Mill distillery on Islay) he was forward-looking in the matter of science, saying of Hastie's work "..we would not be without him. Otherwise, we would be working by the old rule of thumb which is no good.."

Hastie himself was more modest, merely remarking in a lecture to the Institute of Brewing that "the application of science…to the control of pot still distillation processes is still in its infancy after a long series of intermittent attempts to make practical use of laboratory work.."

However, as R B Weir suggests in his *History of the Malt Distillers Association of Scotland* by the early 1920s "In an industry which had been the epitome of technological conservatism scientists slowly began to erode the mysticism that underlay many cherished processes." One might observe that today the various marketing departments spend much time and effort investing in such mysticism – but that would be the subject of a separate article!

Throughout the early part of the 20th century the Distillers Company (DCL, the core of today's Diageo) had been acquiring both patent and pot still distilling capacity, at a time when much of the rest of the industry was in recession. To simplify greatly, much of this was due to their ability to fund these acquisitions from the sale of yeast products and industrial alcohol, which made up as much as two-thirds of their profit. The DCL maintained its own laboratories, researched new markets for alcohol-based products, bought up patents and generally applied the principles of industrial chemistry to developing and diversifying their business.

Other companies, such as Sir Peter Mackie's, were not above their own experimentation. Shortly before they closed the Tullymet distillery in Perthshire, Dewar's engaged what they described as "an eminent analytical chemist" with a view to accelerate the aging of their whisky, ideally "making a 10 year old whisky in one night". Needless to say, the experiments ended in ignominious failure.

So the historical record is patchy. The science of whisky advanced in an erratic and inconsistent manner. How stand matters today?

Strength through cooperation

The current lead on co-operative industry research is taken by the Scotch Whisky Research Institute. Their low public profile and deliberately bland website reflect the fact that the SWRI exists to support its members, who represent more than 90% of the Scotch whisky industry's production, and that the SWRI itself has no consumer role whatsoever.

Its history can be traced back to a predecessor organisation, Pentlands Scotch Whisky Ltd and, even prior to that, the Inveresk laboratories of Arthur D Little Inc, one of the longest-established global consulting firms.

Arthur D Little were working with a number of distillers in the 1970s and early 1980s when it was recognised by John McPhail of Robertson & Baxter Ltd the blenders (part of The Edrington Group) that there would be greater strength in a co-operative, industry-owned organisation. Accordingly, the Arthur D Little interests were acquired by a new company, Pentlands Scotch Whisky and offices established in Slateford Road, Edinburgh.

Pentlands was run by Dr Jim Gray, Dr Jim Swan and Eric Dewar. Dr Swan, who we will meet again, partnered with Dr Harry Riffkin in 1993 to acquire the Glasgow analysts Tatlock & Thomson, and that firm remains active today under Riffkin's management. Pentlands did much work on flavour-related and spirit yield issues but is best-known, at least to consumers, for their pioneering work on the 'whisky wheel', starting around 1979.

This was the first systematic attempt to define the language of whisky tasting: now the accepted way of tabulating aromas and flavours, at the time it was novel. Initially the wheel was intended for industry use only but, with increasing consumer interest and growing connoisseurship a more extensive consumer version was developed in the mid-1980s, by Charles MacLean amongst others (for which we are forever in his debt).

Recognising the need to expand Pentland's work, it grew into the Scotch Whisky Research Institute, established in October 1995 and now located in purpose-built facilities, the construction of which was supported by The Robertson Trust (the charitable trust that is Edrington's ultimate parent).

The SWRI's aims are set out on their website and are as follows:

- Maintaining and improving product quality
- Safeguarding product integrity
- Adding value by enhancing the use of raw materials and improving manufacturing processes
- Providing the understanding to facilitate beneficial changes in manufacturing processes

As they say, "the Institute works closely with Universities, other research facilities and Scotch Whisky companies. It is able to carry out joint pre-competitive research on behalf of all its members as well as specific projects for single companies. Its laboratories are UKAS-accredited to ensure the highest quality in all services."

Key to understanding their work is the phrase "pre-competitive". SWRI work on generic, broad-based programmes and it is for individual companies to pursue their own work independently where they seek (or indeed are seeking) competitive or brand advantage.

For that, apart from the few very large companies who can afford to maintain research facilities, many companies use freelance consultants.

Consultants at work

So that brings us to the hidden men of the whisky world – the consultants who help set up new distilleries; trouble-shoot in existing ones or look at the science of whisky production. Who are they and what exactly do they do?

But, first, if you've worked in any large organisation you'll probably hear the word with a certain foreboding. Consultants are not always everyone's friend. So let's get the jokes out of the way.

"I'm a consultant and I'm here to help you."

"Consultant – one who borrows your watch and charges to tell you the time."

And, of course, the classic light bulb variant.

"Q: How many consultants does it take to change a light bulb?

A: It depends. What was your budget again?"

I should also confess that I've done – and continue to do – my fair share of consulting work myself. In fact, new product development, brand strategy and experiential marketing (visitor centres, to the uninitiated) represent an important part of my life. But it's invisible. Generally, like any consultant, I can't discuss it: if the work is a success the implied bargain is that the client gets the credit and if it's a flop we all quickly distance ourselves from the project!

In the field of marketing there is a great range of consultancy work on offer: PR, corporate and brand strategy, advertising,

Stuart Nickerson - experienced distiller and consultant

Photo: Glenglassaugh Distillery

Dr Jim Swan with one of his clients, Ian Chang from Kavalan

social media, design…the list goes on. But generally these folks are good at promoting themselves, so we'll move on. What interests us are the more shadowy figures working discreetly in the production and distilling field.

In practice, the same names keep coming up: Dr Harry Riffkin of Tatlock & Thomson; Alan Wolstenholme of Caledonian Solutions and Dr Jim Swan.

Stuart Nickerson, currently MD of The Glenglassaugh Distillery Co, is an interesting instance of a former distiller turned consultant who has now returned to running a distillery operation (though he still undertakes a few small projects from time to time).

More visibly, Bill Lark from Australia acts as a kind of 'flying distiller' and advises a number of projects in his native Tasmania and is helping the planning of the proposed Kingsbarns distillery, near St Andrews. This is presently in the fund-raising phase.

Dr Jim Swan is perhaps the most familiar name for a wider audience. He began his career at Arthur D Little, moved to Pentlands, helped Harry Riffkin acquire Tatlock & Thomson and, in 2002, began working totally independently. His work has taken him literally all over the world, though he is perhaps best known for his work at Pen-

deryn in Wales and the Kavalan distillery in Taiwan.

This gives rise to some interesting observations on the state of world whisky that he was able to share with me.

"Whisky is set to grow massively, now that temperature is no longer a barrier to making great whisky. The technology to make the highest quality is now going global and the established players can no longer rest on their laurels."

That may seem controversial, but Dr Swan is not one to mince words. Discussing Scotch whisky and innovation he had this to say.

"In the long, long term I'm concerned over Scotch whisky's future. Despite today's boom and massive growth new competitors will emerge not held back by self-imposed regulation. Increasingly Scotch is tied up in knots where others can explore and experiment."

"Take Maker's Mark 46 as an example. That couldn't be done in Scotch whisky yet is getting a hugely positive reaction from the consumer who is only interested in the taste."

And he went on with a warning about complacency and the challenges that will face established producers.

"China will break into this market with domestically-produced whisky that is very good. We have only to look at what Kavalan have achieved in six years to know that this is true and it represents a huge threat to everything but the very top end brands."

It may only be my opinion but these seem wise words and well worth your attention. Dr Swan has a longer and more distinguished career than many in the global whisky industry and he brings a wide, possibly unique, range of knowledge to bear on the subject. And he's not alone.

Quite independently I spoke to Alan Wolstenholme. His family has a long distilling pedigree (his grandfather worked at Hazelburn and trained Masataka Taketsuru, the 'father' of Japanese whisky). He himself has worked in grain and single malt distilling, starting with DCL's grain distillery at Caledonian, going on to Port Dundas, then working for William Grants, ultimately as their Distilling Director and commissioning Kininvie in 1990/91. He started his own consulting practice after further international experience in the biochemical industry. Like Jim Swan, he's very well travelled.

So, when he describes himself as "sort of a 'native guide' to the whisky industry who can help save newcomers time and money", I don't believe he's over-selling himself. Much of his work is with small or aspirant companies, such as the proprietors of the Borders Distilling Company who plan a new distillery (they currently market the Tweeddale Blend). Other projects, at least three at present, are for significantly larger companies where he feels he offers additional focus, an external resource or simply an unbiased view.

Like Jim Swan he sees many changes ahead.

"There is a sea of change coming with the advent of world whiskies from producers not inhibited by tradition or regulation. It's not the volumes they produce that will be significant but their innovative approach."

"The small guys have far fewer resources but an uninhibited and unrestrained creative approach. And there's a growing tendency for larger companies such as William Grant and Diageo to snap up interesting and creative brands such as the Hudson whiskeys and Cabin Fever flavoured whiskey."

And, again like Swan, he calls things as he sees them.

"There are some pretty funky 'non-malt' whiskies due to arrive very soon. Scotland

Scotland needs a vibrant micro-distilling sector, says Alan Wolstenholme of Caledonian Solutions

Reducing carbon emissions through energy efficient production, like here at Roseisle Distillery, is a key trend in the whisky industry

Photo: Diageo

needs a vibrant micro-distilling sector. I've told Alex Salmond [Scotland's First Minister] that!"

I would have happily have paid good money for a ringside seat at that meeting!

"The SWA does great work and I'm privileged to work with them in some areas but I worry that Scotch whisky regulations may be too restrictive and limit real innovation."

Where have we heard that before? But, looking to the future he does see many positive trends.

"Carbon reduction and energy efficiency are key trends. Much of my work is directed to greening the industry and supporting environmental improvement. It's no longer just about cost per litre of spirit. We're coming to realise that there are many costs other than the simple financial ones."

That, in fact, characterises much of the work going on right now in Scotch whisky. The Scotch Whisky Association recently announced stretching commitments to cut fossil fuel use by 80% by 2050, which they calculate will reduce emissions by more than 750,000 tonnes – or the equivalent of taking 235,000 cars off Scotland's roads (that should make the A9 a little safer!).

Much publicity has resulted for Diageo's work at Roseisle and the innovative bio-energy plant at Bruichladdich. It's just the tip of a giant iceberg that will see dramatic changes in whisky production over future decades.

So the future should see a greener and more environmentally responsible industry, backed by well-understood and thoroughly understood science. Organisations such as

the SWRI and the SWA ensure that best practice is widely disseminated and a number of highly qualified and experienced consultants are available to help companies put theory into practice.

For all that huge global challenges remain, as clearly outlined by Messrs Swan and Wolstenholme. Emerging new producers are keen to secure a growing share of new markets and see no reason to be bound by other people's rules.

Back in 1901 Charles Matthews saw science as the "hand maid" of progress. I still find little to argue with in that view. Though the level of expertise in today's industry might amaze Matthews, Nettleton or Hastie all three would soon recognise the underlying and eternal core of the process and, I have no doubt, salute the achievements of those who have followed in their footsteps.

Keeper of the Quaich and Liveryman of the Worshipful Company of Distillers, Ian Buxton is well-placed to write or talk about whisky, not least because he lives on the site of a former distillery!
Ian began work in the Scotch Whisky industry in 1987 and, since 1991, has run his own strategic marketing consultancy business. In addition, he gives lectures, presentations and tastings and writes regular columns for Whisky Magazine, WhiskyEtc, The Tasting Panel, Malt Advocate and various other titles. His most recent books are the two bestsellers; 101 Whiskies To Try Before You Die and 101 World Whiskies To Try Before You Die.

In Search of New Flavours

*It is common knowledge that the lion part
of a whisky's character is shaped in the warehouse during
maturation. Still, there is plenty of space for experimentation
and innovation during the production process.
Ian Wisniewski has met with some producers
who share their secrets.*

Continual experimentation over the past 20 years has led to dynamic innovations in malt whisky. And as up to 70% of a malt's character develops during aging, innovations during the aging process have been a primary focus. The result is an amazing choice of malts, showcasing the influence of various cask types.

But alongside innovations during aging, more distilleries are also experimenting during the production process, and distilling parcels of new make spirit that differ from the norm. Fascinating in its own right, this also of course provides a different starting point for aging, and results in mature malts that show another side of a distillery's house style.

"We are always experimenting to see how each stage of the production process influences the new make spirit character, and we have the facilities to do a lot of experiments under lab conditions, without producing at a distillery. Experiments come from a number of different imperatives, including flavour development and yield of spirit, as different departments in the company have their own parameters. Changing the character of the distillate is a complex challenge. It won't necessarily work the first time you do it, and can tie up valuable production time," says Nick Morgan, Head of Whisky Outreach, Diageo.

The barley factor

When considering each stage of the production process, fermentation and distillation are automatically considered 'creative,' being a direct influence on spirit character. Meanwhile, milling and mashing tend to be perceived as 'practical,' promoting efficiency rather than influencing spirit character.

Similarly, malted barley is generally considered a practicality, and effectively a source of starch that provides alcohol rather than flavour, although malted barley also contributes cereal notes to the spirit character.

Distillers can choose from various barley varieties that have distinguishing features, which includes a range of harvest dates, different yields per acre and varying yields of spirit per tonne. But whether a barley variety can contribute any individual notes to the spirit character beyond generic cereal notes has been a long running debate. Some say no. Some say definitely, yes.

Ewen Mackintosh, Director - Whisky Supply, Gordon & MacPhail

Photo: Gordon & MacPhail

Benromach distillery, for example, has produced batches of spirit using different barley varieties as part of its Origins Series (launched in 2008). The concept of this series was to release small batches of malt whisky that demonstrate how changes to the production process, including the barley variety, can influence the final flavour profile. Two different varieties were used, with Batch 1 using Golden Promise and Batch 3 using Optic.

"We kept everything except the barley variety absolutely consistent, which included peating the barley to 12 ppm, so the only thing that changed was the barley variety. The new make spirit produced from both varieties had the Benromach fingerprint, which is a perfumed, floral, malty, toasted character. However, Golden Promise also delivered an extra level of character, with oily, buttery, creamyness, while Optic had a slightly fruitier, sharper citrus note," says Ewen Mackintosh, Director - Whisky Supply, Gordon & MacPhail, the independent bottler which owns Benromach distillery.

Another barley variety, Minstrel, also makes a difference at The Macallan. And it's not a variety that will be appearing at any other distillery. Minstrel is exclusive to The Macallan, which owns the world rights to this variety in partnership with Simpson's Malt.

"We include malt from Minstrel in every mash, with Minstrel usually 40% of the

Dr Bill Crilly, Technical Support Manager at Edrington

Photo: The Edrington Group

blend. We also lay down some spirit every year distilled entirely from Minstrel cultivated on The Macallan farm, which totals a couple of hundred tons a year. There is a subtle difference in the new make spirit character. Regular Macallan spirit is rich, with a medium sweetness at the top end, while the 100% Minstrel spirit is slightly sweeter at the top end, slightly more oily, and with slightly more nuttiness at the bottom end," says Dr Bill Crilly, technical support manager of the Edrington Group, which owns The Macallan.

Frank McHardy, Director of Production at Springbank Distillery

Photo: Springbank Distillers

Another option is focusing on provenance. Springbank, for example, distills batches of new make spirit from barley with a specific local provenance. This has been on-going since 1999 (restarting a tradition that was put 'on hold' in the mid-1960s), with the spirit aged in different cask types, including bourbon and sherry, and eventually marketed as a Local Barley bottling.

A specific variety from a single farm within an 8 mile radius of the distillery is selected each year, and reference to the variety and farm will probably be specified on the bottle label. Examples of the barley types grown were Bere in 2006, Heart in 2007, Optic in 2008, Westminster in 2009 and Belgravia in 2010.

"We malt all our barley on the premises, and the production process is exactly the same with locally grown barley distilled as Springbank spirit, which is lightly peated. There usually is a difference in the spirit yield from locally grown barley, and it can be much lower than that attained from our normal barley sources. The new make spirit from local barley also shows a slight increase in sweetness. The regular Springbank new make spirit has always had a hint of salt, and with local barley spirit this is complemented by some extra underlying sweetness. This hint of extra sweetness is quite noticeable at the end of the taste," says Frank McHardy, director of production at Springbank Distillery.

The next production run is all set for the following year.

"This year, 2012, we have some 20 acres of Bere barley being grown for us on a farm at Machrihanish, which, in the early part of the 19th century used to be owned and farmed by a member of the Mitchell family, the founders of Springbank Distillery. We're hoping to get a good crop, and this barley will be malted early in 2013 before being distilled during May 2013. Spirit from this distillation will be matured for 15 years and is intended to be used during 2028 to celebrate the 200th anniversary of the founding of Springbank Distillery in 1828," says Frank McHardy.

A variation on the barley theme is the way the malt is kilned during the malting process, with high roast chocolate malt, for example, having its own technical specification.

"Rather than the usual kilning regime, when the temperature is gradually increased

Bill Lumsden, Head of Distilling and Whisky Creation, Glenmorangie company - producers of both Glenmorangie and Ardbeg

to a maximum of around 80 degrees centigrade in order to dry the malt, high roast chocolate malt sees the temperature dramatically increased to around 250 degrees centigrade. This gives it a right old roast, and it comes out looking and smelling like coffee beans. In fact, I got the idea from coffee and the different flavours that roasting can bring out," says Dr Bill Lumsden, head of distilling and whisky creation, Glenmorangie.

A key aspect of kilning is that gradually increasing the temperature, up to a strict limit, dries the malt without damaging the enzymes (which are very sensitive to heat) within the malt. This is vital as the enzymes play a key role during mashing, by converting starches within the malt into sugars. However, roasting the malt at such a high temperature has a significant effect on the enzymes.

"There is zero enzyme potential in high roast chocolate malt, which means that you can't distill 100% high roast chocolate malt, it accounts for about 35-40% of the malt bill and is mixed with the 'regular' malt. Additionally, a lot of the starch caramelises during kilning, so there's also a loss in the level of fermentable sugars, which dramatically reduces the yield of new make spirit," says Dr Bill Lumsden.

The usual spirit cut was maintained when distilling batches of the high roast chocolate malt, enabling a direct comparison to be made with the usual new make spirit.

"The new make spirit using high roast chocolate malt has a very spicy, earthy, toasty character, compared to the usual Glenmorangie new make spirit which has great delicacy and finesse with lots of floral, apple and pear notes," says Dr Bill Lumsden.

An inevitable question is how the character of high roast chocolate malt spirit develops during aging?

"The new make spirit is not very chocolatey, but the mature product is very chocolatey. It's aged in first fill and second fill bourbon barrels as well as sherry casks, and some of the wood extractives are complexing with other products to bring out these chocolatey notes. In theory I could bottle mature malt whisky produced from the high roast chocolate malt, but it's too earthy, spicy and full on. However, it is currently part of the recipe for Glenmorangie Signet, which is very much part of the core Glenmorangie range, and it's also possible that it will be used in other expressions," says Dr Bill Lumsden.

Another aspect of the malting process is of course peating, with phenolic characteristics directly influencing the spirit character.

Various distilleries have been experimenting with peating levels, though any change in the usual regime raises a key consideration.

"We've been producing batches of heavily peated spirit at all our distilleries for some time now. Although we refer to heavily peated spirit, it's not as simple as that, as we've got to find a peating level that will be taken on by each whisky in a positive way. We have to make sure the whisky will retain its core attributes, and have a range of complexity when peated, so that we can lay the spirit down using different types of wood. And then it takes years of experimenting, to see how they all develop," says Richard Paterson, master blender of Whyte & Mackay, whose portfolio of distilleries includes Isle of Jura, Dalmore, Fettercairn, Tamnavulin and Invergordon.

Meanwhile, distilleries producing heavily peated malt, such as Ardbeg, are also distilling batches of unpeated spirit, which gives an insight into the house style 'beneath' the peat (as phenolics can easily mask various lighter nuances).

"The level of fruity notes in Ardbeg's new make spirit is as high as in Glenmorangie, but you don't pick it up as much under the peat. However, we also produce batches of Kildalton spirit each year at Ardbeg, which is unpeated, and all the fruity flavours show clearly," says Dr Bill Lumsden.

Similarly, Caol Ila has produced batches of unpeated spirit that provide a different perspective.

"Caol Ila new make spirit is very fruity, and without the peat you can get right inside the fruity character, uninhibited by smoke. Distillery character is very important for us, and we want to give the distillery character room to express itself," says Nick Morgan.

Milling and mashing

Milling and mashing are typically perceived (or even dismissed) as merely practical stages that optimize the conversion of starch into sugars, and consequently maximise the spirit yield.

The milling specification is typically 20% husk, 70% grits (also known as 'middles') and 10% flour ('fines'), collectively called grist. These percentages provide an ideal surface area for the hot water to work on during mashing, which enables the maximum amount of sugar to be extracted from the grist in the minimum amount of time.

The grist 'formula' is also a case of balancing various factors. For example, it's easier for the hot water to penetrate the flour and convert starches into sugars compared to penetrating the grist (which is less broken down than the flour) and the husk. However, too high a level of flour can create a lumpy paste in the mash tun, and limit drainage. A higher percentage of husk improves drainage, but above a certain level the extraction of sugars and consequently the yield of alcohol is affected, as this would mean reducing the percentage of flour and grits which are easier for the water to penetrate (than the husk).

Consequently, it's vital that the milling specification remains consistent. However, as barley is an agricultural product and cannot be 100% consistent, the usual milling spec may have to be adapted in order to achieve the usual result.

"Separate batches of malt throughout the year can have a different corn size, particularly when moving from one variety to another, or one harvest to another. This means milling has to be constantly monitored and the milling specification may have to be adjusted to compensate for any differences in corn size, otherwise the malt can behave differently during mashing. This is very important as if you don't get the usual conversion during mashing you won't get the usual flavour, which shows that milling is an indirect influence on spirit character," says Alan Winchester, master distiller, The Glenlivet.

The wort (i.e. sugary liquid produced by mashing) can be either clear or cloudy, with cloudyness created by tiny particles of flour suspended within the wort after draining from the mashtun.

Whether the wort is clear or cloudy is determined by two factors, the level of flour in the milling specification and by the way mashing is conducted. The greater the degree of stirring during mashing, and the larger the drainage slits at the base of the mashtun, the higher the level of solids draining through, and consequently the cloudier the wort.

Most distilleries have cloudy wort, which includes varying levels of cloudyness, while other distilleries prefer a cloudy wort.

"There's no doubt that cloudy wort influences the balance of the new make spirit

Tall stills, like those at Glenmorangie will create a lighter whisky compared to the shorter stills of Ardmore

character, promoting a higher perception of cereal and nutty notes rather than sweet notes. Cloudy wort contains a higher range of congeners (i.e. flavour compounds) across the board than clear wort, but in a sensory evaluation, the heavier notes mask the lighter notes," says Dr Bill Crilly.

Fermentation is a fascinating process renowned for creating a range of flavours in the wort, including fruity notes, though fermentation is also a practical stage during which sugars are converted into alcohol.

Fermentation times are typically between 36-100 hours. Most of the alcohol production and development of lighter flavours is achieved in 36 hours. Allowing fermentation to continue for longer allows an additional, broader range of flavour compounds to be produced.

"Playing with fermentation times can have a huge influence. Longer fermentation means you can get a lot more fruityness, a shorter fermentation can give you more nutty, cereal, grassy notes," says John Campbell, distillery manager, Laphroaig.

Distillation

Distillation subsequently allows the distiller to select which of the flavour compounds created during fermentation are included in the new make spirit. The first distillation establishes the parameters of the spirit character, with the second distillation defining the flavour profile.

"Distillation gives you the greatest opportunity to influence the style of spirit you produce, as the distillation process has the most dials you can turn," says Ewen Mackintosh.

These options include the degree of reflux, for example, which determines the ratio of lighter and richer flavour compounds within the spirit character. The degree of reflux is determined by a number of factors, including the size and shape of the stills, and the rate of distillation.

Taller, slimmer stills generally promote a lighter spirit character, while shorter, rounder stills promote a higher percentage of richer flavours. This is because richer flavour compounds have a higher boiling point than lighter flavour compounds, and as heavier flavour compounds ascend the neck of the still the temperature becomes relatively cooler (the taller the still the more the temperature reduces), which sees heavier flavour compounds condensing on the neck of the still, and returning to the boil pot (base) of the still.

However, increasing the rate of distillation also increases the volume of vapours in the still, which in turn raises the temperature of

Roseisle Distillery is equipped with a mix of copper condensers (left) and stainless steel condensers (right)

the copper surface and results in less reflux, allowing a greater proportion of richer flavour compounds to ascend the neck and reach the condensor. The increased volume of vapours also means less contact between the vapours and the copper surface (where condensation occurs), and again this means less reflux.

The spirit cut is another critical factor, enabling the distiller to select the range of characteristics within the new make spirit. Distillers typically start collecting spirit at around 75% abv, and stop collecting when the distillate reaches a strength of around 65% abv. Lighter, fruitier notes initially come through in the spirit cut, and as the alcoholic strength of the spirit reduces progressively richer flavours come through.

"At Laphroaig we've been producing an experimental spirit called Ardenstiel, for use in the Teacher's blend, with Ardenstiel distilled from unpeated malt, rather than the heavily peated malt used for Laphroaig. We've been distilling Ardenstiel for the past four years, though it's a continuation rather than an innovation, as Ardenstiel was produced up until the 1960s-70s, then ceased in the 1980s-90s, and started again in 2009," says John Campbell.

When producing Ardenstiel the usual distillation regime used to produce Laphroaig is modified. So, let's first recap on how Laphroaig is distilled.

"We have one large still, which produces a new make spirit with more grainy, cereal notes rather than fruit. This is a contrast to the spirit from our small stills, which has a sweet, fruity character, even though the spirit cut for the big and the small stills is the same when we're producing Laphroaig. The difference in spirit character between the large and the small stills is down to running the big still faster, so there's less reflux, and a greater proportion of richer flavours make it through to the condenser. We blend these two styles of spirit together for aging," says John Campbell.

Small but significant changes to the usual distillation regime provide Ardenstiel with a separate identity.

"We slow the rate of distillation down in the big still, in order to get more reflux, which lowers the level of cereal notes and increases the level of lighter, fruity notes. We also change the cut points, we start collecting spirit at a slightly higher strength to get more fruity notes, with the spirit cut for Ardenstiel being from 72% abv down to 60% abv, compared to the usual spirit cut for Laphroaig which is 71-60.5% abv. But

John Campbell, Distillery Manager at Laphroaig

Photo: Laphroaig

even that small difference in the spirit cut is enough to make a huge difference in the character of the spirit," says John Campbell.

The type of condensers used also influence the spirit character.

At Roseisle, for example, some stills are fitted with two sets of shell and tube condensers, and the vapours can be channelled into either simply by turning a valve. One condenser is 'conventional' in the sense that the vapours condense entirely within copper pipes, while the other condenser is fitted entirely with stainless steel pipes, and consequently the vapours have no contact with copper. The copper absorbs sulphur compounds, which provide a rich range including meaty, rubbery, vegetal notes. As these 'big' notes can easily mask lighter notes such as fruityness, reducing the level of sulphur compounds allows lighter notes to show.

"Spirit from the stainless steel condensers retains the sulphur compounds, and although this means loosing some of the grassy, fruity top notes which show in the spirit from the copper condensers, sulphur compounds are also building blocks that promote a much richer and complex range of flavours. These sulphur compounds are subsequently removed during the aging process, through evaporation from the cask, and through absorption by the charred layer. However, the result is a mature spirit that has a more complex mix of fruits, compared to the mature spirit from the copper condensers which has more grassy and fruity top notes.

The option of producing two different styles of spirit adds to our inventory for blending purposes," says Douglas Murray, Diageo's process technology manager.

Distillation is clearly a very influential stage, and tempting though it is to try and rank distillation against other aspects of production, and establish a definitive hierarchy, this is very difficult. Ultimately, every stage of the production process can be considered equally important, in the sense that each stage is dependent on the successful outcome of the preceding stage.

Clearly, the production process provides various opportunities for innovation, and the benefits of doing this can be immense.

"Innovation can reward loyal consumers and intensify their affection for a brand, while also bringing more people into your brand. And exclusive bottlings, which are out of reach of many consumers, can also have a halo effect, enhancing and bolstering perceptions of a brand," says Nick Morgan.

However, getting innovation wrong can entail significant risks.

"Consumers in their head intuitively know what a brand is all about, and they know if innovation feels right. If it doesn't feel right then there's a risk of undermining the reputation of your product, as well as consumer loyalty to it," adds Nick Morgan.
Clearly, whether to innovate, and how best to do this, is a vital decision. So, what is such a decision based on ?

"It's a case of intuition and concrete research, though many people are now happier to use intuition based on their extensive experience, rather than always looking at quantitative research or focus groups to back something up," says Nick Morgan.

Ian Wisniewski is a food, drink and travel writer and broadcaster specialising in spirits. He contributes to various publications, including Whisky Magazine, and has written 8 books on drinks, including Classic Malt Whisky. He is a regular visitor at malt whisky distilleries in Scotland, and also distilleries in various other countries, as he is fascinated by the production process. He is also chairman of the vodka judges for the International Spirits Challenge, and frequently conducts tutored tastings

A World in Motion

*Emerging whisky from new territories
is threatening to turn the world of whisky on its head
– and there may be some bumpy times ahead along the way.*
Dominic Roskrow reports

As whisky warehouses go, this has to be one of the most unusual. It's a cave with a sealable door at the end of a rocky track and you must brave choking dust and searing heat to reach it.

The cask stands alone in the shade of the cave's interior, and a Rabbi stands close by. He is here to make sure that everything is kosher and to give proceedings his blessing. The cask is from Scotland but it has travelled here under three years old, so at the moment its contents cannot be called whisky under European definitions and it will never be able to call itself Scotch. It will be matured here in Israel, though it cannot really be called Israeli whisky either. But it will eventually be sold as full bodied, full flavoured whisky at a strength in excess of 60% ABV, and if it's anything like the last bottling over here, it will have those whisky enthusiasts lucky enough to taste it, reaching for the superlatives.

A few thousand miles North and our whisky cruise is weaving its way through floating ice. Below decks whisky enthusiasts from across Sweden are tasting some of the world's finest whiskies. But one curio has caught the eye – and the palate: it's a murky dark brown colour, tastes of plums and peat,

and it comes from BOX distillery, the world's most northerly distillery. What makes it truly amazing, however, is the fact that it is only 120 days old. It shouldn't have this taste or colour – maturation this far north in Sweden should be slow and stately. It hasn't been, and the reason? Hungarian oak casks.

Set the dials to the other side of the world, to the southern part of the southern hemisphere, as far removed from the north of the northern hemisphere as it's just about possible to go, and Peter Bignell is dabbling.

He doesn't have access to Hungarian oak – though heaven only knows what would happen if he did – and he's using port wood instead. In it he's placing rye spirit made from rye grown on his farm and distilled in a home-made still which looks like a cross between a shaggy R2D2, a dustbin, and the sort of thing they come up with in the weaker episodes of Robot Wars. This is Belvedere, a one man distilling operation on Tasmania, Australia, and despite the mad scientist element of the whisky's creation, after just a few months it's starting to taste pretty darn good.

World distillers offer us an exciting future then, but the potential path forward is fraught with challenges and controversy. And eventually, the whisky world order as

The still room of Yuan Shan Distillery,
the home of Kavalan single malt

we know it could be rocked. Melodramatic? Maybe, but already ominous clouds are gathering on the horizon. Whisky operates under a cosy consensus between the big five whisky making nations. For years now it's been accepted in Europe that whisky must be three years old, and Japan, America and Canada have recognised and actively supported that definition.

But in America there's a revolution going on. More than 400 craft distillers are ripping up the rule books. They're making 12 month and 18 month old single malt whisky and maturing it in all sorts of weird and wonderful woods. And there are new producers here who are questioning whether their new malt products should be excluded from Europe, citing unfair trade restrictions. With an increasing number of whiskies coming from territories where maturation times are greatly reduced by climatic temperature and humidity – Australia, India and Taiwan for instance – who's to say what sort of pressure new world distilleries will bring to bear, purely through the force of their numbers? And what if America's traditional bourbon industry came over to join them? After all, while Kentucky respects the Scottish and European rules, bourbon is bourbon after just a minute in the cask, and straight bourbon needs only two years of barrel ageing. Already the American Distilling Institute and the large craft distillers such as Tuthilltown, now owned by William Grant, are starting to ask some serious questions. For the time being, though, they remain theoretical and beyond the scope of this article. For now.

"Rest of the world" is not enough

What is beyond dispute, however, is that it's no longer okay to dismiss whisky from outside the big five whisky producing countries as one category called 'rest of the world.'

There are now at least 15 distilleries in Australia, eight of them in Tasmania alone; Germany, Austria and Switzerland can boast dozens between them, though some are tiny or are making the odd barrel of whisky in addition to their normal array of fruit liqueurs and genevers; even Sweden has 14 distilleries now.

To do world whisky justice in 2013 you need to view it on three separate and distinct levels.

Firstly, there are the frontline world producers which have effectively earned the right to be categorised with any other major whisky player. These distilleries – which include Penderyn in Wales, Mackmyra in Sweden, Amrut in India, Three Ships in South Africa, Lark and Sullivan's Cove in Australia, St George's in England and increasingly Kavalan in Taiwan – are exporting across the world, making crucial decisions as to which markets to target, deciding where to focus resources and contemplating how rapidly they should expand.

The second tier are the distilleries which are at the stage of just bottling their first whiskies but have yet to grow to a sufficient size or quality to export to any great extent. Nant or Overeem in Australia would fall into this category, as would Draymans in South Africa, Spirit of Hven in Sweden and Glann ar Mor in France. You could also add in scores of craft distillers in America. Some, such as Tuthilltown in New York, are in the process of moving up from the second to the first level.

And finally there are the new distillers who have yet to distill. Some will do so for a local market and a few close friends, others will do so to grow to a moderate but manageable size, happy to remain a one or two person craft operation. Some, though, will feed the whisky supply chain and a decade from now, will be mixing it with the big boys at the top level.

It all seems so simple and logical when written down in a feature such as this, doesn't it? But it's anything but. Growth is a painful, often scary process, and big hurdles stand between a farm distillery and an international malt producer. When the world comes calling, for instance, how does the enthusiast who made malt in his back shed divide his time? Does he carry on distilling, focus on business, or set out across the world as an ambassador for his brand, leaving the making of the whisky in someone else's hands? Decisions, decisions! So, where are the main world players today? Here's what's happening with a few of them.

Mackmyra, Sweden

If you want proof that world whisky from non-traditional areas can play in the premier league look no further than Mackmyra, and the opening of a second distillery a year ago. When the two distilleries are operating, Mackmyra can make 1.1 million litres of spirit – as much as many Scottish distilleries.

Part of Mackmyra´s brand new gravitation distillery

And when you consider that nearly all of this is going in to malt production – as opposed to the 10% that goes in to single malt in Scotland – that's some operation.

"The distillery is located on a new site about 15 minutes from Mackmyra Bruk where the old distillery is located," says founder and managing director Magnus Dandanell. "The new site is called Mackmyra Whisky Village and is built to give a new and unique visiting experience."

Mackmyra has fallen in to a steady pattern of regular bottlings, annual specials, and intense and exciting 'one off' Moment bottlings. Now the company is seeking to develop further afield, too.

"Our market is still Sweden and the Nordic countries, but most countries in Europe are interesting for us," says Magnus Dandanell. "For example The Whisky Shop in the United Kingdom now sells our whisky in their 20 shops all over the UK. We're also working (in a small scale) in New York with our distributor Opici. In Canada, both LCBO in Ontario and the SAQ in Quebec are selling our whisky."

Mackmyra is enjoying its status as a leading acolyte for new world whisky.

"We have never felt being treated as a threat, more with interest and with growing respect. It is maybe because our startup has helped to increase the overall malt whisky interest especially in the Nordic countries, but from now hopefully elsewhere. And that we will be internationally recognized as a distillery in the front line of new world whisky."

Kavalan, Taiwan

The whirlwind rise of Kavalan has been truly amazing, and while the whiskies the Taiwanese have launched have been uniformly excellent, there are many cynics who believe that the trajectory is unsustainable and the distillery will crash and burn. Only time will tell, but for the time being, you ignore this distillery at your peril.

After two years of accolades and high scores – the last batch this writer scored, all hit the 90 plus mark – the company is starting to put some roots down in China. Now on the verge of releasing its eight and ninth releases, Kavalan believes much of its future lies in Asia, but Europe and America are within its sights, too.

"As we are targeting the Chinese market at present, we have just opened a whole new showroom in Shanghai, exhibiting our whole range of products," says marketing manager Joanie Tseng. "Besides that, we are preparing to release new whiskies matured in select casks which will definitely satisfy the Chinese palates."

The malt whisky range from Kavalan - soon to be expanded by two more expressions

There are plans for a European and American push very soon but Kavalan is in a special position. Unlike many new producers it has the backing of international company King Car.

"We run a very complex business but that is not a big problem for us. King Car Group already runs its businesses in several fields: beverages, food, biotechnology, aquaculture, and others." says Tseng. "We are able to use the available resources and at the same time recruit new staff and set up new departments to handle the extra business. It has always been an ongoing process of business for King Car. We hope to be producing for America and Europe very soon, and our aim is to continue to produce top quality whisky for these markets."

Sullivan's Cove, Tasmania

In relative terms Australian distiller Sullivan's Cove is an old timer. In 2012 the distillery bottled a 12 year old, and perhaps more importantly it completed its transition from average producer to premium one. With lots of hard work done behind the scenes, it is starting to reap the rewards. Owner Patrick Maguire explains.

"Sales are rapidly increasing as the brand gathers momentum," he says. "I'm not really surprised as we have worked very hard over

the past few years to create that interest, so to put it in a different light, I am encouraged rather than surprised at how things are going. Things have been moving rapidly here this year. On the production side we bottled our first 12 year which is shaping up to be spectacular."

Australia remains the dominant market for Sullivan's Cove, but that is set to change.

"I can see Australia being eclipsed in the coming years as our presence in France, Belgium, Holland and Canada grows," says Maguire. "We sent our first shipment to the US this year and we are working on further developing Asia as a key market. Europe is important for

us both from a sales perspective, as it has the potential for good volumes, and also from a marketing perspective to build credibility in the eyes of the more brand focussed Asian consumer."

Maguire thinks that some world producers have now earned the right to be taken seriously, and certainly he perceives a change from other markets towards Sullivan's Cove.

"We are being taken far more seriously and I find that we are beginning to be seen as a genuine competitor. There is a huge market and demand for single malt whisky and we are working toward fulfilling our potential in our niche."

Amrut, India

The huge wave of accolades that Amrut has won in recent years has meant huge problems keeping up with demand. So much so that it'll be well in to 2013 before the company gets back on

"We are trying to get back on track with our stock," says global brand ambassador Ashok Chokalingam. "We are distilling more continuously than in the past."

Amrut is one of the more ambitious distillers, and is setting itself no limits:

"We see some opportunities in different parts of the world. Each market is a different ball game. We predict the European market will be very organic and steady growth over the years to come. We also predict America's, both south and north, will be key in the future."

"Considering the relative success of the new world whiskies, perhaps Amrut is the one which suffered a lot. Our Chairman Neel was patient and determined in-spite of the fact that we made a loss for the first six years since launching Amrut Single Malt in the global markets. Importantly, he has given total freedom to both the Sales & Marketing and Production team at the distillery. One of the reasons why we are increasingly successful is that philosophy of the top management at Amrut. I think we have far more better synchronisation and understanding between Production and Marketing at Amrut which is the key. Also we are, perhaps, the only new world whisky company that faces such a bureaucratic nightmare and red tape in India as compared to our counter parts in other parts of the world."

"We were not treated very seriously in the beginning, but I think they can not ignore us any more. We have crossed that line. Making this momentum a commercially successful venture is another issue."

Photo: Amrut Distilleries Ltd.

Surrinder Kumar, Vice President for Operations at Amrut, examining a sample from the warehouse

Tuthilltown, United States

Tuthilltown is at the forefront of craft distilling in America. It makes bourbon, rye and a corn whiskey in addition to single malt whiskey, and its success among the glitterati of Manhattan has caught the eye of William Grant & Sons who have gone in to partnership with it. But innovation remains key.

"The distillery is a work in progress in every sense," says Gable Erenzo, who is one of the founders. "The education continues. Experimentation in process and product development is encouraged."

When it comes to thinking out of the box, Tuthilltown's your distillery. Sonic maturation anybody?

"Our whiskey enjoys a 'sonic maturation' technique while aging, resting in oak while heavy bass beat music is played in the room, vibrating the liquid inside the casks to increase interaction between the oak and the spirit."

Tuthilltown is aimed unapologetically at the cool fashion set, but Erenzo believes the appeal's widening.

"We target consumers of descerning taste, 25 to 40 year old, mainly male spirits drinkers," he says. "Women increasingly are coming to Hudson because of its generally drinkable quality. This is a premium spirit."

"We are in a constant state of expansion and development of new products. The market for aged spirits and craft spirits is growing. Our retail sales have grown considerably as visitor traffic increases. We believe it is possible for a small entrepreneurial effort to succeed in the artisan spirits production business. Innovation should not be a dirty word for whiskey making. Tradition should teach by example, not by constraining creativity. We do not accept the notion of 'thinking outside of the box', because there is NO box."

Bakery Hill, Australia

If ever a distillery operating out on a limb in the remotest of locations has balled to survive, it's Bakery Hill, the distillery run by David Baker in Victoria, Australia. A one person operation, Baker has had to metaphorically sail the ship, navigate dangerous waters and work tirelessly to avoid taking on too much

Gable Erenzo is the Brand Ambassador for Tuthilltown Spirits

Photo: Tuthilltown Spirits

Increasing demand forces David Baker of Bakery Hill to concentrate on the domestic market at the moment

water. Cash flow problems, sourcing raw material and meeting demand expectations have meant never a dull moment for Baker but he's confident that he's moving in the right direction.

"We continue to produce our malts to a standard we are all absolutely delighted with," he says. "Producing enough for future sale is our greatest issue in that what is distilled today must be held for eight or nine years before it can be realized. To do this, a huge number of casks need to be held at any one time all placing a strain on the cash flow. To this end an investment programme has been commenced to provide the necessary funds for ongoing production."

"One of the other concerns brought about by an eight or nine year maturation period is being able to supply the ever growing demand for our malts. Previously we have had the luxury of exporting a number of pallets to France, Germany and Sweden but local demand has increased to such an extent that it is this local market which is predominantly taking all available stocks."

With peated and unpeated whiskies and an exceptional core malt, Bakery Hill is focusing on the Australian market for the time being. Baker says that the change in attitude towards the distillery domestically has been a real plus.

"Over the last three years the most surprising thing has been the way the local Australian public has warmed to our malts," he says. "When we commenced our local sales and marketing programme demand was extremely limited, but over the next three or four years the demand for our expressions has outstripped supply many times over. The growing local demand has completely stopped our ability in continuing the export market for the foreseeable future."

Dominic Roskrow is a freelance whisky writer. He edits Whiskeria and Whiskeria on line as well as his his own online magazines World Whisky Review and Still Crazy. He is a regular writer and reviewer for Whisky Advocate, spcialising in World Whisky. He is the business development director for The Whisky Shop chain and recently set up the Craft Distillers' Alliance, for which he is a director. He has been writing about drinks for 20 years and has just completed his sixth book, The Whisky Opus, published in September 2012. He lives in Norfolk, home of England's first malt whisky distillery, and is married with three children and is one of the few people in the world to be both a Keeper of the Quaich and a Kentucky Colonel.

The Born (and bred) Identity

With every Scotch whisky being made from the same ingredients, an identity must be created for the brand to separate it from its competitors. The creation process can sometimes be more complicated than the whisky production itself as evidenced by Neils Ridley´s report from the inner sanctum of some of the producers.

We've all been there and done it. Stood, bolt upright, in awe at the sight of row-upon-row of achingly beautiful bottles, lining almost every wall of your friendly neighbourhood dealer, sorry, whisky retailer. Each logo and label evoking a different feeling; a tantalising insight into the spirit within, each graceful and curvaceous bottle shape hinting at the uniqueness of the mouthwatering prospect that is to come – should you decide to take one home for the night.

Yes, this does sound a little graphic and given a few salacious tweaks, it could perhaps double as a passage in one of Charles Bukowski's trashy, but profoundly observational short stories about the author's sexual peccadillos as a barfly, but at its heart is something inescapable. Like it or not, we are all bound by our susceptibility to whisky branding. Perhaps it happens from the moment the cork is removed and the first mouthful is either savoured and revered, or quickly swallowed and forgotten. But somehow, whisky, unlike any other spirit has a sense of attached personality – a voice – an identity.

But the striking thing is that across Scotland, our cherished, unique single malts are of course all cut from practically the same cloth: water, barley and yeast. Throw in some contact with a bit of copper and oak and you have a product that whilst is widely identifiable as Scotch whisky, is now made in over 20 countries. Yet despite this, each identifiable whisky brand uses a parlance of so many distinctly different factors to create a unique 'liquid language'. Can any other spirit lay claim to such diversity when it comes to communicating with its consumers?

Let's consider the analogy of the humble motorcar for a second. Each one has four wheels, (ok, unless it's a three-wheeled Reliant Robin...) a steering wheel, an engine and a seat. They function in the same way, i.e. to commute from point A to B. Yet there exists the compact and affordable Fiat 500 and the ballsy, expensive-yet-highly-desirable Ferrari F40 and we obsess about their individuality and core messages, despite the underlying similarities. Does the same thing apply to whisky? And is this why some distilleries have lasted, developing strong brand identities, where others have failed because of a lack of an identity and a resilient core message?

"Brand identity is a clearly understandable proposition for consumers that is based on a set of truths around the brand in question, which can be interpreted and translated into both above and below the line communication," explains Doctor Nick Morgan, Head of Whisky Outreach at Diageo and the man previously tasked with collating the plethora of historical branding materials at Diageo's extensive archives. "The key word here is truth. If you accept my view that you have these created brand identities, they have to be based on truths, otherwise they aren't going to be compelling to consumers."

"If you look to the world of single malts: Glenfiddich, The Glenlivet, The Macallan and The Singleton are definitely brands, which have been invested in for a long time," continues Morgan. "Then you have what I would call 'product led' brands, such as Lagavulin – with a very strong liquid identity. Then there are just products, which don't have any discernable brand identity. The principle thing is that if it's a brand, it's been created deliberately – if it's a product brand it is something, which simply exploits truths that already exist."

When the whisky is the starting point

Looking at the heart of any single malt brand – the liquid – is it fair to say that 'distillery character' should be the starting point that defines a brand message?

"Generally, if you take a more pragmatic, realistic view of the world, certain brands have got a great big truth about them, which comes directly from the liquid, explains Neil Macdonald, Brand Director for Chivas Brothers, whose portfolio includes some of the biggest discernable whisky brands in the world, from The Glenlivet to Chivas Regal. "Laphroaig's is that you either love its peatiness – or you hate it," he smiles. "The Glenlivet's is that it is the 'Original of the Originals'. You can move away from this if you like, but it tends to be the thing that always brings people back and what they want to talk about. When you stick to that centre of gravity, it probably does mean that it is liquid led."

Imagine hypothetically for a minute that you were a distillery owner and were tasked with re-branding a famous whisky, bringing its flagging sales base and reputation kicking and screaming into the 21th Century. What would you do?

Back in the real world, Gerry Tosh, Brand Controller at Highland Park, faced this exact scenario nearly a decade ago and the gloves were well and truly off. The powers that be had granted Tosh and his team carte blanche to reinvent the brand, including the slightly alarming proposition of even changing the name and the profile of the liquid itself.

"It certainly gives you a sense of fear," he laughs "as anything you do will really change how everything is viewed in the future. We asked all the big questions that needed to be asked – to shape our thoughts. Basically the board said that 'this brand needs to move' – you can do anything you like within reason, but challenge every single thing that you think needs looking at – even if it has 200 years of heritage attached. If you think that some of it needs to be abandoned, go ahead, but equally if you think there's something that hasn't been focused on from the past that could work, go with that."

"Taking the name for starters, the bottom line is that it became quite obvious that Highland Park is actually a great name," explains Tosh. "It's easily understood and pronounceable – not just in English but in other languages. If we were called Ghàid-healtachd-bruich or something equally unpronounceable it might have some resonance on the west coast of Scotland, but in China, it adds an extra level of difficulty for the brand."

When it came to the brand's now iconic logo, Gerry and his team made some surprising discoveries. "We started going through the symbolism behind the brand; the old

Gerry Tosh (far right), Brand Controller for Highland Park, at the launch of Thor in Stockholm in February 2012 accompanied by a Viking and Martin Markvardsen, Edrington's Brand Ambassador for the Nordics.

Photo: The Edrington Group

letter 'H', which adorned the bottle and you kind of think that you'll discover that it's 230 years old and something that Magnus Eunson scratched into a cellar door. Then you find out that it was made up by some 17 year-old guy in the 1970's, who'd never even been to Orkney! That's when you realise your playing field is laid out in front of you. We went with the typography of the sign above the distillery gates, which has been there for 200 years – why invent something that doesn't need to be invented, when you already have the perfect answer."

Does Gerry feel that the liquid has to be the most relevant piece in the branding jigsaw?

"Well, the one thing we haven't changed and something that we never would, although we were told we could reformu-late if we wanted to, is the whisky itself. The marketing messages are now hopefully more in tune with the whisky we make and this has to be one of the key points in any re-branding exercise."

One aspect that seemingly helps to affirm any brand identity is the geography, the people and of course, the stories behind

the spirit – and Scotch whisky clearly has all three of these in abundance. Highland Park have perhaps focused their brand messages on their Nordic heritage more so than ever with several of the latest releases: from the Inga Saga-influenced Magnus series to the recent Valhalla Collection, in particular Thor, the whisky itself mirroring the characteristics of the god itself and perhaps the first time that a particular whisky has been given its own personality. I ask Gerry which came first - the idea to create Thor, or the liquid itself?

"There are hundreds, if not thousands of stories around the islands, from the first and second World Wars, the Neolithic age or the Picts, to the Viking influenced Sagas," he points out. "It's about picking the stories that best represent the islanders, the whisky and the history of the distillery. The Orkney Inga Sagas lent themselves to three distinct bottlings and the Valhalla Collection does the same – Thor is such a universally well-known character, yet is unquestionably a Viking and links perfectly to the Norse elements of Highland Park. The idea and the story would usually come before the whisky's creation, but for the first time, we asked Max to capture the character of

51

The dramatic landscape of Isle of Skye has been an inspiration when promoting the island's only distillery - Talisker

the god in the whisky, which was a real challenge, but with this approach you give people the chance to be really creative. Doing 300 bottles from a single cask is relatively easy, but to try and physically create the flavour of a god in whisky form – I can't imagine that conversation would come up in many distilleries around the world!"

Geography shapes the brand

Whilst Gerry and his team have a very clear set of directions for the brand including a meeting point between the geography, history and sociology of the Orkney islands, one aspect that a number of distilleries and their associated marketing teams seem to love is that of 'terroir', which features firmly in the imagery and brand messages of the likes of Bruichladdich, Jura and Talisker.

I ask Nick Morgan whether Talisker's brand strapline – 'Made By The Sea' was relatively easy to construct, given the more compelling landscape of Skye, than that which surrounds, say Glenkinchie.

"Let's say that it is easier to create an identity with Talisker or Lagavulin than it would be with Pittyvaich," he explains. "The reason for this is that a brand like Talisker has bags of product truth about it. Every single malt comes from somewhere but not every single malt comes from somewhere

as dramatic and evocative as Skye or Islay, rich in authentic heritage and tradition with truly inspirational landscapes. The products are also very distinctly flavoured in themselves, so if you can't get this type of brand going, you shouldn't be in a marketing job. If you go to Speyside where you have 40-odd distilleries within a small geographical area, it is much tougher to form a distinct identity, once someone has claimed some aspect – for instance the River Spey, no one can really go any where near it."

For Mark Reynier, the idea of making whisky in a compelling landscape is the sole brand identity for Bruichladdich.

"How can you 'position' a brand?" he points out. "To me, it is or it isn't. We don't try – we DO it! You can look back and for years, we've been 'sold to' by marketing and ad men – look at the programme Mad Men for how this has happened and I think this is why we're now experiencing a kick back and a growth of things like the Slow Food Movement and the Campaign for Real Ale, because people have had enough. They want something that's honest. This doesn't apply to everyone, but when you relate it to whisky, because the category of single malt hasn't been around for that long, consumers are thirsting for information and knowledge – especially if it's real and genuine."

Does Mark feel that being viewed as 'fiercely independent' also gives a sense of truth to the brand identity of Bruichladdich? "I think we've shown that you can run a distillery employing local people, working with locally grown barley and still make money, being as real and independent as you can be. With the resources available to some of the other Islay distillers, such as Ardbeg, it sometimes feels like they have created a 'brand vibe' around the spirit. The other point is that we've defined ourselves differently to larger distilleries, where the processing of barley has become a commodity and the whisky making is done in what are internally known as 'plants' rather than distilleries. The 'Chocolate Box' image is often used to sell the romance of whisky with little or no provenance whatsoever. When we make whisky we're prepared to pay a premium for locally grown barley, which in turn helps the local farmers in Scotland – that way, everyone is happy."

Looking at the aesthetic Bruichladdich have gone with, it would be easy to say they are the masters at creating a product, which stands out on the shelves (and surely the only bottle to be covered from head to toe in turquoise). For their closest rivals, Ardbeg, there seems to be a strong link between building brand loyalty (look no further than the rabid activity of the Ardbeg Committee) and demonstrating a free-wheeling spirit to the marketing messages around the brand. One only needs look at the pictures from the latest Feis Ile open day on Islay and the wacky events Ardbeg are now famous for organising to see that they are building a brand identity based on the social aspects of the brand.

One issue that brand owners perhaps face is the prospect of trying to establish brand identities for less well-known distilleries, that don't have any overt 'brand truths', yet can't be as outgoing and uncompromising as either Bruichladdich or Ardbeg.

"Well," explains Neil Macdonald, "consider Longmorn for an example. We realised that this was perhaps a 'secret brand' – the story is that outside of their own distilleries, Longmorn is often the second favourite single malt for a large number of distillers and distillery managers. We aimed to promote the secrecy angle, for instance, the leather coaster on the base of the bottle, so it doesn't make a noise when you put it on

Photo: Bruichladdich

Mark Reynier, the man behind the ressurection of Bruichladdich

the table. Almost subliminally, we wanted to promote the idea that this was a malt that needed to be discovered or recommended, that will never be advertised – the expert's choice, or malt's best kept secret."

Glenfarclas, under the watchful eye of the Grants, have created a distinctly family-orientated brand identity, which surrounds the portfolio (especially from the perspective of the Family Cask series.) Yet the brand's independent spirit can seemingly attract allies from some very unlikely places, such as the Swedish metal band In Flames. The singer Anders Fridén (a self confessed Glenfarclas fan) recently co-hosted a series of tastings with Robert Ransom, Director of Sales and Marketing.

"What, you might wonder, appeals about Glenfarclas to a heavy metal star?" wrote Ransom on the Glenfarclas blogsite. "Well, Anders Fridén admires our spirit of independence, the Grant family's passion for doing things their way. He sees parallels with the way In Flames has carved their niche."

Different views of a brand

So it would appear that despite the best efforts of the marketeers to target a certain group of drinkers, it doesn't always go according to plan.

"Most of us marketeers tend to be absolutely full of ourselves most of the time," laughs Neil Macdonald. "We have this view that we micromanage and control the communications strategy that consumers see every part of and love. The realism is that we don't. Brands exist in your mind and mine, and we all have a different view, ba-

Glenfiddich's One Day You Will-campaign

an underlying sense of 'aspiration' in the advertising slogan. Does Jamie think that the campaign adheres well to the original ethic of independence that the Grant family established back in the day?

"The whole reason we have the current marketing campaign is based on William Grant's lifestyle," he points out. "There is a book written by Francis Collinson [who was an indirect family member of the Grants] in the 1970's called *The Life and Times Of William Grant* which outlined some key decisions and driving ambitions of the grant family. One Day You Will definitely reflects the Grant and Gordon side of the family, who have driven our business forward."

So does the message translate internationally – or does Jamie think that the sheer size of the brand has given the campaign more gravitas?

"We've been very careful with this campaign. The idea was to develop something that would work on a global scale so that it would be successful in every country we were working in. In the UK we used a mountaineering image, giving consumers the idea that success can be measured by doing a bit more with their free time, whereas in Asia, they have more career-focused aspirations. The challenge we had in places like France and Sweden was that you can't 'order' someone to do something through an advert," he continues. "So 'One Day You Will' wouldn't work. In the end, the French markets went with the phrase 'the spirit of the pioneer' (L'Espirit Pionnier)"

Be it 'Age Matters', (Chivas) 'vintages', (The Glenrothes) perceived 'luxury', (The Macallan, The Dalmore) or aspirational figures (Johnnie Walker) brand identity isn't something that can be invented over night. It takes time and considerable financial investment to engender a set of values into a brand's target audience, building confidence and loyalty along the way.

"Johnnie Walker is a brand, which has been consistently invested in for over 150 years – which makes it a brand with 150 years of brand identity," explains Nick Morgan. But as we discovered from the

sed on the snippets we absorb from around the world that we process differently, based on our likes and dislikes etc."

When it comes to a global branding strategy, one particularly noteworthy case study is Glenfiddich's 'One Day You Will' campaign, which sought to re-energise the brand's core beliefs and key flavour profiles after a number of years in the shadows, despite their obvious worldwide appeal.

"I think that Glenfiddich has lacked a real brand identity for a number of years," explains Brand Ambassador Jamie Milne. "The company, marketing team and management became aware of this about three years ago, that there was a need to come up with a brand image that was, in their words, 'motivating'. When the One Day You Will campaign came out [huge adverts with visual representations of 'tasting notes' across magazines and billboards] it was really designed to get people thinking about whisky in a very different way," he continues.

Alongside the message of what flavours to expect in the whisky, there also seems to be

Highland Park scenario, just because a brand happens to be old, with oodles of juicy brand truths and truckloads of heritage, it doesn't necessarily mean it is relevant any more.

Another brand currently analysing their brand identity is blended whisky Cutty Sark, which has for the past four decades sailed into the doldrums of also-ran blends, but is set for a major reinvention later this year. I ask current captain of the ship Brand Controller Jason Craig how important is a retention of the past when looking to move forward and does one have to be ruthless to successfully rebrand.

"There's a fine balance of keeping your past 'relevant' and just keeping your past for the sake of it and it's this relevance, which was our biggest concern when re-launching Cutty Sark," he explains. "The first thing we did was to re-draw the Cutty Sark Logo, which was last done in the 1950's" [readers may note a stronger wind in the sails, than the previous clipper, indicating the progress of the brand.]

"As a brand guardian, you have to have one eye on where you've been and the heritage, but equally one eye on the future too," he continues. "The style of the Ferrari cars across the last 60 years may have changed but they are all underpinned by the same principles: great engines, surrounded by beauty – the heart of the 'prancing horse'. Art as opposed to Science. The same rules apply to the branding of a whisky and a lot of campaigns these days focus more on the aesthetic or art, rather than the science or 'the liquid' itself. In my opinion, this is why the blended category has lost its appeal, as most campaigns lack any real substance."

So where do we go in the future with brand identity? Whereas in the past decade, we're used to the phrase 'here today, gone tomorrow', we're rapidly entering an age where it is more 'here today, gone today', heightened by the advent of online promotion and interest from social media, particularly Twitter. Have brand owners ever felt the need to jump on the passing bandwagon, just because others have?

"Originality is one thing, but if you keep going on about the same things, you become a boring old fart eventually," thinks Neil Macdonald. "The important thing is to keep people engaged with your core beliefs."

Photo: The Edrington Group

Jason Craig, Brand Controller Cutty Sark

As the man currently in charge of The Glenlivet's branding, I ask Macdonald whether he believes its creator, George Smith, would think the contemporary brand identity is true to his initial vision, when he set the distillery up over 170 years ago.

"This was something very pertinent to us when we expanded the distillery several years back," he explains. "I feel less of a brand manager, more of a custodian and I'd like to think that if George were here today he'd be delighted by the fact that the whisky style that he pioneered over a century ago is still enjoyed by an audience, especially from the global interest the brand has, not just in the parish of the distillery. I call it my 'What Would George Do' moment... hopefully he wouldn't shoot me with his pistols!"

Neil Ridley is a regular contributor to Whisky Magazine and Imbibe, and he is also the co-editor of irreverent whisky blog www. caskstrength.net, recently nominated for several online awards. As well as being Drinks Editor for The Chap, Neil has written articles on whisky and other spirits for Aston Martin Magazine and The Evening Standard, as well as providing his opinion on tasting panels for the likes of The Spirits Business and the World Whisky Awards.

Feel the Burn

What does regenerating a cask mean and what does it do to the whisky inside? How does the industry deal with this natural resource to make it last longer? And when is a cask finally exhausted? Here is Jonny McCormick to answer all your questions.

This is a story about the sustainability of whisky casks; examining what it takes to equip the industry with new ones and what happens when we try to make the existing ones last a little longer.

For me, the cask perfectly encapsulates the magic of single malt whisky. Simultaneously, it provides a protective shell, nurturing encasement and a means of convenient transportation. This achievement is simply accomplished by slim arced staves compressed in place and tightly bound by circumferential metal hoops.

On one hand, it represents womb-like safety, the spirit's cocoon, but it's far from sleeping. Locked inside, chemical reactions abound continuously. The spirit saturates the woody layers, seeking out yielding fibres, pushing ever deeper, prospecting for gold as the evocative colour evolves over months and years like an autumn sunset. This slumbering metamorphic vessel harbours the gestation of new liquid thrills. But be patient. As the seasons whirl passed, the spirit naturally expands and contracts within the timber, as vital as cool air drawn in and out of your lungs. Capacity wanes over years, robbed by celestial evaporation in exchange for oxygen replenishment to drive on the maturing spirit. Eventually, it will join hundreds of thousands of other whisky casks scheduled to be extricated from their resting places, lowered from their racks by mechanical lifts or tugged from their row in a dunnage warehouse, muscled to the ground and compliantly rolled out into the sunlight.

Bungs are pulled expeditiously and cast aside for tipping. A glistening spillage seeps across the dry exterior adjacent to the bung hole before the cask rolls again, yielding a sudden urgency of amber liquid gushing forth as the contents disgorge. The cask now an empty hollowness, spent.

At any given time, there are millions of casks being used by the Scotch whisky industry and they are an important and costly resource for distilleries. Cooperage prices for casks have risen over the last decade, driven by a multitude of factors beyond the price hikes in raw materials; firstly, servicing the rising demand of production increases as whisky stocks are laid down for new whisky consumers in old and new territories by existing distillers, secondly, some additional need for casks for maturation by new distillers and thirdly, competition from new and reinvigorated markets outside Scotland for

Is it sustainable?

To try to put figures in context, it's time for some back of the envelope calculations. It has been estimated that the volume of wood used during cask production is 0.222m³ for a barrel and 0.372m³ for a hogshead (allowing for off cuts and wastage during manufacture). Researchers at the Scotch Whisky Research Institute have calculated that approximately a tenth of all the whisky casks emptied each year are replaced, so there's a need for 340,000 new barrels annually (or ~250,000 hogsheads).

That is going to require 75,500m³ of oak logs (93,000m³ for hoggies). That's difficult to visualise, so to determine if this is sustainable, let's figure out how much forestry land that's going to take. The amount of timberland required depends on its productivity, which is the volume of usable timber that can be harvested from each acre (1 acre is 0.4 hectare). According to the Forest Oak Resources of the United States report (2007), the average timberland productivity is 50-84 cubic feet per acre (1.4-2.4m³ per acre). This means it would take 32,000-53,000 acres at this productivity to yield enough wood for those barrels, and 39,000-66,000 acres for the hoggies. To put it another way, this equates to about 17-28,000 football pitches for the barrels alone (the reports may be American, but we're talking soccer pitches here). Is there enough woodland to provide this?

Quercus alba is the well-known Latin name of the white oak Eastern hardwood used for making barrels. Oak makes up more than 30% of all the hardwood volume in the United States. According to the National Report on Sustainable Forests 2010, timber production capacity in the U.S. is stable and sustainable, based on the available area for timberland, some 514 million acres, remaining steady. In fact, these areas have seen an increase in timber stocking over the last few years.

Obviously, not all timber is suitable for making casks; it takes the properties of white oak because of the tyloses (occlusions in the vessels running through oak which prevent leakage through a stave). *Quercus* species such as white oak, swamp white oak, bur oak, swamp chestnut oak and chinkapin oak are categorised as select white oak and there are over 34 billion cubic feet of growing stock and it's a figure that has

Bill Lumsden, Head of Distilling and Whisky Creation at Glenmorangie Company

maturation of whisk(e)y and other non-whisky spirits from rum to tequila.

Fundamentally, how much wood does it take to make a barrel?

"If you've got a good quality, fairly old mature oak tree (and by that I mean 100-150 years old) with a straight trunk and very few branch points, you can maybe get four or five barrels from it. If you've got one less than 100 years old, then you may only be able to make two or three" advises Dr Bill Lumsden, Head of Distilling and Whisky Creation at The Glenmorangie Company.

"By the time you strip off the bark, take off the sapwood, get into the heartwood, cut it out, have it quarter-sawn and such like, so much of the tree is discarded. That's the one thing that amazed me when I went to Tonnellere Françoise Frère in Burgundy who are my main suppliers of Sauternes casks. However, they use all the bark in a wood fired boiler to generate energy and use the larger chippings for toasting the barrels, so everything is used to make it as sustainable as possible."

Staves awaiting assembly at Speyside Cooperage (top) and a cooper making sure the staves fit to avoid any leakage (bottom).

Gary Taylor charring a cask at Speyside Cooperage (top) and a filled warehouse at Pulteney distillery (bottom).

Robot in action at Diageo's Cambus Cooperage.

the number of barrels that are manufactured in the United States each year, it's hundreds of thousands" confirms Lumsden. "But the vast majority of it goes for construction. If there any sustainability issues, it's not us [The Scotch Whisky Industry] that's causing it."

One common misconception is that The Glenmorangie Company own their own oak forest in the Ozark Mountains.

"That's not the way it works in the U.S.A. The trees are owned by the State and you have to bid for them. We never had one and that's straight from the horse's mouth. I go to the Ozark Mountains for two reasons; I go because I often vary things and try different woods, and I go because I like it. I only discovered recently that the lumbering of the forest is not just desirable, it's utterly imperative" highlights Lumsden.

"The forestry manager from the Missouri Department of Conservation told me they have to thin the trees out because otherwise, they'll not get healthy strong trees. She said, that for every tree felled, up to 50 acorns will seed themselves in the ground and it's a great way of regenerating the forest. So we believe the whole thing is sustainable."

A Close Shave

Cask regeneration is not new, but advances in coopering technology and scientific understanding of the results are giving producers new options when creating their whiskies.

There are two obvious facts; practically, cask regeneration prolongs the useful lifespan of a cask, putting off the day when it's scrapped, and economically, it's far cheaper than buying a new one. The internal char layer becomes less effective at erasing the immature characteristics with each use of the cask and wood compounds diminish as the spirit needs to push deeper in to each stave to extract them which slows maturation.

So what criteria are used to determine when a cask is exhausted and suitable for regeneration?

"Basically, we bring in casks from the disgorging unit that have been rejected by the tint meter," shares Tom Duncan, Cooperage Business Leader at Diageo's Cambus Cooperage. Cask exhaustion is analogous to a used teabag being repeatable squeezed to make progressively weaker cups of

increased by 570 million cubic feet per year over the past decade.

There are 139 million acres of oak-hickory forests in the Eastern USA, 95% of which are suitable as timberland so on the face of it, this should cover it even though the wood for the cooperages is more likely to come from logging areas in the vicinity. However, for quality barrels to be constructed from wood from mature trees, it is realised that only 4% of this stock is actually more than 100 years old, and therefore the kind of mighty oaks we want for coopering.

With this in mind, to make these barrels would utilise 0.6-1.0% of the aged oak-hickory timberland (and 0.7 – 1.2% for the hogsheads). Over the next twenty years, that 0.6% accumulates to 640,000 acres but over that same timeline, an additional 15 million acres of oak-hickory will have matured beyond a century.

In reality, suitable younger trees are also felled, so it is fair to say that the proportion of the wood harvested for cooperage purposes is small and sustainable.

"Which is correct, less than 1% actually goes to the cooperage industry which is a staggering statistic when you think about tea – with the tint meter judging when it's failed.

"We then remove both cask ends and end hoops. The cask is placed on a conveyor to the shaving machine and we shave 2-3mm off the cask which takes us back to the fresh wood. The cask is picked up by robots and placed in the charring area where the burners are set to high fire for two minutes. The cask will be ejected and taken to the far end of the process for final assembly. The components are matched by RFID tagging [Radio-Frequency Identification] so we're guaranteed that the same cask shells are meeting up with the same cask ends and hoops again."

Cambus cooperage will handle 250,000 casks per annum with 165,000 being regenerated casks and bourbon rebuilds forming the remaining third. Cask shaving not only removes the previous internal surface char, but it should expose new wood ready for a fresh burn.

The internal research at Diageo has found that their 2-3mm shave produces the best balance of a good char on new wood without over thinning the staves or compromising load bearing so that regeneration can be a repeatable process. Older techniques such as the wire flail were less precise as Tom Duncan explains.

"I've been with Diageo for 20 years and since I came here they were flailing casks. Our old process at Carsebridge Cooperage was to brush the cask with a wire flail machine and then put the cask on to the fire. The cooper would decide if it the char was heavy enough or not. If it wasn't heavy enough, he would put it back on again. Although we were still getting a quality cask, there wasn't the consistency there. We now take temperature readings from the flue where the cask is being fired, so we have a much more consistent refill cask coming off the new system."

He estimates that an ex-bourbon cask may achieve a lifespan of 30 years with two fills for grain spirit maturation each decade between each regeneration process. Dechar-rechar cask trials with grains whisky have found much higher maturation characteristics (such as spice, wood, sweetness and dried fruit) and diminished new make characteristics (such as feints, sulphur, cereal, soap and oils) after three years compared to a refill cask.

However, certain desirable flavour components such as the oak lactones (which can form the coconut flavours in whiskies from fresh ex-bourbon barrels) and the hydrolysable tannins will have been removed by the previous uses of the cask (leading to its exhaustion) and simply cannot be regenerated unless shaving cuts deeper than the tidemark of the whisky's penetration into the wood.

Other treatments developed by the wine industry for the preparation of casks for regeneration are under investigation such as sonicating the cask by ultrasound which improves the micro-environment and increases access to the oak or by using salt catalysts (so called cask curing) before charring which leads to a greater release of wood extractives.

However, the use of such techniques is not explicitly permissible under the current Scotch Whisky Association regulations. If you get the opportunity to look at some individual staves, you will notice the tidemark of penetration which represents the attenuation of the spirit's removal of wood extractives and colour. The extent of this penetration is dependent on a number of factors including the species of oak, the tightness of the grain (which equates to slow growth and a more open structure), whether it's been air-seasoned as opposed to kiln-dried, and the initial heat treatment.

The difference between charring and toasting

Charring and toasting are different processes and can be easily confused. Charring involves applying a direct heat, typically a gas burner, until the cask shell ignites for a couple of minutes which can result in some of the flavour compounds being vaporised, whereas in toasting, the wood is heated over a longer period of time at much lower temperatures, usually over a fire of oak chips for anything between 10-20 minutes.

Alternatives to traditional toasting over oak chips (which can lead to a greater toast level for either cask ends near the flames and less at the bilge) include methods such as gas burners, convection heaters and infrared heaters, a technique pioneered at the Brown-Forman Cooperage, where staves are evenly toasted by sitting on a conveyor like sliced bread on a hotel toaster.

Bearing in mind these variables, it is not

Cask ends in the yard at Speyside Cooperage

Casks ends can account for 20-25% of the internal surface area, and replacing these could assist maturation without the need to thin the staves. Undoubtedly, fitting new heads on the cask can bring exciting additional flavours and if you need convincing, try the contemporary bottlings of Spice Tree from Compass Box Whisky Co., where new heads of heavily toasted French sessile oak *Quercus petraea* (often used for wine barrels) have been added for additional maturation.

However, cooperages dealing with large-scale cask regeneration typically replace their old cask heads as they make the best fit, and new ends add to the production costs. Tom Duncan knows the difference this makes to his operating margins.

"We're producing a rejuvenated cask for £22.37 and that's compared to £60 for an ex-bourbon rebuild cask. Obviously, the bourbon cask is more expensive because it's got new cask ends, new hoop iron plus it's got to go through a steaming process. On a rejuvenation cask, all we really have is labour and energy costs."

Cask regeneration is an exciting and changing part of the industry where research is leading developments although changing aspects that can produce good colour and mature whisky characteristics in a shorter timeframe in a refurbished cask is attractive to the bottom line as well. However, this does not eliminate the need to source high quality new wood whilst ensuring environmental sustainability which now like never before, remains a priority for the Scotch Whisky Industry.

surprising to note the different tidemark of penetration in every stave you examine. In cross-section, some look like they have barely nibbled the surface, whilst others have commanded more than half the stave depth. As each cask will have staves from several different trees, applying a consistent shave depth to all casks is going to produce different results; some may cut deep enough to go back to the new wood, other may not.

Using carborundum brushes which strip off the char and scrape a few millimetres into the wood is an alternative method with less consistency than the precision shaving. It's a manageable inconsistency if the end flavour profile still produces the desired result for the blender. Wood research suggests that better results may be produced from re-toasting rather than re-charring the cask or a combination of both.

This is regeneration, not resurrection. Exposed new wood does not replicate characteristics of the internal surface of ex-bourbon barrels when first filled with spirit. However, different does not mean poorer, just different and it's not the only way of introducing new wood.

Whisky writer & photographer Jonny McCormick specialises in the scientific and technical facets of whisky production, branding, packaging and articulating aspects of the secondary market for rare single malt whiskies. He is the creator of the Whisky Magazine Index and the Whisky Advocate Auction Index and his work has appeared in a range of publications including Whisky Advocate (formerly Malt Advocate), Whisky Magazine, The Keeper, Whiskeria, Whisky Magazine & Fine Spirits (France) and Fine Spirits magazine (Italy).

Working on the Frontline

IF YOU WANT TO TAKE THE TEMPERATURE of the whisky business – where it stands today and, more importantly, where it´s heading – who should you talk to? Well, who better than the people working on the frontline? The ones that are the closest to the customers, with an ear to the ground picking up the latest trends. We decided to ask some of the Brand Ambassadors, Whisky Retailers and Whisky Evangelists for their views on the whisky business based on their encounters with consumers all over the world.

Donald Colville

Born in Scotland's historic whisky capital, Campbeltown, Donald has spent all his working life in

the whisky industry. In 2003 he returned to Campbeltown to work for Springbank. Since 2008, he is working for Diageo where he is responsible for supporting the development of all of Diageo's Single Malt Scotch Whiskies. Donald was appointed Global Scotch Whisky Ambassador in 2010.

Ian Logan

Having originally joined Pernod Ricard (Campbell Distillers) in 1998, Ian rejoined the company in

2004 to take up the role of International Brand Ambassador at Chivas Brothers. His first job involving whisky was working for a wholesaler in South West Scotland starting there in 1987. Today, Ian is based in the heart of Speyside at Strathisla and The Glenlivet Distilleries.

Eddie Ludlow

Eddie is the founder, along with this wife Amanda, of The Whisky Lounge. Formed in 2008 with

the express purpose of 'Bringing Whisky to the People', the company now organises and hosts 9 Whisky Festivals in the UK as well as dozens of smaller scale tastings around the country. Prior to that, Eddie was the UK Brand Ambassador for Ardbeg and Glenmorangie.

Julia Nourney

Julia is an independent spirits expert with whisky and various other spirits as her main topics. In ad-

dition to offering tastings and seminars, she also works as a freelance writer for magazines, as a spirit-related travel guide and does consultancy for distilleries. She has been a jury member at many spirit competitions and was awarded "Whisky Expert" by the Glenfiddich Distillery in 2007.

Jamie Milne

The son of a distillery Exciseman, Jamie lived beside Cameronbridge and then in Keith and

spent his childhood exploring distilleries with his father. He retained an interest in whisky and distilleries throughout his adult life, running private tasting sessions and working briefly with Glenfiddich in Australia, before taking on the role of UK Glenfiddich Ambassador early in 2010.

Mahesh Patel

Mahesh has been a passionate whisky collector for twenty years and he regularly travels Scotland,

searching for new bottlings. Over the years he has built an extensive network in the whisky industry. Since two years he is hosting a whisky show in Las Vegas - The Nth Ultimate Whisky Experience and has also created his own brand, Sirius, with single cask bottlings of old and rare whiskies.

Johanna Ngoh

Johanna has been writing about whisky since 2002 online at www.singleminded.ca and in print.

She is the executive producer of Spirit of Toronto Whisky Gala, Canada's largest whisky show now in its 9th year. She is known to be an independent and outspoken reviewer of the whisky business and was last year shortlisted for Whisky Magazine´s Whisky Ambassador of the World award.

Duncan Ross

Duncan has been in the drinks business since 1994 when he started with Threshers Wine Shop in

Newcastle. He then moved to London in 1998 to work in the Whiskies of the World shop in Heathrow T1 then Milroy's of Soho. Royal Mile Whiskies captured him for their London shop in 2002 and since 2007 he is working for The Whisky Exchange at Vinopolis in London.

DONALD: As the Scotch Whisky industry grows with so many emerging markets looking to explore new flavours and experiences, we have to look at all age groups and demographics and not just focus on one. However, from my recent experience I am seeing more 25 to 35 year olds enjoying and appreciating Scotch Whisky and also looking to better understand it.

IAN: Whisky in general is doing very well against "white Spirits", look at the success of Chivas Regal in China, Jameson in the US, The Glenlivet in Taiwan as examples. Whisky is one of the truly aspirational drinks in the world and is at the core of spirit growth in many countries around the world.

EDDIE: Whisky will always suffer when it comes to struggling for the attention of young people versus 'trendier' spirits. However, young people are discovering it for themselves and showing real interest in a product that has true credentials and not just the spawn of a misguided product development team. With the recent movement towards products with actual provenance and tangible quality, I believe whisky is deservedly riding the crest of a fresh wave and, if I may say so, our festivals over the last few years have evidenced this, with the average age of visitors falling to around 30 to 34.

JAMIE: There are definitely more young people coming to whisky festivals and tastings around the UK. And not just younger men – women are taking a much greater interest in the wonderful world of whisky, which I think changes the dynamic of a tasting for the better and opens up more discussion on aromas, flavours, people, places and memories.

JOHANNA: Whisky has made significant in-roads with the twentysomething year old demographic, perhaps more than the industry realizes. Without a doubt brand education has been the key, engaging the intellect as well as the palate, with flavour and fact rather than the kind of lifestyle marketing favoured by vodka and rum. These twentysomethings make up a significant percentage of our show's attendance and it is not unusual to see 2 and 3 generations of the same family coming to the show together. The challenge in retaining the interest of these younger consumers will be in offering a quality-price ratio comparable to premium rums now that this sector has taken off.

JULIA: Do we really want to put whisky in a competition with spirits like vodka? Whisky has always been a high price product within the premium segment and this is what young people know it for. They are the future consumers and we should not damage this image thoughtlessly, especially because it would also damage the image current consumers have of whisky.

MAHESH: The challenge to draw the younger consumer to whisky will always be there, simply because others spirits and in particular vodka, have much lower price points and are highly mixable. Younger people will always go for volume drinking at an affordable price. Having said this I see the tied turning towards whisky products. More and more people under thirty attend tasting events; I see a huge whisky mixology culture opening up in the US; TV series like 'Mad Men' are also influencing this group and in the emerging markets like China, India and Russia, whisky attracts the younger drinker – it is the premium spirit drink of choice.

DUNCAN: I have found that young consumers are more prepared to experiment with less traditional drinks (vodka) and will 'Give it a try" and this has meant that they are being introduced to whisky, in all formats, much earlier in their drinking experience and are liking what they find. They also don't mind the pricing points as they understand it takes time to make.

DONALD: I hope so, there would not be the passion for Scotch Malt Whisky if it was not for the pioneering work of our industry forefathers who put Scotch Whisky on the map through blending. I find it hard to compare the two as they are different products but I will describe it in the way of an analogy: Blending is like an orchestra; the master blender or conductor must take each section of the orchestra and make a very impactful piece of music. Each different piece will involve more or less of certain sections. On the other hand you have a Single Malt Scotch Whisky – who in this analogy would be a lead violinist – the diversity of sounds, stories and emotion that can come from one person with one violin can be incredible and those skills can be easily added to the orchestra when needed.

IAN: Blended whisky offers peace of mind for so many whisky drinkers around the world, a comfort and a confidence in what they are drinking.

To compare a blend such as Ballantine's against a malt such as The Glenlivet is very tricky, both are whiskies but different styles. Blends offer a versatility that cannot be found in malts. A true connoisseur appreciates both!

EDDIE: It will change as the average age of whisky-drinkers in general comes down. The current generation of whisky fans (me included) have grown up with the mantra of 'malts are best' and 'blends are the enemy' ringing in their ears and it is going to take a bit of time for this to sort itself out. Going forward It really is about how the industry as a whole chooses to represent itself and to extol the virtues of all styles of whisky.

JAMIE: I think there is still a commonly held perception that "malts are better than blends", which I don't believe is true. We're already seeing a shift in people's awareness and interest in taste and flavour – and a well-made blend can bring together many more flavours than a single malt, especially a single-cask single malt. Quite a few producers have been extending their range of blends, so we're seeing a wider choice from brands and independents alike.

JOHANNA: At this year's Spirit of Toronto I presented a masterclass of fairly exclusive whiskies – Lagavulin Jazz, Nikka Coffey Malt, Glen Flagler – that started out with a blind sample of Dewar's White Label. No one attending guessed this to be a blend – including a brand ambassador – which tells me that perception is the biggest challenge facing blended Scotch among single malt drinkers. That said, the staggering quality of the Compass Box range and newer brands such as Black Bull is forcing this group to rethink their attitude towards blends, and I suspect they will continue to do so as the price of single malt whisky approaches the ridiculous.

JULIA: The evolution of a whisky drinker is usually from an occasional Blend drinker to a knowledgeable Single Malt lover. Especially in these times of diversity and individual likes, some of the more open-minded give blended whiskies a second chance and they are often not disappointed. I think they have learned that a blend can be a very good and affordable choice for the small day-to-day enjoyments, interrupted by some exceptional Single Malt bottlings for special occasions.

MAHESH: Traditionally the hard-core single malt drinkers have treated blended whisky as inferior to malts and would not even consider them in their cabinet. In recent years some great blends have come onto the market, which I see many of these guys drinking and considering. I try to encourage my fellow whisky drinkers to be open minded towards all whisky products and regularly host blind whisky tastings, with single malts, blends and single grains. It has been very interesting to see how many of these groups have appreciated the blends and the single grains.

DUNCAN: I think quite recently the major drinks companies have altered their focus product wise. The demand for malt whisky is still there but the skills of the blender should also be looked upon as an art that takes years to develop. The blend is still the 'base', maybe it needs sexing up a bit or an indication of value for money.

> The last couple of years has seen a debate in the whisky business between those who advocate that age is a determining factor of quality and those that are opposed. Is the purchase decision of the general consumer influenced by the age on the label and are they willing to pay the price for aged expressions?

DONALD: I am seeing a change in this away from age being a deciding factor. To me age has never been a deciding factor on quality – older is not necessarily better. It's what happens in the cask during maturation that can make the whisky wonderful. Diageo holds the largest stock of maturing Scotch Whisky in the world, and even we are still building our knowledge on maturation. The quality of the liquid and the skill used in making it is what makes Scotch Whisky great not simply because it has been aged for many years.

IAN: We actually did some research that found it was the third most important factor after the brand and the taste. Maturation, age, when done correctly, adds complexity and depth that cannot be achieved in a younger whisky so if you know what you are looking for you can appreciate whisky at another level and when we taste expressions of The Glenlivet from say the 18 year old through to the 25 year old and even older Cellar Collections, the reaction to the taste and the deeper level of complexity is fantastic!

EDDIE: I believe this is an education issue and, again, has to be an industry-led initiative. We all know that age is not necessarily a factor in determining quality but we need everyone behind it. The general consumer in the UK is still relatively naive with regards whisky in general and it is up to all of us to ensure their heads are not filled with untruths based upon cynical marketing campaigns supporting sales requirements.

JAMIE: Bearing in mind this question is phrased around "the general consumer" – I think he or she would probably still make the assumption that "older is better" and this may well influence purchasing decisions. Regarding price – I still feel that scotch whisky is massively undervalued when compared with other spirits, such as cognacs and designer vodkas. An 18yo single malt is guaranteed to be at least 18 years old. Yet they're often priced below younger cognacs and day-old white spirits. So, although the general consumer may be willing to pay more for older expressions, I'm not sure they're paying what those expressions are truly worth, and this has to change.

JOHANNA: As anyone who has worked at a whisky festival knows well, the vast majority of consumers are interested in the "oldest whisky you've got" and among this group an age statement will always have the final say in assessing the quality of a whisky, whether real or imagined. Witness my local market where Ardbeg 10 year old sells for $100 – and many happily pay this price! By contrast, our liquor monopoly recently offered a bottling of Kavalan Soloist for pre-order at over $200 and most enthusiasts scoffed. So there is most definitely a glass ceiling for the price of NAS whiskies, but the quality-price ratio still plays a significant factor in the purchase decision, the Compass Box range being a case in point.

JULIA: Long matured products of high age will always have their place in a premium market but the great success of recent products without any age statement already shows a huge progress. The group of people buying these products is likely to grow but it all depends on education. The general consumer still needs an age statement for orientation and it will probably take another generation to change this habbit.

MAHESH: The general whisky consumer is totally influenced by the age statement. To them the older a whisky is, the better it is and more exclusive, and they will pay for it. Another group that will pay for the age on a bottle is the collector. This person is more educated on whisky and is willing to pay the premium for rarity, limited edition and the potential appreciation value of the individual whisky. Now the whisky connoisseur is a person who will not solely base their decision on age. For this group, it is about the whisky itself, how good it tastes.

DUNCAN: Ageism in whisky will always be about. The public need to be educated to the fact that older whiskies are not necessarily better whiskies. There are younger brands about that I feel are overpriced and the use of NAS (Non-age Statement) products is a simple way to mystify the buying public. Some work young, some need time. Explore!

It seems that the number of new releases of wood finishes keeps decreasing every year now. Does this reflect the consumers behaviour? Have they become less interested in enhanced malt whiskies?

DONALD: For me it comes down to my previous point of understanding wood better. Realistically the previous contents deliver a small percentage of the finished flavour. The type of oak is what really imparts the defining flavour – European red oak is where you get those lovely rich fruits, dark bitter chocolate notes and from American white oak you expect toffee, butter and vanilla.

IAN: Apart from 1-2 exceptions Chivas Brothers have never really gone down the lines of finishing. The process certainly served its purpose in re-invigorating the category but over the years only the most succesful have survived. The occasional very limited bottling still comes along but the plethora of choice from the 1990's and early 2000's has certainly diminished.

EDDIE: They have become more of the 'norm' for sure and I think that there are at least as many as there have ever been – they just are not talked about with the same enthusiasm on release. Certain sectors of consumers are probably 'bored' of them, but the general consumer is still playing catch-up and many are still discovering finishing.

JAMIE: I'm not sure I agree, as I still see lots of distillers releasing new cask finishes or multi-maturations, including our own brands. I think consumers have more interest in taste and flavour, and how those flavours are created. Cask finishes offer a way of tweaking flavours in directions that can't be achieved using "traditional" bourbon or sherry casks – and I think this offers other avenues for interested consumers to explore.

JOHANNA: Too much choice leeds to frustration and ultimately dissatisfaction. While variety may be the spice of life, some distillers went too far, losing sight altogether of their core range while changing their wood finish as one changes their underwear. Although one appreciates the challenge of managing both cash flow and inventory, from a consumer perspective the end result was an identity crisis. Many consumers view single malts as a pure and unadulterated product from a single point of origin. While the occasional cask finish can be fun and fanciful, a sustained onslaught of tarted-up whiskies becomes overwhelming and exhausting.

JULIA: Consumers have probably been a bit confused with so many new releases coming into the market every year. And they were probably a bit frustrated about buying a big number of bottles to be up-to-date. It is quite likely that they sometimes were also concerned about the price-quality ratio of some of these whiskys. So it is easy to understand that more consumers are now going "back to the roots" and are interested in trying the "house style" without any finishes first.

MAHESH: I, and fellow whisky connoisseurs, constantly try to seek out newer products to sample, and as single malts have gained popularity, the industry has reacted by creating new trends like 'wood finishing' to keep the category fresh and appealing. You will continue to see wood finished whiskies in the future, but not so many, simply because this trend has peaked and the industry is working towards new, exciting themes. Non-chill filtration seems to be gaining ground as well as un-aged expressions.

DUNCAN: I think the use of 'Finishes, Enhancements, ACEing etc' has diminished someways but it will never truly vanish as many companies are looking to innovate in some other manner, usually involving wood. There are core brands that thrive on the use of finishing so unless there is a change in company policy the use of second or third wood will continue. Finishing isn't finished!

If you were to meet a person saying I´ve never really given whisky a chance – what would be your best way of introducing him or her to the world of whisky?

DONALD: Start light, so as to not scare their palate to much – a Dalwhinnie served over ice with maybe a splash of water to allow the flavours to develop is perfect. Over time we can get them to the more powerful flavours like Talisker and Lagavulin. However some people never make it that far. It's very personal and you have to let the individual make their own journey but I would always start with a light un-peated Scotch whisky.

IAN: Water!!! I am quite sure if you talk to any of my fellow Ambassadors in the industry they will all come across the notion that whisky should be drunk straight. Watching the moment of enlightenment when a new drinker adds water to the whisky is great fun. Beyond that a taste of The Glenlivet 18 usually does the trick.

EDDIE: I would first of all gauge as to whether that person is mentally prepared and ready to open their minds through their taste-buds. There is no point banging your head off a brick wall. If they are, then often in a dinner situation I would suggest trying an appropriate whisky with dessert. If that goes as it should then you should have them 'hooked' by the end of the night and have changed their life. I should, but I don't charge them for this!

JAMIE: You can't help someone take a bold first step unless you understand a little about them. So I always ask what whisky they've tried, how long ago, what else they drink – wine, beer, spirits (with or without mixers). Many newcomers or people who have tried it but "don't like it" may not quite realise that it's quite different to drink wine or a mixed drink at under 20%abv versus a neat single malt, even one at 40%, let alone cask strength. The industry, and many enthusiasts, have long held that whisky and water *dinnae gang thegither*. I think dilution with water (or soda) can offer many people a way of accessing the flavours of whisky without the perceived alcohol burn.

JOHANNA: Truth be told, the Spirit of Toronto Whisky Gala was designed with this kind of person in mind, the one who was curious but never had the opportunity to approach whisky in an accessible, conducive setting. From the outset we've stayed away from billing ourselves as a whisky festival for fear of intimidating those who picture themselves surrounded by anoraks comparing notes on whiskies peated to 1000ppm. Our approach has been to provide a relaxed, elegant venue with excellent food and live jazz whereby newcomers are afforded the opportunity to explore the world of whisky. Our masterclass series is a key component of this formula, with first time whisky drinkers seated next to seasoned connoisseurs, and these sessions are sold out within hours.

JULIA: Don´t try to influence this person with your own preferences by offering him or her only the whiskies you like most! I think it is fairer and more likely to find a new whisky lover if you serve a range of whiskies of various styles – maybe even from all over the world – to let her/him make up his/her own mind! Surprises will be guaranteed!

MAHESH: The single most off putting thing about whisky to a newbie is the 'nose-burn' experience when they try something very crude and strong in alcohol. So what I generally do is to gently coach this person to appreciating whisky. I introduce a very light soft whisky like a Lowland or Speyside (Auchentoshan or Glen Grant), add water to it first and then let them nose it and taste.
I encourage them to use this technique to explore several other expressions and then I ask them to experience all of them neat. Once they graduate from the lighter whiskies they can move up to the big Highland and Islay whiskies.

DUNCAN: I have to do this almost every day, some say start with a blend or a lowlander to ease them in slowly, other will go straight for an Islay, and love it. If you can give them an accurate description of the product then people will 'Give it a go' especially if you have an open bottle of the product in question. You describe, they choose.

Is there such a thing as whisky for women or is it just a male chauvinist way of looking at it?

DONALD: Not at all – more and more women are speaking about whisky and breaking down those once male dominated opinions about whisky. Most women I meet at events enjoy Lagavulin as much as a group of men so the attitude of some whiskies being a "women's dram" is ridiculous and out dated. Enjoying whisky isn't a gender thing but a people thing!

IAN: Personally I don't believe that such a thing exists as a whisky for women. Male or female, anyone who is interested in whisky will be open-minded enough to try many options and you are just as likely to find a woman drinking the big peated Islay whiskies as you will find them with a more delicate lowland.

EDDIE: I don't believe there is such a thing as a whisky only for women and long may that ring true. I think, again, it is a question of engaging with the consumer and being honest with them, not patronising. Too many times we have seen really laughable and sometimes offensive attempts at attracting women into the catgory. They are, and they will continue, discovering it for themselves with help from us, with the same nurturing and treatment given as to anyone entering the whisky world for the first time.

JAMIE: Um... I know several women who would take great offence at the very mention of this idea, so I think it's outdated. Every brand will have a core market of "current drinkers", but surely we're all making whisky that can be enjoyed by anyone? You only have to look at the rising number of women making, marketing, drinking and writing about whisky to see that we're now at the stage where anyone – young, old, male, female – can pick up a glass and not feel as though they're out of place. Exciting times!

JOHANNA: Ah, the woman and whisky question again! While I appreciate the need for marketing types to keep busy, I'm surprised to hear that this outdated old nugget is still being bandied about. Truthfully the only thing more disconcerting than this sort of gender-based nonsense is the "I am woman hear me roar" variety of bloggers and self-promoters who think being a woman who likes whisky is a novelty. The almost 50% female attendance at this year's Spirit of Toronto tells a very different story. Thankfully, from what I can tell, they are there to learn and enjoy themselves rather than make a political statement.

JULIA: More and more women like peaty and smoky whiskies – preferably at cask strength! Is this what men call a "woman´s drink"? More and more men like liqueurs! Is this what men call a "man´s drink"? If yes, then I am fine with these categories!

MAHESH: I am a strong proponent of encouraging women to enjoy whisky. There are more and more women attending tasting events, and this is really helped by the fact that there are some very knowledgeable, passionate women who work in the business and promote the product. At our inaugural whisky show in Las Vegas, I introduced a special event entitled 'Women and Whisky' which was a big hit.

DUNCAN: Women and whisky have been intertwined for years, it was my mother that introduced me to malt whisky (Lagavulin) and she drank many varieties. There are some whiskies that almost have a feminine touch to them but I for one don't use that as a selling aid. As long as they don't put pictures of Brad Pitt or Justin Bieber on bottles I will continue to sell them to everyone.

> *Trying to tell people how they should drink their whisky has always been a controversial issue. Is there any danger in simply saying "Drink it the way you enjoy it"?*

DONALD: I wouldn't tell you how to drink your morning coffee so why should I tell you how to drink your Scotch whisky. Yes, in a structured environment like a lab, then you use the correct glassware, serve at room temperature, analyze the colour, nose and palate etc. If you are sitting at home relaxing, why not add water and ice, or even a splash ginger ale? Yes you may lose a bit of the overall flavour composition but you still have a great drink to relax with.

IAN: Yes, drink it the way you enjoy it but be aware of what you may be missing out on. It´s important to clarify the difference between nosing (and tasting) as against drinking. Nosing is all about the aromas and tastes while drinking is as much about the company, location or how you feel at the time. I am a traditionalist and it´s always water for me.

EDDIE: Absolutely not! We are here to guide, not to lay down rules. An intelligent person will respond far better to being suggested to and then making up their own mind. We have a responsibility to ensure preconceptions are a thing of the past and the only way to do this is to allow and encourage experimentation and freedom of choice. As long as we follow this rule and we show how whisky reacts to water, ice and whatever else – in a positive or negative fashion – we will hopefully provide the consumer with his or her own ideas on how they want to drink whisky.

JAMIE: There's a world of difference between "drinking" and "tasting". We taste to learn and we drink for pleasure. So "tasting" whisky with ice, cola or soda probably isn't the best way to understand the aromas and flavours in that whisky. But if that's what gives you pleasure then it's your drink, so you drink it the way you enjoy it!

JOHANNA: So long as it is not ice or cola being mixed in to my Springbank then I see no danger at all!

JULIA: There is no danger at all. The way people enjoy their whisky has mainly to do with their personal background and cultural history. Nevertheless it is probably helpful to introduce consumers to recommendable techniques to appreciate their whisky even more. At the end of the day they will find out what is best for them.

MAHESH: No! I do not think there is a danger in this. Whisky is a drink made to be enjoyed and everyone's level of enjoyment is different. If you have paid for it, it is yours to enjoy. As a whisky connoisseur I recommend that people try their whisky neat and with a little water to open up the flavors, but I strongly disagree with other experts who try to force people to always drink whisky neat. This approach only pushes new people away from whisky.

DUNCAN: You can't change people's habits easily. If you suggest an alternate way to their norm it may work or it may backfire. There will always be a percentage of the whisky drinking public who will not change and you shouldn't try to force that. Given the opportunity most people are generally prepared to experiment. If you start to dictate drinking methodology the pleasure of drinking the product disappears.

> **Finally, if you were to pick out one whisky trend that will hit us within the near future – what would that be?**

DONALD: More bottlings that don't carry an age statement. Bottling Scotch Whiskies without an age statement isn't about sending young stock out there; it's about taking away the barrier of the age statement and allowing the amazing master blenders and distillers of our industry to produce something incredible. I was once told by a blender that putting an age statement on a bottle was the equivalent to telling Picasso to paint only in Blue! He would make something incredible but think what he could have done with a full array of colours.

IAN: Innovation.... as you look around the globe there are so many new things happening. From the micro-distilling in the US to the success of Japanes whiskies or Indian whiskies to the on-going resurgence of Irish whiskies. Whisky is made across the world now and each new brand brings something new to the table.

EDDIE: A trend is just that. Something that for a short period aims to change the direction of the industry in either a small or large way. I think whisky is too established to allow itself to alter course too dramatically and long may that continue. However, the most important trend, if you can call it that, is for small independent distilleries popping up, seemingly all over the place. This is fantastic news for the category and as long as the quality of these products is good, I have high hopes for the longevity for such projects.

JAMIE: Craft distilling has already taken off in other countries around the world and, although craft UK gins have exploded in recent years, I would love to see a similar growth of craft whisky distilling in the UK. We have a few already, and more on the way, but it's not quite a trend yet.

JOHANNA: The recent proliferation of "instant internet experts" blogging and tweeting about whisky will continue to grow, along with the misinformation that goes with it. While much of the industry now clamours to get on this social media bandwagon, one wonders if it will ultimately find them flailing about in a "rather noisy and smelly souk", to paraphrase whisky's most famous blogger!
Also of note is that while Irish whiskey has enjoyed a veritable renaissance over the past year, American and Canadian whisky won't be far behind. While perhaps not as complex as single malt Scotch, all three of these styles can offer consumers a rich and densely flavoured profile for a significantly lower price, and I see younger whisky drinkers in particular comparison shopping across all styles.

JULIA: For Scotch Whisky I see a trend of multi-cask-maturation. There have been a few releases already which showed great complexity and aromatic richness. So I think the idea of getting the best out of many casks of different origin will be a promising enhancement.
For other countries than Scotland and Ireland I see a trend of whisk(e)y made from aberrating raw material like rye, spelt or wheat together with their malted variations rye malt, spelt malt, wheat malt and others.

MAHESH: Single malts exploded in popularity about twentyfive years ago, and they continue to gain momentum, particularly with the emerging markets. However I think that the next trend is going to be single grain and single aged grain whiskies. They have been very popular at all my tasting events with great reviews. Also given the fact that more women and younger people are getting involved with whisky, this category will gain speed, simply because they are unbiased and open to try different products.

DUNCAN: This is quite fascinating. We live in a world where many countries now produce a 'whisky' of some type. The global potential for these products is limited and some may choose to stay small and local but other may well wish to become international. It needs the large companies to lend a helping hand in marketing these emerging brands for them to succeed. There is enough room in the whisky world for many players but not all players win.

Malt distilleries
of Scotland and Ireland

On the following pages,128 Scottish and Irish distilleries are described in detail. Most are active, while some are mothballed, decommissioned or demolished.

Long since closed distilleries from which whisky is very rare or practically unobtainable are described at the end together with four new and upcoming distilleries.

Japanese malt whisky distilleries are covered on pp. 220-227 and distilleries in other countries on pp. 228-259.

Distilleries that are about to be built or have not left the planning phase yet are treated in the part The Whisky Year That Was (pp. 269-272).

Explanations

Owner:
Name of the owning company, sometimes with the parent company within brackets.

Region/district:
There are four formal malt whisky regions in Scotland today; the Highlands, the Lowlands, Islay and Campbeltown. Where useful we mention a location within a region e.g. Speyside, Orkney, Northern Highlands etc.

Founded:
The year in which the distillery was founded is usually considered as when construction began. The year is rarely the same year in which the distillery was licensed.

Status:
The status of the distillery's production. Active, mothballed (temporarily closed), closed (but most of the equipment still present), dismantled (the equipment is gone but part of or all of the buildings remain even if they are used for other purposes) and demolished.

Visitor centre:
The letters (vc) after status indicate that the distillery has a visitor centre. Many distilleries accept visitors despite not having a visitor centre. It can be worthwhile making an enquiry.

Address:
The distillery's address.

Tel:
This is generally to the visitor centre, but can also be to the main office.

website:
The distillery's (or in some cases the owner's) website.

Capacity:
The current production capacity expressed in litres of pure alcohol (LPA).

History:
The chronology focuses on the official history of the distillery and independent bottlings are only listed in exceptional cases. They can be found in the text bodies instead.

Tasting notes:
For all the Scottish and Irish distilleries that are not permanently closed we present tasting notes of what, in most cases, can be called the core expression (mainly their best selling 10 or 12 year old).

We have tried to provide notes for official bottlings but in those cases where we have not been able to obtain them, we have turned to independent bottlers.

The whiskies have been tasted by *Gavin D Smith* (GS) and *Dominic Roskrow* (DR), well-known and experienced whisky profiles who, i.a., were assigned to write the 6th edition of Michael Jackson's Malt Whisky Companion.

There are also tasting notes for japanese malts and these have been prepared by Chris Bunting.

All notes have been prepared especially for Malt Whisky Yearbook 2013.

Brief distillery glossary

A number of terms occur throughout the distillery directory and are briefly explained here. We can recommend for example *A to Z of Whisky* by Gavin D Smith for more detailed explanations.

Blended malt
A type of whisky where two or more single malts are blended together. The term was introduced a few years ago by SWA to replace the previous term vatted malt. The term is controversial as those who oppose the use of it are of the opinion that it can be confused with 'blended whisky' where malt and grain is blended.

Cask strength
It has become increasingly common in recent times to bottle malt whisky straight from the cask without reducing the alcohol contents to 40, 43 or 46%. A cask strength can be anything between 40 to 65% depending on how long the cask has been matured.

Chill-filtering
A method used for removing unwanted particles and, especially used to prevent the whisky from appearing turbid when water is added. Some producers believe that flavour is affected and therefore avoid chill-filtering.

Continuous still
A type of still used when making grain whisky. The still allows for continuous distillation and re-distillation. Can also be called column still, patent still or Coffey still.

Cooling
The spirit vapours from the stills are cooled into liquids usually by a shell and tube condenser, but an older method (worm tubs) is still in use at some distilleries.

Dark grains
The draff and pot ale from the distillation process is used for making fodder pellets, so-called dark grains.

Drum maltings
The malting method used on all major malting sites today.

Dunnage warehouse
Also called traditional warehouse. The walls are made of stone and the floors of earth. The casks (up to three) are piled on top of each other.

Floor maltings
The traditional method of malting the barley on large wooden floors. This method is only used by a handful of distilleries today.

Lyne arm
The lyne arm leads the spirit vapours from the wash or spirit still to the condenser. The angle of the lyne arm has great significance for reflux and the final character of the whisky.

Mash tun
The procedure after the malt has been milled into grist is called the mashing. The mash tun is usually made of cast iron or stainless steel, but can sometimes be made of wood. The grist is mixed with hot water in order to release the sugars in the barley. The result is the wort which is drawn off through a perforated floor into the underback. The mashed grains in the mash tun are called draff and are then used for making animal feed.

Pagoda roof
A roof shaped as a pagoda which was built over the kiln to lead the smoke away from the drying peat. The pagoda roof was invented by the famous architect Charles Doig. These days pagoda roofs provide mainly aesthetical value as the majority of distilleries usually buy their malt elsewhere.

Peat
A soil layer consisting of plants which have mouldered. Used as fuel in drying the green malts when a more or less peaty whisky is to be produced. In other cases the kiln is usually heated by oil or gas.

PPM
Abbreviation for Parts Per Million. This is used to show the amount of phenols in the peated malt. Peated Islay whisky usually uses malt with 40-60 ppm, which is reduced to 10-20 ppm in the new make spirit.

Purifier
A device used in conjunction with the lyne arm which cools heavier alcohols and lead them back to the still. A handful of distilleries use this technique to make a lighter and cleaner spirit.

Racked warehouse
A modern warehouse with temperature control and built-in shelves. Casks can be stored up to a height of 12.

Reflux
When the heavier vapours in the still are cooled and fall back into the still as liquids. The amount of reflux obtained depends on the shape of the still and the angle of the lyne arm. A distillation process with high reflux gives a lighter, more delicate spirit while a small amount of reflux gives a more robust and flavour-rich whisky.

Saladin box
A method of malting barley which replaced floor maltings. It was invented by the Frenchman Charles Saladin in the late 19th century and was introduced in Scottish distilleries in the 1950s. The only distillery using the method today is Tamdhu.

Shell and tube condenser
The most common method for cooling the spirit vapours. It is a wide copper tube attached to the lyne arm of the still. Cold water is led through a number of smaller copper pipes and cools the surrounding vapours.

Spirit still
The second still, usually a little smaller that the wash still. The low wines are collected in the spirit still for redistilling. Alcohol increases to 64-68% and unwanted impurities disappear. It is only the middle fraction of the distillate (the cut or the heart) which is utilized.

Vatted malt
See blended malt.

Washback
Large tubs of stainless steel or wood in which fermentation takes place. Yeast is added to the worts and the sugars change into alcohol. The result is a wash with an alcoholic content of 6-8% which is then used for distillation.

Wash still
The first and usually largest of the stills. The wash is heated to the boiling point and the alcohol is vaporized. The spirit vapours are cooled in a condenser and the result is low wines with an alcohol content of c 21%.

Worm tub
An older method for cooling the spirit vapours in connection with distilling. This method is still used in approximately ten distilleries. The worm tub consists of a long, spiral-shaped copper pipe which is submerged in water in a large wooden tub, usually outdoors. The spirit vapours are led through the copper spiral so they can condense.

Aberfeldy

Owner:		Region/district:
John Dewar & Sons (Bacardi)		Eastern Highlands

Founded:	Status:	Capacity:
1896	Active (vc)	3 500 000 litres

Address: Aberfeldy, Perthshire PH15 2EB

Tel:	website:
01887 822010 (vc)	www.dewarswow.com

History:

1896 – John and Tommy Dewar embark on the construction of the distillery, a stone's throw from the old Pitilie distillery which was active from 1825 to 1867. Their objective is to produce a single malt for their blended whisky - White Label.

1898 – Production starts in November.

1917-19 – The distillery closes.

1925 – Distillers Company Limited (DCL) takes over.

1972 – Reconstruction takes place, the floor maltings is closed and the two stills are increased to four.

1991 – The first official bottling is a 15 year old in the Flora & Fauna series.

1998 – Bacardi buys John Dewar & Sons from Diageo at a price of £1,150 million.

2000 – A visitor centre opens and a 25 year old is released.

2005 – A 21 year old is launched in October, replacing the 25 year old.

2009 – Two 18 year old single casks are released.

2010 – A 19 year old single cask, exclusive to France, is released.

2011 – A 14 year old single cask is released.

Aberfeldy 12 year old

GS – Sweet, with honeycombs, breakfast cereal and stewed fruits on the nose. Inviting and warming. Mouth-coating and full-bodied on the palate. Sweet, malty, balanced and elegant. The finish is long and complex, becoming progressively more spicy and drying.

DR – The nose is a mix of fresh and clean barley, honey and a hint of smoke. The honey carries through to the palate and the pleasant finish is shaped by a touch of smoke and peppery spice.

Ten years ago, sales of Aberfeldy single malt were negligible, but since then the owners have increased their efforts to promote the brand and it now sells around 300,000 bottles per year. But the focus remains on the blended Scotch for which Aberfeldy is the signature malt, namely Dewar's White Label. Since 1986 it has been the number one blended Scotch in USA but there are reasons for concern. Last year, all the top 12 blended Scotch brands increased their volumes except for two – J&B and Dewar's. Twelve years ago global sales of the brand was 42 million bottles and in 2011 it was down to 38 million. And furthermore, blended Scotch, especially the cheaper expressions, are showing a declining trend in America. That is also why Dewar's are paying more attention to the more exclusive 12 year old version and also introduced an 18 year old a couple of years ago.

Aberfeldy is not just an essential part of the Dewar's blend. The distillery illustrates the heritage dating back to the Dewar brothers who built it and this heritage is also emphasized by Dewar's World of Whiskies, an excellent visitor centre where you can bottle and buy your own exclusive Aberfeldy.

The equipment at Aberfeldy consists of a stainless steel mash tun, eight washbacks made of Siberian larch and two made of stainless steel. The fermentation time varies between 65 and 88 hours. To achieve the desired character, the distillation in the four stills is slow with quite long foreshots (25 minutes) in the spirit stills. As from 2012 the distillery will be working a 7-day week producing 2,8 million litres of alcohol.

The core range consists of *12* and *21 year old*. Single casks also appear from time to time. In 2011 it was a *14 year old single bourbon cask* with three years in a sherry hogshead and 2012 saw the release of a *16 year old finished in a Sassicaia cask*.

12 years old

Meet the Manager

CAROL MORE
DISTILLERY MANAGER, ABERFELDY DISTILLERY

When did you start working in the whisky business and when did you start at Aberfeldy?

I started in the whisky industry in January 2002 and came to Aberfeldy distillery in 2008.

Had you been working in other lines of business before whisky?

I had a variety of other jobs ranging from an au pair in France to a subscriptions manager for a Writing Magazine but nothing I could really get my teeth into!

What kind of education or training do you have?

I have an HND in Business Studies with languages (French and German) which I completed when I left school. Since joining John Dewar & Sons I have completed the General Certificate in Distilling, more recently a Diploma in Distilling and in additional a number of health & safety qualifications.

Describe your career in the whisky business.

My career began in 2002 as Administrator at Royal Brackla distillery. My interview for the position was the first time I had set foot inside a distillery. In 2005 I moved on to being Trainee Production Manager which involved spending time at each of the other Dewars' distilleries, being involved in various projects and basically gaining more experience in the more technical side to distilling. In 2008 I was seconded to Aberfeldy Distillery covering for the Production Manager, Paul Lobar for around 10 months and in 2009 this role became permanent.

What are your main tasks as a manager?

Everything that happens on site falls under my remit, apart from the Visitor Centre, Dewars World of Whisky, which is run separately. My main task in overseeing the production process – everything from raw materials in to new make spirit out, and ensuring we meet our annual production targets. Aberfeldy is very busy site – we have an effluent treatment plant on site where washing waters from the mash house, spent lees from the stillhouse and foul condensate from the evaporator plant are processed. We also have an evaporator plant for processing pot ale into pot ale syrup. Health and safety matters, customs issues, contractor control, keeping an

eye on budgets, ensuring co-products are produced in accordance to FEMAS guidelines and contracts.

What are the biggest challenges of being a distillery manager?

Juggling all the hats that I need to wear!

What would be the worst that could go wrong in the production process?

Having a major breakdown which would entail a loss of production, resulting in not being able to fulfil the year's spirit requirements.

How would you describe the character of Aberfeldy single malt?

Floral notes of heather and the sweetness of honey, develops with rich notes of vanilla and toasted cereals – very drinkable!

What are the main features in the process at Aberfeldy, contributing to this character?

We aim to get the washbacks switching during fermentation, run the spirit stills at a slow, steady distillation rate when they are on spirit to increase copper contact.

What is your favourite expression of Aberfeldy and why?

I love the 21 year old Aberfeldy. Lovely dram, easy to drink.

If it were your decision alone – what new expression of Aberfeldy would you like to see released?

I'd like to see more single cask bottlings of Aberfeldy. There have been a few limited edition cask strength bottlings over the last couple of years that have proved to be very popular.

If you had to choose a favourite dram other than Aberfeldy, what would that be?

Dewars 12 or a Dewars 18 year old.

What are the biggest changes you have seen the past 10 years in your profession and do you see any major changes in the next 10 years to come?

More paperwork, more emphasis on energy savings and reducing water usage.

Do you have any special interests or hobbies that you pursue?

I used to call the evaporator plant my hobby! I like cooking and baking, although not for myself – when I have visitors I do enjoy putting on a feast. Normally cook something with a Chinese slant and enjoy experimenting with new recipes. I have also just taken up cycling again – Aberfeldy is a lovely location so I just need some decent weather to benefit from the lovely scenery we have around here.

You have a magnificent visitor centre focused on Dewar's blended Scotch. Do you sometimes feel that Aberfeldy single malt doesn't get the attention it deserves?

No I think it is important the visitors learn the connection between the distillery and Dewar's. The visitors have the option of tasting the 12 year old Single Malt at the dramming bar and now the visitor centre have two self-fill stations where visitors can fill their own bottle of Aberfeldy Cask Strength single malt.

You have six warehouses on site that are no longer used for storage. How are they used today?

A variety of uses – we use part of one as a storage area for spares, the evaporator plant is hidden away in the middle warehouses where we process our pot ale and turn into pot ale syrup which is sold for animal feed. The old filling store is part of the visitor centre tour and part of one of the warehouses has recently been refurbished to tell the maturation story on the tour.

Aberlour

Owner:
Chivas Brothers Ltd
(Pernod Ricard)

Region/district:
Speyside

Founded: **Status:**
1826   Active (vc)

Capacity:
3 700 000 litres

Address: Aberlour, Banffshire AB38 9PJ

Tel:
01340 881249

website:
www.aberlour.com

History:

1826 – James Gordon and Peter Weir found the first Aberlour Distillery.

1827 – Peter Weir withdraws and James Gordon continues alone.

1879 – A fire devastates most of the distillery. The local banker James Fleming constructs a new distillery a few kilometres upstream the Spey river.

1892 – The distillery is sold to Robert Thorne & Sons Ltd who expands it.

1898 – Another fire rages and almost totally destroys the distillery. The architect Charles Doig is called in to design the new facilities.

1921 – Robert Thorne & Sons Ltd sells Aberlour to a brewery, W. H. Holt & Sons.

1945 – S. Campbell & Sons Ltd buys the distillery.

1962 – Aberlour terminates floor malting.

1973 – Number of stills are increased from two to four.

1975 – Pernod Ricard buys Campbell Distilleries.

2000 – Aberlour a´bunadh is launched. A limited 30 year old cask strength is released.

2001 – Pernod Ricard buys Chivas Brothers from Seagrams and merges Chivas Brothers and Campbell Distilleries under the brand Chivas Brothers.

2002 – A new, modernized visitor centre is inaugurated in August.

2008 – The 18 year old is also introduced outside France.

Aberlour 12 year old

GS – The nose offers brown sugar, honey and sherry, with a hint of grapefruit citrus. The palate is sweet, with buttery caramel, maple syrup and eating apples. Liquorice, peppery oak and mild smoke in the finish.

DR – The nose combines horse chestnut casing then sweet melon and fresh spearmint, the taste is beautifully fresh and clean, with mint and gentle fruit.

Aberlour is a well-known single malt, no doubt about that, but being owned by Chivas Brothers means that it will always be the little brother of megastar Glenlivet. Regardless, Aberlour is one of the most sold malts in the world and the 2.6 million bottles sold in 2011 gives the brand a number 6 spot on the global sales chart. The number one market, by far, is France where it is the most sold Scotch single malt, but it has also become highly popular in the USA, the UK and in the duty free market.

Aberlour distillery lies on the outskirts of the town with the same name and the first building you see from the road is the 5-star visitor centre. Only around 6,000 visitors come every year, but Aberlour was one of the first distilleries to start concentrating on exclusive quality tours, instead of catering for the masses.

The distillery is equipped with one 12 tonnes semi-lauter mash tun, six stainless steel washbacks (painted white) and two pairs of stills. One of the wash stills was replaced in June 2011. There are five warehouses on site (three racked and two dunnage) but only two racked, holding a total of 27,000 casks, are used for maturation. About half of the production is used for single malts. The packaging of the whole range was upgraded in 2010 to achieve a more consistent look.

The core range of Aberlour includes a *10 year old* (sherry/bourbon), a *12 year old Double Cask* matured, a *16 year old Double Cask* matured, an *18 year old* and *a'bunadh*, of which there are 41 batches that have been launched up to and including August 2012. In France, a *10 year old Sherry Cask Finish* and the *15 year Cuvée Marie d'Ecosse* are available. Two 'exclusives' are available for the duty free market – a *12 year old sherry matured* and a *15 year old Double Cask matured*. A new version of the *12 year old*, this time *non chill-filtered*, was introduced to the French market at the beginning of 2012 and was later also launched in the USA.

12 years old

Allt-a-Bhainne

Owner:	Region/district:
Chivas Brothers Ltd (Pernod Ricard)	Speyside

Founded:	Status:	Capacity:
1975	Active	4 000 000 litres

Address: Glenrinnes, Dufftown, Banffshire AB55 4DB

Tel:	website:
01542 783200	-

History:

1975 – The distillery is founded by Chivas Brothers, a subsidiary of Seagrams, in order to secure malt whisky for its blended whiskies. The total cost amounts to £2.7 million.

1989 – Production has doubled.

2001 – Pernod Ricard takes over Chivas Brothers from Seagrams.

2002 – Mothballed in October.

2005 – Production restarts in May.

Few places in Scotland are as beautiful as the area in the Cromdale Hills between Tomintoul and Dufftown. A part of it consists of the Glen of the Livet named after the river which blends into the Avon while meandering its way towards the coast. The star distillery in this part of Scotland is Glenlivet but there are a few considerably less famous distilleries in the area, of which Allt-a-bhainne is one. Built in the mid 1970s this has always been a producer of malt whisky for blends and in particular 100 Pipers, a brand introduced in 1966 by the legendary Sam Bronfman of Seagrams. The idea was to challenge the big sellers on the American market at that time and 40 years of constant rising sales-figures followed. The last few years have been challenging and during 2011 (when 20 million bottles were sold, particularly in Thailand) 100 Pipers was one of the few brands that decreased their sales.

The distillery is equipped with a traditional mash tun with rakes and ploughs. The rest of the equipment consists of eight stainless steel washbacks and two pairs of stills. The distillery is a busy place working 7 days a week with 25 mashes resulting in 4 million litres of alcohol per year. Chivas Brothers has no distillery on Islay so, to cover their need of peated whisky for their blends, they need to resort to other solutions. During the last few years 50% of the production at Allt-a-bhainne has therefore been peated spirit with a phenol content in the malted barley of 10ppm. The whisky is transported by lorry to a facility in Keith for filling. In order to make the distillery more energy efficient, thermal compressors were installed in 2011, similar to the other distilleries in the Chivas group.

There are no official bottlings of Allt-a-Bhainne and according to Chivas Brothers there are no plans for any either. Independent bottlings can be found, though, in the form of Deerstalker 12 year old from Aberko.

Deerstalker 12 year old

GS – Cereal and toffee on the sherbety nose, with mildly metallic notes. The palate is light, with fresh fruits. Medium length and warming in the finish.

DR – Autumn fields and damp hay on the nose, a richer, sweeter earth and heathery taste on the palate and a gentle rounded finish.

Deerstalker 12 year old

Ardbeg

Owner:
The Glenmorangie Co
(Moët Hennessy)

Region/district:
Islay

Founded: **Status:** **Capacity:**
1815   Active (vc)   1 150 000 litres

Address: Port Ellen, Islay, Argyll PA42 7EA

Tel: **website:**
01496 302244 (vc)   www.ardbeg.com

History:
1794 – First record of a distillery at Ardbeg. It was founded by Alexander Stewart.

1798 – The MacDougalls, later to become licensees of Ardbeg, are active on the site through Duncan MacDougall.

1815 – The current distillery is founded by John MacDougall, son of Duncan MacDougall.

1853 – Alexander MacDougall, John's son, dies and sisters Margaret and Flora MacDougall, assisted by Colin Hay, continue the running of the distillery. Colin Hay takes over the licence when the sisters die.

1888 – Colin Elliot Hay and Alexander Wilson Gray Buchanan renew their license.

1900 – Colin Hay's son takes over the license.

1959 – Ardbeg Distillery Ltd is founded.

1973 – Hiram Walker and Distillers Company Ltd jointly purchase the distillery for £300,000 through Ardbeg Distillery Trust.

1974 – Widely considered as the last vintage of 'old, peaty' Ardbeg. Malt which has not been produced in the distillery's own maltings is used in increasingly larger shares after this year.

1977 – Hiram Walker assumes single control of the distillery. Ardbeg closes its maltings.

1979 – Kildalton, a less peated malt, is produced over a number of years.

1981 – The distillery closes in March.

1987 – Allied Lyons takes over Hiram Walker and thereby Ardbeg.

It is hard to imagine that this iconic distillery with its devoted followers around the world was on the verge of being demolished in 1996. The distillery suffered under the ownership of Hiram Walker and then Allied until Glenmorangie came to the rescue and bought it in 1997.

In autumn 2011, Ardbeg distillery was invited to take part in a spectacular 2-year experiment in space! Vials of Ardbeg-crafted molecules were sent up to the International Space Station by a Soyuz rocket from Baikanor in Kazakhstan. The goal is to study the change that these molecules undergo at zero-gravity compared to control samples in warehouse 3 at the distillery on Islay.

The distillery is equipped with a stainless steel semilauter mash tun, six washbacks made of Oregon pine with a fermentation time of 55 hours and one pair of stills. The single malt from Ardbeg is by all definitions heavily peated, but compared to the other two Kildalton distilleries, Lagavulin and Laphroaig, it doesn't come off as smoky. One of the reasons is that the purifier which is connected to the spirit still increases the reflux and adds a fruity note and also that the spirit run is already cut at 62,5% to avoid the most pungent types of phenols. During 2012, the distillery will be running a 5-day week with 12 mashes and around 1 million litres in the year.

The core range consists of the *10 year old, Uiegedail, Blasda* and *Corryvreckan*. Blasda, which is lightly peated (8ppm), was first released in 2008. The peatiest ever release from Ardbeg, is *Supernova* and was released for the first time in early 2009. Its phenol level was well in excess of 100ppm. The second edition, *Supernova 2010*, was released in May 2010. Limited releases in 2010 and 2011 included *Rollercoaster*, a vatting of one cask from each year between 1997 and 2006 and *Ardbeg Alligator*, where some of the whisky had been matured in heavily charred barrels. To celebrate the space experiment mentioned earlier, a limited *Ardbeg Galileo* was released in September 2012. It is a 12 year old and a combination of different casks, all filled in 1999. The core element in the whisky comes from Marsala casks. In common with all the other distilleries on Islay, Ardbeg releases a special bottling every year in connection with the Islay Festival. In 2012 it was a little special as the owners had decided that 2nd of June henceforth should be called Ardbeg Day. So, this year's Feis Ile bottling was also named *Ardbeg Day*. It is a blend of two vintages matured in ex-bourbon casks and then finished for six months In sherry casks.

History (continued):

1989 – Production is restored. All malt is taken from Port Ellen.

1996 – The distillery closes in July and Allied Distillers decides to put it up for sale.

1997 – Glenmorangie plc buys the distillery for £7 million (whereof £5.5 million is for whisky in storage). On stream from 25th June. Ardbeg 17 years old and Provenance are launched

1998 – A new visitor centre opens.

2000 – Ardbeg 10 years is introduced. The Ardbeg Committee is launched and has 30 000 members after a few years.

2001 – Lord of the Isles 25 years and Ardbeg 1977 are launched.

2002 – Ardbeg Committee Reserve and Ardbeg 1974 are launched.

2003 – Uigeadail is launched.

2004 – Very Young Ardbeg (6 years) and a limited edition of Ardbeg Kildalton (1300 bottles) are launched. The latter is an un-peated cask strength from 1980.

2005 – Serendipity is launched.

2006 – Ardbeg 1965 and Still Young are launched. Distillery Manager Stuart Thomson leaves Ardbeg after nine years. Almost There (9 years old) and Airigh Nam Beist are released.

2007 – Ardbeg Mor, a 10 year old in 4.5 litre bottles is released.

2008 – The new 10 year old, Corryvreckan, Rennaissance, Blasda and Mor II are released.

2009 – Supernova is released, the peatiest expression from Ardbeg ever.

2010 – Rollercoaster and Supernova 2010 are released.

2011 – Ardbeg Alligator is released.

2012 – Ardbeg Day and Galileo are released.

Ardbeg 10 year old

GS – Quite sweet on the nose, with soft peat, carbolic soap and Arbroath smokies. Burning peats and dried fruit, followed by sweeter notes of malt and a touch of liquorice in the mouth. Extremely long and smoky in the finish, with a fine balance of cereal sweetness and dry peat notes.

DR – Intense smoke and tar on the nose but with some distinctive sweet lemon notes, a mouth-coating palate with honeyed but firey peat, completely balanced and impressive, and a long smoke tail at the finish.

Uigeadail

Ardbeg Day

Galileo

10 years old

Corryvreckan

Ardmore

Owner:
Beam Global
Spirits & Wine

Region/district:
Highland

Founded: **Status:**   **Capacity:**
1898   Active   5 200 000 litres

Address: Kennethmont,
Aberdeenshire AB54 4NH

Tel: **website:**
01464 831213   www.ardmorewhisky.com

History:
1898 – Adam Teacher, son of William Teacher, starts the construction of Ardmore Distillery which eventually becomes William Teacher & Sons´ first distillery. Adam Teacher passes away before it is completed.

1955 – Stills are increased from two to four.

1973 – A visitor centre is constructed.

1974 – Another four stills are added, increasing the total to eight.

1976 – Allied Breweries takes over William Teacher & Sons and thereby also Ardmore. The own maltings (Saladin box) is terminated.

1999 – A 12 year old is released to commemorate the distillery's 100th anniversary. A 21 year old is launched in a limited edition.

2002 – Ardmore is one of the last distilleries to abandon direct heating (by coal) of the stills in favour of indirect heating through steam.

2005 – Jim Beam Brands becomes new owner when it takes over some 20 spirits and wine brands from Allied Domecq for five billion dollars.

2007 – Ardmore Traditional Cask is launched.

2008 – A 25 and a 30 year old are launched.

Ardmore Traditional

GS – A nose of smoked haddock and butter, plus sweet, fruity malt and spices. Sweet and initially creamy on the palate, spices, peat smoke, tobacco and vanilla emerge and blend together. The finish is long and mellow.

DR – Unique and remarkable mix of burnt meat savouriness on the nose, and a delicatessen of flavours on the palate, smoked vanilla, burnt fruit and a distinctive and highly addictive sweet and savoury mix towards the peated finish.

Ardmore has in recent years been launched as a single malt, but even so, it is the distillery's main task to produce whisky for the owner´s big seller – the blended Scotch Teacher´s. In 2011, the brand sold just over 24 million bottles (an increase by 9%) but the biggest achievement was that it took the No. 1 position in India from Johnnie Walker. In December 2011, a 25 year old version of Teacher´s blend, the oldest so far, was launched to further point out how important the Indian market is. At the same time, a Teacher´s Highland Single Malt (obviously from Ardmore) was released.

Ardmore has always been known to use peated malt (12-14 ppm) but there is also an unpeated version being produced, called Ardlair, which is used by other companies as a blending malt. For 2012 the share of Ardlair will equate to about 30% of the total amount.

Ten years ago, Ardmore was one of the last distilleries in Scotland to abandon the practise of directly firing the stills using coal. Such a dramatic change can easily change the character of the whisky and the owners had to put in a lot of work changing other parameters such as the cut points of the spirit distillation in order to maintain the style.

The distillery is equipped with a large (12.5 tonnes) cast iron mash tun, 14 Douglas fir washbacks and four pairs of stills equipped with sub-coolers to give more copper contact.

At the moment, Ardmore is doing 24 mashes per week resulting in 5,2 million litres. Mostly ex bourbon barrels are filled, but a few Pedro Ximenez sherry, port and cognac casks can also be found in the warehouses.

The core expression is the un-chill filtered *Traditional* with no age statement, but generally made up using a range of ex-bourbon casks from six to thirteen years old. After vatting, it is filled into quarter casks where it is allowed to mature for another year before being bottled. In 2008 a *25 year old* was launched for UK and duty free, while a *30 year old* was released for the American market.

Ardmore Traditional Cask

Arran

Owner: Region/district:
Isle of Arran Distillers   Islands (Arran)

Founded: Status: Capacity:
1993   Active (vc)   750 000 litres

Address: Lochranza, Isle of Arran KA27 8HJ

Tel: website:
01770 830264   www.arranwhisky.com

History:
1993 – Harold Currie founds the distillery.

1995 – Production starts in full on 17th August.

1996 – A one year old spirit is released.

1997 – A visitor centre is opened by the Queen.

1998 – The first release is a 3 year old.

1999 – The Arran 4 years old is released.

2002 – Single Cask 1995 is launched.

2003 – Single Cask 1997, non-chill filtered and Calvados finish is launched.

2004 – Cognac finish, Marsala finish, Port finish and Arran First Distillation 1995 are launched.

2005 – Arran 1996 and two finishes, Ch. Margaux and Grand Cru Champagne, are launched.

2006 – After an unofficial launch in 2005, Arran 10 years old is released as well as a couple of new wood finishes.

2007 – Four new wood finishes and Gordon´s Dram are released.

2008 – The first 12 year old is released as well as four new wood finishes.

2009 – Peated single casks, two wood finishes and 1996 Vintage are released.

2010 – A 14 year old, Rowan Tree, three cask finishes and Machrie Moor (peated) are released.

2011 – The Westie, Sleeping Warrior and a 12 year old cask strength are released.

2012 – The Eagle and The Devil´s Punch Bowl are released.

Arran 14 year old

GS – Very fragrant and perfumed on the nose, with peaches, brandy and ginger snaps. Smooth and creamy on the palate, with spicy summer fruits, apricots and nuts. The lingering finish is nutty and slowly drying.

DR – The precocious ten year old becomes a testy teenager. If the 12 year old was a diversion this is right on track - with sweet, fresh and zesty nose, and rich creamy and rounded palate defined by vanilla, lemon and cream soda. The finish is long and full.

It is difficult to regard Arran distillery as anything but a newcomer to the business , after all, it started production as late as 1995. If you look at what they have accomplished during that time however, it seems as they´ve been around for a long time. They have an interesting range of whiskies with an 18 year old due in two years. Some 60,000 visitors come to Lochranza every year and last year the company made a profit of £250,000 with a turnover of more than £3 million and 180,000 bottles sold.

The distillery is equipped with a semi-lauter mash tun, five Oregon pine washbacks (the last one installed in 2012) and two stills. One dunnage warehouse holds 3,000 casks and there is a racked warehouse with a similar capacity. A third, palletised warehouse was taken into use in May 2012. The total production capacity is 750,000 litres and the plan for 2012 is to do 400,000 litres. For many years now, the distillery has been producing a share of peated spirit every year. For 2012 it will be 40,000 litres from malt peated to 20ppm which will be used for future releases of Machrie Moor. For this once they also produce 20,000 litres of heavily peated spirit (50ppm).

The core range consists of The Arran Malt Original (destined for select markets and without age statement), 10, 12 cask strength and 14 years old and finally Robert Burns Malt. The last one used to be 5 years old but it was re-launched in September 2012, bottled at 43% instead of 40% and included some older whiskies as well. Limited releases for 2012 are The Eagle from 1999 (the final release from the Icons series which started in 2009), The Devil´s Punch Bowl which is a vatting of some of their oldest casks – selected by their Master Distiller and Blender James MacTaggart and bottled at cask strength – and the third edition of the peated Machrie Moor. Finally, the single malt range is completed with three different cask finishes – Amarone, Port and Sauternes. The distillery also produces two blends (Robert Burns and Lochranza) and a cream liqueur called Arran Gold.

14 years old

Auchentoshan

Owner:
Morrison Bowmore
(Suntory)

Region/district:
Lowlands

Founded: 1823
Status: Active (vc)
Capacity: 1 750 000 litres

Address: Dalmuir, Clydebank, Glasgow G81 4SJ

Tel: 01389 878561
website: www.auchentoshan.com

History:

1800 – First mention of the distillery Duntocher, which may be identical to Auchentoshan.

1823 – An official license is obtained by the owner, Mr. Thorne.

1903 – The distillery is purchased by John Maclachlan.

1923 – G. & J. Maclachlan goes bankrupt and a new company, Maclachlans Ltd, is formed.

1941 – The distillery is severely damaged by a German bomb raid.

1960 – Maclachlans Ltd is purchased by the brewery J. & R. Tennant Brewers.

1969 – Auchentoshan is bought by Eadie Cairns Ltd who starts major modernizations.

1984 – Stanley P. Morrison, eventually becoming Morrison Bowmore, becomes new owner.

1994 – Suntory buys Morrison Bowmore.

2002 – Auchentoshan Three Wood is launched.

2004 – More than a £1 million is spent on a new, refurbished visitor centre. The oldest Auchentoshan ever, 42 years, is released.

2006 – Auchentoshan 18 year old is released.

2007 – A 40 year old and a 1976 30 year old are released.

2008 – New packaging as well as new expressions - Classic, 18 year old and 1988.

2010 – Two vintages, 1977 and 1998, are released.

2011 – Two vintages, 1975 and 1999, and Valinch are released.

2012 – Six new expressions are launched for the Duty Free market.

The sales figures for Auchentoshan single malt has increased steadily over the last few years and during 2011 well over 600,000 bottles were sold. The increased demand has now forced the owners to increase production and for 2012 they will be doing 13 mashes per week which will yield 1,6 million litres of alcohol for the year – by far the highest production level for the last 20 years.

Auchentoshan is the only distillery in Scotland doing 100% triple distillation. This procedure means, among other things, having a very narrow spirit cut. At Auchentoshan they start collecting the middle cut at 82% and stop at 80%, long before any other distillery starts collecting. It gives a very fruity and clean spirit which is then diluted to the usual 63,5% before going into cask. The equipment consists of a semilauter mash tun, seven Oregon pine washbacks and three stills. Auchentoshan also has an exquisite visitor centre in a very contemporary style which includes a wooden bar, shaped like a circle.

The core range consists of *Classic, 12 years, Three Wood, 18 years* and *21 years*. The owner of Auchentoshan, Morrison Bowmore, is one of the producers who invests heavily in the duty free market and during 2012 they launched no less than six new expressions; *Springwood* (40%, no age statement, bourbon matured), *Heartwood* (43%, no age statement, bourbon/oloroso), *Cooper's Reserve* (46%, 14 years old, bourbon/oloroso), *Silveroak* (51,5%, Vintage 1991, bourbon/oloroso), *Solera* (48%, older whiskies, different types of oak with a finish in Pedro Ximenez casks) and, finally, a *Vintage 1974. Select* (no age statement) has been moved to the duty free range. The most recent limited releases (from 2011) were *1975 bourbon* maturation and *1999 Bordeaux wine* maturation. Finally, there is the *Valinch*, basically a cask strength, unchillfiltered version of the Classic, which is released in a new version every year which coincides with the Auchentoshan Festival in June.

Auchentoshan 12 year old

GS – The nose features fruit & nut chocolate, cinnamon and oak. Smooth and sweet in the mouth, with citrus fruits and cloves. Drying gently in a gingery finish.

DR – Toffee, rose water and Milk Chocolate Crisp on the nose, grape and crisp apple on the palate before a spicy fruity interplay in a lengthy finish.

12 years old

An Introduction to Whisky Cocktails

Some years ago, mixing drinks with single malt whisky was more or less considered a mortal sin. Well not anymore - on the contrary, skilled bartenders around the world excel with new creations involving malts. To let you try the same at home, we asked Ryan Chetiyawardana to share a few tips.

Whisky cocktails are often greeted with hesitation – be it from those who do drink whisky, or by those who don't drink whisky. For those who don't drink whisky, they fear the flavours will be too dominant, and the drinks will be strong, rich and 'old fashioned'. For those who drink whisky, they worry the cocktail will detract from the whisky's qualities, and mask the nuances.

As with whisky itself, there are a huge range of cocktails, and the best will play up to the intrinsic character of the base spirit. Crucially, I have introduced many more staunch whiskyphobics to the wonderful range of flavours that can be found in single malts using cocktails, and I couldn't have done this by simply asking them to taste the spirit individually.

A good cocktail is balanced, and suited to an occasion. Sometimes you need a bright, lifting drink, other times you need something rich and warming. With the plethora of styles found in single malts - ranging from light and floral through to dry and heavily peated - the spirit is adapt at creating a huge style of drinks that can be enjoyed in many different scenarios. Similarly, as there are so many flavours contained in each drop, a cocktail is perfect for opening out different notes of a whisky showcasing a different facet to suit your mood.

As a starting suggestion, I'd recommend focussing on a particular note you really enjoy in a certain spirit and couple this with something that will emphasise and bolster this detail. The key is balance though, so getting to grips with a few basics is key to making sure you make the most of your creation. I've included a few suggestions that will help:

Paisley Pattern

A simple twist on the hi-ball that creates a wonderfully refreshing drink perfect for summer. It lifts the spice from the whisky and draws out the flavours so they last on the tongue.

40ml Great King Street
10ml Elderflower cordial
Sprig of Tarragon
Lemon Zest
1 dash grapefruit bitters
Soda

Build whisky, bitters and cordial over cubed ice in a sling glass. Stir, add more ice, tarragon and top with soda. Garnish with a lemon zest

Whisky Sour

Sometimes the simplest drinks are the best. The classic whisky sour is a wonderfully refreshing drink that's great for pulling apart the flavours of the base spirit. The key is balance, but experiment with switching the base malt, and also matching different souring agents, different bitters and different sweeteners.

50ml Balvenie Doublewood
25ml lemon juice
25ml egg white
15ml sugar syrup
2 dashes angostura bitters

Shake all ingredients without ice, shake hard with cubed ice and double strain into a chilled cocktail glass (or over ice if you prefer). Garnish with an orange zes

The Monarch

Based around one of my favourite malts to mix- Talisker. The absinthe is almost sub-strata; more there to lift some of the fruit and pepper notes. A simple, classic leaning combination that is both clean and uplifting.

40ml Talisker 10
15ml Lillet Blanc

Ryan Chetiyawardana is an award winning bartender and Creative Director of Mr Lyan. He has been involved in the international cocktail scene for many years, helping to develop some of the UK's best bars including Bramble, 69 Colebrooke Row and The Whistling Shop. He is currently exploring creative consultancy for cocktails and product development. www.sipstir.co.uk

Dash sugar syrup
Absinthe rinse

Stir over cubed ice, and double strain into a small, chilled cocktail glass rinsed with absinthe. Garnish with a mint sprig.

Ceres Joker

A rich, fireside drink, that nonetheless is fresh and clean. Centered around Dalmore 15 to showcase its sherried character but create an approachable drink, brilliant for bringing new whisky drinkers into the fold. In the bar, I garnished this with a burnt twist (a fused, lemon-scented balloon) to mimic the slight gunpowder note sometimes found in sherry casked whiskies.

25ml Dalmore 15
25ml Sloe Gin
15ml Sugar syrup (2parts sugar dissolved in 1 part water)
3 dashes Ginger bitters
25ml egg white

Shake all ingredients without ice, then shake hard over cubed ice. Double strain into a chilled cocktail glass and garnish with a lemon twist and a few drops of ginger bitters on the top.

Auchroisk

Owner: Diageo

Region/district: Speyside

Founded: 1974

Status: Active

Capacity: 5 000 000 litres

Address: Mulben, Banffshire AB55 6XS

Tel: 01542 885000

website: www.malts.com

History:
1972 – Building of the distillery commences by Justerini & Brooks (which, together with W. A. Gilbey, make up the group IDV) in order to produce blending whisky. In February the same year IDV is purchased by the brewery Watney Mann which, in July, merges into Grand Metropolitan.

1974 – The distillery is completed and, despite the intention of producing malt for blending, the first year's production is sold 12 years later as single malt thanks to the high quality.

1986 – The first whisky is marketed under the name Singleton.

1997 – Grand Metropolitan and Guinness merge into the conglomerate Diageo. Simultaneously, the subsidiaries United Distillers (to Guinness) and International Distillers & Vintners (to Grand Metropolitan) form the new company United Distillers & Vintners (UDV).

2001 – The name Singleton is abandoned and the whisky is now marketed under the name of Auchroisk in the Flora & Fauna series.

2003 – Apart from the 10 year old in the Flora & Fauna series, a 28 year old from 1974, the distillery's first year, is launched in the Rare Malt series.

2010 – A Manager's Choice single cask and a limited 20 year old are released.

2012 – A 30 year old from 1982 is released.

Auchroisk 10 year old
GS – Malt and spice on the light nose, with developing nuts and floral notes. Quite voluptuous on the palate, with fresh fruit and milk chocolate. Raisins in the finish.

DR – Young and zesty and citrusy on the nose, warming tangerine and citrus fruits and a touch of salt on the palate, medium long malty finish.

When Auchroisk distillery was built in 1974, the Scotch whisky industry was filled with optimism. No less than 16 distilleries were opened from 1960 to 1975 and only three were closed in the same period. But things changed – the demand decreased, a whisky loch was created and during the 1980s no distilleries were opened but 17 were closed – all of them permanently with the exception of Glenglassaugh.

Auchroisk distillery is equipped with a 12 tonnes stainless steel semilauter mash tun, eight stainless steel washbacks and four pairs of stills. The spacious still house, with four stills on each side, was a role model for the still house at the latest of Diageo´s distilleries, Roseisle. Auchroisk is the location for maturing whiskies from many other Diageo distilleries and also for part of the blending. In order to achieve this there are ten huge, racked warehouses with the capacity of storing 250,000 casks.

The character of Auchroisk new-make used to be nutty but changed in 2011/2012 to become green and grassy. Although this is something that a producer never would do with a distillery marketed mainly as a single malt, it is not uncommon with whiskies destined to become a part of a blend. It all depends on which type the producer requires in the interim. To achieve the new character, they have changed to a clear wort and the fermentations are now longer, 75 hours compared to the previous 48 hours. The distillery is now working 24/7 which means a production of 5 million litres of alcohol during 2012.

Apart from producing whisky, mainly for the J&B blend, Auchroisk is also a backup for production of Gordon´s gin, should any problems occur at Cameronbridge distillery.

The core range from Auchroisk is simply the *10 year old Flora & Fauna* bottling. Recently though, the distillery has become better known. First in 2010 when a *20 year old* from 1990 was launched and later, in 2012, when a *30 year old*, the oldest Auchroisk ever released by the owners, was launched as a part of the Special Releases.

30 years old

Aultmore

Owner:
John Dewar & Sons
(Bacardi)

Region/district:
Speyside

Founded: **Status:** **Capacity:**
1896   Active   3 030 000 litres

Address: Keith, Banffshire AB55 6QY

Tel: **website:**
01542 881800   -

History:
1896 – Alexander Edward, owner of Benrinnes and co-founder of Craigellachie Distillery, builds Aultmore.

1897 – Production starts.

1898 – Production is doubled; the company Oban & Aultmore Glenlivet Distilleries Ltd manages Aultmore.

1923 – Alexander Edward sells Aultmore for £20,000 to John Dewar & Sons.

1925 – Dewar's becomes part of Distillers Company Limited (DCL).

1930 – The administration is transferred to Scottish Malt Distillers (SMD).

1971 – The stills are increased from two to four.

1991 – UDV launches a 12-year old Aultmore in the Flora & Fauna series.

1996 – A 21 year old cask strength is marketed as a Rare Malt.

1998 – Diageo sells Dewar's and Bombay Gin to Bacardi for £1,150 million.

2004 – A new official bottling is launched (12 years old).

Aultmore 12 year old

GS – Gentle spice and fudge notes on the fragrant nose. Fresh fruits and restrained vanilla in the mouth. Nutty and drying in a medium-length finish.

DR – Orange blossom and flowers on the nose, lemon and lime Starburst on the palate, with late sherbet spicy and drying and more-ish finish. Altogether, zesty and very pleasant.

Aultmore distillery is part of Dewar's – a company that was founded as early as 1846. By 1900 the company had grown considerably and sold one million gallons of whisky for the first time and in 1906 their famous brand, White Label, was established. At that time the company, together with John Walker & Co. and James Buchanan & Co., were referred to as "The Big Three". In order to minimize the large costs of marketing and advertising, which was a consequence of tough competition, a merger between the three giants was already discussed in 1909 but without effect. When consumption fell in the 1920s, the situation became more acute and, finally in 1925, The Big Three joined forces with DCL which had already been formed in 1877 by six grain distilleries. DCL then came to dominate the market for many years and became the foundation for today's Diageo.

Aultmore distillery was built as early as 1896 but when you travel the A96 and look to your left, a mile before you reach Keith, you see a very modern, shining, white, complex of buildings. The distillery was completely rebuilt at the beginning of the 1970s and nothing is left of the old buildings.

Since 2008 production has been running seven days a week which, for 2012, means 2,6 million litres of alcohol. A Steinecker full lauter mash tun, six washbacks made of larch and two pairs of stills are operated. The stillhouse control system was modernised in 2008. All the warehouses were demolished in 1996; in fact, Dewar's no longer has any maturation capacity at any of its distilleries. Aultmore was one of the first distilleries to build a dark grains plant in order to process pot ale and draff into cattle feed.

It became operational in 1977 but closed again in 1985. It then reopened in 1989 but was finally taken out of production in 1993. Most of the output is used in Dewar's blended whiskies, but a *12 year old* official bottling has been for sale since 2004.

12 years old

Balblair

Owner:
Inver House Distillers
(Thai Beverages plc)

Region/district:
Northern Highlands

Founded: 1790
Status: Active (vc)
Capacity: 2 000 000 litres

Address: Edderton, Tain, Ross-shire IV19 1LB

Tel: 01862 821273
website: www.balblair.com

History:

1790 – The distillery is founded by John Ross.

1836 – John Ross dies and his son Andrew Ross takes over with the help of his sons.

1872 – New buildings replace the old.

1873 – Andrew Ross dies and his son James takes over.

1894 – Balnagowan Estate signs a new lease for 60 years with Alexander Cowan. He builds a new distillery, a few kilometres from the old.

1911 – Cowan is forced to cease payments and the distillery closes.

1941 – Balnagowan Estate goes bankrupt and the distillery is put up for sale.

1948 – The lawyer Robert Cumming from Keith buys Balblair for £48,000.

1949 – Production restarts.

1970 – Cumming sells Balblair to Hiram Walker.

1988 – Allied Distillers becomes the new owner through the merger between Hiram Walker and Allied Vintners.

1996 – Allied Domecq sells the distillery to Inver House Distillers.

2000 – Balblair Elements and the first version of Balblair 33 years are launched.

2001 – Thai company Pacific Spirits (part of the Great Oriole Group) takes over Inver House.

2004 – Balblair 38 years is launched.

2005 – 12 year old Peaty Cask, 1979 (26 years) and 1970 (35 years) are launched.

2006 – International Beverage Holdings acquires Pacific Spirits UK.

2007 – Three new vintages replace the entire former range.

2008 – Vintage 1975 and 1965 are released.

2009 – Vintage 1991 and 1990 are released.

2010 – Vintage 1978 and 2000 are released.

2011 – Vintage 1995 and 1993 are released.

2012 – Vintage 1975, 2001 and 2002 are released. A visitor centre is opened.

There is a hive of activities going on at Balblair distillery at the moment. First of all, a new, elegant and very contemporary visitor centre and shop was inaugurated in late 2011. Secondly, the distillery was one of three to be featured in the new film by Ken Loach, The Angel's Share, and finally, a new washback will be installed during 2012 which will increase the capacity by another 200,000 litres of alcohol.

The equipment consists of a stainless steel mash tun, six Oregon pine washbacks and one pair of stills. There is actually a third still but it has not been used since 1969 and will be demounted to leave room for the additional washback. The spirit is matured in eight dunnage warehouses with a capacity of 26,000 casks. The production has increased to 21 mashes per week which means that they have now reached their capacity of 1,8 million litres of alcohol. After the new washback is in place, its capacity will be 2 million litres.

Since 2011, part of the production has been heavily peated spirit. During 2012 they will produce approximately 200,000 litres with a phenol specification of 52ppm in the barley.

Since the transition to vintages five years ago, sales have increased steadily and during 2011, 75,000 bottles were sold. The current core range consists of three vintages – *1975* (which replaced the 1978 in 2012), *1989* and *2002* (replacing the *2001* in August 2012). Most of the Balblair releases are from bourbon barrels but the 1975 vintage has been drawn from sherry butts although made of American oak. For the duty free market a new *1996* was released in 2012 and there was also a limited release of *1997* for select markets in autumn 2012. Last, but not least, if you go to the distillery you can bottle your own exclusive *Balblair 1992* in the distillery shop – the only place where this will be available. It is a cask strength (60,9%) while the core range is bottled at 46% without chill filtration.

Balblair 2002

Balblair 2001

GS – Lemonade, vanilla, allspice and developing milk chocolate caramel on the nose. The palate is sweet and spicy, with tangerines, eating apples, toffee, and milk chocolate. Cocoa powder in the spicy, relatively lengthy finish.

Meet the Manager

JOHN MACDONALD
DISTILLERY MANAGER, BALBLAIR DISTILLERY

When did you start working in the whisky business and when did you start at Balblair distillery?

Started in the business in September 1989 and came to Balblair in 2006.

Had you been working in other lines of business before whisky?

I came out of college to take "a year out" and worked in the stores of a supermarket for 12 months.

What kind of education or training do you have?

I did a year in college studying communications and publicity and have since done an HNC in Business Administration. As far as the whisky business is concerned the vast majority has been hands on experience.

Describe your career in the whisky business.

I started my whisky career as a warehouseman at Glenmorangie Distillery in 1989. I knocked on the manager's door as I'd heard there was a job going. I knew the manager (Ian MacGregor) for a long time and the interview consisted of one question "Do you want water in that?". My reply was "yes please" and I started the next Monday. My route to management has been a traditional one. From warehousing I moved to the Mill room, then to the Mash House, Still House and then became Assistant Manager. When the Manager's position arose at Balblair it was too good an opportunity to ignore. I was absolutely ecstatic to be offered the role.

What are your main tasks as a manager?

There are many tasks as a manager these days but the main one is to oversee the day to day running of the distillery and to ensure that we continue to make a high quality whisky.

What are the biggest challenges of being a distillery manager?

To me it's dealing with ever changing and ever increasing bureaucracy.

What would be the worst that could go wrong in the production process?

To lose anything down the drain!

How would you describe the character of Balblair single malt?

All the expressions display wonderful fruity characteristics with a touch of spice which vary from vintage to vintage. They all retain the production flavours even after very long maturations which balance beautifully with the cask driven flavours.

What are the main features in the process at Balblair distillery, contributing to this character?

The emphasis at Balblair is on quality not quantity. We use high quality malt and have a long mashing cycle – 6.25 hours. Due to the deep mash bed and slow drain a great deal of fats that are present in malt will remain in the mash tun and will not be transferred to the washbacks. Fats can mask flavours created during fermentation and this is one of the reasons why Balblair displays its very fruity, flavoursome style.

What is your favourite expression of Balblair and why?

I really enjoy the Vintage 2001 as I think it epitomises Balblair. Fruity, full-bodied, smooth, satisfying and complex.

If it were your decision alone – what new expression of Balblair would you like to see released?

It will be shortly!! I'll leave you in suspense but you will not be disappointed.

If you had to choose a favourite dram other than Balblair, what would that be?

That's a hard question as there are so many fine whiskies out there. If push came to shove I would probably plump for a Pulteney 17 yo.

What are the biggest changes you have seen the past 10 years in your profession?

Demand for the product.

Do you see any major changes in the next 10 years to come?

Energy saving has become increasingly important in the last few years and I think we'll see more emphasis on developing ways to do this.

Do you have any special interests or hobbies that you pursue?

I am a huge music fan and I play the guitar very badly.

Balblair distillery came into the limelight last year in a rather unexpected way. What was that?

Balblair became a film set last year as part of Ken Loach's "The Angels' Share". They chose the distillery for its natural charm and magnificent surroundings. Some of the guys managed to get small roles in it too. The film is great and the distillery looked wonderful on the big screen. It was a pleasure to have them all here and we became good friends with a lot of the cast and crew. Everybody was very relaxed and friendly.

You have also just recently opened a visitor centre and a shop. What do you hope will come out of that?

The shop and visitor centre are things I have pushed for since I became manager here and last year it came to fruition. Our intention is for visitors to have a pleasurable experience and not just to get them round and get them to the till. We want people to enjoy their time here and of course enjoy the whisky. The best PR you can get is word of mouth.

Most distillery managers are not involved in the selection of which casks to be bottled. How is it at Balblair?

To be involved in the selection process of casks for vintages is a pleasure and an honour for me and was something I was asked to be involved in when I became manager. My nose must work!!

Balmenach

Owner:
Inver House Distillers
(Thai Beverages plc)

Region/district:
Speyside

Founded: 1824
Status: Active
Capacity: 2 800 000 litres

Address: Cromdale, Moray PH26 3PF

Tel: 01479 872569
website: www.inverhouse.com

History:

1824 – The distillery is licensed to James MacGregor who operated a small farm distillery by the name of Balminoch.

1897 – Balmenach Glenlivet Distillery Company is founded.

1922 – The MacGregor family sells to a consortium consisting of MacDonald Green, Peter Dawson and James Watson.

1925 – The consortium becomes part of Distillers Company Limited (DCL).

1930 – Production is transferred to Scottish Malt Distillers (SMD).

1962 – The number of stills is increased to six.

1964 – Floor maltings replaced with Saladin box.

1992 – The first official bottling is a 12 year old.

1993 – The distillery is mothballed in May.

1997 – Inver House Distillers buys Balmenach from United Distillers.

1998 – Production recommences.

2001 – Thai company Pacific Spirits takes over Inver House at the price of £56 million. The new owner launches a 27 and a 28 year old.

2002 – To commemorate the Queen's Golden Jubilee a 25-year old Balmenach is launched.

2006 – International Beverage Holdings acquires Pacific Spirits UK.

2009 – Gin production commences.

Deerstalker 18 year old

GS – An intriguing and inviting nose, with herbal notes, eucalyptus, heather and hints of sherry. Rich and warming on the palate, big-bodied, with well harmonised malt and sherry flavours prevailing. The finish is long and sophisticated.

DR – Pine needles, lemon and grapefruit and flu powder on the nose, rich sherry and a trace of sulphur on the palate, with savoury lemon and a traces of peat. A medium and citrusy finish.

Unlike the other four distilleries in the Inver House group, the owners have decided not to bottle Balmenach as a single malt. One reason is that no stocks of mature whisky were included in the deal when the distillery was bought in 1997 from United Distillers. Another reason is that the company´s Master Blender, Stuart Harvey, wants to utilise as much as possible of this excellent blending malt to create body and depth in the Hankey Bannister blend which the company acquired in 1988. The five different versions of Hankey Bannister together sells 2,4 million bottles.

A semi-lauter gear was fitted into the old cast iron mash tun in 2006 and there are also six washbacks made of Douglas fir with a 52 hour fermentation period and three pairs of stills connected to worm tubs for cooling the spirit vapours. The distillery has recently increased production and is now working a 7 day week, doing 20 mashes per week and 2,8 million litres of alcohol annually. The three dunnage warehouses hold 9,500 casks at the moment. The character of Balmenach is quite heavy, something that the worm tubs, with less copper contact, is responsible for.

Since 2009, apart from whisky, gin has been produced at Balmenach distillery. A gin still from the 1920s has been installed in the old filling room. Purchased neutral spirit is pumped through a vaporiser and then to the berry chamber where the vapours travel upwards passing through five trays with 11 different kinds of botanicals (among others heather, rowan berry, apples and coriander) and finally end up in the condenser. In the first year, 6,000 litres of Caorunn gin were made increasing it to 20,000 litres in 2012 which means just 20 days of production.

The only "official" bottling of the whisky so far is the 12 year old Flora & Fauna from the previous owner and this is now becoming increasingly difficult to find. There are, however, other Balmenach on the market. One is produced by an independent company called Aberko in Glasgow under the name Deerstalker 18 years.

Deerstalker 18 years

Balvenie

Owner:
William Grant & Sons

Region/district:
Speyside

Founded: **Status:**
1892   Active (vc)

Capacity:
5 600 000 litres

Address: Dufftown, Keith,
Banffshire AB55 4DH

Tel:
01340 820373

website:
www.thebalvenie.com

History:
1892 – William Grant rebuilds Balvenie New House to Balvenie Distillery (Glen Gordon was the name originally intended). Part of the equipment is brought in from Lagavulin and Glen Albyn.

1893 – The first distillation takes place in May.

1957 – The two stills are increased by another two.

1965 – Two new stills are installed.

1971 – Another two stills are installed and eight stills are now running.

1973 – The first official bottling appears.

1982 – Founder's Reserve, in an eye-catching Cognac-reminiscent bottle, is launched.

1990 – A new distillery, Kininvie, is opened on the premises.

1996 – Two vintage bottlings and a Port wood finish are launched.

2001 – The Balvenie Islay Cask, with 17 years in bourbon casks and six months in Islay casks, is released.

2002 – Balvenie releases 83 bottles of a 50 year old that has been in sherry casks since January 1952. Recommended price £6,000 a bottle.

2004 – The Balvenie Thirty is released to commemorate Malt Master David Stewart's 30th anniversary at Balvenie.

2005 – The Balvenie Rum Wood Finish 14 years old is released.

2006 – The Balvenie New Wood 17 years old, Roasted Malt 14 years old and Portwood 1993 are released.

2007 – Vintage Cask 1974 and Sherry Oak 17 years old are released.

2008 – Signature, Vintage 1976, Balvenie Rose and Rum Cask 17 year old are released.

2009 – Vintage 1978, 17 year old Madeira finish, 14 year old rum finish and Golden Cask 14 years old are released.

2010 – A 40 year old, Peated Cask and Carribean Cask are released.

2011 – Second batch of Tun 1401 is released.

2012 – A 50 year old and Doublewood 17 years old are released.

The Balvenie Doublewood 12 year old

GS – Nuts and spicy malt on the nose, full-bodied, with soft fruit, vanilla, sherry and a hint of peat. Dry and spicy in a luxurious, lengthy finish.

DR – Red fruits and berries, a hint of smoke on the nose, on the palate mouth filling, rich and fruity and, surprisingly, with a peat presence. Lots of sherry and some toffee in the finish.

The longest serving Scotch Malt Master, David Stewart, celebrated 50 years at The Balvenie distillery in 2012 and he has become one of the most respected craftsmen in the whisky industry. During his career, David estimates that he has nosed over 400,000 whisky casks! To celebrate and honour David, an extremely limited (only 88 bottles) 50 year old Balvenie was released in September.

Balvenie is one of few distilleries still doing some of their own maltings. Around 15% of requirements are produced every week. Except for their own maltings the distillery also has its own coppersmith and cooperage. The distillery is equipped with a full lauter mash tun, nine wooden and five stainless steel washbacks. The number of wash stills was increased to five and spirit stills to six, divided into two still rooms in 2008, when the facilities were expanded. For 2012, the production plan is 22 mashes per week, which means 80% of full capacity. Both bourbon (80%) and sherry casks (20%) are used.

A total of 200,000 cases were sold in 2011 which gives Balvenie the 10th spot on the global sales list. The core range consists of *Doublewood 12 years old, Signature 12 years, Single Barrel 15 years, Portwood 21 years, 30 year old* and the *40 year old*. Batch 4 and 5 of the latter were released in 2012. A new addition to the core range was released in September 2012 in the shape of a *Doublewood 17 years old*. Apart from the aforementioned *50 year old*, recent limited bottlings include *The Balvenie Peated cask 17 year old*, the US exclusive rum finish *Caribbean Cask*, *14 year old Cuban Selection* for the French and Taiwanese markets and *Tun 1401*. The last one was first released in autumn 2010 and was made up of six different barrels (both sherry and bourbon) from 1966 to 1988. Batch number 4, 5 and 6 were all released in 2012 in various markets and a special *Tun 1858* was reserved for Taiwan.

The Duty Free range consists of *Peated Cask, Portwood 21 years* bottled at higher strength and the *14 year old Golden Cask*.

Doublewood 17 years

Ben Nevis

Owner: **Region/district:**
Ben Nevis Distillery Ltd   Western Highlands
(Nikka, Asahi Breweries)

Founded: **Status:**   **Capacity:**
1825   Active (vc)   1 800 000 litres

Address: Lochy Bridge, Fort William PH33 6TJ

Tel: **website:**
01397 702476   www.bennevisdistillery.com

History:

1825 – The distillery is founded by 'Long' John McDonald.

1856 – Long John dies and his son Donald P. McDonald takes over.

1878 – Demand is so great that another distillery, Nevis Distillery, is built nearby.

1908 – Both distilleries merge into one.

1941 – D. P. McDonald & Sons sells the distillery to Ben Nevis Distillery Ltd headed by the Canadian millionaire Joseph W. Hobbs.

1955 – Hobbs installs a Coffey still which makes it possible to produce both grain and malt whisky.

1964 – Joseph Hobbs dies.

1978 – Production is stopped.

1981 – Joseph Hobbs Jr sells the distillery back to Long John Distillers and Whitbread.

1984 – After restoration and reconstruction totalling £2 million, Ben Nevis opens up again.

1986 – The distillery closes again.

1989 – Whitbread sells the distillery to Nikka Whisky Distilling Company Ltd.

1990 – The distillery opens up again.

1991 – A visitor centre is inaugurated.

1996 – Ben Nevis 10 years old is launched.

2006 – A 13 year old port finish is released.

2007 – A 1992 single cask is released.

2010 – A 25 year old is released.

2011 – McDonald's Traditional Ben Nevis is released.

At one time there were three operational distilleries in Fort William – Glenlochy, Nevis and Ben Nevis. The first one closed in the early 1980s, while Ben Nevis is currently still producing. The Nevis distillery was built in 1878 by the owner of Ben Nevis, Donald P McDonald, in order to keep up with the increasing demand for Long John´s Dew of Ben Nevis. Nevis continued to produce until 1908 and thereafter it was only the warehouses that were used. Ben Nevis distillery faced some difficulties during the 1980s and was actually closed for the larger part of the decade. In 1989 it was taken over by Japanese Nikka Whisky and has been distilling ever since.

Ben Nevis is equipped with one lauter mash tun, six stainless steel washbacks and two made of Oregon pine and two pairs of stills. Fermentation is 48 hours in the steel washbacks and the spirit is destined to become either single malt or part of the Dew of Ben Nevis blend.

In the wooden washbacks, fermentation time is 96 hours and this version is sent as newmake directly to the owners, Nikka, in Japan. It is used there at a very young age in the popular blend Nikka Black (or just Black as it was renamed in 2009). At the moment, the distillery is doing nine mashes per week, which equals 800,000 litres per year. Ben Nevis had produced peated whisky for some time but stopped six years ago.

Since 1996 the core of the range has been a *10 year old*. Some one-off bottlings have appeared at regular intervals, such as a *13 year old Port finish* the *1992 single cask*. In 2010, a limited release was made of a *25 year old* which sold out quickly. It had spent the first 12 years in a fresh bourbon cask that was then re-racked to a fresh sherry cask. *McDonald's Traditional Ben Nevis*, an attempt to replicate the style of Ben Nevis single malt from the 1880s, was quickly sold out, but another batch is expected during 2012. The character is peatier than the core 10 year old version.

Ben Nevis 10 year old

GS – The nose is initially quite green, with developing nutty, orange notes. Coffee, brittle toffee and peat are present on the slightly oily palate, along with chewy oak, which persists to the finish, together with more coffee and a hint of dark chocolate.

DR – Grape skins, over-ripe pear on the nose, baked apple and liquorice roots on the palate, pleasant malty finish.

10 years old

BenRiach

Owner:
Benriach Distillery Co

Region/district:
Speyside

Founded: **Status:** **Capacity:**
1897   Active   2 800 000 litres

Address:
Longmorn, Elgin, Morayshire IV30 8SJ

Tel: **website:**
01343 862888   www.benriachdistillery.co.uk

History:

1897 – John Duff & Co founds the distillery.

1899 – Longmorn Distilleries Co. buys the distillery.

1903 – The distillery is mothballed.

1965 – The distillery is reopened by the new owner, The Glenlivet Distillers Ltd.

1978 – Seagram Distillers takes over.

1983 – Seagrams starts producing a peated Benriach.

1985 – The number of stills is increased to four.

1994 – The first official bottling is 10 years old.

1999 – The maltings is decommissioned.

2002 – The distillery is mothballed in October.

2004 – Intra Trading, buys Benriach together with the former Director at Burn Stewart, Billy Walker. The price is £5.4 million.

2004 – Standard, Curiositas and 12, 16 and 20 year olds are released.

2005 – Four different vintages are released in limited editions - 1966, 1970, 1978 och 1984.

2006 – Sixteen new releases, i.a. a 25 year old, a 30 year old and 8 different vintages.

2007 – A 40 year old and three new heavily peated expressions are released.

2008 – New expressions include a peated Madeira finish, a 15 year old Sauternes finish and nine single casks.

2009 – Two wood finishes (Moscatel and Gaja Barolo) and nine single casks are released.

2010 – Triple distilled Solstice and heavily peated Horizons are released.

2011 – A 45 year old and 12 vintages are released.

2012 – Septendecim 17 years, Vestige 46 years and ten new vintages are released. The maltings are working again.

BenRiach 12 year old

GS – Malt, orange and pineapple on the nose, floral with vanilla notes. Soft fruits, brittle toffee and honey on the smooth palate, with a finish of spicy milk chocolate.

DR – Classic Speyside nose, with a rich blend of fruits, vanilla and honey. On the palate ripe fruits are balanced by crisp barley and sweet honey, and the finish is balanced, rounded and pleasant.

The owners of BenRiach and GlenDronach, with Billy Walker at the helm, are among the ones with the most aggressive approach in the Scotch whisky industry and there is no sign that they will lay off that approach. On the contrary, in March 2012 they secured a £27m funding from Royal Bank of Scotland, which will be used for "further acquisitions" and to invest in new stock.

The traditional way of producing malted barley for whisky production, was for every distillery to have its own malting floors. Currently there are only six distilleries in Scotland practising this method, but soon this group will be expanding with yet another one – BenRiach. Their floor malting stopped in 1999 having run for 101 years, and for several years now they have talked about reopening the facility. All the engineering was complete by summer 2012, a test run was made during autumn and the plan is to start malting part of the requirement in spring 2013.

BenRiach distillery is equipped with a traditional cast iron mash tun with a stainless steel shell, eight washbacks made of stainless steel with a fermentation time between 72 and 96 hours and two pairs of stills. The production for 2012 will be 2 million litres of alcohol (which includes 250,000 litres of peated spirit and 25,000 triple distilled) with 60% being sold to Chivas Brothers for their blends.

The core range of BenRiach is *Heart of Speyside* (no age), *12, 16, 20, 25* and *30 years old* in what the distillery calls Classic Speyside style and *Birnie Moss, Curiositas 10 year old*, the new *Septendecim 17 years* and *Authenticus* which is now a 25 year old (used to be 21) as the peated varieties. There are six different *wood finishes (12-16 years)* and in 2010 two specials were released – *Horizons*, a 12 year old triple distilled and *Solstice*. The latter was replaced in 2012 with a 17 year old. In June 2012 a batch of ten different *single casks* from *1976 to 1990* were released and by the end of the year, *Vestige 46 year old* from the distillery's oldest stock was launched.

12 year old

Benrinnes

Owner: Diageo

Region/district: Speyside

Founded: 1826 **Status:** Active **Capacity:** 3 500 000 litres

Address: Aberlour, Banffshire AB38 9NN

Tel: 01340 872600 **website:** www.malts.com

History:

1826 – The first Benrinnes distillery is built at Whitehouse Farm by Peter McKenzie.

1829 – A flood destroys the distillery.

1834 – A new distillery, Lyne of Ruthrie, is constructed a few kilometres from the first one. The owner, John Innes files for bankruptcy and William Smith & Company takes over.

1864 – William Smith & Company goes bankrupt and David Edward becomes the new owner.

1896 – Benrinnes is ravaged by fire which prompts major refurbishment. David Edward dies and his son Alexander Edward takes over.

1922 – John Dewar & Sons takes over ownership.

1925 – John Dewar & Sons becomes part of Distillers Company Limited (DCL).

1955/56 – The distillery is completely rebuilt.

1964 – Floor maltings is replaced by a Saladin box.

1966 – The number of stills doubles to six.

1984 – The Saladin box is taken out of service and the malt is purchased centrally.

1991 – The first official bottling from Benrinnes is a 15 year old in the Flora & Fauna series.

1996 – United Distillers releases a 21 year old cask strength in their Rare Malts series.

2009 – A 23 year old (6,000 bottles) is launched as a part of this year's Special Releases.

2010 – A Manager's Choice 1996 is released.

Benrinnes 15 year old

GS – A brief flash of caramel shortcake on the initial nose, soon becoming more peppery and leathery, with some sherry. Ultimately savoury and burnt rubber notes. Big-bodied, viscous, with gravy, dark chocolate and more pepper. A medium-length finish features mild smoke and lively spices.

DR – Cucumber, water melon and some caramel on the nose, sherried and full palate with some figs and harsher notes. The finish is medium long and complex.

Benrinnes distillery, situated at the foot of the mountain with the same name, has been in Diageo's (or their precursors) ownership for soon to be 100 years, but the distillery we see today was built as late as the 1950s. The whisky from Benrinnes has always been considered as one of the best by blenders and its meaty, sulphury style contributes with body and intensity to many blended whiskies. The spirit vapours are cooled using worm tubs with a minimum of copper contact and since copper helps to reduce the amount of sulphur, Benrinnes new-make will retain its pungent style. A sulphury new-make needs time to mature and consequently the single malt is not bottled by the owners before it reaches the age of 15 years.

The distillery is equipped with an 8,5 tonnes stainless steel lauter mash tun, eight washbacks made of Oregon pine and six stills. For a long time the stills were run three and three, instead of in pairs. This technique is reminiscent of Springbank's partial triple distillation and was probably adopted in connection with rebuilding the distillery in 1955. For the last couple of years, though, this has changed and two wash stills are now feeding four spirit stills; two of which were originally the intermediate stills. Worm tubs are used for condensation. From January 2012, the distillery has gone from a 5-day week to a 7-day week. This means that the fermentation time now is a constant 65 hours, while previously, long fermentations (up to 105 hours) took place as well. The total volume for 2012 is expected to be 3,5 million litres of alcohol with 21 mashes per week.

The lion's share of Benrinnes' production is used in blended whiskies – J&B, Johnnie Walker and Crawford's 3 Star – and there is only one official single malt, the *Flora & Fauna 15 years old*. In autumn 2009, a *23 year old* from 1985 was released as part of Diageo's annual Special Releases and in May 2010 came another new release, a *Manager's Choice* from *1996*, drawn from a refill bourbon cask.

Flora & Fauna 15 years old

Benromach

Owner: Gordon & MacPhail

Region/district: Speyside

Founded: 1898   **Status:** Active (vc)   **Capacity:** 500 000 litres

Address: Invererne Road, Forres, Morayshire IV36 3EB

Tel: 01309 675968   **website:** www.benromach.com

History:

1898 – Benromach Distillery Company starts the distillery.

1911 – Harvey McNair & Co buys the distillery.

1919 – John Joseph Calder buys Benromach and sells it to recently founded Benromach Distillery Ltd owned by several breweries.

1931 – Benromach is mothballed.

1937 – The distillery reopens.

1938 – Joseph Hobbs buys Benromach through Associated Scottish Distillers and sells it on to National Distillers of America (NDA).

1953 – NDA sells Benromach to Distillers Company Limited (DCL).

1966 – The distillery is refurbished.

1968 – Floor maltings is abolished.

1983 – Benromach is mothballed in March.

1993 – Gordon & McPhail buys Benromach from United Distillers.

1998 – The distillery is once again in operation. A 17 year old is released to commemorate this and the distillery's 100th anniversary.

1999 – A visitor centre is opened.

2004 – The first bottle distilled by the new owner is released under the name 'Benromach Traditional' in May. Other novelties (although distilled in UD times) include a 21 year Tokaji finish and a Vintage 1969.

2005 – A Port Wood finish (22 years old) and a Vintage 1968 are released together with the Benromach Classic 55 years.

2006 – Benromach Organic is released.

2007 – Peat Smoke, the first heavily peated whisky from the distillery, is released.

2008 – Benromach Origins Golden Promise is released.

2009 – Benromach 10 years old is released.

2010 – New batches of Peatsmoke and Origins are released.

2011 – New edition of Peatsmoke, a 2001 Hermitage finish and a 30 year old are released.

Benromach 10 year old

GS – A nose that is initially quite smoky, with wet grass, butter, ginger and brittle toffee. Mouth-coating, spicy, malty and nutty on the palate, with developing citrus fruits, raisins and soft wood smoke. The finish is warming, with lingering barbecue notes.

DR – Lemon custard creams, apricots and then pine table polish on the nose, spicy virgin oak, refreshing sharp barley and pine needles on the palate, and a complex and intriguing spicy and wood shaving finish.

The worst fear for an independent bottler would, of course, be to run out of whisky. In older days, these companies had no distillery of their own and had to rely on producers for their stock. As the demand for single malts increased, it became necessary for the independents to secure their own production through purchasing a distillery. First up was perhaps the most prestigious company of them all, Gordon & MacPhail who already purchased Benromach in 1993 and restarted the production five years later.

Benromach is the smallest working distillery in Speyside and is equipped with a very small (1.5 tonnes) semi-lauter mash tun with a copper dome. There are four washbacks made of larchwood from the old washbacks and resized to accommodate 11,000 litres with a long fermentation time that varies between 72 and 120 hours. Finally, there is one pair of stills that were custom made when they took over the distillery. Only two people are employed in the production and, although it has the capacity to produce 500,000 litres per annum, the output for 2012 is approximately 130,000 litres of alcohol with small batches being peated. Almost the entire production is destined to be sold as single malt and only a very small amount is used for Gordon & MacPhail blends.

The core range consists of *Traditional* (around 6 years old), *10 year old* (released in 2010), *Cask Strength* (currently a 2001 vintage), *25 year old, 30 year old* (released in 2011), *Vintage 1969* and *Classic 55 years old*. There are also special editions; *Organic* – the first single malt to be fully certified organic by the Soil Association and now available in a *Special Edition* which has been matured in virgin American oak casks, *Peatsmoke* – produced using peated barley with the fifth batch released in 2012 and *Origins* – three batches highlighting how differences in the process produce different whiskies. Limited editions released in 2012 include a new version of a *Sassicaia wood finish*.

10 year old

Bladnoch

Owner:
Co-ordinated
Development Services

Region/district:
Lowlands

Founded: 1817
Status: Active (vc)
Capacity: 250 000 litres

Address: Bladnoch, Wigtown,
Wigtonshire DG8 9AB

Tel: 01988 402605
website: www.bladnoch.co.uk

History:

1817 – Brothers Thomas and John McClelland found the distillery.

1825 – The McClelland brothers obtain a licence.

1878 – John McClelland's son Charlie reconstructs and refurbishes the distillery.

1905 – Production stops.

1911 – Dunville & Co. from Ireland buys T. & A. McClelland Ltd for £10,775. Production is intermittent until 1936.

1937 – Dunville & Co. is liquidated and Bladnoch is wound up. Ross & Coulter from Glasgow buys the distillery after the war. The equipment is dismantled and shipped to Sweden.

1956 – A. B. Grant (Bladnoch Distillery Ltd.) takes over and restarts production with four new stills.

1964 – McGown and Cameron becomes new owners.

1966 – The number of stills is increased from two to four.

1973 – Inver House Distillers buys Bladnoch.

1983 – Arthur Bell and Sons take over.

1985 – Guiness Group buys Arthur Bell & Sons which, from 1989, are included in United Distillers.

1988 – A visitor centre is built.

1993 – United Distillers mothballs Bladnoch in June.

1994 – Raymond Armstrong from Northern Ireland buys Bladnoch in October.

2000 – Production commences in December.

2003 – The first bottles from Raymond Armstrong are launched, a 15 year old cask strength from UD casks.

2004 – New varieties follow suit: e. g. 13 year olds 40% and 55%.

2008 – First release of whisky produced after the take-over in 2000 - three 6 year olds.

2009 – An 8 year old of own production and a 19 year old are released.

2011 – Distiller's Choice is released.

2012 – Peated Distiller's Choice is released.

Bladnoch 8 year old

GS – Bright, fresh and citric, with lemon, cereal, soft toffee and nuts on the nose. Medium in body, the palate is gingery and very lively, with vanilla, hot spices and hazelnuts. The finish offers persistently fruity spice.

Bladnoch is the southernmost of the Scottish distilleries, situated a mile outside Wigtown. The distillery's fate appeared to be sealed when it was mothballed by United Distillers (later Diageo) in 1993. However, along came Raymond Armstrong, a builder from Northern Ireland, who bought it with the reservation from Diageo that it should not be used for whisky production. In 2000, after lobbying from Armstrong and the local community, Diageo gave permission for Bladnoch to start producing again.

Armstrong commenced the resurrection and in December 2000 the first distillation was made. The distillery is equipped with a stainless steel semi-lauter mash tun, six washbacks made of Oregon pine (of which only three are in use) and one pair of stills. Due to the increase in production costs (barley, casks and fuel), the owners took a decision in 2009 to cease production for the time being. According to Armstrong, the intention is to start distilling again during 2012. Of the 11 warehouses on site, Bladnoch uses only one for its own purposes while the others are rented to other distilleries. The latter is also an important contribution to finances of the business. Nearly 50,000 casks from other companies are stored at Bladnoch which yields a yearly income of more than £500,000.

Until four years ago, all official bottlings came from the previous owner's production. These included 13 to 19 year olds but, in spring of 2010, a couple of 20 year olds were also released. In 2008 the first release from stock distilled under the current ownership appeared. Three *6 year old cask strengths* were released – a bourbon matured, a sherry matured and one lightly peated from a bourbon barrel. All these have since appeared in older versions with a *10 year old* lightly peated and sherry matured, as well as an *11 year old* sherry matured being released in spring/summer 2012. The range has mostly been about single casks bottled but the first step to a core range was made in 2011, when *Distiller's Choice* with no age statement, bottled at 46%, was launched. This was followed up in 2012 with a *Peated Distiller's Choice*.

8 year old

Blair Athol

Owner:
Diageo

Region/district:
Eastern Highlands

Founded: **Status:**   **Capacity:**
1798   Active (vc)   2 500 000 litres

Address: Perth Road, Pitlochry,
Perthshire PH16 5LY

Tel: **website:**
01796 482003   www.malts.com

History:
1798 – John Stewart and Robert Robertson found Aldour Distillery, the predecessor to Blair Athol. The name is taken from the adjacent river Allt Dour.

1825 – The distillery is expanded by John Robertson and takes the name Blair Athol Distillery.

1826 – The Duke of Atholl leases the distillery to Alexander Connacher & Co.

1860 – Elizabeth Connacher runs the distillery.

1882 – Peter Mackenzie & Company Distillers Ltd of Edinburgh (future founder of Dufftown Distillery) buys Blair Athol and expands it.

1932 – The distillery is mothballed.

1933 – Arthur Bell & Sons takes over by acquiring Peter Mackenzie & Company.

1949 – Production restarts.

1973 – Stills are expanded from two to four.

1985 – Guinness Group buys Arthur Bell & Sons.

1987 – A visitor centre is built.

2003 – A 27 year old cask strength from 1975 is launched in Diageo's Rare Malts series.

2010 – A distillery exclusive with no age statement and a single cask from 1995 are released.

Blair Athol 12 year old

GS – The nose is mellow and sherried, with brittle toffee. Sweet and fragrant. Relatively rich on the palate, with malt, raisins, sultanas and sherry. The finish is lengthy, elegant and slowly drying.

DR – The nose is rich and full, with orange and citrus fruit. The palate, too, is big and chunky, with some tannin and spice in the mix, and with water, parma violet notes.

Blair Athol distillery in Pitlochry in Perthshire is the spiritual home of Bell's blended Scotch - the number one whisky in the UK, a position which was reached as early as 1978. Today, every fifth bottle of blended whisky sold in the UK is Bell's. The struggle to achieve this position started already in 1933 when prohibition was repealed in the USA. All the big companies were in the starting blocks ready to gain market shares. For Bell's, this meant that they had to purchase two distilleries, Blair Athol and Dufftown, simultaneously to ensure the supply of malt whisky for their blends. Five years later Inchgower was purchased. Today, Bell's is the 8th best selling Scotch in the world (and the third biggest in the Diageo stable after Johnnie Walker and J&B) with 30 million bottles sold in 2011. Important markets, apart from the UK, are Scandinavia, South Africa and Spain. The range of Bell's was expanded in 1993 from Original to also include an 8 year old and again in 2003 when the blended malt Special Reserve was launched. For the greater part of the summer in 2010 Blair Athol distillery was closed for refurbishing and the equipment now consists of an 8 tonnes semi-lauter mash tun, six washbacks made of stainless steel (used to be four wooden and four made of steel) and two pairs of stills. The distillery is running seven days a week with 16 mashes giving a production of 2,5 million litres of spirit. The part of the spirit which goes into Bell's is matured mainly in bourbon casks while the rest is matured in sherry casks. Blair Athol also has an excellent visitor centre and it is Diageo's third busiest after Talisker and Oban, attracting almost 40,000 visitors per year.

The only official bottling used to be the *12 year old Flora & Fauna*. In 2010, a *first fill sherry* bottled at *cask strength* and without age statement was also released as a distillery exclusive. A couple of months earlier, a *single cask* distilled in *1995* was released as part of the Manager's Choice series.

Distillery Exclusive no age

Bowmore

Owner:
Morrison Bowmore
Distillers (Suntory)

Region/district:
Islay

Founded: **Status:**   **Capacity:**
1779   Active (vc)   2 000 000 litres

Address: School Street, Bowmore, Islay,
Argyll PA43 7GS

Tel: **website:**
01496 810441   www.bowmore.com

History:
1779 – Bowmore Distillery is founded by
John Simpson and becomes the oldest Islay
distillery.

1837 – The distillery is sold to James and
William Mutter of Glasgow.

1892 – After additional construction, the
distillery is sold to Bowmore Distillery
Company Ltd, a consortium of English
businessmen.

1925 – J. B. Sheriff and Company takes over.

1929 – Distillers Company Limited (DCL) takes
over.

1950 – William Grigor & Son takes over.

1963 – Stanley P. Morrison buys the distillery
for £117,000 and forms Morrison Bowmore
Distillers Ltd.

1989 – Japanese Suntory buys a 35% stake in
Morrison Bowmore.

1993 – The legendary Black Bowmore is
launched. The recommended price is £100
(today it is at least ten times that if it can be
found). Another two versions are released
1994 and 1995.

1994 – Suntory now controls all of Morrison
Bowmore.

1995 – Bowmore is nominated 'Distiller of the
Year' in the International Wine and Spirits
competition.

In 2007, the owners of Bowmore made two decisions that
boosted sales of the single malt – first of all, they made a
complete revamp of the whole range and, secondly, they
decided that the duty free market was the way to increase
figures. Up until then, considerably less profitable bulk
sales and selling through supermarkets had been in focus.
The effect came quickly and during 2011 Bowmore single
malt sold almost 2 million bottles of which almost 90% was
exported.

At the beginning of 2012, Morrison Bowmore hired Rachel
Barrie, one of the most respected whisky blenders in the
industry. She had then worked several years at Glenmorangie Co. and was responsible for creating several of the
successful Glenmorangie and Ardbeg expressions.

Bowmore is one of few Scottish distilleries with its own
malting floor, with 40% of the malt requirement produced
in-house. The remaining part is bought from Simpsons.
Both parts have a phenol specification of 25ppm and are
mixed before mashing. The distillery has a stainless steel
semi-lauter mash tun, six washbacks of Oregon pine and
two pairs of stills. 27,000 casks are stored in two dunnage
and one racked warehouse. The building closest to the sea,
dating back to the 1700s, is probably the oldest whisky warehouse still in use in Scotland. In 2012 they will be doing
12-13 mashes per week and 1,7 million litres per year.

The core range for domestic markets includes *Legend* (no
age), *12 years, Darkest 15 years, 18 years* and *25 years*.
The duty free line-up contains *Surf, Enigma, Mariner* (15
years old) and *17 year old*. During 2012, another three
expressions were added to the range; *100 Degrees Proof*
(replacing the Bowmore Cask Strength and bottled at
57,1%), *Springtide* (matured in Oloroso casks and bottled
at 54,9%) and finally *Vintage 1983* (from a single hogshead
and bottled at 55,6%). Limited releases for 2011 were
Vintage 1982, the third edition of *Tempest* and batch two
of *Laimrig*. In 2012 the 4th edition of *Tempest* and a further
release of *Laimrig* were launched. The latter has matured
in ex-bourbon casks with an added finish in Oloroso sherry
butts. The Tempest will also be launched in the US market
but, since another company already owns the US trademark
for that name, the owners have asked their customers,
through a contest, to choose between two names - Dorus
Mor or Whirlpool. Finally, a *Small Batch Reserve* (40%) was
released in May 2012 for the UK market and a *30 year old
Bowmore Sea Dragon* was launched in Asia to celebrate the
Year of the Dragon.

History (continued):

1996 – A Bowmore 1957 (38 years) is bottled at 40.1% but is not released until 2000.

1999 – Bowmore Darkest with three years finish on Oloroso barrels is launched.

2000 – Bowmore Dusk with two years finish in Bordeaux barrels is launched.

2001 – Bowmore Dawn with two years finish on Port pipes is launched.

2002 – A 37 year old Bowmore from 1964 and matured in fino casks is launched in a limited edition of 300 bottles (recommended price £1,500).

2003 – Another two expressions complete the wood trilogy which started with 1964 Fino - 1964 Bourbon and 1964 Oloroso.

2004 – Morrison Bowmore buys one of the most outstanding collections of Bowmore Single Malt from the private collector Hans Sommer. It totals more than 200 bottles and includes a number of Black Bowmore.

2005 – Bowmore 1989 Bourbon (16 years) and 1971 (34 years) are launched.

2006 – Bowmore 1990 Oloroso (16 years) and 1968 (37 years) are launched. A new and upgraded visitor centre is opened.

2007 – Dusk and Dawn disappear from the range and an 18 year old is introduced. New packaging for the whole range. 1991 (16yo) Port and Black Bowmore are released.

2008 – White Bowmore and a 1992 Vintage with Bourdeaux finish are launched.

2009 – Gold Bowmore, Maltmen´s Selection, Laimrig and Bowmore Tempest are released.

2010 – A 40 year old and Vintage 1981 are released.

2011– Vintage 1982 and new batches of Tempest and Laimrig are released.

2012 – 100 Degrees Proof, Springtide and Vintage 1983 are released for duty free.

Bowmore 12 year old

GS – An enticing nose of lemon and gentle brine leads into a smoky, citric palate, with notes of cocoa and boiled sweets appearing in the lengthy, complex finish.

DR – Rich peat and seaweed and the merest hint of characteristic palma violets on the nose, smoked fish in butter, menthol cough sweets and lemon on the palate, sweet peat in the finish.

Springtide

100 Degrees Proof

Bowmore Tempest
3rd edition

12 years old

15 years old Darkest

Mariner

Braeval

Owner:
Chivas Brothers Ltd
(Pernod Ricard)

Region/district:
Speyside

Founded:
1973

Status:
Active

Capacity:
4 000 000 litres

Address: Chapeltown of Glenlivet,
Ballindalloch, Banffshire AB37 9JS

Tel:
01542 783042

website:
-

History:
1973 – The Chivas and Glenlivet Group founds Braes of Glenlivet, the name which will be used for the first 20 years. The Glenlivet, Tomintoul and Tamnavulin are the only other distilleries situated in the Livet Glen valley. Production starts in October.

1975 – Three stills are increased to five.

1978 – Five stills are further expanded to six.

1994 – The distillery changes name to Braeval.

2001 – Pernod Ricard takes over Chivas Brothers.

2002 – Braeval is mothballed in October.

2008 – The distillery starts producing again in July.

Deerstalker 10 year old

DR – Grass and violin bow on the nose, zippy sherbet and citrus fruit on the palate, with a clean and refreshing finish.

The isolated Braes where Braeval distillery (or Braes of Glenlivet as it is sometimes called) was a haven for illicit distillers from the 1780s to the early 1800s and the whisky was smuggled out of the valley along narrow paths. At one time over 200 illicit stills were operating in this wild and beautiful part of the glen. Today there are three marked trails (Smuggler´s Trails) which are named after famous people who have a connection to the area. One of the trails starts just outside Braeval distillery and is named after Malcolm Gillespie, an exciseman (or gauger as it was sometimes called) who was wounded no less than 42 times in the line of duty. Braeval distillery is both impressive and surprisingly handsome, despite that it was built to function as a typical working distillery. It is also the highest situated distillery in Scotland at 1665 feet above sea level, beating Dalwhinnie by almost 100 feet. When Braeval was built in the mid 1970s, a new type of efficient mash tun (the lauter tun) had already been introduced at other distilleries. It was therefore surprising that the new distillery (as well as its sister distillery Allt-a-Bhainne) was equipped with the old fashioned type of mash tun with rakes. The equipment consists of a new Briggs mash tun (installed in 2012) of the same highly efficient type as Glenlivet, only slightly smaller. There are also thirteen washbacks made of stainless steel and six stills. There used to be four pairs but now each of the two wash stills serves two spirit stills. The capacity is 25 mashes per week and since there are no warehouses on site, the spirit is tankered away for filling and storage.
The whole production is used for blended Scotch and there are no official bottlings. Independent bottler, Aberko Ltd., have two versions from the distillery in their range of Deerstalker single malts – a 10 year old and a 15 year old.

Deerstalker 10 year old

New Websites To Watch

recenteats.blogspot.com
The proper name for this blog is Sku´s Recent Eats and the man behind it is Steve Ury who is an old-timer amongst bloggers (he started in 2007). He gets his inspiration from many walks of life, so don´t be surprised if you find yourself reading about Hawaiian food or tequila. Steve has a great sense of humour and is known to be quite outspoken. The blog also includes a remarkable list of American Whiskey Distilleries & Brands which is very up-to-date.

spiritsjournal.klwines.com
K&L Wines is a well-known, California-based wine and spirits retailer with stores in San Francisco, Hollywood and Redwood City, but that´s not why they are listed here. One of the staff, David Driscoll, is responsible for the company´s Spirits Journal - a very well written, entertaining and frequent revue of the latest whiskies (and other spirits) but also about the business as an entity.

www.whisky-distilleries.net
To do a website with information on all the distilleries in Scotland, not just in text but accompanied by numerous photos, seems like an impossible task, but Ernst"Ernie" Scheiner has come a long way. Born in Austria, Eddie has made Scotland his second home and has frequently guided parties around the distilleries. The Gateway to Distilleries is constantly being up-dated and more distilleries from other parts of the world will soon be included.

www.whiskymarketplace.co.uk
This great site, with the eminent Stuart Robson as blog editor, can be divided into three parts. First and foremost, it includes well written reviews of daily drams, as well as rare bottlings. Next is Whisky Finder, an elegant and easy-to-navigate price comparison site with over 8,000 whiskies and, finally, Whisky Marketplace TV, a high quality video podcast which we will hopefully see more of in the future.

Some Old Favourites

www.maltmadness.com
Our all-time favourite with something for everyone. Managed by malt maniac Johannes van den Heuvel.

www.maltmaniacs.net
A bunch of knowledgeable whisky lovers dissect, debate, attack and praise the phenomena of the whisky world.

www.whiskyadvocateblog.com
John Hansell is well situated with his contacts in the business to write a first class blog on every aspect of whisky.

www.whiskyfun.com
Serge Valentin, one of the Malt Maniacs, is almost always first with well written tasting notes on new releases.

www.nonjatta.blogspot.com
A blog by Chris Bunting with a wealth of interesting information on Japanese whisky as well as Japanese culture.

www.whiskyreviews.blogspot.com
Ralfy does this video blog with tastings and field reports in an educational yet easy-going and entertaining way.

www.caskstrength.net
Joel and Neil won a Drammie Award for this blog and deservedly so. Initiated, entertaining and well written.

www.edinburghwhiskyblog.com
Lucas and Chris review new releases, interview industry people and cover various news from the whisky world.

www.whiskycast.com
The best whisky-related podcast on the internet and one that sets the standard for podcasts in other genres as well.

www.whiskywhiskywhisky.com
An active forum for whisky friends with lots of daily comments on new whiskies, industry news, whisky events etc.

www.whiskyintelligence.com
The best site on all kinds of whisky news. The first whisky website you should log into every morning!

www.whisky-news.com
Apart from daily news, this site contains tasting notes, distillery portraits, lists of retailers, events etc.

www.dramming.com
Takes a wide-angle view of the whisky world including trip reports, whisky ratings, whisky business, articles etc.

www.guidscotchdrink.com
Tasting notes is one part of this site but the highlights are the many comments on current events and trends.

www.whiskyforum.se
Swedish whisky forum with more than 1,800 enthusiasts. Excellent debate as well as more than 2,000 tasting notes.

www.whisky-pages.com
Top class whisky site with features, directories, tasting notes, book reviews, whisky news, glossary and a forum.

www.whiskynotes.be
This blog is almost entirely about tasting notes (and lots of them, not least independent bottlings) plus some news.

www.whiskyforeveryone.com
Educational site, perfect for beginners, with a blog where both new releases and affordable standards are reviewed.

blog.thewhiskyexchange.com
Tim Forbes from The Whisky Exchange writes about new bottlings as well as the whisky industry in general.

www.ardbegproject.com
A temple for those of you who want to know everything about Ardbeg distillery and, especially, all the bottlings.

www.whiskymag.com
The official website of the printed 'Whisky Magazine'. A very active whisky forum with over 3000 members.

www.whisky-distilleries.info
A great site that is absolutely packed with information about distilleries as well as history and recent bottlings.

www.connosr.com
This whisky social networking community is a virtual smorgasbord for any whisky lover!

www.jewmalt.com
An excellent blog by Joshua Hatton who also acts as an independent bottler, check out www.singlecasknation.com.

www.canadianwhisky.org
Davin de Kergommeaux presents reviews, news and views on all things Canadian whisky. High quality content.

www.whiskyisrael.co.il
Gal Granov is definitely one of the most active of all bloggers. Well worth checking out daily!

www.thebalvenie.com
One of few company websites that is actually good, mainly for The Whisky Academy - see for yourself and learn.

www.thewhiskywire.com
Steve Rush mixes reviews of the latest bottlings with presentations of classics plus news, interviews etc.

Bruichladdich

Owner:
Rémy Cointreau

Region/district:
Islay

Founded: 1881
Status: Active (vc)
Capacity: 1 500 000 litres

Address: Bruichladdich, Islay, Argyll PA49 7UN

Tel: 01496 850221
website: www.bruichladdich.com

History:
1881 – Barnett Harvey builds the distillery with money left by his brother William III to his three sons William IV, Robert and John Gourlay.

1886 – Bruichladdich Distillery Company Ltd is founded and reconstruction commences.

1889 – William Harvey becomes Manager and remains on that post until his death in 1937.

1929 – Temporary closure.

1936 – The distillery reopens.

1938 – Joseph Hobbs, Hatim Attari and Alexander Tolmie purchase the distillery for £23 000 through the company Train & McIntyre.

1938 – Operations are moved to Associated Scottish Distillers.

1952 – The distillery is sold to Ross & Coulter from Glasgow.

1960 – A. B. Grant buys Ross & Coulter.

1961 – Own maltings ceases and malt is brought in from Port Ellen.

1968 – Invergordon Distillers take over.

1975 – The number of stills increases to four.

1983 – Temporary closure.

1993 – Whyte & Mackay buys Invergordon Distillers.

1995 – The distillery is mothballed in January.

1998 – In production again for a few months, and then mothballed.

2000 – Murray McDavid buys the distillery from JBB Greater Europe for £6.5 million.

For several years now, the owners of Bruichladdich have been courted by companies wanting to buy the distillery, but Mark Reynier and company have always declined. In July 2012, they finally accepted an offer from the French spirits group, Rémy Cointreau, and the distillery changed hands for a sum of £58m. The new owners last year sold its champagne division and had been looking to complement its portfolio. Selling the distillery now was probably good timing. Sales increased by 20% during 2011, reaching 200,000 bottles and the goal is set on reaching a turnover of £10m for 2012. Sales efforts so far have been concentrated on the traditional European and American markets but the time has now come for the company to explore emerging markets in Asia and eastern Europe.

The distillery is equipped with a cast iron, open mash tun from 1881, six washbacks of Oregon pine and two pairs of stills. They have also installed the only functioning Lomond still in the industry which was brought to Bruichladdich from Inverleven distillery. The still is being used for the production of Botanist Gin, a new addition to Bruichladdich´s range. The yearly production at Bruichladdich is 800,000 litres of alcohol and all whisky produced is based on Scottish barley, 40% of which comes from Islay.

There are three main lines in Bruichladdich's production; unpeated *Bruichladdich*, moderately peated *Port Charlotte* and the heavily peated *Octomore*. The owners have over the years released an astonishing amount of bottlings but a core range is now emerging; *Laddie Classic* (no age statement), *Laddie Ten* (the first 10 year old from the current owner´s production), *Organic* and *Organic MV* (both from organic barley grown on Islay), *Rocks, 16 year old Bourbon, 17 year old Rum* and *21 year old*. Some of the previous expressions, *Links, Infinity, Waves* and *Peat*, have now been discontinued. Limited releases during 2012 include the 22 year old *Black Art 3* (a combination of bourbon casks and various wine casks), *Islay Barley Dunlossit* (which follows on last year´s *Islay Barley 2004*) and *DNA4* (in a series of very rare and old expressions). Other releases during 2012 were *Laddie 16* and *22 years* to complement the Classic and the 10 year old. Port Charlotte was first released as a five year old and 2012 saw the release of *Port Charlotte 10 year old* which will now become a core expression. The same happened for Octomore with the release of a *10 year old* but two limited versions were also launched - *Comus* (with a finish in Chateau d´Yquem casks) and *5_169*. Finally, the first whisky made from the old barley variety, *Bere*, was released in September as a *6 year old*.

History (continued):

2001 – Jim McEwan from Bowmore becomes Production Director. The first distillation (Port Charlotte) is on 29th May and the first distillation of Bruichladdich starts in July. In September the owners' first bottlings from the old casks are released, 10, 15 and 20 years old.

2002 – The world's most heavily peated whisky is produced on 23rd October when Octomore (80ppm) is distilled.

2003 – Bruichladdich becomes the only distillery on Islay bottling on-site. It is awarded Distillery of the Year for the second time and launches the golf series, Links, 14 years old.

2004 – Second edition of the 20 year old (nick-named Flirtation) and 3D, also called The Peat Proposal, are launched.

2005 – Several new expressions are launched - the second edition of 3D, Infinity (a mix of 1989, 1990, 1991 and Port Charlotte), Rocks, Legacy Series IV, The Yellow Submarine and The Twenty 'Islands'.

2006 – Included in a number of new releases in autumn is the first official bottling of Port Charlotte; PC5.

2007 – New releases include Redder Still, Legacy 6, PC6 and an 18 year old.

2008 – More than 20 new expressions including the first Octomore, Bruichladdich 2001, PC7, Golder Still and two sherry matured from 1998.

2009 – New releases include Classic, Organic, Black Art, Infinity 3, PC8, Octomore 2 and X4+3 - the first quadruple distilled single malt.

2010 – PC Multi Vintage, Organic MV, Octomore/3_152, Bruichladdich 40 year old are released.

2011 – The first 10 year old from own production is released as well as PC9, Octomore 4_167, Ancien Regime and Rennaisance.

2012 – Ten year old versions of Port Charlotte and Octomore are released as well as Laddie 16 and 22, Bere Barley 2006, Black Art 3 and DNA4. Rémy Cointreau buys the distillery.

Port Charlotte 10   Octomore Comus   Bere Barley 2006

Black Art 3

The Laddie 16   The Laddie Ten

Bruichladdich 12 year old

GS – A light, elegant nose of fresh fruit and vanilla fudge. Medium-bodied, smooth, and malty. Becoming nuttier. Spicy oak in the finish.

DR – Very welcoming mix of melon, grape and pear on the nose, and over-ripe peach, soft melon and other sweet fruits on the palate, with a delightful clean and fresh finish.

Port Charlotte PC8

GS – A big hit of sweet peat and malt on the nose. Liquorice and a hint of rubber when water is added. Quite dry on the slightly peppery palate; sweeter and fruitier when diluted. Lingering ash notes in the lengthy, plain chocolate finish.

DR – Classic Port Charlotte peaty smoky nose, but a maturer note on the palate. It's big and bold with citrus fruits, but with sweet honeycomb and Horlicks malt drink in the mix. The peat coats the mouth and lingers on.

Bunnahabhain

Owner:
Burn Stewart Distillers
(CL Financial)

Region/district:
Islay

Founded: **Status:** **Capacity:**
1881 Active (vc) 2 500 000 litres

Address: Port Askaig, Islay, Argyll PA46 7RP

Tel:
01496 840646

website:
www.bunnahabhain.com

History:
1881 – William Robertson of Robertson & Baxter, founds the distillery together with the brothers William and James Greenless, owners of Islay Distillers Company Ltd.

1883 – Production starts in earnest in January.

1887 – Islay Distillers Company Ltd merges with William Grant & Co. in order to form Highland Distilleries Company Limited.

1963 – The two stills are augmented by two more.

1982 –The distillery closes.

1984 – The distillery reopens. A 21 year old is released to commemorate the 100th anniversary of Bunnahabhain.

1999 – Edrington takes over Highland Distillers and mothballs Bunnahabhain but allows for a few weeks of production a year.

2001 – A 35 year old from 1965 is released in a limited edition of 594 bottles during Islay Whisky Festival.

2002 – As in the previous year, Islay Whisky Festival features another Bunnahabhain – 1966, a 35 year old in sherry casks. Auld Acquaintance 1968 is launched at the Islay Jazz Festival.

2003 – In April Edrington sells Bunnahabhain and Black Bottle to Burn Stewart Distilleries (C. L. World Brands) at the princely sum of £10 million. A 40 year old from 1963 is launched.

2004 – The first limited edition of the peated version is a 6 year old called Moine.

2005 – Three limited editions are released - 34 years old, 18 years old and 25 years old.

2006 – 14 year old Pedro Ximenez and 35 years old are launched.

2008 – Darach Ur is released for the travel retail market and Toiteach (a peated 10 year old) is launched on a few selected markets.

2009 – Moine Cask Strength is released during Feis Isle.

2010 – The peated Cruach-Mhòna and a limited 30 year old are released.

2012 – A 40 year old is released.

Bunnahabhain 12 year old
GS – The nose is fresh, with light peat and discreet smoke. More overt peat on the nutty and fruity palate, but still restrained for an Islay. The finish is full-bodied and lingering, with a hint of vanilla and some smoke.

DR – Ginger and barley candy on the nose, then sweet and sour mix on the palate, lots of sweetness but with a distinctive savoury and earthy undertow.

For a long time Bunnahabhain has been one of few Islay whiskies that has been unpeated, but since the late 1990s a peated version has also been produced. During 2012 peated production will be 20% of the total. In order to get less of the fruity esters and more of the heavier phenols, the cut points during the spirit distillation are lowered from the ordinary 73/62 to 71/60.

The distillery is equipped with a 12,5 tonnes traditional stainless steel mash tun, six washbacks made of Oregon pine and two pairs of stills. The washbacks are huge (110,000 litres) but are only filled with 66,000 litres of wort. The fermentation time varies from 48 hours up to 110 hours. The stills are also quite big but only filled to 47% which gives more copper contact for the spirit and a lighter whisky. The production for 2012 will be 1,3 million litres.

Bunnahabhain single malt is an important part of the owner's blended Scotch Black Bottle but more and more effort has been put into building the single malt brand as well. The core range consists of *12, 18* and *25 years old*. A mix of bourbon and sherry casks are used – for the 12 year old it is 25% ex sherry and 75% ex bourbon, for the 18 year old the ratio is 40/60 and for the 25 year old 10/90. Part of the core range is also a 10 year old version of the peated Bunnahabhain called *Toiteach*. There are also two travel retail exclusives. The first, released in 2008, is *Darach Ur* with no age statement and in 2010, *Cruach-Mhòna* was released. The latter is a peatier version of Toiteach made up from young, heavily peated Bunnahabhain matured in ex bourbon refill casks along with 20-21 years old matured in ex sherry butts. For Islay Festival 2012, a *12 year old* with a finish in *Amontillado* casks was launched. In autumn 2012, finally, a rare *40 year old* was released. The last time that happened was in 2003.

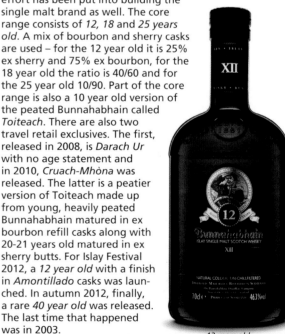

12 years old

Bushmills

Owner:
Diageo

Region/district:
N Ireland (Co. Antrim)

Founded: **Status:**   **Capacity:**
1784   Active (vc)   4 500 000 litres

Address: 2 Distillery Road, Bushmills,
Co. Antrim BT57 8XH

Tel:
028 20731521

website:
www.bushmills.com

History:

1608 – James I issues Sir Thomas Philips a licence for whiskey distilling.

1784 – The distillery is formally registered.

1885 – Fire destroys part of the distillery.

1890 – S.S. Bushmills, the distillery's own steamship, makes its maiden voyage across the Atlantic to deliver whiskey to America and then heads on to Singapore, China and Japan.

1923 – The distillery is acquired by Belfast wine and spirit merchant Samuel Wilson Boyd. Anticipating the end of US prohibition, he gears Bushmills up for expansion and increases production.

1939-1945 – No distilling during the war. The distillery is partly converted to accommodate American servicemen.

1972 – Bushmills joins Irish Distillers Group which was formed in 1966. Floor maltings ceases.

1987 – Pernod Ricard acquires Irish Distillers.

1996 – Bushmills 16 years old is launched.

2005 – Bushmills is sold to Diageo at a price tag of €295.5 million as a result of Pernod Ricard's acquisition of Allied Domecq.

2007 – The 40 year old cast iron mash tun is replaced by a new one of stainless steel at a cost of £1.4m.

2008 – Celebrations commemorate the 400th anniversary of the original license to distil, granted to the area in 1608.

2012 – Bushmills Irish Honey is released.

Bushmills 10 year old

DR – Autumn orchard of over-ripe apples on the nose, soft red apples and pear on the palate, soft sweetie finish.

A few years ago, Diageo set up two goals for Bushmills Irish whiskey. In 2012 it would sell 1 million cases and in the following years it would challenge Jameson for the number one spot on the sales list. Those were tough goals and unsurprisingly the first wasn't achieved and the second seems unlikely. In 2011/2012, Bushmills sold around 650,000 cases while Jameson reached almost 4 million. In between the two brands we have Tullamore Dew with 700,000 cases sold during 2011. In order to speed up the sales volumes, Bushmills introduced a honeyed version, Bushmills Irish Honey and at the same time launched a completely revised web site in order to appeal more to younger drinkers and less to the "stereotypical 30+ whiskey drinker."

Diageo have clearly shown that Bushmills is a brand they will invest in and since the take-over in 2005, no less than £10 million has flowed into the distillery, resulting in a new mash tun, new stills, more warehouses and a new bottle design. Bushmills now has ten stills and since 2008, the production runs seven days a week which means 4.5 million litres a year. Two kinds of malt are used, one unpeated and one slightly peated. The distillery uses triple distillation, which is the traditional Irish method. It is worth noting though, that this practise wasn't used at Bushmills until the 1930s. For many years the owners have claimed in their marketing that Bushmills distillery is the oldest in the world, dating back to 1608. This is not entirely true as the license issued by James I that year was for the district and not a specific distillery. Bushmills' core range of single malts consists of a *10 year old*, a *16 year old Triple Wood* with a finish in Port pipes for 6-9 months and a *21 year old* finished in Madeira casks for two years. There is also a *12 year old Distillery Reserve* which is sold exclusively at the distillery and the *1608 Anniversary Edition*. Black Bush and Bushmills Original are the two main blended whiskeys in the range. Bushmills is open to the public and the visitor centre receives more than 100,000 visitors per year.

10 years old

Caol Ila

Owner: Diageo   **Region/district:** Islay

Founded: 1846   **Status:** Active (vc)   **Capacity:** 6 500 000 litres

Address: Port Askaig, Islay, Argyll PA46 7RL

Tel: 01496 302760   **website:** www.malts.com

History:

1846 – Hector Henderson founds Caol Ila.

1852 – Henderson, Lamont & Co. is subjected to financial difficulties and Henderson is forced to sell Caol Ila to Norman Buchanan.

1863 – Norman Buchanan encounters financial troubles and sells to the blending company Bulloch, Lade & Co. from Glasgow.

1879 – The distillery is rebuilt and expanded.

1920 – Bulloch, Lade & Co. is liquidated and the distillery is taken over by Caol Ila Distillery.

1927 – DCL becomes sole owners.

1972 – All the buildings, except for the warehouses, are demolished and rebuilt.

1974 – The renovation, which totals £1 million, is complete and six new stills are installed.

1999 – Experiments with a completely unpeated malt are performed.

2002 – The first official bottlings since Flora & Fauna/Rare Malt appear; 12 years, 18 years and Cask Strength (c. 10 years).

2003 – A 25 year old cask strength is released.

2005 – A 25 year old Special Release is launched.

2006 – Unpeated 8 year old and 1993 Moscatel finish are released.

2007 – Second edition of unpeated 8 year old.

2008 – Third edition of unpeated 8 year old.

2009 – The fourth edition of the unpeated version (10 year old) is released.

2010 – A 25 year old, a 1999 Feis Isle bottling and a 1997 Manager's Choice are released.

2011 – An unpeated 12 year old and the unaged Moch are released.

2012 – An unpeated 14 year old is released.

Caol Ila 12 year old

GS – Iodine, fresh fish and smoked bacon feature on the nose, along with more delicate, floral notes. Smoke, malt, lemon and peat on the slightly oily palate. Peppery peat in the drying finish.

DR – Barbecued fish and seaweed on the nose, oily bacon-fat, squeezed lemon and sweet smoke on the palate, immensely satisfying citrusy seaside barbecue of a finish.

Diageo, the owners of Caol Ila, also have three of the biggest blends in their portfolio (Johnnie Walker, J&B and Bell's) and a fair amount of peated malt is needed for them. Lagavulin is too important as a single malt in its own right so the owners put their trust in Caol Ila to cover their need. With the upgrade in 2011, the capacity increased to a staggering 6,5 million litres per year and trials doing unpeated Caol Ila have also been suspended since 2005 as demand is for peated whisky. Due to the upgrade, the distillery was closed from summer 2011 to beginning of November. During that time two more washbacks were installed as well as a new 13 tonnes full lauter mash tun. A new control system was installed in the still house and the total investment amounted to £3.5m. Apart from the new mash tun, the equipment now consists of ten wooden washbacks and three pairs of stills. During 2012 the distillery will be operating 49 weeks, doing 28 mashes per week which amounts to 6,5 million litres of alcohol.

It is interesting to compare the taste of Caol Ila with Lagavulin. Both use malted barley with the same phenol content but Caol Ila single malt has a much more subdued peatiness. One reason for this is that at Caol Ila they don't fill the stills as much (only around 50%) which increases the copper contact. The different cut points during the spirit run is another factor. Caol Ila starts at 75% catching a lot of the fruity esters and already stops at 65% thus avoiding the heavier phenols. Corresponding figures for Lagavulin are 72% and 59% giving the whisky a more pungent character. The core range consists of *12* and *18 years old*, *Distiller's Edition Moscatel* finish and *Cask Strength*, but was extended with a *25 year old* in 2010. In 2011, *Caol Ila Moch*, the first official bottling from the distillery without an age statement or distillation year, was released. The first *14 year old* of the unpeated Caol Ila was released in 2012 and, in conjunction with the 2012 Islay Festival, an *11 year old*, drawn from a single sherry butt, was launched.

Caol Ila 14 years unpeated

Cardhu

Owner:
Diageo

Region/district:
Speyside

Founded: **Status:**   **Capacity:**
1824   Active (vc)   3 400 000 litres

Address:
Knockando, Aberlour, Moray AB38 7RY

Tel:
01479 874635 (vc)

website:
www.discovering-distilleries.com

History:

1824 – John Cumming applies for and obtains a licence for Cardhu Distillery.

1846 – John Cumming dies and his son Lewis takes over.

1872 – Lewis dies and his wife Elizabeth takes over.

1884 – A new distillery is built to replace the old.

1893 – John Walker & Sons purchases Cardhu for £20,500 but the Cumming family continues operations. The whisky changes name from Cardow to Cardhu.

1908 – The name reverts to Cardow.

1960-61 – Reconstruction and expansion of stills from four to six.

1981 – The name changes to Cardhu.

1998 – A visitor centre is constructed.

2002 – Diageo changes Cardhu single malt to a vatted malt with contributions from other distilleries in it.

2003 – The whisky industry protests sharply against Diageo's plans.

2004 – Diageo withdraws Cardhu Pure Malt.

2005 – The 12 year old Cardhu Single Malt is relaunched and a 22 year old is released.

2009 – Cardhu 1997, a single cask in the new Manager's Choice range is released.

2011 – A 15 year old and an 18 year old are released.

Cardhu 12 year old

GS – The nose is relatively light and floral, quite sweet, with pears, nuts and a whiff of distant peat. Medium-bodied, malty and sweet in the mouth. Medium-length in the finish, with sweet smoke, malt and a hint of peat.

DR – Honeycomb and chocolate Crunchie bar on the nose, fluffy over-ripe apples, toffee, boiled sweets on the palate, delightful clean and crisp finish.

Cardhu distillery is the spiritual home of Johnnie Walker - the world's best selling blended Scotch. In 2011, no less than 215 million bottles were sold. The core range of the brand is Red Label, Black Label, Double Black (a peatier version, introduced in 2010), Gold Reserve, Platinum (an 18 year old launched in late 2011) and Blue Label. There is also a blended malt called Green Label which is about to be withdrawn from all markets except Taiwan. A range of extremely rare and limited versions include King George V (launched in 2007), John Walker (from 2010 and just 330 bottles), Johnnie Walker XR (a 21 year old from 2010) and finally the Diamond Jubilee bottling – 60 decanters with whiskies all distilled in 1952 and released in 2012.

Cardhu is very beautifully situated on a hill alongside the B9102 in Speyside with a lovely view towards Benrinnes. The distillery is equipped with an 8 tonnes stainless steel full lauter mash tun, ten washbacks (six made of Scottish larch, two of stainless steel and two of Douglas fir), all with a fermentation time of 64 hours and three pairs of stills. During 2012, Cardhu will be working a seven-day week with a production of 3,4 million litres of alcohol. On site are five dunnage warehouses with 7,500 casks maturing.

The biggest market for Cardhu is by far Spain and France, but a couple of years ago it was re-introduced in the USA where it was hugely popular in the 1980s and 90s.

For several years, the core range was just the *12 year old*. In 2011, however, two more expressions were released in the core markets (France and Spain) by way of a *15* and an *18 year old*. Since 2006 there is also a *Special Cask Reserve* with no age statement in these two countries. A *single cask* from *1997* was released in autumn 2009 as part of the new series Manager's Choice.

15 years old

Clynelish

Owner:
Diageo

Region/district:
Northern Highlands

Founded: **Status:**   **Capacity:**
1967   Active (vc)   4 800 000 litres

Address: Brora, Sutherland KW9 6LR

Tel:
01408 623003 (vc)

website:
www.malts.com

History:
1819 – The 1st Duke of Sutherland founds a distillery called Clynelish Distillery.

1827 – The first licensed distiller, James Harper, files for bankruptcy and John Matheson takes over.

1846 – George Lawson & Sons become new licensees.

1896 – James Ainslie & Heilbron takes over.

1912 – James Ainslie & Co. narrowly escapes bankruptcy and Distillers Company Limited (DCL) takes over together with James Risk.

1916 – John Walker & Sons buys a stake of James Risk's stocks.

1931 – The distillery is mothballed.

1939 – Production restarts.

1960 – The distillery becomes electrified.

1967 – A new distillery, also named Clynelish, is built adjacent to the first one.

1968 – 'Old' Clynelish is mothballed in August.

1969 – 'Old' Clynelish is reopened as Brora and starts using a very peaty malt.

1983 – Brora is closed in March.

2002 – A 14 year old is released.

2006 – A Distiller's Edition 1991 finished in Oloroso casks is released.

2009 – A 12 year old is released for Friends of the Classic Malts.

2010 – A 1997 Manager's Choice single cask is released.

Diageo are trying to increase their whisky production wherever they can at the moment and Clynelish is no exception. Already in 2008 the capacity was increased by adding another two washbacks. During 2012, by adding one mash per week and shortening the silent season, they will be doing 4,8 million litres of alcohol – an increase of 15% compared to last year. They assume that the extra volume will become necessary in years to come, as the sales of Johnnie Walker Gold Label, where Cynelish is the signature malt, increases. The 18 year old version of Gold Label will be phased out during 2012 but, instead, Gold Label Reserve (without age statement and including some younger whiskies) will take its place after a 5 year trial period in south-east Asia.

Clynelish is a modern distillery which was built right next to the much older Brora (which used to be called Clynelish) in 1967. The two distilleries were operating together for 14 years but the character of the single malts are completely different, with Brora being much more peated (at least some of the bottlings). Clynelish is equipped with a cast iron full lauter mash tun from 1967 (probably due for replacement in the near future), eight wooden washbacks, two stainless steel washbacks installed in 2008 and three pairs of stills (with the spirit stills being larger than the wash stills). Most of the production at Clynelish is matured elsewhere and some 6,000 casks are stored in the old Brora warehouses.

The Clynelish single malt sells around 100,000 bottles per year. Official bottlings include a *14 year old* and a *Distiller's Edition* with an *Oloroso Seco* finish. The first distillery shop exclusive, an *American oak cask strength*, was released in 2008. In 2009 another addition was made to the range, a *12 year old* for Friends of the Classic Malts and in 2010 a *single cask* (first fill bourbon) distilled in *1997* was released as part of the Manager's Choice series.

Clynelish 14 year old

GS – A nose that is fragrant, spicy and complex, with candle wax, malt and a whiff of smoke. Notably smooth in the mouth, with honey and contrasting citric notes, plus spicy peat, before a brine and tropical fruit finish.

DR – Fresh green fruit and unripe melon on the nose, sweet almost fizzy lemon sherbet on the palate, a wispy hint of peat and pepper, and satisfying and balanced finish.

14 years old

Cooley

Owner:
Beam Inc.

Region/district:
Ireland (County Louth)

Founded: **Status:** **Capacity:**
1987 Active 3 250 000 litres

Address: Riverstown, Cooley, Co. Louth

Tel: **website:**
+353 (0)42 9376102 www.cooleywhiskey.com

History:
1987 – John Teeling purchases Ceimici Teo Distillery in Dundalk. Previously it has produced spirits in column stills (e. g. vodka) and is now renamed Cooley Distillery.

1988 – Willie McCarter acquires part of A. A. Watt Distillery and the brand Tyrconnell and merges with Teeling. Teeling simultaneously buys decommissioned Locke's Kilbeggan Distillery.

1989 – A pair of pot stills is installed for production of both malt and grain whiskey.

1992 – Locke's Single Malt, without age statement, is launched as the first single malt from the distillery. Cooley encounters financial troubles and and stops production.

1995 – Finances improve and production resumes.

1996 – Connemara is launched.

2000 – Locke's 8 year old single malt is launched.

2003 – The Connemara 12 year old is launched.

2006 – Five Connemara Single Casks from 1992 are released.

2007 – Kilbeggan distillery is reopened.

2009 – New packaging for the Connemara range and release of the first in The Small Batch Collection.

2010 – The heavily peated Connemara Turf Mor is released.

2011 – Connemara Bog Oak is released.

2012 – The company is bought by Beam Inc.

Connemara 12 year old
DR – Soft fruit and tarry peat on the nose, then fluffy red apples, toffee and smoke intriguingly mixed into an unusual and very enticing whole. Smoke in the finish.

Irish whiskey as a category has enjoyed a tremendous increase in sales during the last years and it was probably only a matter of time before one of the big companies would try to buy Cooley distillery, the only independently owned whiskey producer in the country. It finally happened in December 2011 when it was announced that Beam Inc. had bought the distillery for $95m. The co-founder of Cooley, John Teeling, later left the company, together with his eldest son, Jack, while the younger son, Stephen, still works for the company with global marketing. A large part of Cooley's production has been sold to other companies and supermarkets, but Beam announced that this will cease in order to concentrate on their own brands instead. Operating both pot stills and column stills at Cooley, means that they can produce both malt and grain whiskey. The equipment consists of one mash tun, four malt and six grain washbacks all made of stainless steel, two copper pot stills and two column stills. During 2011 they were distilling more or less at full capacity which equals 650,000 litres of malt spirit and 2.6 million litres of grain spirit. At the moment, there are more than 60,000 casks in the warehouses.

The Cooley range of whiskies consists of several brands. *Connemara* single malts, which are all more or less peated, consist of a *no age*, a *12 year old*, a *cask strength*, *sherry finish* and the heavily peated *Turf Mor*. The latter two are part of a series of limited expressions called The Small Batch Collection. A new member of this range for 2011, replacing the sherry finish, was *Bog Oak* with the whiskey maturing in 2000 year old oak found in the Irish bog. The rest of Cooley's single malt range includes *Tyrconnel no age*, *Tyrconnel 15 year old single cask* and *Tyrconnel wood finishes*, as well as *Locke's 8 years old*.

A number of blended whiskeys are also produced, as is a single grain, *Greenore 8 years old*. An *18 year old* version of the latter was recently released.

Connemara 12 years old

Cragganmore

Owner:		Region/district:
Diageo		Speyside

Founded:	Status:	Capacity:
1869	Active (vc)	2 200 000 litres

Address: Ballindalloch, Moray AB37 9AB

Tel:	website:
01479 874700	www.malts.com

History:

1869 – John Smith, who already runs Ballindalloch and Glenfarclas Distilleries, founds Cragganmore.

1886 – John Smith dies and his brother George takes over operations.

1893 – John's son Gordon, at 21, is old enough to assume responsibility for operations.

1901 – The distillery is refurbished and modernized with help of the famous architect Charles Doig.

1912 – Gordon Smith dies and his widow Mary Jane supervises operations.

1917 – The distillery closes.

1918 – The distillery reopens and Mary Jane installs electric lighting.

1923 – The distillery is sold to the newly formed Cragganmore Distillery Co. where Mackie & Co. and Sir George Macpherson-Grant of Ballindalloch Estate share ownership.

1927 – White Horse Distillers is bought by DCL which thus obtains 50% of Cragganmore.

1964 – The number of stills is increased from two to four.

1965 – DCL buys the remainder of Cragganmore.

1988 – Cragganmore 12 years becomes one of six selected for United Distillers´ Classic Malts.

1998 – Cragganmore Distillers Edition Double Matured (port) is launched for the first time.

2002 – A visitor centre opens in May.

2006 – A 17 year old from 1988 is released.

2010 – Manager´s Choice single cask 1997 and a limited 21 year old are released.

Cragganmore 12 year old

GS – A nose of sherry, brittle toffee, nuts, mild wood smoke, angelica and mixed peel. Elegant on the malty palate, with herbal and fruit notes, notably orange. Medium in length, with a drying, slightly smoky finish.

DR – The nose has honey, soft fruits and sweet spring meadow notes and is very inviting, and on the palate soft barley, summer fruits and a sweetness lead up to an almost tangy finish.

If you look closely at the label of a bottle of Cragganmore single malt, there is a small picture of a steam locomotive. This is a reminder that the distillery was the first to make use of the railway in the Highlands. Cragganmore was actually built in the same year that the Strathspey Railway was opened. One of the people who took initiative for the new means of transportation was Sir George Macpherson-Grant, a railroad enthusiast and owner of the Ballindalloch Estate, where the distillery is situated. The railway closed in 1968 but part of it has been re-opened by railway enthusiasts. Cragganmore is equipped with a 6,8 tonnes stainless steel full lauter mash tun. There are also six washbacks (two of them being replaced in 2012) made of Oregon pine with a 50-60 hour fermentation time and two pairs of stills. The two spirit stills are peculiar with flat tops, which had already been introduced in the times of the founder, John Smith. As if that was not enough, the unusually T-shaped lyne arms increase the reflux which, together with the long fermentation time, sets the character of the spirit. The stills are attached to cast iron worm tubs on the outside for cooling the spirit vapours. Part of the production matures in four dunnage warehouses on site. The distillery is currently doing 16 mashes per week and thanks to a shorter silent season, it will mean a production of 2,2 million litres during 2012.

For the past decade the sales of Cragganmore single malt has been stable at around 350,000 bottles per year and it also plays an important part in two blended whiskies; Old Parr and White Horse.

The main part of production is used for Old Parr which was first introduced in 1909 and which is now very popular in Japan and Latin America. The core range is made up of a 12 year old and a Distiller's Edition with a finish in Port pipes. Two new limited bottlings appeared in 2010; a single sherry cask distilled in 1997 released as part of the Manager´s Choice series and a 21 year old launched as a part of the yearly Special Releases.

12 years old

Craigellachie

Owner:
John Dewar & Sons
(Bacardi)

Region/district:
Speyside

Founded: **Status:** **Capacity:**
1891   Active   4 000 000 litres

Address: Aberlour, Banffshire AB38 9ST

Tel: **website:**
01340 872971   -

History:
1891 – The distillery is built by Craigellachie–Glenlivet Distillery Company which has Alexander Edward and Peter Mackie as part-owners. The famous Charles Doig is the architect.

1898 – Production does not start until this year.

1916 – Mackie & Company Distillers Ltd takes over.

1924 – Peter Mackie dies and Mackie & Company changes name to White Horse Distillers.

1927 – White Horse Distillers are bought by Distillers Company Limited (DCL).

1930 – Administration is transferred to Scottish Malt Distillers (SMD), a subsidiary of DCL.

1964 – Refurbishing takes place and two new stills are bought, increasing the number to four.

1998 – United Distillers & Vintners (UDV) sells Craigellachie together with Aberfeldy, Brackla and Aultmore and the blending company John Dewar & Sons to Bacardi Martini.

2004 – The first bottlings from the new owners are a new 14 year old which replaces UDV's Flora & Fauna and a 21 year old cask strength from 1982 produced for Craigellachie Hotel.

Sir Peter Mackie, one of the most colourful characters in Scottish history of whisky, was involved in founding Craigellachie distillery in 1891. He had joined his uncle's firm trading in wines and spirits a decade before and helped him establish what would become one of the most well-known brands in the business, White Horse. The name is derived from a legendary inn at Edinburgh that had been within the family since 1650. Peter Mackie, or Restless Peter as he was sometimes known, was famous for always speaking his mind. In 1909 Lloyd George propagated his People's Budget in which the reforms for the weakest in society would be financed through a 30% increase of the tax for whisky (not for beer and wine!). Mackie got upset and retaliated with the comment "What can one expect of a Welsh country solicitor being placed, without any commercial training, as Chancellor of the Exchequer in a large country like this?"

The Craigellachie distillery and the surrounding village take its name from the huge cliff which dominates the landscape and actually means "rocky hill". The village dates back to the mid 18th century with the distillery being built around a century and a half later.

The distillery is equipped with a modern Steinecker full lauter mash tun, installed in 2001, which replaced the old open cast iron mash tun. There are also eight washbacks made of larch with a fermentation time of 56-60 hours and two pairs of stills. The spirit vapours from the stills are condensed through worm tubs. The tub itself (in Craigellachie's case made out of cast iron) can last for many years but the worms (the copper pipes where the spirit is condensed) need to be replaced every 5 to 10 years. Production during 2012 will be 21 mashes per week – the equivalent of 3,4 million litres of alcohol.

Most of the production goes into Dewar's blends but a *14 year old* has been on the market since 2004 and this is the only official bottling.

Craigellachie 14 year old

GS – Citrus fruits, cereal and even a whiff of smoke on the nose. Comparatively full-bodied, with sweet fruits, malt and spice on the palate, plus earthy notes and a touch of liquorice in the slightly smoky and quite lengthy finish.

DR – Intriguing and deep mix of light fruits on the nose, a spicy bite then clean and smooth mouth feel, and a soft finish.

14 years old

Dailuaine

Owner:		Region/district:
Diageo		Speyside

Founded:	Status:	Capacity:
1852	Active	5 200 000 litres

Address: Carron, Banffshire AB38 7RE

Tel:	website:
01340 872500	www.malts.com

History:

1852 – The distillery is founded by William Mackenzie.

1865 – William Mackenzie dies and his widow leases the distillery to James Fleming, a banker from Aberlour.

1879 – William Mackenzie's son forms Mackenzie and Company with Fleming.

1891 – Dailuaine-Glenlivet Distillery Ltd is founded.

1898 – Dailuaine-Glenlivet Distillery Ltd merges with Talisker Distillery Ltd and forms Dailuaine-Talisker Distilleries Ltd.

1915 – Thomas Mackenzie dies without heirs.

1916 – Dailuaine-Talisker Company Ltd is bought by the previous customers John Dewar & Sons, John Walker & Sons and James Buchanan & Co.

1917 – A fire rages and the pagoda roof collapses. The distillery is forced to close.

1920 – The distillery reopens.

1925 – Distillers Company Limited (DCL) takes over.

1960 – Refurbishing. The stills increase from four to six and a Saladin box replaces the floor maltings.

1965 – Indirect still heating through steam is installed.

1983 – On site maltings is closed down and malt is purchased centrally.

1991 – The first official bottling, a 16 year old, is launched in the Flora & Fauna series.

1996 – A 22 year old cask strength from 1973 is launched as a Rare Malt.

1997 – A cask strength version of the 16 year old is launched.

2000 – A 17 year old Manager's Dram matured in sherry casks is launched.

2010 – A single cask from 1997 is released.

2012 – The production capacity is increased by 25%.

Due to the continuing growth of demand for Scotch whisky, many producers are looking to increase production capacity wherever they can. Dailuaine distillery is no exception and another two additional washbacks will increase their production by 25% to 5,2 million litres of alcohol. A new operating system for the whole site will furthermore be installed as well as a new cooling tower. Adjacent to the distillery lies a dark grains plant processing draff and pot ale into cattle feed and a bioplant. The latter will be upgraded during 2012 to a state-of-the-art plant which takes care of the spent lees and wastewater not just from Dailuaine, but also from a number of Diageo's other distilleries in the area. The £9.5m investment is a part of the company's efforts to increase energy efficiency and to reduce the carbon footprint.

The distillery, nicely tucked away by the Spey River, is equipped with a stainless steel full lauter mash tun, eight washbacks made of larch, plus two new stainless steel ones placed outside and three pairs of stills. All the condensers are made of copper but, until a few years ago, some of them were made of stainless steel to help achieve a sulphury style of new make. Since then the style has changed and they are now alternating between nutty and green/grassy. This was done by choosing either a clear or a cloudy wort, changing the fermentation time in the washbacks and the way the stills are run during distillation. At the beginning of 2012 the production had increased to 7 days with 23 mashes per week. There are also eight magnificent granite warehouses but the last time they were used for storing whisky was in 1989.

Dailuaine is one of many distilleries whose main task is to produce malt whisky to become part of a blended Scotch. The only official bottling is the *16 year old* in the *Flora & Fauna* series. In April 2010 a limited ex-sherry single cask from *1997* was released as part of the Manager's Choice series.

Flora & Fauna 16 years old

Dailuaine 16 year old

GS – Barley, sherry and nuts on the substantial nose, developing into maple syrup. Medium-bodied, rich and malty in the mouth, with more sherry and nuts, plus ripe oranges, fruitcake, spice and a little smoke. The finish is lengthy and slightly oily, with almonds, cedar and slightly smoky oak.

DR – Rich and full nose, with plum, apricot jam and some treacle toffee. The palate is very full, rich, rounded and sweet with apricot and red berries. The finish is medium, fruity and sweet.

Meet the Manager

HAZEL EADIE
SITE OPERATIONS MANAGER, DAILUAINE DISTILLERY

When did you start working in the whisky business and when did you start at Dailuaine?

I started in the whisky business in January 2011 and Dailuaine is my first distillery.

Had you been working in other lines of business before whisky?

I worked in the chemical industry manufacturing fungicides.

What kind of education or training do you have?

I have extensive management training within the chemical sector, but no formal brewing and distilling to date.

What are your main tasks as a manager?

Managing the manufacture and quality of New Make Spirit for the production of Scotch whisky.

What are the biggest challenges of being a distillery manager?

You have a lot of 'plates to spin' but the biggest challenge is increase production without compromising quality to meet the ever increasing global demand for Scotch.

What would be the worst that could go wrong in the production process?

Other than health and safety issues, my biggest nightmare would be running out of the natural spring water that is crucial to the manufacturing process. Most problems can be managed, but a mild winter and no rain could impact the supply.

How would you describe the character of Dailuaine single malt?

Dailuaine 16 year old Flora and Fauna bottling has a rich colour. It has a slightly smoky note and sweet taste from maturation in sherry casks.

What are the main features in the process at Dailuaine, contributing to this character?

Most of the Spirit produced at Dailuaine is matured specifically for blending into one of the many Scotch products that Diageo if famous for. The main features which contribute to character are how the malt is mashed, how long the fermentation time and copper contact in the stills are, and of course the sherry casks give Dailuaine 16 year old its distinctive rich colour and sweet taste.

If it were your decision alone – what new expression of Dailuaine would you like to see released?

A special bottling to celebrate the expansion would be nice or to see Dailuaine 16 year old added to Diageo classic malts selection would be an honour.

If you had to choose a favourite dram other than Dailuaine, what would that be?

It would have to be Mortlach, it has similar qualities to Dailuaine, and also shares the name of my daughter's school.

What are the biggest changes you have seen the past 5 years in your profession?

The biggest change has been the shift in demand for Scotch. With emerging markets and growth in Asia and South America, it's been a wonderful boost for an industry that has in the past resulted in the closure of distilleries. We are now seeing significant investment in expanding existing distilleries and Diageo is also planning to build at least one new malt whisky distillery. There has also been a massive shift in being both more environmentally efficient and energy efficient which is demonstrated in the investment in the industry over the last few years. My distillery resides in Speyside, an area of breathtaking natural beauty and we have a responsibility to exist in harmony.

Do you see any major changes in the next 10 years to come?

Diageo has recently announced a huge investment in Scotch whisky on the back of growth in global markets. This will see a number of major expansions at distilleries across Scotland. Much of that will be focused on Speyside and Dailuaine will be one of the distilleries to benefit from the investment.

Do you have any special interests or hobbies that you pursue?

My 5 year old daughter Emily keeps me pretty busy, but in my free time, I like to go to the cinema, take my dog for walks, and have dinner with friends and family.

You haven´t been in the whisky business very long. Why did you decide to change career?

The whisky industry attracted me as during times of financial austerity, it is bucking the trend in terms of the investment. It is a healthy growing business and the science in making whisky, as well as the history of my site is fascinating.

During the last years Dailuaine has been producing three distinctively different styles of malt whisky. Why is that?

Like the vast majority of malt distilleries in Scotland, Dailuaine exists primarily to supply malt whisky for blending. By adjusting elements of the distillation and maturation process we are able to produce different characters of spirit and this adds to the breadth of inventory from which our Master Blenders can draw when producing blends such as Johnnie Walker.

Do you have any plans for the beautiful warehouses since they are no longer used to store whisky?

At the moment there is no plans for the warehouses to be brought back into use. They are architecturally beautiful, as well as the main office with its distinctive turrets, and the only plans are to maintain that beauty.

Dalmore

Owner: Whyte & Mackay Ltd (United Spirits)

Region/district: Northern Highlands

Founded: 1839 **Status:** Active (vc) **Capacity:** 3 700 000 litres

Address: Alness, Ross-shire IV17 0UT

Tel: 01349 882362 **website:** www.thedalmore.com

History:

1839 – Alexander Matheson founds the distillery.

1867 – Three Mackenzie brothers run the distillery.

1886 – Alexander Matheson dies.

1891 – Sir Kenneth Matheson sells the distillery for £14,500 to the Mackenzie brothers.

1917 – The Royal Navy moves in to start manufacturing American mines.

1920 – The Royal Navy moves out and leaves behind a distillery damaged by an explosion.

1922 – The distillery is in production again.

1956 – Floor malting replaced by Saladin box.

1960 – Mackenzie Brothers (Dalmore) Ltd merges with Whyte & Mackay and forms the company Dalmore-Whyte & Mackay Ltd.

1966 – Number of stills is increased to eight.

1982 – The Saladin box is abandoned.

1990 – American Brands buys Whyte & Mackay.

1996 – Whyte & Mackay changes name to JBB (Greater Europe).

2001 – Through management buy-out, JBB (Greater Europe) is bought from Fortune Brands and changes name to Kyndal Spirits.

2002 – Kyndal Spirits changes name to Whyte & Mackay.

2004 – A new visitor centre opens.

2007 – United Spirits buys Whyte & Mackay. 15 year old, 1973 Cabernet Sauvignon and a 40 year old are released.

2008 – 1263 King Alexander III and Vintage 1974 are released.

2009 – New releases include an 18 year old, a 58 year old and a Vintage 1951.

2010 – The Dalmore Mackenzie 1992 Vintage is released.

2011 – More expressions in the River Collection and 1995 Castle Leod are released.

2012 – The visitor centre is upgraded and Constellaton Collection is launched.

Dalmore 12 year old

GS – The attractively perfumed nose offers sweet malt, thick cut orange marmalade, sherry and a hint of leather. Full-bodied, with an initially quite dry sherry taste, though sweeter sherry develops in the mouth, along with spice and balancing, delicate, citrus notes. The finish is lengthy, with more spices, ginger, lingering Seville oranges and vanilla.

DR – Orange jelly and squidgy fruit on the nose, an impressive full confectionery and fruit salad taste on the softest of peat beds, and a wonderful and warming finish.

A completely upgraded visitor centre and shop was opened in summer 2011 at Dalmore. It is very elegant and contemporary and with excellent exhibitions showing, i. a. the importance of the wood. One of the best features is the opportunity for the visitor to nose the different steps in the distillation process from the first drops from the wash still down to the feints. The distillery is equipped with a semi-lauter mash tun, eight washbacks made of Oregon pine and four pairs of stills. The spirit stills have water jackets which allows cold water to circulate between the reflux bowl and the neck of the stills, thus increasing the reflux. Two weeks per year, a heavily peated spirit is produced using a total of 800 tonnes of malt peated at 50 ppm. The owners expect to produce 3,7 million litres during 2012. Dalmore has become known for some very exclusive bottling in the last couple of years and has continued along that route during 2012. For Duty Free, a series of 21 different whiskies distilled between 1964 and 1992 was released. The price for all 21 bottles (called *Constellation Collection*) was £158,000 and the owners plan to release 20,000 bottles over the next five years. Another expression was *Zenith* with just one bottle for sale at Whisky Shop through an auction. The oldest whisky in the bottle was distilled in 1926. Finally, in summer 2012, 1,000 bottles of the 30 year old Dalmore *Ceti* were released. The core range consists of *12, 15, 18 year old, 1263 King Alexander III* and *Cigar Malt* (replacing Gran Reserva). In 2011 a *Distillery Exclusive 1995* was released to be sold at the distillery only. A range called Mackenzie was introduced in 2010 to help raise funds to restore the clans castle. The first two expressions were *Mackenzie* and *Castle Leod* and in 2012 the third, *Cromartie* with an Oloroso finish, was released. Another range where part of the profit is donated is *The Rivers Collection* to help support the conservation of the rivers in Scotland.

12 years old

Dalwhinnie

Owner:
Diageo

Region/district:
Northern Highlands

Founded: **Status:**   **Capacity:**
1897   Active (vc)   2 200 000 litres

Address: Dalwhinnie, Inverness-shire PH19 1AB

Tel: **website:**
01540 672219 (vc)   www.malts.com

History:

1897 – John Grant, George Sellar and Alexander Mackenzie from Kingussie commence building the facilities. The first name is Strathspey and the construction work amounts to £10,000.

1898 – Production starts in February. The owner encounters financial troubles after a few months and John Somerville & Co and A P Blyth & Sons take over in November and change the name to Dalwhinnie.

1905 – America's largest distillers, Cook & Bernheimer in New York, buys Dalwhinnie for £1,250 at an auction. The administration of Dalwhinnie is placed in the newly formed company James Munro & Sons.

1919 – Macdonald Greenlees & Willliams Ltd headed by Sir James Calder buys Dalwhinnie.

1926 – Macdonald Greenlees & Williams Ltd is bought by Distillers Company Ltd (DCL) which licences Dalwhinnie to James Buchanan & Co.

1930 – Operations are transferred to Scottish Malt Distilleries (SMD).

1934 – The distillery is closed after a fire in February.

1938 – The distillery opens again.

1968 – The maltings is decommissioned.

1986 – A complete refurbishing takes place.

1987 – Dalwhinnie 15 years becomes one of the selected six in United Distillers´ Classic Malts.

1991 – A visitor centre is constructed.

1992 – The distillery closes and goes through a major refurbishment costing £3.2 million.

1995 – The distillery opens in March.

1998 – Dalwhinnie Distillers Edition 1980 (oloroso) is introduced for the first time. The other five in The Classic Malts, each with a different finish, are also introduced as Distillers Editions for the first time.

2002 – A 36 year old is released.

2003 – A 29 year old is released.

2006 – A 20 year old is released.

2010 – A Manager´s Choice 1992 is released.

2012 – A 25 year old is released.

Dalwhinnie 15 year old

GS – The nose is fresh, with pine needles, heather and vanilla. Sweet and balanced on the fruity palate, with honey, malt and a very subtle note of peat. The medium length finish dries elegantly.

DR – Full honey and sweet peat on the nose, a rich creamy mouthfeel and a delicious honey and exotic fruits mix all layered on soft peat foundations.

Dalwhinnie is one of Diageo´s best selling single malts (actually number four after Cardhu, Talisker and Lagavulin) and sold around 900,000 bottles in 2011. The exquisite location on the outskirts of the Cairngorm wilderness on the A9 and the fact that it is one of the original six Classic Malts should generate considerably more visitors than the 20,000 yearly visitors. One way could be to make it the spiritual home of Buchanan´s blended Scotch. One could do so much more to show the connection between the blend and one of its signature malts than just putting a sign on the wall. The biggest market for Buchanan´s is Venezuela and Mexico, but also the USA where it is currently the fastest growing blend. Global sales in 2011 was close to 20 million bottles which is an increase by 15% from the previous year. Dalwhinnie distillery is equipped with a full lauter mash tun, six wooden washbacks and just the one pair of stills. From the stills, the lyne arms lead out through the roofs to the wooden wormtubs outside. The style they are looking for in the newmake is sulphury – something that will disappear when it is ready to be bottled.

This character is enhanced by the lack of copper contact in the wormtubs but also through the wide spirit cut (the part of the distillation which goes into casks to mature). At Dalwhinnie they start collecting the spirit at 75% and don´t stop until it has reached 59% in order to catch the heavier congeners. In keeping with most distilleries in the Highlands, Dalwhinnie is using very lightly peated malt (1-2ppm) but do it in a rather special way. They buy unpeated malt as well as malt with a 15-20ppm specification. The two batches are then mixed at the distillery before mashing in order to get the exact specification every time.

The core range is made up of a *15 year old* and a *Distiller's Edition*. In autumn 2012 a *25 year old* matured in rejuvenated American oak hogsheads was launched as a part of the Special Releases.

25 years old

Deanston

Owner: Burn Stewart Distillers (C L Financial)

Region/district: Eastern Highlands

Founded: 1965 **Status:** Active (vc) **Capacity:** 3 000 000 litres

Address: Deanston, Perthshire FK16 6AG

Tel: 01786 843010 **website:** www.deanstonmalt.com

History:

1965 – A weavery from 1785 is transformed into Deanston Distillery by James Finlay & Co. and Brodie Hepburn Ltd (Deanston Distillery Co.). Brodie Hepburn also runs Tullibardine Distillery.

1966 – Production commences in October.

1971 – The first single malt is named Old Bannockburn.

1972 – Invergordon Distillers takes over.

1974 – The first single malt bearing the name Deanston is produced.

1982 – The distillery closes.

1990 – Burn Stewart Distillers from Glasgow buys the distillery for £2.1 million.

1991 – The distillery resumes production.

1999 – C L Financial buys an 18% stake of Burn Stewart.

2002 – C L Financial acquires the remaining stake.

2006 – Deanston 30 years old is released.

2009 – A new version of the 12 year old is released.

2010 – Virgin Oak is released.

2012 – A visitor centre is opened.

Deanston 12 year old

GS – A fresh, fruity nose with malt and honey. The palate displays cloves, ginger, honey and malt, while the finish is long, quite dry and pleasantly herbal.

DR – Fresh and young crystallized barley on the nose with some cut hay and grass. On the palate it's a fruit sandwich, with orange and yellow fruits at first, then a cough candy honey and aniseed centre, and orange marmalade late on. The finish is intensely fruity with some spice.

From May 2012 it is possible to visit Deanston distillery close to Doune in Perthshire. A new, excellent visitor centre was opened and part of the tour includes a film from the 1920s which is projected on a huge, white distillery wall showing one of the water wheels (at that time the biggest in Europe) in action. A total of 8 wheels were demounted by 1937 but were replaced by turbines and Deanston is the only Scottish distillery that is self-sufficient as regards electricity. Originally a weavery built in 1785, Deanston was transformed into a distillery in 1965. Most of the buildings are new but there is an amazing weaving shed from the 19th century which is now being used as a warehouse. The equipment consists of a traditional open top cast iron mash tun, eight stainless steel washbacks and two pairs of stills with ascending lyne arms. During 2012, the distillery will be doing 11 mashes per week and producing 2,3 million litres of alcohol. Starting in 2000, a small part of organic spirit has been produced yearly. The single malt from Deanston has no artificial colouring and it is also unchillfiltered. The master blender and distillery director Ian MacMillan, started years ago trying to recreate the character of Deanston as it used to be – fruity and estery. To achieve this, he introduced low gravity worts, longer fermentations and slower distillation. In 2012, Deanston was featured as one of three distillery locations in Ken Loach´s new film The Angel´s Share.

The core range is a *12 year old* and *Virgin Oak*. The latter is a non-age statement malt with a finish in virgin oak casks. There is also a *30 year old* exclusive to the USA as well as a *12 year old* bottling for *Marks & Spencer*. The first version of *Organic Deanston* (a 10 year old), will be released in 2013. For those of you who travel to the distillery there is a reward in the form of three distillery exclusive bottlings – *Toasted Oak*, *Spanish Oak* and the limited *1974 Vintage*.

12 years old

Meet the Manager

CALLUM FRASER
DISTILLERY MANAGER, DEANSTON DISTILLERY

When did you start working in the whisky business and when did you start at Deanston?

1990 was when I started at Deanston and in the whisky industry.

Had you been working in other lines of business before whisky?

I trained as a Master Baker.

What kind of education or training do you have?

I have been trained by our Master Distiller/Blender Ian MacMillan who has nearly forty years experience in the industry. He progressed me through all operational aspects of the distilling process to become the Distillery Manager in 2006.

Describe your career in the whisky business.

Started at Deanston in October 1990 as a Mashman working my way through all processes. Becoming Chargehand in 2000, Assistant Manager in 2003 and Distillery Manager in 2006.

What are your main tasks as a manager?

Ensuring that our product remains at the high standards that we have set, looking after our employees and Health and Safety on site as well ensuring that the distillery is looking at its best for our visitors.

What are the biggest challenges of being a distillery manager?

Everyday something different can happen, this is what makes this job so interesting.

What would be the worst that could go wrong in the production process?

Fires and Distilleries don't go well together so that would be a fear.

How would you describe the character of Deanston single malt?

Light, Fruity and Sweet - a perfect all round whisky.

What are the main features in the process at Deanston, contributing to this character?

Our water source is from the foot of Ben Ledi in Scotland's national park, it runs over granite rock which makes it very soft and unpeated. We also have long fermentations that give us a nice fruity character. Our still shape creates a nice reflux action during distillation giving a light spirit.

What is your favourite expression of Deanston and why?

Our 12 year old is a fantastic dram but the 1975 bottled for the opening of our Visitor Centre is out of this world.

If it were your decision alone – what new expression of Deanston would you like to see released?

I would like to see many new expressions being released in the coming years, similar in style to the La Panto Brandy Cask bottling that we have done recently.

If you had to choose a favourite dram other than Deanston, what would that be?

Tobermory 15 years is an all time great whisky but I feel that Bunnahabhain 18 year old just beats it.

What are the biggest changes you have seen the past 10 years in your profession?

The industry is for ever changing and modernising, computers seem to be taking over in some distilleries where as at Deanston we still pride ourselves in our traditional methods.

Do you see any major changes in the next 10 years to come?

Whisky will continue to open new markets across the globe becoming available in places never dreamed of before.

Do you have any special interests or hobbies that you pursue?

I like to go running to wind down and gather my thoughts after a day at the distillery.

You recently opened up a visitor centre and shop. What do you think that will mean to the distillery?

It will only help the distillery and put it on the whisky map. The visitor centre has been created in the old Mill Canteen area, and has been designed in keeping with the traditional hand crafted way in which we still produce our whisky at Deanston, while at the same time remembering the Cotton Mill and the heritage of the village.

You are producing all the electricity you need at the distillery yourselves. How did that start?

Deanston was originally a cotton mill and had the biggest water wheels in Europe. When these were removed in 1937 they were replaced with two water driven turbines. These are still in operation today and the surplus power that we generate is exported into the National Grid.

Deanston is one of few distilleries in Scotland producing spirit from organically grown barley? Please tell me some more about that.

We have been distilling Organic Whisky for one week per year since 2000. We were amongst the first to do so in the industry and are really excited about the end product. It is typical Deanston style, but due to the process used and the cask type it has it own very unique character. We have still to decide its release date.

Dufftown

Owner:
Diageo

Region/district:
Speyside

Founded: 1896
Status: Active
Capacity: 5 800 000 litres

Address: Dufftown, Keith, Banffshire AB55 4BR

Tel: 01340 822100
website: www.malts.com

History:

1895 – Peter Mackenzie, Richard Stackpole, John Symon and Charles MacPherson build the distillery Dufftown-Glenlivet in an old mill.

1896 – Production starts in November.

1897 – The distillery is owned by P. Mackenzie & Co., who also owns Blair Athol in Pitlochry.

1933 – P. Mackenzie & Co. is bought by Arthur Bell & Sons for £56,000.

1968 – The floor maltings is discontinued and malt is bought from outside suppliers. The number of stills is increased from two to four.

1974 – The number of stills is increased from four to six.

1979 – The stills are increased by a further two to eight.

1985 – Guinness buys Arthur Bell & Sons.

1997 – Guinness and Grand Metropolitan merge to form Diageo.

2006 – The Singleton of Dufftown 12 year old is launched as a special duty free bottling.

2008 – The Singleton of Dufftown is made available also in the UK.

2010 – A Manager's Choice 1997 is released.

Dufftown distillery is Diageo's third largest after Roseisle and Caol Ila and lays nestling at the foot of a hill in the town bearing the same name.

The distillery was partly rebuilt after an explosion in the mill in 1999. Today it is equipped with a 13 tonnes full lauter mash tun, 12 stainless steel washbacks and three pairs of stills in a very tiny still house. All stills also have sub coolers. The style of Dufftown single malt is somewhat green and grassy which is achieved by a clear wort and long fermentation (75 hours). The spirit is pumped through a 500 metre long pipe (which also crosses a road!) to the filling station and warehouses which are situated where the now demolished Pittyvaich distillery used to be.

On the site is also an evaporator plant and a bio plant. In the first mentioned the pot ale (being the residue from the wash still) is transformed into 140 tonnes of syrup every week, which then goes to the farmers to be spread on the fields. The bio plant takes care of the spent lees, the very last part of the spirit distillation. These mainly consist of water but also a certain amount of copper that needs to be separated before being released into the cycle of nature again. The two plants don't just service Dufftown but also the neighbouring distilleries of Mortlach and Glendullan.

Dufftown has been working 24/7 since 2007 and during 2012 they will be doing 23 mashes per week giving 5,7 million litres of alcohol.

About 97% of the production goes into blended whiskies, especially Bell's. The core range consists of *Singleton of Dufftown 12, 15* and *18 year old* which used to be available only in Duty Free but can now be found in domestic European markets. A higher proportion of European oak has been used for the Singleton version compared to the old *Flora & Fauna 15 year old* which can still be found.

Singleton of Dufftown 12 year old

GS – The nose is sweet, almost violet-like, with underlying malt. Big and bold on the palate, this is an upfront yet very drinkable whisky. The finish is medium to long, warming, spicy, with slowly fading notes of sherry and fudge.

DR – Honeycomb and tinned peach and apricot in syrup on the nose, sharp and spicy clean barley on the palate, with some bitter orange notes towards the finish.

The Singleton of Dufftown

Edradour

Owner:
Signatory Vintage
Scotch Whisky Co. Ltd

Region/district:
Eastern Highlands

Founded: **Status:**   **Capacity:**
1825   Active (vc)   90 000 litres

Address: Pitlochry, Perthshire PH16 5JP

Tel:
01796 472095

website:
www.edradour.com

History:
1825 – Probably the year when a distillery called Glenforres is founded by farmers in Perthshire.

1837 – The first year Edradour is mentioned.

1841 – The farmers form a proprietary company, John MacGlashan & Co.

1886 – J. G. Turney & Sons acquires Edradour through its subsidiary William Whitely & Co.

1922 – William Whiteley buys the distillery. The distillery is renamed Glenforres-Glenlivet.

1975 – Pernod Ricard buys Campbell Distilleries.

1982 – Campbell Distilleries (Pernod Ricard) buys Edradour and builds a visitor centre.

1986 – The first single malt is released.

2002 – Edradour is bought by Andrew Symington from Signatory for £5.4 million. The product range is expanded with a 10 year old and a 13 year old cask strength.

2003 – A 30 year old and a 10 year old are released.

2004 – A number of wood finishes are launched as cask strength.

2006 – The first bottling of peated Ballechin is released.

2007 – A Madeira matured Ballechin is released.

2008 – A Ballechin matured in Port pipes and a 10 year old Edradour with a Sauternes finish are released.

2009 – Fourth edition of Ballechin (Oloroso) is released.

2010 – Ballechin #5 Marsala is released.

2011 – Ballechin #6 Bourbon and a 26 year old PX sherry finish are released.

2012 – A 1993 Oloroso and a 1993 Sauternes finish as well as the 7th edition of Ballechin (Bordeaux) are released.

One might wonder why a big company as Pernod Ricard (through their subsidiary Campbell Distillers) even bothered buying such a small distillery as Edradour back in 1982, but even to a big shot like that the location was probably hard to resist. Just a stone´s throw from the busy A9 between Edinburgh and Inverness, it was the perfect place to build a visitor centre which was exactly what the new owners did the very same year. Twenty years later, it may have been the same reasons behind the final decision when Andrew Symington took over ownership. He had already considered Ardbeg, Glenturret and Glencadam but settled for Edradour. Every year, almost 100,000 visitors find their way to a distillery which has preserved its heritage and artisanal nature.

The distillery is equipped with an open, traditional cast iron mash tun from 1910 with a mash size of only 1,15 tonnes. The two washbacks are made of Oregon pine and the two stills are connected to a more than 100 year old wormtub. In 2012 they will be doing 6 mashes per week and 120,000 litres of alcohol in the year. During the last few years, part of the production has been heavily peated and during 2012 this part will be about 20,000 litres.

The core expression is the *10 year old* and *Caledonia Selection*. A large number of single casks, vintages and wood finishes have been released in addition to this. A series of wood finishes was commenced in 2004. The most recent ones have been *Chateau Neuf du Pape, Sauternes, Moscatel, Sassicaia, Port* and *Marsala*. In 2012 two distillery exclusives were released – a *1993 Oloroso* and a *1993 Sauternes* finish, both bottled at cask strength. Another side of the range from Edradour are the peated whiskies under the name *Ballechin*. The first release was in 2006 and edition number 7, a *Bordeaux cask matured*, appeared in summer 2012. The phenol specification for the malt used for Ballechin is 50ppm.

Caledonia 12 years old

Edradour 10 year old

GS – Cider apples, malt, almonds, vanilla and honey ar present on the nose, along with a hint of smoke and sherry. The palate is rich, creamy and malty, with a persistent nuttiness and quite a pronounced kick of slightly leathery sherry. Spices and sherry dominate the medium to long finish.

DR – Lemon and lime, rich fruits and some mint on the nose, sharp grape, berries and honey on the palate, and a lingering and pleasant fruity finish with hints of smoke.

Fettercairn

Owner:
Whyte & Mackay Ltd
(United Spirits)

Region/district:
Eastern Highlands

Founded: **Status:**   **Capacity:**
1824   Active (vc)   2 300 000 litres

Address: Fettercairn, Laurencekirk,
Kincardineshire AB30 1YB

Tel: **website:**
01561 340205   www.fettercairndistillery.co.uk

History:
1824 – Sir Alexander Ramsay founds the distillery.

1830 – Sir John Gladstone buys the distillery.

1887 – A fire erupts and the distillery is forced to close for repairs.

1890 – Thomas Gladstone dies and his son John Robert takes over. The distillery reopens.

1912 – The company is close to liquidation and John Gladstone buys out the other investors.

1926 –The distillery is mothballed.

1939 – The distillery is bought by Associated Scottish Distillers Ltd. Production restarts.

1960 – The maltings discontinues.

1966 – The stills are increased from two to four.

1971 – The distillery is bought by Tomintoul-Glenlivet Distillery Co. Ltd.

1973 – Tomintoul-Glenlivet Distillery Co. Ltd is bought by Whyte & Mackay Distillers Ltd.

1974 – The mega group of companies Lonrho buys Whyte & Mackay.

1988 – Lonrho sells to Brent Walker Group plc.

1989 – A visitor centre opens.

1990 – American Brands Inc. buys Whyte & Mackay for £160 million.

1996 – Whyte & Mackay and Jim Beam Brands merge to become JBB Worldwide.

2001 – Kyndal Spirits, a company formed by managers at Whyte & Mackay, buys Whyte & Mackay from JBB Worldwide.

2002 – The whisky changes name to Fettercairn 1824.

2003 – Kyndal Spirits changes name to Whyte & Mackay.

2007 – United Spirits buys Whyte & Mackay. A 23 year old single cask is released.

2009 – 24, 30 and 40 year olds are released.

2010 – Fettercairn Fior is launched.

2012 – Fettercairn Fasque is released.

Fettercairn Fior

GS – A complex, weighty nose of toffee, sherry, ginger, orange and smoke. More orange and smoke on the palate, with a sherried nuttiness and hints of treacle toffee. Mild, spicy oak and a touch of liquorice in the lengthy finish.

DR – A big whisky from the off, earthy and rustic on the nose, with bitter orange, cocoa, nuts and burnt toffee on the nose, full mouth feel with toasty orange marmalade, chocolate and peat. The finish includes wood, burnt toffee and spice.

Whyte & Mackay is one of the more prominent members of the Scotch whisky business but during the first 80 years they did not even have their own distillery. It was not until 1960 that Dalmore was acquired and 13 years later they purchased Fettercairn. Later on Invergordon grain distillery, Jura and Tamnavulin were added to the portfolio. The last one, together with Fettercairn, has been the backbone of the bulk whisky side of the company, producing whisky aimed for Tesco, Asda and many other customers. This aspect of the business has now been toned down which has given Fettercairn a chance to show its qualities as a single malt during the last three years.

Fettercairn distillery is equipped with a traditional mash tun with rakes made of cast iron, eight washbacks made of Douglas fir and two pairs of stills. One of the spirit stills was replaced in 2010 and the other in 2011. One feature makes it unique among Scottish distilleries – cooling water is allowed to trickle along the spirit still necks and is collected at the base for circulation towards the top again, in order to increase reflux and thereby produce a lighter and cleaner spirit. There are 14 dunnage warehouses on site holding 32,000 casks with the oldest dating from 1962. For 2012 the production is 24 mashes per week, reaching 2 million litres of alcohol for the year of which 200,000 litres are heavily peated (55ppm in the barley).

The range was revamped in 2009 with the introduction of three old Fettercairn single malts (*24, 30* and *40 year olds*) and one year later the new core malt, *Fettercairn Fior*, saw the light of day replacing the 12 year old. Fior is a blend of whiskies of different age and 15% of the contents is made up by heavily peated whisky. By the end of 2011 another whisky without age statement was launched as an exclusive for Tesco. It is called *Fettercairn Fasque* and contains slightly older whiskies than Fior and only 5% is peated whisky. During the last couple of years there has also been two single cask bottlings available only at the distillery - an *18 year old* and a *13 year old*.

Fettercairn Fior

Glenallachie

Owner:
Chivas Brothers
(Pernod Ricard)

Region/district:
Speyside

Founded: **Status:** **Capacity:**
1967 Active 4 200 000 litres

Address: Aberlour, Banffshire AB38 9LR

Tel: **website:**
01542 783042 -

History:
1967 – The distillery is founded by Mackinlay, McPherson & Co., a subsidiary of Scottish & Newcastle Breweries Ltd. William Delmé Evans is architect.

1985 – Scottish & Newcastle Breweries Ltd sells Charles Mackinlay Ltd to Invergordon Distillers which acquires both Glenallachie and Isle of Jura.

1987 – The distillery is decommissioned.

1989 – Campbell Distillers (Pernod Ricard) buys the distillery, increases the number of stills from two to four and takes up production again.

2005 – The first official bottling for many years is a Cask Strength Edition from 1989.

Glenallachie distillery was built during one of the biggest whisky booms ever – the 1960s. All regulations from the war had ceased to exist and the demand for Scotch exploded, especially in the USA. From 1960 to 1968 when Glenallachie was founded, no less than four grain distilleries and seven malt distilleries were built in Scotland. That doesn't include another four which were built within existing grain distilleries but later closed.

Glenallachie distillery, just outside Aberlour and in the shadow of Ben Rinnes, is equipped with a 9.4 tonnes semi-lauter mash tun, eight stainless steel washbacks (two of which were installed in autumn 2011) and two pairs of stills. The wash stills are lantern-shaped while the spirit stills are of the onion model. All four stills are unusually connected to horizontal tube condensers, rather than vertical ones.

Thanks to the new washbacks, the production capacity has increased by 30% to 4.2 million litres. The spirit is filled into bourbon casks and matured in 12 racked and two palletised warehouses.

The most important role for the whisky from Glenallachie is to be the backbone of one of the best selling blends in the world, Clan Campbell. It was established during the 1930s by Campbell Distillers, but it wasn't until Pernod Ricard took over the brand that sales escalated. By 1985 Clan Campbell was one the best selling Scotch whiskies in France and today it sells more than 20 million bottles globally. Currently, the only official bottling from Glenallachie is *16 year old cask strength* matured in first fill Oloroso casks and released in 2005. This has been for sale at Chivas' visitor centres, together with the other releases in the cask strength range.

Glenallachie 16 year old 56,7%

GS – Major Sherry influence right through this expression, starting with warm leather and a hint of cloves on the fragrant nose, progressing through a Christmas pudding palate, featuring sultanas, dates and lots of spice, to a lengthy, sherried, leathery finish.

1989 16 years old

Glenburgie

Owner:
Chivas Brothers
(Pernod Ricard)

Region/district:
Speyside

Founded: 1810
Status: Active
Capacity: 4 200 000 litres

Address: Glenburgie, Forres,
Morayshire IV36 2QY

Tel: 01343 850258
website: -

History:

1810 – William Paul founds Kilnflat Distillery. Official production starts in 1829.

1870 – Kilnflat distillery closes.

1878 – The distillery reopens under the name Glenburgie-Glenlivet, Charles Hay is licensee.

1884 – Alexander Fraser & Co. takes over.

1925 – Alexander Fraser & Co. files for bankruptcy and the receiver Donald Mustad assumes control of operations.

1927 – James & George Stodart Ltd buys the distillery which by this time is inactive.

1930 – Hiram Walker buys 60% of James & George Stodart Ltd.

1936 – Hiram Walker buys Glenburgie Distillery in October. Production restarts.

1958 – Lomond stills are installed producing a single malt, Glencraig. Floor malting ceases.

1981 – The Lomond stills are replaced by conventional stills.

1987 – Allied Lyons buys Hiram Walker.

2002 – A 15 year old is released.

2004 – A £4.3 million refurbishment and reconstruction takes place.

2005 – Chivas Brothers (Pernod Ricard) becomes the new owner through the acquisition of Allied Domecq.

2006 – The number of stills are increased from four to six in May.

The single malt from Glenburgie is one of the most important parts of the Ballantine´s blend. Spirits worldwide are classified according to price. Ballantine´s has an impressive range starting with Finest which is considered a Premium blend. This is followed by the 12 year old (Super Premium), the 17, 21 and 30 year old (Ultra Premium) and finally the most recently released – the 40 year old that falls under the category Prestige blends. Ballantine´s were among the first to introduce aged expressions and as early as 1927 there were both the 17 and the 30 year old on the market. Ballantine´s Finest was introduced in 1910 and by then, the now famous square bottle was already in use.

A decision was made in 2003 by the owners at the time, Allied Domecq, to refurbish Glenburgie distillery, but it didn´t stop at that. The old distillery was simply knocked down and a new one was built on the same site. The distillery is now equipped with a 7,5 tonne full lauter mash tun, 12 stainless steel washbacks and three pairs of stills. All the equipment fits on one level in one gigantic room. Most of them are new but four stills, the mill and the boiler were brought in from the old distillery. The only remaining building of the original distillery is the custom´s house which is now used as a tasting room. The majority of the production is filled into bourbon casks and part thereof are matured in four dunnage, two racked and two palletised warehouses.

A single malt from Glenburgie, named Glencraig, can still be found on the market. It came into being by Hiram Walker's experimenting with Lomond stills in the fifties. Glenburgie's first Lomond still was a small model, originating in Dumbarton. It was replaced in 1958 by a pair of full-size Lomond stills and it is the make from these stills that received the name Glencraig.

The only official bottling of Glenburgie single malt is a *15 year old cask strength* with the current edition distilled in 1994.

15 years old cask strength

Glenburgie 10 year old G&M

GS – Fresh and fruity on the nose, with toasted malt and a mildly herbal note. Soft fruits and mild oak on the palate, while the finish is subtly drying, with a touch of ginger.

DR – Classic sherry, barley and prickly wood on the nose, sweet and gentle red berry on the palate, and a warming mouth-filling soft and pleasant finish.

Glencadam

Owner: **Region/district:**
Angus Dundee Distillers   Eastern Highlands

Founded: **Status:**   **Capacity:**
1825   Active   1 300 000 litres

Address: Brechin, Angus DD9 7PA

Tel: **website:**
01356 622217   www.glencadamdistillery.co.uk

History:

1825 – George Cooper founds the distillery.

1827 – David Scott takes over.

1837 – The distillery is sold by David Scott.

1852 – Alexander Miln Thompson becomes the owner.

1857 – Glencadam Distillery Company is formed.

1891 – Gilmour, Thompson & Co Ltd takes over.

1954 – Hiram Walker takes over.

1959 – Refurbishing of the distillery.

1987 – Allied Lyons buys Hiram Walker Gooderham & Worts.

1994 – Allied Lyons changes name to Allied Domecq.

2000 – The distillery is mothballed.

2003 – Allied Domecq sells the distillery to Angus Dundee Distillers.

2005 – The new owner releases a 15 year old.

2008 – A re-designed 15 year old and a new 10 year old are introduced.

2009 – A 25 and a 30 year old are released in limited numbers.

2010 – A 12 year old port finish, a 14 year old sherry finish, a 21 year old and a 32 year old are released.

2012 – A 30 year old is released.

Glencadam 10 year old

GS – A light and delicate, floral nose, with tinned pears and fondant cream. Medium-bodied, smooth, with citrus fruits and gently-spiced oak on the palate. The finish is quite long and fruity, with a hint of barley.

DR – Fruity and treacle toffee nose, sweet, fruity and with uncluttered malt on the palate, and a clean medium long fruity finish.

Not too long ago, Glencadam had three other distilleries operating in the vicinity along the East coast of Scotland – one in the same town, Brechin, (North Port distillery) and two in nearby Montrose (Glenesk and Lochside), but the last one closed in 1992. The owner of Glencadam, Angus Dundee Distillers, was founded by Terry Hillman who, at the age of 79, is still the chairman of the company. The daily business, however, is run by his two children, Tania and Aaraon, and in 2011 the company had a turnover of £45m. The core of the business is to produce and sell blended Scotch and they have a huge range of brands in their portfolio. One being Charles Hamilton under whose name, Angus Dundee, at the beginning of 2012 launched a new range of four malt whiskies from each of the main whisky producing areas – Islay, Highland, Lowland and Speyside.

Today, Glencadam is not only a busy distillery, but also hosts a huge filling and bottling plant with 16 large tanks for blending malt and grain whisky. Angus Dundee is responsible for 4-5% of the total export of Scotch and 3,8 million litres per year can be blended at Glencadam.

The distillery is equipped with a 5 tonnes traditional cast iron mash tun from the eighties. There are six stainless steel washbacks (four with wooden tops and two with stainless steel ones) with a fermentation time of 52 hours and one pair of stills. The external heat exchanger on the wash still is from the fifties and perhaps the first in the business. The distillery is currently working seven days a week, which enables 16 mashes per week and 1,3 million litres of alcohol per year.

On site are two dunnage warehouses from 1825, three from the 1950s and one modern, racked.

The core range consists of a *10 year old*, a *15 year old* and the recently introduced *21 year old*. Limited editions released in 2010 included two finishes (a *12 year old port* and a *14 year old Oloroso sherry*) and a *32 year old single cask*. This was followed by a *30 year old* released in June 2012.

21 years old

Glendronach

Owner:
Benriach Distillery Co

Region/district:
Speyside

Founded: Status: Capacity:
1826   Active (vc)   1 400 000 litres

Address: Forgue, Aberdeenshire AB54 6DB

Tel: website:
01466 730202   www.glendronachdistillery.com

History:
1826 – The distillery is founded by a consortium. James Allardes is one of the owners.

1837 – The major part of the distillery is destroyed in a fire.

1852 – Walter Scott (from Teaninich) takes over.

1887 – Walter Scott dies and Glendronach is taken over by a consortium from Leith.

1920 – Charles Grant buys Glendronach for £9,000 and starts production three months later.

1960 – William Teacher & Sons buys the distillery.

1966-67 – The number of stills is increased to four.

1976 – A visitor centre is opened.

1976 – Allied Breweries takes over William Teacher & Sons.

1996 – The distillery is mothballed.

2002 – Production is resumed on 14th May.

2005 – Glendronach 33 years old is launched. The distillery closes to rebuild from coal to indirect firing by steam. Reopens in September. Chivas Brothers (Pernod Ricard) becomes new owner through the acquisition of Allied Domecq.

2008 – Pernod Ricard sells the distillery to the owners of BenRiach distillery.

2009 – Relaunch of the whole range - 12, 15 and 18 year old including limited editions of a 33 year old and five single casks.

2010 – A 31 year old, a 1996 single cask and a total of 11 vintages and four wood finishes are released. A visitor centre is opened.

2011 – The 21 year old Parliament and 11 vintages are released.

2012 – Recherché 44 years and a number of vintages are released.

Glendronach Original 12 year old

GS – A sweet nose of Christmas cake fresh from the oven. Smooth on the palate, with sherry, soft oak, fruit, almonds and spices. The finish is comparatively dry and nutty, ending with bitter chocolate.

DR – Sherry, red berries, vanilla and traces of mint-flavoured toffee on the nose, an intriguing palate of cranberry and blueberry, a peaty carpet and some pepper, and a medium savoury and peaty finish.

When the owners of BenRiach acquired GlenDronach, their second distillery in 2008, they bought a slightly neglected brand. Pernod Ricard, the previous owners, had concentrated on other brands in their portfolio (for example Glenlivet and Aberlour). On the other hand, the distillery had been known for decades to produce a sherry matured Speysider of high quality and the brand had many followers around the world. This was also evident in the rapidly increasing sales figures as almost 200,000 bottles were sold during 2011.

The distillery equipment consists of a small (3,7 tonnes) cast iron mash tun with rakes, nine washbacks where six are made of Oregon pine, while the final three were recently replaced using Scottish larch, two wash stills with heat exchangers and two spirit stills. Glendronach was the last Scottish distillery to fire the stills with coal. This traditional process continued until September 2005 when indirect heating using steam coils replaced it.

The new owners took possession of 9,000 casks of whisky when they bought the distillery which are now maturing in three dunnage and three racked warehouses. Some 50% of the production is aimed for its own releases and the rest will be sold to Pernod Ricard for their blended whiskies.

The core range is the 8 (Octarine), 12 (Original), 15 (Revival), 18 (Allardice) and 31 year old (Grandeur). In September 2011 the range was expanded to include a 21 year old (Parliament). There are four wood finishes (Virgin Oak, Sauternes, Moscatel and Tawny Port) all 14 or 15 years old. In line with the last couple of years, several single casks (all sherry) were also released in 2012; in June five vintages from 1971 to 1993 and a couple of months later another five vintages, 1972 to 1994. All but one (Moscatel 1989) were sherry maturations for which GlenDronach have become famous. Towards the end of 2012 a real gem was released by way of the 44 year old Recherché – a single Oloroso sherry butt and the oldest still left in the warehouses.

Parliament 21 years old

Glendullan

Owner: Diageo

Region/district: Speyside

Founded: 1897 **Status:** Active **Capacity:** 3 700 000 litres

Address: Dufftown, Keith, Banffshire AB55 4DJ

Tel: 01340 822100 **website:** www.malts.com

History:

1896-97 – William Williams & Sons, a blending company with Three Stars and Strathdon among its brands, founds the distillery.

1902 – Glendullan is delivered to the Royal Court and becomes the favourite whisky of Edward VII.

1919 – Macdonald Greenlees buys a share of the company and Macdonald Greenlees & Williams Distillers is formed.

1926 – Distillers Company Limited (DCL) buys Glendullan.

1930 – Glendullan is transferred to Scottish Malt Distillers (SMD).

1962 – Major refurbishing and reconstruction.

1972 – A brand new distillery, accommodating six stills, is constructed next to the old one and both operate simultaneously during a few years.

1985 – The oldest of the two distilleries is mothballed.

1995 – The first launch of Glendullan in the Rare Malts series becomes a 22 year old from 1972.

2005 – A 26 year old from 1978 is launched in the Rare Malts series.

2007 – Singleton of Glendullan is launched in the USA.

Singleton of Glendullan 12 year old

GS – The nose is spicy, with brittle toffee, vanilla, new leather and hazelnuts. Spicy and sweet on the smooth palate, with citrus fruits, more vanilla and fresh oak. Drying and pleasingly peppery in the finish.

DR – The nose has a mix of fruits including grapefruit melon and even banana, the taste is moreish, with the citrus and melon notes coming through. Warm and pleasant finish.

The effect of the water on the taste of the whisky is sometimes debated. The most common perception is that as long as it is clean, it does not add anything to the final taste. There are, however, those who claim that hard water tends to add some fruity notes to the spirit. The majority of Scottish distilleries use soft water but a handful put their trust in hard water, as for example Glenmorangie and Glendullan. In Glendullan´s case the water passes a limestone quarry right behind the distillery and the calcium that is picked up on the way to the distillery may contribute to the character of the whisky.

The Glendullan distillery that opened in 1896 is not the one producing today; a new Glendullan was built in 1972 next to the old one. The two were operated in parallel for a few years until 1985 when the old distillery closed. It is now used as a workshop for Diageo´s distillery engineering team. The old distillery was equipped with one pair of stills with a capacity of one million litres a year. During the 13 years when they were both distilling, the whisky from the two was vatted together before bottling. The new distillery is equipped with a full lauter stainless steel mash tun from Abercrombies, installed in 2010. The equipment also consists of 8 washbacks made of larch and three pairs of stills. The distillery is working a five day week so there will be both short fermentations (65 hours) and long fermentations during the weekends (100 hours). The plan for 2012 is to do 15 mashes per week which means a production of 3,7 million litres of alcohol for the year.

The core range consists of *Singleton of Glendullan 12 year old* which is aimed at the American market. Previously there has also been a *12 year old* in the *Flora & Fauna* series which can still be found. In 2010, a *single cask* from *1995* was released as part of the Manager´s Choice series.

The Singleton of Glendullan

The old distillery

Glen Elgin

Owner:
Diageo

Region/district:
Speyside

Founded: **Status:** **Capacity:**
1898 Active 2 500 000 litres

Address: Longmorn, Morayshire IV30 3SL

Tel:
01343 862100

website:
www.malts.com

History:
1898 – The bankers William Simpson and James Carle found Glen Elgin.

1900 – Production starts in May but the distillery closes just five months later.

1901 – The distillery is auctioned for £4,000 to the Glen Elgin-Glenlivet Distillery Co. and is mothballed.

1906 – The wine producer J. J. Blanche & Co. buys the distillery for £7,000 and production resumes.

1929 – J. J. Blanche dies and the distillery is put up for sale again.

1930 – Scottish Malt Distillers (SMD) buys it and the license goes to White Horse Distillers.

1964 – Expansion from two to six stills plus other refurbishing takes place.

1992 – The distillery closes for refurbishing and installation of new stills.

1995 – Production resumes in September.

2001 – A 12 year old is launched in the Flora & Fauna series.

2002 – The Flora & Fauna series malt is replaced by Hidden Malt 12 years.

2003 – A 32 year old cask strength from 1971 is released.

2008 – A 16 year old is launched as a Special Release.

2009 – Glen Elgin 1998, a single cask in the new Manager´s Choice range is released.

Glen Elgin 12 year old

GS – A nose of rich, fruity sherry, figs and fragrant spice. Full-bodied, soft, malty and honeyed in the mouth. The finish is lengthy, slightly perfumed, with spicy oak.

DR – Ginger, crystallised barley sweet and a complex array of fruit on the nose, a beautiful balanced taste with light fruit, sweet spice and a zesty freshness and mouth filling finish.

A handful of Diageo´s distilleries were chosen to have an upgrade during 2012 so that they would be prepared to meet the estimated demand for Scotch whisky in a couple of years´ time. Glen Elgin was one of them and an extension of the existing tun room was made during summer and in September, an additional three washbacks made of larch were in place, thus increasing the capacity by 50%. After that the site moved from a 5 day operation to 7 days which meant 16 mashes per week and 2,5 million litres in the year. A mixture of short (76 hours) and long (120 hours) fermentations has also changed to a fixed 90 hours.

The distillery is equipped with an 8,2 tonnes Steinecker full lauter mash tun from 2001, nine washbacks made of larch and six small stills that stand in line in the still house. The stills, with their slightly descending lyne arms, are connected to six wooden worm tubs placed in the yard. The wormtubs and the small stills would suggest that the spirit from Glen Elgin is heavy and robust while, in fact, it is light and fruity. This is due to the long fermentation of a clear wort and, not least, the slow distillation.

The whisky from Glen Elgin has for a long time been an essential part of the blended whisky, White Horse. Introduced in 1890, the brand is currently selling 12 million bottles per year, especially in Japan, Brazil, Africa and USA.

In 2001, Glen Elgin was launched as a part of the Flora & Fauna series, but was replaced the year thereafter by a new *12 year old* in what was then called "Hidden Malts". Three limited editions have also been released: a *19 year old* in 2000, a *32 year old* in 2003 and, finally, a *16 year old* was launched in 2008. In autumn of 2009, a *single cask* from *1998* was released as part of the new series Manager´s Choice.

12 years old

Whisky Tapas - the Perfect Match

Whisky and food might mean cooking with whisky. But in the case of Chris Pepper of Whiskykoch in Germany it means to cook accompanying the whisky, in fact, translating the aromas and tastes on the plate. Here are a few good tips how you can do it at home.

As we know each whisky differs from another. There would be no need to have about 90 different distilleries in Scotland if they all churned out a uniform product, would there? I must admit, that I always find it a missed opportunity, when I read "whisky sauce" or "marinated in" on a restaurant menu. The unique attributes of the whisky are pushed somewhere into the background where they will have to shout to be heard.

Why not change this round? Let the whisky be the star and, above all, the inspiration – the food can play the supporting roll. My approach would always be to translate the aromas and tastes on the plate; therefore I never cook with, but to the whisky. This is not as difficult as you might think. It takes a wee bit of planning, a good nose and some self-belief, but is very enjoyable and can sometimes lead to some unexpected and pleasurable results.

The starting point is of course the whiskies. Tasting or rather nosing the whiskies is very important. Don't take anything for granted. Just because it is an Islay whisky does not mean it is just peaty. There will also be other tastes and aromas. From the tasting notes you can now create your menu, whether it be for a finger-food and tapas style evening or a full blown five course meal, all you need are

your tasting notes. They will guide you in the right direction, no matter how obscure they may seem. What I dare to do, and you might, too, is to have the whiskies in a different order then you might expect it from a regular tasting. You may choose a peaty, smoky whisky for a starter or main being followed by a soft and creamy or fruity one for the dessert. Combining whisky with food allows this.

Here are a few very general suggestions for tapas style nibbles which you can use as a starting point. If you want the perfect match, take a closer look into each whisky.

Smoky Islay whiskies
Combine well with strong flavours: strong cheeses, smoked fish, salty foods, olives, strongly flavoured meats.
For example; King Prawns with Olives to go with a lightly smoky Islay or Smoked Mackerel Dumplings with Spring Onions and a Mustard Sauce with a heavier smoked Islay.

Malty Highlanders
Creamy cheeses, black olives, gently spiced dishes.
For example; a warm Garam Masala spiced Chicken and Red Pepper Salad accompanying a spicy full-bodied Highland or a Pancake stuffed with sundried Tomatoes and Black Olive Cream to go with a creamy, malty, olivy northern Highlander.

Speysiders
Good with salads with flowery, herbal notes.
For example; a Strawberry and Black Pepper Salad with Taragon and Sweetleaf with a red wine finish Speyside or Toasted Baguette with an Orange-Herb-Topping with a very zitrusfruity, but also herbal Speyside whisky.

Sherry cask whiskies
Spicy food (not too hot), also dried fruit, nuts and chocolate.
For example; an Aubergine and Prune Soup with Balsamico Cream

Whiskykoch is a combined whisky shop and restaurant in Darmstadt, Germany run by trained chef Chris Pepper and his wife Marion. Resulting from his passion for his profession and of course for his hobby whisky, Chris successfully combines whisky and food for regular events. What started as a rough idea with friends during a tasting session on Islay, turned into a business in 2007.
www.whiskykoch.de

with a first fill cask strength whisky or a Coffee Crème with Nutmeg-Sherry-Raisins with a lightly woody but also creamy and typically raisiny sherry matured cask.

Bourbon cask whiskies
Fresh and exotic fruit, gentle spices.
For example; an Exotic Bread and Butter Pudding with Pineapple and Dried Mangos or an apricot/rosmary muffin with a waxy and exotic fruit bourbon maturated whisky.

Older whiskies
Tend to go well with more subtle flavours, understatement is usually called for. Subtle flavours could be aubergine versus fennel (Aubergine Mousse), vanilla versus nutmeg, banana versus lemon (Banana Soufflé with Vanilla Sauce).

Have fun choosing the whiskies, tasting and combining with food. It can open up new opportunities for whisky enthusiasts or get the most ardent non-whisky drinker interested.

Glenfarclas

Owner:
J. & G. Grant

Region/district:
Speyside

Founded: **Status:**
1836   Active (vc)

Capacity:
3 400 000 litres

Address: Ballindalloch, Banffshire AB37 9BD

Tel:
01807 500257

website:
www.glenfarclas.co.uk

History:

1836 – Robert Hay founds the distillery on the original site since 1797.

1865 – Robert Hay passes away and John Grant and his son George buy the distillery for £511.19s on 8th June. They lease it to John Smith at The Glenlivet Distillery.

1870 – John Smith resigns in order to start Cragganmore and J. & G. Grant Ltd takes over.

1889 – John Grant dies and George Grant takes over.

1890 – George Grant dies and his widow Barbara takes over the license while sons John and George control operations.

1895 – John and George Grant take over and form The Glenfarclas-Glenlivet Distillery Co. Ltd with the infamous Pattison, Elder & Co.

1898 – Pattison becomes bankrupt. Glenfarclas encounters financial problems after a major overhaul of the distillery but survives by mortgaging and selling stored whisky to R. I. Cameron, a whisky broker from Elgin.

1914 – John Grant leaves due to ill health and George continues alone.

1948 – The Grant family celebrates the distillery's 100th anniversary, a century of active licensing. It is 9 years late, as the actual anniversary coincided with WW2.

Since 1865, when John Grant took over the lease of Rechlerich farm and bought Glenfarclas, this distillery has been in the hands of the same family. At the moment it is run by the 5th generation through the Chairman, John Grant, and the 6th generation, George Grant, who is working as Director of Sales. One might assume that with a history like that, the company would be pretty conservative. Two random incidents prove the opposite – in the 1960s they launched Glenfarclas 105, the world´s first commercially available cask strength whisky and in 2010 they released two bottlings together with a Swedish heavy metal band.

The distillery is equipped with a 16,5 tonnes semi-lauter mash tun and twelve stainless steel washbacks. The three pairs of stills are some of the biggest in Scotland and the wash stills are equipped with rummagers. This is a copper chain rotating at the bottom of the still to prevent solids from sticking to the copper, something that otherwise easily happens when you have a direct fired still. There are 30 dunnage warehouses on-site which hold more than 50,000 casks. Glenfarclas uses an unusually large share of sherry butts, mainly Oloroso. Glenfarclas has recently increased their production rate and during 2012 they will do 12 mashes per week for 41 weeks which will amount to 3,4 million litres of alcohol.

The Glenfarclas core range consists of *10, 12, 15, 21, 25, 30* and *40 years old* as well as the *105 Cask Strength*. There is also a *17 year old* destined for the USA, Japan and the Duty Free market. Also in the core range, is the lightly sherried *Glenfarclas Heritage* without age statement. It was originally launched for the French hypermarket trade but is now also available in several other countries. There have also been bottlings of Heritage at 60% and limited vintage versions. Limited releases during 2011 were *175th Anniversary* containing whiskies from six decades dating back to the 1950s and *Chairman´s Reserve*, made up of four casks that, combined, have matured for 175 years. Special versions of the 175th Anniversary have also been released in Sweden and Taiwan. Limited bottlings in 2012 include the oldest whisky ever released by the owners – a *58 year old* single sherry cask with 400 bottles destined for Poland, but also available through Master of Malt. Another old bottling was the *43 year old* with some of the maturation in a cognac cask, a first for the owners. There is also a *20 year old* version of the *Glenfarclas 105*. The owners will continue to release bottlings in their *Family Casks* series with vintages from 1952 to 1996. So far, nine releases totalling 102 casks have been released.

History (continued):

1949 – George Grant senior dies and sons George Scott and John Peter inherit the distillery.

1960 – Stills are increased from two to four.

1968 – Glenfarclas is first to launch a cask-strength single malt. It is later named Glenfarclas 105.

1972 – Floor maltings is abandoned and malt is purchased centrally.

1973 – A visitor centre is opened.

1976 – Enlargement from four stills to six.

2001 – Glenfarclas launches its first Flower of Scotland gift tin which becomes a great success and increases sales by 30%.

2002 – George S Grant dies and is succeeded as company chairman by his son John L S Grant

2003 – Two new gift tins are released (10 years old and 105 cask strength).

2005 – A 50 year old is released to commemorate the bi-centenary of John Grant´s birth.

2006 – Ten new vintages are released.

2007 – Family Casks, a series of single cask bottlings from 43 consecutive years, is released.

2008 – New releases in the Family Cask range. Glenfarclas 105 40 years old is released.

2009 – A third release in the Family Casks series.

2010 – A 40 year old and new vintages from Family Casks are released.

2011 – Chairman´s Reserve and 175th Anniversary are released.

2012 – A 58 year old and a 43 year old are released

105 Cask Strength (Duty Free version)

43 years old Cognac cask

105 Cask Strength 20 years old

Glenfarclas 10 year old

GS – Full and richly sherried on the nose, with nuts, fruit cake and a hint of citrus fruit. The palate is big, with ripe fruit, brittle toffee, some peat and oak. Medium length and gingery in the finish.

DR – Creamy sherry and bitter oranges on the nose, rich fruit cake and red berries on the palate with a pleasant spice and barley interplay and long and warming finish.

10 years old

12 years old

The Family Casks 1959

127

Glenfiddich

Owner:
William Grant & Sons

Region/district:
Speyside

Founded: **Status:**
1886   Active (vc)

Capacity:
12 000 000 litres

Address: Dufftown, Keith, Banffshire AB55 4DH

Tel:
01340 820373 (vc)

website:
www.glenfiddich.com

History:
1886 – The distillery is founded by William Grant, 47 years old, who had learned the trade at Mortlach Distillery. The equipment is bought from Mrs. Cummings of Cardow Distillery. The construction totals £800.

1887 – The first distilling takes place on Christmas Day.

1892 – William Grant builds Balvenie.

1898 – The blending company Pattisons, largest customer of Glenfiddich, files for bankruptcy and Grant decides to blend their own whisky. Standfast becomes one of their major brands.

1903 – William Grant & Sons is formed.

1957 – The famous, three-cornered bottle is introduced.

1958 – The floor maltings is closed.

1963 – Glenfiddich becomes the first whisky to be marketed as single malt in the UK and the rest of the world.

1964 – A version of Standfast's three-cornered bottle is launched for Glenfiddich in green glass.

1969 – Glenfiddich becomes the first distillery in Scotland to open a visitor centre.

1974 – 16 new stills are installed.

2001 – 1965 Vintage Reserve is launched in a limited edition of 480 bottles. Glenfiddich 1937 is bottled (61 bottles).

Five years ago a campaign called "Every Year Counts" was launched to make Glenfiddich the first single malt brand to reach the magical number – one million sold cases (12 million bottles) in a year. But then came the recession and sales figures dropped. In 2010 they were on track again and finally in 2011 the owners could report 1,03 million cases sold! Glenfiddich has been an unthreatened number one on the list since many years back and are still way ahead of Glenlivet and Macallan who both sell approximately 700,000 cases per year.

Glenfiddich distillery is equipped with two big, stainless steel, full lauter mash tuns (11,2 tonnes) and 24 Douglas fir washbacks with a fermentation time of 66 hours. One still room holds 5 wash and 10 spirit stills and the other 5 and 8 respectively. The wash stills are all onion-shaped while half of the spirit stills are of the lantern model and the rest have a boiling ball. All the stills in still house No. 1 are internally fired using steam coils for the past two years. The stills in still house No. 2, however, are still directly fired using gas. The production was increased two years ago and they now make 12 million litres of alcohol in a year.

Glenfiddich´s core range consists of *12, 15* (used to be called Solera Reserve and is still blended using a solera system), *18, 21* (also called Gran Reserva, repackaged in 2012 and finished in rum casks), *Rich Oak 14 year old* and *15 year old Distillery Edition* (formerly 15 yo cask strength) bottled at 51%. Some older expressions have also been released during the years – *30, 40* and *50 years old*. A new range called Age of Discovery was introduced in 2011 with a *19 year old Madeira* finish which was followed up with a *19 year old Bourbon cask* maturation. To start with, the latter will only be sold through Duty Free, but will become available in domestic markets towards the beginning of 2013. The first vatted *Vintage Reserve* (from *1974*) was released in late 2011 and early 2012 saw the *Malt Master´s Edition* – double matured in both bourbon and sherry casks. To celebrate the 125th anniversary of the first distillation, Glenfiddich single malt (at least 14 years old) was finished in 11 new American oak casks and then sold exclusively in the USA. The programme, called *Cask of Dreams*, is now being repeated for the Canadian market as well. The 12 year old *Glenfiddich Millenium Vintage* was launched for Duty Free in July 2012 and, finally, to celebrate the 110th birthday of Janet Sheed Roberts (William Grant´s granddaughter), 15 bottles from a *1955 European oak cask* were sold at auctions with all proceeds being donated to charity.

History (continued):

2002 – Glenfiddich Gran Reserva 21 years old, finished in Cuban rum casks is launched. Caoran Reserve 12 years is released. Glenfiddich Rare Collection 1937 (61 bottles) is launched and becomes the oldest Scotch whisky on the market.

2003 – 1973 Vintage Reserve (440 bottles) is launched.

2004 – 1991 Vintage Reserve (13 years) and 1972 Vintage Reserve (519 bottles) are launched.

2005 – Circa £1.7 million is invested in a new visitor centre.

2006 – 1973 Vintage Reserve, 33 years (861 bottles) and 12 year old Toasted Oak are released.

2007 – 1976 Vintage Reserve, 31 years is released in September.

2008 – 1977 Vintage Reserve is released.

2009 – A 50 year old and 1975 Vintage Reserve are released.

2010 – Rich Oak, 1978 Vintage Reserve, the 6th edition of 40 year old and Snow Phoenix are released.

2011 – 1974 Vintage Reserve and a 19 year old Madeira finish are released.

2012 – Cask of Dreams and Millenium Vintage are released.

Glenfiddich 12 year old

GS – Delicate, floral and slightly fruity on the nose. Well mannered in the mouth, malty, elegant and soft. Rich, fruit flavours dominate the palate, with a developing nuttiness and an elusive whiff of peat smoke in the fragrant finish.

DR – Classic rich fruit and peerless clean barley nose, fruit bowl and sharp malt palate and pleasant and warming lengthy finish.

Malt Master's Edition   *21 years old Gran Reserva*   *Age of Discovery 19 years Bourbon*

12 years old   *Rich Oak*   *18 years old*

Glen Garioch

Owner:
Morrison Bowmore
(Suntory)

Region/district:
Eastern Highlands

Founded: **Status:** **Capacity:**
1797   Active (vc)   1 000 000 litres

Address: Oldmeldrum, Inverurie,
Aberdeenshire AB51 0ES

Tel:
01651 873450

website:
www.glengarioch.com

History:
1797 – Thomas Simpson founds Glen Garioch.

1837 – The distillery is bought by John Manson & Co., owner of Strathmeldrum Distillery.

1908 – Glengarioch Distillery Company, owned by William Sanderson, buys the distillery.

1933 – Sanderson & Son merges with the gin maker Booth's Distilleries Ltd.

1937 – Booth´s Distilleries Ltd is acquired by Distillers Company Limited (DCL).

1968 – Glen Garioch is decommissioned.

1970 – It is sold to Stanley P. Morrison Ltd.

1973 – Production starts again.

1978 – Stills are increased from two to three.

1982 – Becomes the first distillery to use gas from the North Sea for heating.

1994 – Suntory controls all of Morrison Bowmore Distillers Ltd.

1995 – The distillery is mothballed in October.

1997 – The distillery reopens in August.

2004 – Glen Garioch 46 year old is released.

2005 – 15 year old Bordeaux Cask Finish is launched. A visitor centre opens in October.

2006 – An 8 year old is released.

2009 – Complete revamp of the range - 1979 Founders Reserve (unaged), 12 year old, Vintage 1978 and 1990 are released.

2010 – 1991 vintage is released.

2011 – Two vintages, 1986 and 1994, are released.

2012 – Vintage 1995 and 1997 are released.

Glen Garioch 12 years old

GS – Luscious and sweet on the nose, focusing on fresh fruits: peaches and pineapple, plus vanilla, malt and a hint of sherry. Full-bodied and nicely textured, with more fresh fruit on the palate, along with spice, brittle toffee and finally quite dry oak notes.

DR – Surprisingly floral and light on the nose, with fruity sweetness. The taste includes tinned sweet pear, vanilla and caramel with some earthiness as an undercarpet. There is some spice in the finale.

Glen Garioch, situated in the small town of Oldmeldrum west of Aberdeen, is the easternmost distillery in Scotland and one of the oldest. Generally it is said to be founded in 1797 but some evidence shows that it might already have been operational by 1785. The distillery is equipped with a 4,4 tonne full lauter mash tun, eight stainless steel washbacks and one pair of stills. There is also a third still which has not been in use for a long time. The spirit is tankered to Glasgow, filled into casks and returned to be stored in the distillery´s four warehouses. During 2012 the production will be 12 mashes per week (820,000 litres per year) which is an increase compared to last year of more than 40%. The entire range from Glen Garioch was revamped three years ago and, if you pay attention, you will find two different traces in the character of the various expressions. The core bottlings are unpeated, while phenols are easily detected in some of the vintages. The reason for this is that when the distillery was using its own floor maltings (until 1994) the malt was peated with a specification of 8-10 ppm. Around 160,000 bottles were sold during 2011 of which two-thirds were exported. The core range is *1797 Founder´s Reserve* (without age statement) and a *12 year old*, both of them bottled at the rather unusual strength of 48% and non-chillfiltered. There are also a number of limited cask strength vintages released every year. The first three were *1978, 1990* and *1991*. In 2011 two new ones were launched – *1986* and *1994* and 2012 saw the release of a *1995* which was distilled just before the distillery was temporarily closed and a *1997*, drawn from some of the first whisky distilled following the reopening. Finally, there have been some special single casks for selected markets and retailers, for example, a *1971* for The Whisky Exchange and a *1978* for The Whisky Shop.

12 years old

Glenglassaugh

Owner: **Region/district:**
Glenglassaugh Distillery Co   Speyside
(Scaent Group)

Founded: **Status:**   **Capacity:**
1875   Active (vc)   1 100 000 litres

Address: Portsoy, Banffshire AB45 2SQ

Tel: **website:**
01261 842367   www.glenglassaugh.com

History:

1873-75 – The distillery is founded by Glenglassaugh Distillery Company.

1887 – Alexander Morrison embarks on renovation work.

1892 – Morrison sells the distillery to Robertson & Baxter. They in turn sell it on to Highland Distilleries Company for £15,000.

1908 – The distillery closes.

1931 – The distillery reopens.

1936 – The distillery closes.

1957-59 – Substantial reconstruction, including acquisition of new stills, takes place.

1960 – The distillery reopens.

1986 – Glenglassaugh is mothballed.

2005 – A 22 year old is released.

2006 – Three limited editions are released - 19 years old, 38 years old and 44 years old.

2008 – The distillery is bought by the Scaent Group for £5m. Three bottlings are released - 21, 30 and 40 year old.

2009 – New make spirit and 6 months old are released.

2010 – A 26 year old replaces the 21 year old.

2011 – A 35 year old and the first bottling from the new owners production, a 3 year old, are released.

2012 – A visitor centre is inaugurated and Glenglassaugh Revival is released.

Glenglassaugh Revival

GS – Initially, a little mashy, with beer-like aromas. Quite sweet and mildly sherried, with developing roasted malt notes, ginger, hazelnuts and caramel. Medium-bodied, with leather and insistent spice on the palate – majoring in nutmeg and cinnamon. Straightforward in the finish; spicy and nutty.

DR – Sharp, spirity, spicy, vegetal and rootsy on the nose, with green salad notes. Definitely a work in progress. The seedlings of fruit and spice on the palate are there but the dominant notes are young, sappy cereal notes, radish and pepper and rapier-like spirit burn. A medium and peppery finish.

Glenglassaugh was bought and re-opened (after having been closed for 23 years) in 2008 by private investors and included in the deal was stock of 500 casks of mature whisky (from 1963 to 1986). During the time it took for their own spirits to come of age, the sales of the stock generated a turnover of no less than £1m during 2011 and a profit of £100,000. Another part of the business is the sale of a variety of different Octave casks (50 litres), filled with spirit and aged on site for private consumers and whisky clubs. Glenglassaugh has already gained a large amount of devoted followers and in summer 2012 a visitor centre was inaugurated.

The equipment of the distillery consists of a Porteus cast iron mash tun with rakes, four wooden washbacks and two stainless steel ones (although the last two are not being used) and one pair of stills. In 2012 the plan is to do four mashes per week, which translates to just over 200,000 litres of alcohol. The first peated production was done in 2009 and for 2012 around 10% of the production will be peated.

Spring 2012 saw the release of 3 year old *Revival*, the first whisky to be produced by the new owners. The core range also consists of *26 year old* (a vatting of several casks), *aged over 30 years* and *aged over 40 years*. The last two are recurring releases of single casks. Part of the core range are also four spirit drinks (either new make or spirit aged six to twelve months); *Clearac, Blushes, Fledgling XB* and *Peated*. Recent limited releases include a *35 year old* called *The Chosen Few*, a series of four single casks named after previous distillery managers, *The Master Distiller's Selection* (a single cask from 1983) and a number of single cask releases exclusive for certain countries.

Revival

Glengoyne

Owner:
Ian Macleod Distillers

Region/district:
Southern Highlands

Founded: **Status:** **Capacity:**
1833   Active (vc)   1 100 000 litres

Address: Dumgoyne by Killearn,
Glasgow G63 9LB

Tel:
01360 550254 (vc)

website:
www.glengoyne.com

History:
1833 – The distillery is licensed under the name Burnfoot Distilleries by the Edmonstone family.

1876 – Lang Brothers buys the distillery and changes the name to Glenguin.

1905 – The name changes to Glengoyne.

1965-66 – Robertson & Baxter takes over Lang Brothers and the distillery is refurbished. The stills are increased from two to three.

2001 – Glengoyne Scottish Oak Finish (16 years old) is launched.

2003 – Ian MacLeod Distillers Ltd buys the distillery plus the brand Langs from the Edrington Group for £7.2 million.

2004 – A 12 year old cask strength is released.

2005 – Limited editions of a 19 year old, a 32 year old and a 37 year old cask strength are launched.

2006 – Nine "choices" from Stillmen, Mashmen and Manager are released.

2007 – A new version of the 21 year old, two Warehousemen's Choice, Vintage 1972 and two single casks are released.

2008 – A 16 year old Shiraz cask finish, three single casks and Heritage Gold are released.

2009 – A 40 year old, two single casks and a new 12 year old are launched.

2010 – Two single casks, 1987 and 1997, released.

2011 – A 24 year old single cask is released.

Glengoyne 12 year old

GS – Fresh and well-rounded on the nose, with medium sweet aromas suggesting malt, oak, and a hint of sherry. Smooth and delicate on the palate, slightly oaky, with a suggestion of cooking apples. The finish is pleasingly long, with buttery, vanilla notes.

DR – Tinned pear and peach on the nose, crystallised barley, lemon and grapefruit on the palate, and a fruity and peppery finish.

In 2011, the owners of Glengoyne distillery, bought their second distillery – Tamdhu. It will be interesting to see what the new owners will do with this rather neglected brand, especially taking into consideration their success with Glengoyne. Since purchasing the distillery in 2003, sales have increased from 190,000 bottles to 900,000 bottles for 2011! In the last five years, a total of £3m have been invested in the site alone, which was earmarked for new warehouses and an upgraded visitor centre. Glengoyne is now one of the most visited distilleries in Scotland attracting 50,000 people every year. Ian MacLeod Distillers also produces King Robert II, a Scotch blend selling more than 6 million bottles per year. In the year leading up to September 2011, the company could report a 26% increase in sales and pre-tax profits were up by 27% to £5.4m.

Glengoyne distillery is equipped with a traditional mash tun with rakes, six Oregon pine washbacks, one wash still and two spirit stills. In 2012, 13 mashes per week are being made which constitutes 820,000 litres of alcohol. Both short (56 hours) and long (110 hours) fermentations are practised which, together with the exceptionally slow distillation (3 litres per minute), contributes to a subtle and complex character of Glengoyne single malt. All produce destined for single malt sales is stored in two dunnage warehouses, while the part that goes for blending, is stored in four palletised warehouses.

The core range consists of *10, 12, 12 (cask strength), 17* and *21 years old*. The line-up for duty free consists of the unaged *Burnfoot* and *15 year old Distiller's Gold* (replacing 14 year old Heritage Gold). The owners are at the moment preparing a full range repackaging and repositioning of the brand which will take place during 2012/2013. Part of the revamp will be the release of a new *25 year old* and the change of the 12 year old cask strength to an unaged version. A *1990 single cask* exclusive for the UK market was also released in May 2012 under the name Glengoyne Auld Enemy Dram.

12 years old

New Books We Enjoyed

Canadian whisky has finally been rewarded with its own bible. Davin de Kergommeaux has filled this void in the whisky library with his *Canadian Whisky - the Portable Expert*. History, science, anecdotes and tasting notes are entwined in an elegant and authoritative way. Davin masters the subject in great detail and as he himself says in the introduction: "This is a story of Canada."
From Gavin D. Smith and Neil Ridley, comes *Let Me Tell You About Whisky*. It is being labelled as a beginner's guide and some of you may interject: "There are such guides available already!" True, but in an ever-changing world of whisky most of them are outdated. Gavin and Neil not only include exciting new whiskies from all corners of the world, but give advice on how to nose, taste and savour, how to organize a whisky tasting, which glassware to use and how to mix your own whisky cocktails. Gavin D. Smith, together with Dominic Roskrow,

has also been involved in the next book - *The Whisky Opus*. With detailed presentations of the world's 175 best distilleries and 500 tasting notes, this is an essential, modern reference work to the world of whisky. Great photos and maps add even more credibility to this very handy and useful guide.
The last two years has seen a real blockbuster amongst whisky books in the form of Ian Buxton's *101 Whiskies to Try Before You Die*. Ian has now released a sequel, *101 World Whiskies to Try Before You Die*, and is, once again, spoiling us with his witty, lighthearted, yet also very knowledgeable style of writing. Expect to discover whiskies you didn't even know existed!
Finally, a book published in 2005 which is still the ultimate book about Islay, its whiskies and distilleries - *Peat Smoke and Spirit* by Andrew Jefford. Just buy it!

Canadian Whisky - the Portable Expert
ISBN 978-0771027437
Let Me Tell You About Whisky
ISBN 978-1862059658

101 World Whiskies to
Try Before You Die
ISBN 978-0755363193

The Whisky Opus
ISBN 978-1405394741
Peat Smoke and Spirit
ISBN 978-0747245780

Recommended Magazines

Whisky Advocate
www.whiskyadvocate.com

Whisky Magazine
www.whiskymag.com

Whisky Time
www.whiskytime-magazin.com

Der Whisky-Botschafter
www.whiskybotschafter.com

Whisky Passion
www.whiskypassion.nl

Allt om Whisky
www.alltomwhisky.se

Glen Grant

Owner:
Campari Group

Region/district:
Speyside

Founded: 1840
Status: Active (vc)
Capacity: 5 900 000 litres

Address: Elgin Road, Rothes,
Banffshire AB38 7BS

Tel: 01340 832118
website: www.glengrant.com

History:

1840 – The brothers James and John Grant, managers of Dandelaith Distillery, found the distillery.

1861 – The distillery becomes the first to install electric lighting.

1864 – John Grant dies.

1872 – James Grant passes away and the distillery is inherited by his son, James junior (Major James Grant).

1897 – James Grant decides to build another distillery across the road; it is named Glen Grant No. 2.

1902 – Glen Grant No. 2 is mothballed.

1931 – Major Grant dies and is succeeded by his grandson Major Douglas Mackessack.

1953 – J. & J. Grant merges with George & J. G. Smith who runs Glenlivet distillery, forming The Glenlivet & Glen Grant Distillers Ltd.

1961 – Armando Giovinetti and Douglas Mackessak found a friendship that eventually leads to Glen Grant becoming the most sold malt whisky in Italy.

1965 – Glen Grant No. 2 is back in production, but renamed Caperdonich.

Everybody knows that there is a danger in being too dependent of a single market, but nobody knows it better than the owners of Glen Grant whose dominant market for decades has been Italy. In 2010 total sales of Scotch single malt to Italy surged ahead by almost 100%. This was also reflected in Glen Grant´s sales figures with volumes increasing by 32%. In 2011, Scotch single malt in Italy was down by 25% but, in spite of that, Glen Grant managed to withstand and show similar figures as in 2010 thanks to the increase of sales in the duty free segment. The optimism is still at large and the owners, Campari Group, have decided to build a large bottling hall next to the distillery. The hall will be operational from April 2013 and from that date, all Glen Grant expressions will be bottled on site.

The distillery is equipped with a 12,3 tonnes semi-lauter mash tun, ten Oregon pine washbacks with a minimum fermentation time of 48 hours and four pairs of stills. The wash stills are peculiar in that they have vertical sides at the base of the neck and all eight stills are fitted with purifiers. This gives an increased reflux and creates a light and delicate whisky. There have been discussions of a possible capacity expansion by adding another four pairs of stills, but these plans have been put on hold. Production slowed down during 2011 when 2,5 million litres were produced. For 2012, the corresponding figure will be in the region of 3,5-4 million litres.

Bourbon casks are used for maturation and the share of sherry butts is less than 10% (mainly used for the 10 year old). A reconstruction of the visitor centre took place in late 2008 at a cost of £500,000 with The Major´s Coachman's House being converted into a new and very elegant visitor centre. Some 10,000 visitors come here every year, not least to visit the unique garden landscaped by John Grant, known as the Major, in the late 1800s.

Some 50% of the production goes into blended whisky, especially Chivas Regal. The Glen Grant core range of single malts consists of *Major´s Reserve* with no age statement but probably around 7 years old, a *5 year old* sold in Italy only, a *10 year old* and the recently introduced *16 year old*. Recent limited editions include the *170th Anniversary Edition* from 2010 and in summer 2011, 732 bottles of a *25 year old* from sherry butts. The latter was first released in France and then in Asian duty free outlets. In 2012 a *19 year old* single cask called *Distillery Edition* was released, available only at the visitor centre.

History (continued):

1972 – The Glenlivet & Glen Grant Distillers merges with Hill Thompson & Co. and Longmorn-Glenlivet Ltd to form The Glenlivet Distillers. The drum maltings ceases.

1973 – Stills are increased from four to six.

1977 – The Chivas & Glenlivet Group (Seagrams) buys Glen Grant Distillery. Stills are increased from six to ten.

2001 – Pernod Ricard and Diageo buy Seagrams Spirits and Wine, with Pernod acquiring the Chivas Group.

2006 – Campari buys Glen Grant for €115 million in a deal that includes the acquisition of Old Smuggler and Braemar for another €15 million.

2007 – The entire range is re-packaged and re-launched and a 15 year old single cask is released. Reconstruction of the visitor centre.

2008 – Two limited cask strengths - a 16 year old and a 27 year old - are released.

2009 – Cellar Reserve 1992 is released.

2010 – A 170th Anniversary bottling is released.

2011 – A 25 year old is released.

2012 – A 19 year old Distillery Edition is released.

Glen Grant 10 year old

GS – Relatively dry on the nose, with cooking apples. Fresh and fruity on the palate, with a comparatively lengthy, malty finish, which features almonds and hazelnuts.

DR – Sweet banana and toffee, vanilla and pear on the nose, sweet barley, crystallised pineapple on the palate with a touch of honey and finally a cinnamon and spice note at the finish.

16 years old   *25 years old*   *Cellar Reserve 1992*

10 years old   *The Major's Reserve*

Glengyle

Owner:
Mitchell's Glengyle Ltd

Region/district:
Campbeltown

Founded: 2004
Status: Active
Capacity: 750 000 litres

Address: Glengyle Road, Campbeltown, Argyll PA28 6LR

Tel: 01586 551710
website: www.kilkerran.com

History:
1872 – The original Glengyle Distillery is built by William Mitchell.

1919 – The distillery is bought by West Highland Malt Distilleries Ltd.

1925 – The distillery is closed.

1929 – The warehouses (but no stock) are purchased by the Craig Brothers and rebuilt into a petrol station and garage.

1941 – The distillery is acquired by the Bloch Brothers.

1957 – Campbell Henderson applies for planning permission with the intention of reopening the distillery.

2000 – Hedley Wright, owner of Springbank Distillery and related to founder William Mitchell, acquires the distillery.

2004 – The first distillation after reconstruction takes place in March.

2007 – The first limited release - a 3 year old.

2009 – Kilkerran "Work in progress" is released.

2010 – "Work in progress 2" is released.

2011 – "Work in progress 3" is released.

2012 – "Work in progress 4" is released.

Kilkerran Work in Progress IV

GS – Initially, very sweet on the nose, with icing sugar, honey and apple pie. Then caramel and fresh ginger. Relatively full-bodied, with a spicy palate offering vanilla and fudge and just a suggestion of sea salt. Long in the finish, with lingering liquorice and aniseed.

DR – Delicate, fruity, earthy on the nose but not over-aggressive. Peat and industrial oil smoke. Starting to shape up nicely. There's a delightful balance on the palate between delicate tinned fruits, cinnamon and other sweet spice, some toffee notes and a rich, full peat and pepper and exotic spice. Prickly finish, with curry spices.

It is a staggering thought that in Campbeltown, often referred to as the most remote mainland town in Scotland and with 5,500 inhabitants, there once were almost 40 whisky distilleries with 25 operating simultaneously. The most prosperous time for the town was in the Victorian days when shipbuilding, fishing, coal mining and whisky distilling made most of the inhabitants quite prosperous. The downturn came during the first world war and by 1934, when Rieclachan closed, only two distilleries were left – Glen Scotia and Springbank. Seventy years later the number grew to three when Glengyle (also closed in 1925) was re-opened by the owners of Springbank.

When J & A Mitchell bought the closed distillery in 2000, they took care of retaining as many of the original facilities as possible. The boiler house was the only building that had to be constructed. The equipment, however, was gone ever since the distillery had closed way back in 1925, so stills (as well as spirit safe and spirit receivers) had to be bought from another closed distillery, Ben Wyvis. To increase the reflux the body of the stills were reshaped and the lye pipes made slightly ascending. The Boby mill was acquired from Craigellachie and the 4 tonnes semilauter mash tun was made by Forsyth's in Rothes. The four washbacks, with a capacity of 30,000 litres each, are also newly made from boat skin larch. The fermentation time is at least 72 hours, sometimes even longer. Malt is obtained from neighbouring Springbank whose staff also run operations. Although the capacity is 750,000 litres, the plan for 2012 is to produce only 33,000 litres.

The name Kilkerran is used for the whisky as Glengyle was already in use for a vatted malt produced by Loch Lomond Distillers. The first core expression of Kilkerran single malt will be a 12 year old but every year since 2009, the owners have released a limited edition called Work in Progress which will showcase what the distillery is capable of. In June 2012 it was time for the 8 year old Kilkerran Work in Progress 4 and a total of 9,000 bottles were released.

Kilkerran - Work in Progress IV

LOW WINES STILL
CAPACITY 15,000 LITRES

WASH STILL
CAPACITY 18,000 LITRES

Glen Keith

Owner:
Chivas Brothers
(Pernod Ricard)

Region/district:
Speyside

Founded: **Status:** **Capacity:**
1957 Active 6 000 000 litres

Address: Station Road, Keith,
Banffshire AB55 3BU

Tel: **website:**
01542 783042 -

History:
1957 – The Distillery is founded by Chivas
Brothers (Seagrams).

1958 – Production starts.

1970 – The first gas-fuelled still in Scotland is
installed, the number of stills increases from
three to five.

1976 – Own maltings (Saladin box) ceases.

1983 – A sixth still is installed.

1994 – The first official bottling, a 10 year
old, is released as part of Seagram's Heritage
Selection.

2000 – The distillery is mothballed.

2001 – Pernod Ricard takes over Chivas
Brothers from Seagrams.

2012 – The reconstruction and refurbishing of
the distillery begins.

Glen Keith 10 year old
DS – Soft heather and honey on the nose with
a hint of banana. The palate is quite flat and
light and the finish is soft and smooth with a
honeyed aftertaste.

The rumours that we reported about in last year's edition
of Malt Whisky Yearbook proved to be true – Glen Keith
will soon be back as a producing distillery! And not only
that, the capacity will almost double to 6 million litres of
alcohol. The reason for the resurrection of Glen Keith is,
of course, that the owners, Pernod Ricard, have to increase
their stock of malt whisky to satisfy the constantly increasing demand for their blended whiskies, in particular Chivas
Regal and Ballantine´s, in Asia. The work to the distillery
was started during spring 2012, partly by demolishing the
old Saladin maltings. A new, highly efficient Briggs lauter
mash tun will replace the old one and the nine original
Oregon pine washbacks will also be replaced by new ones
made of wood. Six new washbacks made of stainless steel
will moreover be installed. The six stills are the same as
before but new heat recovery technology will be used to
make them more efficient. In addition, they will install
four new malt bins, as well as a new malt intake and the
laboratory will be relocated to another plant. According to
the plans Glen Keith will start producing
again in April 2013.

Glen Keith was built in the late 1950s
on the site of the old Mill of Keith corn
mill and it became a site where many
alternative production methods were
tested. It started with triple distillation,
moved on to distillation of hea-
vily peated whiskies, trials making
malt whisky in a column still and
research on new strains of yeast. It
was also one of the first distilleries
to use microprocessors to control
mashing, milling and distilling.
Even after it was closed in 2000, it
was of importance to the nearby
Strathisla distillery which used the
boiler at Glen Keith and the new-
make from Strathisla was brought
to Glen Keith for filling.

The only official bottling used to
be a *10 year old*. It is no longer
bottled by the owners but can still
be found in some whisky shops.

10 years old

Glenkinchie

Owner: **Region/district:**
Diageo   Lowlands

Founded: **Status:**   **Capacity:**
1837   Active (vc)   2 500 000 litres

Address: Pencaitland, Tranent,
East Lothian EH34 5ET

Tel: **website:**
01875 342004   www.malts.com

History:

1825 – A distillery known as Milton is founded by John and George Rate.

1837 – The Rate brothers are registered as licensees of a distillery named Glenkinchie.

1853 – John Rate sells the distillery to a farmer by the name of Christie who converts it to a sawmill.

1881 – The buildings are bought by a consortium from Edinburgh.

1890 – Glenkinchie Distillery Company is founded. Reconstruction and refurbishment is on-going for the next few years.

1914 – Glenkinchie forms Scottish Malt Distillers (SMD) with four other lowland distilleries.

1939-45 – Glenkinchie is one of few distilleries allowed to maintain production during the war.

1968 – Floor maltings is decommissioned.

1969 – The maltings is converted into a museum.

1988 – Glenkinchie 10 years becomes one of selected six in the Classic Malt series.

1998 – A Distiller's Edition with Amontillado finish is launched.

2007 – A 12 year old and a 20 year old cask strength are released.

2010 – A cask strength exclusive for the visitor centre, a 1992 single cask and a 20 year old are released.

Glenkinchie 12 year old

GS – The nose is fresh and floral, with spices and citrus fruits, plus a hint of marshmallow. Notably elegant. Water releases cut grass and lemon notes. Medium-bodied, smooth, sweet and fruity, with malt, butter and cheesecake. The finish is comparatively long and drying, initially rather herbal.

DR – The nose is light and flowery, with wet meadow notes and cucumber, the palate is pure barley with a touch of star anise spice and an earthy note.

Glenkinchie is one of the original six Classic Malts and also the one that sells the least (around 250,000 bottles per year). The single malt isn't associated with one particular blend like Cardhu (Johnnie Walker), Strathmill (J&B) or Blair Athol (Bell's). Instead, it is part of several of Diageo's blended brands and the company has many. Apart from the three already mentioned (which are also the best-selling) there are a further seven blends each selling more than 5 million bottles every year (Buchanan's, Old Parr, White Horse, Windsor, Black & White, VAT 69 and Haig). Glenkinchie is one of only five distilleries that produce malt whisky in the Lowlands today (Glenkinchie, Auchentoshan, Bladnoch and the two newly constructed Daftmill and Ailsa Bay), but in the second half of the 18th century, the area was more or less the birthplace of commercial whisky distilling in Scotland. By the time Glenkinchie was founded, no less than 115 licensed distilleries were recorded in the Lowlands.

Glenkinchie is equipped with a full lauter mash tun (9 tonnes) and six wooden washbacks. There is only one pair of stills but they are, on the other hand, very big – in fact, the wash still (30,963 litres) is the biggest in Scotland. Steeply descending lyne arms give very little reflux and condensation of the spirit vapours take place in a cast iron worm tub. Since 2008, the distillery has been working 7 days and 14 mashes per week which amounts to 2,5 million litres of alcohol per year. Three dunnage warehouses on site have 10,000 casks maturing, the oldest dating from 1952. The proximity to Edinburgh is one reason why more than 40,000 visitors find their way to the distillery and its excellent visitor centre each year.

The core range consists of a *12 year old* and a *Distiller's Edition 14 years old*. There is also a *cask strength without age statement* sold exclusively at the visitor centre. Recent limited editions include a Manager's Choice *1992 single cask* and a *20 year old* cask strength distilled in 1990, both released in 2010.

12 years old

Glenlivet

Owner:
Chivas Brothers
(Pernod Ricard)

Region/district:
Speyside

Founded: 1824

Status: Active (vc)

Capacity: 10 500 000 litres

Address: Ballindalloch, Banffshire AB37 9DB

Tel: 01340 821720 (vc)

website: www.theglenlivet.com

History:

1817 – George Smith inherits the farm distillery Upper Drummin from his father Andrew Smith who has been distilling on the site since 1774.

1840 – George Smith buys Delnabo farm near Tomintoul and leases Cairngorm Distillery. His son William takes over operations at Upper Drummin.

1845 – George Smith leases three other farms, one of which is situated on the river Livet and is called Minmore.

1846 – William Smith develops tuberculosis and his brother John Gordon moves back home to assist his father. Sales of Smith's Glenlivet increases steadily and neither Upper Drummin nor Cairngorm Distillery can meet demand.

1858 – George Smith buys Minmore farm, which he has leased for some time, and obtains permission from the Duke of Gordon to build a distillery.

1859 – Upper Drummin and Cairngorm close and all equipment is brought to Minmore which is renamed The Glenlivet Distillery.

1864 – George Smith cooperates with the whisky agent Andrew P. Usher and exports the whisky with great success.

1871 – George Smith dies and his son John Gordon takes over.

The struggle for the second place on the global sales list of single malts has been tough for the last ten years with Macallan and Glenlivet taking turns being the number two after the sovereign leader, Glenfiddich. Macallan has a stronghold in Asia while Glenlivet is the number one single malt in the USA (and number five of all Scotch whiskies) where more than 40% of the volume is sold. In 2011 it was Glenlivet's turn to take the lead. The brand showed an impressive increase of almost 15% and sold well over 9 million bottles.

To be able to keep up with the increased demand the owners started a substantial expansion of the distillery in 2009 which was completed during 2010. The end result saw an 80% increase in capacity. After the expansion, the equipment has been divided into two still rooms. In the old, there are eight stills where three of the stills were replaced in 2011. There are also eight wooden washbacks and the old mash tun (which has been mothballed). The new still house has a new, Briggs mash tun with six arms (12.6 tonnes capacity) which is highly efficient, bringing the mashing time down from 6 hours to just over 3 hours. There are also eight new Oregon pine washbacks with a fermentation time of 50 hours and three pairs of stills. The wash stills are heated using external heat exchangers while the spirit stills all have kettles inside. The maximum capacity is 42 mashes per week and 10.5 million litres of alcohol per year.

Glenlivet's core range (or Classic Range as it is called) is the *12 year old, French Oak 15 years, 18 year old, 21 year old Archive* and *Glenlivet XXV*. A special range of unchillfiltered whiskies is called Nadurra and it comes in three expressions; *Nadurra 16 year old* at *cask strength*, the same for duty free but bottled at *48%* and *Nadurra Triumph 1991*. The latter is an 18 year old distilled solely from the Triumph barley variety. Apart from Nadurra, another three expressions are earmarked for the Duty Free market: *First Fill Sherry Cask 12 years old, 15 years old* and (from July 2011) *Glenlivet Master Distiller's Reserve*. A limited edition from 2011 was the *21 year old Glenlivet Founder's Reserve*, released to celebrate the expansion of the distillery. In 2012, the Cellar Collection range was continued with the *1980 Vintage* and the *12 year old Excellence* was released as an exclusive for Hong Kong. A series called *Single Cask Editions* was introduced in 2005 and in 2011/2012 no less than six new bottlings were released aged from 15 to 21 years and from a variety of bourbon and sherry casks; *Guardians, Helios, Josie, Inveravon* (Taiwan only) and *Kilimanjaro* and *Legacy* (both exclusive to Germany).

History (continued):

1880 – John Gordon Smith applies for and is granted sole rights to the name The Glenlivet. All distilleries wishing to use Glenlivet in their names must from now hyphenate it with their brand names.

1890 – A fire breaks out and some of the buildings are replaced.

1896 – Another two stills are installed.

1901 – John Gordon Smith dies.

1904 – John Gordon's nephew George Smith Grant takes over.

1921 – Captain Bill Smith Grant, son of George Smith Grant, takes over.

1953 – George & J. G. Smith Ltd merges with J. & J. Grant of Glen Grant Distillery and forms the company Glenlivet & Glen Grant Distillers.

1966 – Floor maltings closes.

1970 – Glenlivet & Glen Grant Distillers Ltd merges with Longmorn-Glenlivet Distilleries Ltd and Hill Thomson & Co. Ltd to form The Glenlivet Distillers Ltd.

1978 – Seagrams buys The Glenlivet Distillers Ltd. A visitor centre opens.

1996/97 – The visitor centre is expanded, and a multimedia facility installed.

2000 – French Oak 12 years and American Oak 12 years are launched.

2001 – Pernod Ricard and Diageo buy Seagram Spirits & Wine. Pernod Ricard thereby gains control of the Chivas group.

2004 – This year sees a lavish relaunch of Glenlivet. French Oak 15 years replaces the previous 12 year old.

2005 – Two new duty-free versions are introduced – The Glenlivet 12 year old First Fill and Nadurra. The 1972 Cellar Collection (2,015 bottles) is launched.

2006 – Nadurra 16 year old cask strength and 1969 Cellar Collection are released. Glenlivet sells more than 500,000 cases for the first time in one year.

2007 – Glenlivet XXV is released.

2009 – Four more stills are installed and the capacity increases to 8.5 million litres. Nadurra Triumph 1991 is released.

2010 – Another two stills are commissioned and capacity increases to 10.5 million litres. Glenlivet Founder´s Reserve is released.

2011 – Glenlivet Master Distiller´s Reserve is released for the duty free market.

2012 – 1980 Cellar Collection is released.

Glenlivet 12 year old

GS – A lovely, honeyed, floral, fragrant nose. Medium-bodied, smooth and malty on the palate, with vanilla sweetness. Not as sweet, however, as the nose might suggest. The finish is pleasantly lengthy and sophisticated.

DR – Freshly chopped apple, rhubarb and crisp barley on the nose, soft rounded and beautiful mouth feel with green fruit and gooseberries and a delicate, rounded and medium long finish.

18 years old   21 Archive   The Glenlivet XXV   1980 Cellar Collection

Helios 20 years   Kilimanjaro 15 years

12 years old

15 years old   Master Distiller´s Reserve

Glenlossie

Owner: Diageo
Region/district: Speyside

Founded: 1876
Status: Active
Capacity: 1 800 000 litres

Address: Birnie, Elgin, Morayshire IV30 8SS

Tel: 01343 862000
website: www.malts.com

History:
1876 – John Duff, former manager at Glendronach Distillery, founds the distillery. Alexander Grigor Allan (to become part-owner of Talisker Distillery), the whisky trader George Thomson and Charles Shirres (both will co-found Longmorn Distillery some 20 years later with John Duff) and H. Mackay are also involved in the company.

1895 – The company Glenlossie-Glenlivet Distillery Co. is formed. Alexander Grigor Allan passes away.

1896 – John Duff becomes more involved in Longmorn and Mackay takes over management of Glenlossie.

1919 – Distillers Company Limited (DCL) takes over the company.

1929 – A fire breaks out and causes considerable damage.

1930 – DCL transfers operations to Scottish Malt Distillers (SMD).

1962 – Stills are increased from four to six.

1971 – Another distillery, Mannochmore, is constructed by SMD on the premises. A dark grains plant is installed.

1990 – A 10 year old is launched in the Flora & Fauna series.

2010 – A Manager's Choice single cask from 1999 is released.

It is estimated that the Scottish whisky industry produces 1,6 billion litres of pot ale (the remains after the first distillation) and 500,000 tonnes of draff (what is left after the mashing) every year. These by-products can be used to make energy and a lot of focus has been put into that recently. A new bioplant is under construction at Glenlossie (operational by the end of 2012) where draff from 17 Diageo distilleries in the Speyside area will be used as a biomass fuel to produce steam for Glenlossie and Mannochmore distilleries. A similar plant is already taken into use at Roseisle distillery and another is being built at Cameronbridge grain distillery in Fife. These three plants will together reduce annual CO_2 emissions by 75,000 tonnes. The cost for the facility at Glenlossie will be £6m.

Glenlossie distillery, which lies next to the much younger Mannochmore, is equipped with one stainless steel full lauter mash tun (8,2 tonnes) installed in 1992, eight washbacks made of larch and three pairs of stills. The spirit stills are also equipped with purifiers between the lyne arms and the condensers to increase the reflux which gives Glenlossie newmake its light and green/grassy character. Six of the washbacks were replaced in 2010/2011. During 2012 the distillery will be working a five-day week with 12 mashes, resulting in 1,8 million litres of alcohol. Except for the two distilleries and one dark grains plant, the site also holds ten warehouses that can store 200,000 casks of maturing whisky. To Glenlossie Bonds, as it is called, casks are sent from a number of Diageo's distilleries in the vicinity.

The whisky is mainly used for blends, especially Haig – a brand selling around 5 million bottles worldwide but which is not seen as one of Diageo's most famous brands today. During the 1960s and 70s on the other hand, Haig was the brand leader in the UK and the first to sell more than 1 million cases (12 million bottles) in the home market. The only official bottling of Glenlossie available today is a *10 year old*. During 2010 a *first fill bourbon cask* distilled in *1999* was released as a part of the Manager's Choice range.

Glenlossie 10 year old

GS – Cereal, silage and vanilla notes on the relatively light nose, with a voluptuous, sweet palate, offering plums, ginger and barley sugar, plus a hint of oak. The finish is medium in length, with grist and slightly peppery oak.

DR – Powdery and light, with salt and pepper on the nose, big, earthy and spicy palate; savoury and full, with a long and mouth-coating finish.

Flora & Fauna 10 years old

Glen Moray

Owner: **Region/district:**
La Martiniquaise (COFEPP) Speyside

Founded: **Status:**   **Capacity:**
1897   Active (vc)   3 300 000 litres

Address: Bruceland Road, Elgin,
Morayshire IV30 1YE

Tel: **website:**
01343 542577   www.glenmoray.com

History:
1897 – West Brewery, dated 1828, is reconstructed as Glen Moray Distillery.

1910 – The distillery closes.

1920 – Financial troubles force the distillery to be put up for sale. Buyer is Macdonald & Muir.

1923 – Production restarts.

1958 – A reconstruction takes place and the floor maltings are replaced by a Saladin box.

1978 – Own maltings are terminated.

1979 – Number of stills is increased to four.

1992 – Two old stills are replaced by new.

1996 – Macdonald & Muir Ltd changes name to Glenmorangie plc.

1999 – Three wood finishes are introduced - Chardonnay (no age) and Chenin Blanc (12 and 16 years respectively).

2004 – Louis Vuitton Moët Hennessy buys Glenmorangie plc for £300 million and a 1986 cask strength, a 20 and a 30 year old are released.

2005 – The Fifth Chapter (Manager's Choice from Graham Coull) is released.

2006 – Two vintages, 1963 and 1964, and a new Manager's Choice are released.

2007 – The second edition of Mountain Oak is released.

2008 – The distillery is sold to La Martiniquaise.

2009 – A 14 year old Port finish and an 8 year old matured in red wines casks are released.

2011 – Two cask finishes and a 10 year old Chardonnay maturation are released.

2012 – New releases inlude 2003 Chenin Blanc and 25 year old port finish.

Glen Moray 12 year old

GS – Mellow on the nose, with vanilla, pear drops and some oak. Smooth in the mouth, with spicy malt, vanilla and summer fruits. The finish is relatively short, with spicy fruit.

DR – Maltesers and soft vanilla ice cream on the nose, full and rich sweet malt, a touch of vanilla and hints of tannin on the palate and a pleasant and pleasing finish.

With the support of one of the biggest wine & spirits conglomerates in France, COFEPP, Glen Moray has begun to challenge the top producers among single malts in a serious way. In 2011 sales increased by 22% to 720,000 bottles and they are now looking into promoting Glen Moray on a larger scale in the USA through a new distributor. It has also been decided to increase the capacity of the distillery. Two new stills will be installed during 2012 giving the distillery a capacity of 3,3 million litres. A spokesperson for the company has indicated that there is likely to be further expansion in 2013/2014. Part of the extra volume will go into the owner´s two blended whiskies – Label 5 and Sir Edwards – that together sold a total of 46 million bottles during 2012. COFEPP (through Glen Turner Ltd) also runs the huge Starlaw grain distillery (in combination with a maturation, blending and bottling plant) near Bathgate producing 25 million litres of grain whisky per year and there are plans to also build a 5 million litre malt distillery on the site.

Glen Moray distillery is equipped with a stainless steel mash tun, five stainless steel washbacks and two pairs of stills (which will increase to three pairs). In December 2011 one of the wash stills and the pots of the two spirit stills were replaced. Last year 2,3 million litres were distilled, a record for the distillery, and they expect to do the same for 2012. In 2009, the distillery, for the first time, produced a share of whisky from peated malt with around 40ppm phenols. The volume of the first batch amounted to 300,000 litres and for 2012 they will be doing 200,000 litres. It will mainly be used in the owner´s Label 5 blended whisky.

The core range consists of *Classic, 10 year old Chardonnay cask, 12 years old* and *16 years old*. In 2012 a Glen Moray from *2003* with a full maturation in *Chenin Blanc* cask was released as a distillery exclusive and later in the year a *25 year old port finish* was launched.

12 years old

Glenmorangie

Owner:
The Glenmorangie Co
(Moët Hennessy)

Region/district:
Northern Highlands

Founded:
1843

Status:
Active (vc)

Capacity:
6 000 000 litres

Address: Tain, Ross-shire IV19 1PZ

Tel:
01862 892477 (vc)

website:
www.glenmorangie.com

History:
1843 – William Mathesen applies for a license for a farm distillery called Morangie, which is rebuilt by them. Production took place here in 1738, and possibly since 1703.

1849 – Production starts in November.

1880 – Exports to foreign destinations such as Rome and San Francisco commence.

1887 – The distillery is rebuilt and Glenmorangie Distillery Company Ltd is formed.

1918 – 40% of the distillery is sold to Macdonald & Muir Ltd and 60 % to the whisky dealer Durham. Macdonald & Muir takes over Durham's share by the late thirties.

1931 – The distillery closes.

1936 – Production restarts in November.

1980 – Number of stills increases from two to four and own maltings ceases.

1990 – The number of stills is doubled to eight.

1994 – A visitor centre opens. September sees the launch of Glenmorangie Port Wood Finish which marks the start of a number of different wood finishes.

1995 – Glenmorangie´s Tain l´Hermitage (Rhone wine) is launched.

1996 – Two different wood finishes are launched, Madeira and Sherry. Glenmorangie plc is formed.

The Glenmorangie visitor centre and shop was renovated and redesigned during 2011 and arguably it is now one of the top whisky attractions in Scotland (awarded 5 stars from Visit Scotland). There are, for instance, galleries where the visitor can explore Glenmorangie´s history and connection to the landscape and next to the shop there is a great bar with a giant table made of American oak.

The distillery went through a major upgrade and expansion in 2009 and the equipment now consists of a full lauter mash tun with a charge of 9,8 tonnes, 12 stainless steel washbacks with a fermentation time of 52 hours and six pairs of stills. They are the tallest in Scotland and are replicas of old gin type of stills. The still room is one of the most magnificent in Scotland and the recent addition of a stained glass window featuring the Signet panel of the Cadboll Stone by the glass artist John Clark, makes the whole room feel even more like a cathedral than before. Production during 2012 will be 28 mashes per week which equates to 5 million litres in the year. For two of the weeks they will be using chocolate malt – the special variety which is used in the Signet single malt. The whole production is filled into casks on site and most of it is matured on site or nearby. The newmake is always filled into bourbon barrels. For some of the expressions it is later re-racked into different casks for extra maturation.

The core range consists of *Original* (the former 10 year old), *18 year old* and *25 year old*. There are three 12 year old wood finishes: *Quinta Ruban* (port), *Nectar D´Or* (Sauternes) and *Lasanta* (sherry). In 2011 an addition to the range was released in the shape of a *15 year old Nectar d´Or*. It was however withdrawn after just six months. The "old" 15 year old Glenmorangie Sauternes finish could still be found (May 2012) in the distillery shop. Added to the core range are *Astar* and *Signet*. Astar has matured in designer casks while Signet is an unusual piece of work with one portion of the whisky (20%) having been made using chocolate malt. A series of bottlings, called Private Collection, started in 2009 with the release of *Sonnalta PX* and was followed up a year later with lightly peated *Finealta*. In January 2012 the third release in the range was launched, *Artein*, which is a mix of 15 and 21 year old whiskies which have been extra matured in Super Tuscan (Sassicaia) wine casks. In July 2011, *Glenmorangie Pride* was released. This is a 28 year old whisky discovered in the casks in 1999 by Bill Lumsden. He decided to re-rack the whisky into Sauternes barriques for another ten years!

History (continued):

1997 – A museum opens.

2001 – A limited edition of a cask strength port wood finish is released in July, Cote de Beaune Wood Finish is launched in September and Three Cask (ex-Bourbon, charred oak and ex-Rioja) is launched in October for Sainsbury's.

2002 – A Sauternes finish, a 20 year Glenmorangie with two and a half years in Sauternes casks, is launched.

2003 – Burgundy Wood Finish is launched in July and a limited edition of cask strength Madeira-matured (i. e. not just finished) in August.

2004 – Glenmorangie buys the Scotch Malt Whisky Society. The Macdonald family decides to sell Glenmorangie plc (including the distilleries Glenmorangie, Glen Moray and Ardbeg) to Moët Hennessy at £300 million. A new version of Glenmorangie Tain l´Hermitage (28 years) is released and Glenmorangie Artisan Cask is launched in November.

2005 – A 30 year old is launched.

2007 – The entire range gets a complete makeover with 15 and 30 year olds being discontinued and the rest given new names as well as new packaging.

2008 – An expansion of production capacity is started. Astar and Signet are launched.

2009 – The expansion is finished and Sonnalta PX is released for duty free.

2010 – Finealta is released.

2011 – 28 year old Glenmorangie Pride is released.

2012 – Artein is released.

Signet   Astar   Artein

Glenmorangie Original

GS – The nose offers fresh fruits, butterscotch and toffee. Silky smooth in the mouth, mild spice, vanilla, and well-defined toffee. The fruity finish has a final flourish of ginger.

DR – Rounded honey and light tangerine on the nose, much weightier on the palate, with vanilla, honey, oranges and lemons nudging alongside some tannins and soft peat, all coming together in a rich and warming finish.

Original (10 years old)   18 years old   Nectar D´Or

Glen Ord

Owner:
Diageo

Region/district:
Northern Highlands

Founded: 1838

Status: Active (vc)

Capacity: 5 000 000 litres

Address: Muir of Ord, Ross-shire IV6 7UJ

Tel: 01463 872004 (vc)

website: www.malts.com

History:

1838 – Thomas Mackenzie founds the distillery and licenses it to Ord Distillery Co. (Robert Johnstone and Donald MacLennan).

1847 – The distillery is put up for sale.

1855 – Alexander MacLennan and Thomas McGregor buy the distillery.

1870 – Alexander MacLennan dies and the distillery is taken over by his widow who marries the banker Alexander Mackenzie.

1877 – Alexander Mackenzie leases the distillery.

1878 – Alexander Mackenzie builds a new still house and barely manages to start production before a fire destroys it.

1882 – Mackenzie registers the name Glenoran to be used for whisky from Glen Ord.

1896 – Alexander Mackenzie dies and the distillery is sold to the blending company James Watson & Co. for £15,800.

1923 – John Jabez Watson, James Watson's son, dies and the distillery is sold to John Dewar & Sons. The name is changed from Glen Oran to Glen Ord.

1925 – Dewar's joins Distillers Company Limited.

1961 – Floor maltings is abandoned in favour of a Saladin box.

1966 – The two stills are increased to six.

1968 – To augment the Saladin box a drum maltings is built.

1983 – Malting in the Saladin box ceases.

1988 – A visitor centre is opened.

2002 – A 12 year old is launched.

2003 – A 28 year old cask strength is released.

2004 – A 25 year old is launched.

2005 – A 30 year old is launched as a Special Release from Diageo.

2006 – A 12 year old Singleton of Glen Ord is launched.

2010 – A Singleton of Glen Ord 15 year old is released in Taiwan.

2011 – Two more washbacks are installed, increasing the capacity by 25%.

2012 – Singleton of Glen Ord cask strength is released.

Singleton of Glen Ord 12 year old

GS – Honeyed malt and milk chocolate on the nose, with a hint of orange. These characteristics carry over onto the sweet, easy-drinking palate, along with a biscuity note. Subtly drying, with a medium-length, spicy finish.

DR – Red fruits and blackcurrant, mince pies, red apple and sherry on the nose, enjoyable taste of apple, prune and cinnamon, and a delightful and more-ish finish.

When Singleton of Glen Ord was first launched in Taiwan and Korea in 2006, it was an attempt by Diageo to attract consumers aged 25 to 35 to upgrade from blended Scotch to a single malt. Few would have thought that five years later the brand would challenge the top selling malts of the world, selling close to 2 million bottles per year!

The distillery has been upgraded during the last two years starting with a new full lauter mash tun in 2010. The efficient tun has decreased the mashing cycle from 8 hours to 6. At the same time two of the eight Oregon pine washbacks were replaced. In 2011, another two washbacks, this time made from stainless steel, were installed. This increased the maximum capacity to 5,2 million litres of alcohol. The fermentation time is quite long (75 hours) in order to achieve a smooth and delicate character of the spirit. Finally there are three pairs of stills all equipped with after coolers.

The distillery is situated 15 miles west of Inverness in the fertile Black Isle and with one of the best visitor centres in the industry, it is well worth a visit.

A major part of the site is occupied by the Glen Ord Maltings built in 1968. Equipped with 18 drums and with a capacity of 37,000 tonnes per year it produces malt for several other Diageo distilleries.

Singleton of Glen Ord is an exclusive to Southeast Asia (in particular Taiwan and Singapore) but the 12 year old can also be found at the distillery visitor centre. The core expression is the *Singleton of Glen Ord 12 year old*, with a 50/50 mix of sherry and bourbon casks. Other expressions in the range are the *15 year old* and the *18 year old*. There have also been two very limited ones, *32* and *35 year old*, with the last one being relaunched in March 2012. The newest member of the range is a *cask strength*, bottled at 58,1% and released in May 2012.

The Singleton of Glen Ord

Meet the Manager

KIRSTY DAGNAN
SENIOR SITE MANAGER,
GLEN ORD AND TEANINICH DISTILLERIES

When did you start working in the whisky business and when did you start at Glen Ord?

I started in the whisky industry in 2005 and came to Glen Ord in 2010.

Had you been working in other lines of business before whisky?

I started with Diageo straight from University but as part of my degree I worked for GlaxoSmithKline for a year as an Analytical Chemist.

What kind of education or training do you have?

I have a BSc (hons) in Forensic and Analytical Chemistry from the University of Strathclyde in Glasgow.

Describe your career in the whisky business.

I started with Diageo six and a half years ago on their Graduate Scheme. The scheme involved three one year placements. My first placement was working on a variety of projects at Port Dundas Distillery in Glasgow before moving to Speyside to work at Linkwood Distillery as a Site Operations Manager. I then moved to Amsterdam for a year working in Logistics. After Amsterdam I got my first permanent role working as Business Leader for White Spirits and Sweetened Products in the Leven packaging plant in Fife. I was in this role for two years before applying for the position of Senior Site Manager in Malt Distilling. I have been working at Glen Ord for almost 2 years.

What are your main tasks as a manager?

Every day is different which is what I enjoy. Days can vary from dealing with VIP visitors to dealing with breakdowns in the plant. I think it's important to spend as much time as possible in the plant understanding areas for improvement and spending time with my team. My main responsibility is ensuring that each department achieves their targets and that we achieve these is a safe manner.

What are the biggest challenges of being a distillery manager?

I am responsible for the operation of Glen Ord and Teaninich distilleries, Glen Ord Maltings, Glen Ord Visitor Centre and North Engineering Centre. Ensuring I split my time between each area is a big challenge.

What would be the worst that could go wrong in the production process?

Somebody getting hurt at work would be the worst possible thing.

How would you describe the character of Glen Ord single malt?

Well balanced. Rich, smooth and full of character!

What are the main features in the process at Glen Ord, contributing to this character?

We use malted barley from the maltings on site which is the first thing that makes the Singleton of Glen Ord special. We have long fermentations which helps the rich fruitiness develop. Slow distillation with lots of copper contact and hot water condensers keeps the final new make spirit light in character. For maturation we use a combination of American Oak Bourbon casks and European Sherry casks which gives the whisky a perfect balance of rich fruity characteristics coupled with a smooth vanilla sweetness.

What is your favourite expression of Glen Ord and why?

I would have to say the Singleton of Glen Ord 12 year old. It is rich, smooth and sweet - everything you could want in a good dram!

If it were your decision alone - what new expression of Glen Ord would you like to see released?

It would be hard to beat the cask combination that we currently use. It might be interesting to finish the maturation in a different cask type e.g. ex Rum cask so see what impact this would have on the flavour profile.

If you had to choose a favourite dram other than Glen Ord, what would that be?

Apart from Teaninich! My family come from Islay so I am very partial to most of the Islay malts as well.

What are the biggest changes you have seen the past 5 years in your profession?

I haven't really been in the industry for a huge length of time but even I can see the increasing demand for Whisky and the impact this is having on the industry.

Do you see any major changes in the next 10 years to come?

I hope more and more growth!

Do you have any special interests or hobbies that you pursue?

I completed my competent crew qualification in sailing last year and would like to do more but as yet haven't. I am also getting into Mountain biking - living in the highlands there are some fantastic places to explore.

When you started at Glen Ord, you were the youngest distillery manager within Diageo and at the same time the distillery was due for a huge upgrade. Were you prepared for that or do you feel you got a tough start on the job?

I would be lying if I said it wasn't a tough start. It was a very steep learning curve but nearly 2 years down the line I wouldn't change it. I love my job; there are new challenges everyday and lots to learn. It is a fantastic industry to work in and I feel very fortunate.

Was your mind set on the whisky business already when you were studying for your BSc?

I have always had a passion for Malt Whisky, I remember saying to my Mum I would love to be a distillery manager - her response was that I was probably doing the wrong course! I applied for a lot of roles when I was nearing the end of my degree, mostly Chemistry roles. When I went for the interview with Diageo for the graduate scheme I knew I wanted that job - the people and company were fantastic and I could see that there were lots of exciting opportunities.

Glenrothes

Owner: **Region/district:**
The Edrington Group   Speyside
(the brand is owned by Berry Bros)

Founded: **Status:**   **Capacity:**
1878   Active   5 600 000 litres

Address: Rothes, Morayshire AB38 7AA

Tel: **website:**
01340 872300   www.theglenrothes.com

History:
1878 – James Stuart & Co., licensees of Macallan since 1868, begins planning a new distillery in Rothes. Robert Dick, William Grant and John Cruickshank are partners in the company. Stuart has financial problems so Dick, Grant and Cruickshank terminate the partnership, form William Grant & Co. and continue the building of the distillery in Rothes.

1879 – Production starts in May.

1884 – The distillery changes name to Glenrothes-Glenlivet.

1887 – William Grant & Co. joins forces with Islay Distillery Co. (owners of Bunnahabhain Distillery) and forms Highland Distillers Company.

1897 – A fire ravages the distillery in December.

1898 – Capacity doubles.

1903 – An explosion causes substantial damage.

1963 – Expansion from four to six stills.

1980 – Expansion from six to eight stills.

1989 – Expansion from eight to ten stills.

1999 – Edrington and William Grant & Sons buy Highland Distillers.

2002 – Four single cask malts from 1966 and 1967 are launched.

2005 – A 30 year old is launched together with Select Reserve and Vintage 1985.

2006 – 1994 and 1975 Vintage are launched.

2007 – A 25 year old is released as a duty free item.

2008 – 1978 Vintage and Robur Reserve are launched.

2009 – The Glenrothes John Ramsay, two vintages (1988 and 1998), Alba Reserve and Three Decades are released.

2010 – Berry Brothers takes over the brand while Edrington remains owner of the distillery.

2011 – Editor's Casks are released.

Glenrothes Select Reserve

GS – The nose offers ripe fruits, spice and toffee, with a whiff of Golden Syrup. Faint wood polish in the mouth, vanilla, spicy and slightly citric. Creamy and complex. Slightly nutty, with some orange, in the drying finish.

DR – On the nose, oranges dominating a fruit bowl of flavours that includes berries among the citrus. The palate is wonderfully rounded and complete, a masterclass in fruit, wood and spice balance, and the finish is a total joy, perfectly weighted and balanced.

It came as no surprise when Edrington announced that from April 2012, Glenrothes would be working a 7 day week with 50 mashes resulting in 5,2 million litres of alcohol – double the amount compared to 2011. The reason is that Edrington last year sold Tamdhu to Ian Macleod and now have to make up for that loss in volume. The sales of the company's two big blended brands, Famous Grouse and Cutty Sark, are increasing steadily and therefore there is also the need for malt whisky. The situation regarding the ownership at Glenrothes is rather special. The distillery is owned and operated by Edrington but the single malt brand itself is in the hands of Berry Bros & Rudd (BBR). The distillery is equipped with a stainless steel full lauter mash tun from the 1970s – probably one of the first in the business. Ten washbacks made of Oregon pine are in one room, whilst an adjacent modern tun room houses eight new stainless steel washbacks. The wash from the different types of washbacks are always mixed before distillation. With the new 7 day week, all fermentations are 58 hours. The magnificent, cathedral-like still house has five pairs of stills performing a very slow distillation.

The core expression of Glenrothes is the *Select Reserve* without age statement, while it is the vintages that have brought fame to Glenrothes. The most recent vintages are *1988, 1995* and *1998*. In 2009, *Alba Reserve*, matured solely in American Oak refill bourbon casks, was added to the core range. The duty free range include *Robur Reserve, Three Decades* (with whiskies from the seventies, eighties and nineties), a *25 year old* and *Vintage 1991*. In 2010 a limited edition was released, *The Glenrothes John Ramsay*, the last vatting from the now retired Master Blender, John Ramsay. On rare occasions, Glenrothes will release single casks. One such occasion was the launch of the two *Editor's Casks* (selected by four whisky editors) in late 2011, one from 1979 and one from 1996.

1995 Vintage

Glen Scotia

Owner: **Region/district:**
Loch Lomond Distillery Co   Campbeltown

Founded: **Status:**   **Capacity:**
1832   Active   750 000 litres

Address: High Street, Campbeltown, Argyll PA28 6DS

Tel: **website:**
01586 552288   www.glenscotia-distillery.co.uk

History:
1832 – The family Galbraith founds Scotia Distillery (the year 1835 is mentioned by the distillery itself on labels).

1895 – The distillery is sold to Stewart Galbraith.

1919 – Sold to West Highland Malt Distillers.

1924 – West Highland Malt Distillers goes bankrupt and one of its directors, Duncan MacCallum, buys the distillery.

1928 – The distillery closes.

1930 – Duncan MacCallum commits suicide and the Bloch brothers take over.

1933 – Production restarts.

1954 – Hiram Walker takes over.

1955 – A. Gillies & Co. becomes new owner.

1970 – A. Gillies & Co. becomes part of Amalgated Distillers Products.

1979–82 – Reconstruction takes place.

1984 – The distillery closes.

1989 – Amalgated Distillers Products is taken over by Gibson International and production restarts.

1994 – Glen Catrine Bonded Warehouse Ltd takes over and the distillery is mothballed.

1999 – Production restarts 5th May through J. A. Mitchell & Co., owner of Springbank.

2000 – Loch Lomond Distillers runs operations with its own staff from May onwards.

2005 – A 12 year old is released.

2006 – A peated version is released.

2012 – A new range (10, 12, 16, 18 and 21 year old) is launched.

Glen Scotia 12 year old

GS – Initially floral on the nose, then gummy, with spice, citrus fruit and a faintly phenolic note. Quite full-bodied, peaty and nutty on the palate. Lengthy in the mildly herbal finish, with a whiff of smoke.

DR – The nose is of rich fudge and butter, the palate sliced apricot, walnut and fudge, with a medium finish touched with sweet spice.

Photo: © 2005 www.whisky.de

For the past four decades, Glen Scotia has had a history of intermittent production and it has been hard for the owners to come up with relevant stock to create a wide range of bottlings. This autumn however, they have announced that five new expressions will be released – 10, 12, 16, 18 and 21 year old. That is pleasant news from a distillery that has become used to living in the shadow of its Campbeltown cousin, Springbank.

Recently, Glen Scotia was having its biggest upgrade since the 1970s. All six washbacks made of Corten steel were replaced by stainless steel ones, an effluent system to take care of spent lees and pot ale was installed and there are also plans to start using the second warehouse which has been redundant for years! The addition of a newly constructed website clearly shows that the owners have started noticing "the little brother".

Glen Scotia lies hidden away between modern high-rise buildings and it is only the sign at the gate that reveals malt whisky production. The equipment consists of a traditional cast iron mash tun, six new washbacks made of stainless steel and one pair of stills. Fermentation time is usually 48 hours but can be as long as up to five days. During 2012, there will be three mashes per week which will give 130,000 litres of alcohol in the year. Lightly to medium peated barley has been used for two periods per year since 1999. In 2012 the peated production was 23,000 litres.

The core range consists of a *12 year old* but, as mentioned above, there are now plans to introduce another four bottlings. Peated expressions (*6 and 7 year old*) were released in 2006 and 2007 in the owner´s Distillery Select range and some single casks of the unpeated version have also been bottled. Older expressions include a *17 year old* and the occasional *vintage*.

12 years old

Glen Spey

Owner:
Diageo

Region/district:
Speyside

Founded: 1878
Status: Active
Capacity: 1 400 000 litres

Address: Rothes, Morayshire AB38 7AU

Tel: 01340 831215
website: www.malts.com

History:
1878 – James Stuart & Co. founds the distillery which becomes known by the name Mill of Rothes.

1886 – James Stuart buys Macallan.

1887 – W. & A. Gilbey buys the distillery for £11,000 thus becoming the first English company to buy a Scottish malt distillery.

1920 – A fire breaks out.

1962 – W. & A. Gilbey combines forces with United Wine Traders and forms International Distillers & Vintners (IDV).

1970 – The stills are increased from two to four.

1972 – IDV is bought by Watney Mann who is then acquired by Grand Metropolitan.

1997 – Guiness and Grand Metropolitan merge to form Diageo.

2001 – A 12 year old is launched in the Flora & Fauna series.

2010 – A 21 year old is released as part of the Special Releases and a 1996 Manager's Choice single cask is launched.

Glen Spey 12 year old

GS – Tropical fruits and malt on the comparatively delicate nose. Medium-bodied with fresh fruits and vanilla toffee on the palate, becoming steadily nuttier and drier in a gently oaky, mildly smoky finish.

DR – Delicate and floral on the nose, a complex mix of flavours on the palate with orange, citrus fruits, honey, vanilla and cinnamon in the mix.

For more than a century, W & A Gilbey was one of the most influential wine & spirits companies in the world. Today the name is surprisingly unknown except for the gin which still carries the company's name. The two Gilbey brothers (later joined by a third) started as wine merchants in the mid 1800s and soon became involved in all aspects of the alcohol business. They bought three distilleries in Scotland (Glen Spey was first, then came Strathmill and Knockando). They also founded a distillery in Canada which made Black Velvet whisky and Smirnoff vodka, they took over a chateau in Bordeaux and they launched Spey Royal which still is one of Thailand's best-selling blended whiskies. When the company peaked it had 22 distilleries in 18 countries By 1962, the independence of the company was over when they merged with another company and a decade later it was absorbed by Grand Metropolitan and then Diageo.

Glen Spey distillery, hidden away in a side street in Rothes, is equipped with a semi-lauter mash tun, eight stainless steel washbacks and two pairs of stills where the spirit stills are equipped with purifiers to obtain a lighter character of the spirit. The distillery is producing on a 5-day week basis and this means that they practise short fermentations (just 46 hours) during the weekdays and long fermentations (100 hours) over the weekend. To even out the differences in the character, the two versions are always mixed before distillation. For 2012 a production of 1,4 million litres is planned (18 mashes per week).

The Glen Spey malt is, above all, an important ingredient in different blends, not least in Spey Royal. The core expression is the *12 year old Flora & Fauna* bottling. In 2010, two limited releases were made – a *single cask* from new American Oak, distilled in *1996*, was released as a part of the Manager's Choice series and as part of the yearly Special Releases, a *21 year old* with a maturation in ex-sherry American oak was launched.

12 years old

A Quick Guide to Whisky Math

We all know that it takes barley, water and yeast to make a Scotch single malt whisky but have you sometimes wondered just how much is needed? What volumes are we talking about during the whole process? Let's look at a typical mid-sized distillery and see where the calculations will take us.

At this particular distillery, 5 tonnes of malted barley is required every time the mash-tun is filled. Let's use that figure as a starting point to see how many bottles of 12 year old single malt we eventually will end up with.

Now, the first step in the process actually takes place outside the distillery. This is the malting of the barley during which the barley is modified so that it is possible to extract the sugar which later on will be turned into alcohol.

The barley is steeped in water to increase the moisture content of the grain from 14% to the desired 45%. It is also important to know that, due to losses during the process, it takes around 6,6 tonnes of barley to get the 5 tonnes of malted barley that is needed for the mash tun.

For every tonne of barley it takes 4 m³ of water which in this case means 6.6 x 4,000 litres, a total of 26,400 litres.

We have now reached the distillery where the mash tun is charged with 5 tonnes of malted

barley, together with 25,500 litres of water in order to extract the sugar from the barley. The result after a few hours is 22,600 litres of worts and, of course, 5 tonnes of draff. The latter is used for cattle feed while the worts goes into a washback to be fermented, i. e. when the sugars are transformed into alcohol.

During fermentation there is no loss of volume so, in this case, the 22,600 litres give two charges of the wash still (11,300 litres per charge) for the first distillation. After the wash still has been run twice, we end up with a total of 8,000 litres of spirit, or as it is called low wines, with an alcohol strength of around 25%. We also get 14,600 litres of pot ale which again is used to feed the cattle.

What we have now, is 8,000 litres of low wines which is mixed with 4,000 litres of foreshots and feints, the first and the last part of the previous distillation in the spirit still. The 12,000 litres go into the spirit still for the second distillation.

During that distillation you only collect the middle cut for maturation which at this distillery will be 2,800 litres. We also get 4,000 litres of foreshots and feints which will be used for the next distillation plus 5,200 litres of spent lees. The latter part contains no alcohol and forms the residue in the spirit still after the distillation.

The 2,800 litres of spirit has a strength of 68.8%. We add

235 litres of water which gives us 3,035 litres of spirit at the ideal filling strength of 63.5% which will fill either 15 American barrels, 12 hogsheads or 6 sherry butts.

It is now time to put the casks into the warehouse and wait for 12 years before we bottle it. But things are happening during this time as well. Evaporation, or Angel's Share, will create losses of approximately 2% in both volume of water and alcohol of the previous year's content. After 12 years we have 2,340 litres left with a strength of around 55%.

Before we bottle it, we reduce the strength to 40% by adding 880 litres of water and finally we end up with 4,600 70cl bottles of 12 year old whisky, ready to be sold.

All in all, it took 11 litres of water and 1.4 kilos of barley to produce one bottle of whisky, not to mention the 640,000 litres of water that it took to condense the spirit during distillation. But then again, water tends to be "borrowed" and returned to the source after use.

The figures above will serve as an example of how the process works in general. There can be substantial variations between distilleries depending on the alcohol yield from the barley that is used, the distilling regime but also the evaporation during maturation. Under some conditions, the alcohol strength can in fact be higher after 12 years.

Glentauchers

Owner:
Chivas Brothers
(Pernod Ricard)

Region/district:
Speyside

Founded: **Status:**
1897   Active

Capacity:
4 200 000 litres

Address: Mulben, Keith,
Banffshire AB55 6YL

Tel:
01542 860272

website:
-

History:
1897 – James Buchanan and W. P. Lowrie, a whisky merchant from Glasgow, found the distillery.

1898 – Production starts.

1906 – James Buchanan & Co. takes over the whole distillery and acquires an 80% share in W. P. Lowrie & Co.

1915 – James Buchanan & Co. merges with Dewars.

1923-25 – Mashing house and maltings are rebuilt.

1925 – Buchanan-Dewars joins Distillers Company Limited (DCL).

1930 – Glentauchers is transferred to Scottish Malt Distillers (SMD).

1965 – The number of stills is increased from two to six.

1969 – Floor maltings is decommissioned.

1985 – DCL mothballs the distillery.

1989 – United Distillers (formerly DCL) sells the distillery to Caledonian Malt Whisky Distillers, a subsidiary of Allied Distillers.

1992 – Production recommences in August.

2000 – A 15 year old Glentauchers is released.

2005 – Chivas Brothers (Pernod Ricard) become the new owner through the acquisition of Allied Domecq.

Glentauchers 1991 Gordon & MacPhail

GS – Fresh and floral aromas, with sweet fruits and peppery peaches. Medium to full-bodied in the mouth, with cereal and sweet spice. The finish is medium to long.

DR – Deep plum and sherry on the nose, then cocoa and blackcurrant. The palate is soft, with plum, raisin and green banana, and the finish is banana and date cake.

Glentauchers is a distillery where almost everything is done mechanically without the aid of computers. The owners have kept it that way quite intentionally so that new employees can come and learn basic techniques. This is about traditional whisky production, with valves and wheels to be found everywhere.

From the first day until the present, Glentauchers' role has been to produce malt whisky for blends. Founded by whisky baron, James Buchanan, Black & White was obviously the first to rely on Glentauchers for its character. As the owners changed over the years it became signature malt for Teacher's and today it is an integral part of Ballantine's. The distillery is equipped with a 12 tonnes stainless steel full lauter mash tun installed in 2007 with the copper dome from the old mash tun fitted on top. There are six washbacks made of Oregon pine with a fermentation time of 52 hours and tree pairs of stills with sub-coolers fitted in 2007. Since 2006 the distillation is what you would call balanced, i. e. one wash still and one spirit still work together and they have their own designated low wines and feints receiver. The production recently increased from six to seven days, which means 18 mashes per week and a total of 4.2 million litres in a year.

Glentauchers distillery lies on the A95 just a few miles west of Keith and if you continue on that road you reach Mulben where Chivas Brothers has a huge site with bonded warehouses called Malcolmburn. There are 56 in total with 1.25 million casks (20% of the company's total stock in Scotland). Twenty of the warehouses were destroyed under the weight of heavy snow in 2010 and have since been rebuilt.

An official 15 year old was released by Allied Domecq some years ago but the current owners have not yet released any bottlings of Glentauchers.

*Gordon & MacPhail
Glentauchers 1990*

Glenturret

Owner:
The Edrington Group

Region/district:
Eastern Highlands

Founded:
1775

Status:
Active (vc)

Capacity:
340 000 litres

Address: The Hosh, Crieff, Perthshire PH7 4HA

Tel:
01764 656565

website:
www.thefamousgrouse.com

History:
1775 – Whisky smugglers establish a small illicit farm distillery named Hosh Distillery.

1818 – John Drummond is licensee until 1837.

1826 – A distillery in the vicinity is named Glenturret, but is decommissioned before 1852.

1852 – John McCallum is licensee until 1874.

1875 – Hosh Distillery takes over the name Glenturret Distillery and is managed by Thomas Stewart.

1903 – Mitchell Bros Ltd takes over.

1921 – Production ceases and the buildings are used for whisky storage only.

1929 – Mitchell Bros Ltd is liquidated, the distillery dismantled and the facilities are used as storage for agricultural needs.

1957 – James Fairlie buys the distillery and re-equips it.

1959 – Production restarts.

1981 – Remy-Cointreau buys the distillery and invests in a visitor centre.

1990 – Highland Distillers takes over.

1999 – Edrington and William Grant & Sons buy Highland Distillers for £601 million. The purchasing company, 1887 Company, is a joint venture between Edrington (70%) and William Grant (30%).

2002 – The Famous Grouse Experience, a visitor centre costing £2.5 million, is inaugurated.

2003 – A 10 year old Glenturret replaces the 12 year old as the distillery's standard release.

2007 – Three new single casks are released.

Glenturret 10 year old

GS – Nutty and slightly oily on the nose, with barley and citrus fruits. Sweet and honeyed on the full, fruity palate, with a balancing note of oak. Medium length in the sweet finish.

DR – Full and rich honeyed nose, oily and fruity palate with some appealing rootsy savouriness. Something of the farmyard about it. Charming finish.

Glenturret is the spiritual home of Famous Grouse blended Scotch and the excellent Famous Grouse Experience visitor centre celebrates its tenth birthday in 2012, by way of a special Celebration Tour. The range of Famous Grouse has been expanded this year with The Black Grouse Alpha, a peatier version of the Black Grouse and containing some older whiskies. To start off with, it will be reserved for the duty free market. To celebrate the Queen's Diamond Jubilee, a special Famous Jubilee bottling (exclusive to Waitrose) has been created by master blender, Gordon Motion. The range consists of, as before, The Famous Grouse, Black Grouse, Snow Grouse and Naked Grouse. The once so popular Famous Grouse blended malt has now been abandoned in all markets except for Taiwan.

With so much emphasis on Famous Grouse, it is sometimes easy to overlook the Glenturret distillery itself. It is one of the oldest working distilleries in Scotland and a very traditional one at that. The one tonne mash tun is a traditional, open tun with rakes, made of stainless steel but dressed in wood. There are eight Douglas fir washbacks with a minimum fermentation time of 48 hours (but sometimes longer) and finally one pair of stills.

During 2012, there will be 8-10 mashes per week which will give 160,000 litres in the year (circa 50% of the capacity). The main part, 150,000 litres, will be the heavily peated (80ppm in the barley) Ruadh Maor which is used for blended whisky. The remaining 10,000 litres are put aside for Glenturret single malt.

There is only one official bottling in the core range, the *10 year old*. A limited edition of three single casks was released in 2007 and there are plans to do more single cask bottlings in the near future, but nothing has yet been decided.

10 years old

Highland Park

Owner:
The Edrington Group

Region/district:
Highlands (Orkney)

Founded: 1798
Status: Active (vc)
Capacity: 2 500 000 litres

Address: Holm Road, Kirkwall, Orkney KW15 1SU

Tel: 01856 874619
website: www.highlandpark.co.uk

History:
1798 – David Robertson founds the distillery. The local smuggler and businessman Magnus Eunson previously operated an illicit whisky production on the site.

1816 – John Robertson, an Excise Officer who arrested Magnus Eunson, takes over production.

1826 – Highland Park obtains a license and the distillery is taken over by Robert Borwick.

1840 – Robert´s son George Borwick takes over but the distillery deteriorates.

1869 – The younger brother James Borwick inherits Highland Park and attempts to sell it as he does not consider the distillation of spirits as compatible with his priesthood.

1876 – Stuart & Mackay becomes involved and improves the business by exporting to Norway and India.

1895 – James Grant (of Glenlivet Distillery) buys Highland Park.

1898 – James Grant expands capacity from two to four stills.

1937 – Highland Distilleries buys Highland Park.

1979 – Highland Distilleries invests considerably in marketing Highland Park as single malt which increases sales markedly.

Highland Park single malt is one of the most respected Scotch whiskies which is why it seems odd that sales have been more or less consistent around 1,3 million bottles over the last couple of years. The reason is a shortage of stock aged 10-15 years which, in turn, is because of the production being somewhat irregular towards the end of the 1990s. Highland Park 3-12 years old is also needed for the owner´s Famous Grouse blend. Stocks are filling up though and soon we will most likely see sales figures increasing.

To say that Highland Park is peated is correct but rather simplistic. First of all, only part of the malted barley is peated (the 20% which they are malting themselves). Secondly, it has a phenol content of 20-40 ppm (lower than most Islay malts). Finally, because of the lack of trees in Orkney, the peat gives it a distinctly different flavour compared to Islay. The distillery equipment consists of one semi-lauter mash tun, twelve Oregon pine washbacks and two pairs of stills. The mash tun has a 12 tonnes capacity but is only filled at 50%. The reason for that is the washback configuration and also the throughput in the spirit stills. For single malts, ex-sherry casks are used (20% first fill and 80% refill) and the whisky matures in 19 dunnage and four racked warehouses. The plan for 2012 is to produce 2 million litres.

The core range of Highland Park consists of *12, 15, 18, 25, 30, 40* and *50 years old*. Added to the range in 2012, albeit in limited numbers, is the *21 year old*. This was originally released for duty free in 2007 and quickly became very popular. Due to stock shortages, the alcohol strength was then lowered from 47,5% to 40% and eventually it disappeared. Now it is back at its old strength and is still matured mainly in American oak sherry casks. Travel retail exclusives include four different vintages – *1973, 1978* (launched in 2011), *1991* (replacing the 1990) and *2001* (replacing the 1998). Added to the range in 2011, was *Leif Eriksson* which has matured in American oak ex-sherry casks and *Drakkar*, another sherry maturation but using Spanish oak. Both are bottled at 40%. A trilogy of limited releases which started in 2009 was ended in 2011 with the *18 year old Earl Haakon*. They were all bottled at cask strength and the names celebrate the Viking heritage of Orkney. Highlighting the Vikings is also a new range called Valhalla Collection. The first bottling was *Thor*, a 16 year old bottled at cask strength and in the years to follow we can expect to see *Odin, Freya* and *Loki*. Another limited range, *Orcadian Vintages*, started in 2008 with *1968*, followed by *1964* and *1970* and, in autumn 2011, *1971* and *1976*.

History (continued):

1986 – A visitor centre, considered one of Scotland's finest, is opened.

1997 – Two new Highland Park are launched, an 18 year old and a 25 year old.

1999 – Highland Distillers are acquired by Edrington Group and William Grant & Sons.

2000 – Visit Scotland awards Highland Park "Five Star Visitor Attraction".

2005 – Highland Park 30 years old is released. A 16 year old for the Duty Free market and Ambassador´s Cask 1984 are released.

2006 – The second edition of Ambassador´s Cask, a 10 year old from 1996, is released. New packaging is introduced.

2007 – The Rebus 20, a 21 year old duty free exclusive, a 38 year old and a 39 year old are released.

2008 – A 40 year old and the third and fourth editions of Ambassador´s Cask are released.

2009 – Two vintages and Earl Magnus 15 year are released.

2010 – A 50 year old, Saint Magnus 12 year old, Orcadian Vintage 1970 and four duty free vintages are released.

2011 – Vintage 1978, Leif Eriksson and 18 year old Earl Haakon are released.

2012 – Thor and a 21 year old are released.

Vintage 1991   *Thor*   *Vintage 2001*

Highland Park 12 year old

GS – The nose is fragrant and floral, with hints of heather and some spice. Smooth and honeyed on the palate, with citric fruits, malt and distinctive tones of wood smoke in the warm, lengthy, slightly peaty finish.

DR – Honey, peat and marmalade fruit in balance on the nose, then on the palate a big mouth feel with dark chocolate, chilli, sharp barley and honey, concluding with a monster pot pouri of a finish.

18 years old

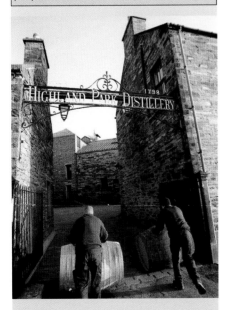

12 years old   *21 years old*

Inchgower

Owner:
Diageo

Region/district:
Speyside

Founded: 1871

Status: Active

Capacity: 2 900 000 litres

Address: Buckie, Banffshire AB56 5AB

Tel: 01542 836700

website: www.malts.com

History:

1871 – Alexander Wilson & Co. founds the distillery. Equipment from the disused Tochineal Distillery, also owned by Alexander Wilson, is installed.

1936 – Alexander Wilson & Co. becomes bankrupt and Buckie Town Council buys the distillery and the family's home for £1,600.

1938 – The distillery is sold on to Arthur Bell & Sons for £3,000.

1966 – Capacity doubles to four stills.

1985 – Guinness acquires Arthur Bell & Sons.

1987 – United Distillers is formed by a merger between Arthur Bell & Sons and DCL.

1997 – Inchgower 1974 (22 years) is released as a Rare Malt.

2004 – Inchgower 1976 (27 years) is released as a Rare Malt.

2010 – A single cask from 1993 is released.

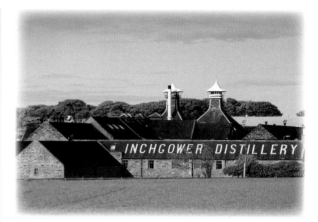

In 2012, Inchgower distillery was closed for 16 weeks because of an extensive upgrade. It was not a matter of installing more stills in order to increase the production. Instead, it was a wide range of unflattering improvements which show just how many steps there are in producing whisky – new features include: the grist handling facility, a hot liquor tank, a spirit receiver, a fully automated control system, a clean-in-place system as well as a mashing machine (the screw where the grist is mixed with the mashing water).

Inchgower belongs to a small group of three coastal distilleries (the other two being Macduff and Glenglassaugh), all situated on the south side of Moray Firth. Both Glenglassaugh and Inchgower were built during the first few years of the 1870s when few other distilleries were founded, but since then their fates go separate ways, Glenglassaugh was closed during long periods of time (often 20 years at a time). In the meanwhile Inchgower has produced steadily, with the exception of WWII. It is difficult to miss Inchgower as it is situated just at the A98 near the small fishing port of Buckie. If one is driving from Elgin towards Banff it is even easier to spot as the name appears on the roof.

The distillery is equipped with a stainless steel semi-lauter mash tun, six washbacks made from Oregon pine (two of them were replaced in 2011 and the other four during 2012) with a fermentation time of 46-54 hours and two pairs of stills. Most of the production is matured elsewhere, but there are also five dunnage and four racked warehouses on site with room for 60,000 casks. Due to the upgrade the distillery will only produce 1,5 million litres of alcohol during 2012.

By far, the greater part of production is being used for Bell's blended whisky. Besides the official *Flora & Fauna 14 years old* there have been a few limited releases. In 2010 a *single sherry cask* distilled in *1993* appeared in the Manager's Choice series.

Inchgower 14 year old

GS – Ripe pears and a hint of brine on the light nose. Grassy and gingery in the mouth, with some acidity. The finish is spicy, dry and relatively short.

DR – Rootsy, fresh cut grass and hay nose, light grassy and hay-like palate, and incredibly delicate barley-like nose, with a very delicate dusting of spice.

*Flora & Fauna
14 years old*

Jura

Owner: **Region/district:**
Whyte & Mackay   Highlands (Jura)
(United Spirits)

Founded: **Status:**   **Capacity:**
1810   Active (vc)   2 200 000 litres

Address: Craighouse, Isle of Jura PA60 7XT

Tel: **website:**
01496 820240   www.isleofjura.com

History:
1810 – Archibald Campbell founds a distillery named Small Isles Distillery.

1853 – Richard Campbell leases the distillery to Norman Buchanan from Glasgow.

1867 – Buchanan files for bankruptcy and J. & K. Orr takes over the distillery.

1876 – The licence is transferred to James Ferguson & Sons.

1901 – The distillery closes and Ferguson dismantles the distillery.

1960 – Charles Mackinlay & Co. embarks on reconstruction and extension of the distillery. Newly formed Scottish & Newcastle Breweries acquires Charles Mackinlay & Co.

1962 – Scottish & Newcastle forms Mackinlay-McPherson for the operation of Isle of Jura.

1963 – The first distilling takes place.

1978 – Stills are doubled from two to four.

1985 – Invergordon Distilleries acquires Charles Mackinlay & Co., Isle of Jura and Glenallachie from Scottish & Newcastle Breweries.

1993 – Whyte & Mackay (Fortune Brands) buys Invergordon Distillers.

1996 – Whyte & Mackay changes name to JBB (Greater Europe).

2001 – The management of JBB (Greater Europe) buys out the company from the owners Fortune Brands and changes the name to Kyndal.

2002 – Isle of Jura Superstition is launched.

2003 – Kyndal reverts back to its old name, Whyte & Mackay. Isle of Jura 1984 is launched.

2004 – Two cask strengths (15 and 30 years old) are released in limited numbers.

2006 – The 40 year old Jura is released.

2007 – United Spirits buys Whyte & Mackay. The 18 year old Delmé-Evans and an 8 year old heavily peated expression are released.

2008 – A series of four different vintages, called Elements, is released.

2009 – The peated Prophecy and three new vintages called Paps of Jura are released.

2010 – Boutique Barrels and a 21 year old Anniversary bottling are released.

2012 – The 12 year old Jura Elixir is released.

Jura 10 year old

GS – Resin, oil and pine notes on the delicate nose. Light-bodied in the mouth, with malt and drying saltiness. The finish is malty, nutty, with more salt, plus just a wisp of smoke.

DR – The nose is sweet condensed milk, the palate an intriguing mix of earthy malt and tangy spice, with a medium sweet and spice finish.

Jura is one of the more difficult distilleries to reach. You have to go by boat to Islay and then take the small ferry across he Sound of Islay to Jura. The production is also relatively small (just over 2 million litres) but none of this seems to stop the brand´s explosive increase in sales. In 2010 it was up by 50% and in 2011 by a further 37%. With a total sales of 1,6 million bottles, Jura is now on the verge of entering into the Top 10. Nearly all of the increase in 2011 went to the UK market where Jura is now the third best selling single malt after Glenfiddich and Glenmorangie.

Jura distillery is equipped with one semi-lauter mash tun, six stainless steel washbacks and two pairs of stills. Until April 2011 they were working a 5 day week with a fermentation time of 60 hours. They have since then increased to a 7 day production and the fermentation time has changed to 54 hours. At the moment they are doing 28 mashes per week producing 2,2 million litres of alcohol in the year. Almost 50% of that is destined to become single malt and is matured in the five racked warehouses on site with the oldest cask being from 1973. Since the restart of the distillery in 1963, Jura single malt has been unpeated, but in 2002 the first expression containing peated whisky was introduced and today they produce peated spirit (55ppm) for eight weeks of the year. The distillery visitor centre was upgraded in 2011 and, in spite of the remote location, almost 10,000 visitors come here annually.

The core range consists of *Origin* (10 years), *Diurach´s Own* (16 years), *Superstition* (13% peated Jura and various casks from 13 to 21 years of age), as well as the peated *Prophecy* which was released in 2009. *Jura Elixir*, a 12 year old matured in both American and European oak, was released in 2012 as an exclusive for Sainsbury´s. Recent limited releases include *1976 Feith A´Chaorainn* and a *1995 Grand Cru Classé*, the latter being a part of the Boutique Barrels range.

10 years old

Kilbeggan

Owner:
Beam Inc.

Region/district:
Ireland

Founded: **Status:** **Capacity:**
1757   Active (vc)   80 000 litres

Address: Kilbeggan, Co. Westmeath

Tel:
+353 (0)57 933 2183

website: www.kilbegganwhiskey.com

History:
1757 – The distillery is founded by the McManus family.

1794 – The Codd family takes over and capacity is doubled.

1843 – John Locke & Sons buy the distillery.

1954 – Production stops.

1957 – The distillery is officially closed.

1988 – Cooley Distillery plc buys the brand Kilbeggan as well as the old distillery to use it for warehousing.

2007 – The first distillation in the refurbished distillery takes place on 19 March.

2010 – The first single malt since the resurrection is released.

2011 – Kilbeggan 18 year old, a blended whiskey, is released.

2012 – Beam buys Cooley distillery and Kilbeggan. The second edition of Kilbeggan Distillery Reserve is released.

Kilbeggan distillery has now been producing for five years since its sensational re-birth in 2007. It was the owners of Cooley distillery with John Teeling at the forefront, who decided to bring the distillery back to life and it is now the oldest producing whiskey distillery in the world.

The distillery, which lies in the town Kilbeggan on the N6 and just an hour's drive west of Dublin, was bought by John Teeling and his Cooley Distillery way back in 1988. Eventually, the new owner decided to reinstate the distillery to its former glory and to start distilling again. Meanwhile, a blended Kilbeggan whiskey, a brand taken over simultaneously with the distillery, was selling with great success.

In December 2011, Cooley Distillery was taken over by Beam Inc. and they are now also the owners of Kilbeggan. It is no secret that Beam´s biggest interest lies in the Kilbeggan blended whiskey brand which is very popular in the USA. Since most of the production for the Kilbeggan blend is confined to Cooley distillery in Riverstown, it remains to be seen what will now happen to Kilbeggan distillery. Some fears have been expressed that it will be used as a visitor centre and spiritual home of the brand with very little production going on.

At the moment, the distillery is equipped with a wooden mash tun, four Oregon pine washbacks and two stills with one of them being 180 years old. The production at the distillery spans over a wide range of techniques and whiskey varieties including malt whiskey, pure pot still whiskey (malted and unmalted barley mixed), rye whiskey from pot stills and triple distillation.

The first single malt whiskey release (a *3 year old* bottled at 40%) from the new production came in June 2010 and a second batch, *5 years old*, was released in 2012. The blended range of *Kilbeggan* includes a *no age statement*, a *15 year old* and, since early 2011, an *18 year old*. There has also been a release of Poitín (unaged spirit) under the name of Cooley but distilled at Kilbeggan.

*Kilbeggan
Distillery Reserve*

Kilbeggan Distillery Reserve
GS – Highly individualistic on the nose. Oily and herbal, with tarragon, warm leather, paper gum, and even violets. The palate is quite delicate, yet far from fragile, with gentle leather and developing fruity spices. Drying in a medium-length finish.

Kilchoman

Owner:
Kilchoman Distillery Co.

Region/district:
Islay

Founded: 2005
Status: Active (vc)
Capacity: 120 000 litres

Address: Rockside farm, Bruichladdich, Islay PA49 7UT

Tel: 01496 850011
website: www.kilchomandistillery.com

History:
2002 – Plans are formed for a new distillery at Rockside Farm on western Islay.

2005 – Production starts in June.

2006 – A fire breaks out in the kiln causing a few weeks' production stop but malting has to cease for the rest of the year.

2007 – The distillery is expanded with two new washbacks.

2009 – The first single malt, a 3 year old, is released on 9th September followed by a second release.

2010 – Three new releases and an introduction to the US market. John Maclellan from Bunnahabhain joins the team as General Manager.

2011 – Kilchoman 100% Islay is released as well as a 4 year old and a 5 year old.

2012 – Machir Bay, the first core expression, is released together with Kilchoman Sherry Cask Release and the second edition of 100% Islay.

Kilchoman Machir Bay

GS – A nose of sweet peat and vanilla, undercut by brine, kelp and black pepper. Filled ashtrays in time. A smooth mouthfeel, with lots of nicely-balanced citrus fruit, peat smoke and Germolene on the palate. The finish is relatively long and sweet, with building spice, chili and a final nuttiness.

DR – Down by the seaside after a storm, with salt and fresh seaweed in the breeze, chimney smoke drifting. On the palate the distillery hits its stride, with sweet honey and lemon, peat smoke and coastal saltiness all in evidence. Nice balance between sugar and spice. A savoury, earthy, medium long and balanced finish.

Even though Kilchoman is, by far, the youngest distillery on Islay, it seems as if it has been around for more than just seven years. The man behind it, Anthony Wills, together with his team, has managed to come a long way in such a short time with an exciting range of whiskies, a visitor centre attracting 10,000 visitors every year and, not least, having established a foothold on the important US market. In 2011, a total of 55,000 bottles were sold with Ukraine, Russia and South Korea as some of the new markets. Kilchoman has its own floor maltings with a third of the barley requirements coming from fields surrounding the distillery. The malt is peated to 20 to 25 ppm and the remaining malt (50 ppm) is bought from Port Ellen. Other equipment includes a stainless steel semi-lauter mash tun, four stainless steel washbacks and one pair of stills. The distillery is currently running at full capacity which translates to 120,000 litres of alcohol. The spirit is filled into fresh and refill bourbon casks (80%) and fresh sherry butts (20%). The *Inaugural Release*, bourbon-matured for 3 years with a six months Oloroso finish, was launched in September 2009. This was followed up by a number of expressions including *Summer 2010*, the first all-bourbon expression and the first to be sold in the US and *Spring 2011*, the first where both 3 and 4 year old whiskies were vatted. In June 2011 it was time for the first *Kilchoman 100% Islay* where all the barley used, came from its own farm and had been malted at the distillery. This was followed up in September by a *4 year old* from sherry casks and a *5 year old* (2006 Vintage) in November. The first general release in larger quantities from the distillery was *Machir Bay*, which was released in spring 2012. It is a vatting of whiskies from 3 to 5 years old, matured in fresh bourbon barrels and finished in Oloroso sherry butts. More releases during 2012 included *Kilchoman Sherry Cask Release* and the *second edition* of *Kilchoman 100% Islay*.

Machir Bay

Kininvie

Owner:
William Grant & Sons

Region/district:
Speyside

Founded: **Status:**
1990 Active

Capacity:
4 800 000 litres

Address: Dufftown, Keith,
Banffshire AB55 4DH

Tel:
01340 820373

website:
-

History:
1990 – Kininvie distillery is inaugurated on 26th June and the first distillation takes place 18th July.

2001 – A bottling of blended whisky containing Kininvie malt is released under the name Hazelwood Centennial Reserve 20 years old.

2006 – The first expression of a Kininvie single malt is released as a 15 year old under the name Hazelwood.

2008 – In February a 17 year old Hazelwood Reserve is launched at Heathrow's Terminal 5.

When Kininvie was inaugurated in 1990, it was opened by Janet Sheed Roberts, the last surviving granddaughter of William Grant who founded Glenfiddich distillery. Mrs Roberts celebrated her 110th birthday in August 2011 as the oldest woman in Scotland and passed away in April 2012. Kininvie distillery only consists of one still house constructed in white, corrugated metal tucked away behind Balvenie. The owners, William Grant & Sons, built it as a working distillery producing malt whisky for the increasingly popular Grant's blended whiskies. Over the last couple of years, the importance of Kininvie has lessened due to the fact that William Grant opened up Ailsa Bay in 2007 with a capacity of producing over 6 million litres per year. As a result of this there has not been any production at Kininvie since late 2010.

The distillery is equipped with a stainless steel full lauter mash tun which is placed next to Balvenie's in the Balvenie distillery. Ten Douglas fir washbacks can be found in two separate rooms next to the Balvenie washbacks. Three wash stills and six spirit stills are all heated by steam coils.

Kininvie malt whisky is frequently sold to other companies for blending purposes under the name Aldundee. To protect it from being sold as Kininvie single malt, the whisky is always "teaspooned", i. e. a small percentage of Balvenie whisky is blended with the make.

Kininvie malt is mainly used for the Grant's blend but is also a major part of the blended malt, Monkey Shoulder. The first time that Kininvie appeared as an official single malt bottling was in 2006, when a *Hazelwood 15 year old* was launched to celebrate the 105th birthday of Janet Sheed Roberts. In 2008 it was time for a *17 year old* to celebrate her 107th birthday. This was the first to become publicly available as it was sold at Heathrow. A bottling under the name Hazelwood 110 was given to employees of Wm Grant in 2011 to celebrate Mrs. Roberts' 110th birthday, but this was a blend and not a single malt.

Hazelwood Reserve 17 year old
GS – New leather and creamy nougat on the nose. Developing molasses notes with time. Rich, leathery and spicy on the palate, with oranges and milk chocolate. Lengthy and elegant in the finish.

*Hazelwood Reserve
17 years old*

Knockando

Owner:
Diageo.

Region/district:
Speyside

Founded: **Status:**   **Capacity:**
1898   Active   1 400 000 litres

Address: Knockando, Morayshire AB38 7RT

Tel: **website:**
01340 882000   www.malts.com

History:
1898 – John Thompson founds the distillery. The architect is Charles Doig.

1899 – Production starts in May.

1900 – The distillery closes in March and J. Thompson & Co. takes over administration.

1904 – W. & A. Gilbey purchases the distillery for £3,500 and production restarts in October.

1962 – W. & A. Gilbey merges with United Wine Traders (including Justerini & Brooks) and forms International Distillers & Vintners (IDV).

1968 – Floor maltings is decommissioned.

1969 – The number of stills is increased to four.

1972 – IDV is acquired by Watney Mann who, in its turn, is taken over by Grand Metropolitan.

1978 – Justerini & Brooks launches a 12 year old Knockando.

1997 – Grand Metropolitan and Guinness merge and form Diageo; simultaneously IDV and United Distillers merge to United Distillers & Vintners.

2010 – A Manager´s Choice 1996 is released.

Knockando 12 year old

GS – Delicate and fragrant on the nose, with hints of malt, worn leather, and hay. Quite full in the mouth, smooth and honeyed, with gingery malt and a suggestion of white rum. Medium length in the finish, with cereal and more ginger.

DR – Beeswax, honey and gentle peat on the nose, the palate is altogether bolder, with pepper and earthy peat in evidence mixing it with very sweet crystallised barley and a sweet and rounded finish.

The blended Scotch J&B consists of 42 different whiskies and at the very heart of the whisky you will find Knockando single malt. J&B was introduced to the Spanish market in 1962 and today it is the market leader. Knockando single malt was established as a brand around the same time in southern Europe with Spain and, in particular, France becoming strongholds for the brand. With 650,000 bottles, Knockando today is Diageo´s 7th best selling single malt. The distillery is equipped with a semi-lauter mash tun, eight Douglas fir washbacks and two pairs of stills. Knockando´s nutty character, a result of the cloudy worts coming from the mash tun, has given it its fame. However, in order to balance the taste, the distillers also wish to create the typical Speyside floral notes by using boiling balls on the spirit stills to increase reflux.

Knockando has always worked a five-day week with 16 mashes per week, 8 short fermentations (48 hours) and 8 long (104 hours). In 2012 this will mean a production of 1,4 million litres of alcohol. The spirit is tankered away to Auchroisk and Glenlossie and some of the casks are returned to the distillery for maturation in two dunnage and two racked warehouses. There is a fifth warehouse called Ultima, named after the legendary J&B Ultima blend which was released in 1994, where whiskies from 128 distilleries (116 malts and 12 grains) were blended together. One cask from each distillery is still kept in this warehouse.

Since the 1970s, Knockando single malt has been bottled according to vintage and without any age statement, but of late, bottles on all markets show both vintage and age on the labels. The core range consists of four expressions, all of them a mix of bourbon and sherry maturation; *12 year old, 15 year old Richly Matured, 18 year old Slow Matured* and the *21 year old Master Reserve*. The 15 year old was destined for the French market but will now be available in more markets which will include Italy, Germany, Spain and Switzerland. In autumn of 2011 a *25 year old* matured in first fill European oak was released as part of the Special Releases range.

12 years old

Knockdhu

Owner:
Inver House Distillers
(Thai Beverages plc)

Region/district:
Highland

Founded: 1893
Status: Active
Capacity: 1 750 000 litres

Address: Knock, By Huntly,
Aberdeenshire AB54 7LJ

Tel: 01466 771223
website: www.ancnoc.com

History:

1893 – Distillers Company Limited (DCL) starts construction of the distillery.

1894 – Production starts in October.

1930 – Scottish Malt Distillers (SMD) takes over production.

1983 – The distillery closes in March.

1988 – Inver House buys the distillery from United Distillers.

1989 – Production restarts on 6th February.

1990 – First official bottling of Knockdhu.

1993 – First official bottling of An Cnoc.

2001 – Pacific Spirits purchases Inver House Distillers at a price of $85 million.

2003 – Reintroduction of An Cnoc 12 years.

2004 – A 14 year old from 1990 is launched.

2005 – A 30 year old from 1975 and a 14 year old from 1991 are launched.

2006 – International Beverage Holdings acquires Pacific Spirits UK.

2007 – anCnoc 1993 is released.

2008 – anCnoc 16 year old is released.

2011 – A Vintage 1996 is released.

2012 – A 35 year old is launched.

An Cnoc 12 year old

GS – A pretty, sweet, floral nose, with barley notes. Medium bodied, with a whiff of delicate smoke, spices and boiled sweets on the palate. Drier in the mouth than the nose suggests. The finish is quite short and drying.

DR – Complex and layered nose, with delicate peat, green fruits and pear. On the palate, full savoury peatiness then tingling yellow fruity follow through and fairydust finale.

Photo: Bill Bain, Bodies of Banff

To the casual visitor, the work at a distillery can appear to be rather mundane with mashing, fermentation and distillation as the main parts of the production. But behind that lies a lot of work and technical equipment that demand careful planning and review. At the big producers there are designated technical teams dealing with such matters. At the smaller distilleries however, you can come across distillery managers who are constantly trying to find new ways to save energy and increase efficiency. Gordon Bruce at Knockdhu, for example, is one of them and his efforts do not just save money because, as he himself says, being fiscally efficient and being green are closely related. One of his latest projects is digging a wetland area where he can take care of spent lees from the distillation on site, instead of sending them by truck to a bioplant.

Knockdhu distillery is equipped with a 5 tonnes stainless steel lauter mash tun, six washbacks made of Oregon pine and one pair of stills. The distillery is running at full capacity which for 2012 means 1,75 million litres of alcohol. The share of peated production makes up 35% of the total production. The phenol specification of the barley is 40-50ppm. The spirit is filled mainly into bourbon casks with an additional 15% of sherry butts. The casks are stored in one racked and three dunnage warehouses of which one had to be rebuilt (with beautiful stained-glass windows) after it collapsed during heavy snowfalls in 2010.

The biggest markets for AnCnoc are UK, USA, Sweden and Germany and 180,000 bottles were sold in 2011. The core range consists of *12* and *16 year old*. Every year a new vintage is released and for 2011 it was a *1996 vintage* which was replaced by a *1998* in 2012. Later that year it was time for a *35 year old* – the oldest expression yet to be released by the owner. During 2012, InverHouse also commissioned the illustrator, Peter Arkle, to produce a series of limited edition packaging for a new *AnCnoc without age statement* which is a vatting of fino sherry casks aged 6 to 12 years.

35 years old

Lagavulin

Owner: Diageo   **Region/district:** Islay

Founded: 1816   **Status:** Active (vc)   **Capacity:** 2 350 000 litres

Address: Port Ellen, Islay, Argyll PA42 7DZ

Tel: 01496 302749 (vc)   **website:** www.malts.com

History:
1816 – John Johnston founds the distillery.

1825 – John Johnston takes over the adjacent distillery Ardmore founded in 1817 by Archibald Campbell and closed in 1821.

1835 – Production at Ardmore ceases.

1837 – Both distilleries are merged and operated under the name Lagavulin by Donald Johnston.

1852 – The brother of the wine and spirits dealer Alexander Graham, John Crawford Graham, purchases the distillery.

1867 – The distillery is acquired by James Logan Mackie & Co. and refurbishment starts.

1878 – Peter Mackie is employed.

1889 – James Logan Mackie passes away and nephew Peter Mackie inherits the distillery.

1890 – J. L. Mackie & Co. changes name to Mackie & Co. Peter Mackie launches White Horse onto the export market with Lagavulin included in the blend. White Horse blended is not available on the domestic market until 1901.

1908 – Peter Mackie uses the old distillery buildings to build a new distillery, Malt Mill, on the site.

When peated whisky had its big consumer breakthrough in the 1990s, Lagavulin single malt was in the lead. The past decade, however, was characterized by a decrease in sales volumes and the brand has fallen from seventh to thirteenth place globally. The main reason for this was a shortage of mature whisky due to a temporary, lower production pace in the mid-eighties. However, it looks as if the brand is bouncing back now as evidenced by the increase in volume during 2011, being up by 17% to 1.3 million bottles – the best sales figure for the brand since 2000 and also the largest gain by any of the big, peated brands during 2011.

Lagavulin distillery is also famous for another distillery, Malt Mill, which was built on the same site in 1908 by Peter Mackie. He got into a feud with the neighbouring distillery Laphroaig over a distribution agreement and decided to try and replicate their whisky with the produce from Malt Mill. He never succeeded – the distillery closed in 1962 and allegedly there are only two bottles left in the world of Malt Mill single malt. An even rarer version is the world's only bottle of Malt Mill new make which, since summer 2012, is on display at Lagavulin visitor centre.

The distillery is equipped with a stainless steel full lauter mash tun, ten washbacks made of larch and two pairs of stills. The spirit stills are filled to 95% of its capacity during distillation which is very unconventional. The result is that the spirit vapour's diminished contact with the copper, produces a more robust spirit. Operations have run 24 hours a day, seven days a week, for some time now to keep up with demand. This means 28 mashes per week and 2,35 million litres of spirit. Bourbon hogsheads are used almost without exception for maturation and all of the new production is stored on the mainland. There are only around 16,000 casks on Islay, split between warehouses at Lagavulin, Port Ellen and Caol Ila.

The core range of Lagavulin consists of *12 year old cask strength*, *16 year old* and the *Distiller's Edition*, a Pedro Ximenez sherry finish. In 2010 a distillery exclusive bottling, available only at the distillery, was added to the range which basically is a slightly older, cask strength version of the Distiller's Edition. The Islay Festival special release for 2012 was a *14 year old* from a refill sherry butt, bottled at cask strength. As in recent years, a new edition of the *12 year old* was released in autumn 2012 as a Special Release together with a *21 year old* from first fill sherry casks. This was only the second time the owners had released a 21 year old Lagavulin.

History (continued):

1924 – Peter Mackie passes away and Mackie & Co. changes name to White Horse Distillers.

1927 – White Horse Distillers becomes part of Distillers Company Limited (DCL).

1930 – The distillery is administered under Scottish Malt Distillers (SMD).

1952 – An explosive fire breaks out and causes considerable damage.

1960 – Malt Mills distillery closes and today it houses Lagavulin's visitor centre.

1974 – Floor maltings are decommisioned and malt is bought from Port Ellen instead.

1988 – Lagavulin 16 years becomes one of six Classic Malts.

1998 – A Pedro Ximenez sherry finish is launched as a Distillers Edition.

2002 – Two cask strengths (12 years and 25 years) are launched.

2006 – A 30 year old is released.

2007 – A 21 year old from 1985 and the sixth edition of the 12 year old are released.

2008 – A new 12 year old is released.

2009 – A new 12 year old appears as a Special Release.

2010 – A new edition of the 12 year old, a single cask exclusive for the distillery and a Manager's Choice single cask are released.

2011 – The 10th edition of the 12 year old cask strength is released.

2012 – The 11th edition of the 12 year old cask strength and a 21 year old are released.

Lagavulin 12 year old

GS – Soft and buttery on the nose, with dominant, fruity, peat smoke, grilled fish and a hint of vanilla sweetness. More fresh fruit notes develop with the addition of water. Medium-bodied, quite oily in texture, heavily smoked, sweet malt and nuts. The finish is very long and ashy, with lingering sweet peat.

DR – A monster truck nose with rich smoke, lychee and unripe pear, with prickly smoke and banana skin notes on the palate, and a superb long dark chocolate and smoky finish.

21 years old   *Distiller's Edition*

16 years old   *12 years old (11th ed.)*   *Distillery Exclusive no age*

Laphroaig

Owner:		Region/district:
Beam Global Spirits & Wine		Islay

Founded:	Status:	Capacity:
1810	Active (vc)	3 300 000 litres

Address: Port Ellen, Islay, Argyll PA42 7DU

Tel:	website:
01496 302418	www.laphroaig.com

History:

1810 – Brothers Alexander and Donald Johnston found Laphroaig.

1815 – Official year of starting.

1836 – Donald buys out Alexander and takes over operations.

1837 – James and Andrew Gairdner found Ardenistiel a stone's throw from Laphroaig.

1847 – Donald Johnston is killed in an accident in the distillery when he falls into a kettle of boiling hot burnt ale. The Manager of neighbouring Lagavulin, Walter Graham, takes over.

1857 – Operation is back in the hands of the Johnston family when Donald's son Dugald takes over.

circa 1860 – Ardenistiel Distillery merges with Laphroaig.

1877 – Dugald, being without heirs, passes away and his sister Isabella, married to their cousin Alexander takes over.

1907 – Alexander Johnston dies and the distillery is inherited by his two sisters Catherine Johnston and Mrs. William Hunter (Isabella Johnston).

1908 – Ian Hunter arrives in Islay to assist his mother and aunt with the distillery.

1924 – The two stills are increased to four.

Laphroaig single malt is a hugely popular whisky, not least evidenced by their fan club, Friends of Laphroaig, which now stands at more than 500,000 members. The club's 18th birthday was celebrated in May with a special bottling of Cairdeas (see below). Another reason for celebrating was that the sales figures for 2011 for the first time broke the 200,000 cases barrier (nearly 2,5 million bottles sold). This means that Laphroaig is still the number one selling Islay single malt and has been since 2001.

Laphroaig is one of very few distilleries with its own maltings. Four malting floors hold 7 tonnes each and together account for 15% of its requirements. Another 70% comes from Port Ellen maltings on Islay, while 15% are imported from the mainland. Own malt and malt from different suppliers is always blended before mashing. During the floor malting, peat is used at a very low temperature at the beginning of the kilning, which adds to the special character of Laphroaig. The own malt has a phenol specification of 60ppm.

The distillery is equipped with a stainless steel full lauter mash tun and six washbacks that are also made of stainless steel. Three years ago the manager, John Campbell, introduced smaller mashes (5,5 tonnes instead of 8,5) in order to increase flexibility and capacity. Two mashes will now fill one washback which gives five wash still charges. The distillery uses an unusual combination of three wash stills and four spirit stills and the spirit is matured in three dunnage and five racked warehouses. During 2012, they will be working full time producing 3,3 million litres of alcohol.

The core range consists of *10 year old, 10 year old cask strength, Quarter Cask, 18 year old* and *25 year old*. A new addition to the core range from September 2011 was *Triple Wood*. To replace Triple Wood in travel retail came another triple matured expression, *Laphroaig PX*, without age statement but made up of whiskies between 5 and 10 years old with a maturation both in hogsheads and quarter casks and with a finish in Pedro Ximenez sherry casks. Since 2008, the special bottling in conjunction with Feis Isle has been a variety of Cairdeas. The festival bottling for 2012 was no exception; *Cairdeas Origin* is a mix of whiskies between 13 and 21 years and 7 year old whisky matured in quarter casks. Like many other producers, Laphroaig also released a *Diamond Jubilee* version in 2012 - an *18 year old* bottled at 48%. Finally, an exclusive for Sweden and the Viking Line was *Brodir*, a 13 year old which had matured in three different types of casks.

History (continued):

1927 – Catherine Johnston dies and Ian Hunter takes over.

1928 – Isabella Johnston dies and Ian Hunter becomes sole owner.

1950 – Ian Hunter forms D. Johnston & Company

1954 – Ian Hunter passes away and management of the distillery is taken over by Elisabeth "Bessie" Williamson, who was previously Ian Hunters PA and secretary. She becomes Director of the Board and Managing Director.

1967 – Seager Evans & Company buys the distillery through Long John Distillery, having already acquired part of Laphroaig in 1962. The number of stills is increased from four to five.

1972 – Bessie Williamson retires. Another two stills are installed bringing the total to seven.

1975 – Whitbread & Co. buys Seager Evans (now renamed Long John International) from Schenley International.

1989 – The spirits division of Whitbread is sold to Allied Distillers.

1991 – Allied Distillers launches Caledonian Malts. Laphroaig is one of the four malts included.

1994 – HRH Prince Charles gives his Royal Warrant to Laphroaig. Friends of Laphroaig is founded.

1995 – A 10 year old cask strength is launched.

2001 – 4,000 bottles of a 40 year old, the oldest-ever Laphroaig, are released.

2004 – Quarter Cask, a mix of different ages with a finish in quarter casks (i. e. 125 litres) is launched.

2005 – Fortune Brands becomes new owner.

2007 – A vintage 1980 (27 years old) and a 25 year old are released.

2008 – Cairdeas, Cairdeas 30 year old and Triple Wood are released.

2009 – An 18 year old is released.

2010 – A 20 year old for French Duty Free and Cairdeas Master Edition are launched.

2011 – Laphroaig PX and Cairdeas - The Ileach Edition are released. Triple Wood is moved to the core range and replaced in duty free by Laphroaig PX.

2012 – Brodir and Cairdeas Origin are launched.

Laphroaig 10 year old

GS – Old-fashioned sticking plaster, peat smoke and seaweed leap off the nose, followed by something a little sweeter and fruitier. Massive on the palate, with fish oil, salt and plankton, though the finish is quite tight and increasingly drying.

DR – Salt, peat, seawood and tar in a glorious and absorbing nose, then structured and rock like barley with waves of tarry peat washing over them, then a long phenolic and peaty finish.

18 years old

Cairdeas Master Edition

Triple Wood

10 years old

10 years old cask strength

Quarter Cask

167

Linkwood

Owner:		Region/district:
Diageo		Speyside
Founded:	**Status:**	**Capacity:**
1821	Active	3 750 000 litres

Address: Elgin, Morayshire IV30 3RD

Tel:	website:
01343 862000	www.malts.com

History:

1821 – Peter Brown founds the distillery.

1868 – Peter Brown passes away and his son William inherits the distillery.

1872 – William demolishes the distillery and builds a new one.

1897 – Linkwood Glenlivet Distillery Company Ltd takes over operations.

1902 – Innes Cameron, a whisky trader from Elgin, joins the Board and eventually becomes the major shareholder and Director.

1932 – Innes Cameron dies and Scottish Malt Distillers takes over in 1933.

1962 – Major refurbishment takes place.

1971 – The two stills are increased by four. Technically, the four new stills belong to a new distillery sometimes referred to as Linkwood B.

1985 – Linkwood A (the two original stills) closes.

1990 – Linkwood A is in production again for a few months each year.

2002 – A 26 year old from 1975 is launched as a Rare Malt.

2005 – A 30 year old from 1974 is launched as a Rare Malt.

2008 – Three different wood finishes (all 26 year old) are released.

2009 – A Manager's Choice 1996 is released.

Linkwood 12 year old

GS – Floral, grassy and fragrant on the nutty nose, while the slightly oily palate becomes increasingly sweet, ending up at marzipan and almonds. The relatively lengthy finish is quite dry and citric.

DR – Sweet and squidgy with over-ripe melon and soft pear on the nose, and a delightful palate of marzipan, vanilla, green apples and a touch of spice. The finish is balanced, pleasant and very enticing.

Linkwood distillery, situated on the outskirts of Elgin, is now back in full production after having been closed from February to July 2011. The reason for the standstill was a major upgrade with a new full lauter mash tun replacing the old cast iron one, parts of the stills being replaced, as well as the installation of new control systems in both the mash house and the still house. As if that wasn't enough there are discussions regarding increasing the capacity by almost 50% to 5,5 million litres, but the final decision has not yet been taken. During 2012 they will be doing 15 mashes per week and 3,75 million litres in the year.

The only buildings left from the 1820s when the distillery was built are the kiln and the malt barn. The distillery is divided into two sites with the old one housing six smaller washbacks still being used for production. The two stills and the wormtub, however, have not been used since 1996. In the new building (from 1971) there is the mash tun, five wooden washbacks with a fermentation time of 75 hours and two pairs of stills with the spirit stills slightly larger than the wash stills. The owners try to achieve a light and delicate newmake through a very clear wort, long fermentation, slow distillation and by not filling the stills too much, which gives a lot of copper contact. The beautiful dam at the distillery is used for condensing only; the process water comes from springs near Millbuies Loch.

Linkwood has always been popular with the blenders and plays an important role in major brands such as Johnnie Walker and White Horse. The core expression is a *12 year old Flora & Fauna*. In 2008 a limited edition of three unusual *26 year old* bottlings were released. For the last 14 years, all of them finished in three different types of casks - *port, rum* and *sweet red wine*. A 15 year old Linkwood from independent bottler Gordon & MacPhail is also widely available.

12 years old

Loch Lomond

Owner:	Region/district:
Loch Lomond Distillery Co.	Western Highlands

Founded:	Status:	Capacity:
1965	Active	4 000 000 litres

Address: Lomond Estate, Alexandria G83 0TL

Tel:	website:
01389 752781	www.lochlomonddistillery.com

History:

1965 – The distillery is built by Littlemill Distillery Company Ltd owned by Duncan Thomas and American Barton Brands.

1966 – Production commences.

1971 – Duncan Thomas is bought out and Barton Brands reforms as Barton Distilling (Scotland) Ltd.

1984 – The distillery closes.

1985 – Glen Catrine Bonded Warehouse Ltd buys Loch Lomond Distillery.

1987 – The distillery resumes production.

1993 – Grain spirits are also distilled.

1997 – A fire destroys 300,000 litres of maturing whisky.

1999 – Two more stills are installed.

2005 – Inchmoan and Craiglodge are officially launched for the first time. Both are 4 years old from 2001. Inchmurrin 12 years is launched.

2006 – Inchmurrin 4 years, Croftengea 1996 (9 years), Glen Douglas 2001 (4 years) and Inchfad 2002 (5 years) are launched.

2010 – A peated Loch Lomond with no age statement is released as well as a Vintage 1966.

Inchmurrin 12 year old

GS – Malt and spicy oranges on the nose; newly-opened glossy magazines. The palate is lively and spicy with notes of caramel, fudge and honey. Fudge and spice persist in the medium-length finish.

The very first distillery with the name Loch Lomond was built in 1814 but only lasted three years. Almost 150 years later the current distillery was founded although not on the same site. The current owners, headed by the whisky tycoon, Sandy Bulloch, entered the arena in 1985 when they took over the distillery. Sandy had in the 1950s built up a chain of wine and spirit shops and, in order to supply them, he then acquired a wholesale company (Wm Morton). With an increasing amount of own bottlings, he decided that they also needed a bottling plant and founded Glen Catrine Bonded Warehouse. Finally, in the 1980s, when finding stock of whisky to buy, it became necessary to add a production plant to the company and Loch Lomond distillery was bought.

Loch Lomond distillery has a most unusual set-up of equipment. One full lauter mash tun complemented by ten 25,000 litres and eight 50,000 litres washbacks, are all made of stainless steel. Going on to the stills it becomes fascinating. First of all, there are two traditional copper pot stills. Then there are four copper stills where the swan necks have been exchanged with rectifying columns which enable making different types of spirit in the same stills. Furthermore, there is one Coffey still used for continuous distillation where, for example, the Rhosdhu single malt is produced. As this was not enough, an additional distillery with continuous stills producing grain whisky is housed in the same building. For the grain side of production there are twelve 100,000 litres and eight 200,000 litres washbacks. The total capacity is 4 million litres of malt spirit and 18 million litres of grain.

Loch Lomond produces a broad range of whiskies. The core range of malts is *Loch Lomond Blue Label* (no age statement), *Black Label* (18 year old), *Green Label* (peated) and *Loch Lomond 1966*. From time to time, they also release other expressions in their Distillery Select range; *Inchmurrin, Rhosdhu, Inchmoan, Craiglodge, Croftengea, Glen Douglas* and *Inchfad*.

Inchmurrin 12 years old

Longmorn

Owner:
Chivas Brothers
(Pernod Ricard)

Region/district:
Speyside

Founded: 1894
Status: Active
Capacity: 4 400 000 litres

Address: Longmorn, Morayshire IV30 8SJ

Tel: 01343 554139
website: -

History:
1893 – John Duff & Company, which founded Glenlossie already in 1876, starts construction. John Duff, George Thomson and Charles Shirres are involved in the company. The total cost amounts to £20,000.

1894 – First production in December.

1897 – John Duff buys out the others and founds Longmorn Distillery.

1898 – John Duff builds another distillery next to Longmorn which is called Benriach (at times aka Longmorn no. 2). Duff declares bankruptcy and the shares are sold by the bank to James R. Grant.

1970 – The distillery company is merged with The Glenlivet & Glen Grant Distilleries and Hill Thomson & Co. Ltd. Own floor maltings ceases.

1972 – The number of stills is increased from four to six. Spirit stills are converted to steam firing.

1974 – Another two stills are added.

1978 – Seagrams takes over through The Chivas & Glenlivet Group.

1994 – Wash stills are converted to steam firing.

2001 – Pernod Ricard buys Seagram Spirits & Wine together with Diageo and Pernod Ricard takes over the Chivas group.

2004 – A 17 year old cask strength is released.

2007 – A 16 year old is released replacing the 15 year old.

2012 – Production capacity is expanded.

Longmorn 16 year old
GS – The nose offers cream, spice, toffee apples and honey. Medium bodied in the mouth, with fudge, butter and lots of spice. The finish is quite long, with oak and late-lingering dry spices.

DR – Cut flowers and mixed fruit on the nose, rounded and full fruit and honey with some wood and spice adding complexity, long and rich finish.

For Longmorn distillery, 2012 turned out to be a year of refurbishing and expansion. The old tun room was demolished and a new tun room, as well as a mash house was built on the northern side of the still houses. A new Briggs full lauter mash tun, the same size as the old, traditional one, was installed. Seven of the eight old stainless steel washbacks were moved to the new tun room and an additional three were installed. External heat exchangers have been installed on the four wash stills, as well as new draff storage. Official capacity figures have not been released but the whole investment will increase the output by 25% to 4.4 million litres of alcohol per year.

Longmorn distillery has a place not only in Scottish whisky history but also the Japanese. The father of the Japanese whisky industry, Masataka Taketsuru, not only came to Scotland in 1918 to study chemistry, but also to practise at Scottish distilleries. Longmorn was one of the few that accepted him as an intern in 1919 and fifteen years later Yoichi was built more or less as a replica of Longmorn. It is one of five single malt brands the owners Pernod Ricard are investing in. They have nine additional malt distilleries whose main purpose is to serve the company's blended whiskies. Pernod Ricard is the third largest producer of wine and spirits in the world (in terms of volume) and of their total sales of Scotch whisky, single malt accounts for 5% compared to their arch rival, Diageo, with a 2.5% single malt share.

Longmorn has always had a symbiotic relationship with Ben-Riach distillery and the last one was actually named Longmorn 2 when it was built. Even today, Longmorn supplies BenRiach with water from boreholes and also takes care of the effluent. The core range is the *16 year old* and there is also *17 year old cask strength* for sale at Chivas´ visitor centres.

16 years old

Macallan

Owner:
Edrington Group

Region/district:
Speyside

Founded: 1824
Status: Active (vc)
Capacity: 9 400 000 litres

Address: Easter Elchies, Craigellachie, Morayshire AB38 9RX

Tel: 01340 871471
website: www.themacallan.com

History:
1824 – The distillery is licensed to Alexander Reid under the name Elchies Distillery.

1847 – Alexander Reid passes away and James Shearer Priest and James Davidson take over.

1868 – James Stuart takes over the licence. He founds Glen Spey distillery a decade later.

1886 – James Stuart buys the distillery.

1892 – Stuart sells the distillery to Roderick Kemp from Elgin. Kemp expands the distillery and names it Macallan-Glenlivet.

1909 – Roderick Kemp passes away and the Roderick Kemp Trust is established to secure the family's future ownership.

1965 – The number of stills is increased from six to twelve.

1966 – The trust is reformed as a private limited company.

1968 – The company is introduced on the London Stock Exchange.

1974 – The number of stills is increased to 18.

1975 – Another three stills are added, now making the total 21.

1979 – Allan Schiach, descendant of Roderick Kemp, becomes the new chairman of the board after Peter Schiach.

1984 – The first official 18 year old single malt is launched.

1986 – Japanese Suntory buys 25% of Macallan-Glenlivet plc stocks.

Saleswise, things are going well for Macallan, to say the least. An increase in volume in 2010 by 15% was followed up by a further 9% during 2011. The brand now sells more than 9 million bottles. Asia accounts for more than half of that and sales in the USA has started to increase again after the recent economic downturn.

Since 2008 the production takes place in two separate plants. The number one plant holds one full lauter mash tun, 16 stainless steel washbacks, five wash stills and ten spirit stills. The number two plant is comprised of one semi-lauter mash tun (6 tonnes), six new wooden washbacks, two wash stills and four spirit stills. Macallan was one of very few distilleries in Scotland that was still heating their stills by direct fire. However, since 2010, all stills are indirectly fired using steam. Warehouse capacity has increased over the last years and there are now 16 dunnage and 23 racked warehouses with another two due to be completed by the end of 2012. The distillery will be doing 66 mashes per week, resulting in 9,4 million litres. There has been talk about increasing the production capacity and the fact is that two new washbacks will be installed during 2012.

Since 2004, the Macallan core range has been divided into Sherry Oak (exclusively matured in ex-sherry casks) and Fine Oak (a combination of ex-sherry and ex-bourbon). In June 2012 the owners surprised the market when they declared that another range of whiskies without age statements would be added to the assortment. The first in the new range (called *The Macallan 1824 Series*) is *Gold*, due for release in the UK in autumn 2012 and later in Canada. This will be followed in 2013 by *Amber* (released in 50 markets but not the UK), *Sienna* and *Ruby*. After the release of the new series, the *Sherry Oak* range will still consist of *10, 15, 18, 25* and *30 year old* while *Fine Oak* consists of *12, 15, 17, 18, 21, 25* and *30 year old*. In some markets, these expressions will be removed and replaced with the 1824 series. The duty free range, named *The Macallan 1824 Collection*, holds five expressions; *Select Oak, Whisky Maker´s Edition, Estate Reserve, Oscuro* and the new *The Macallan Limited Release MMXII* which replaced the *MMXI* in 2012. A single cask available only at the distillery was released in 2012 - the 14 year old *Easter Elchies Cask Selection*. There is also *The Fine & Rare range* – vintages from 1926 to 1989. A cooperation with crystal maker Lalique, has so far resulted in four rare bottlings, the last one a *60 year old* released in 2011. Other recent limited editions include *Master of Photography 3* and *The Macallan Diamond Jubilee*.

History (continued):

1996 – Highland Distilleries buys the remaining stocks. 1874 Replica is launched.

1999 – Edrington and William Grant & Sons buys Highland Distilleries (where Edrington, Suntory and Remy-Cointreau already are shareholders) for £601 million. They form the 1887 Company which owns Highland Distilleries with 70% held by Edrington and 30% by William Grant & Sons (excepting the 25% share held by Suntory).

2000 – The first single cask from Macallan (1981) is named Exceptional 1.

2001 – A new visitor centre is opened.

2002 – Elegancia replaces 12 year old in the duty-free range. 1841 Replica, Exceptional II and Exceptional III are also launched.

2003 – 1876 Replica and Exceptional IV, single cask from 1990 are released.

2004 – Exceptional V, single cask from 1989 is released as well as Exceptional VI, single cask from 1990. The Fine Oak series is launched.

2005 – New expressions are Macallan Woodland Estate, Winter Edition and the 50 year old.

2006 – Fine Oak 17 years old and Vintage 1975 are launched.

2007 – 1851 Inspiration and Whisky Maker´s Selection are released as a part of the Travel Retail range. 12 year old Gran Reserva is launched in Taiwan and Japan.

2008 – Estate Oak and 55 year old Lalique are released.

2009 – Capacity increased by another six stills. The Macallan 1824 Collection, a range of four duty free expressions, is launched. A 57 year old Lalique bottling is released.

2010 – Oscuro is released for Duty Free.

2011 – Macallan MMIX is released for duty free.

2012 – Macallan Gold, the first in the new 1824 series, is launched.

Oscuro

Whisky Maker´s Edition

Select Oak

Fine Oak 17 yo

1949 vintage

Estate Reserve

The Macallan Gold

18 years old

25 years old

30 years old

Macallan 12 year old Sherry Oak

GS – The nose is luscious, with buttery sherry and Christmas cake characteristics. Rich and firm on the palate, with sherry, elegant oak and Jaffa oranges. The finish is long and malty, with slightly smoky spice.

DR – Unmistakenly the sherried version of The Macallan, with a classic red berry and orange mix. The palate is plummy, with intense sherry and some toffee and cocoa notes. The finish is medium long sweet and fruity.

Macallan 12 year old Fine Oak

GS – The nose is perfumed and quite complex, with marzipan and malty toffee. Expansive on the palate, with oranges, marmalade, milk chocolate and oak. Medium in length, balanced and comparatively sweet.

DR – Vanilla, butterscotch, satsumas and orange candy on the nose, mixed grapefruit, orange and other fruits on the palate and then a big dash of spice, and a reasonably long and balanced mix of fruit and spice in the finish.

Macduff

Owner:
John Dewar & Sons Ltd
(Bacardi)

Region/district:
Highlands

Founded: **Status:**
1962   Active

Capacity:
3 340 000 litres

Address: Banff, Aberdeenshire AB45 3JT

Tel:
01261 812612

website:
-

History:
1962 – The distillery is founded by Marty Dyke, George Crawford and Brodie Hepburn (who is also involved in Tullibardine and Deanston). Macduff Distillers Ltd is the name of the company.

1963 – Production starts.

1965 – The number of stills is increased from two to three.

1967 – Stills now total four.

1972 – William Lawson Distillers, part of General Beverage Corporation which is owned by Martini & Rossi, buys the distillery from Glendeveron Distilleries.

1990 – A fifth still is installed.

1992 – Bacardi buys Martini Rossi (including William Lawson) and transfers Macduff to the subsidiary John Dewar & Sons.

Glen Deveron 10 year old

GS – Sherry, malt and a slightly earthy note on the nose. Smooth and sweet in the mouth, with vanilla, spice and a hint of smoke. Sweet right to the finish.

DR – The nose is a mix of crisp barley, orange, hay and a trace of smoke, and on the palate an oily and fruity combination beautifully coats the mouth before giving way to a pepper, savoury and astringent finish.

Even though Glen Deveron single malt (the official brand name of whisky from Macduff distillery) sells over 300,000 bottles per year, the focus is on the blended Scotch, William Lawson's. The brand was first registered as Lawson's in 1889 by William Lawson, manager of the blending company, E & J Burke. In 1963 the brand name was acquired by Martini & Rossi and changed to William Lawson's and in 1972 Macduff distillery was added to the business. Twenty years later, Bacardi became the new owner of both the blend and the distillery. Sales of William Lawson's is concentrated to France, Russia and, especially, Mexico – the second biggest market in Latin America for Scotch whisky. During 2011 William Lawson's was the fastest growing whisky brand in the world – up a staggering 35% and now selling almost 28 million bottles, which gives the brand spot number 11 on the list of most sold Scotch whiskies.

Macduff has a beautiful location on the eastern outskirts of Banff on the Moray Firth coast. The distillery is equipped with a very efficient 6-roller Bühler Miag mill from 2007, a stainless steel semi-lauter mash tun, nine washbacks made of stainless steel and the rather unusual set-up of five stills (two wash stills and three spirit stills). The fifth still was installed in 1990. In order to fit the stills into the still room, the lyne arms on four of the stills are bent in a peculiar way and on one of the wash stills it is U-shaped. Because of limited space, they have chosen to have vertical condensers on the wash stills but horizontal condensers on the spirit stills. For maturation, a mix of sherry and bourbon casks is used but nothing is maturing on site, even though they have seven large warehouses. In 2012 the distillery will be producing 2,8 million litres of alcohol.

The most common official bottling of Glen Deveron is the *10 year old* but there is also a *15 year old* to be found. Older versions of *8* and *12 year olds* are also available.

10 years old

Meet the Manager

STEPHEN BURNETT
DISTILLERY MANAGER, MACDUFF DISTILLERY

When did you start working in the whisky business and when did you start at Macduff?

I started work in the whisky industry at Macduff Distillery in 1990.

Had you been working in other lines of business before whisky?

After leaving school I served an apprenticeship as a Painter & Decorator, working in the industry for six years.

What kind of education or training do you have?

I was educated locally at Banff Academy. I started working at Macduff Distillery in 1990, firstly in cask preparation & warehousing (cask disgorging & filling). At the time there were three cooper's employed at the distillery. After a couple of years I learnt the mashing and distilling processes providing shift cover as when required. I also worked as a shift operator in the Syrup Evaporation Plant for a number of years.

Describe your career in the whisky business.

In 1999 I started as a trainee with John Dewar & Sons carrying out various duties and tasks within their five distilleries, (Aberfeldy, Aultmore, Craigellachie, Macduff and Royal Brackla). I was also fortunate to be part of the project teams who installed the two new mashtuns at Craigellachie and Aultmore Distilleries.

What are your main tasks as a manager?

Maintaining the quality and consistency of the new make spirit and running the distillery safely and as efficiently as possible ensuring the distillery is fully compliant in all aspects of Health & Safety, HMR&C and SEPA.

What are the biggest challenges of being a distillery manager?

Running the distillery as safely and efficiently maintaining a consistent high quality spirit and satisfying all legislative demands.

What would be the worst that could go wrong in the production process?

The priority is the health and safety of the individuals who work at the distillery and also any contractors or visitors attending site. I would hate for anyone to get injured whilst on site. Buildings and plant can be replaced.

How would you describe the character of Glen Deveron single malt?

Overtones of nut oil with a complex fruity background giving way to an estery nose and notes of fresh plum. Dry finish with a subtle hint of wood.

What are the main features in the process at Macduff, contributing to this character?

At Macduff there are two wash stills with vertical condensers and three spirit stills with horizontal condensers and sub coolers. Maturation takes place off site.

What is your favourite expression of Glen Deveron and why?

I like the Glen Deveron 10 year old which is a dram that could be taken at any time regardless of the occasion.

If it were your decision alone – what new expression of Glen Deveron would you like to see released?

I would let others make that decision, I'm happy just trying their creations.

If you had to choose a favourite dram other than Glen Deveron, what would that be?

Aberfeldy 12 year old or Aultmore 12 year old.

What are the biggest changes you have seen the past 10 years in your profession?

Process automation and the company's drive to reduce its carbon footprint through reducing its energy and water consumption. Also the emergence of new whisky markets.

Do you see any major changes in the next 10 years to come?

Continually investment in energy and environmental projects, further developments in Bio-technology, with further reductions in our carbon footprint without affecting the quality or character of the new make spirit. Hopefully continued growth in the whisky industry with emerging and existing markets.

Do you have any special interests or hobbies that you pursue?

When possible I enjoy cycling. I used to play quite a lot of golf but I haven't had the opportunity to play lately.

Why are the official single malt bottlings from Macduff called Glen Deveron?

Macduff Distillery sits on the banks of the River Deveron

You have seven large warehouses on site but none of them are used for maturing whisky. Why is that?

John Dewar & Sons have heavily invested in two warehousing complex's in Central Scotland. Westthorn was redeveloped and the company is currently developing a site at Poniel. The warehouses at Macduff were emptied a number of years ago as it wasn't cost effective to redevelop them.

Single malt from Macduff plays an important part in the William Lawson's blended Scotch. What does it contribute to the flavour of the blend and could it be replaced without changing the character?

Body and complex fruity notes. Macduff is the heart of the William Lawson's blend - you can't replace that.

Mannochmore

Owner:
Diageo

Region/district:
Speyside

Founded: 1971
Status: Active
Capacity: 3 450 000 litres

Address: Elgin, Morayshire IV30 8SS

Tel: 01343 862000
website: www.malts.com

History:
1971 – Scottish Malt Distillers (SMD) founds the distillery on the site of their sister distillery Glenlossie. It is managed by John Haig & Co. Ltd.

1985 – The distillery is mothballed.

1989 – In production again.

1992 – A Flora & Fauna series 12 years old becomes the first official bottling.

1997 – United Distillers launches Loch Dhu – The Black Whisky which is a 10 year old Mannochmore. A 22 year old Rare Malt from 1974 and a sherry-matured Manager's Dram 18 years are also launched.

2009 – An 18 year old is released.

2010 – A Manager's Choice 1998 is released.

Mannochmore 12 year old
GS – Perfumed and fresh on the light, citric nose, with a sweet, floral, fragrant palate, featuring vanilla, ginger and even a hint of mint. Medium length in the finish, with a note of lingering almonds.
DR – Buttery, with lemon, sweet dough and floral notes on the nose, oily, malty and floral on the palate and with a relatively short finish.

Optimism was great in the Scotch whisky industry at the beginning of the 1970s. The demand, not least in the USA, had increased steadily every decade since the end of WWII. The producers had to act to keep up with demand and one way was to build a new distillery on the site of an old one and run them simultaneously. In most cases the older distillery closed within a couple of years; Clynelish/Brora (new distillery opened 1968 with the old closing 1983), Teaninich (1970/1984), Linkwood (1971/1996) and Glendullan (1972/1985). An exception was the construction of Mannochmore on the grounds of Glenlossie in 1971. Except for Mannochmore being closed for a couple of years, both distilleries continued to produce during the hardships of the 1980s up until today. The workforce used to alternate between the two distilleries with each distillery being in production for half a year at a time, but since 2007, both distilleries are producing all year round.

Next to Mannochmore lies a dark grains plant which processes draff and pot ale from 21 different distilleries. Draff is the residue from the mashing of the malt and the pot ale is the left over from the wash stills after distillation. The pot ale is processed into a heavy syrup using evaporators, while moisture is extracted from the draff. The two are then mixed together, dried, formed into pellets and sold as animal feed.

Mannochmore is equipped with a large cast iron lauter mash tun (11,1 tonnes) which is probably due for a replacement during 2013, eight washbacks made of larch and three pairs of stills, with the spirit stills being larger than the wash stills.

The core range of Mannochmore is just a *12 year old Flora & Fauna*. In 2009, a limited *18 year old* matured in re-charred sherry casks, bourbon casks and new American Oak casks was released and in 2010 it was time for a sherry matured *single cask* from *1998* in the Manager's Choice range.

Flora & Fauna 12 years old

Miltonduff

Owner:
Chivas Brothers
(Pernod Ricard)

Region/district:
Speyside

Founded: **Status:** **Capacity:**
1824   Active   5 500 000 litres

Address: Miltonduff, Elgin,
Morayshire IV30 8TQ

Tel: **website:**
01343 547433   -

History:
1824 – Andrew Peary and Robert Bain
obtain a licence for Miltonduff Distillery.
It has previously operated as an illicit farm
distillery called Milton Distillery but changes
name when the Duff family buys the site it is
operating on.

1866 – William Stuart buys the distillery.

1895 – Thomas Yool & Co. becomes new part-
owner.

1936 – Thomas Yool & Co. sells the distillery to
Hiram Walker Gooderham & Worts. The latter
transfers administration to the newly acquired
subsidiary George Ballantine & Son.

1964 – A pair of Lomond stills is installed to
produce the rare Mosstowie.

1974-75 – Major reconstruction of the
distillery.

1981 – The Lomond stills are decommissioned
and replaced by two ordinary pot stills, the
number of stills now totalling six.

1986 – Allied Lyons buys 51% of Hiram Walker.

1987 – Allied Lyons acquires the rest of Hiram
Walker.

1991 – Allied Distillers follow United Distillers´
example of Classic Malts and introduce
Caledonian Malts in which Tormore, Glendronach and Laphroaig are included in addition
to Miltonduff. Tormore is later replaced by
Scapa.

2005 – Chivas Brothers (Pernod Ricard)
becomes the new owner through the
acquisition of Allied Domecq.

The single malts from Miltonduff and Glenburgie have
been at the very core of each bottle of Ballantine´s at least
since 1936. It was then that Hiram Walker, the largest
distiller in Canada at the time, bought the two distilleries.
One year earlier they had acquired the Ballantine´s brand.
Since then, the blend and the two distilleries have changed
hands on two occasions – in 1987 when Hiram Walker was
swallowed up by Allied Distillers and in 2005 when the
current owner, Pernod Ricard, took over. For many years,
Ballantine´s was the global number three Scotch whisky but
managed to surpass J&B in 2007 and is now second to Johnnie Walker. In 2011, 78 million bottles were sold which was
an increase by 5% compared to the year before.

The distillery is equipped with an 8 tonne full lauter mash
tun which, when producing at full capacity, performs 40
mashes a week. There are no less than 16 stainless steel
washbacks and three pairs of stills. A balanced distillation
similar to that of, for example, Glen-
burgie, incorporating one wash and
one spirit still working in tandem and
served by a designated feints and low
wines receiver, was introduced in autumn 2009. Several racked warehouses
on the site hold a total of 54,000 casks.
Miltonduff is one of a handful of distilleries which used Lomond stills for
a period of time. The idea behind
it was to produce several types
of malt whisky with the same
still. Miltonduff had Lomond
stills installed in 1964, but by
1981 they were rebuilt as ordinary stills as the trials had not
been completely successful. The
Lomond still malt was named
Mosstowie and can, with a bit
of luck, still be found. A 1979
bottling was released by Signatory in late 2010.
The most recent official bottling of Miltonduff is a *1992,
19 years old*, which was
released in Chivas Brothers´
cask strength series.

18 years old cask strength

Mortlach

Owner:
Diageo

Region/district:
Speyside

Founded: Status: Capacity:
1823   Active   3 800 000 litres

Address: Dufftown, Keith,
Banffshire AB55 4AQ

Tel: website:
01340 822100   www.malts.com

History:
1823 – The distillery is founded by James Findlater.

1824 – Donald Macintosh and Alexander Gordon become part-owners.

1831 – The distillery is sold to John Robertson for £270.

1832 – A. & T. Gregory buys Mortlach.

1837 – James and John Grant of Aberlour become part-owners. No production takes place.

1842 – The distillery is now owned by John Alexander Gordon and the Grant brothers.

1851 – Mortlach is producing again after having been used as a church and a brewery for some years.

1853 – George Cowie joins and becomes part-owner.

1867 – John Alexander Gordon dies and Cowie becomes sole owner.

1895 – George Cowie Jr. joins the company.

1897 – The number of stills is increased from three to six.

1923 – Alexander Cowie sells the distillery to John Walker & Sons.

1925 – John Walker becomes part of Distillers Company Limited (DCL).

1930 – The administration is transferred to Scottish Malt Distillers (SMD).

1964 – Major refurbishment.

1968 – Floor maltings ceases.

1996 – Mortlach 1972 (23 years) is released as a Rare Malt. The distillery is renovated at a cost of £1.5 million.

1998 – Mortlach 1978 (20 years) is released as a Rare Malt.

2004 – Mortlach 1971, a 32 year old cask strength is released.

2009 – Mortlach 1997, a single cask in the new Manager's Choice range is released.

The robust and flavourful single malt from Mortlach distillery has many fans. This became apparent when it was virtually impossible to get hold of it a few years back, since it was needed for the evermore popular Johnnie Walker Black Label. Its popularity is nothing new though. Already in the 1860s when the distillery was owned by John Gordon, Mortlach was sold in Leith and Glasgow under the name of "The Real John Gordon". Mortlach was the first of the famous seven Dufftown distilleries to be built and for some time William Grant was the manager before he left in order to set up Glenfiddich a few miles to the north.

The distillery is equipped with a 12 tonnes full lauter mash tun and six washbacks made of larch which each holds 90,000 litres, but are charged with 55,000 litres of wort. In the still house there are six stills in various sizes with slightly descending lyne arms. The distillation process at Mortlach, sometimes called partial triple distillation, is unique in Scotland. There are three wash stills and three spirit stills where the No. 3 pair act as a traditional double distillation. The low wines from wash stills No. 1 and 2 are directed to the remaining two spirit stills according to a certain distribution. In one of the spirit stills, called Wee Witchie, the charge is redistilled twice and with all the various distillations taken into account, it can be said that Mortlach is distilled 2,8 times. The importance of the distilling regime is evidenced by a sign in the still house saying: "You need to have one run of spirit from the Wee Witchie in every filling to give Mortlach its true character". All spirit is condensed using five worm tubs made of larch and one made of stainless steel, which adds to the powerful character. The plans for 2012 are to do 16 mashes per week and 3,8 million litres of alcohol per year. On the site are six beautiful dunnage warehouses holding 9,000 casks.

The only official core bottling of Mortlach is the 16 year old Flora & Fauna. In 2009, a Mortlach 1997 single cask was released in the new range Manager's Choice.

Flora & Fauna 16 years old

Oban

Owner:
Diageo

Region/district:
Western Highlands

Founded: 1794

Status: Active (vc)

Capacity: 780 000 litres

Address: Stafford Street, Oban, Argyll PA34 5NH

Tel: 01631 572004 (vc)

website: www.malts.com

History:

1793 – John and Hugh Stevenson found the distillery on premises previously used for brewing.

1794 – Start of operations.

1820 – Hugh Stevenson dies.

1821 – Hugh Stevenson's son Thomas takes over.

1829 – Bad investments force Thomas Stevenson into bankruptcy. His eldest son John takes over operations at the distillery.

1830 – John buys the distillery from his father's creditors for £1,500.

1866 – Peter Cumstie buys the distillery.

1883 – Cumstie sells Oban to James Walter Higgins who refurbishes and modernizes it.

1898 – The Oban & Aultmore-Glenlivet Co. takes over with Alexander Edwards at the helm.

1923 – The Oban Distillery Co. owned by Buchanan-Dewar takes over.

1925 – Buchanan-Dewar becomes part of Distillers Company Limited (DCL).

1930 – Administration is transferred to Scottish Malt Distillers (SMD).

1931 – Production ceases.

1937 – In production again.

1968 – Floor maltings ceases and the distillery closes for reconstruction.

1972 – Reopening of the distillery.

1979 – Oban 12 years is on sale.

1988 – United Distillers launches Classic Malts. Oban 14 year is selected to represent Western Highlands.

1989 – A visitor centre is built.

1998 – A Distillers' Edition is launched.

2002– The oldest Oban (32 years) so far is launched in a limited edition of 6,000 bottles.

2004 – A 20 year old cask strength from 1984 (1,260 bottles) is released.

2009 – Oban 2000, a single cask in the new Manager's Choice range is released.

2010 – A no age distillery exclusive is released.

Oban 14 year old

GS – Lightly smoky on the honeyed, floral nose. Toffee, cereal and a hint of peat. The palate offers initial cooked fruits, becoming spicier. Complex, bittersweet, malt, oak and more gentle smoke. The finish is quite lengthy, with spicy oak, toffee and discreet, new leather.

DR – A mixed nose of heather, honey, pineapple and nuts, a perfectly balanced mix of grapey fruit, pineapple chunks, roast nuts and smoky undertow, and a rounded and fruity finish, drying and more-ish.

Most of the distilleries in Scotland reserve a smaller or larger quantity of their production to become part of various blends but Oban doesn't. The reason partly being that Oban single malt is very popular, not least in the US market, but also that the distillery has a very low capacity – it is in fact one of the ten smallest in Scotland. Hence it is not strange that the owners are trying everything within their power to increase production without compromising the character of the whisky. Through a reduced silent season in 2012 they have successfully increased by 10% to 780,000 litres of alcohol.

Oban is one of the original six Classic Malts and it sells around 780,000 bottles per year, which makes it the fifth best selling single malt in the company and the biggest seller of all Diageo malts in the USA. The distillery, which is the second smallest in the Diageo group after Royal Lochnagar, is equipped with a 6,5 tonnes traditional stainless steel mash tun with rakes, four washbacks made of European larch and one pair of stills. Attached to the stills is a rectangular, stainless steel double worm tub to condensate the spirit vapours. One washback will fill the wash still twice. However, the character of Oban single malt is dependent on long fermentations (110 hours), hence they can only manage six mashes per week (five longs and one short).

Oban wasn't much more than a fishing village when the Stevenson brothers founded the distillery in 1794 but it began to flourish soon thereafter. The distillery boasts one of the best visitor centres in the business with more than 30,000 visitors every year.

The core range consists of two expressions – a *14 year old* and a *Distiller's Edition* with a montilla fino sherry finish. In 2010 a *distillery exclusive bottling*, available only at the distillery, was released. It is finished in fino sherry casks and has no age statement. Older limited editions include a *32 year old*, a *20 year old* and, exclusive to the American market (8,700 bottles), an *18 year old* released in 2008.

14 years old

Pulteney

Owner:	Region/district:
Inver House Distillers (Thai Beverages plc)	Northern Highlands

Founded:	Status:	Capacity:
1826	Active (vc)	1 800 000 litres

Address: Huddart St, Wick, Caithness KW1 5BA

Tel:	website:
01955 602371	www.oldpulteney.com

History:

1826 – James Henderson founds the distillery.

1920 – The distillery is bought by James Watson.

1923 – Buchanan-Dewar takes over.

1925 – Buchanan-Dewar becomes part of Distillers Company Limited (DCL).

1930 – Production ceases.

1951 – In production again after being acquired by the solicitor Robert Cumming.

1955 – Cumming sells to James & George Stodart, a subsidiary to Hiram Walker & Sons.

1958 – The distillery is rebuilt.

1959 – The floor maltings close.

1961 – Allied Breweries buys James & George Stodart Ltd.

1981 – Allied Breweries changes name to Allied Lyons after the acquisition of J Lyons in 1978.

1995 – Allied Domecq sells Pulteney to Inver House Distillers.

1997 – Old Pulteney 12 years is launched.

2001 – Pacific Spirits (Great Oriole Group) buys Inver House at a price of $85 million.

2004 – A 17 year old is launched.

2005 – A 21 year old is launched.

2006 – International Beverage Holdings acquires Pacific Spirits UK.

2009 – A 30 year old is released.

2010 – WK499 Isabella Fortuna is released.

2012 – A 40 year old and WK217 Spectrum are released.

Pulteney is the most northerly distillery on the Scottish mainland and is situated in the small town of Wick (c 7,000 inhabitants). This was once the busiest herring port in Europe. Old Pulteney (as the whisky from Pulteney distillery is called), together with Speyburn, are the most successful of Inver House´s single malts.

The old semi-lauter mash tun made of cast iron was replaced in July 2012 with a stainless steel semi-lauter tun with the same mash size, 5 tonnes. There are six washbacks, five made of Corten steel and one of stainless steel and one pair of stills. The wash still is equipped with a huge ball creating added reflux. The spirit still is equipped with a purifier (which hasn´t been used for years) and both stills use stainless steel worm tubs for condensing the spirit. For 2012, there will be 16 mashes per week, which is the equivalent of 1,4 million litres of alcohol.

The interest for Old Pulteney single malt has increased considerably over the last decade, especially in the UK, USA and Sweden. In 2011, more than 400,000 bottles were sold which is an increase of 75% compared to ten years ago.

The core range is made up of *12, 17, 21* and *30 years old*, the last one released in 2009 as the oldest Old Pulteney so far. Three years later (in 2012) it was time for an even older expression – a *40 year old*. It is a marriage of two casks from 1968 and the plan was to already release it by 2011, but getting the exclusive packaging ready delayed the launch. 2010 saw the first release of a Duty Free exclusive from Pulteney, the non-aged *WK499 Isabella Fortuna*, named after one of Wick´s two remaining herring drifters. Shortly thereafter, the *WK209 Good Hope* was released. The final release in this "boat series" of malts was *WK217 Spectrum*, launched in 2012 as a duty free item. A *Vintage 2000* has been released exclusively in France and there is also a *1997 single bourbon cask* only available at the distillery.

Old Pulteney 12 year old

GS – The nose presents pleasingly fresh malt and floral notes, with a touch of pine. The palate is comparatively sweet, with malt, spices, fresh fruit and a suggestion of salt. The finish is medium in length, drying and decidedly nutty.

DR – Honey and lemon lozenges on the nose, sweet citrus fruits, chunky malt and some traces of sea brine on the palate, an amusing sweet and sour two step at the finish.

12 years old

Royal Brackla

Owner:
John Dewar & Sons
(Bacardi)

Region/district:
Highlands

Founded: 1812
Status: Active
Capacity: 4 000 000 litres

Address: Cawdor, Nairn, Nairnshire IV12 5QY

Tel: 01667 402002
website: -

History:
1812 – The distillery is founded by Captain William Fraser.

1835 – Brackla becomes the first of three distilleries allowed to use 'Royal' in the name.

1852 – Robert Fraser & Co. takes over the distillery.

1898 – The distillery is rebuilt and Royal Brackla Distillery Company Limited is founded.

1919 – John Mitchell and James Leict from Aberdeen purchase Royal Brackla.

1926 – John Bisset & Company Ltd takes over.

1943 – Scottish Malt Distillers (SMD) buys John Bisset & Company Ltd and thereby acquires Royal Brackla.

1966 – The maltings closes.

1970 – Two stills are increased to four.

1985 – The distillery is mothballed.

1991 – Production resumes.

1993 – A 10 year old Royal Brackla is launched in United Distillers' Flora & Fauna series.

1997 – UDV spends more than £2 million on improvements and refurbishing.

1998 – Bacardi–Martini buys Dewar's from Diageo.

2004 – A new 10 year old is launched.

The gentle and fruity character of Royal Brackla single malt makes it a perfect part of any blended whisky. A number of related factors during production work together to create that particular flavour; clear wort, long fermentations (72 hours), long foreshots (30 minutes), a slow distillation and ascending lyne arms on the stills to create as much reflux as possible during the distillation. Almost the entire output is used by the owners for their blends, Dewar's in particular, and even if they would want to release more single malt they don't have any stock older than 14 years. When Dewar's bought the distillery from Diageo in 1998, no maturing whisky was included in the deal.

Royal Brackla was founded in 1812 and they are celebrating 200 years of existence. Another event to celebrate was that in 1835 the distillery was the first to be given a royal warrant by King William IV and the whisky became known as "The King's Own Whisky".

Royal Brackla 10 year old

GS – An attractive malty, fruity, floral nose, with peaches and apricots. Quite full-bodied, the creamy palate exhibits sweet malt, spice and fresh fruit. The finish is medium to long, with vanilla and gently-spiced oak.

DR – Pineapple and citrus fruits on the nose, candy barley, melon and pleasant sweet spice on the palate, medium sweet finish with a trace of green melon.

The distillery, beautifully situated just south of Nairn and Moray Firth, was completely refurbished by the previous owners, Diageo, in the 1990s and from the still house you have a great view through the glazed curtain walls towards the dam for the cooling water. The equipment consists of a big (12.5 tonnes) full lauter mash tun from 1997. There are six wooden washbacks (but with stainless steel tops) and another two made of stainless steel which are insulated because they are placed outside. Finally, there are two pairs of stills. At the moment the distillery is running at full capacity, which means 17 mashes per week and 4 million litres of alcohol per year. This makes it the biggest distillery in the Dewar's group. Today's core range consists of a *10 year old* and a limited edition of a *25 year old*. There have been indications from the owners though, that the range is about to be expanded, probably during 2012 in order to celebrate the distillery's 200th anniversary.

10 years old

Royal Lochnagar

Owner:
Diageo

Region/district:
Eastern Highlands

Founded: **Status:**
1845   Active (vc)

Capacity:
500 000 litres

Address: Crathie, Ballater,
Aberdeenshire AB35 5TB

Tel: **website:**
01339 742700   www.malts.com

History:

1823 – James Robertson founds a distillery in Glen Feardan on the north bank of River Dee.

1826 – The distillery is burnt down by competitors but Robertson decides to establish a new distillery near the mountain Lochnagar.

1841 – This distillery is also burnt down.

1845 – A new distillery is built by John Begg, this time on the south bank of River Dee. It is named New Lochnagar.

1848 – Lochnagar obtains a Royal Warrant.

1882 – John Begg passes away and his son Henry Farquharson Begg inherits the distillery.

1896 – Henry Farquharson Begg dies.

1906 – The children of Henry Begg rebuild the distillery.

1916 – The distillery is sold to John Dewar & Sons.

1925 – John Dewar & Sons becomes part of Distillers Company Limited (DCL).

1963 – A major reconstruction takes place.

2004 – A 30 year old cask strength from 1974 is launched in the Rare Malts series (6,000 bottles).

2008 – A Distiller´s Edition with a Moscatel finish is released.

2010 – A Manager´s Choice 1994 is released.

Royal Lochnagar 12 year old

GS – Light toffee on the nose, along with some green notes of freshly-sawn timber. The palate offers a pleasing and quite complex blend of caramel, dry sherry and spice, followed by a hint of liquorice before the slightly scented finish develops.

DR – Rich fruit and honey on the nose, sophisticated mix of crystal barley, chunky fruit and delicious peat base and a warming and rounded finish.

Even though Royal Lochnagar is Diageo´s smallest distillery, the single malt that is produced is of vital importance as a signature malt in a couple of high end blended whiskies, namely Johnnie Walker Blue Label and Windsor. The latter, introduced in 1996, is the leading brand in Korea and is becoming increasingly more popular in China. The whisky sells almost 12 million bottles per year and, together with Johnnie Walker Black Label, form Diageo´s weapon against its competitor, Chivas Regal, with it´s dominant position in the Southeast Asian market.

Royal Lochnagar lies in beautiful surroundings with Royal Deeside and the imposing Lochnagar mountain to the south and Balmoral, the Queen´s summer residence, just a stone´s throw to the north.

The nine hour mashing is done in batches of 5,4 tonnes in an open, traditional cast iron mash tun using rakes. Fermentation takes place in two wooden washbacks, with short fermentations of 67 hours and long of 107 hours. The long fermentation helps create the light character that the owners are looking for. The two stills are quite small with a charge in the wash still of 6,100 litres and 4,000 litres in the spirit still. The cooling of the spirit vapours takes place in cast iron worm tubs. The whole production is filled on site (mostly into European oak casks) with around 1,000 casks stored in the only warehouse (which previously was used for the maltings) and the rest is sent to Glenlossie for maturation. Because of the continued success for the Windsor blend, production has increased since last year. Five mashes per week during 2012 will result in 500,000 litres of pure alcohol.

The pretty visitor centre attracts 10,000 visitors a year, a figure that could easily be quadrupled if it had been more accessible to one of the main roads.

The core range consists of the *12 year old* and *Selected Reserve*. The latter is a vatting of selected casks, usually around 18-20 years of age. There is also a *Distiller´s Edition* with a second maturation in Muscat casks. In 2010 a *single cask* distilled in *1994* was released as part of the Manager´s Choice series.

12 years old

Meet the Manager

JACKIE ROBERTSON
SITE OPERATION MANAGER, ROYAL LOCHNAGAR DISTILLERY

When did you start working in the whisky business and when did you start at Royal Lochnagar?

I started in the whisky business in 2006 and I came to Lochnagar in February 2012.

Had you been working in other lines of business before whisky?

Prior to joining the whisky industry I was manager in some of Scotland's top Country House Hotels. I also had my own restaurant for approx 3 years.

What kind of education or training do you have?

I left school at 18 and went on to college to study Hotel and Catering, but for my current role Diageo has provided the training required, both on the job and external courses. I have also had the opportunity to meet and work with some of the best distillers and managers in the whisky industry and glean some of my knowledge from them.

Describe your career in the whisky business.

I started in the whisky business as Brand Home Manager at Dalwhinnie Distillery in 2006. This role was very customer focused, managing the visitor experience and the team responsible for delivering an exceptional experience for our visitor. I then moved on to the production side based at various sites, including Glenlossie and Cardhu. After a short break working in the great Scottish outdoors I returned to Diageo to become Site Operations Manager at Lochnagar

What are your main tasks as a manager?

First and foremost is Safety, to ensure that everyone goes home safely every day. Also maintaining our spirit quality is a key focus on a day to day basis as there are many factors that can impact on this.

What are the biggest challenges of being a distillery manager?

Producing the right spirit for Royal Lochnagar in the given time frames, safely, cost effectively and consistently.

What would be the worst that could go wrong in the production process?

First and foremost someone being injured whilst working or visiting the distillery.

How would you describe the character of Royal Lochnagar single malt?

We produce a light grassy character at the distillery, which is quite unusual for a site that has worm tub condensers, they are usually associated with distilleries that produce heavier characters eg Dalwhinnie.

What are the main features in the process at Royal Lochnagar, contributing to this character?

Our mix of long and short fermentations, the long copper conversation with the stills/worms and running our worms hot are the key factors in producing our grassy character.

What is your favourite expression of Royal Lochnagar and why?

Royal Lochnagar Distillers Edition because it has more spice on the palate, ginger, cinnamon and when you add a dash of water the 12 year old character is there with a hint of dryness and fresh apples.

If it were your decision alone – what new expression of Royal Lochnagar would you like to see released?

Royal Lochnagar is typically bottled as a 12 year old and also as the highly prized 'Select Reserve', there have also been bottlings of 23, 24 and 30 year old Royal Lochnagar Rare Malt. But if I could choose a new expression it would be one that is older or in a different type of cask.

If you had to choose a favourite dram other than Royal Lochnagar, what would that be?

That is difficult but if you really twist my arm I would have to say, when available, Oban 32 year old.

What are the biggest changes you have seen the past 10 years in your profession?

Probably the technology available to us now and also compliance requirements.

Do you see any major changes in the next 10 years to come?

I think the key area, as well as increasing production to meet the emerging markets, will be about continuing to protect the environment and reduce our carbon footprint.

Do you have any special interests or hobbies that you pursue?

I spend a lot of my time hill walking, cycling, skiing and more recently learning to play golf. I also enjoy travelling and experiencing different countries and cultures.

Royal Lochnagar distillery is also used for educational purposes. Please tell me more.

Royal Lochnagar Distillery is the Brand Home of Malt Whisky for Diageo and we host the Malt Advocates Course here for both internal personnel and our business clients. This is an intensive week long course supported by both myself and other industry experts, providing an in depth look at the process and what influences the character of our malts during the different stages of production, also looking at the impact of the cask during maturation.

How was it coming from the marketing side (for example at Dalwhinnie) to the production side here at Lochnagar?

The role of a Brand Home Manager over the last few years has changed, and although the main part is the visitor side of the business, the Brand Home Manager now play a part in supporting the Site Operations Manager and this was how I initially became interested in the operations role, but it was a dilemma as I also enjoy the customer side of the business. Lochnagar with Production and the Malt Advocates course gives me a perfect balance.

Scapa

Owner:
Chivas Brothers
(Pernod Ricard)

Region/district:
Highlands (Orkney)

Founded: 1885

Status: Active

Capacity: 1 500 000 litres

Address: Scapa, St Ola, Kirkwall,
Orkney KW15 1SE

Tel: 01856 876585

website: www.scapamalt.com

History:
1885 – Macfarlane & Townsend founds the distillery with John Townsend at the helm.

1919 – Scapa Distillery Company Ltd takes over.

1934 – Scapa Distillery Company goes into voluntary liquidation and production ceases.

1936 – Production resumes.

1936 – Bloch Brothers Ltd (John and Sir Maurice) takes over.

1954 – Hiram Walker & Sons takes over.

1959 – A Lomond still is installed.

1978 – The distillery is modernized.

1994 – The distillery is mothballed.

1997 – Production takes place a few months each year using staff from Highland Park.

2004 – Extensive refurbishing takes place at a cost of £2.1 million. Scapa 14 years is launched.

2005 – Production ceases in April and phase two of the refurbishment programme starts. Chivas Brothers becomes the new owner.

2006 – Scapa 1992 (14 years) is launched.

2008 – Scapa 16 years is launched.

Scapa 16 year old

GS – The nose offers apricots and peaches, nougat and mixed spices. Pretty, yet profound. Medium-bodied, with caramel and spice notes in the mouth. The finish is medium in length and gingery, with fat, buttery notes emerging at the end.

DR – Sweet baked banana in cream with shortbread on the nose. The taste is a delightful mix of sweet and sour, with sugar and salt sparring but kept apart by green and orange fruit. There's a late sharper note towards lengthy fruit finish.

One may wonder why two distillers (Townsend and Macfarlane) based in Glasgow decided to build a distillery in Orkney. Especially in the 1880s when the islands appeared much more remote than today. One can, however, state that the stunning location, with its marvellous view of the Scapa Bay, can be matched only by a few Scottish distilleries.

The equipment consists of a new semi-lauter mash tun installed in 2004 and eight washbacks. Four of them (installed in 1968) are made of stainless steel, while the old ones (1955) are made of Corten steel. Scapa probably has the longest fermentation time of any distillery in Scotland. All the washbacks are filled and left for up to 160 hours before distillation begins. The wash still is of Lomond type with the rectification plates removed, while the spirit still is of a traditional onion design. Both stills are equipped with purifiers. Distillation takes place from Monday to Wednesday, resulting in a production of about 400,000 litres of alcohol and the entire output is destined for single malts. There are three dunnage and three racked warehouses, but only the latter are in use today.

Scapa malt is not what you would expect from an island malt. There is nothing heavy, nothing pungent and definitely no peat – it is a gentle and fruity dram. Part of the explanation for that is its very long fermentation process. With the exception of a few, new "boutique" distilleries, it is very rare to come across a site where the whole production is destined to become single malt. Oban is one and so is Scapa. With the distillery having been more or less closed between 1994 and 2004, inventory has been an issue for the owners. The Scapa core range at the moment is just the *16 year old*, while limited editions include a *25 year old* from 1980 and a *Vintage 1992*. There is also a *19 year old cask strength* distilled in 1993, sold exclusively at Chivas' visitor centres.

16 years old

Speyburn

Owner:
Inver House Distillers
(Thai Beverages plc)

Region/district:
Speyside

Founded: 1897
Status: Active
Capacity: 2 000 000 litres

Address: Rothes, Aberlour,
Morayshire AB38 7AG

Tel: 01340 831213
website: www.speyburn.com

History:

1897 – Brothers John and Edward Hopkin and their cousin Edward Broughton found the distillery through John Hopkin & Co. They already own Tobermory. The architect is Charles Doig. Building the distillery costs £17,000 and the distillery is transferred to Speyburn-Glenlivet Distillery Company.

1916 – Distillers Company Limited (DCL) acquires John Hopkin & Co. and the distillery.

1930 – Production stops.

1934 – Productions restarts.

1962 – Speyburn is transferred to Scottish Malt Distillers (SMD).

1968 – Drum maltings closes.

1991 – Inver House Distillers buys Speyburn.

1992 – A 10 year old is launched as a replacement for the 12 year old in the Flora & Fauna series.

2001 – Pacific Spirits (Great Oriole Group) buys Inver House for $85 million.

2005 – A 25 year old Solera is released.

2006 – Inver House changes owner when International Beverage Holdings acquires Pacific Spirits UK.

2009 – The un-aged Bradan Orach is introduced for the American market.

2012 – Clan Speyburn is formed.

Speyburn 10 year old

GS – Soft and elegant on the spicy, nutty nose. Smooth in the mouth, with vanilla, spice and more nuts. The finish is medium, spicy and drying.

DR – Sweet malt nose, then one of the sweetest and most easy-drinking of all malts, with the faintest touch of smoke in the mix. Like eating a bag of sugar.

Even though Speyburn sells half a million bottles per year and is the number five single malt brand in USA by volume, not much is spoken about the brand. This is now about to change. The owners have launched a new packaging and a new website and they have also created a whole new community called Clan Speyburn which can be reached on the website. There will also be exclusive offers of single cask bottlings for the members called Clan Casks.

The brand's success in USA can probably be explained by the fact that Inver House had American owners for the first 24 years. Publicker Industries founded the company in 1964 and the connections that were established during these years led to an agreement in 1993 with Barton Brands to distribute Speyburn single malt on the American market. The agreement with Barton expired in 2009 and Speyburn is now sold through a subsidiary of Thai Beverages.

Speyburn distillery is equipped with a stainless steel mash tun which replaced the old cast iron tun in 2008. There are six washbacks of which two were changed to Oregon pine in 2010, while the others are made of larch. Finally, there is one wash still (17,300 litres) and one spirit still (13,200 litres) using stainless steel worm tubs with 104 metre long copper tubes for cooling.

There are three dunnage warehouses with 5,000 casks where the spirit intended for bottling as single malt is maturing. In 1900, Speyburn was the first distillery to abandon floor malting in favour of a new method – drum malting. In the late sixties, the malting closed and ready malt was bought instead, but the drum maltings are still there to see, protected by Historic Scotland.

The core range of Speyburn single malt is the *10 year old* and *Bradan Orach* without age statement. There is also a limited *25 year old* which was released in a new version in 2012. In late 2012 the first of the Clan casks for members was released – a *1975 PX sherry single cask*.

10 years old

Speyside

Owner:
Speyside Distillers Co.

Region/district:
Speyside

Founded: 1976

Status: Active

Capacity: 600 000 litres

Address: Glen Tromie, Kingussie
Inverness-shire PH21 1NS

Tel: 01540 661060

website: www.speysidedistillery.co.uk

History:
1956 – George Christie buys a piece of land at Drumguish near Kingussie.

1957 – George Christie starts a grain distillery near Alloa.

1962 – George Christie (founder of Speyside Distillery Group in the fifties) commissions the drystone dyker Alex Fairlie to build a distillery in Drumguish.

1986 – Scowis assumes ownership.

1987 – The distillery is completed.

1990 – The distillery is on stream in December.

1993 – The first single malt, Drumguish, is launched.

1999 – Speyside 8 years is launched.

2000 – Speyside Distilleries is sold to a group of private investors including Ricky Christie, Ian Jerman and Sir James Ackroyd.

2001 – Speyside 10 years is launched.

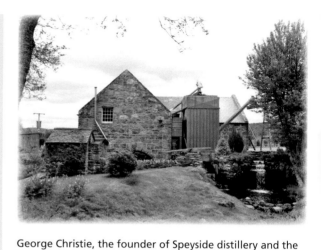

Speyside 12 year old

GS – A nicely-balanced nose of herbs and toasted barley. Medium-bodied, with a suggestion of peat, plus hazelnuts and oak. Toffee and orange notes in the lingering finish.

DR – Rootsy damp straw nose, a sharp and clean barley delivery on the palate with an earthy, peaty undertow, and a willowy, nutty savoury finish.

George Christie, the founder of Speyside distillery and the last whisky baron, passed away last April. He was in his mid-nineties and lived just up the road from the distillery. A former submarine captain, he started buying and selling whisky in the 1950s. At the same time he founded his own grain distillery, North of Scotland, with a production of 13 million litres per year. He sold it to DCL (later Diageo) in the 1980s and they closed it down. By then he had already started the construction of Speyside distillery and he also continued his business as a blender and bottler.

Speyside produces on a small-scale and is set in beautiful surroundings. No wonder then that the production people from BBC chose Speyside distillery to act as Lagganmore distillery in their television series, Monarch of the Glen, from the early 2000. The distillery is equipped with a semi-lauter mash tun, four stainless steel washbacks and one pair of stills. There are no warehouses on site. Instead, the spirit is tankered away to the company´s bonded warehouses in Glasgow. The total production for 2012 will be around 430,000 litres of alcohol and they will also do three weeks of peated production with a malt specification of 50ppm. The owners are also discussing the possibility of installing a small grain still as well, but nothing has yet been decided.

Speyside produces three brands of single malt; *Speyside* with the core range of *12 and 15 year old*, *Drumguish* and the quaint and almost black *Cu Dubh*. Apart from the distillery at Drumguish, there is a diverse range of activities at the company´s base in Rutherglen, Glasgow. Cask warehousing, a bottling plant and a blending operation are all found here. A range of 20 brands of blended whiskies are produced as well as two ranges of single malts from other distilleries – Scott's Selection and Private Cellar. The total number of staff is 80 and exports go to more than 100 countries with the US and the Far East as top markets.

12 years old

Whisky Chronology

continued on page 193

1644 The Scottish parliament instates a new law on Excise Duty to be paid for each pint of aqua vitae that is produced.

1698 Berry Bros. is founded.

1756 Arthur Guinness Son & Co. is established.

1774 A law prohibiting wash stills less than 400 gallons and spirit stills less than 100 gallons is passed.

1784 The Wash Act is introduced to encourage legal distilling in the Highlands.

1805 Seager Evans (producer of gin) is formed.

1814 Matthew Gloag embarks on a career as a whisky merchant in Perth.

1814 The Excise Act states that the smallest size of a Highland still is to be 500 gallons.

1816 The Small Stills Act states that the smallest allowed size of a still is 40 gallons in all of Scotland.

1820 John Walker establishes himself as a grocer and wine and spirits merchant in Kilmarnock.

1823 An Excise Act states that a licence is required to suppress illicit distilling.

1826 Robert Stein invents a patent still for continuous distilling.

1827 George Ballantine becomes established as a grocer and wine merchant in Edinburgh.

1828 J. & A. Mitchell & Co. (Springbank) is founded.

1830 Aenas Coffey patents an improved version of Robert Steins patent still which is named Coffey still.

1830 William Teacher obtains a liquor licence for a shop in Glasgow.

1831 Justerini & Brooks is formed.

1841 James Chivas forms a company in Aberdeen.

1842 William Cadenhead Ltd is formed.

1846 John Dewar is established as a wholesale wine and spirit merchant in Perth.

1853 Andrew Usher & Co. starts to produce blended whisky.

1857 Walter and Alfred Gilbey start their career as wine merchants in London.

1857 Joseph Seagram & Sons is founded.

1857 William and Robert Hill join forces with William Thomson and found Hill Thomson & Co.

1858 James and John Chivas found Chivas Brothers.

1860 Roberston & Baxter is established.

1865 Eight Lowland grain distilleries form Scotch Distillers Association.

1865 The passing of The Blending Act allows for malt and grain whisky being blended.

1869 W. P. Lowrie & Co. is founded.

1870 Greenlees Brothers is established.

1874 The North of Scotland Malt Distillers Association is founded.

1875 William Teacher founds William Teacher & Sons.

1877 Distillers Company Limited (DCL) is founded by six grain distilleries.

1882 James Whyte and Charles Mackay found Whyte & Mackay.

1885 The North British Distillery Co. is formed.

1886 Alexander Walker brings in his sons to the company and founds John Walker & Sons Ltd.

1886 William Grant and Sons is founded.

1887 Highland Distillers is founded.

1888 John Alicius Haig founds Haig & Haig Ltd.

1890 Mackie & Co. is established.

1893 McDonald & Muir is founded.

1895 Gordon & MacPhail is founded.

1895 Arthur Bell & Sons is founded.

1896 Matthew Gloag & Son establish The Grouse.

1898 The Pattison crash.

1906 Buchanan takes over W. P. Lowrie.

1907 Robertson & Baxter buys Haig & Haig.

1914 Scottish Malt Distillers is founded.

1915 Buchanan and Dewars merge into Scotch Whisky Brands.

1915 Immature spirits act requires that whisky must be bonded for two years prior to bottling.

1916 The bonding time is increased to three years.

1917 The Whisky Association, a predecessor to SWA, is formed.

1919 James Barclay and R. A. McKinlay acquire Ballantines.

1919 Scotch Whisky Brands becomes Buchanan & Dewar.

1919 John Haig & Co. and Andrew Usher & Co. join DCL.

1920 Prohibition is introduced in the United States.

1922 Roberston & Baxter is acquired by DCL, Walker and Buchanan-Dewar.

1924 Sir Peter Mackie dies and the company changes name to White Horse Distillers.

1925 The Big Amalgamation – DCL merges with Buchanan-Dewar and Walker.

1925 DCL acquires W. P. Lowrie & Co.

1925 DCL buys Scottish Malt Distillers.

1926 Pot-Still Malt Distillers replaces North of Scotland Malt Distillers Association.

1927 DCL acquires White Horse Distillers.

1928 Distillers Corporation of Canada buys Joseph E. Seagram & Sons.

1933 The Prohibition ends in USA.

1934 Arthur Bell & Sons buys P. Mackenzie & Co.

1935 William Sanderson & Son merges with Booth's Distillers.

1935 Hiram Walker acquires George Ballantine & Son.

1936 Seager Evans buys W. H. Chaplin and the brand Long John.

1936 Lundy & Morrison buys Chivas Bros.

1937 Hiram Walker (Scotland) is formed.

1942 Scotch Whisky Association (SWA) is formed.

1949 Lundie & Morrison sells Chivas Bros to Robert Brown & Co. (subsidiary of Seagrams).

1950 Seagrams buys Strathisla and transfers administration to Chivas Brothers.

1950 Douglas Laing & Co. is founded.

1951 Morrison Bowmore Distillers Ltd is founded.

1952 George & G. J. Smith Ltd and J. & J. Grant form The Glenlivet & Glen Grant Distillers Ltd.

1952 Justerini & Brooks merges with Twiss, Browning & Hallowes and form United Wine Traders.

1956 Inver House is founded.

1956 Seager Evans is acquired by Schenley Industries Inc.

1958 Watney Mann is formed through merger between Watney, Coombe Reid & Co. and Mann, Crossman & Paulin Ltd.

1960 Edrington Holdings is formed.

1960 Whyte & Mackay merges with Mackenzie Brothers and takes over Dalmore Distillery.

1961 Ind Coope, Tetley Walker and Ansells form Ind Coope Tetley Ansell (later to become Allied Breweries).

Springbank

Owner: **Region/district:**
Springbank Distillers   Campbeltown
(J & A Mitchell)

Founded: **Status:**   **Capacity:**
1828   Active (vc)   750 000 litres

Address: Well Close, Campbeltown,
Argyll PA28 6ET

Tel: **website:**
01586 551710   www.springbankdistillers.com

History:
1828 – The Reid family, in-laws of the Mitchells (see below), founds the distillery.

1837 – The Reid family encounters financial difficulties and John and William Mitchell buy the distillery.

1897 – J. & A. Mitchell Co Ltd is founded.

1926 – The depression forces the distillery to close.

1933 – The distillery is back in production.

1960 – Own maltings ceases.

1969 – J. & A. Mitchell buys the independent bottler Cadenhead.

1979 – The distillery closes.

1985 – A 10 year old Longrow is launched.

1987 – Limited production restarts.

1989 – Production restarts.

1992 – Springbank takes up its maltings again.

1997 – First distillation of Hazelburn.

1998 – Springbank 12 years is launched.

1999 – Dha Mhile (7 years), the world's first organic single malt, is released.

2000 – A 10 year old is launched.

2001 – Springbank 1965 'Local barley' (36 years), 741 bottles, is launched.

2002 – Number one in the series Wood Expressions is a 12 year old with five years on Demerara rum casks. Next is a Longrow sherry cask (13 years). A relaunch of the 15 year old replaces the 21 year old.

2004 – J. & A. Mitchell's main owner, Hedley Wright, reopens Glengyle Distillery. Springbank 10 years 100 proof is launched as well as Springbank Wood Expression bourbon, Longrow 14 years old, Springbank 32 years old and Springbank 14 years Port Wood.

On the site of an illicit still run by Archibald Mitchell, Springbank was founded by Archibald's father-in-law in 1828. A few years later, the Mitchell family became the owners of the distillery and the status quo has remained ever since which makes Springbank the oldest distillery in Scotland owned by the same family. The Mitchell family were involved in at least four other distilleries in Campbeltown, all of them now closed except for the resurrected Glengyle. Springbank single malt has for many decades had a solid reputation among blenders as one of the best whiskies on the market but the interest from the consumers is more recent. The company had financial problems during the 1980s and the distillery was closed for most part of the decade. There was a turnaround in the 90s and Springbank's ranking today, as producers of one of the most respected malts, is largely as a result of the good work done by two former distillery managers – John McDougall and Frank McHardy (who still works for the company).

The distillery is equipped with an open cast iron mash tun, six washbacks made of Scandinavian larch, one wash still and two spirit stills. The wash still is unique in Scotland, as it is fired by both an open oil-fire and internal steam coils. Ordinary condensers are used to cool the spirit vapours, except in the first of the two spirit stills, where a worm tub is used. Springbank is unique in Scotland as they malt their whole need of barley using their own floor maltings. Springbank produces three distinctive single malts with different phenol contents in the malted barley. Springbank is distilled two and a half times (12-15ppm), Longrow is distilled twice (50-55 ppm) and Hazelburn is distilled three times and unpeated. Currently around 100,000 litres are produced in a year at Springbank.

The core range of Springbank distillery is *Springbank 10, 15* and *18 years, Springbank 12 year old cask strength* (released in batches) and *Springbank CV*. Longrow is represented by *Longrow* (formerly known as Longrow CV), the *18 year old* and the new *Longrow Red*. The latter (released in September 2012) has been matured for 7 years in refill bourbon and then another 4 years in Australian Cabernet Sauvignon casks. Finally there is *Hazelburn CV, 8* and *12 years old*. Recent limited editions include *Longrow 14 year old Burgundy finish, Springbank Rundlets & Kilderkins* and *Springbank 21 years old*. The last one will be released again in January 2013. The Springbank Society bottling for 2012 was a *14 year old* matured for 7 years in a port cask and the rest of the time in a bourbon cask. Finally, a *Springbank Calvados finish* was released in late 2012.

History (continued):

2005 – Springbank 21 years is released. The first version of Hazelburn (8 years) is released. Longrow Tokaji Wood Expression is launched.

2006 – Longrow 10 years 100 proof, Springbank 25 years, Springbank 9 years Marsala finish, Springbank 11 years Madeira finish and a new Hazelburn 8 year old are released.

2007 – Springbank Vintage 1997 and a 16 year old rum wood are released.

2008 – The distillery closes temporarily. Three new releases of Longrow - CV, 18 year old and 7 year old Gaja Barolo.

2009 – Springbank Madeira 11 year old, Springbank 18 year old, Springbank Vintage 2001 and Hazelburn 12 year old are released.

2010 – Springbank 12 year old cask strength and a 12 year old claret expression together with new editions of the CV and 18 year old are released. Longrow 10 year old cask strength and Hazelburn CV are also new.

2011 – Longrow 18 year old and Hazelburn 8 year old Sauternes wood expression are released.

2012 – New releases include Springbank Rundlets & Kilderkins, Springbank 21 year old and Longrow Red.

Longrow Red   Hazelburn 12 years old   Springbank 21 years old

Springbank 10 year old

GS – Fresh and briny on the nose, with citrus fruit, oak and barley, plus a note of damp earth. Sweet on the palate, with developing brine, nuttiness and vanilla toffee. Long and spicy in the finish, with more salt, coconut oil and drying peat.

DR – Raw vegetables, damp leaves, autumn forest, traces of smoke fire. Wonderful and challenging on the palate with gooseberry, apple, pear, greek yoghurt, oil, smoke and chili. Complex, tingling, savoury delight. Spicy, earthy, savoury and fun in the finale, coating the mouth.

Longrow (NAS)

GS – Initially slightly gummy on the nose, but then brine and fat peat notes develop. Vanilla and malt also emerge. The smoky palate offers lively brine and is quite dry and spicy, with some background vanilla and lots of ginger. The finish is peaty with persistent, oaky ginger.

DR – Slightly vegetal, oily and industrial, with pepper and smoke. Much better on the palate than the nose. Big fishy peaty earthy taste with gooseberry and grape, chili pepper and fresh salad. Rapier sharp in the mouth with big flavours. A long finish, with pepper and peat.

Hazelburn 12 year old

GS – A highly aromatic nose, featuring nutty toffee, sherry, dried fruits and dark chocolate. The palate is rich and spicy, with cocoa, coffee, ginger and sweeter notes of caramel and orange marmalade. Long and spicy in the finish, with more caramel, coffee, chocolate and oak notes.

DR – Rich and fruity nose of nectarine, peach, plums and some nuttiness. On the palate rich plums, red berries, dry sherry and drying tannins, with an intense rich and fruity finish.

Springbank 10 years old   Longrow (former CV)

Strathisla

Owner:
Chivas Brothers
(Pernod Ricard)

Region/district:
Speyside

Founded: 1786
Status: Active (vc)
Capacity: 2 400 000 litres

Address: Seafield Avenue, Keith,
Banffshire AB55 5BS

Tel: 01542 783044
website: www.maltwhiskydistilleries.com

History:

1786 – Alexander Milne and George Taylor found the distillery under the name Milltown, but soon change it to Milton.

1825 – MacDonald Ingram & Co. purchases the distillery.

1830 – William Longmore acquires the distillery.

1870 – The distillery name changes to Strathisla.

1880 – William Longmore retires and hands operations to his son-in-law John Geddes-Brown. William Longmore & Co. is formed.

1890 – The distillery changes name to Milton.

1940 – Jay (George) Pomeroy acquires majority shares in William Longmore & Co. Pomeroy is jailed as a result of dubious business transactions and the distillery goes bankrupt in 1949.

1950 – Chivas Brothers buys the run-down distillery at a compulsory auction for £71,000 and starts restoration.

1951 – The name reverts to Strathisla.

1965 – The number of stills is increased from two to four.

1970 – A heavily peated whisky, Craigduff, is produced but production stops later.

2001 – The Chivas Group is acquired by Pernod Ricard.

Strathisla 12 year old

GS – Rich on the nose, with sherry, stewed fruits, spices and lots of malt. Full-bodied and almost syrupy on the palate. Toffee, honey, nuts, a whiff of peat and a suggestion of oak. The finish is medium in length, slightly smoky and a with a final flash of ginger.

DR – Rich, full and fruity nose with lots of barley, then barley, currants and a touch of oak, peat and pepper, concluding with a complex and intriguing finish.

When you arrive at Strathisla distillery you get the feeling that you have ended up in a model railway landscape with the beautiful buildings, perfectly manicured lawns and the spinning waterwheel. No wonder a lot of people find it the most picturesque distillery in Scotland. It is also the spiritual home of Chivas Regal where Strathisla plays the part of the signature malt. The famous blend is the market leader in Asia and sales have increased by no less than 26% from 2009 to 2011 when it sold almost 60 million bottles. That puts the brand in fourth place on the list of most sold Scotch whiskies and displaces J&B to fifth place.

The distillery is one of the oldest in Scotland and has from time to time operated under the name Milton distillery. Its real time of glory began in 1950 when Seagram´s bought the run-down distillery at a compulsory auction. The previous owner, Jay Pomeroy, had over several years sold large parts of the stock without paying tax and was subsequently jailed. The distillery was renovated and some years later, an excellent visitor centre was built which today attracts nearly 15,000 visitors per year.

Strathisla distillery is equipped with a 5 tonnes traditional cast iron mash tun with a raised copper canopy, ten washbacks made of Oregon pine with a 48 hour fermentation and two pairs of stills. The wash stills is of lantern type with descending lyne arms and the spirit stills have boiling balls and the lyne arms are slightly ascending. The spirit produced at Strathisla is piped to nearby Glen Keith distillery for filling or to be tankered away. A small amount is stored on site in two racked and one dunnage warehouse.

Pernod Ricard has only released two official bottlings of Strathisla, the *12 year old* and a *cask strength* (currently a 14 year old from 1997) which is sold only at the distillery.

12 years old

Meet the Manager

TREVOR BUCKLEY
DISTILLERY OPERATIONS MANAGER
- THE GLENLIVET, ALLT-A-BHAINNE AND BRAEVAL

When did you start working in the whisky business and when did you start at Strathisla?

I have been working in the whisky business since 1987 and became operations manager at Strathisla in 2008.

Had you been working in other lines of business before whisky?

When I left school I wanted to work in the golfing industry and was fortunate to get an apprentice greenkeepers job at my local golf course in Huntly. I attended Elmwood College in Fife which specialises in Greenkeeping. After 3 years of apprenticeship I qualified as a greenkeeper.

What kind of education or training do you have?

I left school with a handful of "O" levels. When I started working in the whisky industry I started in the cooperage painting cask ends and since then I have been trained and worked in all areas of the process including floor maltings.

Describe your career in the whisky business.

I started at Ardmore Distillery in 1987 where I worked in the filling store painting cask ends. I remember thinking to myself at the time "why do they paint those nice wooden barrels". Fortunately, before he let me loose with a paint brush, the head warehouseman did explain that it was only the cask ends that had to be painted. During the next few years I progressed through the various jobs at the distillery from cooperage, warehousing, evaporator plant and then on to the milling, mashing and fermentation processes. In the late eighties I moved to Glendronach as a stillman operating coal fired stills. I also had spells of Brewer at a number of distilleries within Allied. In 2005 I became distillery team leader at Aberlour, Glenallachie and Tormore distilleries until I was promoted to my current role of distillery operations manager in 2007 where I have managed Glentauchers, Strathisla and Tormore distilleries. I am currently managing The Glenlivet, Allt a' Bhainne and Braeval distilleries.

What are your main tasks as a manager?

My main tasks are to ensure that my sites make the quantity of spirit required and at the right quality and to ensure that all standards within our company are met or exceeded where possible, when doing this all legislative requirements must be met at all times to protect our business and the environment.

What are the biggest challenges of being a distillery manager?

Because this is an age old industry, the end result of the process hasn't changed over the years but the technology has, keeping up with the latest technology is very challenging for the future of our distilleries and keeping up with ever tightening energy and environmental targets.

What would be the worst that could go wrong in the production process?

I think fire would be the worst nightmare especially with highly flammable liquids and dust on site.

How would you describe the character of Strathisla single malt?

Very sweet with a citrus note on the nose, baked fruits and slight malt on the palate with a fruity/spicy finish.

What are the main features in the process at Strathisla, contributing to this character?

The conventional mashtun, wooden washbacks and the very short neck stills all contribute to the character of Strathisla along with very carefully chosen wood for the maturation.

What is your favourite expression of Strathisla and why?

The Strathisla 12yo does it for me being smooth, slightly malty, sweet with a hint of sherry.

If it were your decision alone – what new expression of Strathisla would you like to see released?

A double matured 15yo, 1st fill bourbons and 2nd fill Sherry casks.

If you had to choose a favourite dram other than Strathisla, what would that be?

It undoubtedly has to be The Glenlivet 18yo with its concentrated fruity and rich spicy notes. Beautiful!

What are the biggest changes you have seen the past 10 years in your profession?

Increase of whisky sales around the world is always a welcome change for the better. An emphasis on heat recovery and energy efficient plants have resulted in the biggest changes during the last 10 years.

Do you see any major changes in the next 10 years to come?

I think it will be more of the same with legislation getting tighter. With the price of raw materials ever increasing, the main focus will be to continue to run the distilleries as cost effective as possible without having a negative effect on spirit quality, health & safety and the environment.

Do you have any special interests or hobbies that you pursue?

I try and get onto the golf course as much as possible. Spending time with my family and cooking dinner at the weekends then relaxing with a dram of The Glenlivet 18yo.

You recently got the job as distillery manager of Glenlivet. Is it a special feeling to be responsible for such an iconic distillery?

All those years ago on a freezing February morning in 1987 painting cask ends, I never once thought that this is where I would be today. When I was appointed manager of The Glenlivet I felt very privileged to be the manager of a distillery that is testimony to the great George Smith's legacy. Every day at The Glenlivet is a "school day" as there is so much history attached to this truly great distillery.

What are the characteristics of Strathisla single malt that makes it such an important part of the Chivas Regal blend?

With the natural sweetness of a Strathisla single malt this assists in defining the character of the Chivas Regal blend.

Strathmill

Owner: **Region/district:**
Diageo   Speyside

Founded: **Status:**   **Capacity:**
1891   Active   2 300 000 litres

Address: Keith, Banffshire AB55 5DQ

Tel: **website:**
01542 883000   www.malts.com

History:
1891 – The distillery is founded in an old mill from 1823 and is named Glenisla-Glenlivet Distillery.

1892 – The inauguration takes place in June.

1895 – The gin company W. & A. Gilbey buys the distillery for £9,500 and names it Strathmill.

1962 – W. & A. Gilbey merges with United Wine Traders (including Justerini & Brooks) and forms International Distillers & Vintners (IDV).

1968 – The number of stills is increased from two to four and purifiers are added.

1972 – IDV is bought by Watney Mann which later the same year is acquired by Grand Metropolitan.

1993 – Strathmill becomes available as a single malt for the first time since 1909 as a result of a bottling (1980) from Oddbins.

1997 – Guinness and Grand Metropolitan merge and form Diageo.

2001 – The first official bottling is a 12 year old in the Flora & Fauna series.

2010 – A Manager's Choice single cask from 1996 is released.

Strathmill 12 year old

GS – Quite reticent on the nose, with nuts, grass and a hint of ginger. Spicy vanilla and nuts dominate the palate. The finish is drying, with peppery oak.

DR – Butterscotch and summer flowers mixed with lemon flu powder, and some powdery, talc-like notes on the nose, the palate has some apricot and peach fruits before a wave of salt and pepper and a spicy conclusion.

The whisky from Strathmill is one of the key malts for the J&B blend which is Diageo´s second biggest Scotch whisky brand. As recently as 2009, it was also the third biggest Scotch in the world but in 2010 it lost that place to Grant´s. Just one year later it was surpassed by Chivas Regal and so it now holds the fifth place. The reason for the decline is the economic downturn in its main market, Spain. Four years in a row now, exports of bottled blended Scotch to Spain has gone down by a total of 40%. During the same period the sales of J&B has decreased by 20% from 70 million bottles to 57 million. Their slump has been eased slightly thanks to a strong performance in France.
Strathmill is neatly tucked away right next to the River Isla which flows through Keith. The distillery is equipped with a stainless steel semi-lauter mash tun and six stainless steel washbacks with a combination of short (60 hours) and long (120 hours) fermentations. There are two pairs of stills and Strathmill is one of a select few distilleries using purifiers on the spirit stills. This device is mounted between the lyne arm and the condenser and acts as a mini-condenser, allowing the lighter alcohols to travel towards the condenser and forcing the heavier alcohols to go back into the still for another distillation. The result is a lighter and fruitier spirit. In Strathmill´s case both purifiers and condensers are fitted on the outside of the still house to optimize energy savings. One mash (9 tonnes) will fill one washback with 44,000 litres of wort and one washback will fill the two wash stills twice. For 2012 the production has been increased and they are doing 11 mashes per week (still working five days) producing around 2,1 million litres of pure alcohol. The spirit is tankered away to Auchroisk for filling and some of the casks find their way back for storage in two racked and five dunnage warehouses.
The only official bottling was a *12 year old* in the Flora & Fauna series until 2010, when a *single cask* distilled in *1996* was released as part of the Manager's Choice series.

Flora & Fauna 12 years

Whisky Chronology

continued from page 187

continued from page 187

1962 United Wine Traders merges with W. A Gilbey and forms United Distillers & Vintners.

1963 Ind Coope Tetley Ansell changes name to Allied Breweries.

1964 Inver House Distillers becomes a subsidiary to Publicker Industries.

1965 Invergordon Distillers is formed.

1969 Allied Breweries buys Alexander Stewart & Son.

1969 Seager Evans changes name to Long John International.

1970 Highland Distilleries Co. buys Matthew Gloag & Son Ltd.

1970 Hill Thomson merges with Glenlivet & Glen Grant Distilleries and form The Glenlivet Distilleries.

1972 International Distillers & Vintners (IDV) is bought by Watney Mann.

1972 Watney Mann is bought by Grand Metropolitan.

1973 House of Fraser buys Whyte & Mackay.

1974 Lonhro buys Whyte & Mackay.

1975 Pernod Ricard buys Campbell Distillers.

1975 Schenley sells Long John International to Whitbread & Company.

1976 Allied Brewers takes over William Teacher & Sons.

1978 Seagram buys the Glenlivet Distillers Limited.

1978 Allied Breweries buys J. Lyons.

1981 Allied Breweries changes name to Allied-Lyons.

1983 Grand Met buys International Distillers & Vintners (IDV).

1985 Scottish & Newcastle Breweries sells their whisky division to Invergordon Distillers.

1985 Guinness Group buys Bell's for £356 million.

1986 DCL sells A. & A. Crawford to Whyte & Mackay.

1986 Allied Lyons buys 51% of Hiram Walker Gooderham & Worts.

1987 Guinness buys DCL, who merges with Arthur Bell to become United Distillers, for £2,35bn.

1987 Louis Vuitton and Moët Hennessy merge into LVMH.

1988 Andrew Symington and his brother Brian found Signatory Vintage Scotch Whisky.

1987 Allied Lyons buys the remaining 49% of Hiram Walker Gooderham & Worts.

1988 Allied Distillers becomes a new

subsidiary to Allied Lyons and is made up of Ballantine, Long John International, Stewarts of Dundee and William Teacher.

1988 United Distillers launches 'The Classic Malts'.

1988 Management buy-out of Inver House from Publicker Industries.

1989 Lonhro sells Whyte & Mackay to Brent Walker.

1989 Whitbread's wine & spirits division is acquired by Allied Lyons for £545 million.

1989 Management buys out Invergordon Distillers from Hawker Siddely.

1990 Fortune Brands (then called American Brands) buys Whyte & Mackay from Brent Walker for £165 million.

1990 Guinness and LVMH in 12% cross-shareholding.

1991 Allied Lyons buys Long John from Whitbread.

1993 United Distillers sells Benromach to Gordon & MacPhail.

1993 Whyte & Mackay (Fortune Brands) buys Invergordon Distillers for £382 million.

1994 Allied Lyons acquires Pedro Domecq and changes name to Allied Domecq plc.

1995 Blackadder International is founded by Robin Tucek and John Lamond.

1996 Highland Distilleries buys Macallan-Glenlivet plc.

1996 Whyte & Mackay changes name to JBB (Greater Europe).

1997 Guinness and Grand Metropolitan form Diageo. United Distillers and International Distillers & Vintners (IDV), merge and form United Distillers & Vintners (UDV).

1997 Fortune Brands transfers administration of Whyte & Mackay to Jim Beam Brands.

1997 Glenmorangie plc buys Ardbeg distillery for £7 million.

1998 Diageo sells Dewars and Bombay to Bacardi for £1 150 million.

1998 Highland Distilleries changes name to Highland Distillers Ltd.

1999 Edrington Group and William Grant & Sons buy Highland Distillers for £601 million. Grant and Edrington form 1887 Company, owned 70% by Edrington and 30% by Grant.

1999 Gordon & MacPhail introduces their 'Rare Old Series'.

2000 Allied Domecq suggests Diageo

that they jointly acquire Seagram Spirits & Wine, but Diageo declines.

2001 Pernod Ricard and Diageo buy Seagram Spirits & Wine from Vivendi Universal for £5.7bn.

2001 Pacific Spirits, owned by Great Oriole Group, buys Inver House Distillers at a price tag of £56m.

2001 West LB bank and management buy out the Fortune Brands subsidiary JBB (Greater Europe) for £208 million in October. The new company is called Kyndal.

2001 Chivas Brothers and Campbell Distillers form Chivas Brothers.

2001 Murray McDavid buys Bruichladdich from Whyte & Mackay.

2002 Trinidad-based venture capitalists CL Financial buys Burn Stewart Distillers for £50 million.

2003 Kyndal changes name to Whyte & Mackay.

2003 Robert Tchenguiz owns 35% of Whyte & Mackay while West LB holds 21%.

2004 Glenmorangie plc buys Scotch Malt Whisky Society.

2004 Ian Bankier, formerly Burn Stewart Distillers, buys Whisky Shop retail chain for £1,5m.

2004 Moët Hennessy buys Glenmorangie plc for £300m.

2005 Pernod Ricard buys Allied Domecq.

2005 Pernod Ricard sells Bushmills to Diageo.

2006 Pernod Ricard sells Glen Grant distillery to Campari.

2007 United Spirits buys Whyte & Mackay.

2008 Glenmorangie sells Glen Moray distillery to La Martiniquaise, Pernod Ricard sells Glendronach distillery to BenRiach and Glenglassaugh distillery is sold to Sceant Group for £5m.

2010 William Grant & Sons buys the spirit and liqueur part of C&C Group (with i. a. Tullamore Dew and Carolans). Berry Bros sells Cutty Sark to Edrington who, in turn, sells Glenrothes single malt to Berry Bros.

2011 Edrington sells Tamdhu distillery to Ian Macleod Distillers. Tullibardine is sold to Picard Vins & Spiritueux. Beam Inc buys Cooley Distillers

2012 Rémy Cointreau buys Bruichladdich distillery.

Talisker

Owner:
Diageo

Region/district:
Highlands (Skye)

Founded: 1830

Status: Active (vc)

Visitor centre: 2 600 000 litres

Address: Carbost, Isle of Skye,
Inverness-shire IV47 8SR

Tel: 01478 614308 (vc)

website: www.malts.com

History:

1830 – Hugh and Kenneth MacAskill, sons of the local doctor, found the distillery.

1848 – The brothers transfer the lease to North of Scotland Bank and Jack Westland from the bank runs the operations.

1854 – Kenneth MacAskill dies.

1857 – North of Scotland Bank sells the distillery to Donald MacLennan for £500.

1863 – MacLennan experiences difficulties in making operations viable and puts the distillery up for sale.

1865 – MacLennan, still working at the distillery, nominates John Anderson as agent in Glasgow.

1867 – Anderson & Co. from Glasgow takes over.

1879 – John Anderson is imprisoned after having sold non-existing casks of whisky.

1880 – New owners are now Alexander Grigor Allan and Roderick Kemp.

1892 – Kemp sells his share and buys Macallan Distillery instead.

1894 – The Talisker Distillery Ltd is founded.

1895 – Allan dies and Thomas Mackenzie, who has been his partner, takes over.

1898 – Talisker Distillery merges with Dailuaine-Glenlivet Distillers and Imperial Distillers to form Dailuaine-Talisker Distillers Company.

1916 – Thomas Mackenzie dies and the distillery is taken over by a consortium consisting of, among others, John Walker, John Dewar, W. P. Lowrie and Distillers Company Limited (DCL).

Starting with the Talisker 10 year old in the beginning of 2012, the design of labels and cartons have been revamped to better express Talisker´s maritime connection and the rugged beauty of Isle of Skye. This was something that impressed Alfred Barnard already in 1887 when he wrote his famous *The Whisky Distilleries of the United Kingdom.* He is almost lost for words when he writes "It would be difficult to describe this romantic, wild and mountainous island." It is hard not to agree with him and the fact that 55,000 visitors come to the distillery every year speaks for itself. The popularity of the single malt has also increased rapidly in recent years and in 2011 1.4 million bottles were sold.

The malt comes from Glen Ord maltings peated at 18-20 ppm which gives a phenol content of 5-7 ppm in the new make. This means that the whisky definitely has a peated touch but not as much as most Islay malts for example. The distillery is equipped with a stainless steel lauter mash tun with a capacity of 8 tonnes, eight washbacks and five stills – two wash stills and three spirit stills, all of them connected to wooden wormtubs. The wash stills are equipped with a special type of purifiers, using the colder outside air, and have a u-bend in the lyne arm. The purifiers and the odd bend of the lyne arms give more copper contact and increase the reflux during distillation. This gives the spirit a light fruitiness while the use of wormtubs create body and depth.

The fermentation time is quite long (65-75 hours) and the middle cut from the spirit still is collected between 76% and 65% which gives a medium peated spirit. A large part of the phenol compounds occur late in the middle cut and distilleries known for heavily peated malts won´t cut until much later (55-60%). Only a small part of the produce (mostly refill bourbon) is matured on the island while the rest is tankered and taken to the mainland for storage. The distillery is currently running at full capacity.

Talisker's core range consists of 10 *year old, 18 year old,* a *Distiller's Edition* with an Amoroso sherry finish and *Talisker 57° North.* Limited releases of *25* and *30 year old* used to appear in Diageo´s annual Special Releases but will now be available on a regular basis although still limited. In autumn 2012 a *35 year old* from American and European refill casks was launched, the oldest limited release from the distillery.

History (continued):

1928 – The distillery abandons triple distillation.

1930 – Administration of the distillery is transferred to Scottish Malt Distillers (SMD).

1960 – On 22nd November the distillery catches fire and substantial damage occurs.

1962 – The distillery reopens after the fire with five identical copies of the destroyed stills.

1972 – Malting ceases and malt is now purchased from Glen Ord Central Maltings.

1988 – Classic Malts are introduced, Talisker 10 years included. A visitor centre is opened.

1998 – A new stainless steel/copper mash tun and five new worm tubs are installed. Talisker is launched as a Distillers Edition with an amoroso sherry finish.

2004 – Two new bottlings appear, an 18 year old and a 25 year old.

2005 – To celebrate the 175th birthday of the distillery, Talisker 175th Anniversary is released. The third edition of the 25 year old cask strength is released.

2006 – A 30 year old and the fourth edition of the 25 year old are released.

2007 – The second edition of the 30 year old and the fifth edition of the 25 year old are released.

2008 – Talisker 57° North, sixth edition of the 25 year old and third edition of the 30 year old are launched.

2009 – New editions of the 25 and 30 year old are released.

2010 – A 1994 Manager's Choice single cask and a new edition of the 30 year old are released.

2011 – Three limited releases - 25, 30 and 34 year old.

2012 – A limited 35 year old is released.

Talisker 10 year old

GS – Quite dense and smoky on the nose, with smoked fish, bladderwrack, sweet fruit and peat. Full-bodied and peaty in the mouthy; complex, with ginger, ozone, dark chocolate, black pepper and a kick of chilli in the long, smoky tail.

DR – Grilled oily fish in lemon oil, on the nose, dry salt and pepper on the palate, peat and pepper in a tastebud treat of a finish.

57° North   *25 years old
7th edition*   *35 years old*

10 years old   *18 years old*   *Distiller's Edition 1992*

Tamdhu

Owner:
Edrington Group

Region/district:
Speyside

Founded: **Status:** **Capacity:**
1896　　Active　　4 000 000 litres

Address: Knockando, Aberlour,
Morayshire AB38 7RP

Tel: **website:**
01340 872200　　-

History:
1896 – The distillery is founded by Tamdhu
Distillery Company, a consortium of whisky
blenders with William Grant as the main
promoter. Charles Doig is the architect.

1897 – The first casks are filled in July.

1898 – Highland Distillers Company, which has
several of the 1896 consortium members in
managerial positions, buys Tamdhu Distillery
Company.

1911 – The distillery closes.

1913 –The distillery reopens.

1928 – The distillery is mothballed.

1948 – The distillery is in full production again
in July.

1950 – The floor maltings is replaced by
Saladin boxes when the distillery is rebuilt.

1972 – The number of stills is increased from
two to four.

1975 – Two stills augment the previous four.

1976 – Tamdhu 8 years is launched as single
malt.

2005 – An 18 year old and a 25 year old are
released.

2009 – The distillery is motballed.

2011 – The Edrington Group sells the distillery
to Ian Macleod Distillers.

2012 – Production is resumed.

Tamdhu (no age statement)
DR – Something of a rollercoaster ride. Ripe
fruit salad in juice and syrup on the nose,
crystallised barley, fruit flavoured sherbet,
sharp pepper, nuts and peat on the palate and
a spicy finish.

When the Edrington Group announced in November 2009
that Tamdhu distillery was to be mothballed (stop the
production but leave the equipment intact), it came as a
surprise. All the other big companies were gearing up accordingly to meet the increased demand of their blended
whiskies. Considering that Edrington have both Famous
Grouse and Cutty Sark in their portfolio, one would have
thought that they would do the same, but apparently they
relied on the three big ones in the group (Macallan, Glenrothes and Highland Park) to fill the needs. In summer 2011
it was announced that Ian Macleod Distillers had bought
the distillery. In January 2012 they restarted production
but also took a decision not to use the Saladin maltings on
the site. The new owners have a very experienced manager
at Tamdhu, Sandy Coutts, who has held
various positions at the distillery since 1970
(but at times also at Glenrothes).

The distillery is equipped with a 12 tonne
semilauter mash tun, nine Oregon pine
washbacks and three pairs of stills. All the
washbacks are from 1973 and two of them
were replaced in summer 2012. There are
four dunnage and one racked warehouse
on site and the idea is to mature all spirit
destined to be sold as single malt on
site while the rest is tankered away.
Sherry butts will mainly be used for
the single malts while bourbon barrels are reserved for the spirit going
to blends. The plan for 2012 is to
produce 1,9 million litres of alcohol.
It remains to be seen what the new
owners will do in terms of new
bottlings but a re-launch of the brand
is expected early in 2013. Apparently Tamdhu will be positioned as a
premium malt and to do this, Ian Macleod Distillers have brought in Good
Agency who were also involved with
the re-launch of Glengoyne. Edrington rarely made too much of a fuss
with Tamdhu and the official range
only consisted of a *non-aged version*.
In 2005 an *18* and a *25 year old* were
introduced and there has also been a
10 year old.

*Gordon & MacPhail
Tamdhu 8 years old*

Tamnavulin

Owner: Whyte & Mackay (United Spirits)

Region/district: Speyside

Founded: 1966   **Status:** Active   **Capacity:** 4 000 000 litres

Address: Tomnavoulin, Ballindalloch, Banffshire AB3 9JA

Tel: 01807 590285   **website:** -

History:

1966 – Tamnavulin-Glenlivet Distillery Company, a subsidiary of Invergordon Distillers Ltd, founds Tamnavulin.

1993 – Whyte & Mackay buys Invergordon Distillers.

1995 – The distillery closes in May.

1996 – Whyte & Mackay changes name to JBB (Greater Europe).

2000 – Distillation takes place for six weeks.

2001 – Company management buy out operations for £208 million and rename the company Kyndal.

2003 – Kyndal changes name to Whyte & Mackay.

2007 – United Spirits buys Whyte & Mackay. Tamnavulin is opened again in July after having been mothballed for 12 years.

Tamnavulin 12 year old

GS – Delicate and floral on the nose, with light malt and fruit gums. Light to medium bodied, fresh, malty and spicy on the palate, with a whiff of background smoke. The finish is medium in length, with lingering spice, smoke, and notes of caramel.

DR – Wet hay, celery and cucumber on the nose and a delightful exotic fruit and citrus taste and a satisfying and pleasant finish.

Tamnavulin distillery was founded by Invergordon Distillers upon initiative from one of the most influential persons in the Scotch whisky business – Dr. Chris Greig. He had just joined the company (in 1966) and contributed to both the expansion and the modernisation of the entire industry during the following 30 years. He led the management buyout of the company in 1988 and was the managing director until Whyte & Mackay took over in 1994. During his tenure the production at Invergordon grain distillery was expanded and they also bought Tullibardine, Jura and Bruichladdich distilleries. Dr. Greig passed away in February 2012 at the age of 77.

Shortly after Dr. Greig had left the company in 1994, Tamnavulin was mothballed and remained closed for 12 years with the exception of 2000 when it was temporarily re-opened and 400,000 litres were produced. The distillery is now producing at more or less full capacity doing 21 mashes per week during 2012, accounting for 3,9 million litres. A heavily peated whisky (55ppm) has also been pro-duced during part of the year since 2010. The distillery is equipped with a full lauter mash tun with 10,5 tonnes capacity, eight washbacks (four of them made of stainless steel and the rest of Corten steel) with a maturation time of 48 hours and three pairs of stills. Two racked warehouses (10 casks high) on site have a capacity of 34,250 casks with the oldest ones dating back to 1967, but several of the casks are from other distilleries. Two hundred casks are filled every week on site, while the rest of the production is tankered to Invergordon for filling.

Almost the whole production goes to blended whiskies and the only standard release of Tamnavulin, for quite some time now, has been a *12 year old*. A number of aged Stillman's Dram have also been launched, the most recent being a *30 year old*.

12 years old

Teaninich

Owner: Diageo

Region/district: Northern Highlands

Founded: 1817   **Status:** Active   **Capacity:** 4 400 000 litres

Address: Alness, Ross-shire IV17 0XB

Tel: 01349 885001   **website:** www.malts.com

History:

1817 – Captain Hugh Monro, owner of the estate Teaninich, founds the distillery.

1831 – Captain Munro sells the estate to his younger brother John.

1850 – John Munro, who spends most of his time in India, leases Teaninich to the infamous Robert Pattison from Leith.

1869 – John McGilchrist Ross takes over the licence.

1895 – Munro & Cameron takes over the licence.

1898 – Munro & Cameron buys the distillery.

1904 – Robert Innes Cameron becomes sole owner of Teaninich.

1932 – Robert Innes Cameron dies.

1933 – The estate of Robert Innes Cameron sells the distillery to Distillers Company Limited.

1970 – A new distillation unit with six stills is commissioned and becomes known as the A side.

1975 – A dark grains plant is built.

1984 – The B side of the distillery is mothballed.

1985 – The A side is also mothballed.

1991 – The A side is in production again.

1992 – United Distillers launches a 10 year old Teaninich in the Flora & Fauna series.

1999 – The B side is decommissioned.

2000 – A mash filter is installed.

2009 – Teaninich 1996, a single cask in the new Manager´s Choice range is released.

Teaninich 10 year old

GS – The nose is initially fresh and grassy, quite light, with vanilla and hints of tinned pineapple. Mediumbodied, smooth, slightly oily, with cereal and spice in the mouth. Nutty and slowly drying in the finish, with pepper and a suggestion of cocoa powder notes.

DR – All about the barley this one, with clean, sweet ginger barley on the nose, and a clean and crealy palate with some orange and other citrus notes. Pleasant, clean and impressive with a wave of spices late on.

Of the many distilleries which once operated in the vast area north of Inverness, few survived into the 20th century. Not counting the ones that are still active, it was only six that were still producing after 1900 – Ben Morven (closed in 1911) situated up north in Caithness, Brora (1983) next to Clynelish and Pollo (1903), Glenskiach (1926) and the two Ben Wyvis sites (1926 and 1976), all four in the Alness area close to Dalmore and Teaninich. The last mentioned is the second oldest of the surviving distilleries (Balblair was founded 27 years earlier) and at one time, back in the 1970s, it was one of the largest distilleries in Scotland with a capacity of 6 million litres.

Unlike Dalmore, the second malt distillery in Alness, Teaninich cannot boast with a splendid location at the sea. On the contrary, it lies in the rather unromantic Teaninich Industrial Estate just south of the village. Instead, the distillery is exciting for other reasons. Two elements in the production process of Teaninich differ from that of all other Scottish distilleries. The malt is ground into a very fine flour without husks in an Asnong hammer mill. Once the grist has been mixed with water, the mash passes through a Meura 2001 mash filter and the wort is collected. Water is added for a second time in the filter and a second run of mash is obtained. The procedure is repeated three times until a washback is filled. Besides the mash filter the distillery is equipped with 10 washbacks, eight made of larch and two of stainless steel, and six stills. The fermentation time in the washbacks is 75 hours. There are no warehouses on site; instead 4-5 tankers leave the distillery each week for filling elsewhere. Twenty mashes are done per week, amounting to 4,4 million litres which is more or less its maximum capacity. Teaninich is mainly produced to be a component of Johnnie Walker blended whiskies. The only official bottling used to be a *10 year old* in the Flora & Fauna series until autumn of 2009, when a Teaninich 1996 single cask was released in the new range Manager´s Choice.

Flora & Fauna 10 years old

Tobermory

Owner: **Region/district:**
Burn Stewart Distillers   Highland (Mull)
(C L Financial)

Founded: **Status:**   **Capacity:**
1798   Active (vc)   1 000 000 litres

Address: Tobermory, Isle of Mull,
Argyllshire PA75 6NR

Tel: **website:**
01688 302647   www.burnstewartdistillers.com

History:
1798 – John Sinclair founds the distillery.

1837 – The distillery closes.

1878 – The distillery reopens.

1890 – John Hopkins & Company buys the distillery.

1916 – Distillers Company Limited (DCL) takes over John Hopkins & Company.

1930 – The distillery closes.

1972 – A shipping company in Liverpool and the sherrymaker Domecq buy the buildings and embark on refurbishment. When work is completed it is named Ledaig Distillery Ltd.

1975 – Ledaig Distillery Ltd files for bankruptcy and the distillery closes again.

1979 – The estate agent Kirkleavington Property buys the distillery, forms a new company, Tobermory Distillers Ltd and starts production.

1982 – No production. Some of the buildings are converted into flats and some are rented to a dairy company for cheese storage.

1989 – Production resumes.

1993 – Burn Stewart Distillers buys Tobermory for £600,000 and pays an additional £200,000 for the whisky supply.

2002 – Trinidad-based venture capitalists CL Financial buys Burn Stewart Distillers for £50m.

2005 – A 32 year old from 1972 is launched.

2007 – A Ledaig 10 year old is released.

2008 – A limited edition Tobermory 15 year old is released.

Tobermory 10 year old
GS – Fresh and nutty on the nose, with citrus fruit and brittle toffee. A whiff of peat. Medium-bodied, quite dry on the palate with delicate peat, malt and nuts. The finish is medium to long, with a hint of mint and a slight citric tang.

DR – Barley and crystal ginger on the nose, but the palate carries this, with a nice oily mouth feel, and creamed fruits giving way to a sharper spicier conclusion.

Ledaig 10 year old
GS – The nose is profoundly peaty, sweet and full, with notes of butter and smoked fish. Bold, yet sweet on the palate, with iodine, soft peat and heather. Developing spices. The finish is medium to long, with pepper, ginger, liquorice and peat.

DR – Peat and smoke on the nose, more fruity and malty on the palate but with a definite tarry heart, and then gristly smoke in the finish.

Even if the Isle of Mull has been inhabited since 5,000 BC, the main town, Tobermory, wasn't founded until 1788. It was actually created by British Fisheries Society in an attempt to attract the people working on the land to become fishermen. It never turned out the way they planned, instead during some years kelp was harvested for the use of manufacturing soap and glass. For many years now, tourism (not least ecotourism due to the island's amazing wildlife) has been the main source of income.

The distillery was built ten years after the town was founded which makes it one of the oldest distilleries in Scotland. It has alternatingly been called Tobermory and Ledaig and single malt is released under both names with Ledaig being reserved for the peated versions with a phenol content of 30-40ppm. Peat was used in the old days but was re-introduced in 1996 when Burn Stewart's Master Blender, Ian Macmillan, decided to recreate the old style of Tobermory single malt.

The distillery is equipped with a traditional cast iron mash tun, four wooden washbacks and two pairs of stills with unusual S-shaped lyne arms to increase the reflux. Storage space is small and most produce is sent to Deanston distillery for maturation. During 2012 there will be five to six mashes per week resulting in almost 700,000 litres of alcohol. There is a 50/50 split in total production between peated Ledaig and unpeated Tobermory. Mashing and fermentation of Ledaig is similar to Tobermory's, but the spirit run has a lower cut-off point in order to collect the peaty flavours.

The core range from Tobermory distillery is *10* and *15 year old Tobermory* and *10 year old Ledaig*. Previously there have been plenty of limited releases of Ledaig and also a *32 year old Tobermory* from 2005. The release of a *40 year old Ledaig* has already been announced for early 2013 and there have also been rumours about a new 15 year old.

10 years old

Tomatin

Owner:
Tomatin Distillery Co
(Takara Shuzo Co. Ltd., Kokubu & Co., The
Marubeni Corporation)

Region/district:
Highland

Founded: 1897
Status: Active (vc)
Capacity: 5 000 000 litres

Address: Tomatin, Inverness-shire IV13 7YT

Tel: 01463 248144 (vc)
website: www.tomatin.com

History:
1897 – The Inverness businessmen behind Tomatin Spey Distillery Company found Tomatin.

1906 – Production ceases.

1909 – Production resumes through Tomatin Distillers Co. Ltd.

1956 – Stills are increased from two to four.

1958 – Another two stills are added.

1961 – The six stills are increased to ten.

1964 – One more still is installed.

1974 – The stills now total 23 and the maltings closes.

1985 – The distillery company goes into liquidation.

1986 – Two long-time customers, Takara Shuzo Co. and Okara & Co., buy Tomatin through Tomatin Distillery Co. Tomatin thus becomes the first distillery to be acquired by Japanese interests.

1997 – Tomatin Distillery Co buys J. W. Hardie and the brand Antiquary.

1998 – Okura & Co, owners of 20% of Tomatin Distillery, is liquidated and Marubeni buys out part of their shareholding.

2004 – Tomatin 12 years is launched.

2005 – A 25 year old and a 1973 Vintage are released.

2006 – An 18 year old and a 1962 Vintage are launched.

2008 – A 30 and a 40 year old as well as several vintages from 1975 and 1995 are released.

2009 – A 15 year old, a 21 year old and four single casks (1973, 1982, 1997 and 1999) are released.

2010 – The first peated release - a 4 year old exclusive for Japan.

2011 – A 30 year old and Tomatin Decades are released.

Tomatin 12 year old

GS – Barley, spice, buttery oak and a floral note on the nose. Sweet and medium-bodied, with toffee apples, spice and herbs in the mouth. Medium-length in the finish, with sweet fruitiness.

DR – Strawberry cream and raspberry ripple ice cream and pecan on the nose, delicate zesty barley on the palate, with a sweet citrus and powdery spice mix contributing to a very welcoming finish. More-ish.

The owners of Tomatin distillery has set out a course that will lead to reduced sales of bulk whisky to other companies and instead invest in their own brands – Tomatin single malt and the two blends The Antiquary and Talisman. In order to ease the transformation they changed bank during spring 2012 to HSBC which, given its global presence, could make the company's entry into emerging markets like China, India and Brazil easier. They have already come a long way establishing the single malt in their main markets (USA, Germany, France, Japan and Sweden) and sales increased in 2011 by 36% to 280,000 bottles.

For a brief period in the 1970s, Tomatin was the largest distillery in Scotland. Today the equipment consists of one 8 tonne stainless steel mash tun, 12 stainless steel washbacks with a fermentation time from 57 to 110 hours and six pairs of stills (only four of the spirit stills are used). There is another mash tun in place with the side taken out which allows the visitors to see inside, both above and below the plates. During 2012 they will produce 1,8 million litres of alcohol of which a smaller part will be peated and this year slightly higher than before (around 30ppm).

There are 12 racked and two dunnage warehouses (where whisky destined to be bottled as single malts are maturing) holding 170,000 casks. The distillery also has a cooperage with two coopers working.

In 2012 the distillery's visitor centre was refurbished at a cost of £150,000 and the owners hope to attract 20,000 visitors during the year.

The core range of single malts consists of 12, 15, 18 and 30 year old. *Tomatin Decades*, a limited edition, was released in 2011 to celebrate Douglas Campbell's 50th year at Tomatin and the whisky contains single malt from each decade that Douglas has worked at the distillery. In spring 2012 came another limited bottling – a *15 year old* with a maturation in a combination of bourbon and Tempranillo wines casks and bottled at 52%.

12 years old

Tomintoul

Owner: **Region/district:**
Angus Dundee Distillers   Speyside

Founded: **Status:**   **Capacity:**
1964   Active   3 300 000 litres

Address: Ballindalloch, Banffshire AB37 9AQ

Tel: **website:**
01807 590274   www.tomintouldistillery.co.uk

History:

1964 –The distillery is founded by Tomintoul Distillery Ltd, which is owned by Hay & MacLeod & Co. and W. & S. Strong & Co.

1965 – On stream in July.

1973 – Scottish & Universal Investment Trust, owned by the Fraser family, buys the distillery. It buys Whyte & Mackay the same year and transfers Tomintoul to that company.

1974 – The two stills are increased to four and Tomintoul 12 years is launched.

1978 – Lonhro buys Scottish & Universal Investment Trust.

1989 – Lonhro sells Whyte & Mackay to Brent Walker.

1990 – American Brands buys Whyte & Mackay.

1996 – Whyte & Mackay changes name to JBB (Greater Europe).

2000 – Angus Dundee plc buys Tomintoul.

2002 – Tomintoul 10 year is launched.

2003 – Tomintoul 16 years is launched.

2004 – Tomintoul 27 years is launched.

2005 – A young, peated version called Old Ballantruan is launched.

2008 – 1976 Vintage and Peaty Tang are released.

2009 – A 14 year old and a 33 year old are released.

2010 – A 12 year old Port wood finish is released.

2011 – A 21 year old, a 10 year old Ballantruan and Vintage 1966 are released.

2012 – Old Ballantruan 10 years old is released.

Tomintoul 10 year old

GS – A light, fresh and fruity nose, with ripe peaches and pineapple cheesecake, delicate spice and background malt. Medium-bodied, fruity and fudgy on the palate. The finish offers wine gums, mild, gently spiced oak, malt and a suggestion of smoke.

DR – Toffee and fruit on the nose then an easy, pleasant rounded and sweet barley taste before a gently fading finish.

Today, Tomintoul distillery is operated by Angus Dundee Distillers but, at one time in the1980s, it was owned by one of the biggest and most diverse conglomerates in the UK at the time – Lonhro. Their business operations included such diverse fields as mining, agriculture, newspaper publishing, hotels, engineering and wine and spirits.

Tomintoul may not be the prettiest distillery in Scotland but it lies in beautiful surroundings a few miles southeast of Glenlivet. The owners, Angus Dundee Distillers, is one of Scotland´s biggest exporters of whisky with a huge range of blended whisky. In 2003 they built their own blend centre at Tomintoul with 14 whisky storage vats, in order to handle the large production. Three of them (100,000 litre each) were built as late as 2012. Angus Dundee also bought a plant for warehousing in Coatbridge from Dewar´s in 2011 and, by the end of that year, they had installed a new bottling line there as well. Prior to that all bottlings were done by third parties.

Tomintoul distillery is equipped with a 11.6 tonnes semi lauter mash tun, six washbacks, all made of stainless steel and with a fermentation time of 54 hours, and two pairs of stills. There are currently 15 mashes per week, which means that capacity is used to its maximum, and the six racked warehouses have a storage capacity of 116,000 casks. The malt used for mashing is lightly peated, but for three weeks this year, heavily peated (55 ppm) malt will be used for the peated range.

The owners have invested heavily in recent years to establish Tomintoul as a single malt. The core range of Tomintoul consists of *10, 14, 16* and *21 years old*. The peaty side of Tomintoul is represented by *Old Ballantruan, Peaty Tang* (a vatting of 4-5 year old peated Tomintoul and 8 year old unpeated Tomintoul) and the latest addition, *Old Ballantruan 10 years* old, launched in May 2012. Older, limited editions have included a *12 year old portwood finish*, the *1976 Vintage*, a *33 year old* and a *12 year old Oloroso finish*.

16 years old

Tormore

Owner:
Chivas Brothers
(Pernod Ricard)

Region/district:
Speyside

Founded: **Status:** **Capacity:**
1958 Active 4 900 000 litres

Address: Tormore, Advie, Grantown-on-Spey, Morayshire PH26 3LR

Tel: **website:**
01807 510244 -

History:
1958 – Schenley International, owners of Long John, founds the distillery.

1960 – The distillery is ready for production.

1972 – The number of stills is increased from four to eight.

1975 – Schenley sells Long John and its distilleries (including Tormore) to Whitbread.

1989 – Allied Lyons (to become Allied Domecq) buys the spirits division of Whitbread.

1991 – Allied Distillers introduce Caledonian Malts where Miltonduff, Glendronach and Laphroaig are represented besides Tormore. Tormore is later replaced by Scapa.

2004 – Tormore 12 year old is launched as an official bottling.

2005 – Chivas Brothers (Pernod Ricard) becomes new owners through the acquisition of Allied Domecq.

2012 – Production capacity is increased by 20%.

Tormore 12 year old
GS – Caramel on the nose, with hints of lemon and mint, mildly spicy, gentle and enticing. Good weight of body, and a creamy, honeyed mouth feel. Fudge and mixed spices, notably ginger, dry in the increasingly complex finish.
DR – A perfumey and delicate smell on the nose and soft but pleasant palate with macaroni cake and toasted almond in the mix, and a soft fading finish.

From the outside, Tormore is without a shadow of a doubt, the oddest-looking distillery in Scotland. When it was built in the 1950s it was decided by the owners that it should become a showpiece. The famous architect, Sir Albert Richardson, was called in and the result is magnificent – from the green copper roofs to the elegant, barred windows. You can enjoy it from the A95 in the middle of Speyside but, unfortunately, they do not accept visitors. The bushes in front of the buildings are cut in various shapes, i. a. stills, and a beautiful path leads up to the water source on the back of the distillery.

Tormore was closed from November 2011 to January 2012 for an upgrade of the distillery. Three more washbacks were installed in a separate building (with a clock tower at the top) and this means that the production capacity has increased by 20% to almost 5 million litres of alcohol. The beautiful still room was also refurbished and all stills now have external heaters instead of steam coils inside the stills, thus reducing the energy needed by 15%. The equipment consists of one stainless steel full lauter mash tun, 11 stainless steel washbacks and four pairs of stills.

To achieve the light character of the whisky which characterises Tormore, all stills are equipped with copper purifiers which lead the spirit vapours back into the stills for another distillation before condensing. Clear worts and slow distillation also add to make a fruity and clear spirit.

The spirit is tankered away to Keith Bonds or another Chivas Bros facility for filling in ex-bourbon casks. Part of it returns to the distillery for maturation in a combination of six palletised and racked warehouses.

Nearly everything that is produced at Tormore goes into a variety of blended Scotch and there is only one official bottling, a *12 year old* which was introduced in 2004/5.

12 years old

Tullibardine

Owner:
Picard Vins & Spiritueux

Region/district:
Highlands

Founded: 1949 **Status:** Active (vc) **Capacity:** 2 700 000 litres

Address: Blackford, Perthshire PH4 1QG

Tel: 01764 682252 **website:** www.tullibardine.com

History:
1949 – The architect William Delmé-Evans founds the distillery.

1953 – The distillery is sold to Brodie Hepburn.

1971 – Invergordon Distillers buys Brodie Hepburn Ltd.

1973 – The number of stills increases to four.

1993 – Whyte & Mackay (owned by Fortune Brands) buys Invergordon Distillers.

1994 – Tullibardine is mothballed.

1996 – Whyte & Mackay changes name to JBB (Greater Europe).

2001 – JBB (Greater Europe) is bought out from Fortune Brands by management and changes name to Kyndal (Whyte & Mackay from 2003).

2003 – A consortium buys Tullibardine for £1.1 million. The distillery is in production again by December. The first official bottling from the new owner is a 10 year old from 1993.

2004 – Three new vintage malts are launched.

2005 – Three wood finishes from 1993, Port, Moscatel and Marsala, are launched together with a 1986 John Black selection.

2006 – Vintage 1966, Sherry Wood 1993 and a new John Black selection are launched.

2007 – Five different wood finishes and a couple of single cask vintages are released.

2008 – A Vintage 1968 40 year old is released.

2009 – Aged Oak is released.

2011 – Three vintages (1962, 1964 and 1976) and a wood finish are released.

Tullibardine Aged Oak

GS – The nose exhibits barley, light citrus fruits, pear drops, marzipan and cocoa. Oily in the mouth, slightly earthy, with Brazil nuts and developing vanilla and lemon on the palate. The finish is drying and slightly woody, with lingering spices.

DR – Syrupy fruit and honey-filled lemon lozenges on the nose, a light and creamy ginger barley core on the palate, with some wood. Oak and fruit dominate a medium finish.

For the past couple of years there have been rumours that Tullibardine distillery was up for sale. In November 2011 those rumours became true when the family-owned French wine and spirits group, Picard Vins & Spiritueux, based in Burgundy, bought the company for an undisclosed amount. Picard had purchased whiskey during three years from Tullibardine but wished to obtain a stronger position within the Scotch whisky segment. Picard started as a wine dealer in 1951 but it wasn't until the 1990s that the business was expanded with spirits. Four years ago they purchased the Highland Queen brand, a three year old blend, from Glenmorangie and today the company has over 400 employees. Tullibardine distillery is situated in the village of Blackford on the A9 between Perth and Stirling, with a large commercial outlet next door. Together they attract no less than 130,000 visitors every year. The equipment consists of a stainless steel semi-lauter mash tun, nine stainless steel washbacks and two pairs of stills. In 2012 the owners expect to run at full capacity, which means 24 mashes per week resulting in 2,7 million litres of alcohol in the year. Around 70% of the production is tankered away while 30% is filled on site, some of it to be matured in the one racked warehouse. There used to be more warehouses but they have all become part of the adjacent shopping centre.

A clear wort, wide stills with a lot of copper contact and slightly ascending lyne arms giving plenty of reflux, contribute to the light and delicate character of Tullibardine single malt. Since 2011 all single malts (except single casks) are bottled at 46% and un-chillfiltered.

The core range is *Aged Oak* (a blend of whiskies from 2004 and 2005) and vintages from 1988 and 1993. There are also five different *cask finishes (sherry, port, rum, banyuls* and *sauternes)*. The cask finishes are all non-aged. Limited releases from 2011 include *1962, 1964* and *1976 vintages*, together with a *1992 wood finish* from *Chateau Lafite* casks. The oldest whisky in the warehouse is a quarter cask from 1952.

Aged Oak

Meet the Manager

JOHN BLACK
DISTILLERY MANAGER, TULLIBARDINE DISTILLERY

When did you start working in the whisky business and when did you start at Tullibardine?

I started in the whisky business at Cardhu distillery in 1958 and came to Tullibardine in 2003.

Had you been working in other lines of business before whisky?

No, started when I left school.

What kind of education or training do you have?

I have been very fortunate having worked in a malt barn, a cooperage and all distilling processes.

Describe your career in the whisky business.

I was born into it, quite literally! I was born in a cottage in the grounds of Cardow (Cardhu) Distillery in Speyside. My dad worked there all his life and I grew up playing around the old whisky stills, and giving the Distillery Manager a hard time. I officially started my long career in the industry at Cardhu in 1958, working in the malt barns, cooperage and as a Stillman or Mashman over a 10 year period. I then moved onto various other distilleries between 1969 and 1985 namely Glenburgie, Miltonduff, Ardbeg, Auchentoshan, Glenburgie, Glencadam and Balblair in various distilling roles. My first Distillery Manager post was at Pulteney in 1986 where I stayed until 1990. From there I moved to Imperial, Tormore, and Ardmore and then returned to Miltonduff, Glenburgie then onto Scapa which saw me through the next decade. In 2000 I decided to change direction and organised whisky tours and hosted nosings and tastings. In 2003, finally, I became the manager at Tullibardine.

What are your main tasks as a manager?

My main areas of responsibility are overseeing the production process, selecting good quality casks to use for filling, managing the maturing spirit in the bond.

What are the biggest challenges of being a distillery manager?

The main challenges are making sure the quality of the malted malt and yeast being used are the best and that there is sufficient, good quality water. Also that the operators are doing their jobs properly and above all complying with HMRC, SEPA and Scottish Water.

What would be the worst that could go wrong in the production process?

The worst thing that can happen is if there is a problem with the equipment or human error that would result in product loss.

How would you describe the character of Tullibardine single malt?

Tullibardine is a very easy drinking malt with a lovely sweet, rich and fruity palate. A mellow whisky!

What are the main features in the process at Tullibardine, contributing to this character?

The type of malted barley and yeast which we use plays a huge part in the flavour as well as distilling control and cask selection.

What is your favourite expression of Tullibardine and why?

My favourite Tullibardine expression has to be the 1988 which is an excellent blend of sherry and bourbon casks which creates a fruity, well balanced whisky.

If it were your decision alone – what new expression of Tullibardine would you like to see released?

If I had sole decision on a Tullibardine new expression as a new product I would go for a 20yo similar to the current 1988.

If you had to choose a favourite dram other than Tullibardine, what would that be?

I would have to opt for something from Cardhu, as this was the very first whisky I ever tasted.

What are the biggest changes you have seen the past 10 years in your profession?

During my career I have had to deal with many changes. In particular the introduction of the computer and other new technologies in the distilleries. Many distilleries are just more or less production plants without their own malting and warehouses. I have noticed big changes in the industry over the past decade, especially the acquisition by the French of maltings, malt and grain distilleries plus cooperages.

Do you see any major changes in the next 10 years to come?

I foresee the necessity over the next decade for higher volumes of production to meet world demand for Scotch whisky.

Do you have any special interests or hobbies that you pursue?

In 1993 I purchased a 1973 Volkswagen Beetle, which I have been restoring for a number of years as time allows me. When the restoration is complete it will be known as "The Whisky Bug". Also, I love to collect anything whisky orientated – memorabilia, books, whisky etc, plus gardening, golfing and socialising. I think I need more hours in the day!

What made you decide to start working at Tullibardine even though you had decided to take an early retirement?

In 2003 Douglas Ross, one of the Directors of a consortium that had recently bought the mothballed distillery, called me and asked me whether I was interested in a job at Tullibardine. They were looking for experienced people in production and I agreed to help them out independently. It was always my intention to stay for a short time then return to what I was doing before, and here I am almost a decade later!

Tullibardine single malt has mostly been about vintages rather than a specific age. Why is that?

People often ask that question and it was decided to do this as a point of difference from the previous Tullibardine. It has proved popular with people who have special birthdays, particular anniversaries or to commemorate the birth of a child.

The really new ones!

Ailsa Bay

Owner:		Region/district:
William Grant & Sons		Lowlands
Founded:	**Status:**	**Capacity:**
2007	Active	6 250 000 litres
Address:		**Tel:**
Girvan, Ayrshire KA26 9PT		01465 713091

Commisioned in September 2007, it only took nine months to build this distillery on the same site as Girvan Distillery near Ayr on Scotland´s west coast. It is equipped with a 12.5 tonne full lauter mash tun and 12 washbacks made of stainless steel. Each washback will hold 50,000 litres and fermentation time is between 72 and 78 hours. There are eight stills, made according to the same standards as Balvenie's, with one pair having stainless steel condensers instead of copper. That way, they have the possibility of making batches of a more sulphury spirit if desired. A unique feature is the octangular spirit safe which sits between the two rows of stills. Each side corresponds to one specific still. Another feature is the preheater for the wash. By using this technique at Ailsa Bay, the wash enters the still preheated at 60° C. To increase efficiency and to get more alcohol, high

gravity distillation is used. The wash stills are heated using external heat exchangers but they also have interior steam coils. The spirit stills are heated by steam coils. The distillery is currently working at full capacity which means 25 mashes per week and 6.25 million litres of alcohol in the year. Four different types of spirit are produced; one lighter and sweeter, one heavier and two peated with the peatiest having a malt specification of 50ppm. A majority of the casks (60-70%) used for maturation, are refill bourbon casks and the rest is made up of first fill bourbon and sherry casks.

Abhainn Dearg

Owner:		Region/district:
Mark Tayburn		Islands (Isle of Lewis)
Founded:	**Status:**	**Capacity:**
2008	Active	c 20 000 litres
Address:		
Carnish, Isle of Lewis, Outer Hebrides HS2 9EX		
Tel:	**website:**	
01851 672429	www.abhainndearg.co.uk	

When Kilchoman Distillery opened on Islay in 2005 it became the westernmost distillery in Scotland. This did not last for long though, three years later, in September 2008, spirit flowed from a newly constructed distillery in Uig on the island of Lewis in the Outer Hebrides. The Gaelic name of this distillery is Abhainn Dearg which means Red River, and the founder and owner is Mark "Marko" Tay-burn who was born and raised on the island. Very little was known about Abhain Dearg until it was suddenly ready and producing.

Part of the distillery was converted from an old fish farm while some of the buildings are new. There are two 500 kg mash tuns made of stain-less steel and two 7,500 litre washbacks made of Douglas fir with a fermentation time of 4 days. The two stills are modelled after an old, illicit still which is now on display at the distillery. The wash still has a capacity of 2,112 litres and the spirit still 2,057 litres. Both have very long necks and steeply

descending lye pipes leading out into two wooden worm tubs. To start with Marko is using ex-bourbon barrels for maturation but is planning for ex-sherry butts as well. Some 50 tonnes of malted barley is imported while 5 tonnes is grown locally and slightly peated. This year over ten acres of the Golden Promise variety were planted. In 2010, 10,000 litres of spirit was distilled.

The first limited release, in October 2011, was a 3 year old unpeated whisky and beginning of 2012 a cask strength version (58%) was released.

Roseisle

Owner:	Region/district:	
Diageo	Highlands	
Founded:	**Status:**	**Capacity:**
2009	Active	12 500 000 litres
Address:		**Tel:**
Roseisle, Morayshire IV30 5YP		01343 832100

The planning for a new mega distillery at Roseisle, a few miles west of Elgin, commenced in early 2006, and in October 2007 it was approved by Moray Council. The first test run from one pair of stills was in February 2009 and from August that year it was more or less in full production. The distillery is located on the same site as the already existing Roseisle maltings.

Due to the large capacity, the distillery has three malt bins each holding 115 tonnes of malted barley. The distillery is equipped with two stainless steel mash tuns with a 12 tonnes charge each. There are 14 huge (116,000 litres) stainless steel washbacks and two full mashes feed one washback which feeds all seven wash stills. There is a total of 14 stills with the wash stills being heated by external heat exchangers while the spirit stills are heated using steam coils. The spirit vapours are cooled through copper condensers but on three spirit stills and three wash stills there are also stainless steel condensers attached, that you can switch to for a more sulphury spirit. All stills are equipped with flanges in four places for easier maintenance. The stills were manufactured by Diageo´s own coppersmiths at Abercrombies, Alloa. The whole distillery can work with just two operators but in spite of hi tech and computers, one operator opens up the man doors on the stills after each run, in order for the copper to rejuvenate for 30 minutes. During 2012 they will be doing 46 mashes per week which means 10 million litres of alcohol, but there is a possibility of increasing it to 12.5 million litres.

The total cost for the distillery was £40m and how to use the hot water in an efficient way was very much a focal point from the beginning. For example, Roseisle is connected by means of two long pipes with Burghead maltings, 3 km north of the distillery. Hot water is pumped from Roseisle and then used in the seven kilns at Burghead and cold water is then pumped back to Roseisle. The pot ale from the distillation will be piped into anaerobic fermenters to be transformed into biogas and the dried solids will act as a biomass fuel source. The biomass burner on the site, producing steam for the distillery, covers 72% of the total requirement. Furthermore, green technology has reduced the emission of carbon dioxide to only 15% of an ordinary, same-sized distillery.

The distillery has won several awards for its ambition towards sustainable production. In 2012 it was named one of the world´s most hi-tech distilleries by Popular Mechanics magazine due to its commitment to renewable energy.

At the moment they are producing two styles of spirit at Roseisle – heavy Speyside and light Speyside. So far no peated spirit has been distilled. For the heavy style a fermentation time of 50-60 hours is used and for the lighter style, 75 hours. Twelve road tankers per week transport the spirit to Cambus for filling and maturation.

Daftmill

Owner:	Region/district:	Founded:
Francis Cuthbert	Lowlands	2005
Status:	**Capacity:**	**website:**
Active	c 65 000 litres	www.daftmill.com
Address:		**Tel:**
By Cupar, Fife KY15 5RF		01337 830303

Permission was granted in 2003 for a steading at Daftmill Farmhouse in Fife, just a few miles west of Cupar and dating back to 1655, to be converted into a distillery. Contrary to most other new distilleries selling shares in their enterprise, Francis Cuthbert funded the entire operation himself. The first distillation was on 16th December 2005 and around 20,000 litres are produced in a year.

It is run as a typical farmhouse distillery. The barley, which recently changed from Optic to Publican and for 2012 to Concerto, is grown on the farm and they also supply other distilleries, such as Macallan to mention but one. Of the total 800 tonnes that Francis harvests in a year, around 100 tonnes are used for his own whisky. The malting is done without peat at Crisp's in Alloa. The equipment consists of a one tonne semi-lauter mash tun with a copper dome, two stainless steel washbacks with a fermentation between 72 and 100 hours and one pair of stills with slightly ascending lyne arms. The equipment is designed to give a lot of copper contact, a lot of reflux. The wash still has a capacity of 3,000 litres and the spirit still 2,000 litres.

Francis Cuthbert's aim is to do a light, Lowland style whisky similar to Rosebank. In order to achieve this they have very short foreshots (5 minutes) and the spirit run starts at 78% to capture all of the fruity esters and already comes off at 73%. The spirit is filled mainly into ex-bourbon casks, always first fill, but there are also a few sherry butts in the two dunnage warehouses.

Taking care of the farm obviously prohibits Francis from producing whisky full time. His silent season is during spring and autumn when work in the fields take all of his time. Whisky distillation is therefore reserved for June-August and November-February. During that period he manages to do 2-4 mashes per week.

It could have been possible to launch a 3 year old whisky already in December 2008, but Francis himself says that the first release is still a good few years away.

Distilleries per owner

c = closed, d = demolished, mb = mothballed, dm = dismantled

Diageo
Auchroisk
Banff (d)
Benrinnes
Blair Athol
Brora (c)
Bushmills
Caol Ila
Cardhu
Clynelish
Coleburn (dm)
Convalmore (dm)
Cragganmore
Dailuaine
Dallas Dhu (c)
Dalwhinnie
Dufftown
Glen Albyn (d)
Glendullan
Glen Elgin
Glenesk (dm)
Glenkinchie
Glenlochy (d)
Glenlossie
Glen Mhor (d)
Glen Ord
Glen Spey
Glenury Royal (d)
Inchgower
Knockando
Lagavulin
Linkwood
Mannochmore
Millburn (dm)
Mortlach
North Port (d)
Oban
Pittyvaich (d)
Port Ellen (dm)
Rosebank (c)
Roseisle
Royal Lochnagar
St Magdalene (dm)
Strathmill
Talisker
Teaninich

Pernod Ricard
Aberlour
Allt-a-Bhainne
Braeval
Caperdonich (c)
Glenallachie
Glenburgie
Glen Keith
Glenlivet
Glentauchers
Glenugie (dm)
Imperial (c)
Inverleven (d)
Kinclaith (d)
Lochside (d)
Longmorn

Miltonduff
Scapa
Strathisla
Tormore

Edrington Group
Glenrothes
Glenturret
Highland Park
Macallan

Inver House (Thai Beverage)
Balblair
Balmenach
Glen Flagler (d)
Knockdhu
Pulteney
Speyburn

John Dewar & Sons (Bacardi)
Aberfeldy
Aultmore
Craigellachie
Macduff
Royal Brackla

**Whyte & Mackay
(United Spirits)**
Dalmore
Fettercairn
Jura
Tamnavulin

William Grant & Sons
Ailsa Bay
Balvenie
Glenfiddich
Kininvie
Ladyburn (dm)

Beam
Ardmore
Cooley
Kilbeggan
Laphroaig

**Glenmorangie Co.
(Moët Hennessy)**
Ardbeg
Glenmorangie

Morrison Bowmore (Suntory)
Auchentoshan
Bowmore
Glen Garioch

**Burn Stewart Distillers
(CL Financial)**
Bunnahabhain
Deanston
Tobermory

Loch Lomond Distillers
Glen Scotia
Littlemill (d)
Loch Lomond

Angus Dundee Distillers
Glencadam
Tomintoul

J & A Mitchell
Glengyle
Springbank

Benriach Distillery Co.
Benriach
Glendronach

Ian Macleod Distillers
Glengoyne
Tamdhu

Campari Group
Glen Grant

Isle of Arran Distillers
Arran

**Signatory Vintage
Scotch Whisky Co.**
Edradour

**Tomatin Distillery Co.
(Marubeni Europe plc)**
Tomatin

J & G Grant
Glenfarclas

Rémy Cointreau
Bruichladdich

**Co-ordinated
Development Services**
Bladnoch

Gordon & MacPhail
Benromach

**Glenglassaugh Distillery Co
(Scaent Group)**
Glenglassaugh

La Martiniquaise
Glen Moray

**Ben Nevis Distillery Ltd
(Nikka)**
Ben Nevis

Picard Vins & Spiritueux
Tullibardine

Speyside Distillers Co.
Speyside

Kilchoman Distillery Co.
Kilchoman

Cuthbert family
Daftmill

Mark Tayburn
Abhainn Dearg

Closed
Distilleries

Convalmore Distillery

Brora

Owner:		Region/district:
Diageo		Northern Highlands
Founded:	Status:	Capacity:
1819	Closed	

History:
1819 – The Marquis of Stafford, 1st Duke of Sutherland, founds the distillery as Clynelish Distillery.

1827 – The first licensed distiller, James Harper, files for bankruptcy and John Matheson takes over.

1828 – James Harper is back as licensee.

1834 – Andrew Ross takes over the license.

1846 – George Lawson & Sons takes over.

1896 – James Ainslie & Heilbron takes over and rebuilds the facilities.

1912 – James Ainslie & Co. narrowly escapes bankruptcy and Distillers Company Limited (DCL) takes over together with James Risk.

1916 – John Walker & Sons buys a stake of James Risk's stocks.

1925 – DCL buys out Risk.

1930 – Scottish Malt Distillers takes over.

1931 – The distillery is mothballed.

1939 – Production restarts.

1960 – The distillery becomes electrified (until now it has been using locally mined coal from Brora).

1967 – A new distillery is built adjacent to the first one, it is also named Clynelish and both operate in parallel from August.

1968 – 'Old' Clynelish is mothballed in August.

1969 – 'Old' Clynelish is reopened as Brora and starts using a very peaty malt over the next couple of years

1983 – Brora is closed in March.

1995 – Brora 1972 (20 years) and Brora 1972 (22 years) are launched as Rare Malts.

1996 – Brora 1975 (20 years) is launched as a Rare Malt.

1998 – Brora 1977 (21 years) is launched as a Rare Malt.

2001 – Brora 1977 (24 years) is launched as a Rare Malt.

2002 – A 30 year old cask strength is released in a limited edition.

2003 – Brora 1982 (20 years) is launched as a Rare Malt.

2011 – The 10th release of Brora – a 32 year old.

2012 – The 11th release of Brora – a 35 year old.

Although founded under the name Clynelish distillery in 1819, it is under the name Brora that the single malt has enjoyed its newfound fame during the past two decades. The whisky has mostly appealed to peat freaks around the world but, for the first 140 years, it actually wasn't that peated. In 1967 DCL decided to build a new, modern distillery on the same site. This was given the name Clynelish and it was decided the old distillery should be closed. Shortly after, the demand for peated whisky, especially for the blend Johnnie Walker, increased and the old site re-opened but now under the name Brora and the "recipe" for the whisky was changed to a heavily peated malt. This continued from 1969 to 1973 and after that the peatiness was reduced, even if single peated batches turned up until the late seventies.

Brora closed permanently in 1983 but the buildings still stand next to the new Clynelish. The two stills, the feints receiver, the spirit receiver and the brass safe remain, while the warehouses are used for storage of spirit from Clynelish. The first distillery was built in the time referred to as the Highland Clearances. Many land-owners wished to increase the yield of their lands and consequently went into large-scale sheep farming. Thousands of families were ruthlessly forced away and the most infamous of the large land-owners was the Marquis of Stafford who founded Clynelish (Brora) in 1819.

Since 1995 Diageo has regularly re-leased different expressions of Brora in the *Rare Malts* series. The latest, which also became the last, appeared in 2003. In 2002 a new range was created, called *Special Releases* and bottlings of Brora have appeared ever since. In autumn 2011 it was a *32 year old* and by autumn 2012 the time had come for the 11th expression, a *35 year old* and the oldest ever distillery bottling of Brora. Very few independent bottlings of Brora turn up nowadays. The latest was a 28 year old from Douglas Laing in 2009.

35 years old

Banff

Owner:	Region:	Founded:	Status:
Diageo	Speyside	1824	Demolished

Banff's tragic history of numerous fires, explosions and bombings have contributed to its fame. The most spectacular incident was when a lone Junkers Ju-88 bombed one of the warehouses in 1941. Hundreds of casks exploded and several thousand litres of whisky were destroyed. The distillery was closed in 1983 and the buildings were destroyed in a fire in 1991. The distillery was owned for 80 years by the Simpson family but when their company filed for bankruptcy in 1932, it was sold to Scottish Malt Distillers which later would be a part of Diageo. When the distillery was at its largest it produced 1 million litres per year in three pairs of stills.

Recent bottlings:
There has only been one official Rare Malts bottling from 2004. A number of expressions from the seventies have been released recently; Dewar Rattray 1975, Douglas Laing 1971, Duncan Taylor 1975 and a 36 year old from 1975 from Douglas Laing.

Caperdonich

Owner:	Region:	Founded:	Status:
Chivas Bros	Speyside	1897	Closed

The distillery was founded by James Grant, owner of Glen Grant which was located in Rothes just a few hundred metres away. Five years after the opening, the distillery was shut down and was re-opened again in 1965 under the name Caperdonich. In 2002 it was mothballed yet again, never to be re-opened. Parts of the equipment were dismantled to be used in other distilleries within the company. In 2010 the distillery was sold to the manufacturer of copper pot stills, Forsyth´s in Rothes, who already had business adjacent to it. In the old days a pipe connected Caperdonich and Glen Grant for easy transport of spirit, ready to be filled.

Recent bottlings:
An official cask strength was released in 2005. Recent bottlings from independents are a 14 year old distilled in 1996 from Cadenheads, a 15 year old (1995) from Dewar Rattray and a 28 year old (1982) released by Douglas Laing.

Coleburn

Owner:	Region:	Founded:	Status:
Diageo	Speyside	1897	Dismantled

Like so many other distilleries, Coleburn was taken over by DCL (the predecessor of Diageo) in the 1930s. Although the single malt never became well known, Coleburn was used as an experimental workshop where new production techniques were tested. In 1985 the distillery was mothballed and never opened again. Two brothers, Dale and Mark Winchester, bought the buildings in 2004 with the intention of transforming the site into an entertainment centre. After a lengthy process, they were granted planning permission in 2010 and the reconstruction work, transforming it into a 60-bedroom hotel and a spa, has commenced.

Recent bottlings:
There has only been one official Rare Malts bottling from 2000, while Independent bottlings are also rare. One of the latest was a 36 year old released in 2006 by Signatory.

Convalmore

Owner:	Region:	Founded:	Status:
Diageo	Speyside	1894	Dismantled

This distillery is still intact and can be seen in Duff-town next to Balvenie distillery. The buildings were sold to William Grant´s in 1990 and they now use it for storage. Diageo, however, still holds the rights to the brand. In the early 20th century, experimental distilling of malt whisky in continuous stills (the same method used for producing grain whisky) took place at Convalmore. The distillery closed in 1985. One of the more famous owners of this distillery was James Buchanan who used Convalmore single malt as a part of his famous blend Black & White. He later sold the distillery to DCL (later Diageo).

Recent bottlings:
The latest bottling from the owners was a 28 year old released in 2005. The latest independent bottling was a 32 year old from 1975 released by Douglas Laing in 2007.

Dallas Dhu

Owner:	Region:	Founded:	Status:
Diageo	Speyside	1898	Closed

Dallas Dhu distillery is located along the A96 between Elgin and Inverness and is still intact, equipment and all, but hasn´t produced since 1983. Three years later, Diageo sold the distillery to Historic Scotland and it became a museum which is open all year round. One of the founders of the distillery, Alexander Edwards, belonged to the more energetic men in the 19th century Scotch whisky business. Not only did he start Dallas Dhu but also established Aultmore, Benromach and Craigellachie and owned Benrinnes and Oban. For a period, the malt whisky from Dallas Dhu, was a part of the immensely popular blended Scotch, Roderick Dhu.

Recent bottlings:
There are two Rare Malts bottlings from Diageo, the latest in 1997. The latest from independents is a 1979 released by Gordon & Macphail and there have also been a few releases for Historic Scotland – the current owners.

Glen Albyn

Owner:	Region:	Founded:	Status:
Diageo	N Highlands	1844	Demolished

Glen Albyn was one of three Inverness distilleries surviving into the 1980s. Today, there is no whisky production left in the city. The first forty years were not very productive for Glen Albyn. Fire and bankruptcy prevented the success and in 1866 the buildings were transformed into a flour mill. In 1884 it was converted back to a distillery and continued producing whisky until 1983 when it was closed by the owners at the time, Diageo. Three years later the distillery was demolished.

Recent bottlings:
Glen Albyn has been released as a Rare Malt by the owners on one occasion. It is rarely seen from independents as well but recently a 1976 was released by Gordon & Macphail.

Glenesk

Owner: *Region:*   *Founded:*   *Status:*
Diageo   E Highlands   1897   Demolished

Few distilleries, if any, have operated under as many names as Glenesk; Highland Esk, North Esk, Montrose and Hillside. The distillery was one of four operating close to Montrose between Aberdeen and Dundee. Today only Glencadam remains. At one stage the distillery was re-built for grain production but reverted to malt distilling. In 1968 a large drum maltings was built adjacent to the distillery and the Glenesk maltings still operate today under the ownership of Boortmalt, the fifth largest producer of malt in the world. The distillery building was demolished in 1996.

Recent bottlings:
The single malt from Glen Esk has been bottled on three occasions as a Rare Malts, the latest in 1997. It is also very rare with the independent bottlers. Last time it appeared was in 2007 when Duncan Taylor released a 26 year old distilled in 1981.

Glenlochy

Owner: *Region:*   *Founded:*   *Status:*
Diageo   W Highlands   1898   Demolished

Glenlochy was one of three distilleries in Fort William at the beginning of the 1900s. In 1908 Nevis merged with Ben Nevis distillery (which exists to this day) and in 1983 (a disastrous year for Scotch whisky industry when eight distilleries were closed), the time had come for Glenlochy to close for good. Today, all the buildings have been demolished, with the exception of the kiln with its pagoda roof and the malt barn which both have been turned into flats. For a period of time, the distillery was owned by an energetic and somewhat eccentric Canadian gentleman by the name of Joseph Hobbs who, after having sold the distillery to DCL, bought the second distillery in town, Ben Nevis.

Recent bottlings:
Glenlochy has occurred twice in the Rare Malts series. Recent independent bottlings are rare; a 49 year old from 2003 by Douglas Laing and a 24 year old released by Duncan Taylor in 2005.

Glen Mhor

Owner: *Region:*   *Founded:*   *Status:*
Diageo   N Highlands   1892   Demolished

Glen Mhor is one of the last three Inverness distilleries and probably the one with the best reputation when it comes to the whisky that it produced. When the manager of nearby Glen Albyn, John Birnie, was refused to buy shares in the distillery he was managing, he decided to build his own and founded Glen Mhor. Almost thirty years later he also bought Glen Albyn and both distilleries were owned by the Birnie family until 1972 when they were sold to DCL. Glen Mhor was closed in 1983 and three years later the buildings were demolished. Today there is a supermarket on the site.

Recent bottlings:
Glen Mhor has appeared on two ocasions as Rare Malts. A couple of years ago three 27 year olds all distilled in 1982 were released by Signatory, Berry Brothers, Cadenheads and Douglas Laing and from the latter also a 32 year old distilled in 1975

Glenury Royal

Owner: *Region:*   *Founded:*   *Status:*
Diageo   E Highlands   1825   Demolished

Glenury Royal did not have a lucky start. Already a few weeks after inception in 1825, a fire destroyed the whole kiln, the greater part of the grain lofts and the malting barn, as well as the stock of barley and malt. Just two weeks later, distillery worker James Clark, fell into the boiler and died after a few hours. The founder of Glenury was the eccentric Captain Robert Barclay Allardyce, the first to walk 1000 miles in 1000 hours in 1809 and also an excellent middle-distance runner and boxer. The distillery closed in 1983 and part of the building was demolished a decade later with the rest converted into flats.

Recent bottlings:
Bottled as a Rare Malt on three occasions. Even more spectacular were three Diageo bottlings released 2003-2007; two 36 year olds and a 50 year old. In early 2012 a 40 year old was released. There are few independent bottlings, the latest being a 32 year old released in 2008 by Douglas Laing.

Imperial

Owner: *Region:*   *Founded:*   *Status:*
Chivas Bros   Speyside   1897   Closed

Rumours of the resurrection of this closed distillery have flourished from time to time during the last decade. Six years ago, the owner commissioned an estate agent to sell the buildings and convert them into flats. Shortly after that, Chivas Bros withdrew it from the market. Most of the equipment is still there, even though there was an attempt in 2009, which failed, to loot the distillery. In over a century, Imperial distillery was out of production for 60% of the time, but when it produced it had a capacity of 1.6 million litres per year. If rumours have it right and Chivas Bros restart Glen Keith, it will mean that Imperial is the last of their distilleries to remain closed.

Recent bottlings:
The 15 year old official bottling is hard to find these days but independents are more frequent. Douglas Laing, Signatory and Duncan Taylor all made releases in 2012 of Imperial distilled in 1995.

Littlemill

Owner: *Region:*   *Founded:*   *Status:*
Loch Lomond   Lowlands   1772   Demolished
Distillery Co.

Until 1992 when production stopped, Littlemill was Scotland's oldest working distillery and could trace its roots back to 1772, possibly even back to the 1750s! Triple distillation was practised at Littlemill until 1930 and after that some new equipment was installed, for example, stills with rectifying columns. The stills were also isolated with aluminium. The goal was to create whiskies that would mature faster. Two such experimental releases were Dunglas and Dumbuck. In 1996 the distillery was dismantled and part of the buildings demolished and in 2004 much of the remaining buildings were destroyed in a fire.

Recent bottlings:
This is one of the few closed distilleries where official bottlings are released regularly. The official 12 year old is now closer to 19 years! A 21 year old was released in 2012 by Hart Brothers to celebrate the Queens Diamond Jubilee.

Lochside

Owner: *Region:*   *Founded:*   *Status:*
Chivas Bros E Highlands 1957   Demolished

Originally a brewery for two centuries, In the last 35 years of production Lochside was a whisky distillery. The Canadian, Joseph Hobbs, started distilling grain whisky and then added malt whisky production in the same way as he had done at Ben Nevis and Lochside. Most of the output was made for the blended whisky Sandy MacNab´s. In the early 1970s, the Spanish company DYC became the owner and the output was destined for Spanish blended whisky. In 1992 the distillery was mothballed and five years later all the equipment and stock were removed. All the distillery buildings were demolished in 2005.

Recent bottlings:
There are no recent official bottlings. A handful of independent bottlings, however, appeared in 2010/2011 as well as an unusual Lochside single blend (malt and grain distilled at the same distillery) which was distilled in 1965 and released by Adelphi in 2011.

Photo: © 2005 www.whisky.de

Millburn

Owner: *Region:*   *Founded:*   *Status:*
Diageo   N Highlands 1807   Dismantled

The distillery is the oldest of those Inverness distilleries that made it into modern times and it is also the only one where the buildings are still standing. It is now a hotel and restaurant owned by Premier Inn. With one pair of stills, the capacity was no more than 300,000 litres. The problem with Millburn distillery was that it could never be expanded due to its location, sandwiched in between the river, a hill and the surrounding streets. It was bought by the London-based gin producer Booth´s in the 1920s and shortly after that absorbed into the giant DCL. In 1985 it was closed and three years later all the equipment was removed.

Recent bottlings:
Three bottlings of Millburn have appeared as Rare Malts, the latest in 2005. Other bottlings are scarce. The most recent was a 33 year old distilled in 1974, released by Blackadder.

North Port

Owner: *Region:*   *Founded:*   *Status:*
Diageo   E Highlands 1820   Demolished

The names North Port and Brechin are used interchangeably on the labels of this single malt. Brechin is the name of the city and North Port comes from a gate in the wall which surrounded the city. The distillery was run by members of the Guthrie family for more than a century until 1922 when DCL took over. Diageo then closed 21 of their 45 distilleries between 1983 and 1985 of which North Port was one. It was dismantled piece by piece and was finally demolished in 1994 to make room for a supermarket.The distillery had one pair of stills and produced 500,000 litres per year.

Recent bottlings:
North Port was released as a Rare Malt by Diageo twice and in 2005 also as part of the Special Releases (a 28 year old). Independent bottlings are very rare - the latest (distilled in 1981) was released by Duncan Taylor in 2008.

Port Ellen

Owner:		Region/district:
Diageo		Islay
Founded:	**Status:**	**Capacity:**
1825	Dismantled	

History:
1825 – Alexander Kerr Mackay assisted by Walter Campbell founds the distillery. Mackay runs into financial troubles after a few months and his three relatives John Morrison, Patrick Thomson and George Maclennan take over.

1833 – John Ramsay, a cousin to John Morrison, comes from Glasgow to take over.

1836 – Ramsay is granted a lease on the distillery from the Laird of Islay.

1892 – Ramsay dies and the distillery is inherited by his widow, Lucy.

1906 – Lucy Ramsay dies and her son Captain Iain Ramsay takes over.

1920 – Iain Ramsay sells to Buchanan-Dewar who transfers the administration to the company Port Ellen Distillery Co. Ltd.

1925 – Buchanan-Dewar joins Distillers Company Limited (DCL).

1929 – No production.

1930 – Administration is transferred to Scottish Malt Distillers (SMD) and the distillery is mothballed.

1967 – In production again after reconstruction and doubling of the number of stills from two to four.

1973 – A large drum maltings is installed.

1980 – Queen Elisabeth visits the distillery and a commemorative special bottling is made.

1983 – The distillery is mothballed.

1987 – The distillery closes permanently but the maltings continue to deliver malt to all Islay distilleries.

1998 – Port Ellen 1978 (20 years) is released as a Rare Malt.

2000 – Port Ellen 1978 (22 years) is released as a Rare Malt.

2001 – Port Ellen cask strength first edition is released.

2011 – The 11th release of Port Ellen - a 32 year old from 1979.

2012 – The 12th release of Port Ellen - a 32 year old from 1979

When Port Ellen closed in 1983 it was one of three Islay distilleries owned by Diageo (then DCL). The other two were Lagavulin and Caol Ila who had been operating uninterruptedly for many years. Port Ellen, mothballed since 1930, had only been producing for 16 years since re-opening, which made it easy for the owners to single out which Islay distillery was to close when malt whisky demand decreased. It was also the smallest of the three, with an annual output of 1.7 million litres of alcohol. The stills were shipped abroad early in the 1990s, possibly destined for India, and the distillery buildings were destroyed shortly afterwards. The whisky from Port Ellen is so popular, however, that rumours of distilling starting up again, do flourish from time to time.

Today, the site is associated with the huge drum maltings that was built in 1973. It supplies all Islay distilleries and a few others, with a large proportion of their malt. There are seven germination drums with a capacity of handling 51 tonnes of barley each. Three kilns are used to dry the barley and for every batch, an average of 6 tonnes of peat are required which means 2,000 tonnes per year. The peat was taken from Duich Moss until 1993 when conservationists managed to obtain national nature reserve status for the area in order to protect the thousands of Barnacle Geese that make a stop-over there during their migration. Nowadays the peat is taken from nearby Castlehill.

Besides a couple of versions in the *Rare Malts* series, Diageo began releasing one official bottling a year in 2001 and in autumn 2012 it was time for the 12th release – a *32 year old* from refill American oak and refill European oak, distilled in 1979. Port Ellen is a favourite with independent bottlers as well. Some of the most recent ones are two from 1982 released by Old Bothwell and a 32 year old distilled in 1979 from Douglas Laing.

32 years old

Pittyvaich

Owner:	Region:	Founded:	Status:
Diageo	Speyside	1974	Demolished

The life span for this relatively modern distillery was short. It was built by Arthur Bell & Sons on the same ground as Dufftown distillery which also belonged to them and the four stills were exact replicas of the Dufftown stills. Bells was bought by Guinness in 1985 and the distillery was eventually absorbed into DCL (later Diageo). For a few years in the 1990s, Pittyvaich was also a back up plant for gin distillation (in the same way that Auchroisk is today) in connection with the production of Gordon´s gin having moved from Essex till Cameronbridge. The distillery was mothballed in 1993 and has now been demolished.

Recent bottlings:
An official 12 year old Flora & Fauna can still be obtained and in 2009 a 20 year old was released by the owners. Recent independents include an 18 year old from Douglas Laing and a 23 year old rum finish by Cadenheads, both released in 2008.

Rosebank

Owner:	Region:	Founded:	Status:
Diageo	Lowlands	1798	Dismantled

When Rosebank in Falkirk was mothballed in 1993, there were only two working malt distilleries left in the Lowlands – Glenkinchie and Auchentoshan. The whisky from the distillery has always had a great amount of supporters and there was a glimmer of hope that a new company would start up the distillery again. At the beginning of 2010 though, most of the equipment was stolen and furthermore, Diageo has indicated that they are not interested in selling the brand. The buildings are still intact and most of them have been turned into restaurants, offices and flats. The whisky from Rosebank is triple distilled.

Recent bottlings:
The official 12 year old Flora & Fauna is still released and in autumn 2011 a 21 year old Special Release appeared. Four independent bottlings, all distilled in 1990, were released in 2011 by Ian Macleod, Cadenheads, Murray McDavid and Douglas Laing.

St Magdalene

Owner:	Region:	Founded:	Status:
Diageo	Lowlands	1795	Dismantled

At one time, the small town of Linlithgow in East Lothian had no less than five distilleries. St Magdalene was one of them and also the last to close in 1983. The distillery came into ownership of the giant DCL quite early (1912) and was at the time a large distillery with 14 washbacks, five stills and with the possibility of producing more than 1 million litres of alcohol. Ten years after the closure the distillery was carefully re-built into flats, making it possible to still see most of the old buildings, including the pagoda roofs.

Recent bottlings:
These include two official bottlings in the Rare Malts series. In 2008/2009 a handful of independent releases appeared, all of them distilled in 1982 and released by Ian MacLeod, Douglas Laing, Blackadder, Signatory and Berry Brother. The latest were two 28 year olds from Douglas Laing and Mackillop´s released in 2011.

Ben Wyvis

Owner: Whyte & Mackay *Region:* N Highlands *Founded:* 1965 *Status:* Dismantled

The large grain distillery, Invergordon, today producing 36 million litres of grain whisky per year, was established in 1959 on the Cromarty Firth, east of Alness. Six years later a small malt distillery, Ben Wyvis, was built on the same site with the purpose of producing malt whisky for Invergordon Distiller´s blends. The distillery was equipped with one mash tun, six washbacks and one pair of stills. Funnily enough the stills are still in use today at Glengyle distillery. Production at Ben Wyvis stopped in 1976 and in 1977 the distillery was closed and dismantled.

Bottlings:
There have been only a few releases of Ben Wyvis. The first, a 27 year old, was released by Invergordon in 1999, followed by a 31 year old from Signatory in 2000 and finally a 37 year old from Kyndal (later Whyte & Mackay) in 2002. It is highly unlikely that there will be more Ben Wyvis single malt to bottle.

Inverleven

Owner: Chivas Bros *Region:* Lowlands *Founded:* 1938 *Status:* Demolished

Dumbarton was the largest grain distillery in Scotland when it was built in 1938. It was mothballed in 2002 and finally closed in 2003 when Allied Domecq moved all their grain production to Strathclyde. On the same site, Inverleven malt distillery was built, equipped with one pair of traditional pot stills. In 1956 a Lomond still was added and this still (with the aid of Inverleven´s wash still), technically became a second distillery called Lomond. Inverleven was mothballed in 1991and finally closed. The Lomond still is now working again since 2010 at Bruichladdich distillery.

Bottlings:
The first official bottling of Inverleven came as late as in 2010 when Chivas Bros released a 36 year old in a new range called Deoch an Doras. The latest independent was a 34 year old released by Signatory in 2011. The whisky from the Lomond still was bottled in 1992 by the Scotch Malt Whisky Society.

Glen Flagler / Killyloch

Owner: Inver House *Region:* Lowlands *Founded:* 1964 *Status:* Closed

In 1964 Inver House Distillers was bought by the American company, Publicker Industries, and that same year they decided to expand the production side as well. Moffat Paper Mills in Airdrie was bought and rebuilt into one grain distillery (Garnheath) and two malt distilleries (Glen Flagler and Killyloch). A maltings was also built which, at the time, became the biggest in Europe. The American interest in the Scotch whisky industry faded rapidly and Killyloch was closed in 1975, while Glen Flagler continued to produce for another decade.

Bottlings:
Glen Flagler was bottled as an 8 year old by the owners in the 70s. The next release came in the mid 1990s when Signatory released both Glen Flagler and Killyloch (23 year old) and finally in 2003 when Inver House bottled a Glen Flagler 1973 and a Killyloch 1967. A peated version of Glen Flagler, produced until 1970, was called Islebrae.

Kinclaith

Owner: Chivas Bros *Region:* Lowlands *Founded:* 1957 *Status:* Demolished

This was the last malt distillery to be built in Glasgow and was constructed on the grounds of Strathclyde grain distillery by Seager Evans (later Long John International). Strathclyde still exists today and produces 40 million litres of grain spirit per year. Kinclaith distillery was equipped with one pair of stills and produced malt whisky to become a part of the Long John blend. In 1975 it was dismantled to make room for an extension of the grain distillery. It was later demolished in 1982.

Bottlings:
There are no official bottlings of Kinclaith. The latest from independents came in 2005 when Duncan Taylor and Signatory both released 35 year old bottlings. Older releases include a 32 year old from Gordon & MacPhail released in 1996 and a 20 year old from Cadenheads in 1985.

Glenugie

Owner: Chivas Bros *Region:* E Highlands *Founded:* 1831 *Status:* Demolished

Glenugie, positioned in Peterhead, was the most Eastern distillery in Scotland, producing whisky for six years before it was converted into a brewery. In 1875 whisky distillation started again, but production was very intermittent until 1937 when Seager Evans & Co took over. Eventually they expanded the distillery to four stills and the capacity was around 1 million litres per year. After several ownership changes Glenugie became part of the brewery giant, Whitbread, in 1975. The final blow came in 1983 when Glenugie, together with seven other distilleries, was closed never to open again.

Bottlings:
The first official bottling of Glenugie came as late as in 2010 when Chivas Bros (the current owners of the brand) released a 32 year old single sherry cask in a new range called Deoch an Doras. Recent independent bottlings include a 33 year old with 8 years Oloroso finish from Signatory, released in 2011.

Ladyburn

Owner: W Grant & Sons *Region:* Lowlands *Founded:* 1966 *Status:* Dismantled

In 1963 William Grant & Sons built their huge grain distillery in Girvan in Ayrshire. Three years later they also decided to build a malt distillery on the site which was given the name Ladyburn. The distillery was equipped with two pairs of stills and they also tested a new type of continuous mashing. The whole idea was to produce malt whisky to become a part of Grant´s blended whisky. The distillery was closed in 1975 and finally dismantled during the 1980s. In 2008 a new malt distillery opened up at Girvan under the name Ailsa Bay.

Bottlings:
The latest official bottling from the owners was a 27 year old distilled in 1973 and released in 2001. Independent bottlings have appeared occasionally, sometimes under the name Ayrshire. The most recent was a 36 year old, released by Signatory in 2012.

Single malts from Japan

by Nicholas Coldicott

Hakushu Distillery

I have a small bottle of Mascot Whisky at home. You might not have heard of it. It was produced in 1911 by Ota Shoten, a company that dabbled in various beverages.

It's not clear how Ota made the drink. The label offers no clues. But we can be sure they didn't malt, mash and distill. The early 20th century was a wild time in Japan's whisky history. The government was issuing whisky licenses, but nobody was using them to make the drink we know. There are stories of companies relabeling Scotch, adding caramel to shochu, or mixing a frightening jumble of spirits and chemicals. But companies such as Ota, Eigashima Shuzo and Suntory don't reminisce about these early efforts.

The age of authentic Japanese whisky began in 1923 when Suntory founder Shinjiro Torii and sake brewer's son-turned-whisky apprentice Masataka Taketsuru built a distillery in Yamazaki, near Kyoto. Which means 2013 is the industry's 90th anniversary. It reaches the milestone in rather good shape. Domestic consumption is rising steadily, export markets are opening fast, and juries keep furnishing Japan's distillers with trophies.

Nikka and Suntory took a title apiece at the World Whiskies Awards 2012. Nikka's Taketsuru 17 years old was named best pure malt, and Suntory's Yamazaki 25 years old took the single malt trophy. But it wasn't the silverware that showed how far they've come; it was the muted reaction to the news.

Back in 2008, when a Yoichi 20 years old and Hibiki 30 years old took the single malt and blended titles at the WWAs, editors leapt at the story. It was classic underdog stuff; the little whisky distillers that could, with echoes of the 1976 Judgement of Paris when Californian winemakers gave the French a surprise.

This year, the tone was different. If media outlets reported the story, they gave it little space or spin. It was the fourth time in five years that Japan's leading distillers both won major WWA titles. It would have been more newsworthy if they'd flown home empty handed.

The silverware seems to be spurring interest abroad. Suntory aims to triple its sales in France, Europe's biggest whisky market, over the next three to four years. They've set a target of around 10,000 cases. They also signed a distribution deal with Champagne house Laurent Perrier, which gives us a clue who they're aiming at.

Nikka Whisky is doing even better there. Its European distributor, La Maison du Whisky, expects to sell 25,000 cases in France in 2012, and another 12,500 elsewhere in Europe. La Maison's Nick Sikorski says France is a natural fit for Japanese whisky because the people "know about food and drink and are prepared to pay for quality." Last year they bottled 8 casks of Japanese whisky; next year they'll bottle 16.

Both Nikka and La Maison have hinted that they're preparing to have a crack at the US market. They'll be following Suntory, who now have all three major brands on sale Stateside. Suntory marketing spokesperson Midori Takahashi says ever-rising sales of the 12 year old Yamazaki and Hibiki persuaded them to launch the Hakushu version in late 2011 and sales for the first 12 months beat their target. In the short-term, it's likely to be supply, not demand, that dictates how much Hakushu crosses the Pacific.

Domestically, whisky consumption leveled off in 2011 after three years of growth, but that could be viewed as a triumph given the challenges of a year that saw an earthquake, tsunami and nuclear accident. Asahi, owner of Nikka Whisky, says that while the Great East Japan Earthquake hurt demand for most of its drinks, its domestic whisky segment grew by 1 percent. Early estimates for the industry as a whole suggest sales rose again in 2012.

Japan is still a highball nation. Whisky sodas have moved out of the izakaya and into homes, supermarkets and convenience stores, paying dividends for campaign mastermind Suntory as well as its rivals. But Suntory's aim has always been to turn highball fans into single malt drinkers, and it unveiled its latest stepping stones in May 2012. The company added Hakushu and Yamazaki bottles with no age statements to its line-up, in both 700ml and budget-friendly 350ml bottles.

A company press release made their motivations clear: "With an eye toward further increasing the number of whisky fans, the new lineup will be launched … so that consumers who first gained a taste for whisky through the whisky highball can now become acquainted with premium whisky."

The original highball campaign showed Suntory as masters of marketing; we should all be watching now to see if they can forge a new audience for single malts.

New Faces

The revitalized Japanese whisky industry has roused some sleeping distillers. Hombo Shuzo's Shinshu is back after a 19-year break. It began distilling again in early 2011 and released its first new make spirit the following year. Luckily they have stock in the warehouse and revenue from their wine, shochu, umeshu and brandy businesses to keep them in business while the whisky matures. These other business interests also mean that Hombo can afford to stay micro.

The White Oak distillery has never stopped making whisky, but only since 2007 has it been selling single malts. They have always focused on young blends, which means they don't have a warehouse full of well-aged whisky, but after a series of successful short-run single malt bottlings under the brand name "Akashi", White Oak has launched a single malt with no age statement that it says will be a long-term offering.

Distilling at White Oak is still a rare event, limited to just two or three weeks per year (the rest of the calendar is devoted to making sake, shochu, wine or umeshu), but the new focus on premium whisky is encouraging.

Japan's newest distillery, Chichibu, is unique for Japan in that its owner doesn't make any other kind of drink. Nikka, Suntory, Hombo, Eigashima and Kirin all have a diverse portfolio, but Chichibu makes whisky and only whisky.

To survive the difficult first decade, owner Ichiro Akuto can sell the stock he bought from his family's defunct Hanyu distillery. And Akuto isn't planning to wait ten years before building a core range. His first three releases were all three year-olds, but deceptively complex and mature tasting. High-end department store Takashimaya bottled a heavily peated Chichibu that had aged just two years in new American oak. It was the colour of old Sauternes and presented by the retailer not as a new-distillery curiosity but as a fine single malt to sip with a cigar.

Akuto says most upcoming Chichibu releases will be around 5-7,000 bottles, split evenly between domestic and export markets.

The only bad news of the year was confirmation that the Karuizawa distillery has been dismantled. The whisky has built a cult status thanks largely to the efforts of distributor Number One Drinks and retailers La Maison du Whisky and The Whisky Exchange, but it wasn't enough to tempt owners Kirin to revive the dormant distillery.

Sometime late in 2012, Number One will release around 50 bottles of whisky from a 52 year old cask of Karuizawa. The price, rarity and flavour should guarantee plenty of media coverage, making the defunct distillery more famous than ever.

The price and rarity also guarantee that almost nobody will get to try the drink; all but the most curious buyers will surely keep the bottles as an investment and a piece of Japanese whisky history.

Speaking of whisky history, I opened that bottle of Mascot while writing this report. The drink has a nice, malty aroma. On the palate, it starts out sweet, quickly collapses into a biting acid, and made me worryingly delirious with just one sip. We've come a long way in 90 years.

Nicholas Coldicott is the former editor-in-chief of Eat magazine, former drink columnist for The Japan Times and former contributing editor at Whisky Magazine Japan. He currently works for Japan's national broadcaster, NHK, and writes a drink column for CNNgo.com.

Chichibu

Owner: Venture Whisky   **Founded**: 2008
Location: Saitama Prefecture
Capacity: 80,000 litres
Malt whisky range: Three limited releases.

Photo: William Robb

You could call Chichibu a craft distiller, but that wouldn't convey the hold this distillery has on Japan's malt lovers. Nor the expectations. Chichibu may be Japan's newest distillery, but it comes with some heritage. Owner Ichiro Akuto hails from a sake-making family. They branched out into whisky in the 1980s, just as the market began shrinking. The family held on for nearly two decades, then turned off the stills in 2000 and dismantled the distillery four years later. Ichiro kept the stock and began issuing it as single cask releases. The Ichiro's Malt series gained a cult following and each release sold fast. As his inventory dwindled, Akuto decided to build a new distillery just northwest of Tokyo.

Chichibu's most unusual features are the washbacks made from Japan's mizunara wood. They're the most visible manifestation of Akuto's aim to keep things local. He uses both local and imported barley, plans to open a malt house, and is experimenting with Japanese peat. He's even asked a local cooper to teach his team to make barrels. The stills are small with steep arms for a rich spirit. The distillate is aged, without temperature controls, in Chichibu's seesawing climate. Akuto says the fluctuations let the casks breathe more deeply and speed up the aging process.

His first whisky proper, Chichibu The First, was aged for 3 years in ex-bourbon casks. It came out, and sold out, in 2011. Half the 7,400 bottle run was exported, half sold at home. The second release, Chichibu The Floor Malted, reached shelves in spring 2012. Distilled from barley that Akuto malted on a visit to England's Malt Stars, it was another signal that he's aiming to master all the skills of the trade. The third release, Chichibu The Peated, will be around three years old and bottled at 50.5%. It's due in late 2012, and the 5,000 bottle run will again be split evenly between the domestic and export market.

Tasting note:
Chichibu The Peated
A full-bodied, meaty, peaty nose, much more than you would expect from the age. Sweeter on the palate, with nougat, vanilla and an elegant, inter grated smokiness. With water, develops a creamy texture. A fairly long finish.

Fuji Gotemba

Owner: Kirin Holdings   **Founded**: 1973
Location: Shizuoka Prefecture
Capacity: 12,000,000 litres (including grain whisky)
Malt whisky range: Fujisanroku 18 years old.

It was just 12 years ago that each of Japan's three beverage behemoths owned a pair of whisky distilleries apiece and Japanese whisky was still in the shadow of its Scotch, Irish and American forefathers. So much has changed since then, but only one company seems to have gone backwards. Kirin mothballed its Karuizawa distillery in 2001 and focused on its workhorse at the foot of Mount Fuji. Kirin, Seagram, Chivas and Four Roses teamed up to open Fuji Gotemba the same year as Suntory switched on the stills at Hakushu. The two have followed very different paths. Hakushu has built a fan base and a trophy cabinet for its single malts, but slashed production since the '80s when it was the world's largest distillery.

Fuji Gotemba has toiled quietly in the background, and whisky fans may be surprised to learn that it vies with Glenfiddich for the title of world's biggest whisky distillery. It has pot and column stills to produce malt and grain whisky. Most of its output goes into low-end blends Emblem, Boston Club, Ocean Lucky Gold and Robert Brown. There's also a blended Fujisanroku 50 Degrees that has thrived in the highball era, and just one single malt: Fujisanroku 18 years old. Unlike other Japanese distilleries, Fuji Gotemba sticks exclusively to one kind of wood: American oak. Kirin wanted easy warehouse management, but they sacrificed much of the depth and variety that has made Japanese whisky so successful. Ironically, it's the late Karuizawa that's carved itself a spot in the export market, thanks to a handful of enthusiastic retailers and an indie bottler. Fujisanroku hasn't officially made it overseas yet. Kirin has the production capacity and name recognition to make an impact on the global whisky market, but it doesn't have the rich inventory or, seemingly, the inclination.

Meet the Manager

ICHIRO AKUTO
OWNER AND MANAGER, CHICHIBU DISTILLERY

Photo: William Rob...

Tell us about your career before you started Chichibu Distillery?

I graduated from the Tokyo University of Agriculture in 1988. My major was fermentation and distillation. I worked for Suntory as a brand manager of imported liquor, mainly whisky, and a sales representative. I then joined my father's company, Toa Shuzo, which produced sake, wine, shochu and other spirits, including whisky. I worked at Karuizawa in 2006, then at Benriach in 2007. In 2008, we were licensed to manufacture whisky and started to distill.

How did you research how to open a distillery?

I visited as many distilleries as possible, especially small ones. I thought they would help me learn how to set up and operate a small distillery. I went to Kilchoman, Edradour, Benromach, Daftmill, BenRiach, Cornish Cyder Farm, Somerset Distillery, Penderyn, Karuizawa and so on. It was really helpful to learn to install equipment and make spirits when I worked at Karuizawa and Benriach. Usually you don't have to care about the piping between vessels, but it's important for a craft whisky founder to know about it.

What was the hardest part about building a distillery?

Probably finance. The whisky market was dramatically shrinking around the time I tried to set up the distillery in 2007. And it takes a long time to mature whisky and put it on the market.
At first, it was hard for me to persuade all parties, such as bank people and land owners, to understand the whisky business. I told them how nice whiskies are, and explained that the overseas market was increasing. Even in the domestic market, I was confident because I observed young people and ladies enjoying single malt whiskies in bars.
The statistics showed that overall whisky consumption was shrinking, but the single malt market had been increasing for a decade. Finally, I succeeded in getting them to understand the whisky business.

You've been studying malting. When will you start malting at Chichibu?

We've already started test malting at Chichibu. In a year, I would like to start full-scale malting.

How big is your team?

We have seven people working full time and four part timers so far.

We're only 3 releases along, but do you have an idea about a Chichibu whisky character?

Chichibu is well matured for its age. The spirit is round, soft and fruity, with a little spiciness. I guess our whisky facility makes a lot of flavours, and as a result it tastes rounded.

How many types of cask are you using at Chichibu?

In total, more than 20 types. We're using sherry butts, port pipes, bourbon hogsheads, bourbon barrels, Cognac casks, Madeira casks, red wine casks, rum casks, white oak virgin casks, mizunara casks, chibidaru (our original quarter casks) and more. We'll use each cask for first, second or third fills.

Do you have a favourite Ichiro's Malt?

It's difficult to say, because all of them are like my children. I can't rank them. But I like the Chichibu ones, although they are young. I like to imagine their future.

If you had to choose a favourite dram other than Chichibu or Hanyu, what would it be?

My favourite changes often in accordance with my physical condition and atmosphere. I like Islay ones when I'm excited. I like soft and mild whisky, like Speyside ones such as Glenmorangie, Glenlivet and Glenfiddich, especially matured in bourbon casks, when I am deliberating about something. When I succeed in something important, I like to drink very old sherry-matured ones.

How do you imagine Chichibu 15 years from now?

We don't have to be a big company.

We'll just keep focusing on the basics, from malting to aging. In the future, I'd like to have our own cooperage. We studied with a local cooper who is over 80 years old and has nobody to succeed him. We decided to be his successor. We've already made casks by ourselves and are using them for maturation. And the most important thing is that we will enjoy Chichibu 15 years old with a lot of whisky lovers.

Have you been surprised by the kind of people buying Ichiro's Malts?

One guy came to Chichibu all the way from Sweden to buy two bottles he doesn't have. He'd collected most of our whiskies. But we don't have stock at our distillery, so he travelled around retailers in Tokyo and finally got one at a liquor shop and the other through a web-site. I was surprised by his enthusiasm.

How do you spend time when you're not making or promoting whisky?

I used to enjoy marine sports such as windsurfing, sailing and scuba diving. But I'm happy concentrating on making whisky now. I like to go to bars when I'm tired with something. When I'm happy with something, I like to go to bars, too. And I live in a mountainous area with nice rivers, so fishing might be good as my next hobby.

Hakushu

Owner: Suntory *Founded*: 1973
Location: Yamanashi Prefecture
Capacity: Undisclosed (estimated 3,000,000 litres)
Malt whisky range: Hakushu Single Malt NAS, 10, 12,
18 and 25 years old plus regular limited releases.

In late 2011, Hakushu finally arrived in the US. Suntory launched the 12 years old after Yamazaki 12 and the blended Hibiki 12 had established Suntory's whisky reputation Stateside. A company spokesperson says first-year demand surpassed expectations and the company increased the US allotment from 300 cases to 320. For 2012, they are expecting to ship 650 cases.

Domestically, Suntory added a no-age statement single malt to the Hakushu line-up, with predicted sales of 10,000 cases in 2012. The company has also made the 10 and 12 year olds the focus of a single malt highball campaign as it tries to nudge consumers upmarket from the blended highballs that re-energized Japan's whisky market.

To cope with the surging demand, Suntory spent around 100 million yen (US$80 million) to boost the distillery's capacity by around 10 percent. They added four washbacks, bringing the total to 18. This comeback is great news for what was once the world's biggest distillery. In the giddy 1980s, when whisky consumption was peaking in Japan, Hakushu had two stillhouses and 36 stills. Now it has 12 stills in one building. Those stills come in all manner of shapes. The malt can be unpeated, peated or heavily peated. Suntory periodically releases a limited run of heavily peated Hakushu (as well as bourbon barrel and sherry cask expressions).

The distillery stands more than 700 metres above sea level in the Japanese Alps. The marketing makes much of Hakushu's verdant setting, and the whisky does seem to have sucked flavours straight from its forested surroundings.

Tasting note:
Hakushu 12 year old
A clean nose of pepper and wood shavings. On the palate, forest floor, bamboo, pepper, fresh apple, with an elegant smokiness. The pepper stays with the long finish.

Hanyu

Owner: Toa Shuzo *Founded*: 1941
Location: Saitama Prefecture
Capacity: Dismantled
Malt whisky range: A wide variety of limited single cask, single malt and other bottlings.

Ichiro Akuto wanted to work for the Yamazaki distillery, but when he joined Suntory they had him marketing import liquor instead. It may not have been his dream job, but perhaps the experience paid off. He has proven adept at marketing the stock from his family's late Hanyu distillery. Most of the casks have been bottled as part of the Ichiro's Malt Card Series. Each release features a different playing card on the label. The device helps consumers remember their favourites, makes single-cask whiskies approachable for neophytes, and encourages completists to buy every release.

Akuto also showed himself to be a fan of finishes, using mizunara and wood that once held Madeira, cream sherry, oloroso, Pedro Ximenez, port, cognac or bourbon among other styles. Hanyu's old stock is disappearing fast, but it's not done yet. Akuto says there are still around 140 casks and some will reach the market in 2013, though nothing has been fixed at time of writing. He says there will only be a small number of single cask releases in the future, but far more vatted or blended whiskies as he looks to stretch the stock. He has already released a vatting of whiskies from Hanyu and his new Chichibu distillery, under the name Ichiro's Malt Double Distilleries, as well as two expressions of Ichiro's Malt and Grain, described as a "worldwide blend" using stock from three continents.

The most recent pure Hanyu releases are the Eight of Clubs (a cask-strength 23-year-old aged in a hogshead and finished in an American oak puncheon), and the Nine of Clubs (a 20 year old aged in a hogshead and finished in a bourbon barrel). The organizers of the Tokyo International Bar Show also bottled a 12 year old finished in a quarter cask.

Tasting note:
Ichiro's Malt Four of Spades
(Distilled 2000, bottled 2010;
Hogshead with mizunara finish)
A nose of spice and cypress. More prickly and spicy on the palate, with ginger and a pleasant bitterness. Ends long and dry.

Karuizawa

Owner: Kirin Holdings   **Founded**: 1956
Location: Nagano Prefecture
Capacity: Dismantled
Malt whisky range: Single cask and Asama pure malt.

The stills have gone, the plot's been sold, the distillery is dead. Yet 2013 could be one of Karuizawa's most interesting years. The U.K.-based Number One Drinks bought the last few hundred barrels from Japanese drink giant Kirin in 2011 and has begun furnishing the world with single cask and vatted malts. Number One has been championing Karuizawa whisky for several years. Its Noh and Vintage releases put the then-mothballed distillery back in the spotlight. So it's fitting and reassuring that they'll be the people handling its legacy. According to Number One director David Croll, around two thirds of the stock will be single cask releases, and the remaining third will be vattings.

They're starting with a two-pronged attack. At the headline end of the spectrum, the oldest (and most expensive) Japanese single malt is slated to appear in late 2012. It sat 52 years in a 250-litre sherry cask and is everything Karuizawa is known for: so deep and sherried it's like drinking a gentleman's library, all mahogany, leather and shoe polish.

That release will do nothing to placate those who grumble that Karuizawa whisky is expensive. But the pure malts might. Number One hired a pair of blenders to create a recipe from the distillery's final vintages. They vatted 77 casks, then tipped the result back into sherry butts and shipped them to the Chichibu distillery for further aging. The first release appeared in mid-2012 under the name Asama. Expect the rest to trickle out in various guises. The pure malts will challenge established notions of Karuizawa price and flavour. Perhaps Number One Drinks' greatest achievement will be to show that it was a multifaceted distillery that should never have closed.

Tasting note:
Asama Vatted Malt
The nose is straightforward baked apple pie, crust and all. On the tongue, it's toast and cereal at first, with a salty licorice coming later. Oily, with a short finish.

Miyagikyo

Owner: Nikka Whisky   **Founded**: 1969
Location: Miyagi Prefecture
Capacity: 5,000,000 litres
Malt whisky range: NAS, 10, 12, 15 years old and occasional 20 years and single cask releases.

Nikka's second distillery, in chronology and reputation, deserves a lot more attention than it gets. For one thing, without Miyagikyo, Nikka couldn't make its Taketsuru pure malt, the whisky that can't stop winning awards. This is the graceful beauty that tames the Yoichi beast. And while it isn't as decorated as Yoichi, Miyagikyo has been picking up some medals recently. The 10, 12 and 15 year olds all won silvers at the International Spirits Challenge 2012. The distillery has eight pot stills and two sets

of Coffey stills. It produces both malt and grain spirit, and sometimes sends malt through its Coffey stills. The Coffey malt can finish up vatted with pot still malt or bottled on its own as a single cask release. Coffey grain bottlings also appear from time to time, as one did in September 2012 as a Europe-only release for La Maison du Whisky. As with Nikka's other distillery, this was the creation of Masataka Taketsuru, who searched Japan for a location with the perfect humidity, geology, air purity and access to water. Miyagikyo fitted the bill perfectly. It's surrounded by mountains and sandwiched by rivers. It's also close to the heart of the 2011 disaster, but only suffered minor damage. The distillery has gone by the names Sendai and Sakunami. It became Miyagikyo in 2001, just as the world was starting to pay attention to Japanese whisky.

Tasting note:
Miyagikyo 12 year old
A nose of persimmon, vanilla fudge and tobacco. It's chewy in the mouth, and moves from dense autumn fruit into creamy chocolate and leather. The finish is long, long, long.

Shinshu

Owner: Hombo Shuzo **Founded**: 1985
Location: Nagano Prefecture
Capacity: 25,000 litres
Malt whisky range: Mars Maltage 3 plus 25 pure malt, Komagatake 10 years old pure malt, and occasional single cask releases.

Japan's most elevated distillery sits 798 meters up in the central Japanese Alps. Its owner, Hombo Shuzo, began life in 1872 as a cotton processing company. It branched out into shochu in 1909, then added a whisky license forty years later. Over the years they've had three whisky distilleries, first on their home turf of Kagoshima, using tiny cylindrical stills, barely larger than a washing machine. In 1969, they asked Kiichiro Iwai to design a distillery in Yamanashi Prefecture, west of Tokyo. Iwai was one of the men who backed Nikka Whisky founder Masataka Taketsuru's pivotal 1918 research trip to Scotland, and he based the distillery on Taketsuru's report. They moved the operation to Shinshu in 1985, but just 7 years later they halted production as whisky sales plummeted.

Now that whisky drinking is back, so is Shinshu. Hombo dusted off the equipment and began distilling again in February 2011. Though their Mars brand name is most associated with blends, they say they plan to focus on single malts this time around. They issued 1,000 bottles of new make spirit in 2012, but haven't made plans for further releases. In the meantime, they're tapping their old stock. A 20 years old single cask whisky from the first Shinshu era will reach consumers in 2013. There's also a pair of pure malts. Komagatake 10 years old uses Yamanashi and Shinshu whisky. Mars Maltage 3 plus 25 is a drink that reflects Hombo's winding history. The company vatted 3 year old whiskies from the Kagoshima and Yamanashi distilleries, then returned it to wood for another 25 years at Shinshu. Hombo uses a variety of wood, including sherry butts, bourbon barrels, mizunara and ex-cognac casks.

Tasting note:
Mars Maltage 3 plus 25 pure malt
The aromatic nose made me think of Gewürztraminer with its Turkish Delight and marzipan. There's also a touch of rubber. On the tongue, lavender, vanilla and raisins. Medium, subtle finish.

White Oak Distillery

Owner: Eigashima Shuzo **Founded**: 1919
Location: Hyogo Prefecture
Capacity: 60,000 litres
Malt whisky range: NAS, limited 14, 15 years old Akashi single malts.

White Oak is, technically, Japan's oldest distillery. It received its whisky license in 1919, four years before Yamazaki was built. But current president Mikio Hiraishi says "we may have been selling whisky, but weren't distilling malt until the 1960s." When White Oak finally started running stills, they focused on lower shelf blends. The first single malt didn't arrive until 2007. But over the last 5 years, they've released 5, 8, 12 and 14 years old single malts under their Akashi brand. They use lightly peated malt (5ppm) and age it in either Spanish or American oak. Sadly, most of those releases have run dry. Happily, there are new styles to take their place.

A no age statement Akashi appeared in September 2012 and Hiraishi says this will be one of White Oak's core products. A revised version of the 14 years old will appear in late 2012. The first spent 18 months finishing in French oak that once held white wine. The next release will spend only six months in the wine cask. More intriguingly, White Oak's oldest single malt to date will debut in spring 2013. It's almost certainly the first whisky to be finished in Japan's konara oak, (*Quercus serrata*). Like its more famous cousin mizunara (*Quercus mongolica*), konara is leaky. And konara trees are short. All in all, far from ideal for casks. But the owner of White Oak, used to produce shochu in Oita Prefecture, where it's not unusual to age the Japanese spirit in konara. So they had a little leaky wood to hand. Eigashima has also been making sake for centuries, and drew on that experience when they began distilling malt. Most Japanese distilleries source dry yeast from Scotland, but Eigashima makes a liquid starter. They say it's a faster and smoother method of fermenting, but since it's the only method they've ever used, they aren't sure what effect it has on the flavour.

Tasting note:
Akashi non-age statement single malt
The sweet raisin juice nose reveals a sherry cask influence, but it's light on the palate and the bourbon wood pokes through with biscuits and pine.

Yamazaki

Owner: Suntory **Founded**: 1923
Location: Osaka Prefecture
Capacity: Undisclosed (estimated 3,500,000 litres)
Malt whisky range: NAS, 10, 12, 18, 25 years old and regular limited bottlings.

Yamazaki distillery had a good year. In March, its 25 years old was crowned Best Single Malt at the World Whiskies Awards. It's the first time a distillery has taken the title twice in succession (a Yamazaki 1984 won the previous year). The following month, the 18 years old took double gold at the San Francisco World Spirits Competition, then gold at the International Spirits Challenge in August. Suntory added to the core range for the first time in 14 years. The new no-age statement is a fraction cheaper than the 10 years old. The company aims to shift 20,000 cases in the first year. For drinkers with deeper pockets, Suntory released a Yamazaki 50 years old for the third time at the tail end of 2011. Despite the million yen price tag, all 150 bottles sold out within the week.

Last year we reported a warning by Suntory Global Brand Ambassador Mike Miyamoto that Yamazaki supplies might not be able to meet global demand. This year, a spokesperson for the company says only that they're carefully managing their marketing, and the strategy for Europe and the US is to "communicate the value of Japanese whisky, rather than selling a large quantity."

The distillery has 12 pot stills of vastly different shapes, some using direct heat, some using steam. The warehouse holds several hundred thousand casks – ex-sherry, ex-bourbon, mizunara and new wood – with various levels of charring. The result is a distillery capable of producing a spectrum of flavours. As Dave Broom noted in his *World Atlas of Whisky*, Yamazaki 18 years old isn't just a 12 years old that spent an extra 6 years in the warehouse – Suntory has the variety of stock to create a whole different recipe

Tasting note:
Yamazaki 18 year old
A lovely warm fruity nose, quite inky too. On the tongue, a big sherry flavour, dates and rich raisins. It gradually develops a floral spice, perhaps from mizunara, before a long, spicy finish.

Yoichi

Owner: Nikka Whisky **Founded**: 1934
Location: Hokkaido
Capacity: 2,000,000 litres
Malt whisky range: NAS, 10, 12, 15, 20 years old and occasional single cask releases.

You can tell a lot about Masataka Taketsuru from just a glance at the notes he took while working at Scotland's Longmorn, Hazelburn and Bo'ness distilleries. The immaculate handwriting, the diagrams so detailed you can see each bricks and rivet, the carefully spaced, perfectly straight lines representing the sea on his maps. Taketsuru was a man of detail and precision. And Yoichi, on the coast of the northernmost island of Hokkaido, is where he built a distillery to match his meticulous character.

Yoichi has always been Japan's most traditional distillery. It's the only one in Japan that heats its stills with coal. Those six stills are fairly straight to create the kind of bold spirit that Taketsuru must have been drinking in Scotland. The varying angles of the lyne arms offer some diversity, as do the differing peat levels (0ppm, 4ppm and 35-50ppm). The on-site cooperage works with new oak, sherry butts and bourbon barrels. It was a Yoichi that first scored global headlines for Japanese whisky. The 10 years old won "Best of the Best" at the 2001 World Whisky Awards. Since then the distillery has built an enviable collection of medals and trophies, including a World's Best Single Malt title for a limited release 20 years old at the WWAs in 2008.

Tasting note:
Yoichi 15 year old
A wonderful aroma of campfires, brazil nuts and dried figs. In the mouth, it's oily and a little salty, with a big body. Buttered nuts, chocolate and more dried fruit. It's got smoke, but doesn't punch you with phenol. Wonderfully balanced.

Distilleries
around the globe

Casey Overeem from Overeem Distillery, Tasmania

The number of malt whisky producers from parts of the world other than Scotland and Ireland increases month by month and this trend is especially seen in USA. Ten years ago, Bill Owens founded The American Distilling Institute in order to promote the movement of craft distilling. Ever since, Bill has published a yearly list of distillers in North America. In the first Directory, 69 producers were listed and in the 2012 edition, this number had increased to no less than 301 craft distillers in USA and an additional 16 in Canada. The majority of these do not produce malt whisky but the number of new distilleries since last year is, none-theless, impressive.

Now, it is often said that innovation in the whisky industry comes from these small, artisan producers and that the big guys had better watch out being cemented in the old traditional ways. That is not entirely true. Within the large established companies, there are plenty of innovative people who try out new methods, but the thing is that we rarely hear about them because that kind of information is business sensitive in a highly competitive industry. Having said that, it is also true that new ideas and experiments from the big members of the business tend to be about producing whisky in a more cost efficient way, rather than bringing unorthodox products on the shelves.

Many of the new distillers either come from the beer business or the wine industry and with them they often bring new, innovative ideas and are not prevented by budgets or share holders from putting these ideas to the test. One of these guys is Chip Tate, the owner of Balcones Distillery in Texas. He obviously sees rules and boundaries as something that should be broken and crossed. He uses figs and honey for his Rumble, was the first to use the native Hopi blue corn for his Baby Blue and when he produces his Brimstone Smoked Whisky he doesn´t use peat to dry the malted barley, but treats the liquid spirit with the smoke from Texas scrub oak. The rest of the world are starting to take notice of Chip and his peers and the fact that Balcones was presented with an Icons of Whisky Distillery award by Whisky Magazine in late 2011 bears testimony to that.

In other parts of the world, new whisky distilleries are established and every country has its own way of doing it. In Sweden, for example, there are ten distilleries producing malt whisky and more will follow during 2013. With few exceptions, these pioneers don´t have any experience of wine, beer or spirits production. More often they are enthusiasts that have fallen in love with whisky to the extent that they find themselves compelled to producing it with the aid of experienced consultants. These enterprises are also almost enti-rely dedicated to malt whisky produc-tion and usually produce from around 100,000 up to 1 million litres per year.

This is rarely the case in Central Euro-pe where distillers in Germany, Austria and Switzerland often are family-owned companies which have been established in the 19th century and where the third or fourth generations have added a small share of whisky production to the traditional distillation of various spirits from fruits and berries. Noticeable exceptions are, among others, Slyrs and Blaue Maus in Germa-ny and Roggenhof in Austria – all three completely devoted to whisky produc-tion and in larger volumes.

But there are even bigger distilleries to be found and with a possibility to challenge the established producers in the near future – both in terms of quality and volumes. I´m talking about Kavalan in Taiwan and Amrut in India, two distilleries that have impressed fastidious whisky drinkers around the world with their products. And in the UK, Penderyn in Wales and St George´s in England have quickly created a fan base of dedicated customers.

EUROPE

Austria

DISTILLERY: Waldviertler Roggenhof, Roggenreith
FOUNDED: 1995
OWNER/MANAGER: Johann & Monika Haider
www.roggenhof.at

In the small village of Roggenreith in northern Austria, Johann and Monika Haider have been distilling whisky since 1995. In 2005, they opened up a Whisky Experience World with guided tours, a video show, whisky tasting and exhibitions. Six years later, more than 75,000 visitors find their way to the distillery every year. Roggenhof was the first whisky distillery in Austria and over the years production has increased to currently reach 30,000 litres. The capacity is 100,000 litres annually. The wash is allowed to ferment for 72 hours before it reaches either of the two 450 litre Christian Carl copper stills. The desired strength is reached in one single distillation, thanks to the attached column.

The new make is filled in casks made of the local Manhartsberger Oak adding a slight vanilla flavour and left to mature for three years. When the casks are used a second time, the whisky matures for five years. The casks are used a third time, but only after dismantling, shaving and charring before filling. Spirit on third fill casks is expected to mature for 12-18 years. Two single malts made of barley are available: Gersten Malzwhisky J. H. (light malt) and Gersten Malzwhisky J. H. Karamell (dark, roasted malt). There are also three different rye whiskies.

DISTILLERY: Reisetbauer, Kirchberg-Thening
FOUNDED: 1994 (whisky since 1995)
OWNER/MANAGER: Julia & Hans Reisetbauer
www.reisetbauer.at

This is a family-owned farm distillery near Linz in northern Austria specialising in brandies and fruit schnapps. Since 1995, a range of malt whiskies are also produced. The distillery is equipped with five 350 litre stills. All stills are heated, using hot water rather than steam, which, according to Hans Reisetbauer, allows for a more delicate and gentle distillation. The 70 hour-long fermentation takes place in stainless steel washbacks. Approximately 20,000 litres of pure alcohol destined for whisky making are produced annually, using local barley to make the unpeated malt. Casks are sourced locally from the best Austrian wine producers.

The current range of whiskies includes a 7 year old single malt which consists of a vatting of whiskies aged in casks that have previously contained Chardonnay and Trockenbeerenauslese. There is also a12 year old (the first for Austria) which has undergone maturation in Trockenbeerenauslese barrels.

DISTILLERY: Destillerie Weutz, St. Nikolai im Sausal
FOUNDED: 2002
OWNER/MANAGER: Michael & Brigitte Weutz
www.weutz.at

This family distillery, initially producing schnapps and liqueur from fruits and berries, is situated in Steiermark in the south of Austria. In 2004 Michael Weutz started cooperation with the brewer Michael Löscher and since then Weutz has added whisky to its produce based on the wash from the brewery. The business grew quickly and in 2006 the distillery moved to a bigger location.

Since 2004, 14 different malt whiskies have been produced. Some of them are produced in the traditional Scottish style: Hot Stone, St. Nikolaus and the peated Black Peat. Others are more unorthodox, for example Green Panther, in which 5% pumpkin seeds are added to the mash, and Franziska based on elderflower. Annual production is currently at approximately 14,000 litres and for maturation casks made of French Limousin and Alliere oak are used.

DISTILLERY: Old Raven, Neustift
FOUNDED: 2004
OWNER/MANAGER: Andreas Schmidt
www.oldraven.at

In 1999, Andreas Schmidt opened up his Rabenbräu brewery on their family estate. Five years later a distillery was added, located in what used to be a Hungarian customs house before 1914. More than 250,000 litres of beer are produced yearly and the wash from the brewery is used for distillation of the 2,000 litres of single malt whisky every year. Old Raven, which is triple distilled, comes in three expressions – Old Raven, Old Raven Smoky and Old Raven R1 Smoky. The last one was filled into a PX sherry cask which had been used to mature Islay whisky. The first whisky was released in 2009 as a 5 year old.

DISTILLERY: Broger Privatbrennerei, Klaus
FOUNDED: 1976 (whisky since 2008)
OWNER/MANAGER: Broger family
www.broger.info

Like many other distilleries in Central Europe, Broger is producing whisky to supplement the distillation and production of eau de viex, in Broger´s case, from apples and pears. For their whisky, peated malt is bought from Crisp in the UK and unpeated malt from Germany. The distillery is equipped with a 1,000 litre mash tun, a 150 litre Christian Carl still and a 1,000 litre washback with a four to five day fermentation time. The total volume of whisky produced in a year is 700 litres. A large variety of casks are used for maturation (bourbon, sherry, port and sauternes) and the sizes vary from 25 litres up to 250 litres. The first release was a three and a half year old single malt in autumn 2011 and the next release is expected to be a smoked malt (not peated but smoked using beech wood).

Bruno and Eugen Broger from Broger Privatbrennerei

Andreas Schmidt from Old Raven Distillery

DISTILLERY: Wolfram Ortner Destillerie, Bad Kleinkirchheim
FOUNDED: 1990
OWNER/MANAGER: Wolfram Ortner
www.wob.at

Fruit brandies of all kinds make up the bulk of Wolfram Ortner´s produce, as well as cigars, coffee and other luxuries. For the last years he has also been producing malt whisky. New oak of different kinds (Limousin, Alolier, Nevers, Vosges and American) is used for the maturation process. His first single malt, WOB DÖ MALT Vergin, began selling in 2001 and an additional product line, in which Ortner mixes his whisky with other distillates such as orange/moscatel, is called WOB Marriage.

Belgium

DISTILLERY: The Owl Distillery, Grâce Hollogne
FOUNDED: 1997
OWNER/MANAGER: Etienne Bouillon (manager), Christian Polis & Pierre Roberti
www.belgianwhisky.com
www.thebelgianowl.com

In October 2007, Belgium's first single malt 'The Belgian Owl', was released. The next bottling came in 2008 but was exclusively reserved for private customers. The first commercial bottling was introduced in November 2008. A limited cask strength expression, 44 months old, was released in 2009 and more cask strength versions have followed. The distillery is equipped with a mash tun holding 4.1 tonnes per mash, one washback with a fermentation time of 60-100 hours and, until recently, one wash still (550 litres) and one spirit still (450 litres). The demand for The Belgian Owl single malt has grown dramatically and the owners were forced to increase capacity. Instead of having new stills manufactured, the decision was made to buy two stills (11,000 and 8,000 litres respectively) that had previously been used at the now demolished Caperdonich distillery in Rothes, Speyside. At the same time, production moved to a new location in Ferme de Goreux, close to where their barley is grown.

Etienne Bouillon, owner of The Owl Distillery

DISTILLERY: Het Anker Distillery, Blaasfeld
FOUNDED: 1369 (whisky since 2003)
OWNER/MANAGER: Charles Leclef (owner)
www.hetanker.be

Seven years ago the producer of the quality beer Gouden Carolus, Brouwerij Het Anker, and its owner, Charles Leclef, decided to find out how whisky, distilled from the brewery's wash, would taste. Distillation of the spirits was tasked to nearby genever distiller, Filliers, and was done in a genever column still. The result was Gouden Carolus Single Malt – the third Belgian malt whisky to reach the market after Belgian Owl and Goldlys. The first 3,000 bottles were released in January 2008.

No new releases were made in 2009. Instead, Leclef concentrated on the next step in the project, namely, building a distillery of his own with pot stills. The location chosen was not at the brewery in Mechelen, but at Leclef´s family estate, Molenberg, at Blaasfeld. Leclef is the fifth generation of a family that long since has been involved in distilling genever and brewing beer. The distillery started producing in October 2010. The stills have been made by Forsyth´s in Scotland with a wash still of 3,000 litre capacity and a spirit still of 2,000 litres. The wash for the distillation is made at the brewery in Mechelen and it is basically a Gouden Carolus Tripel beer without hops and spices and with a fermentation time of four to five days. Around 100,000 litres of alcohol are produced per year and the first release will be in December 2013.

Czech Rebublic

DISTILLERY: Gold Cock Distillery
FOUNDED: 1877
OWNER/MANAGER: Rudolf Jelinek a.s
www.rjelinek.cz

The distilling of Gold Cock whisky started already in 1877. Gold Cock was originally a malt whisky made from abundnt local barley. Now it is produced in two versions – a 3 year old blended whisky and a 12 year old malt. Production was stopped for a while but after the brand and distillery were acquired by R. Jelinek a.s., the leading Czech producer of plum brandy, the whisky began life anew. The malt whisky is double distilled in 500 litre traditional pot stills. The new owner has created a small whisky museum which is also home to the club Friends of Gold Cock Whisky with private vaults, where any enthusiast can store his bottlings of Gold Cock.

Denmark

DISTILLERY: Braunstein, Køge
FOUNDED: 2005 (whisky since 2007)
OWNER/MANAGER: Michael & Claus Braunstein
www.braunstein.dk

Denmark's first micro-distillery was built in an already existing brewery in Køge, just south of Copenhagen. Unlike many other brewery/whisky distillery enterprises around the world, the owners consider the whisky production to be on equal terms with beer production, even in financial terms.

The wash, of course, comes from the own brewery. A Holstein type of still, with four plates in the rectification column, is used for distillation and the spirit is distilled once. For five winter months, peated whisky (+60ppm) is produced, while the rest of the year is devoted to unpeated varieties. Peated malt is bought from Port Ellen, unpeated from Simpsons, but as much as 40% is from ecologically grown Danish barley. The lion's share of the whisky is stored on ex-bourbon (peated version) and first fill Oloroso casks (unpeated) from 190 up to 500 litres.

The Braunstein brothers filled their first spirit casks in 2007 and have produced 50,000 litres annually since then. Their first release and the first release of a malt whisky produced in Denmark was in 2010 – a 3 year old single Oloroso sherry cask called Edition No. 1 which was followed the same year by Library Collection 10:1, bottled at 46%. The first Braunstein whisky from 100% ecologically grown barley, was released as Edition No. 3 in 2011 and in 2012 came Library Collection 12:1, sherry matured with a sauternes finish, and Library Collection 12:2 and Edition No. 4 – both bourbon matured and peated.

DISTILLERY: Stauning Whisky, Stauning
FOUNDED: 2006
OWNER/MANAGER: Stauning Whisky A/S
www.stauningwhisky.dk

The first Danish purpose-built malt whisky distillery entered a more adolescent phase in May 2009, after having experimented with two small pilot stills bought from Spain. Two, new Portuguese-made stills of 1,000 and 600 litres respectively were installed and the distillery was able to produce 6,000 litres of alcohol annually. In 2012 another couple of stills were installed which increased the capacity to 12-15,000 litres.

The aim has always been to be self-sustaining and Danish barley is bought and turned into malt on an own malting floor. The germinating barley usually has to be turned 6-8 times a day, but Stauning has constructed an automatic "grain turner" to do the job. Two core expressions were decided on – Peated Reserve and Traditional Reserve – and the peat for the first one is acquired from one of few remaining peat bogs in Denmark. In June 2012 the first edition of the two versions were released with slightly more than 700 bottles of each. A further

variety, a rye whisky made from 100% malted rye, is also made and the third bottling (Third Solution) was launched in June.

DISTILLERY: Ørbæk Bryggeri, Ørbæk
FOUNDED: 1997 (whisky since 2007)
OWNER/MANAGER: Niels and Nicolai Rømer
www.oerbaek-bryggeri.nu

Niels Rømer and his son, Nicolai, have run Ørbæk Brewery since 1997 on the Danish island of Fyn. It is now one of many combinations of a micro-brewery and a micro-distillery where the wash from the brewery is used to produce whisky. In June 2009 the first barrels of Isle of Fionia single malt were filled and the first release was made exactly three years later. The whisky, in common with Ørbæk's beer, is ecological and two different expressions are produced – Isle of Fionia and the peated Fionia Smoked Whisky. It is matured in ex-bourbon barrels from Jack Daniels and ex-sherry casks. In April 2011, the Rømer family announced that they had plans to open yet another distillery in Nyborg, some 10 miles from the existing plant. An old railway workshop was bought and if everything goes according to plan, the new distillery could open in 2013.

DISTILLERY: Fary Lochan Destilleri, Give
FOUNDED: 2009
OWNER/MANAGER: Jens Erik Jørgensen
www.farylochan.dk

This is the second, purpose-built whisky distillery in Denmark to come on stream and, just like the first, Stauning, it is situated in Jutland. The first cask was filled in December 2009 and the owner has recently increased the production from 6,000 bottles per year to 10,000. The actual capacity of the distillery is 12,000 bottles.

Jørgensen imports most of the malted barley from the UK, but he also malts some Danish barley by himself. A part of his own malted barley is dried using nettles instead of peat to create a special flavour. This is a well-known technique used in Denmark to produce smoked cheese. After mashing, it is fermented for five days in a 600 litre stainless steel washback. Distillation is performed in two traditional copper pot stills from Forsyth's in Scotland – a 300 litre wash still and a 200 litre spirit still. The spirit is matured in ex-bourbon barrels, some of which have been remade into quarter casks. The first release (750 bottles very lightly smoked) is expected to take place in autumn 2013.

First releases of Isle of Fionia and Stauning

Jens Erik Jørgensen in the Fary Lochan still room

DISTILLERY: Trolden Distillery, Kolding
FOUNDED: 2011
OWNER/MANAGER: Michael Svendsen
www.trolden.com

The distillery is a part of the Trolden Brewery which started in 2005. Michael Svendsen, the owner, uses the wash from the brewery and ferments it for 4-5 days before a double distillation in a 325 litre alembic pot still. The spirit is filled in bourbon casks and production is quite small as brewing beer is the main task. The first release of the whisky will be in December 2014.

England _____

DISTILLERY: St. George´s Distillery,
Roudham, Norfolk
FOUNDED: 2006
OWNER/MANAGER: The English Whisky Co.
www.englishwhisky.co.uk

St. George´s Distillery near Thetford in Norfolk was started by father and son, James and Andrew Nelstrop, and came on stream on 12th December 2006. This made it the first English malt whisky distillery for over a hundred years. Customers, both in the UK and abroad, have had the opportunity to follow the development of the whisky via releases of new make, as well as 18 months old spirit, both peated and unpeated. These were called Chapters 1 to 4. Finally, in December 2009, it was time for the release of the first legal whisky called Chapter 5 – unpeated and without chill filtering or colouring. This was a limited release but, soon afterwards, Chapter 6 was released in larger quantities. The next expression (Chapter 8) was a limited release of a lightly peated 3 year old, followed in June 2010 by Chapter 9 (with the same style but more widely available). Chapter 7, a 3 year old with 6 months finish in a rum cask, was planned for a launch in spring 2010, but was not released until autumn 2010 together with Chapter 10, which has a sherry cask finish. The next bottling, Chapter 11, appeared in July 2011. This was the heaviest peated expression so far (50ppm) while Chapters 8 and 9 had a phenol content of 32ppm. Chapter 11 is between 3 and 4 years old and has matured in bourbon casks. Cask strength versions of Chapter 6 and 11 were launched in September 2012 and one month later saw the release of the sherry cask matured Chapter 12. The owners have also announced that Chapters 14 and

Chapter 12 - the latest release from St George´s Distillery

15 are likely to be released in spring 2013 and these will be the first readily available classic and peated 5 year old malts. In between the Chapter releases there are also very limited bottlings of the so called Founder´s Private Cellar. Another limited edition was introduced in 2012 in the shape of Distiller´s Elect where the whisky has been selected by Senior Distiller David Fitt.

Around 55,000 bottles were sold in 2011 and important markets are Benelux, France, Scotland, Japan, Singapore and England. Plans are now to expand into USA, China and India.

The distillery is equipped with a stainless steel semi-lauter mash tun with a copper top and three stainless steel washbacks with a fermentation time of 85 hours. There is one pair of stills, the wash still with a capacity of 2,800 litres and the spirit still of 1,800 litre capacity. First fill bourbon barrels are mainly used for maturation but the odd Sherry, Madeira and Port casks have also been filled. Non-peated malt is bought from Crisp Malting Group and peated malt from Simpson´s Malt in Berwick-upon-Tweed. Around 60% of production is unpeated and the rest is peated. Recently, a bottling line was installed, giving St. George's the possibility to bottle using its own water source. The capacity is 800 bottles per day. Around 120,000 bottles will be produced during 2012.

Finland _____

DISTILLERY: Teerenpeli, Lahti
FOUNDED: 2002
OWNER/MANAGER: Anssi Pyysing
www.teerenpeli.com

The first Teerenpeli Single Malt was sold as a 3 year old in late 2005, though solely at the owner's restaurant in Lahti. Four years later, the first bottles of a 6 year old were sold in the Teerenpeli Restaurants and later that year also in the state owned ALKO-shops. In spring 2011, it was time for an 8 year old, which was introduced at Whisky Live in London. This is a mix of whisky from both bourbon and sherry casks. The owner has plans for a 100% sherry matured version called Distiller´s Choice Kaski which will be released in 2013.

Teerenpeli is equipped with one wash still (1,500 litres) and one spirit still (900 litres) and the average fermentation time in the washback is 70 hours. Lightly peated malt obtained locally is used and the whisky matures in ex-sherry and ex-bourbon casks from Speyside Cooperage. 7,500 bottles are produced annually. In August 2010 a new mash tun was installed and later that month a new visitor centre was opened.

France _____

DISTILLERY: Glann ar Mor, Pleubian, Bretagne
FOUNDED: 1999
OWNER/MANAGER: Jean Donnay
www.glannarmor.com

The owner of Glann ar Mor Distillery in Brittany, Jean Donnay, already started his first trials back in 1999. He then made some changes to the distillery and the process and regular production commenced in 2005. The distillery is very much about celebrating the traditional way of distilling malt whisky. The two small stills are directly fired and Donnay uses worm tubs for condensing the spirit. He practises a long fermentation in wooden washbacks and the distillation is very slow. For maturation, first fill bourbon barrels and ex-Sauternes casks are used and when the whisky is bottled, there is neither chill filtration nor caramel colouring. The full capacity is 50,000 bottles per year. In 2008 the company opened its new premises, including a larger warehouse and a visitor centre, a couple of miles away from the distillery's location.

There are two versions of the whisky from Glann ar Mor – the unpeated Glann ar Mor matured in bourbon barrels and the peated Kornog matured in either bourbon barrels or Sauternes casks. The first release, in 2008, was a 3 year old Glann ar Mor followed in 2009 by a Kornog bottled at cask strength. The most recent expressions are the bourbon matured Kornog Sant Erwan 2012 bottled at 50% and the second edition of Kornog Sant Ivy at 59,9% There is also a new edition of the unpeated Glann ar Mor Taol Esa 1an Gwech 12 bottled at 46%.

Apart from the Glann ar Mor venture, Jean Donnay has also specialised in double maturation Single Malts. The "Celtique Connexion" range includes whiskies originally distilled and matured in Scotland, then further matured at the company's seaside warehouse. The whiskies can be found at *www.tregorwhisky.com*

DISTILLERY: Distillerie Warenghem,
Lannion, Bretagne
FOUNDED: 1900 (whisky since 1994)
OWNER/MANAGER: Warenghem
www.distillerie-warenghem.com

Leon Warenghem founded the distillery at the beginning of the 20th century but Armorik, the first malt whisky, was not distilled until 1994 and released in 1999. Since 1983 Gilles Leîzour has run the distillery. The Armorik single malt now exists in two versions; a 4 year old that is bottled at 40%, matured in bourbon barrels and finished in sherry casks, and a 7 year old (42%) with a double maturation in fresh oak and sherry butts. Three blended whiskies supplement the range; Whisky Breton W. B., a 3 year old with 25% share of malt, Breizh matured in fresh oak and with a 50% malt content, as well as Galleg, matured in both sherry and bourbon casks and also with a 50% malt content.

DISTILLERY: Distillerie Guillon,
Louvois, Champagne
FOUNDED: 1997
OWNER/MANAGER: Thierry Guillon
www.whisky-guillon.com

Thierry Guillon, originally a wine man, decided in 1997 to begin distilling whisky. Not perhaps a novel idea if it was not for the fact that the distillery is located in the heart

of the Champagne district. But besides champagne this area is also known as a major barley producer in France. In fact, several Scottish maltsters buy barley from this region. Guillon has increased his production steadily and now makes 140,000 bottles a year and has 1,200 casks maturing on site.

The range of single malts is quite large and vary in age between 4 and 10 years. Guillon No. 1, has a particularly interesting maturation process. It is a 5 year old matured in a new oak cask the first year, a whisky barrel the second year, then white wine, red wine and finally the last year in a Port pipe. Apart from single malts there is also a blend in the range, Le Premium Blend, consisting of 50% malt and 50% grain whisky and a whisky liqueur. The whisky is exported to several European countries, as well as to China. There is also a visitor centre, which attracts 15,000 visitors per year.

DISTILLERY: Distillerie Bertrand,
Uberach, Alsace
FOUNDED: 1874 (whisky since 2002)
OWNER/MANAGER: Affiliate of Wolfberger
www.distillerie-bertrand.com

Distillerie Bertrand is an independent affiliate of Wolfberger, the large wine and eaux-de-vie producer. The manager, Jean Metzger, gets his malt from a local brewer and then distils it in Holstein type stills. Two different types of whisky are produced. One is a single malt at 42.2%, non-chill filtered and with maturation in both new barrels and barrels which have previously contained the fortified wine Banyuls. The other is a single cask at 43.8% matured only in Banyuls barrels. The first bottles, aged 4 years, were released in late 2006 and the annual production is around 7,000 bottles with 5,000 bottles currently being sold per year.

Recent new releases include two single casks; the 9 year old L´Ultime matured in a Banyuls cask and the 8 year old V8 which was matured in new French limousin oak.

At the moment, Uberach Single Malt Alsace, a name taken from the village, is only sold in France, Germany, Switzerland, Luxembourg and Andorra.

Germany _____

DISTILLERY: Slyrs Destillerie, Schliersee
FOUNDED: 1928 (whisky since 1999)
OWNER/MANAGER: Florian Stetter
www.slyrs.de

Lantenhammer Destillerie in Schliersee, Bavaria was founded in 1928 and was producing mainly brandy until 1999 when whisky came into the picture, and in 2003 Slyrs Destillerie was founded. The malt, smoked with beech, comes from locally grown grain, and the spirit is distilled twice at low temperatures in the 1,500 litre stills. Maturation takes place in charred 225-litre casks of new American White Oak from Missouri. Recently the owner decided to double the capacity of the distillery. Investments in three new fermentation tanks (washbacks) and a malt silo during 2009/2010 increased the capacity to 60,000 bottles.

The non chill-filtered whisky is called Slyrs after the original name of the surrounding area, Schliers. Around 40,000 bottles are sold annually. The owners are releasing a new "vintage" every spring and they are now selling 2009. In autumn 2011, the range was expanded with a cask strength version bottled at 54.9%. Slyrs whisky is available in several European countries and is also exported to the USA and Australia.

The two versions from Glann ar Mor - Kornog and Glann ar Mor

DISTILLERY: Spreewälder Feinbrand- & Likörfabrik, Schlepzig
FOUNDED: 2004 (whisky production)
OWNER/MANAGER: Torsten Römer
www.spreewaldbrennerei.de

The product range consists of different kinds of beers, eau-de-vie and rum, and since 2004 also malt whisky. The distillery is equipped with a 650 litre still with eight trays in the fractionating column and is fired using gas. The annual production of whisky and rum has now increased to 15,000 litres per year.

French Oak casks, that have previously contained wine made of Sylvaner and Riesling grapes, are used for maturation, as well as new Spessart oak casks. Torsten Römer is also looking for other casks in Germany, France and Spain. Before filling into casks the spirit is left for six months in stainless steel tanks. The whisky, which was first released in December 2007 as a 3 year old, is called Sloupisti. Most of the production is bottled at 40%, but a cask strength bottling was released in autumn 2010.

DISTILLERY: Whisky-Destillerie Blaue Maus, Eggolsheim-Neuses
FOUNDED: 1980
OWNER/MANAGER: Robert Fleischmann
www.fleischmann-whisky.de

This is the oldest single malt whisky distillery in Germany and it celebrated its 25th anniversary in February 2008. The first distillate, never released on the market, was made in 1983. It took 15 years until the first whisky, Glen Mouse 1986, appeared. Fleischmann uses unpeated malt and the whisky matures for approximately eight years in casks of fresh German Oak. A completely new still room is currently under construction. All whisky from Blaue Maus are single cask and with the release of new expressions in 2011, Seute Deern, Elbe 1 and Otto's Uisge Beatha, there are currently ten single malts, the others being Blaue Maus, Spinnaker, Krottentaler, Schwarzer Pirat, Grüner Hund, Austrasier and Old Fahr. Some of them are released at cask strength while others are reduced to 40%. The oldest bottlings are more than 20 years old.

DISTILLERY: Hammerschmiede, Zorge
FOUNDED: 1984 (whisky since 2002)
OWNER/MANAGER: Karl-Theodor and Alexander Buchholz
www.hammerschmiede.de

In common with many other small whisky producers on mainland Europe, Hammerschmiede's main products are liqueurs, bitters and spirits from fruit, berries and herbs. But whisky distilling was embarked on in 2002 and whisky production has now increased to 15% of the total.

The first bottles were released in 2006 under the name Glan Iarran. Today, all whisky produced has changed name to Glen Els. So far, the owners have specialized in single cask releases and this will continue. In autumn 2010, however, the first "distillery edition" of Glen Els was launched. The bottlings for 2012 include the first woodsmoked edition in three different editions – ancient oak, marsala and madeira – and in November another woodsmoked version was released, Alrik, which will become a permanent part of the range with a PX maturation available later in 2012.

DISTILLERY: Bayerwald-Bärwurzerei und Spezialitäten-Brennerei Liebl, Kötzting
FOUNDED: 1970 (whisky since 2006)
OWNER/MANAGER: Gerhard Liebl Jr.
www.bayerischer-whisky.de

In 1970 Gerhard Liebl started spirit distillation from fruits and berries and in 2006 his son, Gerhard Liebl Jr., built a completely new whisky distillery. Leibl Jr. uses 100%

Bavarian malt and the wash is left to ferment for 3-5 days. It is then double distilled in Holstein stills (wash still 400 litres and spirit still 150 litres).

Maturation takes place in first or second fill ex-bourbon barrels, except for whisky destined to be bottled as single casks. Sherry, Port, Bordeaux and Cognac casks are used here. The whisky is non chill-filtered and non-coloured. About 10,000 litres of whisky are produced per year and in 2009 the first 1,500 bottles bearing the name Coillmór were released in three different expressions – American White Oak, Sherry single cask and Bordeaux single cask. Since then, a number of other expressions have been released such as Port single cask and a 5 year old peated version with a maturation in Cognac casks.

DISTILLERY: Preussische Whiskydestillerie, Mark Landin
FOUNDED: 2009
OWNER/MANAGER: Cornelia Bohn
www.preussischerwhisky.de

Cornelia Bohn, one of few female whisky producers in Germany, purchased a closed-down distillery in 2009 in the Uckermark region, one hour's drive from Berlin. The distillery had been operational for 100 years up until WWII when Russian soldiers took it apart and the last copper stills disappeared in the 1950s. She installed a 550 litre copper still with a 4-plate rectification column attached and brought in malt from a malting in Bamberg. Some of the malt is smoked (not peated) using beechwood. The fermentation is done with all the solids from the mashing still left in the washbacks, to get a more full-bodied and robust result. The spirit is distilled five to six times and is then matured in casks made of American oak, as well as the German Spessart oak. Circa 2000 litres per year are produced and the first release of a 3 year old whisky is scheduled for December 2012.

DISTILLERY: Brennerei Höhler, Aarbergen
FOUNDED: 1895 (whisky since 2001)
OWNER/MANAGER: Holger Höhler
www.brennerei-hoehler.de

The main produce from this distillery in Hessen consists of different distillates from fruit and berries. In November

Cornelia Bohn, owner of Preussische Whiskydestillerie

2000, a new 390 litre still with four rectifying plates from Firma Christian Carl was installed. Whisky production commenced thereafter. The first whisky, a bourbon variety, was distilled in 2001 and released in 2004. Since then, Holger Höhler has experimented with different types of grain (rye, barley, spelt and oat). There was a limited release of a single malt in July 2007 and a very limited amount of whisky has been released since then. Until recently, all casks were made from Sessart oak with a storage capacity of between 30 and 75 litres. In spring 2007 Höhler started filling 225 litres barriques.

DISTILLERY: Stickum Brennerei (Uerige),
Düsseldorf
FOUNDED: 2007
OWNER/MANAGER: ObergärigeHausbrauerei GmbH
www.stickum.de

Uerige Brewery, which celebrates its 150th anniversary this year, was completed with a distillery in 2007. The wash comes from their own brewery, of course, and the distillation takes place in a 250 litre column still. For the maturation they use new oak but also bourbon, sherry and port casks. The distillery produces 1,200 litres per year of their whisky BAAS and the first bottling (a 3 year old) was released in December 2010. The whisky is sold in Germany but can also, surprisingly, be found in Whisky Shop in San Francisco (July 2012).

DISTILLERY: Kleinbrennerei Fitzke,
Herbolzheim-Broggingen
FOUNDED: 1874 (whisky since 2004)
OWNER/MANAGER: Fitzke family
www.kleinbrennerei-fitzke.de

The main commerce for this old distillery is the production of schnapps, eau de viex and vodka, but they also distil 900 litres of whisky from different grains. Mashing, fermentation and distillation all take place at the distillery and for maturation they use 30 litres oak casks. For the first six months they use virgin oak and thereafter the spirit is filled into used barrels for another two and a half years. The first release of the Schwarzwälder Whisky single malt was in 2007 and new batches have been launched ever since.

DISTILLERY: Rieger & Hofmeister,
Fellbach
FOUNDED: 1994 (whisky since 2006)
OWNER/MANAGER: Rieger and Hofmeister families
www.rieger-hofmeister.de

Marcus Hofmeister´s stepfather, Albrecht Rieger, started the distillery and when Marcus entered the business in 2006 he expanded it to also include whisky production. The mashing is done in a keg with a mixer, the mash is then fermented in a stainless steel tank for five days before distillation. Marcus selects a middle cut starting at 80% and coming off at 70% and maturation takes place in casks from local wine producers. The first release of this Schwäbischer Whisky was in 2009 and currently there are two expressions in the range - a single malt matured in Pinot Noir casks and a Malt & Grain (50% wheat, 40% barley and 10% smoked barley) from Chardonnay casks.

DISTILLERY: Kinzigbrennerei, Biberach
FOUNDED: 1937 (whisky since 2004)
OWNER/MANAGER: Brosamer family
www.kinzigbrennerei.de

Martin Brosamer is the third generation in the family and he is also the one who expanded the production to include whisky in 2004. The total production of whisky is 2,000 litres annually. In the beginning, Martin filled small casks (50 litres) made of new oak but has progressively moved to larger casks. The first release in 2008 was Badische Whisky, a blend made from wheat and barley. Two years later came Biberacher Whisky, the first single malt and in 2012, the range was expanded with Schwarzwälder Rye Whisky and the smoky single malt Kinzigtäler Whisky.

DISTILLERY: Destillerie Kammer-Kirsch,
Karlsruhe
FOUNDED: 1961 (whisky since 2006)
OWNER/MANAGER: Gerald Erdrich
www.kammer-kirsch.de

Like for so many distilleries, production of spirits from various fruits and berries is the main focus for Kammer-Kirsch and they are especially known for their Kirschwasser from cherries. In 2006 they started a cooperation with the brewery, Landesbrauerei Rothaus, where the brewery

Bottlings from Stickum Brennerei and Rieger & Hofmeister   *Walter Fitzke, owner of Kleinbrennerei Fitzke*

delivers a fermented wash to the distillery and they continue distilling a whisky called Rothaus Black Forest Single Malt Whisky. The whisky was launched in 2009 and every year in March a new batch is released. Bourbon casks are used for maturation and besides the "original" version, there is a special edition with a wood finish. In 2011 a Glendronach sherry cask was used to enhance the whisky and in 2012 it was a Madeira cask. Around 6,000 bottles are produced every year.

Liechtenstein ─────────

DISTILLERY: Brennerei Telser, Triesen
FOUNDED: 1880 (whisky production since 2006)
OWNER/MANAGER: Telser family
www.brennerei-telser.com

The first distillery in Liechtenstein to produce whisky is not a new distillery. It has existed since 1880 and is now run by the fourth generation of the family. Traditions are strong and Telser is probably the only distillery in Europe still using a wood fire to heat the small stills (150 and 120 litres). Like so many other distilleries on mainland Europe, Telser produces mainly spirits from fruits and berries, including grappa and vodka.

For whisky, the distillery uses a mixture of three different malts (some peated) which are fermented and distilled separately. After an extremely long fermentation (lasting 10 days), the spirit is triple distilled (still containing the solids from the mashing and fermentation) and the three different spirits are blended and filled into Pinot Noir barriques and left to mature for a minimum of three years in a 500 year old cellar with an earth floor resembling the dunnage warehouses of Scotland.

The first bottling of Telsington was distilled in May 2006 and released in July 2009. Since then, another four releases have been made, the latest (the 4 year old Telsington IV) in October 2012.

The Netherlands ─────────

DISTILLERY: Zuidam Distillers, Baarle Nassau
FOUNDED: 1974 (whisky since 1998)
OWNER/MANAGER: Zuidam family
www.zuidam.eu

Zuidam Distillers was started in 1974 as a traditional family distillery producing liqueurs, genever, gin and vodka. The first attempts to distil malt whisky took place in 1998, but according to one of the owners, Patrick van Zuidam, the result is not fit for bottling. Instead, the first release was from the 2002 production and it was bottled in 2007 as a 5 year old. In 2009 there were two limited editions of 8 year olds, one matured in new American Oak and one in new French Oak. This year also saw the first bottling of a 5 year old 100% potstill rye whisky. The next release, in 2010, was a peated version of the 5 year old. In 2012, a 12 year old Millstone sherry cask was released together with a new Millstone 100% Rye.

The whisky is double distilled in two 1,000 litre pot stills made by Kothe & Holstein in Germany. The malt is sourced both locally and abroad and there are three stainless steel mash tuns. Fermentation is slow (five days) and takes place at a low temperature. The spirit is matured in new barrels made of American White Oak, but ex bourbon and ex Oloroso sherry casks are also used. Fermentation capacity has recently been increased to cope with the rising demand and in August 2011 the building of additional warehouses was started.

DISTILLERY: Us Heit Distillery, Bolsward
FOUNDED: 2002
OWNER/MANAGER: Aart van der Linde
www.usheitdistillery.nl

This is one of many examples where a beer brewery also contains a whisky distillery. Frysk Hynder, as the whisky is called, was the first Dutch whisky and made its debut in 2005 at 3 years of age. The barley is grown in surrounding Friesland and malted at the distillery. The owner of the brewery and distillery, Aart van der Linde, has even developed a malting technique which he

Telsington IV - the 4th release from Brennerei Telser

Patrick Zuidam from Zuidam Distillers

237

describes on a separate website - *www.mouteryfryslan.nl*. Some 10,000 bottles are produced annually and the whisky is matured in various casks - sherry, bourbon, red wine, port and cognac.

DISTILLERY: Vallei Distilleerderij, Leusden
FOUNDED: 2002 (officially opened 2004)
OWNER/MANAGER: Bert Burger
www.valleibieren.nl

This is the latest addition to Dutch whisky distilleries. Bert Burger buys barley from a local farmer but apart from that he is very much in control of the whole process from malting to bottling. The whisky is double distilled in pot stills and he produces some 2,500 litres per year. The first trials were in 2002 but in 2004 the distillery was officially opened. After a while Burger started bottling his 2 year old spirit as Valley single malt spirit in 40 ml bottles for customers to try. Finally, on 1st December 2007, the first bottles of single malt whisky reached the market as a 3 year old. Other products include whisky liqueur and two kinds of beer.

Spain

DISTILLERY: Distilerio Molino del Arco, Segovia
FOUNDED: 1959
OWNER/MANAGER: Distilerias y Crianza
del Whisky (DYC)
www.dyc.es

Spain´s first whisky distillery is definitely not a small artisan distillery like so many others on these pages. Established by Nicomedes Garcia Lopez already in 1959 (with whisky distilling commencing three years later), this is a distillery with capacity for producing eight million litres of grain whisky and two million litres of malt whisky per year. In addition to that, vodka and rum are produced and there are in-house maltings which safeguard malted barley for the production. The distillery is equipped with six copper pot stills and there are 250,000 casks maturing on site. The blending and bottling plant which used to sit beside the distillery is now relocated to the Anis Castellana plant at Valverde del Majano.

The big seller when it comes to whiskies is a blend simply called DYC which is around 4 years old. It is supplemented by an 8 year old blend and, since 2007, also by DYC Pure Malt, i. e. a vatted malt consisting of malt from the distillery and from selected Scottish distilleries. A brand new expression was also launched in 2009 to commemorate the distillery's 50th anniversary – a 10 year old single malt, the first from the distillery.

DYC has an interesting liaison with a Scottish distillery which dates back to the early seventies. It bought Lochside Distillery north of Dundee in 1973 to safeguard malt whisky requirements and retained it until it stopped production in 1992. During that time DYC was acquired by Pedro Domecq, which, in turn, was acquired by Allied Lyons, which eventually changed its name to Allied Domecq. When the latter was bought by Pernod Ricard in 2005, a small share, including DYC, went to Beam Global.

DISTILLERY: Destilerias Liber, Padul, Granada
FOUNDED: 2001
OWNER/MANAGER: Destilerías y Distribuciones
Liber S.L.
www.destileriasliber.com

This distillery is quite a bit younger than its competitor in Segovia, DYC. Destilerias Liber was founded as late as in 2001 and did not start production until late 2002. Like so many other newly established distilleries, they started distilling rum, marc and vodka - spirits that do not require maturation and can bring in cash to the company almost instantly. For the whisky production, the spirit is double distilled after a fermentation of 48-72 hours. Maturation takes place in sherry casks. The only available whisky on the market is a 5 year old single malt with the name Embrujo de Granada.

Sweden

DISTILLERY: Mackmyra Svensk Whisky, Valbo
FOUNDED: 1999
OWNER/MANAGER: Mackmyra Svensk Whisky AB
www.mackmyra.se

Many in the whisky world have begun to open their eyes to the rapid increase of distilleries in Sweden, and Mackmyra is the one that started it all. The first distillery was built in 1999 and ten years later the company revealed plans to build a brand new facility in Gävle, a few miles from the present distillery at Mackmyra. The distillery was ready in 2012 and the first distillation took place in spring. The total investments, which includes a whisky village to be built within a ten year period, are expected to amount to approximately £50 million and the capacity of the two distilleries is 500,000 litres of alcohol per year. The construction of the new distillery is quite extraordinary and with its 37 metre structure it is perhaps one of the tallest distilleries in the world. The reason for this height is that it is a gravity fed distillery with malt and water coming in at the top of the building and then the entire production process "works itself" downwards to reach the stills at the bottom. In order to finance the expansion, the company raised almost £20 million through loans and a listing on Nasdaq OMX late in 2011.

Mackmyra whisky is based on two basic recipes, one resulting in a fruity and elegant whisky, the other being more peaty. The peatiness does not stem from peat, but from juniper wood and bog moss. The whisky is matured

Special:08 and Brukswhisky (the core expression) from Mackmyra

in a variety of casks, including Swedish oak. The latter is, according to the owners, one of the reasons for the special character of Mackmyra single malt.

The first release in 2006/2007 was a series of six called Preludium. The first "real" launch was in June 2008 – 'Den Första Utgåvan' (The First Edition) and this is still part of the core range. In 2009 Special, a new series of limited editions, was introduced with the latest, Special:08, being launched in May 2012. Another range of limited editions called Moment was introduced in December 2010 and consists of exceptional casks selected by the Master Blender Angela D`Orazio. Eight bottlings have so far been released in that series. The latest was Solsken (Sunshine) and was released in June 2012. A core expression was also launched in 2010, Mackmyra Brukswhisky, with a maturation in first fill bourbon casks, spiced up with sherry casks and Swedish oak and bottled at 41.4%.

Mackmyra has five sites spread around Sweden for the maturation of their whisky; a 50 metre deep, abandoned mine in northern Sweden, an island in the archipelago of Stockholm, one is found along the west coast, another at a castle in the southernmost part of Sweden and (the latest) on the same site as the new distillery.

Currently the whisky is sold in Scandinavia, the UK, Canada (since autumn 2010) and USA (since April 2011). The company has now started to plan for its introduction in China and Taiwan.

DISTILLERY: Spirit of Hven, Hven
FOUNDED: 2007
OWNER/MANAGER: Backafallsbyn AB
www.hven.com

The second Swedish distillery to come on stream, after Mackmyra, was Spirit of Hven, a distillery situated on the island of Hven right between Sweden and Denmark. The first distillation took place in May 2008.

Henric Molin, founder and owner, is a trained chemist and very concerned about choosing the right oak for his casks. The oak is left to air dry for three to five years before the casks are loaned to, especially, wine producers in both the USA and Europe. It is mostly sweet wines that are filled in the casks but dry white wines and bourbon could also be used. Around 70% of the casks are made of American White Oak while the rest are of Spanish Red

Urania - the first whisky release from Spirit of Hven

Oak (Quercus falcata) and (a few percent) of Japanese Mizunara Oak (Quercus mongolica). By 2013, Henric would have built a wood analysis and test centre capable of examining not only 300 hunderd different types of oak, but also monitoring how spirit matures in other types of wood. He is also installing an instrument for performing GCMS (gas chromatography/mass spectrometry) in his laboratory. Using a new application with an upgraded olfactory port, he will, with great accuracy, be able to determine which flavour compounds will appear during the different stages of production.

Part of the barley is malted on site and for part of it he uses Swedish peat, sometimes mixed with seaweed and sea-grass, for drying. The malt is dried for 48 hours using peat smoke and the final 30 hours hot air is used. The distillery is equipped with a 500 kilogram mash tun, six washbacks made of stainless steel and one pair of stills – wash still 2,000 litres and spirit still 1,500 litres. A long fermentation time of 90-120 hours is used in order to achieve a more full flavoured product with high citric notes and a nutty character. The spirit yield at the distillery, 410-420 litres per tonne of malted barley, is quite impressive, given the fact that the distillery is small and part of the production is peated whisky. The yield from his own malted barley is 390 litres. Around 15,000 litres of whisky is distilled per year and other products include rum made from sugar beet, vodka, gin, aquavit and calvados.

The plans are to produce four different types of malt whisky – organic, unpeated, lightly peated and heavily peated. The first release (without age statement) was the lightly peated Urania which was released in January 2012. The next launch isn´t expected until 2013.

DISTILLERY: Smögen Whisky AB, Hunnebostrand
FOUNDED: 2010
OWNER/MANAGER: Pär Caldenby
www.smogenwhisky.se

In August 2010, Smögen Whisky on the west coast of Sweden, produced their first spirit. This project has quietly progressed since 2009 without any drum banging and thus became Sweden's third whisky distillery, following Mackmyra and Spirit of Hven. Pär Caldenby – lawyer, whisky enthusiast and the author of Enjoying Malt Whisky is behind it all. He has designed the facilities himself and much of the equipment is constructed locally. The three washbacks, for example, carry 1,600 litres each and are rebuilt milk tanks. The wash still (900 litres), spirit still (600 litres), spirit safe and the horizontal condensers have all been made by Forsyth's in Scotland. Pär practices a slow distillation with unusually long foreshots (45 minutes) in order not to get a newmake with too many fruity esters. The maturation takes place in casks made of new, toasted French Oak but some of them will also have held sherry. Ex-bourbon barrels made of American white oak and Sauternes cask are also used. The cask size ranges from 28 to 500 litres. Heavily peated malt is imported from Scotland and the vision is to produce an Islay-type of whisky. Some of the batches produced have had a phenol content of almost 100ppm. In summer 2011, the first production from own barley, grown at the distillery, was made. The capacity is 35,000 litres per year and a first release of the whisky may be in spring 2014.

DISTILLERY: Grythyttan Whisky, Lillkyrka
FOUNDED: 2010
OWNER/MANAGER: Grythyttan Whisky AB
www.grythyttanwhisky.se

The company was founded on Benny Borghs initiative in 2007 at a farm dating back to the 13th century, situated about 180 km west of Stockholm. The company has around 800 share-holders and the distillery came on stream in October 2010. In common with most Swedish distilleries, the stills (900 litres wash still and 600 litres spirit still) were made at Forsyth's in Scotland and the three washbacks are made of Oregon pine. The distillery has its own water source and the water is cleaned using reversed osmosis.

Three different malt varieties are used; unpeated Swedish malt and, imported from Scotland, medium peated (16ppm) and heavily peated (50ppm). For maturation ex-sherry casks are used as a first choice, but ex-bourbon barrels from Maker´s Mark, as well as casks which have previously contained sauternes, madeira, cognac and rum, are also used. The capacity of the distillery is 24,000 litres per year. The distillery has a visitor centre and they are also selling new make spirit and future casks. The release date for the first whisky has not yet been decided but meanwhile a vodka has been produced and bottled.

DISTILLERY: **Box Destilleri, Bjärtrå**
FOUNDED: 2010
OWNER/MANAGER: **Ådalen Destilleri AB**
www.boxwhisky.se

The company was founded in 2005 by Mats and Per de Vahl who, during their travels to Scotland, had been inspired to start their own distillery in Sweden. Buildings from the 19th century that had previously been used both as a sawmill and a powerplant, were restructured and equipped with a four-roller Boby mill (being at least 100 years old) from a closed English brewery, a semilauter mash tun with a capacity of 1,5 tonnes and three stainless steel washbacks holding 8,000 litres each and with a fermentation time of two to four days. The wash still (3,800 litres) and the spirit still (2,500 litres) were both ordered from Forsyth´s in Scotland. The first distillation was made in November 2010 and the distillery has a capacity of 100,000 litres.

Box Destilleri will be making two types of whisky – fruity/unpeated and peated. As regards the former, the malted barley comes from Sweden, whereas the peated malt is imported from Belgium where it has been dried using peat from Islay. The distillery manager, Roger Melander, wants to create a new make which is as clean as possible through a very slow distillation process with lots of copper contact in the still. The flavour of the spirit is also impacted by the effectice condensation using the cold water from a nearby river.

A majority of the casks are first fill bourbon in a variety of sizes from 200 litres down to 40 litres. A number of Oloroso casks and virgin oak casks have also been filled, as well as the rather unusual casks made from Hungarian oak. The company has imported and bottled single malts from Scotland to keep up the cash flow until its own whisky has matured. Future casks (39 litres) are being sold and it is also possible to visit the distillery. The first whisky is expected to be bottled sometime in 2014.

DISTILLERY: **Norrtelje Brenneri, Norrtälje**
FOUNDED: 2002 (whisky since 2009)
OWNER/MANAGER: **Richard Jansson**
www.norrteljebrenneri.se

This distillery, situated 70 kilometres north of Stockholm, was founded on a farm which has belonged to the owner´s family for five generations. The production consists mainly of spirits from ecologically grown fruits and berries. Since 2009, a single malt whisky from ecologically grown barley is also produced. The whisky is double distilled in copper pot stills (400 and 150 litres respectively) from Christian Carl in Germany. Most of the production is matured in 250 litre Oloroso casks with a finish of 3-6 months in French oak casks which have previously held the distillery´s own apple spirit. The character of the whisky will be fruity and lightly peated (6ppm) and the first bottling may appear in 2013.

DISTILLERY: **Bergslagens Destilleri, Nora**
FOUNDED: 2011
OWNER/MANAGER: **Lihnell and Lindell families**
www.bergslagensdestilleri.se

One of many new Swedish malt whisky distilleries, Bergslagen Destilleri is aiming for large volumes, at least in Swedish measures. The capacity will be 1,2 million litres of alcohol per year which makes it the largest distillery in Sweden and bigger than, for example, Ardbeg and Glengoyne in Scotland. The distillery is under construction and the first distillation is planned for autumn 2012. The distillery will be equipped with a 2 tonnes mash tun, four 15,000 litre washbacks made of Oregon pine, one wash

Roger Melander, Distillery Manager at BOX Distillery

Bergslagen´s Engelbrekt whisky, made from imported Scotch

still (10,000 litres) and one spirit still (6,000 litres) - both made at Forsyth´s. The plan is to use mainly bourbon and sherry casks and the maturation will take place in a spectacular warehouse, a 40,000 m² cavern which was built by the Swedish government some 60 years ago. The idea was that in the event of a war, the government, the defense command and the royal family would have this as a rescue place and headquarters.

Bergslagens Destilleri is also responsible for the Swedish branch of The Scotch Malt Whisky Society.

DISTILLERY: Gammelstilla Whisky, Torsåker
FOUNDED: 2005
OWNER/MANAGER: Gammelstilla Whisky AB
www.gammelstilla.se

Less than 30 kilometres from the better known Mackmyra lies another distillery since 2011 – Gammelstilla. The company was already founded in 2005 by three friends but today there are more than 200 shareholders. Unlike most of the other Swedish whisky distilleries, they chose to design and build their pot stills themselves. The wash still has a capacity of 500 litres and the spirit still 300 litres and the annual capacity is 20,000 litres per year. The mashing and fermentation takes place in a brewery which has moved into the same facilities. The first distillation took place in April 2012 with a plan to launch the first bottlings in five years.

DISTILLERY: Gotland Whisky, Romakloster
FOUNDED: 2011
OWNER/MANAGER: Gotland Whisky AB
www.gotlandwhisky.se

The company behind this distillery was already founded in 2004 with the intention of building a distillery at a farmstead near Klinte. The plans were changed and it was decided to build the distillery at the present location instead, a decommissioned sugar works south of Visby. The distillery is equipped with a wash still (1,600 litres) and a spirit still (900 litres) - both made by Forsyth´s in Scotland. Gotland Whisky is unique in Sweden because they malt their own barley. The local barley is ecologically grown and the floor malting is made easier through the use of a malting robot of their own construction which turns the barley. The whisky is matured in a warehouse situated four metres underground. The goal is to produce two kinds of single malts, unpeated and peated and the capacity is 60,000 litres per year. The distillery came on stream in May 2012 and the plan is to release the first whisky, under the name Isle of Lime, in 2015.

Switzerland

DISTILLERY: Whisky Castle, Elfingen, Aargau
FOUNDED: 2002
OWNER/MANAGER: Ruedi Käser
www.whisky-castle.com

The first whisky from this distillery in Elfingen, in the north of Switzerland, reached the market in 2004. It was a single malt under the name Castle Hill. Since then the range of malt whiskies has been expanded and today include Castle Hill Doublewood (3 years old matured both in casks made of chestnut and oak), Whisky Smoke Barley (at least 3 years old matured in new oak), Fullmoon (matured in casks from Hungary) and Terroir (4 years old made from Swiss barley and matured in Swiss oak). All these are bottled at 43%. Adding to these are Cask Strength (5 years old and bottled at 58%) and Edition

Käser (71% matured in new oak casks from Bordeaux). For a couple of years now, Käser has also made three special single malts for the cruise ship company, Hapag Lloyd. Two new releases were made in October 2010 – Girl´s Choice, which is a light 3 year old whisky aged in white wine barrels, and Port Cask, which is 4 years old with a full maturation in port pipes and bottled at 50%. One of the latest releases was Chateau with a maturation in Sauternes casks. All released whiskies are unpeated, but some of them have a smoky flavour which derives from the beech wood used to dry the malt. A new distillery was built in 2005 and commissioned in 2006, hence the annual production has increased from 5,000 to 25,000 bottles. Ruedi Käser has also constructed a complete visitor's experience, including a restaurant and a shop.

DISTILLERY: Bauernhofbrennerei Lüthy, Muhen, Aargau
FOUNDED: 1997 (whisky since 2005)
OWNER/MANAGER: Urs Lüthy
www.swiss-single-malt.ch

The farm distillery, Lüthy, in the north of Switzerland, started in 1997 by producing distillates from fruit, as well as grappa, absinthe and schnapps. The range was expanded to include whisky in 2005 which was distilled in a mobile pot still distillery. Lüthy´s ambition is to only use grain from Switzerland in his production. Since it was impossible to obtain peated malt from Swiss barley, he decided to build his own floor maltings in autumn 2009.

The first single malt expression to be launched in December 2008, was Insel-Whisky, matured in a Chardonnay cask. It was followed by Wyna-Whisky from a sherry cask in April 2009 and Lenzburg-Whisky, another Chardonnay maturation and bottled in September 2009. One of the most recent bottlings was Swiss Spelt Ur-Dinkel Whisky, made from spelt and matured in a Pinot Noir cask. The selection is so far limited as only 500-1000 bottles are filled per year.

DISTILLERY: Spezialitätenbrennerei Zürcher, Port, Bern
FOUNDED: 1954 (whisky from 2000)
OWNER/MANAGER: Daniel & Ursula Zürcher
www.lakeland-whisky.ch

The first in the Zürcher family to distil whisky was Heinz Zürcher in 2000, who released the first 1,000 bottles of Lakeland single malt in 2003. Daniel and Ursula Zürcher took over in 2004. They continued their uncle's work with whisky and launched a second release in 2006. The main focus of the distillery is specialising in various distillates of fruit, absinth and liqueur. The latest barrel of Lakeland single malt was released in 2009 as a 3 year old, but the Zürchers are working on the release of older whiskies in the future. The wash for the whisky is bought from Rugenbräu brewery in Interlaken and maturation takes place in Oloroso sherry casks.

DISTILLERY: Brennerei Stadelmann, Altbüron, Luzern
FOUNDED: 1932 (whisky since 2003)
OWNER/MANAGER: Hans Stadelmann
www.schnapsbrennen.ch

Established in the 1930s this distillery was mobile for its first 70 years. The current owner´s grandfather and father would visit farmers and distil local fruits and berries. Hans Stadelmann took over in 1972 and in 2001 decided to build a stationary distillery which would also be suitable for crop distilling. The distillery was equipped with three Holstein-type stills (150-250 litres) and the first whisky was distilled for a local whisky club in 2003. In 2005 the first Luzerner Hinterländer Single Malt was released, although not as a whisky since it was just 1 year old. A year later the first 3 year old was bottled for the whisky club under the name Dorfbachwasser and finally, in 2010, the first official bottling from the distillery in the shape of a 3 year old single malt whisky was released. In autumn 2011, the fourth release was made, a 3 year old matured in a Merlot cask. The first whisky from smoked barley was distilled in 2012.

DISTILLERY: Brauerei Locher, Appenzell,
Appenzell Innerrhoden
FOUNDED: 1886 (whisky since 1998)
OWNER/MANAGER: Locher family
www.säntisspirits.ch, www.saentismalt.ch

This old, family-owned brewery started to produce whisky in 1998 when the Swiss government changed laws and allowed for spirit to be distilled from grain. The whole production takes place in the brewery where there is a Steinecker mash tun holding 10,000 litres. The spirit ferments in stainless steel vats and, for distillation, Holstein stills are used. Brauerei Locher is unique in using old (70 to 100 years) beer casks for the maturation. The production amounts to a couple of thousand bottles per year and at the moment there are three expressions; Säntis, bottled at 40%, Dreifaltigkeit which is slightly peated having matured in toasted casks and bottled at 52% and, finally, Sigel which has matured in very small casks and is bottled at 40%. A new addition for 2012 was Säntis Malt Cask No 1130 bottled at cask strength (64%). The new expression recently won a competition beating such renowned malts as Glenlivet 21 year old Archive.

DISTILLERY: Whisky Brennerei Hollen,
Lauwil, Baselland
FOUNDED: 1999 (for whisky distillation)
OWNER/MANAGER: The Bader family.
www.swiss-whisky.ch, www.single-malt.ch

Since WW1 Switzerland has had a law forbidding the use of staple foods such as potatoes and grain for making alcohol. On 1st July 1999 this was abolished and the spirit streamed through the stills of Holle the very same day making it the first Swiss producer of malt whisky. The whisky is stored on French oak casks, which have been used for white wine (Chardonnay) or red wine (Pinot Noir). Most bottlings are 4 years old and contain 42% alcohol. A 5 year old has also been released, which has had three years in Pinot Noir casks followed by two years in Chardonnay casks. Other expressions include a peated version and a cask strength Chardonnay-matured.

Bader also recently launched what he calls a dessert whisky from a white wine cask as well as his first single grain whisky, and July 2009 saw the release of a 10 year old. Annual production amounts to roughly 30,000 bottles.

DISTILLERY: Destillatia AG (Olde Deer),
Langenthal, Bern
FOUNDED: 2005
OWNER/MANAGER: Hans Baumberger
www.olde-deer.ch

The distillery was built in 2005 under the same roof as the brewery Brau AG Langenthal (already established in 2001). The reason for this co-habitation was to access a wash for distillation and thereby avoiding investments in mashing equipment. The wash (in which both peated and unpeated malt is used) is fermented for five days and after that distilled three times, using a Holstein type of still. The casks are all 225 litres and Swiss oak (Chardonnay), French oak (Chardonnay and red wine) and ex sherry casks are used. The first whisky was produced in 2005 and released in 2008 under the name, Olde Deer. Since then a new 3 year old has been released every year. From June 2010, the whisky can be bought using their on-line shop. Apart from whisky, the distillery also produces rum, whisky liqueur and schnapps.

DISTILLERY: Etter Distillerie, Zug,
FOUNDED: 1870 (whisky since 2007)
OWNER/MANAGER: Etter family
www.etter-distillerie.ch

The distillery was started in 1870 by Paul Etter and has been in the family ever since. Today it is the third and fourth generations who are running it. Their main produce is eaux de vie from various fruits and berries with cherry as their speciality (Kirsch). A sidetrack to the business was entered in 2007 when they decided to distill their first malt whisky. The malted barley was bought from a brewery (Brauerei Baar), distilled at Etter, filled into wine casks and left to mature in moist caves for a minimum of three years. The first release was made in October 2010 under the name Johnett Single Malt Whisky.

DISTILLERY: Brennerei Hagen,
Hüttwilen, Thurgau
FOUNDED: 1999
OWNER/MANAGER: Ueli Hagen
www.distillerie-hagen.ch

A triple distilled malt whisky is, since a few years, produced by Ueli Hagen in the small village of Hüttwilen in the northernmost part of Switzerland. The spirit is matured in bourbon barrels and the first produce was sold in 2002 as a 3 year old. Ueli Hagen produces mainly schnapps and absinth and distills around 300 bottles of malt whisky a year, a number he expects to double. He has recently been experimenting; a few years ago when he was building a new cow shed, he found a 1700 year old oak tree in the ground so he put pieces of the oak into a maturing barrel of spirit and he says it gives the whisky a slightly peated touch.

DISTILLERY: Burgdorfer Gasthausbrauerei,
Burgdorf, Bern
FOUNDED: 1999
OWNER/MANAGER: Thomas Gerber
www.burgdorferbier.ch

The Burgdorfer Single Malt Whisky is an excellent example of the kind of cross-fertilization that more and more breweries are choosing. When a wash is made for beer brewing, it is an excellent opportunity to use the batch (without adding hops) to distil spirit which can be made into whisky. The first whisky from Burgdorfer was released as a five year old in 2006 and it is sold using a kind of subscription system. The customer pays 50 swiss francs for a 50 cl bottle and receives it 5 years later. They produce around 300 bottles annually.

Wales

DISTILLERY: Penderyn Distillery, Penderyn
FOUNDED: 2000
OWNER/MANAGER: Welsh Whisky Company Ltd
www.welsh-whisky.co.uk

In 1998 four private individuals started The Welsh Whisky Company and two years later, the first Welsh distillery in more than a hundred years started distilling.

A new type of still, developed by David Faraday for Penderyn Distillery, differs from the Scottish and Irish procedures in that the whole process from wash to new make takes place in one single still. But that is not the sole difference. Every distillery in Scotland is required by law, to do the mashing and fermenting on site. At Penderyn, though, the wash is bought from a regional beer brewer and transported to the distillery on a weekly basis. The normal procedure at a brewery is to boil the wash to clear it from any lactic acid which can make it appear cloudy. This was a problem for Penderyn as lactic acid creates a second fermentation which is beneficial in a whisky context and adds more taste. Penderyn has solved this by pumping the wash to a heated tank where lactic acid is added before distillation is commenced. The distillery is working 24 hours a day to keep up with the increasing demand and now seems to have reached the capacity ceiling of the current equipment. The plan is now to add two additional stills during 2013 to increase capacity.

The first single malt was launched in March 2004. The core range consists of Penderyn Madeira Finish, Penderyn Sherrywood and Penderyn Peated. Recent limited releases include Rich Madeira (in 2008) and Portwood Single Cask (2009). Two single casks were released in 2010 – one was a 2000 Vintage bourbon-matured and the other an Oloroso sherry maturation. A special version for the French market is Penderyn 41, bourbon matured with a Madeira finish. In 2012 two new bottlings were released; a portwood matured expression bottled at 41% and non chill-filtered and Penderyn Grand Slam 2012 which celebrated the success of Wales rugby team in beating all other nations in the annual six nations tournament.

The main market for Penderyn is UK with 75% of total sales mainly through supermarkets like Asda, Tesco, Sainsbury's and Waitrose. Twenty percent goes on export with France as the biggest market. The turnover for the company in 2010 was £3.1m.

A visitor centre was officially opened by HRH, The Prince of Wales, in June 2008 at a total cost of £850,000 and almost 40,000 visitors come here every year.

Penderyn Grand Slam 2012 and Portwood

NORTH AMERICA

USA

DISTILLERY: Stranahans Whiskey Distillery, Denver, Colorado
FOUNDED: 2003
OWNER/MANAGER: Proximo Spirits
www.stranahans.com

Stranahans, founded by Jess Graber and George Stranahan, became a victim of its own success in 2009. In order to keep up with demand, the owners not only had to find a new location but also needed to bring the mashing in-house instead of being dependent on local breweries. The solution was to move to the closed Heavenly Daze Brewery in Denver in May 2009.

In December 2010, the next significant step in the history of the distillery was taken when the New York based Proximo Spirits (makers of Hangar 1 Vodka and Kraken Rum among others) acquired the company. Their intentions were to increase production even further with the addition of three new stills from Vendome. A surprising decision was also made to withdraw Stranahans Colorado Whiskey from all other markets but Colorado. The owners claim that they want to build up a signficant stock before delivering nationally (and also internationally) again. Jess Graber, the former owner, is still involved in the business as a brand ambassador.

The whiskey is always made in batches and until summer of 2012, 90 batches have been released. Except for the core expression, a single barrel is launched once a year under the name Snowflake. The special release for 2012 was Maroon Bells which had been finished in casks that previously held cherry wine.

STILLERY: Clear Creek Distillery, Portland, Oregon
FOUNDED: 1985
OWNER/MANAGER: Stephen McCarthy
www.clearcreekdistillery.com

Steve McCarthy in Oregon was one of the first to produce malt whiskey in the USA and like many other small distilleries, they started by distilling eau-de-vie from fruit, especially pears, and then expanded the product line into whiskey. They began making whiskey in 1996 and the first bottles were on the market three years later. There is only one expression at the moment, McCarthy's Oregon Single Malt 3 years old. Steve has for a long time hoped to launch an 8 year old, but so far it has simply not been possible to save adequate quantities due to high demand.

The whiskey is reminiscent of an Islay and, in fact, the malt is purchased directly from Islay with a phenol specification of 30-40 ppm. Steve expanded the number of pot stills to four a couple of years ago to try and catch up with demand. Maturation takes place in ex-sherry butts with a finish in new Oregon White Oak hogsheads.

Steve has doubled the production of whiskey every year since 2004 which does not, however, seem to be enough to satisfy demand. He only bottles once a year and the next release is scheduled for February 2013.

DISTILLERY: Charbay Winery & Distillery, St. Helena, California
FOUNDED: 1983
OWNER/MANAGER: Miles and Marko Karakasevic
www.charbay.com

Charbay has a wide range of products: vodka, grappa,

pastis, rum, port and since 1999 also malt whiskey. That was the year when Miles and Marko decided to take 20,000 gallons of Pilsner and double distil it in their Charentais pot still, normally used for distilling, for example, cognac. From this distillation, a 4 year old called Double-Barrel Release One (two barrels) was launched in 2002. There were 840 bottles at cask strength and non-chill filtered. The whiskey is quite unique since a ready beer, hops and all, rather than wash from a brewery is used.

It took six years before Release II appeared in 2008, this time with 22 barrels. In January 2010, a different type of whiskey, Charbay's Doubled & Twisted Light Whiskey designed by Marko Karakasevic, was launched. It was distilled from bottle-ready IPA beer (India Pale Ale), aged for one day in oak barrels and then for six years in stainless steel tanks. The second release of Doubled & Twisted came in summer 2011 and a third in 2012. In October 2011, a 14 month old Charbay IPA Whiskey (the whole maturation in French oak) was released, together with a Charbay IPA Light Whiskey (one day on oak and then filled into stainless steel tank). New releases in 2012 were Charbay R5 Whiskey matured in French oak for 21 months and Charbay R5 Clear Whiskey. R5 stands for the Racer 5 beer from Bear Republic that they are using.

DISTILLERY: Edgefield Distillery,
Troutdale, Oregon
FOUNDED: 1998
OWNER/MANAGER: Mike and Brian McMenamin
www.mcmenamins.com

Brothers Mike and Brian McMenamin started their first pub in Portland, Oregon in 1983. It has now expanded to a chain of more than 60 pubs and hotels in Oregon and Washington. More than 20 of the pubs have adjoining microbreweries (the first opened in 1985) and it is now the fourth-largest chain of brewpubs in the United States.

The chain's first distillery opened in 1998 at their huge Edgefield property in Troutdale and their first whiskey, Hogshead Whiskey (46%), was bottled in 2002. Hogshead is still their number one seller and the production has increased to nearly 70 barrels per year. Starting with the releases in 2012, the character of the whiskey will be more complex and a touch sweeter. The reason for this is that Head Distiller James Whelan back in 2008 started to use three different malted barley recipes for the wash. He also began aging the spirit in both heavy and lightly charred barrels. Another part of the range is the Devil's Bit, a limited bottling released every year on St. Patrick's Day. For 2012 it was a 6 year old "toasted oak finish".

A second distillery was opened in September 2011 at the company's Cornelius Pass Roadhouse location in Hillsboro. A 19th century charentais alambic still has been acquired and the initial focus will be on whiskey and then moving on to brandy and gin. Compared to Edgefield the new distillery are using more wheat, rye and barley combinations and also different barrels. The first release from the Hillsboro distillery was an un-aged whiskey called The White Owl.

DISTILLERY: Dry Fly Distilling, Spokane,
Washington
FOUNDED: 2007
OWNER/MANAGER: Don Poffenroth
& Kent Fleischmann
www.dryflydistilling.com

Dry Fly Distilling started production in autumn 2007 and became the first grain distillery to open in Washington since Prohibition. To ensure a positive cash flow from the start, in common with many other distilleries, vodka and gin were produced. The first batch of malt whisky was distilled in January 2008. The owners expect to make 200-300 cases of malt whisky annually, but the first bottling will probably not be released until 2013/2014.

However, there are a couple of other whiskies in production and one of them is quite unusual – Washington Wheat Whiskey. It was first released in August 2009 and, at that time, it was only the second of this style following Heaven Hill's launch of Bernheim Straight Wheat Whiskey in 2005. In July 2011, Dry Fly Distilling launched the first bourbon ever made in Washington State. It was a 3 year old, the oldest release yet from the owners, made of corn, wheat and malted barley.

The original equipment consisted of one still, a Christian Carl manufactured in Germany. In autumn 2008 another still was installed, as well as two additional fermenters, which raised capacity to 10,000 cases per annum. Another three fermenters were added recently.

DISTILLERY: Eades Distillery,
Lovingston, Virginia
FOUNDED: 2008
OWNER/MANAGER: The Virginia Distillers Co.
www.vadistillery.com

Chris Allwood and his partners spent the first two years of this project to find funding of around $5m to complete their plans for a distillery in Nelson County, Virginia. The plan was originally to start distilling in spring 2009

The more than 100 year old still in Hillsboro

Busy day at Dry Fly Distilling

but, as is often the case, things do take longer time than expected when building a distillery. As of summer 2011, the building is complete and the stills are in place. Phase two is to install all the piping and mechanicals and the plan now is to have whisky in casks by autumn 2012.

The equipment consists of a 2 tonne mash tun, a 10,000 litre wash still and an 8,000 litre spirit still. The malting of locally grown barley will be done on-site. Initial production volumes are expected to be around 2,500 barrels of 200 litres each per year and the spirit will mature mainly in bourbon barrels, but port pipes and wine barrels from local wineries will also be used. It will probably take at least four years before the first bottlings of matured whiskey are for sale.

Meanwhile, the owners have created a series of vatted malt whiskies called "Eades Anticipation Series". The idea is to select two different malts aged anything between 10 and 18 years for each bottling, marry them and then let them go through a second maturation in wine barrels.

DISTILLERY: Prichard´s Distillery, Kelso, Tennessee
FOUNDED: 1999
OWNER/MANAGER: Phil Prichard
www.prichardsdistillery.com

When Phil Prichard started his business in 1999, it became the first legal distillery for 50 years in Tennessee. Today, it is the third largest in the state after giants Jack Daniel's and George Dickel. In 2012 the capacity was tripled with the installation of a new 1,500 gallon mash cooker and three additional fermenters. The plan is to increase the capacity even further by adding a 1,500 gallon wash still and turning the old 550 gallon wash still into a spirit still.

Prichard produces around 20,000 cases per year with different kinds of rum as the main track. The biggest seller, however, is a bourbon-based liqueur called Sweet Lucy which is responsible for 50% of sales. Bourbon and single malt whiskey is also produced and in 2010 the first single malt was released. Prichard´s single malt (which often contains a small percentage of rye) is usually a vatting from barrels of different age (some up to 10 years old) and also a mix of new charred oak and old oak is used. Their bourbon range was expanded in late 2011 with the innovative Double Chocolate Bourbon where Prichard has infused the essence of chocolate beans from a local artisan chocolateer into the bourbon, giving the spirit a mellow (but not sweet) chocolate flavour. Prichard's Distillery's range is sold all across America, in Canada and in eight European countries.

DISTILLERY: Lexington Brewing & Distilling Co., Lexington, Kentucky
FOUNDED: 1999
OWNER/MANAGER: Pearse Lyons
www.lyonsspirits.com

Most of the producers of malt whiskey in the USA have a background in brewing, winemaking or distilling other spirits. This also applies to Lexington Brewing & Distilling Company, as whiskey production is derived from their production of Kentucky Ale. Dr Pearse Lyons' background is interesting – being the owner, the founder and a native of Ireland, he used to work for Irish Distillers in the 1970s. In 1980 he changed direction and founded Alltech Inc, a biotechnology company specializing in animal nutrition and feed supplements. Alltech purchased Lexington Brewing Company in 1999, with the intent to produce an ale that would resemble both an Irish red ale and an English ale. Dr Lyons, holding a PhD in brewing and distilling, obviously knew what he was doing, as the ales became an instant success. In 2008, two traditional copper pot stills from Scotland were installed with the aim to produce Kentucky's first malt whiskey. North American 2-row malted barley is mashed in a lauter mash tun and fermented using a yeast designed by Alltech. The first single malt whiskey was released in August 2010 under the name Pearse Lyons Reserve and in autumn 2011

it was time for a release of their Town Branch bourbon with the rather unusual mash bill of 51% corn and 49% malted barley.

In autumn 2012 the stills were relocated from the brewery to a new stand alone distillery building right across the street. The new distillery, with a capacity of 450,000 litres of pure alcohol per year, will also be a part of the Kentucky Bourbon Trail experience. Two new stills that were made at Vendome Copper and Brass Company in Louisville Kentucky, were shipped to Ireland end of August 2012 to become part of a new distillery located at Carlow Brewing Company in Bagenalstown, Co Carlow.

DISTILLERY: Triple Eight Distillery, Nantucket, Massachusetts
FOUNDED: 2000
OWNER/MANAGER: Cisco Brewers
www.ciscobrewers.com

In 1995 Cisco Brewers was established and five years later it was expanded with Triple Eight Distillery. The base of the whiskey production is, of course, wash from the brewery where Maris Otter barley is used. The first distillation took place as early as ten years ago and the first 888 bottles (5 barrels) were released on 8th August 2008 as an 8 year old. To keep in line, the price of these first bottles was $888. The whiskey is named Notch (as in "not Scotch"). Annual production is approximately 5,000 bottles and the storage is on ex-bourbon casks from Brown Forman (Woodford Reserve) and finished in French Oak.

The Nantucket facility consists of a brewery, winery and distillery. Triple Eight also produces vodka, rum and gin. Whiskey production was moved to a new distillery in May 2007.

DISTILLERY: St. George Distillery, Alameda, California
FOUNDED: 1982
OWNER/MANAGER: Jörg Rupf/Lance Winters
www.stgeorgespirits.com

The distillery is situated in a hangar at Alameda Point, the old naval air station on the San Fransisco Bay. It was founded by Jörg Rupf, a German immigrant who came

Pot still at Lexington Distillery

to California in 1979 and who was to become one of the forerunners when it came to craft distilling in America. In 1996, Lance Winters joined him and today he is Distiller as well as co-owner.

The main produce is based on eau-de-vie from locally grown fruit, and vodka under the brand name Hangar One. Whiskey production was picked up in 1996 and the first single malt appeared on the market in 1999. Like in so many other craft distilleries, the wash is not produced in-house. St George´s obtain their from Sierra Nevada Brewery. Some of the malt used has been dried with alder and beech but is non-peated. Maturation is in bourbon barrels (80%), French Oak (15%) or port pipes (5%). St. George Single Malt used to be sold as three years old, but nowadays comes to the market as a blend of whiskeys aged from 4 to 12 years.

DISTILLERY: RoughStock Distillery,
Bozeman, Montana
FOUNDED: 2008
OWNER/MANAGER: Kari & Bryan Schultz
www.montanawhiskey.com

Unlike many other American micro distilleries relying on obtaining mash from a nearby brewery, RoughStock buys its 100% Montana grown and malted barley and then mill and mash it themselves in a 1,000 gallon mash cooker. The mash is not drained off into a wash, but fermented directly from the mash tun in two 1,000 gallon open top wooden fermenters for 72 hours before double distillation in two Vendome copper pot stills (500 and 250 gallons). Maturation is on a mix of quarter casks and 225 litre barrels made from new American oak. The distillery moved to a new location in early 2011 and one year later two new stills were installed, increasing the capacity significantly.

In September 2009, the first bottles of RoughStock Montana Pure Malt Whiskey, the first legally made whiskey in Montana's history since Prohibition, were released. Since then a single barrel bottled at cask strength has been added (Black Label Montana Whiskey) and apart from whiskey made from 100% malted barley, the product range also includes Spring Wheat Whiskey, Sweet Corn Whiskey and Straight Rye Whiskey,

Products from RoughStock are now available in 40 states, Canada, Europe and Japan.

DISTILLERY: Nashoba Valley Winery,
Bolton, Massachusetts
FOUNDED: 1978 (whiskey since 2003)
OWNER/MANAGER: Richard Pelletier
www.nashobawinery.com

Nashoba Valley Winery lies in the heart of Massachusetts' apple country, just 40 minutes from Boston and is owned by Richard Pelletier since 1995. Although mainly about wines, the facilities have in recent years expanded with a brewery and Massachusetts' first distillery, which holds a farmer's distiller's license. Here Pelletier produces a wide range of spirits including vodka, brandy and grappa.

Since 2003 malt whiskey is also distilled. The malt is imported and the wash is produced in his own brewery. The whiskey is matured in a combination of ex bourbon barrels and American and French Oak casks, which previously have contained wine from the estate.

In autumn 2009, Stimulus, the first single malt was released. The two casks were distilled in 2004. The second release of a 5 year old came in 2010 and it is Richard´s plan to release a 5 year old once a year. At the same time he has also put aside whiskey to be sold as a 10 year old and, eventually, as a 15 year old. The first 10 year old is due in 2014 and during that same year he will also bottle a rye whiskey and a corn whiskey. At the moment they are producing about 20 barrels per year.

DISTILLERY: Tuthilltown Spirits,
Gardiner, New York
FOUNDED: 2003
OWNER/MANAGER: Ralph Erenzo & Brian Lee
www.tuthilltown.com

This is the first whiskey distillery in the State of New York since Prohibition. Just 80 miles north of New York City, Ralph Erenzo and Brian Lee, with the help of six employees produce bourbon, single malt whiskey, rye whiskey, rum and vodkas distilled from local apples. Erenzo bought the 18th century property in 2001 with the intention of turning it into a rock climbers ranch, but neighbours objected. A change in the law in New York State made it possible to start a micro-distillery. Erenzo thus changed direction and started distilling instead. Erenzo and Lee built the distillery, acquired licences and learned the basic craft over the following two years.

Bryan Schultz from RoughStock Distillery

Tuthilltown Distillery

The first products came onto the shelves in 2006 in New York and the range now consists of Hudson Baby Bourbon, made from 100% New York corn and the company's biggest seller by far, Four Grain Bourbon (corn, rye, wheat and malted barley), Single Malt Whiskey (aged in small, new, charred American Oak casks), Manhattan Rye, New York Corn Whiskey, Heart of the Hudson Vodka and Spirit of the Hudson Vodka.

A cooperative venture was announced between Tuthilltown and William Grant & Sons (Grants, Glenfiddich, Balvenie et al) in June 2010, in which W Grants acquired the Hudson Whiskey brand line in order to market and distribute it around the world. Tuthilltown Spirits remains an independent company that will continue to produce the different spirits. The produce from Tuthilltown currently sells in 17 US states, in Europe and in Australia.

In July 2009 the distillery crew hand-harvested the first crop of rye grown at the distillery, and opened for its first public tours. Tuthilltown's new whiskey tasting room and shop are in the barrel room, the first at a distillery in New York since 1919. Private single cask bottling of whiskey is also available to consumers at the distillery.

DISTILLERY: Rebecca Creek Distillery,
San Antonio, Texas
FOUNDED: 2010
OWNER/MANAGER: Steve Ison and Mike Cameron
www.rebeccacreekdistillery.com

With a background in the insurance business, Mike Cameron and Steve Ison started Rebecca Creek Distillery in 2010. Fermenters and a mash system were bought from Newland Systems in Canada and the 3,000 litre copper pot still, together with the column, was made by the well-known Christian Carl in Germany. The malted barley is sourced from Cargill in Sheboygen, Wisconsin and for maturation charred American oak is used.

The first product to be launched was Enchanted Rock Vodka. The first year alone, 30,000 cases of vodka were sold. First whiskey to be released was Rebecca Creek Fine Texas Whiskey, a blended whiskey which was launched in autumn 2011. Steve and Mike plan for a release of their Single Malt Whiskey sometime during 2012.

At the moment, the production capacity for vodka is 100,000 cases per year and for whiskey 10-20,000 cases, but the owners have even bigger plans, namely, to

become the largest craft distillery in North America with a yearly production of 150,000 cases of vodka and 75,000 cases of whiskey.

DISTILLERY: Woodstone Creek Distillery,
Cincinnati, Ohio
FOUNDED: 1999
OWNER/MANAGER: Donald and Linda Outterson
www.woodstonecreek.com

Don and Linda Outterson opened a farm winery in Lebanon, Ohio in 1999 and relocated to the present facilities in 2003 where a distillery was added to the business.

The first whiskey, a five grain bourbon (white and yellow corn, malted barley, malted rye, and malted wheat), was released in July 2008 and the second in November. Both bourbons were made of malted grains (no enzymes), 51% corn, sweet mash and without chill-filtering and colouring. In 2010, the Outtersons released a peated 10 year old single malt from malted barley which they call "The Murray Cask", named after Jim Murray who praised it in his Whisky Bible. In 2012 this was followed up by a 12 year old unpeated single malt whiskey, Ridge Runner (a five-grain bourbon white dog) and a blended whiskey. The last one is made from 5% malted wheat, malted barley and malted rye which is mixed with 95% unmalted wheat distillate. The malted whiskey is 8 years old while the unmalted is 3 years. The reason behind this release was to be able to have something on offer for the customers who wished to purchase a more affordable product.

DISTILLERY: High Plains Distillery,
Atchison, Kansas
FOUNDED: 2004
OWNER/MANAGER: Seth Fox
www.highplainsinc.com

Former process engineer, Seth Fox, is mainly known for his Most Wanted Vodka of which he sells over 13,000 cases a year in Kansas, Missouri and Texas. The product range was expanded in late 2006 also to include a Most Wanted Kansas Whiskey (reminiscent of a Canadian whisky) and Kansas Bourbon Mash. Fox continued in 2007 to produce his first single malt whiskey made from malted barley but it has not been released yet. He also produces Pioneer Whiskey and a premium vodka called Fox Vodka which is filtered five extra times. The two stills were bought second-hand from Surrey in England. When High Plains opened, it was the first legal distillery in Kansas since 1880. In 2009 he expanded the facility in order to accommodate a production of 70-80,000 cases per year, compared to previous 20,000.

DISTILLERY: New Holland Brewing Co.,
Holland, Michigan
FOUNDED: 1996 (whiskey since 2005)
OWNER/MANAGER: Brett VanderKamp, David
White, Fred Bueltmann
www.newhollandbrew.com

This company started as a beer brewery, but after a decade, it opened up a micro-distillery as well and the wash used for the beer is now also used for distilling whiskey. There is a variety of malts for mashing and the house ale yeast is used for fermentation. Until August 2011, the spirit was double distilled in a 225 litre, self-constructed pot still. At that time, the capacity had increased tenfold mainly as a result of the installation of a 3,000-litre still. This still had been built in 1932 and hasn't been used since the early 1940s but was restored.

The first cases of New Holland Artisan Spirits were released in December 2008 and among them were Zeppelin Bend, a 3 year old (minimum) straight-malt whiskey which is now their flagship brand. In autumn 2010, a new series of releases called Brewer's Whiskey began.

Rebecca Creek Distillery

They have all aged in small (five and eight gallon) casks and the first bottling was Double Down Barley, 6 months old. This was followed up in summer 2011 by Malthouse (a mix of three different malted barleys and two malted ryes) and Walley Rye. In autumn 2011 came the next two releases; Ichabod´s Flask and a bourbon. Batch number 2 of Double Down Barley is due for release in spring 2012 and for that, some experimentation has been going on. Toasted staves of different wood other than oak (for example hickory) have been integrated into the casks to see what effect this would have on the whiskey.

DISTILLERY: Corsair Artisan,
        Bowling Green, Kentucky and
        Nashville, Tennessee
FOUNDED: 2008
OWNER/MANAGER: Darek Bell, Andrew Webber
        and Amy Lee Bell
www.corsairartisan.com

The two founders of Corsair Artisan, Darek Bell and Andrew Webber, were based in Nashville when they came up with the idea in 2008 to start up a distillery. At that time Tennessee didn´t allow this, so the first distillery was opened across the border in Bowling Green, Kentucky. Two years later, the legislation in Tennessee had changed and a second distillery and brewery were opened up in Nashville. Apart from producing 16 different types of beer, the brewery is also where the wash for all the whisky production takes place. In Nashville, they also have a 240 gallon antique copper pot still. For those whiskies in the range that require a second distillation, the low wines are taken to Bowling Green and the custom made 50 gallon still from Vendome Copper.

Corsair Artisan has a wide range of spirits, gin, vodka, absinthe, rum and whiskey. So far four types of whiskey have been released – Wry Moon, an unaged 100% rye whiskey, 100% Rye Whiskey (aged two months), Triple Smoke Single Malt Whiskey (made from three different types of smoked malt with an addition of chocolate malt) and Pumpkin Spice Moonshine (a malt whiskey where different spices and pumpkin are added after fermentation). Darek Bell recently published a book (Alt Whiskeys: Alternative Whiskey Recipes and Distilling Techniques for the Adventurous Craft Distiller) describing the experiments at Corsair and also giving recipes for many of the whiskies produced.

DISTILLERY: DownSlope Distilling,
        Centennial, Colorado
FOUNDED: 2008
OWNER/MANAGER: Mitch Abate,
        Matt & Andy Causey
www.downslopedistilling.com

The three founders were brought together by their interest and passion for craft-brewing when they started the distillery in 2008 and in 2009 they finally got their licence to start distilling. The distillery is equipped with two stills – one very elegant, copper pot still made by Copper Moonshine Stills in Arkansas and a vodka still of an in-house design. The first products to be launched in August 2009 were a vodka made from sugar cane and a white rum. More vodkas and rums were to follow and in April 2010 the first whiskey, Double-Diamond Whiskey, was released. It is made from 65% malted barley and 35% rye and matured in three different barrels in a solera style. The first malt whiskey (a single barrel), available only at the distillery, was released in November 2011. The whiskey had spent two years in a burgundy cask. Upcoming special releases will include an all malt Irish style whiskey, a malt/rye whiskey aged in a 40 year old French cognac barrel and an all malt aged as a bourbon in new heavy char American white oak.

DISTILLERY: Copper Fox Distillery,
        Sperryville, Virginia
FOUNDED: 2000
OWNER/MANAGER: Rick Wasmund
www.copperfox.biz

Copper Fox Distillery was founded in 2000 by Rick Wasmund. In 2005 they moved to another site, built a new distillery and began distilling in January 2006.

Rick Wasmund has become one of the most unorthodox producers of single malt. The malted barley is dried using smoke from selected fruitwood but variations of that concept are also used in other places, for example Sweden. It is the maturation process that Rick takes one step further thereby differing from common practice. In every barrel of new make spirit, he adds plenty of hand chipped and toasted chips of apple and cherry trees, as well as oak wood.

Adding to the flavour, Wasmund also believes that this procedure drastically speeds up the time necessary for maturation. In fact, he used to bottle his Wasmund´s Single Malt after just four months in the barrel but the maturation time has nowadays increased to 12-16 months. Every batch ranging from 250 to 1,500 bottles tastes a little different and the distillery is producing around 2,500 bottles every month. Other expressions in the range are Copper Fox Rye Whiskey with a mash bill of 2/3 Virginia rye and 1/3 malted barley and two unaged spirits – Rye Spirit and Single Malt Spirit.

DISTILLERY: Bull Run Distillery,
        Portland, Oregon
FOUNDED: 2011
OWNER/MANAGER: Lee Medoff and
        Patrick Bernards
www.bullrundistillery.com

This is one of the newest distilleries in the USA, founded by former brewer Lee Medoff, an experienced man in the industry. The company was formed in 2010 and in early autumn 2011, it was time for the first distillation. The distillery is equipped with two pot stills (800 gallons each) of Lee´s own design and manufactured locally. The plan to start with, is to use local breweries for the production of the wash but already next year, they may

Triple Smoke from Corsair and Double Diamond from Downslope

be installing their own mashing equipment. Except for Medoyeff Vodka which is already for sale, the distillery will also produce two types of rum from turbinado sugar. However, the main mission of the distillery is whiskey based on 100% malted barley and the first distillation was in February 2012. It will be unpeated with a maturation of at least two years in new American oak barrels.

DISTILLERY: Ballast Point Brewing & Distilling, San Diego, California
FOUNDED: 1996 (whiskey since 2008)
OWNER/MANAGER: Jack White, Yuseff Cherney
www.ballastpoint.com

Building on Jack White's Home Brew Mart, he and Yuseff Cherney founded Ballast Point Brewing Company in 1996. Distilling started in 2008 and it became the first craft distillery in San Diego. The equipment consists of two hybrid pot/column stills - one 200 gallon for gin production and a second 500 gallon for whiskey and rum. The first product to appear on the market was Old Grove gin in August 2009. Three Sheets (white) Rum, Three Sheets Barrel Aged Rum and Fugu Vodka have been released thereafter. Two different whiskeys are produced; a single malt Devil's Share Whiskey and Devil's Share Bourbon, both of them matured in virgin American oak with a heavy (#3) char for a minimum of three years. The owners hope to release the first whiskey at the end of 2012.

DISTILLERY: Rogue Ales & Spirits, Newport, Oregon
FOUNDED: 2009
OWNER/MANAGER: Jack Joyce
www.rogue.com

The company started in 1988 as a combined pub and brewery. Over the years the business expanded and now consists of one brewery, two combined brewery/pubs, two distillery pubs (Portland and Newport) and five pubs scattered over Oregon, Washington and California. The main business is still producing Rogue Ales, but apart from whiskey, rum and gin are also distilled.

Two malt whiskies have been released so far. The first, Dead Guy Whiskey, was launched in December 2009 and is based on five different types of barley. It is distilled twice in a 150 gallon Vendom copper pot still and the spirit is matured for one month in charred barrels made of American Oak. The second expression was released in June 2010 under the name Chatoe Rogue Oregon Single Malt Whiskey. It is made from barley grown on Rogue's own farm in Tygh Valley. The malt is smoked using Oregon Alder wood chips and the spirit is matured for three months. The whiskey can be bought in 30 states in the US and is also exported to Canada, Puerto Rico, Philippines, Japan and Australia.

DISTILLERY: The Solas Distillery, La Vista, Nebraska
FOUNDED: 2009
OWNER/MANAGER: Zac Triemert, Brian McGee, Jason Payne
www.solasdistillery.com

The Solas Distillery, the first licensed distillery in Nebraska since prohibition, can trace its origins back to 2005, when brewer Zac Triemert persuaded his colleagues, Brian McGee and Jason Payne, to set up their own brewery. At first they brewed out of another Omaha brewery. In 2008 their own Lucky Bucket brewery was ready to roll and a year later, at the same premises, a distillery was built. The first product to hit the market in November 2009 was Joss Vodka while the Cuban-style Chava Rum was released in 2011. In February 2010 single malt whiskey was distilled but it will not be ready to bottle until February 2013. Zac Triemert lets the wash ferment for 7 days and then distills it in two copper pot stills from Forsyth's in Scotland.

DISTILLERY: Green Mountain Distillers, Stowe, Vermont,
FOUNDED: 2001
OWNER/MANAGER: Harold Faircloth III, Tim Danahy
www.greendistillers.com

Tim Danahy and Howie Faircloth, previously in the beer brewing business, started Green Mountain Distillers in 2001. It is an unusual distillery in the respect of being Certified Organic. The first product to hit the shelves was Sunshine Vodka in 2004, which became a huge success and was followed in summer 2009 with two new versions – Organic Lemon and Organic Orange. Two years earlier, Green Mountain Distillers had also released Maple Syrup Liqueur. However, a 100% organic malt whiskey has always been on their minds. The first batches were already distilled in September 2004, but unlike many other distillers in the USA, Tim and Howie decided to let it mature for quite a number of years and at the moment there has been no release.

DISTILLERY: Santa Fe Spirits, Santa Fe, New Mexico
FOUNDED: 2010
OWNER/MANAGER: Colin Keegan
www.santafespirits.com

Colin Keegan, originally from Newcastle in England, was working as an architect when he decided to become a distiller of spirits. Santa Fe Spirits is one of only two distilleries in New Mexico and they are the only one producing whiskey. Colin is collaborating with Santa Fe Brewing Company that supplies the un-hopped beer that is fermented and distilled in a 1,000 litre copper still from Christian Carl in Germany. The whiskey gets a hint of smokiness due to a special and (as of yet) undisclosed type of malt. The first product, Silver Coyote released in spring 2011, was an unaged malt whiskey which was followed in November by an apple brandy and in spring 2012 a vodka was launched. The first release of an aged (2 years) malt whiskey is expected for June 2013. Colin's goal is to produce 24,000 bottles of whiskey a year and the same amount of other spirits.

Colin Keegan, owner of Santa Fe Spirits

DISTILLERY: House Spirits Distillery,
Portland, Oregon
FOUNDED: 2004
OWNER/MANAGER: Matt Mount,
Christian Krogstad
www.housespirits.com

This distillery was started in Corvallis in 2004 by two former brewers from Portland, Lee Medoff and Christian Krogstad. A year later, operations were moved to its present location in Portland. In 2010, Lee Medoff left the company to start a new distillery also in Portland, Bull Run Distillery. In the absolute vicinity of House Spirits another five distilleries have been established, producing vodka, gin, rum and brandy and the area is now called Distillery Row. The main products for House Spirits are Aviation Gin and Krogstad Aquavit but there are also big plans for whiskey installed. The first three expressions were released in December 2009. Two of them had been matured for 2 years and 8 months and the third bottling was a white dog. White dog is the non-matured spirit and corresponds roughly to what is called new make in Scotland and poitín in Ireland. More white dog whiskies were released in 2011 and in October 2010 a blended whiskey (40% malted spirits and 60% grain spirits) called Slab Town Whiskey was also released. For the double distillation, a 1,500 litre still is used and the spirit is filled into new charred American oak.

DISTILLERY: Balcones Distillery,
Waco, Texas
FOUNDED: 2008
OWNER/MANAGER: Chip Tate
www.balconesdistilling.com

When this distillery was established the founder, Chip Tate, did not go the usual way by ordering stills from one of the well-known manufacturers but instead went about and built the stills himself. The creativity in doing this is also reflected in the first whiskies that were produced. Chip Tate was the first to use Hopi blue corn for distillation. Four different expressions of blue corn whiskey have been released so far – the first was Baby Blue, bottled at 46%, followed by True Blue which is a cask strength version. The third variety is called Brimstone Smoked Whiskey but the smoky flavours do not derive from drying the grain using smoke but it is, instead, the whisky itself that is treated with smoke from Texas scrub oak. Most recently, Balcones has released True Blue 100, a 100 proof bottling of True Blue. Balcones also produces single malt whiskey from 100% malted barley which was released in autumn 2011. The demand for Balcones whiskies has grown rapidly and Chip Tate hopes to be moving

The first single malt whisky from Balcones

production to a recently acquired 65,000 square foot warehouse in the near future.

DISTILLERY: Immortal Spirits,
Medford, Oregon
FOUNDED: 2008
OWNER/MANAGER: Jesse Gallagher, Enrico Carini
www.immortalspirits.com

So far, this distillery can mainly be seen as a labour of love by two homebrewers, but Jesse and Enrico have their minds set on a proper distillery in the near future. Currently they distil in a 1,200 gallon pot still and an 88 gallon still for limited release runs. Both stills are designed and fabricated by themselves. The wash comes from a local brewery, Standing Stone, and malt whiskey production is limited to one barrel per month. They also distil rum from cane sugar and brandy from a variety of fruits. Jesse and Enrico plan on releasing a small amount of a 2 year old single malt by the end of 2013, whilst the larger part of the production will probably be stored for an additional 6-8 years.

DISTILLERY: Lost Spirits Distillery,
Prunedale, California
FOUNDED: 2009
OWNER/MANAGER: Bryan Davis and Joanne Haruta
www.lostspirits.net

This is a distillery that hasn't made much fuss about itself, even though it has been around for three years. One of the owners, Bryan Davis, has a background as a hobby distiller and the two of them also managed an absinthe distillery in Spain before returning to Monterey County to build their own whisky distillery. And build it they did – all the equipment has been made by them with inspiration taken not least from distilleries on Islay. From the very beginning, their goal was to make peated, single malt whisky. The still is placed outside, surrounded by a Japanese garden but that is not the most peculiar thing about it. It is of a design called log-and-copper which means that it is made of both oak wood and copper. This is an old variety of still that doesn´t exist anymore, except at a rum distillery in Guyana. They are using Canadian peat with explicit chocolate and coffee notes and the fermentation is quite long in order for the wash to enter into the malolactic phase which contributes to the flavour. For maturation, Bryan and Joanne have chosen late harvest Cabernet casks (sweet wine) from Napa Valley and in 2012 the first two expressions were released - Leviathan I (peated at 110ppm) and Seascape (55ppm).

The unique log-and-copper still at Lost Spirits Distillery

DISTILLERY: Westland Distillery,
Seattle, Washington
FOUNDED: 2011
OWNER/MANAGER: Lamb family
www.westlanddistillery.com

Unlike most of the new craft distilleries in the USA producing whiskey, Westland Distillery will not (at least for
the forseeable future) distil other spirits to finance the
early stages of production. At the moment the distillery is
equipped with two 7,000 litre fermenters and one 1,400
litre Christian Carl pot still. The wash comes from a local
brewery and the yearly capacity is 58,000 litres of whiskey. However, from February 2013, they will be working
from a new, expanded facility with their own brewhouse,
five 10,000 litre fermenters, one 7,560 Vendome wash
still and one 5,670 litre Vendome spirit still. The new site
will be able to produce 260,000 litres per year which makes Westland Distillery an unusually large distillery. The
malt for the production is sourced both locally and from
England and the casks are predominantly heavy char new
American oak. Trials are also being conducted with ex-
bourbon, ex-sherry and ex-port casks. The first release of
the single malt is excpected to be by the end of 2013.

DISTILLERY: Hillrock Estate Distillery,
Ancram, New York
FOUNDED: 2011
OWNER/MANAGER: Jeffrey Baker
www.hillrockdistillery.com

Jeffrey Baker seems to have planned this brand-new
distillery ten years ago. That is when he bought the
100-acre farm where the distillery is now situated and
another 100 acres nearby. In 2011 the time was right for
this MD of a banking firm in New York to take the next
step. A 250 gallon pot still was ordered from Vendome,
five fermentation tanks were installed and the first spirit
was distilled in November 2011. What makes this distillery really unique, at least in the USA, is that they are
not just malting their own barley - they are floor malting
it. This technique that has been abandoned even in
Scotland, except for a handful of distilleries. The malt is
dried in a kiln for two to three days and then goes into
the mash tun. The distillery is all about whiskey but no
products have yet been released. The first releases are
expected to be a single malt and a solera aged bourbon,
and rye whiskey is also in the pipeline. To help Jeffrey set
up the distillery and to take on the role as Master Distiller, the legendary David Pickerell of Maker's Mark fame
was called in.

DISTILLERY: High West Distillery,
Park City, Utah
FOUNDED: 2007
OWNER/MANAGER: David Perkins
www.highwest.com

This is probably Utah's first legal distillery since 1870.
Even though it has not been established for more than
four years the owner, David Perkins, has already made
a name for himself mainly because of the releases of
several rye whiskies. None of these have been distilled at
High West distillery though. Perkins has instead bought
casks of mature whiskies and blended them himself. The
first (released in 2008) was Rendezvous Rye, a mix of two
whiskies (16 and 6 years old). Since then, he has also released a 16 year old and a 21 year old rye. The two most
recent bottlings (from summer 2011) were a 12 year old
rye and Double Rye which is a mix of a 2 year old and a
16 year old whiskey. Meanwhile, Perkins has been distilling vodka from oats and he has also released an unaged
oat whiskey from his own production called Western Oat
which contains 85% oats and 15% malted barley.
A single malt from 100% barley is also in the pipeline, In
2012 a rather unique spirit was released, Campfire, which
is a blend of Straight Bourbon, Straight Rye and Blended
Malt Scotch Whiskey.

DISTILLERY: Cedar Ridge Vineyards,
Swisher, Iowa
FOUNDED: 2003
OWNER/MANAGER: Jeff Quint
www.cedarridgedistillery.com

Jeff Quint and his wife Laurie started Cedar Ridge Vineyards in downtown Cedar Rapids in 2003 and expanded
the business soon afterwards to also include a distillery.
After a while they moved to the present location in
Swisher, between Cedar Rapids and Iowa City, where
they now have two stills in the distillery part. The first
spirit produced was Clearheart Vodka that was later
complemented by gin, rum and grappa. The first whiskey,
a bourbon, was released on 1 July 2010. Malt whisky production started in 2003 but so far nothing has been released. However, the plan is to launch the first single malt
towards the end of 2012, followed by a wheat whiskey
in 2013. A huge variety of casks are used at Cedar Ridge
(bourbon, port, rum, brandy and wine) and the idea is to
do a vatting of a selection of casks and then marry them
in a second barrel for a period before bottling.

DISTILLERY: Pinckney Bend Distillery,
New Haven, Missouri
FOUNDED: 2011
OWNER/MANAGER: Jerry Meyer, Tom Anderson,
Ralph Haynes
www.pinckneybend.com

Missouri´s newest craft distillery got their licence in
September 2011 and the three founders all have a long
experience as artisan brewers. Most of the mashing and
fermentation take place at the local Second Shift Brewery
in New Haven but the owners have also installed a small
15 gallon pilot system in order to do a small volume of
mashing and fermentation in-house. At the moment,
they have three small stills made of stainless steel and if
everything goes as planned, a 150 gallon Vendome copper pot still will be ordered in autumn 2012. For maturation, the owners are still experimenting with different
types of casks from 15 gallon barrels to a variety of types
made from Missouri oak. The main purpose for the distillery is to produce malt whiskey, but in order to finance
this, they also distil spirits that don´t require maturation
- gin, vodka and brandies - some of which have already
been released. The first whiskey release will probably be
a white dog for sale only at the distillery.

DISTILLERY: Batch 206 Distillery, Seattle,
Washington
FOUNDED: 2011
OWNER/MANAGER: Jeff Quint
www.batch206.com

A consortium of Seattle business owners started this
distillery in downtown Seattle in 2011 and the first distillation was in February 2012. In November 2011 Rusty
Figgins, known from the Ellensburg distillery which he
had sold, started at Batch 206 as the Master Distiller.
With him he also had his own brand of malt whisky, Gold
Buckle Club which in the future will be produced at this
new distillery under his supervision. The first products
from batch 206 to hit the shelves were Batch 206 Vodka
and Counter Gin. The distillery is also producing bourbon
and rye. For the whiskey, they are doing some of the
mashing themselves but are also working with a brewery
which delivers un-fermented wort. Distillation takes
place in a 1,000-litre pot-and-column still from Kothe in
Germany. Batch 206 distillery produces around 12 barrels
of whiskey every month.

Canada

DISTILLERY: Glenora Distillery,
Glenville, Nova Scotia
FOUNDED: 1990
OWNER/MANAGER: Lauchie MacLean
www.glenoradistillery.com

Situated in Nova Scotia, Glenora was the first malt whisky distillery in Canada. The first launch of in-house produce came in 2000 but a whisky called Kenloch had been sold before that. This was a 5 year old vatting of some of Glenora's own malt whisky and whisky from Bowmore Distillery on Islay. The first expression, a 10 year old, came in September 2000 and was named Glen Breton and this is still the core expression under the name Glen Breton Rare. Since then several expressions have been launched, among them single casks and sometimes under the name Glenora. A new expression, Glen Breton Ice (10 years old), the world's first single malt aged in an ice wine barrel, was launched in 2006. Interest was massive and another release came onto the market in spring of 2007. In 2008 a 15 year old version was available from the distillery only and in 2011 a 17 year old version was released. A 15 year old version of Glen Breton single malt was released under the name Battle of the Glen in June 2010. The release commemorated the distillery's victorious outcome of the ten year-long struggle with Scotch Whisky Association. Finally, a limited 20 year old expression was recently launched for sale at the distillery only.

DISTILLERY: Still Waters Distillery, Concord,
Ontario
FOUNDED: 2009
OWNER/MANAGER: Barry Bernstein, Barry Stein
www.stillwatersdistillery.com

Barry Bernstein and Barry Stein started their career in the whisky business as Canada's first independent bottler, importing casks from Scottish distilleries and selling the whisky across Canada. The next step came in January 2009 when they opened Still Waters distillery in Concord, on the northern outskirts of Toronto. The distillery is equipped with a 3,000 litre mash tun, two 3,000 litre washbacks (with a possible addition of two more during 2012) and a Christian Carl 450 litre pot still. The still also has rectification columns for brandy and vodka production. The plan is to install a second, larger still for wash distillations in a year. The focus is on whisky but Barry and Barry also produce vodka, brandy and gin. Their first release was a triple distilled, single malt vodka and they have also released a Canadian whisky with distillate sourced from other producers. Their first own whisky will probably be launched towards the end of 2012 when it turns 3 years old. Around 50% of the whisky production is from malted barley, while 40% are ryes and 10% corn whisky.

DISTILLERY: Victoria Spirits, Victoria (Vancouver
Island), British Columbia
FOUNDED: 2008 (whisky since 2009)
OWNER/MANAGER: Bryan Murray
www.victoriaspirits.com

This family-run distillery actually has its roots in a winery called Winchester Cellars, founded by Ken Winchester back in 2002. Bryan Murray, the owner of Victoria Spirits, came in as an investor, but soon started to work with Ken on the distilling part of the business. Before Ken left the business in 2008, he took part in introducing Victoria Gin, which currently is the big-selling product with 10,000 bottles a year. The Murray family left the wine part of the business in order to increase the spirits role and the next product on the list was a single malt whisky. The first batch was distilled in late 2009 by Bryan's son, Peter Hunt, using wash from a local brewery owned by Matt Phillips. The still is a 120 litre German-made copper pot-still fired by wood. The whisky will initially be matured in small casks (octaves) made of new American Oak, but old Bourbon barrels will also be used.

DISTILLERY: Shelter Point Distillery, Vancouver
Island, British Columbia
FOUNDED: 2009
OWNER/MANAGER: Andrew Currie,
Jay Oddleifson, Patrick Evans
www.shelterpointdistillery.com

Andrew Currie, who co-founded Arran Distillery in Scotland 18 years ago, and Jay Oddleifson, a former

Barry Stein and Barry Bernstein from Still Waters Distillery

accountant who was the CFO of Mount Washington Alpine Resort, are the men behind Shelter Point Distillery, just north of Comox on Vancouver Island. The buildings were completed in 2009 and in May 2010 all the equipment was in place. That means a one ton mash tun, five washbacks made of stainless steel and one pair of stills (a 5,000 litre wash still and a 4,000 litre spirit still). Both stills and the spirit safe were made by Forsyth´s in Scotland. The idea was to start distillation in September 2010 but federal, provincial and local licensing requirements, multiple inspections and one mechanical complication after another delayed the startup with eight months. Since June 2011 however, they have produced four batches of whisky every week under the supervision of distillery manager Mike Nicholson. There was no distillation during summer 2012 but production was resumed again in September and the owners anticipate to do 60 barrels per month. Twohundred acres of barley is grown on the estate and is expected to be used in the whisky production.

DISTILLERY: Pemberton Distillery, Pemberton, British Columbia
FOUNDED: 2009 (whisky since 2010)
OWNER/MANAGER: Tyler Schramm
www.pembertondistillery.ca

This is one of the most recently established distilleries in Canada. Distilling started in July 2009, with vodka from potatoes being their first product. Almost 98% of all the vodkas of the world are made from grain and Tyler came up with the idea to use potatoes while studying brewing and distilling at the renowned Heriot-Watt University in Edinburgh. The organically grown potatoes are sourced locally, and the distillery itself, is a Certified Organic processing facility. Tyler uses a copper pot still from Arnold Holstein and the first vodka, Schramm Vodka, was launched in August 2009. In June 2010, Tyler started his first trials, distilling a single malt whisky using organic malted barley from the Okanagan Valley. He filled four ex-bourbon barrels with unpeated spirit and another five were filled in 2011. At that time he also produced five barrels of lightly peated new make. The first release of this whisky will probably not take place for another two-three years. In 2012, Pemberton was named one of the five most high-tech distilleries in the world (together with the giants Roseisle and Wild Turkey) by Popular Mechanics Magazine. In Pemberton´s case it was because of its use of geothermal energy to run the distillery.

AUSTRALIA & NEW ZEALAND

Australia

DISTILLERY: Bakery Hill Distillery, North Balwyn, Victoria
FOUNDED: 1998
OWNER/MANAGER: David Baker
www.bakeryhilldistillery.com.au

In 2008 Bakery Hill Distillery, situated northeast of Melbourne, completed the installation of a 2,000 litre brewery and now has total control of all the processes from milling the grain to bottling the matured spirit. During 2009 the brewing part of the production was fine-tuned and Baker's evaluation was that the results

were stunning. The last two years, David has focussed on two things; first, environmental adjustments where the spent grain and pot ale are now sent to Yarra Valley to be used as stock feed and fertiliser instead of just being disposed of and secondly, building stock. The last thing has become more and more important as the interest from the home market has increased rapidly. A couple of years ago, David exported small volumes of his whisky to France, Germany and Sweden but he now sees himself forced to put a stop to that, at least for the time being.

The first spirit at Bakery Hill Distillery was produced in 2000 and the first single malt was launched in autumn 2003. Three different versions are available - Classic and Peated (both matured in ex-bourbon casks) and Double Wood (ex-bourbon and a finish in French Oak). As Classic and Peated are also available as cask strength bottlings, they can be considered two more varieties. Recently David started doing trials with three new wood finishes but an eventual release is still a couple of years away. The whisky is double-distilled in a copper pot still. With the Bakery Hill Distillery being situated in the southern part of Australia, the climate is very different to that of Scotland. The overall ambient temperatures are much higher while the air mass is much drier. These factors influence the rate of flavour development and whisky character, and David Baker is constantly experimenting with a wide variety of oak to find the optimal path.

DISTILLERY: Lark Distillery, Hobart, Tasmania
FOUNDED: 1992
OWNER/MANAGER: Bill Lark
www.larkdistillery.com.au

One can consider Bill Lark to be the father of the modern whisky distilling that we currently see in Australia. In 1992 he was the first person for 153 years to take out a distillation license in Tasmania. Since then he has not just established himself as a producer of malt whiskies of high quality, but has also helped several new distilleries to start up. Recently he co-founded the Tasmanian Distillers Group, together with the five other whisky distilleries on the island.

Bill Lark´s original establishment in Kingston was moved to Hobart in 2001. In 2006 a new distillery was constructed on a farm at Mt Pleasant, 15 minutes' drive from Hobart. The farm grows barley for Cascade Brewery and at the moment that is where Lark Distillery gets its malt from. However, the intention is to set up own floor maltings within two years, thereby enabling them to produce everything in-house, from barley field to bottle, at one site. Not only that – in 2004 they secured their own peat bog at Brown Marsh and in January 2007 they also purchased the cooperage that makes the barrels. All in all, they are now very much in control of the whole chain. The "old site" down in Hobart by the waterfront is now a showcase for the Lark whisky with a shop, café and whisky bar with over 100 different single malts.

The core product in the whisky range is the Single Cask Malt Whisky at 43% but Bill Lark has also released a Distillers Selection at 46% and a Cask Strength at 58%, both of which are also single cask. The range is completed by a malt whisky liqueur called Slainte and a Pure Malt Spirit at 45%. The whisky is double-distilled in a 1,800 litre wash still and a 600 litre spirit still and then matured in 100 litre "quarter casks". An important achievement for Lark distillery in 2011, was when they secured access to high quality port barrels from the world famous Seppeltsfield Wine in Barossa Valley. In 2012 Lark distillery celebrated its 20th anniversary with a unique bottling where samples of the distillery´s first 150 releases were married together in the first barrel of Para Port laid down by Seppeltsfield in 1878!

The demand for Lark single malt has grown rapidly in recent years, also outside of Australia. Through La Maison du Whisky it is selling well in Europe and was also introduced to the American market during 2011.

DISTILLERY: Hellyers Road Distillery,
Burnie, Tasmania
FOUNDED: 1999
OWNER/MANAGER: Betta Milk Co-op
www.hellyersroaddistillery.com.au

Hellyer´s Road Distillery is the largest single malt whisky distillery in Australia with a capacity that allows for 500 casks per year to be produced. The Tasmanian barley is malted at Cascade Brewery in Hobart and peat from Scotland is used for the peated expressions. Batches of 6.5 tonnes of grist are loaded into the mash tun and then the wash is fermented for 65 hours. There is only one pair of stills but they compensate for numbers by size. The wash still has a capacity of 60,000 litres which is twice that of the largest wash still in Scotland at Glenkinchie Distillery. The spirit still's capacity is 30,000 litres and the interesting part here is the really slow distillation. The foreshots take around 4-5 hours and the middle cut will last for 24 hours, which is six to seven times longer compared to practice in Scotland. Maturation takes place in ex-bourbon casks but they also use Tasmanian red wine barrels for part of it.

There are four varieties of Hellyers Road Single Malt Whisky in the range: Original, Slightly Peated, Peated and (the most recent one) Pinot Noir finish with an additional three months maturation in Pinot Noir casks from a Tasmanian winery. In 2012 Hellyers Road celebrated their first 10 years as a working distillery. One of the events was the launch of the distillery´s first 10 year old version of their Original Single Malt.

DISTILLERY: Old Hobart Distillery
Blackmans Bay, Tasmania
FOUNDED: 2005
OWNER/MANAGER: Casey Overeem
www.oldhobartdistillery.com

Even though Casey Overeem did not start his distillery until 2007, he had spent several years experimenting with different types of distillation which were inspired by travels to Norway and Scotland. The distillery (previously known as Overeem Distillery) came on stream in 2007 with assistance from the omnipresent Bill Lark (see Lark distillery) and others. The mashing is done at Lark distillery where Overeem also has his own washbacks and the wash is made to his specific requirement, i. a. with his own yeast. In every mash, a mix of 50% unpeated barley

and 50% slightly peated is used. The peat smoke is added to the barley when it has been malted and not during the drying of the malt which is the most common. The wash is then transported to Old Hobart Distillery where the distillation takes place in two stills (wash still of 1,800 litres and spirit still of 600 litres) made by the Hobart still maker, Knapp-Lewer. The spirit is matured in casks that have previously contained either port, bourbon or sherry. Most of the production is slightly peated and during 2011 Overeem plans to make 5,000 litres with production increasing every year. The first release in November 2011 consisted of four different expressions, all single casks and distilled in 2007; two cask strengths from port and sherry casks and two bottled at 43%, also from port and sherry. Casey is selling the whiskey in Australia but has also been contacted by several European distributors.

DISTILLERY: Tasmania Distillery,
Cambridge, Tasmania
FOUNDED: 1996
OWNER/MANAGER: Patrick Maguire
www.tasmaniadistillery.com

Three generations of whisky can trace its origin to Tasmania Distillery. The first was distilled between 1996 and 1998 and, according to the current owner, Patrick Maguire, the quality is so poor that he does not want to bottle it. The second generation was distilled from November 1999 to July 2001 and is bottled today under the name Sullivan´s Cove. The third generation is the whisky distilled from 2003, until now under Patrick and his three partners' ownership and will not be bottled until it has reached 12 years of age.

The range used to be made up of three different 7 year old whiskies - Sullivan´s Cove Single Cask (used to be bottled at 60% but has changed to around 50%) matured in either bourbon casks or port casks and Sullivan´s Cove Double Cask (40%) which is a marriage of port and bourbon casks. In 2010, the distillery launched its first 10 year old versions of both the bourbon and the port matured and as of 2012 they have now moved up to 12 year old versions.

Tasmania distillery obtains wash from Cascade Brewery located in Hobart, near to the distillery. The whisky is then double distilled, although there is only one still at the distillery. The model is of a French brandy design with a worm condenser attached. 12,000 litres of wash from Cascade make up one production run and it takes five wash runs and two spirit runs to complete the

The range of single malts from Overeem Distillery

process. There is generally one production run every two weeks. Annual production amounts to 120 casks of 200 litres each of non chill-filtered whisky, which is matured in American Oak bourbon casks and French Oak port pipes.

In 2010, Patrick bought a disused train tunnel, a few kilometres from the distillery, in which he plans to stock all whisky from autumn 2011 and, perhaps, in a few years' time build a new distillery. The tunnel provides a cooler and more even temperature, not to be taken on lightly in this part of the world, where great differences in temperature occur during the year.

Apart from Australia, the whisky is available in the UK, Scandinavia, France, Belgium, Holland, Korea, Singapore, Taiwan, Hong-Kong, China, USA and Canada.

DISTILLERY: Nant Distillery, Bothwell, Tasmania
FOUNDED: 2007
OWNER/MANAGER: Keith Batt
www.nantdistillery.com.au

Nant distillery, in Bothwell in the Central Highlands of Tasmania, started when Queensland businessman, Keith Batt, bought the property in 2004. He embarked on refurbishing the Historic Sandstone Water Mill on the estate that was built in 1823 and converted it into a whisky distillery. The first distillation took place in April 2008. Keith's idea is to manage the whole production process on site. Barley has been grown on the estate since 1821 and continues to this day. On the estate there was also a 180 year old water-driven flour mill which is now used for grinding the barley into grist. Keith plans to start with floor malting on the site close to the end of 2012 and peat from the original Nant summer highland grazing property, Lake Echo, will be used in the malting process. The distillery is equipped with a 1,800 litre wash still, a 600 litre spirit still and wooden washbacks are used for the fermentation. Keith uses quarter casks of 100 litres, previously used for port, sherry and bourbon, for maturation. Production is approximately 350 100-litre barrels per year.

In June 2010 the first bottlings from the distillery saw the light of day. The release was split into two different styles – the Blood Tub series with five individual bottlings at 43% from five different 20 litre casks that had previously contained port and a Double Wood bottling, with maturation both in French oak port casks and American oak sherry. A further two releases followed with whisky matured in French oak port and American oak port. The

fourth release was made in August 2011 (American oak port) and in 2012 it was time for the first release of a bourbon matured whisky.

Keith has also expanded the business to include two Nant Whisky Bars - one in Hobart and the other in Brisbane. The bars are dedicated to all things whisky and offer both single malts from Scotland as well as Tasmanian whisky.

DISTILLERY: William McHenry and Sons Distillery, Port Arthur, Tasmania
FOUNDED: 2011
OWNER/MANAGER: William McHenry
www.mchenrydistillery.com.au

William McHenry was working for a biotech company in Sydney in 2006 when he first started considering a distillery of his own. In 2011 the decision was taken and he moved to Tasmania with his family. The copper still was delivered in October of that year and in January 2012 he started distilling.

The distillery is equipped with a 500 litre copper pot still with a surrounding water jacket to get a lighter spirit and the wash is brought in from Cascade brewery. The plan is to do 400 litres of newmake per month and the spirit is filled into first-fill bourbon barrels from maker´s Mark, both 100 and 200 litres. William is hoping for a first release within three to five years. To help with the cash flow, he is producing a triple distilled vodka, gin and sloe gin. He has also released a 10 year old single malt named Three Capes Whisky which he buys from Tasmania Distillery in Cambridge. At latitude 43°, it is the most southerly distillery in Australia and the cool and temperate maritime climate is ideal for a slow maturation for the whisky.

DISTILLERY: Southern Coast Distillers, Adelaide, South Australia
FOUNDED: 2004
OWNER/MANAGER: Ian Schmidt, Tony Fitzgerald, Victor Orlow
www.southerncoastdistillers.com.au

The distillery was started by three friends mainly as a hobby. They built an 80 litre copper pot still but soon moved to a 600 litre still. Later in 2012 the plan is to double the capacity and next year to relocate to a dedicated site which will double the capacity again.

William McHenry (left), owner of William McHenry & Sons Distillery and Ian Schmidt, one of the owners of Southern Coast Distillers

By that time, the owners will give up their current jobs and dedicate themselves to producing whisky full time.

The whisky gets its distinctive, sweet flavour from the Australian peat which contains small quantities of eucalyptus. For maturation, mainly port and sherry casks are used, re-made into 100 litre casks and from both European and American oak. The first release was a 3 year old single cask in 2010 bottled at 46%. Until May 2012, there have been six releases, the last one being a 5 year old from a heavily toasted French oak port cask.

DISTILLERY: Great Southern Distilling Company, Albany, Western Australia
FOUNDED: 2004
OWNER/MANAGER: Great Southern Distilling Company Pty Ltd/Cameron Syme
www.distillery.com.au

This is the only whisky distillery in the western part of Australia. It was built in Albany on the south-western tip of Australia in 2004 with whisky production commencing in late 2005. Throughout the initial years, production of whisky, brandy, vodka and gin took place in a set of sheds on the outskirts of Albany. A move was made in October 2007 to a new, custom-built distillery with a visitor centre on Princess Royal Harbour.

Production takes place in pot stills (one wash still of 1,900 litres and one spirit still of 580 litres) and a 600 litre copper pot antique gin still has also been installed. The fermentation time is unusually long – 7 to 10 days and for maturation a mix of ex-bourbon, ex-house brandy and ex-sherry barrels are used, as well as new and re-shaved/charred American Oak and French Oak casks. Great Southern Vodkas and Gin have been available for sale since October 2006.

The first expression of the whisky, called Limeburners, was released in April 2008 and this is still the core expression from the distillery. In autumn 2010, the first peated version of Limeburners was released. The peat that was been used, had been sourced from the nearby Porongurup ranges. The whiskies are bottled either at barrel strength (63%) or diluted to 43%.

DISTILLERY: Victoria Valley Distillery, Essendon Fields, Melbourne, Victoria
FOUNDED: 2008
OWNER/MANAGER: David Vitale, Lark Distillery et al.
www.victoriavalley.com.au

One of the men behind this distillery is David Vitale who previously worked with sales and marketing at Lark Distilleries in Tasmania. Bill Lark from the aforementioned distillery has also taken part in the start-up of Victoria Valley. The distillery is fitted into an old Qantas maintenance hangar at Essendon Fields, Melbourne's original airport. The stills (an 1,800 litre wash still and a 600 litre spirit still) were bought from Joadja Creek Distillery in Mittagong and contribute to an initial capacity of 20,000 cases of whisky in a year. The target is to increase to 50,000 cases in the future.

David uses a variety of cask sizes for maturation (50, 100 and 200 litres) but all have previously contained sherry. The first whisky, a blend of 12 different casks, was released in Australia in October 2012 under the name Starward.

DISTILLERY: Timboon Railway Shed Distillery, Timboon, Victoria
FOUNDED: 2007
OWNER/MANAGER: Tim Marwood
www.timboondistillery.com

The small town of Timboon lies 200 kilometres southwest of Melbourne. Here Tim Marwood established his combination of a distillery and a restaurant in 2007 in a reno-

vated railway goods shed. Using a pilsner malted barley, Marwood obtains the wash (1,000 litres) from the local Red Duck microbrewery. The wash is then distilled twice in a 600 litre pot still. For maturation, resized (20 litres) and retoasted ex-port, tokay and bourbon barrels are used. The first release of a whisky was made In June 2010.

New Zealand ⸻

DISTILLERY: New Zealand Malt Whisky Co, Oamaru, South Island
FOUNDED: 2000
OWNER/MANAGER: Extra Eight
www.thenzwhisky.com
www.milfordwhisky.co.nz

In 2001, Warren Preston bought the entire stock of single malt and blended whisky from decommissioned Wilsons Willowbank Distillery in Dunedin. The supplies that Preston acquired consisted of, among other things, 400 casks of single malt whisky including production dating back to 1987. Before he bought it, the whisky was sold under the name Lammerlaw, but Preston renamed it Milford. Preston also had plans to build a distillery in Oamaru. In February 2010, however, his company was evicted from its premises and one month later the company was placed in receivership with a debt of NZ$3 million. In October 2010, rescue came in the form of a syndicate of nine international investors led by Tasmanian-based businessman Greg Ramsay who had been involved in the foudning of distilleries in both Australia and Scotland. Their capital injection revived the company and plans to build a distillery still exist. The total cost is expected to be $1.7m and the question remains if the site will be in Dunedin or Oamaru.

With the new ownership, the range of expressions from the old stock has increased and the follwoing bottlings can now be found; Milford Single Malt (10, 15, 18 and 20 years old), South island Single Malt (18 and 21 years), Dunedin Doublewood (6 years in American oak and 4 years in French red wine casks), single casks from 1988, 1989, 1990 and 1993, Diggers & Ditch (a blended malt with whiskies from both New Zealand and Tasmania) and The Water of Leith (a 10 year old blend). The most recent release was a 24 year old from 1987 - the year the All Blacks (the New Zealand national rugby team) won the Rugby World Cup.

ASIA

India ⸻

DISTILLERY: Amrut Distilleries Ltd., Bangalore
FOUNDED: 1948
OWNER/MANAGER: Jagdale Group
www.amrutdistilleries.com
www.amrutwhisky.co.uk

The family-owned distillery, based in Bangalore, south India, started to distil malt whisky in the mid-eighties. More than 36 million litres of spirits (including rum, gin and vodka) is manufactured a year, of which 1 million litres is whisky. Most of the whisky goes to blended brands, but Amrut single malt was introduced in 2004.

It was first introduced in Scotland, can now be found in more than 20 countries and has recently been introduced to the American market. Funnily enough, it took until 2010 before it was launched in India and currently it is only sold in Bangalore. In 2011 total sales on the export market were 10,000 cases and the plan is to sell 15,000 cases in 2013. .

The distillery is equipped with two pairs of stills, each with a capacity of 5,000 litres. The barley is sourced from the north of India, malted in Jaipur and Delhi and finally distilled in Bangalore. The small amount of peated malt that is used, comes from Inverness. Ex bourbon casks are most commonly used for maturation, but sherry casks and casks made of new oak can also be found in the warehouse. The whisky is bottled without chill-filtering or colouring. The conditions for maturation differ much from the Scottish environment. The temperature in the summer is close to 40° C and it rarely falls below 20° C in winter. Hence the much larger evaporation, between 10-16% per year. This, in turn, means that it is not cost efficient to mature the whisky for more than four years. The Amrut family of single malts has grown considerably in recent years and ingenuity is great when it comes to new limited releases. The core range consists of unpeated and peated versions bottled at 46%, a cask strength and a peated cask strength and finally Fusion which is based on 25% peated malt from Scotland and 75% unpeated Indian malt. Special releases include Two Continents, where maturing casks have been brought from India to Scotland for their final period of maturation, Intermediate Sherry Matured where the new spirit has matured in ex-bourbon or virgin oak, then re-racked to sherry butts and with a third maturation in ex-bourbon casks, Kadhambam which is a peated Amrut which has matured in ex Oloroso butts, ex Bangalore Blue Brandy casks and then finally in ex rum casks, Amrut Herald (released in 2011) with four years bourbon maturation in India and a final 18 months on the German island of Helgoland and finally Portonova (also from 2011) with a maturation in bourbon casks, then 9 months in port pipes and back to bourbon casks for the last 8 months. Autumn 2011 also saw the release of new editions of Kadhambam (this time unpeated) and Two Continents.

DISTILLERY: McDowell's, Ponda, Goa
FOUNDED: 1988 (malt whisky)
OWNER/MANAGER: UB Group
www.unitedspirits.in

In 1826 the Scotsman, Angus McDowell, established himself as an importer of wines, spirits and cigars in Madras (Chennai) and the firm was incorporated in 1898. In the same town another Scotsman, Thomas Leishman, founded United Breweries in 1915. Both companies were bought by Vital Mallya around 1950 and today United Breweries (in which the spirits division consists of United Spirits) is the second largest producer of alcohol in the world after Diageo. Vijay Mallya, the son of Vital, is acting as chairman since 1983.

United Spirits have more than 140 brands in their portfolio including Scotch whisky, Indian whisky, vodka, rum, brandy and wine. Since last year, 22 of the brands are so called "millionaire brands", i.e. brands selling more than one million cases a year. The absolute majority of United Spirits' whiskies are Indian whisky, i. e. made of molasses. The major brands in the group are huge sales-wise with McDowell's No.1 whisky as the top seller (16.1 million cases in 2011). Single malt sales are, of course, negligible compared to these figures. McDowell's Single Malt is made at the distillery in Ponda (Goa) and sells some 20,000 cases each year. It has matured for 3-4 years in ex-bourbon casks.

McDowell's launched the world's first diet whisky, McDowell's No.1 Diet Mate, in 2006. It is a blend of whisky and the herb, garcinia, which increases the rate of metabolism. In 2007 United Spirits Limited acquired the Scottish whisky-maker, Whyte & Mackay, (with Whyte & Mackay blends and Dalmore, Jura and Fettercairn distilleries) for £595m.

Pakistan

DISTILLERY: Murree Brewery Ltd., Rawalpindi
FOUNDED: 1860
OWNER/MANAGER: Bhandara family
www.murreebrewery.com

Murree Brewery in Rawalpindi started as a beer brewery supplying the British Army. The assortment was completed with whisky, gin, rum, vodka and brandy. Three single malts have been available for some time; 3, 8 and 12 years respectively. In 2005 an 18 year old single malt was launched and the following year their oldest expression so far, a 21 year old, reached the market. There are also a number of blended whiskies such as Vat No. 1, Lion and Dew of Himalaya.

Company sources mention a supply of half a million litres of whisky in underground storage. The brewery makes its own malt (using both floor maltings and Saladin box) and produces 2.6 million litres of beer every year and approximately 440,000 litres of whisky.

Murree Brewery consists of three divisions – the liquor division (responsible for 70% of income and almost 100% of the profit), Tops division (mainly fruit juices) and a glass division (which manufactures glass containers for the company and other customers).

Muslims are prohibited by their religion to drink alcohol, so it is not surprising that in a country where 97% are Muslims, the whisky market is quite small. Only about 3 million litres per year are sold, mainly to the Christian, Hindu and Parsee minorities.

Amrut Portonova

Taiwan _____

DISTILLERY: Yuan Shan Distillery, Yuanshan,
Yilan County
FOUNDED: 2005
OWNER/MANAGER: King Car Food Industrial Co.
www.kavalanwhisky.com

The first whisky distillery in Taiwan lies in the north-eastern part of the country, in Yilan County, just one hour from Taipei. The area is flat between two mountain ranges and it was built in record time with construction lasting just eight months. The first distillation took place on 11th March 2006.

The distillery is divided into two units, with the first completed in 2006. It is equipped with a semi-lauter stainless steel mash tun with copper top and eight closed stainless steel washbacks with a 60 hour fermentation time. The malted barley is imported with Baird's of Inverness as the main supplier. There are two pairs of lantern-shaped copper stills with descending lye pipes. The capacity of the wash stills is 12,000 litres and of the spirit stills 7,000 litres. After 10-15 minutes of foreshots, the heart of the spirit run takes 2-3 hours. The cut points differ from what is common in Scotland. To capture the sweetness (important to the Chinese consumers), collecting starts at 78% and stops already at 72%. The extreme cut points are also determined by the climate and the quick maturation. The spirit vapours are cooled using tube condensers but due to the hot climate, subcoolers are also used. The total capacity of this unit is 1.3 million litres per year.

The second unit of the distillery was completed in 2008 and consists of a full lauter Steinecker mash tun, 12 stainless steel washbacks and eight Holstein stills. The stills function, unusually enough, in pairs and two pairs have rectification columns with four plates, while the other two pairs have seven plates. This unit, with a 2.6 million litre capacity, is used for spirits other than whisky.

The warehouse is five stories high with the first four floors palletised and the top floor more of a traditional dunnage warehouse. The casks are tied together four and four due to the earthquake risk. The climate in Taiwan is very hot and humid and on the top floors of the warehouse the temperature can reach 42° C. Hence the angel's share is quite dramatic – no less than 15% is lost every year. The warehouse harbours 30,000 casks and there is a need for more warehousing capacity within the near future. The ideal solution would be to build up in the cooler mountains, but in order to do that, the legislation must be changed, as warehousing must currently be in close proximity to the production plant.

The first release of Kavalan (as the whisky from the distillery is called) was in December 2008 and this is now one of the core expressions. In 2009, a port finish version called Concertmaster appeared and later that year, two different single casks were launched – one ex-bourbon and one ex-Oloroso sherry, both bottled at cask strength under the name Solist. A third single cask, this time from a Fino cask, was released just in time for Chinese New Year in 2010. In 2011 the release of single casks continued with Solist Vinho, bottled at 59% and with a maturation in Portuguese wine barriques, and finally a new core expression – King Car Conductor. This was the first whisky from Kavalan to be bottled under the company name and is a mix of eight different types of casks, unchillfiltered and bottled at 46%. Another two expressions have been announced for a release end of 2012. One of them will be exclusively sold at the visitor centre. The recipe of the Classic Kavalan is quite complex and includes six different types of casks - fresh bourbon, fresh sherry, refill bourbon, red wine casks from Spain and two different white wine casks from Portugal.

The most important market apart from Taiwan is mainland China. The strategy is to open up showrooms where visitors can attend master classes, taste the whisky for free and, of course, buy from the whole range. A new showroom was recently opened in Shanghai. Kavalan whisky is exported to Macau, Hong Kong, Malaysia, Japan and, recently, Canada. The owners also plan to launch their whisky in both Europe (starting with the UK) and the USA.

There is an impressive visitor centre on site. No less than one million visitors come here per annum, which is roughly the same number as all Scottish distilleries' visitor centres together. The owning company, King Car Group, with 2,000 employees, was already founded in 1956 and runs businesses in several fields; biotechnology and aquaculture, among others. It is also famous for its canned coffee, Mr. Brown, which is also exported to Europe.

Yuan Shan Distillery in Taiwan - home of Kavalan Single Malt and the Kavalan Concertmaster bottling

SOUTH AMERICA

Argentina

DISTILLERY: La Alazana Distillery, Golondrinas, Patagonia
FOUNDED: 2011
OWNER/MANAGER: Pablo Tognetti, Nestor Serenelli
www.laalazana.whisky.com

The first whisky distillery in Argentina concentrating solely on malt whisky production was founded in 2011 and the distillation started in December that year. Located in the Patagonian Andes in the South of Argentina, it is owned and run by Pablo Tognetti, and old time home brewer, and his son-in-law Nestor Serenelli. The distillery is equipped with a lauter mash tun and four 1,100 litre washbacks all made of stainless steel. The one 550 litre pot still is made of copper and takes care of both distillation runs. A second still will probably be added in the future. The owners are aiming for a light and fruity whisky and for maturation they use a mix of 200 litre toasted Malbec casks and ex-bourbon casks. Following Argentinian legislation, the first whisky could be released after two years, i. e. end of 2013.

AFRICA

South Africa

DISTILLERY: James Sedgwick Distillery, Wellington, Western Cape
FOUNDED: 1886 (whisky production since 1990)
OWNER/MANAGER: Distell Group Ltd.
www.threeshipswhisky.co.za

Distell Group Ltd. was formed in 2000 by a merger between Stellenbosch Farmers' Winery (founded in 1925) and Distillers Corporation (founded in 1945) although the James Sedgwick Distillery was already established in 1886. The company produces a huge range of wines and spirits. One of the most successful brands was introduced in 1989 – Amarula Cream, today the second best-selling cream liqueur in the world.

James Sedgwick Distillery has been the home to South African whisky since 1990. The distillery is currently under major expansion and will, when finished, be equipped with one still with two columns for production of grain whisky, two pot stills for malt whisky and one still with six columns designated for neutral spirit. There are also two mash tuns and 23 washbacks. Grain whisky is distilled for nine months of the year, malt whisky for two (always during the winter months July/August) and one month is devoted to maintenance.

In Distell's whisky portfolio, it is the Three Ships brand, introduced in 1977, that makes up for most of the sales. The range consists of Select and 5 year old Premium Select, both of which are a blend of South African and Scotch whiskies. Furthermore, there is Bourbon Cask Finish, the first 100% South African blended whisky and the 10 year old single malt. The latter was launched for the first time in 2003 and it wasn't until autumn 2010 that the next batch was released. It sold out quickly and another 8,000 bottles were launched in October 2011. Apart from the Three Ships range, Distell also produces two 3 year old blended whiskies – Harrier and Knight. James Sedgwick distillery has the capability of producing both malt and grain whisky and two years ago produced yet another first for South Africa. A "single grain" whisky was released under the name Bain's Cape Mountain Whisky. It is double matured in the same style of cask and, although it has no age statement, it is matured for a minimum of five years.

DISTILLERY: Drayman's Distillery, Silverton, Pretoria
FOUNDED: 2006
OWNER/MANAGER: Moritz Kallmeyer
www.draymans.com

Being a full-time beer brewer since 1997, Moritz Kallmeyer began distilling malt whisky in July 2006. Until last year, production was small, but operations have now been expanded to two pot stills. The new wash still has a capacity of 1,500 litres with the old spirit still holding 800 litres. The spirit still was reconstructed from a stainless steel tank in which perfume was imported. He also believes in letting the wash spend up to ten days in the washback, to allow the malolactic fermentation to transfer its character to the spirit. The whisky matures in French oak casks which have previously held red wine from the Cape area.

Kallmeyer's first whisky was released as a 4 year old in autumn 2010 under the name Drayman's Highveld Single Malt and there has also been the release of a second batch. Kallmeyer works with other distillates as well such as Mampoer, which is a local brandy, a honey liqueur and fruit schnapps. The main source of income, however, comes from production of craft beers.

Kallmeyer is also, together with property lawyer, As Botha, involved in a new whisky venture. The concept consists of a whisky distillery and boutique beer house on an African game farm in the Cradle of Humankind – a World Heritage site in Gauteng.

La Alazana Distillery

James Sedgwick Distillery

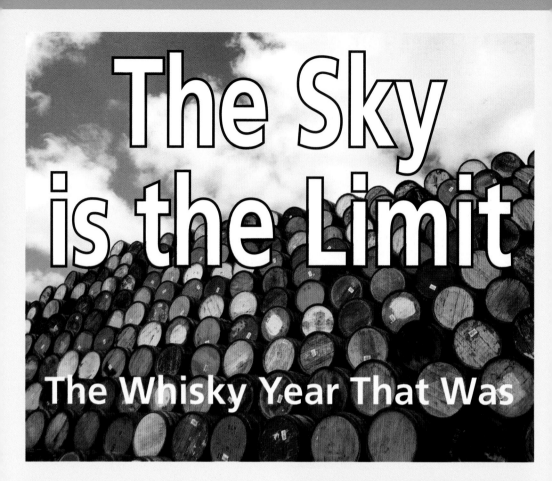

The Sky is the Limit

The Whisky Year That Was

Great expectations for the Scottish whisky industry!

The Scotch whisky industry is absolutely oozing with optimism for the future! Strong figures for 2011, not least in emerging markets, have the producers worried whether the availability of Scotch whisky will be sufficient over the next few years. Most of them are now earnestly investing to increase the capacity in their current distilleries or are planning to open up new ones.

When figures were presented in March 2012, one could note yet another record breaking year. If 2009 was the year of affordable blended whiskies due to the economic crisis and 2010 was characterized by an upswing for single malts and premium blends, then 2011 was a year with considerable upswings in all segments.

The total value of exported Scotch increased by no less than 23% to £4.23bn – of course, a new record! The volume, which decreased last year, was boosted during 2011 and increased by 19% to the equivalent of 1253 million 70 cl bottles, thereby surpassing the previous record. The revenue per bottle for the producers continues to rise. In 2006, they earned £2.38 on average per bottle. The same ratio for 2011 was £3.38.

The picture for 2011, if broken down into malt and blends, is as follows:

SINGLE MALT - EXPORT
Value: +29% to £745m
Volume: +18% to 100m bottles

BLENDED SCOTCH - EXPORT
Value: +28% to £3.33bn
Volume: +16% to 902m bottles

TOTAL SCOTCH - EXPORT
Value: +23% to £4.23bn
Volume: +19% to 1253m bottles

The two top markets are the same as last year – France in terms of volume (57 million litres of pure alcohol, up 25% from last year) and USA in terms of value (£655m, up 31%). But let us analyse the nine different regions to see how they performed. We can start by pointing out that all have increased both in terms of volume, as well as value.

The biggest market by far is still the European Union (excl. UK) where 38% of all Scotch whisky is being exported. If we look at individual countries, it is a mixed bag. Second after France is Germany which has increased its volume by 19%. Other countries which enjoyed double digit gains are Belgium, Estonia, Finland, Latvia, The Netherlands, Norway and Poland. Those countries which have shown a decline are, not surprisingly, found in the Mediterranean area with Greece and Italy decreasing by 25% and 13% respectively. Spain and Portugal managed to hold their positions with volumes similar to 2010.

The major share of the export destined for Eastern Europe and other non EU countries lands in Russia, Turkey and Switzerland. The volume to these regions increased by 31% while the value was up 26%. The figures for the UK (not included in the EU figures) decreased in volume by 6% and blended whisky suffered most while single malts were more or less unchanged.

The second biggest region is Asia, which is also where we find several of the emerging markets where most producers spend the biggest part of their marketing budget. Volumes were up by 21% to 77 million litres of pure alcohol while value increased even more dramatically (+27% to £912m). The most important country in the region, both by value and volume is Singapore, but the country also serves as a hub for further export to neighbouring countries. In the top 10 list by volume, we find India where sales were up 30% and Thailand with a 17% increase. In terms of value Taiwan impresses with an increase of 45% while South Korea was down by 7%. Two other important Asian markets that both increased in terms of volume are China (+12%) and Japan (+56%).

The third biggest region is North America which, in Scotch exporting terms, to 93% consists of USA and Mexico. The value of Scotch sold to the USA increased by 31% to £655m which means that the Americans paid an average of £18 per litre of pure alcohol, while the French paid half, only about £9 per litre.

Next of the regions is Central and South America, a very important (and growing) market for blended Scotch. The region as a whole was up 31% in terms of volume and 38% in terms of value. The two dominant countries are Brazil and Venezuela and both showed impressive increases for volume, as well as value, reaching from 33% to 48%. Brazil is now number 9 on the global value list with Venezuela in tenth place. Venezuela tends to differ greatly from year-to-year and this year's sharp rise can be compared to the decrease of 46% from the previous year.

Scotch whisky sales to Africa increased by 20% in terms of volume and, it is of course South Africa that is the main market with a 75% share. The country now occupies place number 7 on the global volumes list and number 5 on the value list.

Next is the Middle East with a volume increase of 17% and its value has increased by 27%. Some 50% of the volumes go to United Arab Emirates.

The final region is Australasia where Australia accounts for 90% of the total of 8 million litres of alcohol. The increase for 2011 was 6%.

Looking at the figures for the first six months of 2012, it would appear that Scotch whisky has tougher times ahead. Global sales in terms of volume were down by 10% compared to January-June 2011. USA was down by 7% and France by no less than 30%. Very few of the bigger markets

showed positive figures but there was light at the end of the tunnel for the UK where consumption had increased by almost 10%.

The big players

Diageo

When CEO Paul Walsh presented Diageo's full year results in August 2012, he said the company was "on track for medium term targets". For the fiscal year ending 30 June, Diageo reported an increase in net sales by 8% to £10.8bn, while operational profit before exceptional items was up by almost 11% to £3.2bn. Net profit came in considerably lower with an increase of only 2.7%. The main reason for this was the much higher taxation, 33%, compared to last year's 14%. Diageo has been in negotiations with the tax authority during the year which resulted in an exceptional write-off this year of future tax deductions but, on the other hand, made it clear that in future the tax rate will remain steady at approximately 18%.

Paul Walsh - Diageo's CEO

Spirits represent 66% of Diageo's net sales and whisky is 35%. Within the whisky sector, Buchanan's was the shining star during the year with a 24% increase in organic net sales. Other brands that performed well were Bushmill's (+20%) and Johnnie Walker (+15%). The fastest growing for Johnnie Walker comes from the super deluxe versions such as Double Black and Blue Label. Red Label, however, also increased mainly due to campaigns in South Africa and Brazil which targeted the emerging middle classes. Windsor is still the leading Scotch brand in Korea even though net sales declined by 1% due to a problematic spirits market for the whole industry. As we have become accustomed to, J&B showed negative figures (-3%) but, at least, it seems as if the rate of decline is slowing down.

If we look at the different regions, the biggest growth in terms of profit can be found in Latin America and Caribbean (+22%), where

Diageo historically has a strong position. In second place comes Africa (+20%) followed by Asia Pacific (+18%). The more mature markets showed more modest increases – North America (+6%) and Europe (+3%). North America is still by far the most important region for Diageo with net sales of £3,556m and operating profit of £1,343m. Europe comes in second while Asia Pacific is the region with the smallest profit, only £332m. The potential in Asia is huge and the company is putting a lot of effort into increasing their presence in the region, not least in India. Sales growth for Diageo India was 24% with Johnnie Walker Black Label up 40%, VAT 69 by 39% and the new IMFL whisky Rowson´s Reserve, launched in October 2011, also contributed to the sales growth.

Rowson´s Reserve, Diageos´s new Indian whisky

Photo: Diageo

Pernod Ricard

When the CEO of Pernod Ricard presented the company´s results on the 30th of August for the fiscal year ending 30 June 2012, it was overshadowed by the sudden death of the company´s chairman, Patrick Ricard, two weeks earlier. Executive changes were announced which meant that his nephew Alexandre Ricard would take over the dual role of both CEO and chairman from January 2015. Until then, Pierre Pringuet will continue as CEO and Daniéle Ricard, Patrick Ricard´s sister, will act as chairman of the board.

Patrick Ricard, Pernod Ricard´s chairman of the board, passed away in August 2012

Photo: Pernod Ricard

When it comes to their figures they could show an increase in net sales of 7% to €8.22bn while net profits rose by 9% to €1.17bn. Pringuet was satisfied and said: "the group recognised its best growth rates since the 2008 crisis". If we look at the different regions, Asia and Rest of the World (+15%) is still the main driver of growth for the company and it is mainly due to China, India, Vietnam, Taiwan and Travel Retail. The Americas could report a growth of +6%. The USA was up 5% and Brazil 13% while Mexico declined by 12%. Over to the headache of many producers – Europe, which unsurprisingly was a mixed bag. The Mediterranean countries all posted declining figures while sales in Eastern Europe increased by 16%, mainly thanks to Russia and Ukraine. France finally, which makes up 9% of the group´ sales, showed a decline of 1%.

The whisky brands all performed very well with Royal Salute at the top (+20%) followed by Glenlivet (+15%), Jameson (+15%) and Chivas Regal (+7%). Even Ballantine´s managed to surprise on the positive side by showing roughly the same figures as last year. This was a step forward for a brand weighed down by problems, not least in their main market Spain which is struggling with huge finacial difficulties.

United Spirits

In many ways, United Spirits is a company focused on volumes and since early 2011 they are selling more cases than any of its rivals in the spirits business, including Diageo. In terms of value, however, the company still has a long way to go. For the fiscal year ending March 2012, United Spirits Limited (part of the UB Group) could report an increase in net sales of 18% to Rs. 75.42 billion. Behind these figures was a volume of 123 million cases sold. Net profits fell by 10% to Rs. 3.43 billion while operating profits were up by 5.3% to Rs. 10.66 billion.

United Spirits have more than 140 brands in their portfolio including Scotch whisky, Indian whisky, vodka, rum, brandy and wine. Since last year, 22 of the brands are so called "millionaire brands", i.e. brands selling more than one million cases a year. The latest brand to enter the list was a gin, Carew´s Dry. The only competitor able to match United Spirits in this regard, is Pernod Ricard who also has 22 millionaire brands. United Spirits´ biggest brand is McDowell´s No.1 whisky (16.1 million cases) which surpassed Bagpiper during 2011. The fastest growing whisky in the world during 2011 also belongs to United Spirits - Gold Riband, which sold 3 million cases (+36%).

In 2007, United Spirits entered the Scotch whisky market for the first time when Whyte & Mackay was acquired for £595m. Four malt distilleries (Dalmore, Isle of Jura, Fettercairn and Tamnavulin), a bottling-plant and stocks of 115 million litres were included in the deal. There have been rumours during the last year that United Spirits were about to sell Whyte &

Mackay. The reason would be that they needed the money to compensate for losses in the mother company UB Group, in particular from Kingfisher Airlines which is reported to be on the verge of a bankruptcy. Another way to handle the financial difficulties could be to offer Heineken (which already owns a 37,5% stake of United Breweries) a larger part of the company or to team up with either of the two big conglomerates - Diageo or Pernod Ricard. Diageo and United Spirits were already in talks two years ago that led to nothing, but there were signs during spring 2012 that negotiations had started again. Rumours have it that the owner of United Spirits would be willing to sell as much as 27% of the company to Diageo.

Whyte & Mackay
The company has been a subsidiary of Indian United Spirits since 2007 when it was acquired for £595m. Four malt distilleries (Dalmore, Isle of Jura, Fettercairn and Tamnavulin), a grain distillery (Invergordon), a bottling-plant and stocks of 115 million litres were included in the deal.

At that time, Whyte & Mackay were deeply involved in the bulk spirits business, selling huge quantities to supermarkets. From an early stage it was apparent that the new owners had other plans for the company and the transition towards a brand-orientated business was quickly established. Dalmore single malt has become known as a producer of extremely old and rare whiskies while Jura is one of the fastest climbers in terms of volume. Their new brand-orientated direction and strategy has also manifested itself in the last available financial statements for the year ending March 2011. Net sales fell by 20% to £169.5m while net profits tumbled by 54.5% to £10.25m. At the beginning of 2012, a spokesperson for the company said that they were considering expanding the capacity of two of the five distilleries. No time frame was presented and it probably depends on how the mother company of United Spirits (UB Group) actively manages to handle the

financial difficulties brought on by the crisis for Kingfisher Airlines (see United Spirits, page 262)

Morrison Bowmore
Ever since Morrison Bowmore decided a couple of years ago to cut down on the bulk business, selling huge stocks of whisky to the likes of Asda and Tesco, and instead, decided to concentrate on their own brands, profits have increased steadily. The fiscal year for 2011 was no exception – the turnover rose by 7% to £44,6m while pre-tax profits soared by no less than 84% to £6,1m. All their main brands – Bowmore, Auchentoshan, Glen Garioch and McClellands – contributed to the positive result and the focus on the Duty Free segment is of particular importance.

The result has also been impacted by the agreement that was concluded with Drambuie Liqueur Company in early 2010 to provide Drambuie with supply chain services covering whisky procurement, blending, bottling, warehousing and logistics at the plant in Springburn. The same services had previously been supplied by Glenmorangie at their Broxburn facility.

LVMH
LVMH Moët Hennessy Louis Vuitton SA is the world's leading luxury goods vendor. It provides products ranging from champagne and perfumes, to designer handbags and jewellery. The Wines & Spirits business group includes brands such as Moët & Chandon Champagne and Hennessy Cognac, with Glenmorangie and Ardbeg representing Scotch whisky.

One interesting fact is that Diageo owns 34% of the Wine & Spirits division (Moët Hennessy), an arrangement which dates back to 1988 when Guinness (one of the two companies that later formed Diageo) entered into a joint venture with LVMH. Over the last three years there has been lots of speculation about Diageo wanting to acquire the rest of the shares and, in that way, get their hands on a big cognac and champagne

Constellation Collection - the new prestige range from Dalmore

Bill Lumsden explains the high-flying plans for Ardbeg

brand, something that is missing in their portfolio at this point. The only problem is that Bernard Arnault, majority share holder in LVMH and also the richest man in France, seems determined to keep the Wine & Spirits division in the company.

For 2011, LVMH could report a 22% rise in profit from recurring operations to €5263m and an increase in revenue of 16% to €23.7bn.

Wine & Spirits is the second largest division in the company with a turnover of €3524 million (+8%) and profit of €1101 million (+18%). Champagne and cognac are the most important segments of the division with Hennessy being the largest cognac brand in the world by far, selling almost 5 million cases during 2011 and the brand has 47% of the lucrative Chinese market.

Glenmorangie Company
Glenmorangie Company, owner of Glenmorangie and Ardbeg and a subsidiary of LVMH, reported a considerable decrease in the turnover for 2011. The fall was 20% down to £60m while pre-tax profits only went down by 5% to £10.8m. The company decided in 2008 to withdraw from blended whisky and bulk- and third party sales to concentrate solely on single malts and this is one explanation why the figures are still lower than pre 2008. Another reason for last year's slump is also that the total boardroom pay bill increased to £2.5 from £1.1 while the remuneration for an unnamed director increased from £0.5m to £1.7m.

In autumn 2011, the company became involved in a spectacular experiment when vials of Ardbeg-crafted molecules were sent up to the International Space Station. The goal is to study how these molecules interact with oak wood at zero-gravity compared to control samples in warehouse 3 at the distillery on Islay.

Edrington
The figures for the Edrington Group, the world's fourth largest producer of single malt Scotch whisky, for the year that ended 31 March 2012,

showed a decline in comparison to the previous financial year. The turnover increased by just 0.5% to £556m compared to an increase last year by 18%. Profit before tax was up 5,2% to £149m (last year it was +19%). When comparing the figures it should be noted that last year's figures were impacted by the purchase of the Cutty Sark blend in April 2010. The increase in profit for the last three years is nonetheless impressive, up 57%, but also these figures have been influenced by an acquisition of another brand, namely Brugal rum, in late 2008.

Macallan lost volumes in the last year, being surpassed by Glenlivet on the global sales list, although profits from the brand had increased. Highland Park grew both by volume and value, especially in the UK, US and Scandinavia, while the blends were a mixed bag. Famous Grouse increased somewhat, while Cutty Sark volumes declined because of weaker sales in Greece, Spain and Portugal.

Edrington's chief executive, Ian Curle, pointed out that the brand investment for the coming year will be targeted towards emerging markets and will continue to focus on premiumisation. There will also be more investments in markets such as South- East Asia, Russia and the Middle East. The Edrington Group is owned by a charitable trust, The Robertson Trust, which donated £14,6m to charitable causes in Scotland last year.

Gruppo Campari
After a very successful 2010, the Italian group seemed to slow down a little during 2011. Net sales

Bob Kunze-Conzewitz, CEO of Gruppo Campari

increased by almost 10% to €1274m while net profits were up by just 1.4% to €159m (last year profits grew by 14%).

Spirits account for 75% of the group's sales, with Aperol, Campari, SKYY Vodka, Cinzano, Wild Turkey and Glen Grant as the big brands. In terms of regions, the Campari Group concentrates on Italy (one third of the sales), the Americas (one third) and Europe (25%). Sales in the rest of the world (including travel retail) only account for 9% of the total. On the other hand, this was the area where sales increased the most during 2011 (+39%). The growth mainly took place in Australia, South Africa and global travel retail. The company has also declared that they expect to double its sales in India within five years.

In 2009 the sales figures for Glen Grant slowed down by 4%, in 2010 they were up by 9% only to once again slow down in 2011 (+ 1%). The brand is still suffering from a weak Italian market (where Glen Grant for decades has been the biggest single malt).

The Campari Group has spent quite a lot of money over the past couple of years on acquisitions. In 2009 they bought Wild Turkey bourbon at a cost of $581m and in 2010 they paid €128,5m to get Frangelico, Carolans and Irish Mist from William Grant & Sons. They also more than doubled the capacity at Wild Turkey distillery in Kentucky at a cost of $50m and have now decided to build a $44m bottling plant set to open in 2013. In spite of these investments, the company CEO Bob Kunze-Concewitz does not exclude the fact that there will be more acquisitions during 2012.

Matt Shattock, President and CEO of Beam

Ian Macleod Distillers

The family-owned company can look back at three excellent years starting in 2008 when the global economic downturn set in. Those three years have seen sales increase by 50% and pre-tax profit by a staggering 238%. For 2011, the turnover was up by 26% to £43m while pre-tax profit increased by 27% to £5.4m. A strong contributing factor to the good results is the continued success of Glengoyne single malt where sales have doubled since they bought the distillery in 2003. Their second distillery, Tamdhu, was acquired as late as 2011 and to help finance the deal, Ian Macleod Distillers was backed up by a £23m asset-based credit line and a £5m loan from Royal Bank of Scotland. Exports accounted for two-thirds of the company's turnover in 2011 and they also opened up an Indian subsidiary two years ago to gain a position in one of the most important emerging markets for Scotch whisky. Their biggest blended whisky, King Robert II, which sells 500,000 cases per year is already one of the most popular brands in India. The biggest markets for Glengoyne are France, Germany and Scandinavia.

Beam Inc.

For years the American company, Fortune Brands, were active in three very different business areas; Home & Security, Golf and Spirits. The latter has been contained within subsidiary Beam Global Spirits & Wine, with major spirits brands such as Jim Beam, Maker's Mark, Canadian Club, Courvoisier and, in Scotch, Teacher's and Laphroaig. With such a diversified structure, it has been difficult to maintain a decent growth and in 2010, a decision was made to separate the Spirits division from the other two. In 2011, the Golf business was first sold to a Korean group for $1.23bn and in October, Home & Security was spun off. Spirits was left, which now operates under a new name - Beam Inc.

The full year figures for 2011 for Beam is therefore filled with one-off profits and costs and difficult to compare with previous results. Net sales increased by 10% to $2.31bn while net profits rocketed by 88% to $917m. Apart from the separation from the other business areas, the biggest event during 2011 was the acquisition of Cooley Distillery for $95m which marked the company's entry into the lucrative Irish whiskey market.

With the spin-off of the Spirits division, rumours became rife that one of the big companies (most likely Diageo which didn't have a big bourbon brand) would make a bid for Beam Inc. However, during spring 2012, Beam bought Pinnacle vodka and Calico Jack's rum from White Rock Distillers for $605m, matters that would make an acquisition more difficult in the foreseeable future. The volume figures for the Scotch brands have improved in comparison to 2010, with Teacher's increasing by 8% to 2 million cases sold, while Laphroaig is selling around 185,000 cases. In the bourbon category, Maker's Mark (which exceeded one million cases sold for the first time in 2010)

Photo: Beam

continued its ascendency with 1.2 million cases sold during 2011 (+15%).

Inver House Distillers

Last year, Inver House, a subsidiary of ThaiBev, reported an impressive increase in sales (+19%). The full year 2011 was even better with total sales at £80.6m – up by 28%. Net profits were even more impressive with an increase of 70% to £11.6m. All their single malt brands increased but it was a blend, Hankey Bannister, that led the way with a sales jump of 53%, mainly in Eastern Europe and South America.

The big brands

As we've grown accustomed to the last couple of years, most of the fastest growing whiskies in the world are from India. No less than eight of the top ten climbers are Indian with only William Lawson´s and Jameson breaking the tradition. Apart from that it was less polarised compared to 2009 when cheaper whiskies increased due to the recession and 2010 when premium brands recovered market shares. If there was a trend then it was more about the different markets and not the price. Cutty Sark, J&B and Bell´s decreased due to lower demand in Spain and the UK, while, for example Buchanan´s, William Lawson´s and Black & White gained thanks to increased demand in France and Latin America.

In 2011, Glenfiddich managed to do something that no other single malt brand has ever achieved – selling more than 1 million cases in one year.

It ended up at 1,050,000 cases which, of course, meant that the brand still is in the lead on the global sales list. In second and third place, the battle between Macallan and Glenlivet continues unabated. The winner in 2011 was Glenlivet which managed to sell 765,000 cases while Macallan landed around the 700,000 mark. In fourth place is Glenmorangie which has gained significantly over the last couple of years and during 2011 sold 390,000 cases. They were followed by Glen Grant which after having gained well during 2010, decreased last year due to the weak Italian market. Their sales were 265,000 cases. The Singleton came in at fifth place (225,000 cases) but that includes all three versions (Glen Ord, Glendullan and Dufftown). Aberlour followed (with 216,000), then Laphroaig (204,000), Balvenie (199,000) and Cardhu (181,000).

In the blended Scotch segment Johnnie Walker succeeded to strengthen its position even further. Two years ago they had a market share of 17,5% which in 2011 had increased to 19,1%. Total sales of all varieties were 18 million cases – an increase of 6% compared to last year. The number two spot has been held by Ballantine´s since 2007 and last year they managed to sell 6,5 million cases. Sales of Grant´s have been pretty stable the last five years, but thanks to declining volumes of its competitor, J&B, they now occupy the third place with almost 5 million cases sold closely followed by Chivas Regal which sold a few thousand cases less. J&B is now in fifth place with 4,5 million cases thanks to problems experienced in the Spanish market. Dewar´s is next with sales of 3,2 million cases followed by the rapidly increasing William

Johnnie Walker House in Shanghai - the first outside Scotland

Mark Reynier, together with the rest of the shareholders, decided to sell Bruichladdich distillery in summer 2012 to Rémy Cointreau

Peel which increased by 16% to 2,7 million cases. In ninth and tenth place we find Bell's and Label 5, both selling around 2,5 million cases each.

As always, this ranking shows just the Scotch whisky brands. If we look at whiskies produced in North America, the number one spot is held by Jack Daniel's (Tennessee whiskey) with 10,5 million cases, followed by Jim Beam (Bourbon) with 5,9 million cases, Crown Royal (Canadian) 5 million cases, Seagram's 7 Crown (American blended whiskey) 2,4 million cases and Black Velvet (Canadian) with 2,1 million cases.

Finally, let's have a look at the Indian whiskies. This is a category where volumes are really high due to the fact that India is the country where most whisky is consumed. The most popular is Officer's Choice which has made an incredible journey since 2007 with an increase of 150% in five years to 16,5 million cases sold during 2011. McDowell's No. 1 comes in second with 16,1 million cases, while last year's number one, Bagpiper, has slipped to third place selling 16 million cases. One of the big climbers in 2011, Royal Stag, (+20% to 12,5 million cases), comes in at fourth place followed by Old Tavern which increased even more (+22% to 11 million cases).

Changes in ownership
- mergers and acquisitions

In similarity with the previous year, 2012 was not characterized by major structural changes in terms of ownership. Instead, there were three smaller acquisitions that drew attention to themselves.

The acquisition of Tullibardine Distillery by the French wine and spirits group Picard Vins & Spiritueux in November 2011 was the first one. Tullibardine was founded in 1947 and in 1971 it was sold to Invergordon Distillers. They were, in turn, acquired by Whyte & Mackay in 1993 (which was owned by Fortune Brands at that time) and two years later, Tullibardine was closed. In 2003, a consortium consisting of Michael Beamish, Alan Williamson, Douglas Ross and Lastair Russel bought the closed distillery for £1.1m and by the end of that year the distillery was producing again. Rumours have been circulating over the last couple of years that the distillery would be up for sale but in was not until 2011 that a deal came through. The buyer, the family-owned Picard Vins & Spiritueux, was founded in 1951 and is run by the managing director, Gabriel Picard. Their product range includes still and sparkling wines, as well as various spirits. Among their brands is the famous white burgundy Chassagne Montrachet whose castle also serves as the company's head office. Their first contact with the Scotch whisky segment was in 2008 when they bought Highland Queen, a three year old blend, from Glenmorangie. Picard has since three years back also been one of Tullibardine's most important customers. Picard has 400 employees and is operational in 55 countries.

One month later, in December 2011, it was announced that Beam Inc, who recently streamlined its wine and spirits business by breaking away and selling off other parts of the business, had purchased Cooley Distillery in Ireland. The purchase attracted attention since Cooley was the only remaining independent distillery in Ireland with Jameson being owned by Pernod Ricard, Bushmills by Diageo and the Tullamore Dew brand by William Grant & Sons. The deal was worth $95m and although Cooley is a small player with just a 5% share of the total sales in the Irish whiskey category, they have a production capacity that could improve their position in the fast growing segment. The new owners declared that their focus will be on the blended Kilbeggan brand which is already known in the US market. They will also cut down on sales to third-party customers.

The third distillery to change hands was Bruichladdich which was effected in July 2012. The distillery was reopened in 2000 when Mark Reynier and partners bought the distillery from JBB Greater Europe (Beam) for a sum of £6.5m. Reynier and his team soon established themselves as a company going their own way, and their outspokenness was, at times, not appreciated in other parts of the whisky producing community. They managed, however, to build up a loyal customer circuit and even in economic terms the company became successful over time. Several suitors have offered to buy the distillery and the shareholders finally came to a decision regarding a sale of the distillery. The venerable company Rémy Cointreau became the new owners. The French spirits group already has Rémy Martin cognac and Cointreau liqueur in their portfolio and the take-over of Bruichladdich marks the first step into the Scotch whisky category. With their excellent distribution network in Asia, Rémy Cointreau expects a strong growth for Bruichladdich in the increasingly important Asian market. In order to close the deal, Rémy Cointreau had to pay £58m.

Moreover, several of the bigger role-players declared that they didn't rule out mergers or acquisitions in the nearby future. United Spirits showed interest for Teacher's during autumn 2011 but only months thereafter the question was rather if they could hold on to Whyte & Mackay that they purchased in 2007. The reason was that Kingfisher Airlines, included in the parent company UB Group, was on the verge of bankruptcy and one way to solve the situation would be to sell all or parts of Whyte & Mackay. Another way would be to invite a competitor to buy a part of United Spirits and Diageo would be closest at hand since there had previously been negotiations with the Indian company regarding cooperation of some sort.

The Campari group was another of the big companies that declared they would be looking to make an acquisition during 2012. The Italian company bought Glen Grant in 2006 and three years later Wild Turkey, but a spokesperson for the company declared that "Campari is in a good cash position to do a reasonable acquisition".

When Beam Inc. was spun out of Fortune Brands in 2011, many analysts thought there would be a scramble among the other role-players to take over the American company. Many thought that, for example, Diageo, who lacks a big bourbon brand, should be interested in Jim Beam (even though more than one spokesperson within the company has indicated that Jack Daniels, although not technically a bourbon, would be a better choice). Nothing has happened so far and the probability that it will happen within the nearby future diminished as the owners of Beam made several acquisitions from the end of 2011 and during spring 2012. It started with Cooley and continued with the take-over of the Pinnacle vodka brand and the rum Calico Jack's. Apparently Beam Inc. plans to be a force to be reckoned with in the international drinks business, at least for a while yet.

The new kid on the block – flavoured whisky!

It couldn't have escaped anyone that more and more vodkas come in flavoured varieties. One fourth of all vodka sold is flavoured and it comes in many shapes. Some of the more unusual flavours are bubble gum, butterscotch and bacon! It has also been said that vodka is the main threat to the whisky industry in the battle for the young consumers' attention, for the simple reason that the spirit comes in so many flavours. No wonder then that the whisky producers in recent years have decided to jump on the bandwagon too. The first among them was Beam when they introduced their Jim Beam Red Stag in 2009 which was a 4 year old bourbon infused with flavours of Black Cherry. In 2012 the Red Stag range was expanded with a Honey Tea and a Spiced (cinnamon)

Bushmill's Irish Honey ad for the American market

version. Last year sales of Red Stag increased by 58% and it now sells 300,000 cases a year. Other producers were to follow. Wild Turkey launched American Honey (230,000 cases sold in 2011) and Jack Daniel´s released Tennessee Honey which sold a staggering 320,000 cases in its first year (2011). Evan Williams and 7 Crown also have flavoured varieties and the category is now the fastest growing spirits type in the US market. In 2011, the five biggest brands alone sold over 1 million cases. Until recently, this has mostly been a bourbon trend even if there are Canadian examples as well as the spiced Dock No. 57 from Canadian Club and Revel Stoke (which actually started several years ago) with their whisky flavoured with vanilla, coriander and cardamom. In 2011, the trend spread to Ireland when Diageo declared that they would release a honeyed version of their Bushmill´s Irish whiskey and in summer 2012, the company announced that they had acquired Cabin Fever, a maple flavoured whisky, from the Robillard family.

The question is probably not if this trend will continue, but rather if it will affect the position of Scotch whiskies. As it currently stands today, Scotch whisky cannot be flavoured. The Scotch Whisky Association (and EU Spirits Regulation) are very adamant about that. It could neither be called Scotch nor whisky. On the other hand, they have no problem with a flavoured spirit where Scotch whisky has been used as long as it is labelled liqueur. In that case the producer may also refer to Scotch whisky on the label. After all, that has been done for a long time by Drambuie, for instance. Voices within the Scotch whisky industry have requested to allow the rules to be adjusted in favour of allowing flavoured Scotch but, on the other hand, the fear is great that this could prove damaging to the quality perception of Scotch whisky as a category.

New, revived and planned distilleries

Ardnamurchan Distillery
The success for the independent bottler, Adelphi Distillery, (founded in 1993) forced the owners, Keith Falconer and Donald Houston, in 2007 to start planning for increased production either by filling more casks of new-make from other distillers, buying an existing distillery or building their own distillery. They chose the last option and after years of planning, permission was finally granted in April 2012 to commence with the building.

The chosen site at Glenbeg in Ardnamurchan is 1.5 miles west of the company´s headquarter at Glenborrodale Castle and this means that it will become the most westerly distillery in mainland Scotland.

Up to 50% of the barley will be sourced from a farm in West Fife and will be floor malted at the distillery. The distillery will also be equipped with four washbacks, one wash still (10,000 litres) and one spirit still (6,000 litres). The goal is to produce 100,000 litres of alcohol in the first year with a possibility to eventually increase production to

Photo: Adelphi Distillery

Adelphi´s future distillery at Ardnamurchan

300,000 litres. The distillery will also use a wood chip fuelled biomass plant as its main source of fuel. The owners are planning for three different styles of whisky; the first one will be similar to their current brand, Fascadale, which has usually been drawn from bourbon casks from either Talisker or Highland Park. The second style will be more sherried while the third will probably be a heavier peated whisky. Production will start during 2013.

Annandale Distillery

In May 2010 consent was obtained from Dumfries & Galloway Council for the building of the new Annandale Distillery. The old one was closed in 1921 and in December 2008 the site was bought by Professor David Thomson and his wife, Teresa Church, with the aim to resurrect this, the southernmost distillery in Scotland. Work on the restoration began in June 2011 with the two, old sandstone warehouses which will be restored to function as two-level dunnage warehouses. The mash house and the tun room will need a complete reconstruction while a new still house will be built in what used to be the mill house in the Johnnie Walker days David also has plans to start using the old maltings as well, to malt locally sourced barley, but that will probably not be for another five years. Meanwhile, the old maltings with the kiln and original pagoda roof, will house a visitor centre.

As for the equipment (the original ones have all disappeared), this will be made by Forsyth's in Rothes. In 2010, Malcolm Rennie, who managed Kilchoman distillery on Islay, joined the company as Distillery Manager and, together with Jim Swan, he has created the design. The equipment specification, as it currently looks, will be one semi-lauter mash tun (2,5 tonnes) which was installed in summer of 2012, six wooden washbacks (12,000 litres each), one wash still (12,000 litres), one intermediate still and one spirit still (4,000 litres each). The planned output is 250,000 litres per annum. According to David's plans, the first production run could be in December 2012 with the distillery open to public by late spring 2013.

Wolfburn Distillery

In Caithness, a consortium called Aurora Brewing Limited, has ambitious plans to build a distillery which, when completed, will be the most northerly distillery on the mainland (which at the moment is Pulteney in Wick). The owners have chosen a site that is situated 350 metres from the ruins of the old Wolfburn Distillery which was founded in 1821 and closed down during the latter half of the 19th century. The water for the production will also be drawn from the same source – the Wolf Burn. Planning consent was received from the authorities in Caithness in June 2012 and they had, prior to that, already signed a contract with Forsyth's regarding the distillery equipment. Construction work commenced in August and the plan is to start production early in 2013.

Construction work has begun at the Wolfburn Distillery site. This picture was taken end of August 2012.

The distillery will be equipped with a one tonne stainless steel mash tun with a copper canopy, three stainless steel washbacks (6,000 litres each), a 5,500 litres wash still and a 3,600 litres spirit still. The final style of the whisky has not been decided yet, but they will probably be doing both unpeated and peated spirit. The production capacity will be 116,000 litres of pure alcohol annually.

Tullamore Dew Distillery

When William Grant & Sons acquired the second biggest Irish whiskey brand in the world, Tullamore Dew, in 2010, rumours started to flourish that they also planned to build a new distillery . Until the 1950s, Tullamore Dew had been distilled at Daly´s Distillery in Tullamore. When they closed, production was moved to Power´s Distillery in Dublin and later on to Midleton Distillery where it is still produced today. In March 2012, Grant´s could report that they were in the final stages of negotiations to acquire a 58-acre site at Clonminch on the outskirts of Tullamore. Construction of the distillery will start later in 2012 and the combined pot still and malt whiskey distillery should be producing in 2014. The total cost for the new plant will be €35m.

Dingle Distillery

Permission to build a distillery in Dingle, County Kerry, Ireland was applied for in autumn 2008 and was granted in March 2009 by Kerry County Council. The people behind it, Porterhouse Brewing Company and Jerry O´Sullivan, managing director of Southbound Properties, planned to convert an old creamery into a distillery, at a cost of €2.9m. Initially, it was said that the distillery would be up and running in late 2009, but the production process was postponed.

In 2010, the former business partners went their separate ways and Jerry O´Sullivan started planning for a brewery at the old creamery site. In summer 2011 brewing commenced and they also have plans to distil whiskey on site.

The people from Porterhouse Brewing Company, Oliver Hughes and Liam LaHart on the other hand, found a new location, also in Dingle. The plan is now to turn an old saw mill into a whiskey distillery. Two stills manufactured by Forsyth´s were installed in June 2012 and it is hoped that whiskey production will start during autumn.

Kingsbarns Distillery

Kingsbarns Company of Distillers, spearheaded by Greg Ramsay and Doug Clement, are behind the plans to establish a distillery in Fife. Their idea is to build a distillery in the vicinity of St Andrews, home of golf and an area with thousands of visitors each year but lacking a whisky distillery. Greg and Doug have consulted Bill Lark as advisor. He is the owner of Lark Distillery in Tasmania, godfather of modern whisky-making in Australia, and advisor to several other whisky companies in his native Australia. The idea is to convert a farm-stead on the Cambo Estate which has been

home to the Erskine family since 1688 and is owned today by Sir Peter Erskine. The distillery will have one pair of stills (to be built in Tasmania) and the capacity will be around 100,000 litres per year. Planning permission was received in March 2011. After that a second round of share offer to potential investors was released but, due to the current economic climate, this proved harder than anticipated. The company will now try and raise the final £1.8m that is needed through a combination of more funds from the original investors, crowd funding and a possible loan from Scottish Venture Fund.

Falkirk Distillery

The construction of the first distillery in Falkirk, since Rosebank was closed in 1993, came to a halt temporarily in autumn of 2009 after the plans had been approved by the local council in spring of 2009. Objections were raised by Historic Scotland that the distillery would be built too close to the Antonine Wall. The Wall was built in 142 AD to stop Caledonian tribes attacking the Romans and it was given World Heritage Status in 2008. However, in May 2010 Scottish ministers gave the final approval, arguing that the distillery would not interfere with the wall but could boost tourism to the area instead.

Falkirk Distillery Company, owned by Fiona and Alan Stewart, is behind the £5m project. The facilities will include a visitor centre, restaurant and shops, apart from the distillery itself and could create up to 80 jobs. Very little news has come from the company in the last year and it is uncertain how far they have come with their planning.

Barra Distillery

The classic film, Whisky Galore, based on the equally classic novel by Sir Compton Mackenzie, was filmed on the island of Barra in the Outer Hebrides. It is a story of the SS Politician which was stranded in 1941 and 264,000 bottles of whisky which were among her cargo were lost. The island where the ship went missing was in fact Eriskay, a smaller island to the north of Barra, but that did not deter Peter Brown who had moved to Barra from Edinburgh 12 years ago. He wants to build a distillery there and is convinced that the connection with the film location will be favourable for the business.

In November 2005, the Loch Uisge reservoir on the west of the island was acquired in order to secure water supply for the future distillery. Future casks have been sold to the public since early 2008 and most of the plans regarding building and construction are ready. In July 2010, Peter Brown bought all the shares owned by Andrew Currie (of Arran Distillery fame) who had been part of the project since its inception. The original idea was to start building in autumn of 2009, but the recession has made funding difficult and the future for the distillery is now uncertain.

Early plans

Apart from the distilleries (or proposed distilleries) that we have mentioned, there are a few more that are still in the early stages of planning.
Isle of Harris Distillers is planning for a distillery on the Hebridean island of Harris. One of the men behind it is a former director of Glenmorangie, Simon Erlanger, and the distillery will be built at Tarbert. According to Erlanger, £10m is needed of which one-third is already secured by investors. If they manage to raise the rest of the funds, the construction could commence as early as 2013 and the distillery could be up and running by the second half of 2014.

Scottish Development International (SDI) claims that a major Indian spirits producer (not United Spirits) has shown an interest in building a whisky distillery in Scotland to help meet demand for Scotch in the Indian market. So far, no further details have been revealed.

Peter Lavery, lottery millionaire and founder of The Belfast Distillery Company, revealed plans in May 2012 to build a new distillery in Belfast. The idea is to use a part of the former Crumlin Road jail for the whiskey production. If all falls into place this will be the first distillery to operate in Belfast for over 75 years. The whole investment is expected to be around £5m and if everything is going according to plans, the distillery could be producing in 2014. Since 2011, Lavery is already selling whiskey produced elsewhere under the brand name Danny Boy and recently he added another range of 5 and 10 year old whiskeys called Titanic.

The Northern Irish producer of cream liqueurs, Niche Drinks, are looking to build a new plant in Derry for their existing operation and the plans include a new whiskey distillery. Planning approval has been applied for and the total investment will amount to £10m.

Investments

That the whisky producers have a bright view of the future is mirrored in all the reports issued during the year regarding different investments. It became the most obvious at the turn of the month of June when Chivas Brothers announced that they were committed to an annual capital expenditure of £40 million to increase the production capacity. Six days later, Diageo presented a plan to invest over £1 billion in Scotch whisky production over the next five years.

To start with Chivas Brothers, the money will be used for increasing capacity at Glenallachie, Glentauchers, Tormore and Longmorn distilleries. Add to that the re-opening of Glen Keith distillery and the total capacity will increase by 25%. A new bottling hall was opened in Paisley in the summer with emphasis on the prestige and ultra-prestige editions, for instance Chivas Regal 25 year old and Royal Salute. Christian Porta, the chief executive of Chivas Brothers also revealed that they would consider building a new distillery in Scotland if demand continues to rise after Glen Keith has been re-opened.

Diageo´s plans include an increase in capacity at some of their existing distilleries, among others,

Chivas Brothers´ new luxury bottling facility in Paisley

Part of Diageo's warehousing complex in Blackgrange, Alloa

Dailuaine and Glen Elgin. It has also been decided to build a major, new distillery, with a capacity of 13 million litres, at one of three existing sites – Teaninich, Glendullan or Inchgower. And if this was not enough, there are plans for a second new distillery and a possible third if "the 10 percent plus annual sales growth of recent years is sustained for the next three or four years". If a second distillery is built it would mean that within three to five years, Diageo's Scotch whisky production capacity would have increased by 30-40%. Of the £1bn, £500m are earmarked for production while the remaining £500m will cover working capital as the spirit matures. The company says that the investment will create 100 new jobs within the company, another 250 construction jobs during a five-year period and a further 500 jobs in other sectors.

But the investment is not solely about distilling capacity. Warehousing is an essential part of the plan and, apart from the existing warehouses at Blackgrange, Alloa being expanded a completely new warehouse complex with 46 units will be built in Cluny, Fife. At the same time, Diageo has leased a commercial property at Grangemouth near Edinburgh on an eight year rental deal where 140,000 casks will be stored.

The results of investments announced for the last two years are now starting to take shape. At the end of March 2012, the Kilmarnock bottling plant closed and the £86m extension of the existing blending and bottling plant at Leven opened up in the summer. The plant, which opened in 1973, now has 24 production lines with the capacity of producing around 35 million cases of 142 different brands every year. The £10m cooperage in Cambus, which replaces the cooperages in Dundashill and Carsebridge, was officially opened in November 2011. At full production the 40 employees will produce 250,000 casks per year.

In March 2012, William Grant & Sons could confirm what everybody was hoping for – a new distillery for Tullamore Dew situated in Tullamore where the old site (Daly's Distillery) was closed in 1954. William Grant & Sons bought the brand (the number 2 Irish whiskey in the world) in 2010 from C&C Group. The new distillery will be a combination of a pot still distillery and a malt distillery, and construction will begin during 2012. Until now, Tullamore Dew has been produced at Midleton Distillery.

The Campari Group will open a bottling plant both at Glen Grant distillery and at Wild Turkey distillery in Kentucky. The latter means a $44m investment. Both plants will be operational from 2013.

Bottling grapevine

Of all the new bottlings released during 2012, it was a no age statement expression from *Macallan*, named *Gold*, which drew the most attention. This was not because it was rare, expensive or spectacular, but because it was the first sign of a major change for the Macallan range. More versions of the same kind will follow in 2013 (*Amber, Sienna* and *Ruby*) and several markets will, in due time, see the classic Sherry oak and Fine oak series with age statements lessen to a few expressions. Regardless of Macallan's intentions with a move like this, it can't be denied that it makes life a little easier for a producer when their hands are not tied by having to find casks with an exact age in the warehouse. On the other hand, it can also be said that there will be consumers who find it harder to judge if a bottle is price worthy without an age on the label. Macallan, however, are far from being alone about this strategy. The fact that it received so much attention was rather due to that, in this case, the producer has for a long time been famous for a wide range of expressions with an age on the label.

Let's continue with some old bottlings that were released during the year. From *Pulteney* came a long-awaited *40 year old* and the same age was released by the owners of *Bunnahabhain*. Slightly younger but still the oldest bottling so far from the distillery came in the shape of *anCnoc 35 year old*. A thorough search throughout the

The Balvenie 50 years

old bourbon maturation, will start off as a duty free item only to become available in domestic markets next year.

The people of *Highland Park* are proud of the Viking heritage at Orkney and rarely miss an opportunity to express that sentiment. The new range, Valhalla, pays tribute to the old Nordic Gods and first out was *Thor, a 16 year old* bottled at cask strength. To the delight of many, 2012 saw the return of the popular *Highland Park 21 years*, now at the original strength (47,5%). *Glenmorangie* continued their series of bottlings called Private Collection and being the masters of second maturations, the new expression *Artein* was no exception – a mix of 15 and 21 year old whiskies which had been extra matured in Super Tuscan wine casks. Under the supervision of Bill Lumsden, the company also put a new *Ardbeg* on the market under the name *Galileo*.

Jura single malt has enjoyed an incredible success in the last couple of years with sales going through the roof. A new release for 2012 was *Jura Elixir*, a 12 year old released as an exclusive for Sainsbury´s. Whyte & Mackay´s other star distillery, *Dalmore*, continued on their path lined with exclusive and rare bottlings. In the summer, the *30 year old Ceti* was released but it was overshadowed, at least in terms of rarity, by the one bottle of *Zenith* which was offered by Whisky Shop through an auction and expects to be sold for at

warehouses of *BenRiach* and *GlenDronach* resulted in the release of the oldest whisky still in stock at the two distilleries – the *46 year old Vestige* from BenRiach and the *44 year old Recherché* from GlenDronach. To celebrate Malt Master David Stewart´s 50 years working with *The Balvenie*, a very limited *50 year old* bottling was released which, in terms of age, was surpassed only by a *58 year old Glenfarclas*.

As we move on to the younger bottlings *Glenglassaugh* have so far relied on some really old casks from the previous owners for their releases. In 2012 it was time for the first of their own production – a *3 year old* aptly named *Revival*. After a couple of years of limited releases, Anthony Wills of *Kilchoman* launched his first core bottling in larger volumes, *Machir Bay*, a vatting of whiskies from 3 to 5 years old and from *Glengyle* distillery in Campbeltown came *Kilkerran Work In Progress IV* that has now reached the age of 8 years.

Travel retail has been recognised by many producers as one of the most important markets and no-one confirmed this more clearly than Morrison Bowmore. *Three new Bowmores* and no less than *six new Auchentoshans* were soon to be found in the Duty Free shelves. *Laphroaig* delighted their Swedish fans (and there are a few) with *Brodir*, a 13 year old exclusively found onboard the Viking Line ferries. The second expression in *Glenfiddich´s* new series *Age of Discovery, 19 year*

Highland Park Thor

least £150,000. Dalmore also released a series of 21 different whiskies distilled between 1964 and 1992. The price tag for all 21 bottles in the *Constellation Series* is £158,000.

Back on planet Earth, Springbank made a revamp of their range of Longrow single malts which included the introduction of the *Longrow RED*, an 11 year old with the last 4 years in Australian Cabernet Sauvignon casks. The owners also re-launched their famous *21 year old Springbank* which sold out quickly. Another chance will be had in early 2013 when more bottles become available. *Glen Garioch* released more vintages, this time a *1995* which was distilled just before the distillery was temporarily closed and a *1997* from some of the first whisky distilled following the re-opening. From *Glen Moray* came a *25 year old port finish* while *Old Pulteney* launched the final bottling in their boat series – *WK217 Spectrum*. During 2012, InverHouse also commissioned the illustrator, *Peter Arkle*, to produce a series of limited edition packaging for a new *anCnoc* without age statement which is a vatting of fino sherry casks aged 6 to 12 years.

The much anticipated yearly Special Releases from *Diageo* consisted in part of rare bottlings from two closed distilleries – *Brora (35 years)* and *Port Ellen (32 years)*. There were also new bottlings from *Lagavulin (12 and 21 years)*, *Caol Ila (14 years unpeated)* and *Talisker (35 years)*.

Glenfiddich Janet Sheed Roberts Reserve 55 years

Finally, two unusually old versions from *Auchroisk (30 years)* and *Dalwhinnie (25 years)* were also launched.

The acquisition of *Bruichladdich* by French spirits & wine giant, Rémy Cointreau, almost overshadowed a handful of exciting new releases; *Laddie 16* and *22 years old*, 10 year olds of both *Port Charlotte* and *Octomore* and the latter was also represented by *Comus* with a finish in Chateau d`Yquem casks and *5_169* – the most heavily peated Octomore yet.

Isle of Arran distillers released *The Eagle*, the last in their Icons series, as well as *The Devil´s Punch Bowl*, a vatting of some of their oldest casks. *Laphroaig* moved their *Triple Wood* from the duty free segment to the core range and replaced it with *Laphroaig PX* and released a new Cairdeas variety for Feis Ile – *Cairdeas Origin*. *Glenlivet* presented a new *Cellar Collection* bottling, this time a *Vintage 1980* and expanded their *Single Cask Editions* with no less than six new versions aged from 15 to 21 years. From *Glenfiddich* came a new duty free item in the shape of *Glenfiddich Millennium Vintage* and to celebrate the 110th birthday of *Janet Sheed Roberts* (the founder William Grant´s granddaughter), 15 bottles from a 1955 European oak cask were sold at auctions with all proceeds being donated to charity.

anCnoc Peter Arkle limited edition

Independent Bottlers

*The independent bottlers play an important role
in the whisky business. With their innovative bottlings, they increase
diversity. Single malts from distilleries where the owners' themselves decide
not to bottle also get a chance through the independents.
The following are a selection of the major companies.
All tasting notes have been prepared by Dominic Roskrow.*

Gordon & MacPhail............www.gordonandmacphail.com
Established in 1895 the company which is owned by the
Urquhart family still occupies the same premises in Elgin.
Apart from being an independent bottler, there is also
a legendary store in Elgin and, since 1993, an own distillery, Benromach. There is a wide variety of bottlings,
for example *Connoisseurs Choice, Private Collection,
MacPhail's Collection* and *Secret Stills*. Many of the
bottlings have been diluted to 40%, 43% or 46%, but
the series *Cask Strength* obviously, as the name implies,
contains bottlings straight from the cask. Another range
called *Distillery Labels* is a relic from a time when Gordon
& MacPhail released more or less official bottlings for
several producers. The labels are all unique and currently
16 distilleries are represented in the range, some of them
closed. The Gordon & MacPhail warehouses in Elgin
probably contain the largest collection of matured malt
whisky in the world which was a prerequisite for the
2010 launch of the world's oldest single malt ever bottled
– a 70 year old *Mortlach*. This was the first release in a
new range called *Generations* and was followed in 2011
with the release of a *Glenlivet 70 year old*. There are also
large volumes of *Macallan* dating all the way to 1940
enabling the release of a special range of whisky from
this distillery called *Speymalt*. Several
blended whiskies, e. g. *Ben Alder, Glen
Calder* and *Avonside* are also found in
the company's range. To celebrate the
Queen's Diamond Jubilee, a *60 year
old Glen Grant* distilled in 1952 was
released in 2012.

Glentauchers 1991, 43%
Nose: Light, with vanilla, icing sugar
and soft lime.
Palate: Clean, rich and mouth coating,
sweet, with fresh garden herbs,
spearmint, sweet leaf tea and milk
chocolate.
Finish: Sweet with some spice kicking
in. Balanced and pleasant.

Glen Elgin 1996, 46%
Nose: Toffee, honeycomb, grapefruit,
lemon curd.
Palate: A delightful and blemish-free
mix of sweet lemon bonbons, sweet
liquorice and traces of mint. Late on
there's a big pepper hit. Rich, clean
and fresh.
Finish: A long and large cracked
lemon pepper delight.

Berry Bros. & Rudd................................www.bbr.com
Britain's oldest wine and spirit merchant, founded in
1698 has been selling their own world famous blend,
Cutty Sark, since 1923. Berry Brothers had been offering
their customers private bottlings of malt whisky for years,
but it was not until 2002 that they launched *Berry's Own*

Selection of single malt whiskies. Under the supervision
of Spirits Manager, Doug McIvor, some 30 expressions
are on offer every year. Bottling is usually at 46% but
expressions bottled at cask strength are also available.
The super premium blended malt, *Blue Hanger* is also
included in the range. So far, six different releases have
been made, each different from the other. The sixth
edition sets itself apart from the rest as it combines both
sherried malts from Speyside and peated Islay whisky.
In 2012, to commemorate the centenary of the sinking
of Titanic, Berry Brothers released a *Titanic Malt* drawn
from a 1998 cask of Glenrothes.
   In 2010 BBR sold Cutty Sark blended Scotch to
Edrington and obtained *The Glenrothes* single malt in
exchange. A strategic partnership with American Anchor
Distilling Co, best known for Old Potrero
single rye in a whisky context, was announced in 2010. Anchor Distilling will
assist BBR in selling part of their range
in the USA.

Blue Hanger 6ᵗʰ release, 45.6%
Nose: A beguiling and complex nose, with
lots of tropical fruit notes, pineapple,
marmalade and oak – dusky, moody and
seductive.
Palate: Superb. Sweet, soft, balanced
and very fruity, with fresh figs, dates
and polished oak. Very complex, very
stylish, very palatable.
Finish: Long, fruity, oaky and with
marmalade in the mix.

Glen Grant 1974, 49.3%
Nose: Raisins, squiggly grape, soft
plum. Prickly sweet spice – nutmeg
perhaps?
Palate: Intense, rich and full fruit with
a delightful wave of pepper and oak.
Prune juice, orange marmalade, and
some delightful spearmint.
Finish: Wonderfully more-ish mix of
fruit, oak and spice.

Signatory Vintage Scotch Whisky
Founded in 1998 by Andrew and Brian Symington, Signatory lists at least 50 single malts on any one occasion. The
most widely distributed range is *Cask Strength Collection*
which sometimes contains spectacular bottlings from
distilleries which have long since disappeared. Another
range is *The Un-chill Filtered Collection* bottled at 46%.
Andrew Symington bought *Edradour Distillery* from
Pernod Ricard in 2002.

Ian Macleod Distillers...................www.ianmacleod.com
The company was founded in 1933 and is one of the
largest independent family-owned companies within
the spirits industry. Gin, rum, vodka and liqueurs are
found within the range, apart from whisky and they

also own *Glengoyne* and *Tamdhu* distilleries. In total 15 million bottles of spirit are sold per year. Single malt ranges like *The Chieftain's* and *Dun Bheagan* are single casks either bottled at cask strength or (more often) at reduced strength, always natural colour and unchill-filtered. There are two *As We Get It* expressions – Highland and Islay, both 8 year olds. Bottled at 40% are the five *MacLeod's Regional Single Malts* (one for every region and Campbeltown is not included). The blended *Six Isles Single Malt* contains whisky from all the whiskyproducing islands and is bottled at 43%. One of the top sellers is the blended malt *Isle of Skye* with four expressions - *8, 12, 21* and *50 years old*. Finally, *Smokehead*, a heavily peated single malt from Islay, was introduced in 2006. There is also a *Smokehead Extra Black 18 years old* and *Smokehead Extra Rare* (which basically is a 1 litre duty free bottling of the 12 year old).

Isle of Skye 8 year old, 40%
Nose: A light and delicate peat nose, with cracked pepper and some citrus.
Palate: Softer and more rounded than you might expect, but delicately balanced, with cocoa and camp coffee and a late dose of spice.
Finish: Citrusy and peppery, with the spice dominating.

Isle of Skye 12 year old, 40%
Nose: Peat, citrus fruits, with lime, floor polish.
Palate: Balanced between fruit, oak and peat. Delicate but quite complex, and with some astringent notes from old whiskies in the mix.
Finish: Pleasant, medium length, peaty.

Blackadder International ....www.blackadder.se
Blackadder is owned by Robin Tucek, one of the authors of *The Malt Whisky File*. Apart from the *Blackadder* and *Blackadder Raw Cask*, there are also a number of other ranges - *Smoking Islay, Peat Reek, Aberdeen Distillers, Clydesdale Original* and *Caledonian Connections*. One of the latest brands in the Blackadder family is *Riverstown* aiming especillay for the Asian market. The company has also been known for bottling unusual expressions of *Amrut* single malt. All bottlings are single cask, uncoloured and unfiltered. Most of the bottlings are diluted to 43-46% but Raw Cask are always bottled at cask strength. Around 100 different bottlings are launched each year.

Duncan Taylor ....www.duncantaylor.com
Duncan Taylor & Co was founded in Glasgow in 1938 and in 2001, Euan Shand bought the company and operations were moved to Huntly. The company bottles around 200 expressions per year. The range includes *Rarest of the Rare* (single cask, cask strength whiskies of great age from demolished distilleries), *Rare Auld* (single cask, cask strength malts and grains with the vast majority aged over 30 years), *Peerless* (a unique collection of single malts over 40 years old), *NC$_2$* (mainly single casks, 12-17 years, non chill-filtered at 46%), *Battlehill* (younger malts at 43%) and *Lonach* (vattings of two casks from same distillery of the same age to bring them up to a natural strength of over 40%). A new addition to the range is the *Dimensions* collection with single malts and single grains aged up to 39 years and bottled either at cask strength or at 46%. A couple of the most recent are *Blair Athol 22 years, Imperial 16 years* and *Linkwood 25 years*. *Auld Reekie* is a 10 year old vatted malt from Islay, which is similar to *Big Smoke*, although the latter is younger, more peated and available in two strengths, 40% and 60%. In the blended Scotch category, Duncan Taylor is well

represented by the *Black Bull* range. The brand was trademarked already in 1933 and Duncan Taylor took over the brand in 2001. The range consists of a *12 year old* and a *30 year old*, both with a 50/50 malt/grain ratio. New editions to the range are *Black Bull 40 year old* (now with its third edition), containing 90% malt whiskies (i. a. Glen Grant, Highland Park and Caperdonich) and *Black Bull Special Reserve No. 1*.

Another addition to the Duncan Taylor range involves the concept of re-racking the whisky from larger casks (hogsheads or barrels) to the smaller quarter casks (ca 125 litres) or octaves (ca 60 litres). This will speed up the maturation due to the higher whisky to wood ratio, i. e. the whisky is more in contact with the oak. The whisky is allowed to be in the smaller casks for a minimum of 3 months before it is bottled.

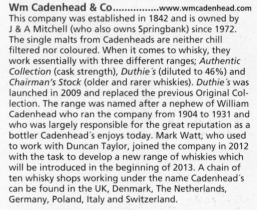

Big Smoke 60, 60%
Nose: To Islay malts what Metallica is to rock music – the full monty, big and full in every way. Peat, iodine and sea spray dominate.
Palate: Needs water but it's a monster malt rich in oil, cough sweet, peat and citrus. Fabulous.
Finish: Long and peaty.

Old Reekie, 46%
Nose: Drifting chimney smoke, damp wood, honeyed lemon.
Palate: Soft and smooth, with a big hit of peat, sweet, yellow fruits and fish shop.
Finish: Long and smoky.

Wm Cadenhead & Co ....www.wmcadenhead.com
This company was established in 1842 and is owned by J & A Mitchell (who also owns Springbank) since 1972. The single malts from Cadenheads are neither chill filtered nor coloured. When it comes to whisky, they work essentially with three different ranges; *Authentic Collection* (cask strength), *Duthie's* (diluted to 46%) and *Chairman's Stock* (older and rarer whiskies). *Duthie's* was launched in 2009 and replaced the previous Original Collection. The range was named after a nephew of William Cadenhead who ran the company from 1904 to 1931 and who was largely responsible for the great reputation as a bottler Cadenhead's enjoys today. Mark Watt, who used to work with Duncan Taylor, joined the company in 2012 with the task to develop a new range of whiskies which will be introduced in the beginning of 2013. A chain of ten whisky shops working under the name Cadenhead's can be found in the UK, Denmark, The Netherlands, Germany, Poland, Italy and Switzerland.

Murray McDavid ....www.murray-mcdavid.com
Established in 1995 by Mark Reynier, Gordon Wright and Simon Coughlin. Murray McDavid makes three to four releases a year, averaging 25 expressions per time. The range is highly selective and all casks are chosen by Jim McEwan who has more than 40 years experience in the whisky industry. Unlike most independent bottlers, the bottlings are vattings of four or five casks (same age) at 46% without chill filtration or tinting. The range can be divided into three categories: – the *Murray McDavid* range, the *Mission* range (unusual aged stock) and, finally, the *Celtic Heartlands* range – exceptionally old or unique casks from the sixties and seventies.

Master of Malt ....www.masterofmalt.com
Master of Malt is one of the biggest whisky retailers in the UK and in 2012 they were awarded Online Retailer of the Year at the World Whiskies Awards. The company also has ranges of its own bottled single malts. One

range is called *Secret Bottlings* and are bottled at 40%. No distillery names appear on the label. Instead, the region is highlighted (50 year old Speyside, 12 year old Lowland etc.). The bottlings are very competitively priced, not least the older ones. Master of Malt also bottles single casks from various distilleries. Some of the latest are a *34 year old Glenturret*, a *21 year old Glen Garioch* and *17 year old Aberlour*. In 2011, Master of Malt invited 10 whisky bloggers to create their own whisky blends. The winning contribution was released in autumn 2011 under the name *St Isidore*. The people behind Master of Malt have also come up with the brilliant idea to sell single malts (and other spirits) in 30 ml bottles. They call it *Drinks by the Dram* and it gives the customer an opportunity to sample a whisky before they buy it. At the moment there are around 500 different drams to choose from, some of them extremely rare whiskies from closed distilleries such as *Brora* and *Linlithgow*.

St Isidore, 41.4%

Nose: Dusty and fruity, with shaved wood, tropical fruits, grape and campfire smoke.
Palate: Rich and creamy, smoky, with vanilla ice cream, sweet, rounded and balanced – some burnt sugar and molasses in the mix. Rum and raisin. Honey.
Finish: Smoke, sweetness and fruit. Big, rounded and warming.

50 year old Speyside 2nd edition, 40%

Nose: Venerable, marmalade fruit, lots of oak, hint of smoke.
Palate: Vanilla, milk chocolate, smoke, oak and caramel. Gloopy, mouth coating and rounded.
Finish: Long, sweet, honey, and intensely fruity with a whisper of smoke.

Compass Box Whisky Co ....www.compassboxwhisky.com

Most people within the whisky industry acknowledge the fact that the cask has the greatest influence on the flavour of whisky, but none more so than the founder and owner of Compass Box, John Glaser. His philosophy is strongly influenced by meticulous selection of oak for the casks, clearly inspired by his time in the wine business. But he also has a lust for experimenting and innovation to test the limits, which was clearly shown when *Spice Tree* was launched in 2005. For an additional maturation, Glaser filled malt whisky in casks prepared with extra staves of toasted French oak suspended within the cask.

The company divides its ranges into a *Signature Range* and a *Limited Range*. *Spice Tree* (a blended malt), *The Peat Monster* (a combination of peated islay whiskies and Highland malts), *Oak Cross* (American oak casks fitted with heads of French oak), *Asyla* (a blended whisky matured in first-fill ex-bourbon American oak) and *Hedonism* (a vatted grain whisky) are included in the former. The Limited range consists of *Hedonism Maximus*, *Peat Monster Reserve* and *Flaming Heart* (a vatting of Highland malts aged in new French oak and heavily peated Islay malts). A new Flaming Heart was released in August 2012 and this time it included whisky matured in sherry casks. Two special versions were released in 2011 to celebrate the 10th anniversary of the company; *Double Single* and *Hedonism*. A third range was added in summer of 2011 when *Great King Street* was launched. The range will offer blended Scotch with a 50% proportion of malt whisky and using new French oak for complexity. The first expression was called *Artist's Blend* and the next bottling (a peated version) is expected in May 2013. Meanwhile,

the first release of a series of limited regional versions of Great King Street was launched in New York end of October 2012. The whisky was called *New York Blend* and had a malt proportion as high as 80%.

Flaming Heart, 48.3% (new edition)

Nose: More seaweed, grungier, and peatier than I remember.
Palate: Big, punky, powerful. A huge hit of spice and peat. Less of the rich, blackcurrant and berry of the past and more in your face smoke and coke. It is, to coin a phrase, a big, peaty monster.
Finish: Long, peaty and full.

Oak Cross, 46% (new edition)

Nose: This new version is very spicy and spiritey with a punchy nose, apple pip and a trace of menthol and blackcurrant.
Palate: Pricklier and more peppery than of old, almost Talisker-like with a big peaty heart. After time cracked lemon pepper comes through, some softer notes. But it never dumbs down. Big and impressive.
Finish: Peaty, peppery, spicy and long.

Adelphi Distillery ....www.adelphidistillery.com

The Adelphi Distillery is named after a distillery which closed in 1902. The company is owned by Keith Falconer and Donald Houston, who recruited Alex Bruce from the wine trade to act as Marketing Director. Their whiskies are always bottled at cask strength, uncoloured and non chill-filtered. Adelphi bottles around 50 casks a year. Unusual for an independent, Adelphi has an on-line shop on their website. The company affords its customers the opportunity to join the Adelphi's Dancey Man Whisky Club which has special offerings for its members, discounts and first choice of the latest releases. A new warehouse was recently constructed on the company's family farm in Fife, including a bonded area and a bottling line. In April 2012, Adelphi Distillery received planning permission to build their own distillery in Ardnamurchan, a couple of miles from the company's office. It will become the most westerly distillery in mainland Scotland and the goal is to produce 100,000 litres per year. Production will start during 2013.

Fascadale, 46%

Nose: Buttery with hints of lemon, some white pepper, marzipan, bakery dough.
Palate: Sharp mouth feel, with pepper and citrus notes, and a gloomy oilyness. Pepper, apple pip and some sweetness.
Finish: Soft and cushion like – seems to pull its punches. Medium in length.

Liddesdale, 46%

Nose: Pruney, autumn leaves, plums, berry compote.
Palate: Rich, fruity, oaky, spicy and with a peaty undercarriage. This is a big sherried whisky with lots of berry fruit notes.
Finish: Berries, peach and apricot. Big and fruity.

Douglas Laing & Co .... www.douglaslaing.com

Established in 1948 by Douglas Laing, it is currently run by his two sons, Fred and Stewart. One of their most talked about ranges is *The Old Malt Cask* which contains rare and old bottlings. More than 100 different expressions can be found regularly in this range where bottlings are diluted to 50%. Some malts are released in an even more exclusive range – *The Old and Rare Selection* (sometimes also referred to as *Platinum Selection*), offered at cask strength. A third range is called *McGibbon's Provenance*, often aged around 10-12 years and almost always diluted to 46%. The *Premier Barrel* range, was initially designed for the gift market and consists of single malts bottled in ceramic decanters.

What started as a one-off with a blend of Macallan and Laphroaig single malts, has now turned into a small range of its own called *Double Barrel*, where only two malts are vatted together and bottled at 46%. In 2009, the company launched *Big Peat*, a vatting of selected Islay malts (among them Ardbeg, Caol Ila, Bowmore and Port Ellen) and also bottled at 46%. A new range, *Director's Cut*, was introduced in November 2011 and includes some spectacular cask strength bottlings of both single malt and single grain whiskies. Some of the most recent are *Caperdonich 30 years*, *Glenlivet 35 years* and, not least, a *50 year old North British single grain*. Douglas Laing & Co also has a range of blended whiskies in which *John Player Special*, *The King of Scots* and *The McGibbon Golf Range* are the biggest sellers.

Clan Denny, 46%

Nose: Big, strong, rich peat and seaweed.
Palate: With a mix of most of Islay's peated offering including Port Ellen, this is intense, smoky, peaty and fruity. Everything has the volume turned up. An Islay greatest hits.
Finish: Unsurprisingly, long and peated.

Double Barrel Ledaig/Bowmore, 46%

Nose: Typically Islay, with peat, swirling smoke, some lemon and traces of seashore.
Palate: Oily damp boathouse, with tarred rope, shellfish, peat, damp wood and grilled fish.
Finish: Medium and peaty.

Dewar Rattray .... www.adrattray.com

This company was founded by Andrew Dewar and William Rattray in 1868. In 2004 the company was revived by Tim Morrison, previously of Morrison Bowmore Distillers and fourth generation descendent of Andrew Dewar, with a view to bottling single cask malts from different regions in Scotland. All whiskies are bottled at cask strength, without colouring or chill filtration. To give customers a choice, a new range of single malts bottled at 46% was recently introduced. A *12 year old* single malt named *Stronachie* is also found in their portfolio. It is named after a distillery that closed in the 1930s. Tim Morrison bought one of the few remaining bottles of Stronachie and found a Highland distillery that could reproduce its character. The distillery in question was shrouded in secrecy until 2010, when it was revealed as Benrinnes in Speyside. Each Stronachie bottling is a batch of 6-10 casks from Benrinnes. The *12 year old* Stronachie was joined in 2010 by another expression – an *18 year old*. In 2011, Dewar Rattray introduced a new range of blended malts. The first was a limited release named *Rattray's Selection Batch 01*, containing whisky from four single sherry butts from Auchentoshan (1991), Balblair (1990), Benrinnes (1989) and Bowmore (1981). The second release, *Cask Islay*, came in October 2011.

It is a blended malt (actually 99.9% single malt), bottled at 46% and the thought is to compete with the likes of Smokehead and Big Peat.

In September 2011, the company opened A D Rattray's Whisky Experience & Shop in Kirkoswald, South Ayrshire. Apart from having a large choice of whiskies for sale, there is a sample room and a cask room. The plan is to have a new spirit collection from every distillery in Scotland and samples from as many different types of casks and ages from as many distilleries as possible. A new expression has also been launched exclusively available at the shop - an *8 year old Glentauchers* from a first fill sherry cask.

Cask Islay, 46%

Nose: Wispy smoke, a splash of seaspray, damp hessian cloth, winter damp leather.
Palate: Classic Islay. A big-hearted sweet and peat combo, with a trace of mint battling to get out, and some peppery toes.
Finish: Long and peaty, oily and seaweedy.

AD Rattray Whisky Experience & Whisky Shop – Malt 1

Nose: Tangerine, with orange syrup and soft toffee. Rounded, sweet and inviting.
Palate: Java coffee, dark chocolate. orange zest, liqueur-like with hints of dusty spice.
Finish: Long and with cherry liqueur, orange and spice. Very pleasant indeed.

Glenkeir Treasures .... www.whiskyshop.com

The Whisky Shop is the biggest whisky retail chain in the UK with 20 shops. The company was founded in 1992 and was bought by the current owner, Ian Bankier, in 2004. Apart from having an extensive range of malt (and other) whiskies, they also select and bottle their own range of single malts called *Glenkeir Treasures*. Once a cask has been chosen it is re-racked into smaller oak casks which are then put out for display in each store. The whisky is bottled to order and the customer can also try the whisky in the shop before buying. Glenkeir Treasures come in three bottle sizes – 10, 20 and 50 cl and is bottled at 40%. The current range consists of *Aberlour 12, Ben Nevis 15, Deanston 12, Isle of Jura 21, Ledaig 9, Linkwood 12* and *Macallan 18 year old*. *Dalmore Zenith*, one of the rarest whiskies in the world (one bottle actually!), was offered through an auction by Whisky Shop in 2012. The oldest whisky in the bottle was from 1926.

Creative Whisky Company .....www.creativewhisky.co.uk

David Stirk, who has worked in the whisky industry for the last 15 years, started the Creative Whisky Co in 2005. He is also author of The Distilleries of Campbeltown and of features in several editions of Malt Whisky Yearbook. Creative Whisky exclusively bottles single casks, divided into three series: The *Exclusive Malts* are bottled at cask strength and vary in age between 8 and 40 years. Around 20 bottlings are made annually. *Exclusive Range* are somewhat younger whiskies, between 8 and 16 years bottled at either 45% or 45.8%. Finally, *Exclusive Casks* are single casks, which have been 'finished' for three months in another cask, e. g. Madeira, Sherry, Port or different kinds of virgin oak. The Creative Whisky Company recently introduced a new beer brand, *Hanley & Stirk*, which is pale ale that has been aged for twelve weeks in a PX sherry cask previously used for Bowmore single malt.

Speciality Drinks.........................www.specialitydrinks.com

Sukhinder Singh, known by most for his two very well-stocked shops in London, The Whisky Exchange, is behind this company. Since 2005 he is also a bottler of malt whiskies operating under the brand name *The Single Malts of Scotland*. He has around 50 bottlings on offer at any time, either as single casks or as batches bottled at cask strength or at 46%. In 2009 a new range of Islay malts under the name *Port Askaig* was introduced, starting with a *cask strength*, a *17 year old* and a *25 year old*. In summer 2011 the 17 year old was replaced by a *19 year old*.

Elements of Islay, a series in which all Islay distilleries are, or will be, represented was introduced around the same time. The list of the product range is cleverly constructed with periodical tables in mind (see www.elements-of-islay.com) in which each distillery has a two-letter acronym followed by a batch number, for example Pe_4 (Port Ellen) and Lg_3 (Lagavulin).

> **Glen Keith 1989 22 Year Old, 50.7%**
> *Nose*: Soft with mandarin, summer fruits cordial, spinet like with liquorice.
> *Palate*: A large dose of fresh and dried pineapple, soft fruits, baked apple and later, liquorice rancho and astringency from the oak. But overall delightful and balanced.
> *Finish*: Big, rich, full and very fruity with a bright, rounded taste.
>
> **Bowmore 1985 26 year old, 54.9%**
> *Nose*: Winey, vines but good to nose. Some waspish, scatty smoke.
> *Palate*: Welcome home, old friend. This is a cask strength and grown up version of the 17 year old from a decade ago. A huge mix of peat and palma violet sweets. It's a classic golden oldie flavour and if you know it and love it, it's here with the volume set to 11.
> *Finish*: Sweet, peat, with smoke in the water.

Scotch Malt Whisky Society ....www.smws.com

The Scotch Malt Whisky Society, established in the mid 1980s and owned by Glenmorangie Co since 2003, has more than 20,000 members worldwide and apart from UK, there are 15 chapters around the world. The idea from the very beginning was to buy casks of single malts from the producers and bottle them at cask strength without colouring or chill filtration. The labels do not reveal the name of the distillery. Instead there is a number but also a short description which will give you a clue to which distillery it is. A Tasting Panel selects and bottles around twenty new casks the first Friday of every month. The SMWS also arranges tastings at their different venues but also at other locations. The society produces an excellent, award winning members magazine called Unfiltered.

The Whisky Agency ....www.whiskyagency.de

The man behind this company is Carsten Ehrlich, to many whisky aficionados known as one of the founders of the annual Whisky Fair in Limburg, Germany. His experience from sourcing casks for limited Whisky Fair bottlings led him to start as an independent bottler in 2008 under the name The Whisky Agency. He is currently working with three ranges; *The Whisky Agency* with five series of whiskies released so far – *Butterflies, Sharks, Fossils, Flowers* and *Liquid Sun* – the names alluding to the motif on the labels, *The Perfect Dram* (three series with four expressions each) and *Specials* with some unusual bottlings, for example a Tomatin 1967 sherry butt.

Wemyss Malts ....www.wemyssmalts.com

This family-owned company, a relatively newcomer to the whisky world, was founded in 2005. The family owns another three companies in the field of wine and gin. Based in Edinburgh, Wemyss Malts takes advantage of Charles MacLean's experienced nose when choosing their casks. There are two ranges; one of which consists of single casks bottled at 46% or 55%. The distillery name is not used on the label, instead, the names are chosen to reflect what the whisky tastes like, for instance, *A Matter of Smoke, A Day At The Coast* and *Strawberry Ganache*. All whiskies are un chill-filtered and without colouring. The other range is made up of blended malts of which there are three at the moment – *Spice King, Peat Chimney* and the recently introduced *The Hive*. When first launched in 2005 they were bottled at the age of 5. Four years later the range was expanded with 8 year olds and in 2010 with 12 year olds. All the blended malts are bottled at 40%. In October 2012, the company released their first premium blended whisky based on a selection of malt and grain whiskies aged a minimum of 15 years. The whisky is named *Lord Elcho* after the eldest son of the 5th Earl of Wemyss.

> **The Hive 12 year old, 40%**
> *Nose*: Acaccia honey, over-ripe peach and apricot.
> *Palate*: A mix of fruits and flowers, with apricot, soft plum and then the honey comes through. Does what it says on the tin. But there's a sting in the tail too.
> *Finish*: Sugar and spice, with the liquid honey matched by pepper.
>
> **Peat Chimney 12 year old, 40%**
> *Nose*: Dusty fire hearth, delicate and sooty, and with traces of gooseberry and lychee.
> *Palate*: Leans more to blend than malt and is perhaps over polite on the peat. Some biting sharp notes, green fruit and smoke.
> *Finish*: Short, with the peat battling it out to the very end.

Malts of Scotland ....www.malts-of-scotland.com

This is one of the more recently established independent bottlers. Thomas Ewers from Germany, bought casks from Scottish distilleries and decided in the spring of 2009 to start releasing them as single casks bottled at cask strength and with no colouring or chill filtration. At the moment he has released circa 70 bottlings from a 5 year old Bunnahabhain to a 38 year old Glengoyne. He also has two expressions called *Glen First Class* (a Glenfarclas) and *Glen Peat Class* (a vatting of Ardbeg, Laphroaig and Bowmore), both bottled at 50%. Another new series is *Amazing Casks*, dedicated to very special and superior casks. According to Ewers, there are several hundreds of casks from more than 60 distilleries maturing in the warehouse.

Scott´s Selection ....www.speysidedistillers.co.uk

Speyside Distillers in Glasgow are the owners of Speyside distillery but also has a wide range of whisky brands in their domains. One of them is *Scott's Selection*, a range of single cask malt whiskies, previously selected by the Master Blender Robert Scott, who is now retired. Emphasis is placed on whisky distilled in the 70's and 80's and some unusual distilleries such as North Port, Linlithgow and Convalmore are represented. Perhaps the most interesting bottling is a single grain, *North of Scotland 1973*.

This was the grain distillery that the founder of Speyside distillery, George Christie, had built in 1958 and has since closed down in 1980. More single grains were released in 2011; Girvan 1964, Invergordon 1964 and the very rare Port Dundas 1965. All the whisky in the Scott's Selection range are bottled without colouring or chill-filtration and at cask strength. There is an additional range of single malts in the company, *Private Cellar*, but these are all diluted to 43%. In addition to single malt Speyside Distillers produces a range of blended whiskies, such as *Glen Ross* and *Scotchguard*.

Mackillop´s Choice .... www.mackillopschoice.com
Mackillop's Choice, founded in 1996, is an independent bottler owned by Angus Dundee Distillers (owner of Tomintoul and Glencadam distilleries). The brand is named after Lorne McKillop who selects the casks. The whole range is single casks with no colouring or chill filtration. Some of the bottlings are at cask strength, while others are diluted to 40 or 43%. Among the latest new bottlings (released in summer 2011) are Bowmore 1989, Mortlach 1987, Tomintoul 1981, Tomatin 1965 and Linlithgow 1982.

The Vintage
Malt Whisky Company .... www.vintagemaltwhisky.com
The Vintage Malt Whisky Co. was founded in 1992 by Brian Crook who previously had twenty years experience in the malt whisky industry. In recent years, Brian has been joined in the company by his son Andrew. The company also owns and operates a sister company called The Highlands & Islands Scotch Whisky Co. The most famous brands in the range are undoubtedly two single Islay malts called *Finlaggan* and *The Ileach*. Other expressions include the blended Highland malt *Glenalmond* and, not least, a wide range of single cask single malts under the name *The Cooper's Choice*. They are bottled at 46% or at cask strength and are all non coloured and non chillfiltered. In 2012, the company launched a range extension called *Cooper's Choice Golden Grains* with a selection of old single grain whiskies from closed distilleries, for example Lochside and Garnheath. The company´s whiskies are today sold in more than 25 countries.

The Ileach, 40%
Nose: Islay with the volume turned up to 11 – peat, fish, oily rope, damp boathouse, sea salt.
Palate: Complex but surprisingly rounded – full, rich, peaty, chili pepper, some drying astringency and green fruit.
Finish: Medium, salt and pepper, sweet with peat.

Finlaggan, 40%
Nose: Rugged, earthy, smoky with an oily grilled fish note.
Palate: A youthful strapping monster of a malt, with sharp, fresh and pungent pettiness and a mouth-coating rich oiliness.
Finish: Long and peaty with wood fire and charcoal.

Sirius .... www.siriuswhiskypurveyors.com
This newly established independent bottler is a boutique brand and not one where we can expect a wide range of releases every year. It is the brainchild of Mahesh Patel, a passionate whisky collector and connoisseur, as well as the founder and CEO of The Nth Ultimate Whisky Experience in Las Vegas. Over the years, Mahesh has established valuable contacts with whisky producers in Scotland enabling him to select and buy rare casks.

Mahesh Patel with his first release of Sirius

Visitors to the Las Vegas show in March 2012, were able to have a sneak preview of the first bottlings which later, in summer 2012, were released to the world through The Whisky Shop chain in the UK. The first range consists of *Dalmore 1967, Fettercairn 1966* and two single grains - *Carsebridge 1965* and *North British 1962*. Mahesh intends to release 5 to 6 new bottlings per year and, in the future, the range will probably be extended to also include rare Japanese whiskies and bourbons.

Meadowside Blending ..... www.meadowsideblending.com
The company may be a newcomer to the family of independent bottlers but the founder certainly isn´t. Donald Hart, a Keeper of the Quaich and co-founder of the well-known bottler Hart Brothers, runs the Glasgow company together with his son. There are two sides to the business – blends sold under the name *The Royal Thistle* where the core expression is a 3 year old, as well as single malts labelled *The Maltman*. Some of the latest single malts include *Ben Nevis 45 year old, Caol Ila 30 year old* and *Mortlach 22 year old*.

Edition Spirits .... www.editionspirits.com
Until now the name Laing has in whisky circles referred to Fred and Stewart Laing, the two brothers in charge of the venerable firm, Douglas Laing & Co. As of 2011 it can just as easily refer to Andrew Laing, Stewart´s son, who has started his own business as an independent bottler. Andrew is concentrating on single casks, preferably quite old and from less known distilleries. Some of his first bottlings under the name *The First Editions*, include *Littlemill 21 years, Tomintoul 44 years, Teaninich 28 years* and *Bladnoch 21 years*. Andrew is already selling his products in Singapore, USA, Canada and Scandinavia.

Jewish Whisky Company .... www.singlecasknation.com
Joshua Hatton and Jason Johnstone-Yellin, two well-known whisky bloggers have, in alliance with Seth Klaskin, taken their first step into the world of whisky bottling. The idea with *Single Cask Nation* somewhat reminds you of Scotch Malt Whisky Society in the sense that you have to become a member of the nation in order to buy the bottlings. You can choose between three different cost levels which will give you various benefits, including one or more bottlings from the current range of whiskies. The first four bottlings that were released in 2012 were *Arran 12 years* from a Pinot Noir cask, a peated *BenRiach 17 years* from a bourbon cask, a *Glen Moray 12 years* bourbon cask and, finally, a *4 year old Kilchoman* also bourbon matured. The range will not be limited to Scotch single malts but will also include for example rye and bourbon in the future.

Whisky Shops

AUSTRIA

Potstill
Strozzigasse 37
1080 Wien
Phone: +43 (0)664 118 85 41
www.potstill.org
Austria's premier whisky shop with over 1100 kinds of which c 900 are malts, including some real rarities. Arranges tastings and seminars and ships to several European countries. On-line ordering.

BELGIUM

Whiskycorner
Kraaistraat 16
3530 Houthalen
Phone: +32 (0)89 386233
www.whiskycorner.be
A very large selection of single malts, no less than 1100 different! Also other whiskies, calvados and grappas. The site is in both French and English. Mail ordering, but not on-line. Shipping worldwide.

Jurgen's Whiskyhuis
Gaverland 70
9620 Zottegem
Phone: +32 (0)9 336 51 06
www.whiskyhuis.be
An absolutely huge assortment of more than 2,000 different single malts with 700 in stock and the rest delivered within the week. Also 40 different grain whiskies and 120 bourbons. Online mail order with shipments worldwide.

Huis Crombé
Engelse Wandeling 11
8500 Kortrijk
Phone: +32 (0)56 21 19 87
www.crombewines.com
A wine retailer with a heritage dating back to 1894 and now covers all kinds of spirits. The whisky range is very nice where a large assortment of Scotch is supplemented with whiskies from Japan, the USA and Ireland to mention a few. Regular tastings in the shop.

CANADA

Kensington Wine Market
1257 Kensington Road NW
Calgary
Alberta T2N 3P8
Phone: +1 403 283 8000
www.kensingtonwinemarket.com
With 400 different bottlings this is the largest single malt assortment in Canada. Also 2,500 different wines. Regular tastings in the shop.

DENMARK

Juul's Vin & Spiritus
Værnedamsvej 15
1819 Frederiksberg
Phone: +45 33 31 13 29
www.juuls.dk
A very large range of wines, fortified wines and spirits. Around 500 single malts. Also a good selection of drinking glasses. On-line ordering. Shipping outside Denmark (except for Scandinavian countries).

Cadenhead's WhiskyShop Denmark
Kongensgade 69 F
5000 Odense C
Phone: +45 66 13 95 05

Silkegade 7, kld
1113 København K
Phone: +45 33 39 95 05
www.cadenheads.dk
Whisky specialist with a very good range, not least from Cadenhead's. Nice range of champagne, cognac and rum. Arranges whisky and beer tastings. On-line ordering with worldwide shipping.

Whiskydirect.dk
Braunstein
Carlsensvej 5
4600 Køge
Phone: +45 7020 4468
www.whiskydirect.dk
On-line retailer owned by Braunstein Distillery. Aside from own produce one can find an assortment of 200 different whiskies, including own single cask bottlings.

Kokkens Vinhus
Hovedvejen 102
2600 Glostrup
Phone: +45 44 97 02 30
www.kokkensvinhus.dk
A shop with a complete assortment of wine, spirit, coffee, tea and delicatessen. More than 500 whiskies are in stock, mostly single malts. They are specialists in independent bottlings. On-line ordering for shipments within Denmark.

ENGLAND

The Whisky Exchange (2 shops)
Unit 7, Space Business Park
Abbey Road, Park Royal
London NW10 7SU
Phone: +44 (0)208 838 9388

The Whisky Exchange
Vinopolis, 1 Bank End
London SE1 9BU
Phone: +44 (0)207 403 8688
www.thewhiskyexchange.com
This is an excellent whisky shop

established in 1999 and owned by Sukhinder Singh. Started off as a mail order business which was run from a showroom in Hanwell, but since some years back there is also an excellent shop at Vinopolis in downtown London. The assortment is huge with well over 1000 single malts to choose from. Some rarities which can hardly be found anywhere else are offered much thanks to Singh's great interest for antique whisky. There are also other types of whisky and cognac, calvados, rum etc. On-line ordering and ships all over the world.

The Whisky Shop
(See also Scotland, The Whisky Shop)
Unit 1.09 MetroCentre
Gateshead NE11 9YG
Phone: +44 (0)191 460 3777

11 Coppergate Walk
York YO1 9NT
Phone: +44 (0)1904 640300

510 Brompton Walk
Lakeside Shopping Centre
Grays, Essex RM20 2ZL
Phone: +44 (0)1708 866255

7 Turl Street
Oxford OX1 3DQ
Phone: +44 (0)1865 202279

3 Swan Lane
Norwich NR2 1HZ
Phone: +44 (0)1603 618284

Unit 7 Queens Head Passage
Paternoster
London EC4M 7DY
Phone: +44 (0)207 329 5117

25 Chapel Street
Guildford GU1 3UL
Phone: +44 (0)1483 450900

Unit 35 Great Western Arcade
Birmingham B2 5HU
Phone: +44 (0)121 212 1815

64 East Street
Brighton BN1 1HQ
Phone: +44 (0)1273 327 962

3 Cheapside
Nottingham NG1 2HU
Phone: +44 (0)115 958 7080

Trentham Shopping Village
Trentham, Stoke on Trent
Staffordshire ST4 8JG
Phone: +44 (0)178 264 4483
www.whiskyshop.com
The first shop opened in 1992 in Edinburgh and this is now the United Kingdom's largest specialist retailer of whiskies with 20 outlets. A large product range with over 700 kinds, including 400 malt whiskies and 140 miniature bottles, as well as accessories and books. The own range 'Glenkeir Treasures' is a

special assortment of selected malt whiskies. On-line ordering and shipping all over the world except to the USA.

Royal Mile Whiskies
3 Bloomsbury Street
London WC1B 3QE
Phone: +44 (0)20 7436 4763
www.royalmilewhiskies.com
The London branch of Royal Mile Whiskies. See also Scotland, Royal Mile Whiskies.

Berry Bros. & Rudd
3 St James´ Street
London SW1A 1EG
Phone: +44 (0)870 900 4300

Berry Bros. & Rudd's Bin End Shop
Hamilton Close, Houndmills
Basingstoke RG21 6YB
Phone: +44 (0)800 280 2440
www.bbr.com/whisky
A legendary shop that has been situated in the same place since 1698. One of the world's most reputable wine shops but with an exclusive selection of malt whiskies. There are also shops in Dublin and Hong Kong specialising primarily in fine wines.

The Wright Wine and Whisky Company
The Old Smithy, Raikes Road, Skipton, North Yorkshire BD23 1NP
Phone: +44 (0)1756 700886
www.wineandwhisky.co.uk
An eclectic selection of near to 1000 different whiskies to choose from. 'Tasting Cupboard' of nearly 100 opened bottles for sampling with hosted tasting evenings held on a regular basis. Great 'Collector to Collector' selection of old and rare whiskies plus a fantastic choice of 1200+ wines, premium spirits and liqueurs. International mail order.

Master of Malt
8a London Road
Tunbridge Wells
Kent TN1 1DA
Phone: +44 (0)800 5200 474
www.masterofmalt.com
Independent bottler and online retailer since 1985. A very impressive range of more than 1,000 Scotch whiskies of which 800 are single malts. In addition to whisky from other continents there is a wide selection of rum, cognac, Armagnac and tequila. The website is redesigned and contains a wealth of information on the distilleries. They have also recently launched "Drinks by the Dram" where you can order 3cl samples of more than 500 different whiskies to try before you buy a full bottle.

Whiskys.co.uk
The Square, Stamford Bridge
York YO4 11AG
Phone: +44 (0)1759 371356
www.whiskys.co.uk
Good assortment with more than 600 different whiskies. Also a nice range of armagnac, rum, calvados etc. On-line ordering, ships outside of the UK.
The owners also have another website, www.whiskymerchants.co.uk with a huge amount of information on just about every whisky distillery in the world and very up to date.

The Wee Dram
5 Portland Square, Bakewell
Derbyshire DE45 1HA
Phone: +44 (0)1629 812235
www.weedram.co.uk
Large range of Scotch single malts (c 450) with whiskies from other parts of the world and a good range of whisky books. Run 'The Wee Drammers Whisky Club' with tastings and seminars. On-line ordering.

Mainly Wine and Whisky
3-4 The Courtyard, Bawtry
Doncaster DN10 6JG
Phone: +44 (0)1302 714 700
www.whisky-malts-shop.com
A good range with c 400 different whiskies of which 300 are single malts. Arranges tastings and seminars. On-line ordering with shipping also outside the UK. Was known as Mainly Malts before they joined with a local wine shop.

Chester Whisky & Liqueur
59 Bridge Street Row
Chester
Cheshire CH1 1NW
Phone: +44 (0)1244 347806
www.chesterwhisky.com
A shop that specialises in single malt Scotch and American, Irish, Japanese and Welsh whisky.There is also a good range of calvados, armagnac and rum and the shop has its own house blend, Chester Cross Blended Scotch Whisky, as well as three casks for tasting and bottling in the store.

Nickolls & Perks
37 Lower High Street, Stourbridge
West Midlands DY8 1TA
Phone: +44 (0)1384 394518
www.nickollsandperks.co.uk
Mostly known as wine merchants but also has a good range of whiskies with c 300 different kinds including 200 single malts. On-line ordering with shipping also outside of UK. Since 2011, Nickolls & Perks also organize the acclaimed Midlands Whisky Festival, see www.whiskyfest.co.uk

Gauntleys of Nottingham
4 High Street
Nottingham NG1 2ET
Phone: +44 (0)115 9110555
www.gauntley-wine.co.uk
A fine wine merchant established in 1880. The range of wines are among the best in the UK. All kinds of spirits, not least whisky, are taking up more and more space and several rare malts can be found. The monthly whisky newsletter by Chris Goodrum makes good reading and there is also a mail order service available.

The Wine Shop
22 Russell Street, Leek
Staffordshire ST13 5JF
Phone: +44 (0)1538 382408
www.wineandwhisky.com
In addition to wine there is a good range of c 300 whiskies and also calvados, cognacs, rums etc. They also stock a range of their own single malt bott-lings under the name of 'The Queen of the Moorlands'. Mailorders by telephone or email for UK delivery.

The Lincoln Whisky Shop
87 Bailgate
Lincoln LN1 3AR
Phone: +44 (0)1522 537834
www.lincolnwhiskyshop.co.uk
Mainly specialising in whisky with more than 400 different whiskies but also 500 spirits and liqueurs and some 100 wines. Mailorder only within UK.

Milroys of Soho
3 Greek Street
London W1D 4NX
Phone: +44 (0)20 7437 2385
www.milroys.co.uk
A classic whisky shop in Soho now owned by the retail wine merchant Jeroboams Group. A very good range with over 700 malts and a wide selection of whiskies from around the world. On-line ordering for shipping within the UK.

Arkwrights
114 The Dormers
Highworth
Wiltshire SN6 7PE
Phone: +44 (0)1793 765071
www.whiskyandwines.com
A good range of whiskies (over 700 in stock) as well as wine and other spirits. Regular tastings in the shop. On-line ordering with shipping all over the world except USA and Canada.

Cadenhead´s Whisky Shop
26 Chiltern Street
London W1U 7QF
Phone: +44 (0)20 7935 6999
www.whiskytastingroom.com
Used to be in Covent Garden but moved and was expanded with a tasting room. One in a chain of shops owned by independent bottlers Cadenhead. Sells Cadenhead's product range and c. 200 other whiskies. Regular tastings and on-line ordering.

Constantine Stores
30 Fore Street
Constantine, Falmouth
Cornwall TR11 5AB
Phone: +44 (0)1326 340226
www.drinkfinder.co.uk
A full-range wine and spirits dealer with a good selection of whiskies from the whole world (around 800 different, of which 600 are single malts).Worldwide shipping except for USA and Canada.

The Vintage House
42 Old Compton Street
London W1D 4LR
Phone: +44 (0)20 7437 5112
www.sohowhisky.com
A huge range of 1400 kinds of malt whisky, many of them rare or unusual. Supplementing this is also a selection of fine wines. On-line ordering with shipping only within the UK.

Whisky On-line
Units 1-3 Concorde House, Charnley Road, Blackpool, Lancashire FY1 4PE
Phone: +44 (0)1253 620376
www.whisky-online.com
A good selection of whisky and also cognac, rum, port etc. On-line ordering with shipping all over the world.

FRANCE

La Maison du Whisky
20 rue d´Anjou
75008 Paris
Phone: +33 (0)1 42 65 03 16

6 carrefour d l´Odéon
75006 Paris
Phone: +33 (0)1 46 34 70 20

(2 shops outside France)

47 rue Jean Chatel
97400 Saint-Denis, La Réunion
Phone: +33 (0)2 62 21 31 19

The Pier at Robertson Quay
80 Mohamed Sultan Road, #01-10
Singapore 239013
Phone: +65 6733 0059
www.whisky.fr
France's largest whisky specialist with over 1200 whiskies in stock. Also a number of own-bottled single malts. La Maison du Whisky acts as a EU distributor for many whisky producers around the world. Four shops and on-line ordering. Ships to some 20 countries.

GERMANY

Celtic Whisk(e)y & Versand
Otto Steudel
Bulmannstrasse 26
90459 Nürnberg
Phone: +49 (0)911 45097430
www.whiskymania.de/celtic
A very impressive single malt range with well over 1000 different single malts and a good selection from other parts of the world. On-line ordering with shipping also outside Germany.

SCOMA - Scotch Malt Whisky GmbH
Am Bullhamm 17
26441 Jever
Phone: +49 (0)4461 912237
www.scoma.de
Very large range of c 750 Scottish malts and many from other countries. Holds regular seminars and tastings. The excellent, monthly whisky newsletter SCOMA News is produced and can be downloaded as a pdf-file from the website. On-line ordering.

The Whisky Store
Am Grundwassersee 4
82402 Seeshaupt
Phone: +49 (0)8801-23 17
www.whisky.de
A very large range comprising c 700 kinds of whisky of which 550 are malts. Also sells whisky liqueurs, books and accessories. The website is a veritable goldmine of information about the whisky business and especially so when it comes to photographs of distilleries. There are 7500 photos of 168 distilleries. On-line ordering.

Cadenhead´s Whisky Market
Luxemburger Strasse 257
50939 Köln
Phone: +49 (0)221-2831834
www.cadenheads.de
This first Cadenhead shop outside of the UK was established in 2001. Good range of malt whiskies (c 350 different kinds) with emphasis on Cadenhead's own bottlings. Other products include wine, cognac and rum etc. Arranges recurring tastings and also has an on-line shop.

Cadenhead´s Whisky Market
Mainzer Strasse 20
10247 Berlin-Friedrichshain
Phone: +49 (0)30-30831444
www.cadenhead-berlin.de
Good product range with c 350 different kinds of malt with emphasis on Cadenhead's own bottlings as well as wine, cognac and rum etc. Arranges recurrent tastings.

Malts and More
Hosegstieg 11
22880 Wedel
Phone: +49 (0)40-23620770
www.maltsandmore.de
Very large assortment with over 800 different single malts from Scotland as well as whiskies from many other countries. Also a nice selection of cognac, rum etc. Orders can be placed on-line or through Email and telephone.

Reifferscheid
Mainzer Strasse 186
53179 Bonn / Mehlem
Phone: +49 (0)228 9 53 80 70
www.whisky-bonn.de
A well-stocked shop which has been listed as one of the best in Germany several times. Aside from a large range of whiskies (among them a good selection from Duncan Taylor), wine, spirit, cigars and a delicatessen can be found. Holds regular tastings.

Whiskywizard.de
Christian Jaudt
Schulstrasse 57
66540 Neunkirchen
Phone: +49 (0)6858-699507
www.whiskywizard.de
Large assortment of single malt (over 500) and other spirits. Only orders on-line, shipping also outside Germany.

Whisky-Doris
Germanenstrasse 38
14612 Falkensee
Phone: +49 (0)3322-219784
www.whisky-doris.de
Large range of over 300 whiskies and also sells own special bottlings. Orders via email. Shipping also outside Germany.

Finlays Whisky Shop
Friedrichstrasse 3
65779 Kelkheim
Phone: +49 (0)6195 9699510
www.finlayswhiskyshop.de
Whisky specialists with a large range of over 700 single malts. Finlays also work as the importer to Germany of Douglas laing, James MacArthur and Wilson & Morgan. There is an impressive listing of 700 bottlings of Port Ellen on the website (The Port Ellen Archive). Shop in Friedrichsdorf as well as on-line orders.

Weinquelle Lühmann
Lübeckerstrasse 145
22087 Hamburg
Phone: +49 (0)40-25 63 91
www.weinquelle.com
An impressive selection of both wines and spirits with over 1000 different whiskies of which 850 are malt whiskies. Also an impressive range of rums. On-line ordering with shipping also possible outside Germany.

The Whisky-Corner
Reichertsfeld 2
92278 Illschwang
Phone: +49 (0)9666-951213
www.whisky-corner.de
A small shop but large on mail order. A very large assortment of over 1600 whiskies. Also sells blended and American whiskies. The website is very informative with features on, among others, whisky-making, tasting and independent bottlers. On-line ordering.

World Wide Spirits
Hauptstrasse 12
84576 Teising
Phone: +49 (0)8633 50 87 93
www.worldwidespirits.de
A nice range of c 500 whiskies with some rarities from the twenties. Also large selection (c 1000) of other spirits.

Whisk(e)y Shop Tara
Rindermarkt 16
80331 München
Phone: +49 (0)89-26 51 18
www.whiskyversand.de
Whisky specialists with a very broad range of, for example, 800 different single malts. On-line ordering.

WhiskyKoch
Weinbergstrasse 2
64285 Darmstadt
Phone: +49 (0)6151 99 27 105
www.whiskykoch.de
Christopher Pepper and his wife Marion own this combination of a whisky shop and restaurant. The shop has a nice selection of single

malts as well as other Scottish products and the restaurant has specialised in whisky dinners and tastings.

Single Malt Collection
(Glen Fahrn Germany GmbH)
Hauptstraße 38
79801 Hohentengen a. H.
Phone: +49 (0)77 42 -857 222
www.singlemaltcollection.com
A very large range of single malts (c 600). Newsletter. On-line orders. Shipping also outside Germany.

Kierzek
Weitlingstrasse 17
10317 Berlin
Phone: +49 (0)30 525 11 08
www.kierzek-berlin.de
Over 400 different whiskies in stock. In the product range 50 kinds of rum and 450 wines from all over the world are found among other products. Mail order is available within Germany.

House of Whisky
Ackerbeeke 6
31683 Obernkirchen
Phone: +49 (0)5724-399420
www.houseofwhisky.de
Aside from over 1,200 different malts also sells a large range of other spirits (including over 100 kinds of rum). On-line ordering with shipping also outside Germany.

Whiskyworld
Ziegelfeld 6
94481 Grafenau / Haus i. Wald
Phone: +49 (0)8555-406 320
www.whiskyworld.de
A very good assortment of more than 1,000 malt whiskies. Also has a good range of wines, other spirits, cigars and books. Also on-line ordering.

World Wide Whisky (2 shops)
Eisenacher Strasse 64
10823 Berlin-Schöneberg
Phone: +49 (0)30-7845010

Hauptstrasse 58
10823 Berlin-Schöneberg
www.world-wide-whisky.de
Large range of 1,500 different whiskies. Arranges tastings and seminars. Has a large number of rarities. Orders via email.

HUNGARY
Whisky Net / Whisky Shop
Kovács Làszlò Street 21
2000 Szentendre

(shop)
Veres Pálné utca 8.
1053 Budapest
Phone: +36 1 267-1588
www.whiskynet.hu
www.whiskyshop.hu
A whisky trader established in 2007. In the shop in downtown Budapest one finds the largest selction of whisky in Hungary. Agents for Douglas Laing, Cadenhead, Bruichladdich and Glenfarclas among others. Also mailorder.

IRELAND
Celtic Whiskey Shop
27-28 Dawson Street
Dublin 2
Phone: +353 (0)1 675 9744
www.celticwhiskeyshop.com
More than 70 kinds of Irish whiskeys but also a good selection of Scotch, wines and other spirits. On-line ordering with shipping all over the world.

ITALY
Cadenhead's Whisky Bar
Via Poliziano, 3
20154 Milano
Phone: +39 (0)2 336 055 92
www.cadenhead.it
This is the tenth and newest addition in the Cadenhead's chain of shops. Concentrating mostly on the Cadenhead's range but they also stock whiskies from other producers.

THE NETHERLANDS
Whiskyslijterij De Koning
Hinthamereinde 41
5211 PM 's Hertogenbosch
Phone: +31 (0)73-6143547
www.whiskykoning.nl
An enormous assortment with more than 1400 kinds of whisky including c 800 single malts. Also whisky-related items like decanters, books etc. Arranges recurring tastings. The site is in Dutch and English. On-line ordering. Shipping all over the world.

Whisky- en Wijnhandel Verhaar
Planetenbaan 2a
3721 LA Bilthoven
Phone: +31 (0)30-228 44 18
www.whiskyshop.nl
A wide selection of wines and spirits with 1300 whiskies of which 1000 come from Scotland. Email orders.

Wijnhandel van Zuylen
Loosduinse Hoofdplein 201
2553 CP Loosduinen (Den Haag)
Phone: +31 (0)70-397 1400
www.whiskyvanzuylen.nl
Excellent range of whiskies (c 1100) and wines. Email orders with shipping to some ten European countries.

Wijnwinkel-Slijterij
Ton Overmars
Hoofddorpplein 11
1059 CV Amsterdam
Phone: +31 (0)20-615 71 42
www.tonovermars.nl
A very large assortment of wines, spirits and beer which includes more than 400 single malts. Arranges recurring tastings. Orders via email.

Van Wees - Whiskyworld.nl
Leusderweg 260
3817 KH Amersfoort
Phone: +31 (0)33-461 53 19
www.whiskyworld.nl
A very large range of 1000 whiskies

including over 500 single malts. On-line ordering.

Wijn & Whisky Schuur
Blankendalwei 4
8629 EH Scharnegoutem (bij Sneek)
Phone: +31 (0)515-520706
www.wijnwhiskyschuur.nl
Large assortment with 1000 different whiskies and a good range of other spirits as well. Arranges recurring tastings. On-line ordering.

Versailles Dranken
Lange Hezelstraat 72-76
6511 Cl Nijmegen
Phone: +31 (0)24-3232008
www.versaillesdranken.nl
A very impressive range with more than 1500 different whiskies, most of them from Scotland but also a surprisingly good selection (more than 60) of Bourbon. Arranges recurring tastings. On-line ordering.

NEW ZEALAND
Whisky Galore
66 Victoria Street
Christchurch 8013
Phone: +64 (3) 377 6824
www.whiskygalore.co.nz
The best whisky shop in New Zealand with 550 different whiskies, approximately 350 which are single malts. The owner Michael Fraser Milne, has also founded The Whisky Guild which has, as one of its aims, to produce exclusive single cask bottlings for members. There is also online mail-order with shipping all over the world except USA and Canada.

POLAND
George Ballantine's
Krucza str 47 A, Warsaw
Phone: +48 22 625 48 32

Pulawska str 22, Warsaw
Phone: +48 22 542 86 22

Marynarska str 15, Warsaw
Phone: +48 22 395 51 60

Francuska str 27, Warsaw
Phone: +48 22 810 32 22
www.sklep-ballantines.pl
These four shops have the biggest assortment in Poland with more than 360 different single malts. Apart from whisky there is a full range of spirits and wines from all over the world. Recurrent tastings are arranged and mail-orders are dispatched.

RUSSIA
Whisky World Shop
9, Tverskoy Boulevard
123104 Moscow
Phone: +7 495 787 9150
www.whiskyworld.ru
Huge assortment with more than 1,000 different single malts, mainly from independent bottlers. It also stocks a selection of rare and old

whiskies. The range is supplemented with a nice range of cognac, armagnac, calvados, grappa and wines. Tastings are also arranged.

SCOTLAND

Gordon & MacPhail
58 - 60 South Street, Elgin
Moray IV30 1JY
Phone: +44 (0)1343 545110
www.gordonandmacphail.com
This legendary shop opened already in 1895 in Elgin. The owners are perhaps the most well-known among independent bottlers. The shop stocks more than 800 bottlings of whisky and more than 600 wines and there is also a delicatessen counter with high-quality products. Tastings are arranged in the shop and there are shipping services within the UK and overseas. The shop attracts visitors from all over the world.

Royal Mile Whiskies (2 shops)
379 High Street, The Royal Mile
Edinburgh EH1 1PW
Phone: +44 (0)131 2253383

3 Bloomsbury Street
London WC1B 3QE
Phone: +44 (0)20 7436 4763
www.royalmilewhiskies.com
Royal Mile Whiskies is one of the most well-known whisky retailers in the UK. It was established in Edinburgh in 1991. There is also a shop in London since 2002 and a cigar shop close to the Edinburgh shop. The whisky range is outstanding with many difficult to find elsewhere. They have a comprehensive site regarding information on regions, distilleries, production, tasting etc. Royal Mile Whiskies also arranges 'Whisky Fringe' in Edinburgh, a two-day whisky festival which takes place annually in mid August. On-line ordering with worldwide shipping.

The Whisky Shop
(See also England, The Whisky Shop)
Buchanan Galleries
220 Buchanan Street
Glasgow G1 2GF
Phone: +44 (0)141 331 0022

17 Bridge Street
Inverness IV1 1HD
Phone: +44 (0)1463 710525

11 Main Street
Callander FK17 8DU
Phone: +44 (0)1877 331936

93 High Street
Fort William PH33 6DG
Phone: +44 (0)1397 706164

Station Road
Oban PA34 4NU
Phone: +44 (0)1631 564409

Unit 14
Gretna Gateway Outlet Village
Gretna DG16 5GG
Phone: +44 (0)1461338004

Unit RU58B, Ocean Terminal
Edinburgh EH6 6JJ
Phone: +44 (0)131 554 8211

Unit 23
Princes Mall
Edinburgh EH1 1BQ
Phone: +44 (0)131 558 7563

28 Victoria Street
Edinburgh EH1 2JW
Phone: +44 (0)131 225 4666
www.whiskyshop.com
The first shop opened in 1992 in Edinburgh and this is now the United Kingdom's largest specialist retailer of whiskies with 20 outlets. A large product range with over 700 kinds, including 400 malt whiskies and 140 miniature bottles, as well as accessories and books. The own range 'Glenkeir Treasures' is a special assortment of selected malt whiskies. On-line ordering and shipping all over the world except to the USA.

Loch Fyne Whiskies
Inveraray
Argyll PA32 8UD
Phone: +44 (0)1499 302 219
www.lfw.co.uk
A legendary shop with an equally legendary owner, Richard Joynson. Joynson is known as a person with a high degree of integrity who does not mince his words on whisky matters. The range of malt whiskies is large and they have their own house blend, the prize-awarded Loch Fyne, as well as their 'The Loch Fyne Whisky Liqueur'. There is also a range of house malts called 'The Inverarity'. On-line ordering with worldwide shipping.

Single Malts Direct
36 Gordon Street
Huntly
Aberdeenshire AB54 8EQ
Phone: +44 (0) 845 606 6145
www.singlemaltsdirect.com
Duncan Taylor, one of Scotland's largest independent bottlers, also has a shop in Huntly. In the assortment is of course the whole Duncan Taylor range but also a selection of their own single malt bottlings called Whiskies of Scotland. Add bottlings from other producers and you end up with a good range of almost 700 different expressions. On-line shop with shipping worldwide. The website has information on whisky production and a very comprehensive glossary of whisky terms.

The Whisky Shop Dufftown
1 Fife Street, Dufftown, Keith
Moray AB55 4AL
Phone: +44 (0)1340 821097
www.whiskyshopdufftown.co.uk
Whisky specialist in Dufftown in the heart of Speyside, wellknown to many of the Speyside festival visitors. More than 500 single malts as well as other whiskies. Arranges tastings as well as special events during the Festivals. On-line ordering with worldwide shipping.

The Scotch Whisky Experience
354 Castlehill, Royal Mile
Edinburgh
Phone: +44 (0)131 220 0441
www.scotchwhiskyexperience.co.uk
The Scotch Whisky Experience is a must for whisky devotees visiting Edinburgh. An interactive visitor centre dedicated to the history of Scotch whisky. This five-star visitor attraction has an excellent whisky shop with almost 300 different whiskies in stock. Reccently, after extensive refurbishment, a brand new and interactive shop was opened. Do not miss the award-winning Amber Restaurant.

Cadenhead's Campbeltown Whisky shop (Eaglesome)
30-32 Union Street
Campbeltown
Argyll PA28 6JA
Phone: +44 (0)1586 551710
www.wmcadenhead.com
One in a chain of shops owned by independent bottlers Cadenhead. Sells Cadenhead's products and other whiskies with a good range of Springbank. On-line ordering.

Cadenhead´s Whisky Shop
172 Canongate, Royal Mile
Edinburgh EH8 8BN
Phone: +44 (0)131 556 5864
www.wmcadenhead.com
The oldest shop in the chain owned by Cadenhead. Sells Cadenhead's product range and a good selection of other whiskies and spirits. Arranges recurrent tastings. On-line ordering.

The Good Spirits Co.
23 Bath Street,
Glasgow G2 1HW
Phone: +44 (0)141 258 8427
www.thegoodspiritsco.com
A newly opened specialist spirits store selling whisky, bourbon, rum, vodka, tequila, gin, cognac and armagnac, liqueurs and other spirits. They also stock quality champagne, fortified wines and cigars.

Whiski Shop
4 North Bank Street
Edinburgh EH1 2LPL
Phone: +44 (0)131 225 1532
www.whiskishop.com
www.whiskirooms.co.uk
A new concept (opened in 2010) located near Edinburgh Castle, combining a shop, a tasting room and a bistro. Also regular whisky tastings. Online mail order with worldwide delivery.

Robbie's Drams
3 Sandgate, Ayr
South Ayrshire KA7 1BG
Phone: +44 (0)1292 262 135
www.robbiesdrams.com
A whisky specialist with over 600 whiskies available in store and over 900 available from their on-line shop, including a large range of Irish, Japanese and American Bourbons. Specialists in single cask bottlings, closed distillery bottlings,

rare malts, limited edition whisky and a nice range of their own bottlings. Worldwide shipping.

The Whisky Barrel
PO Box 23803, Edinburgh, EH6 7WW
Phone: +44 (0)845 2248 156
www.thewhiskybarrel.com
Online specialist whisky shop based in Edinburgh. They stock over 1,000 single malt and blended whiskies including Scotch, Japanese, Irish, Indian, Swedish and their own casks. Worldwide shipping.

The Scotch Malt Whisky Society
www.smws.com
A society with more than 20 000 members worldwide, specialised in own bottlings of single casks and re-lease between 150 and 200 bottlings a year. Orders on-line for members only. Shipping only within UK.

Drinkmonger
100 Atholl Road
Pitlochry PH16 5BL
Phone: +44 (0)1796 470133

11 Bruntsfield Place
Edinburgh EH10 4HN
Phone: +44 (0)131 229 2205
www.drinkmonger.com
Two new shops opened in 2011 by the well-known Royal Mile Whiskies. The idea is to have a 50:50 split between wine and specialist spirits with the addition of a cigar assort-ment. The whisky range is a good cross-section with some rarities and a focus on local distilleries.

Luvian's Bottle Shop (2 shops)
93 Bonnygate, Cupar
Fife KY15 4LG
Phone: +44 (0)1334 654 820

66 Market Street, St Andrews
Fife KY16 9NU
Phone: +44 (0)1334 477752
www.luvians.com
Wine and whisky merchant with a very nice selection of more than 600 malt whiskies.

A.D. Rattray's Whisky Experience & Whisky Shop
32 Main Road
Kirkoswald
Ayrshire KA19 8HY
Phone: +44 (0) 1655 760242
www.adrattray.com
A combination of whisky shop, sample room and educational center owned by the independent bottler A D Rattray. Tasting menus with dif-ferent themes ara available.

Robert Graham Ltd (3 shops)
194 Rose Street
Edinburgh EH2 4AZ
Phone: +44 (0)131 226 1874

Finlay House
10-14 West Nile Street
Glasgow G1 2PP
Phone: +44 (0)141 248 7283

Robert Graham's Treasurer 1874
254 Canongate
Royal Mile
Edinburgh EH8 8AA

Phone: +44 (0)131 556 2791
www.whisky-cigars.co.uk
Established in 1874 this company specialises in Scotch whisky and cigars. They have a nice assortment of malt whiskies and their range of cigars is impressive. On-line ordering with shipping all over the world

Whisky Castle
Main Street
Tomintoul
Aberdeenshire AB37 9EX
Phone: +44 (0)1807 580 213
www.whiskycastle.co.uk
Whisky specialist situated in the heart of malt whisky country. With over 500 single malts, the specialisation is in independent bottlings. There is also a mail order shipping worldwide with the exception of USA.

SOUTH AFRICA

Aficionados Premium Spirits Online
M5 Freeway Park
Cape Town
Phone: +27 21 511 7337
www.aficionados.co.za
An online liquor retailer specialising in single malt whisky. They claim to offer the widest of range of whiskies available in South Africa and hold regular tastings around the country. Shipping only within South Africa.

SWITZERLAND

P. Ullrich AG
Schneidergasse 27
4051 Basel
Phone: +41 (0)61 338 90 91
Another two shops in Basel:
Laufenstrasse 16
Unt. Rebgasse 18
www.ullrich.ch
A very large range of wines, spirits, beers, accessories and books. Over 800 kinds of whisky with almost 600 single malt. On-line ordering. Recently, they also founded a whisky club with regular tastings (www.whiskysinn.ch).

Eddie's Whiskies
Dorfgasse 27
8810 Horgen
Phone: +41 (0)43 244 63 00
www.eddies.ch
A whisky specialist with more than 700 different whiskies in stock with emphasis on single malts (more than 500 different). Also arranges tastings.

World of Whisky
Via dim Lej 6
7500 St. Moritz
Phone: +41 (0)81 852 33 77
www.world-of-whisky.ch
A legendary shop situated in the Hotel Waldhaus Am See which has an also legendary whisky bar, the Devil's Place. The shop stocks almost 1,000 different whiskies and has a good range of other spirits such as rum, cognac and armagnac.

Glen Fahrn (3 shops)
Glen Fahrn N°1 "the origin"
Fahrnstrasse 39
9402 Mörschwil
Phone: +41 (0)71 860 09 87

Glen Fahrn N°2 "the pearl"
Oberdorfstrasse 5
8001 Zürich
Phone: +41 (0)44 520 09 87

Glen Fahrn N°4 "the store"
Glen Fahrn Germany GmbH
Hauptstrasse 38
79801 Hohentengen a.H.
Germany
Phone: +49 (0)7742 857 222
www.glenfahrn.com
A wide range of spirits, fortified wines and champagnes. A large selection of whisky, with over 600 from Scotland. On-line ordering. Ships within Switzerland and to adjacent countries.

Scot & Scotch
Wohllebgasse 7
8001 Zürich
Phone: +41 44 211 90 60
www.scotandscotch.ch
A whisky specialist with a great selection including c 560 single malts. Mail orders, but no on-line ordering.

Angels Share Shop
Unterdorfstrasse 15
5036 Oberentfelden
Phone: +41 (0)62 724 83 74
www.angelsshare.ch
A combined restaurant and whisky shop. More than 400 different kinds of whisky as well as a good range of cigars. Scores extra points for short information and photos of all distilleries. On-line ordering.

USA

Binny's Beverage Depot
5100 W. Dempster (Head Office)
Skokie, IL 60077
Phone:
Internet orders, 888-942-9463 (toll free)
Whiskey Hotline, 888-817-5898 (toll free)
www.binnys.com
A chain of no less than 28 stores in the Chicago area, covering every-thing within wine and spirits. Some of the stores also have a gourmet grocery, cheese shop and, for cigar lovers, a walk-in humidor. The whisk(e)y range is impressive with 700 single malts, 120 bourbons, 40 Irish whiskeys and more. Among other products almost 200 kinds of tequila should be mentioned. Online mail order service.

Park Avenue Liquor Shop
292 Madison Avenue
New York, NY 10017
Phone: +1 212 685 2442
www.parkaveliquor.com
Legendary whisky shop established in 1934. A very large assortment of wine and spirits with 400 different expressions of single malt.

Statistics

Shieldhall Bottling Plant. Photo: Diageo

The following pages have been made possible thanks to kind cooperation from four sources – The IWSR, Euromonitor International, The Scotch Whisky Industry Review and Scotch Whisky Association.

The IWSR
is the leading provider of data on wine, spirits and RTDs. The IWSR's database, essential to the industry, is used by all of the largest multinational wine and spirits companies, as well as many more local companies. The IWSR has a unique methodology which, by tapping into local country expertise, allows them to get closer to what is actually consumed and better understand how markets work. The IWSR conducts face-to-face interviews with 1,200 companies in 115 countries each year, with further input from 350 companies. The IWSR tracks overall consumption and trends at brand, quality and category level for wine, spirits and RTDs, and aims to provide data that is as accurate and detailed as possible. More information can be found on **www.iwsr.co.uk**

Euromonitor International
is the leading provider of global strategic intelligence on consumer markets. For more than 40 years, Euromonitor has published internationally respected market research reports, business reference books and online information systems, providing strategic business intelligence for the world's leading FMCG multinationals.
More information on **www.euromonitor.com**

The Scotch Whisky Industry Review 2012
is written and compiled by Alan S Gray, Sutherlands Edinburgh. It is now in its 34th consecutive year and provides a wealth of unique business critical information on the Scotch Whisky Industry. For more information visit **www.scotchwhiskyindustryreview.com**

Scotch Whisky Association (SWA)
is the trade association for the Scotch Whisky industry. Their main objective is to promote, protect and represent the interests of the whisky industry in Scotland and around the world. They also produce a plethora of statistical material covering production and sales of Scotch whisky. More information can be found on **www.scotch-whisky.org.uk**

Whisk(e)y forecast (volume) by region and sector 2010-2016

= positive volume growth   = negative volume growth

SW=Scotch Whisky, IW=Irish Whiskey, UW=US Whiskey, CW=Canadian Whisky, OW=Other Whisky, TOT=Total.
The figures show CAGR% (Compound Annual Growth Rate) i. e. year-over-year growth rate.

The World

SW	2.9
IW	9.6
UW	2.1
CW	-0.6
OW	7.9
TOT	5.5

Asia Pacific

SW	3.4
IW	9.2
UW	2.9
CW	9.2
OW	8.2
TOT	7.8

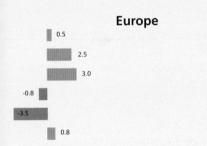

Europe

SW	0.5
IW	2.5
UW	3.0
CW	-0.8
OW	-3.5
TOT	0.8

Africa & Middle East

SW	4.0
IW	3.5
UW	2.8
CW	-0.3
OW	3.5
TOT	3.7

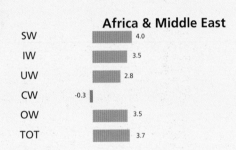

CIS*

SW	15.5
IW	10.1
UW	11.3
CW	7.3
OW	10.5
TOT	14.8

* Russia and other former Soviet Socialist Republic states

Duty Free

SW	4.0
IW	7.6
UW	8.1
CW	0.7
OW	8.1
TOT	4.7

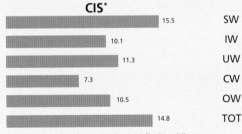

Americas

SW	4.0
IW	18.3
UW	1.3
CW	-0.8
OW	-1.0
TOT	2.2

Rest of the World

SW	0.1
IW	-
UW	5.9
CW	-
OW	2.4
TOT	0.2

Source: © The IWSR 2012

World Consumption of Blended Scotch

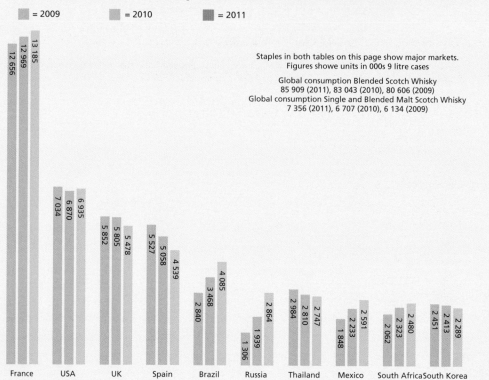

= 2009   = 2010   = 2011

Staples in both tables on this page show major markets.
Figures showe units in 000s 9 litre cases

Global consumption Blended Scotch Whisky
85 909 (2011), 83 043 (2010), 80 606 (2009)
Global consumption Single and Blended Malt Scotch Whisky
7 356 (2011), 6 707 (2010), 6 134 (2009)

France: 12 656, 12 969, 13 185
USA: 7 034, 6 870, 6 935
UK: 5 852, 5 805, 5 478
Spain: 5 527, 5 058, 4 539
Brazil: 2 840, 3 468, 4 085
Russia: 1 306, 1 939, 2 864
Thailand: 2 984, 2 810, 2 747
Mexico: 1 848, 2 233, 2 591
South Africa: 2 062, 2 323, 2 480
South Korea: 2 451, 2 413, 2 289

Source: © The IWSR 2012

World Consumption of Single Malt Scotch

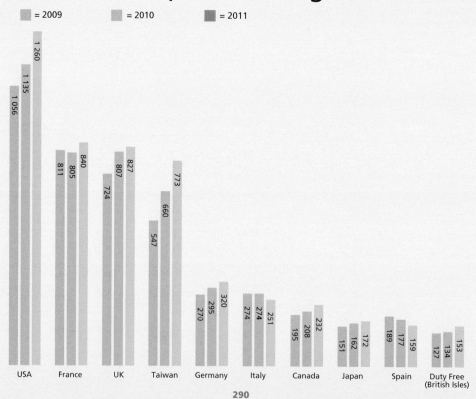

= 2009   = 2010   = 2011

USA: 1 056, 1 135, 1 260
France: 811, 805, 840
UK: 724, 807, 827
Taiwan: 547, 660, 773
Germany: 270, 295, 320
Italy: 274, 274, 251
Canada: 195, 208, 232
Japan: 151, 162, 172
Spain: 189, 177, 159
Duty Free (British Isles): 127, 134, 153

Source: © The IWSR 2012

The Top 30 Whiskies of the World

Sales figures for 2011 (units in million 9-litre cases)

Johnnie Walker (Diageo), Scotch whisky — 18,00
Officer's Choice (Allied Blenders & Distillers), Indian whisky — 16,53
McDowell's No. 1 (United Spirits), Indian whisky — 16,08
Bagpiper (United Spirits), Indian whisky — 15,98
Royal Stag (Pernod Ricard), Indian whisky — 12,49
Old Tavern (United Spirits), Indian whisky — 11,07
Original Choice (John Distilleries), Indian whisky — 10,77
Jack Daniel's (Brown-Forman), Tennessee whiskey — 10,58
Imperial Blue (Pernod Ricard), Indian whisky — 7,17
Ballantine's (Pernod Ricard), Scotch whisky — 6,47
Hayward's (United Spirits), Indian whisky — 6,16
Jim Beam (Beam Inc.), Bourbon — 5,86
Crown Royal (Diageo), Canadian whisky — 5,00
William Grant's (William Grant & Sons), Scotch whisky — 4,97
Chivas Regal (Pernod Ricard), Scotch whisky — 4,89
J&B Rare (Diageo), Scotch whisky — 4,80
Director's Special (United Spirits), Indian whisky — 4,52
8PM (Radico Khaitan), Indian whisky — 4,32
Jameson (Pernod Ricard), Irish whiskey — 3,78
Blenders Pride (Pernod Ricard), Indian whisky — 3,46
Dewar's (Bacardi), Scotch whisky — 3,19
Gold Riband (United Spirits), Indian whisky — 3,07
Director's Special Black (United Spirits), Indian whisky — 2,92
McDowell's Green Label (United Spirits), Indian whisky — 2,92
William Peel (Belvédère), Scotch whisky — 2,90
Kakubin (Suntory), Japanese whisky — 2,50
Bell's (Diageo), Scotch whisky — 2,50
Label 5 (La Martiniquaise), Scotch whisky — 2,50
Seagram's 7 Crown (Diageo), American blended whiskey — 2,40
William Lawson's (Bacardi), Scotch whisky — 2,29

Source: Drinks International, Millionaires Supplement 2012 (Euromonitor International)

Global Exports of Scotch by Region

Volume (litres of pure alcohol)			chg	Value (£ Sterling)			chg
Region	2011	2010	%	Region	2011	2010	%
Africa	19,057,777	15,875,099	20	Africa	224,098,833	212,556,356	5
Asia	76,666,463	63,430,599	21	Asia	911,872,078	716,165,032	27
Australasia	8,321,443	7,849,366	6	Australasia	78,471,748	72,417,272	8
C&S America	45,407,648	34,695,655	31	C&S America	489,279,849	354,561,104	38
Eastern Europe	3,956,298	3,225,658	23	Eastern Europe	48,982,325	43,217,299	13
Europe (other)	6,905,534	5,074,472	36	Europe (other)	77,164,062	56,616,923	36
European Union	132,303,170	114,740,670	15	European Union	1,448,326,333	1,264,914,448	14
Middle East	12,778,425	10,879,453	17	Middle East	151,318,182	119,085,205	27
North America	48,566,887	41,627,083	17	North America	796,247,171	608,256,781	31
Total	353,963,645	297,398,055	19	Total	4,225,760,581	3,447,790,420	23

Source: Scotch Whisky Association

Top 10 Scotch Malt Whisky brands world market share %

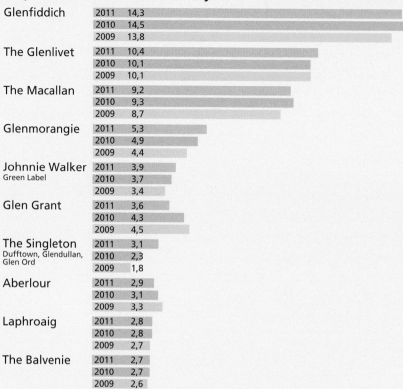

Brand	Year	Share
Glenfiddich	2011	14,3
	2010	14,5
	2009	13,8
The Glenlivet	2011	10,4
	2010	10,1
	2009	10,1
The Macallan	2011	9,2
	2010	9,3
	2009	8,7
Glenmorangie	2011	5,3
	2010	4,9
	2009	4,4
Johnnie Walker Green Label	2011	3,9
	2010	3,7
	2009	3,4
Glen Grant	2011	3,6
	2010	4,3
	2009	4,5
The Singleton Dufftown, Glendullan, Glen Ord	2011	3,1
	2010	2,3
	2009	1,8
Aberlour	2011	2,9
	2010	3,1
	2009	3,3
Laphroaig	2011	2,8
	2010	2,8
	2009	2,7
The Balvenie	2011	2,7
	2010	2,7
	2009	2,6

Top 10 Scotch Blended Whisky brands world market share %

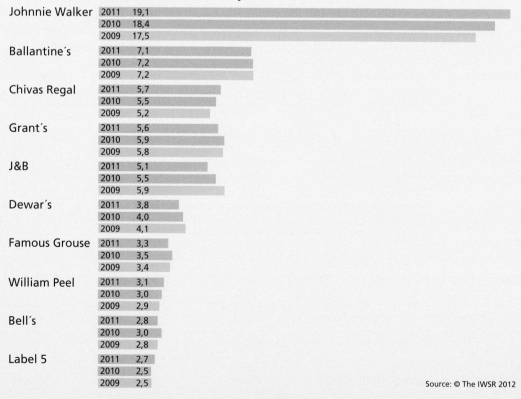

Brand	Year	Share
Johnnie Walker	2011	19,1
	2010	18,4
	2009	17,5
Ballantine's	2011	7,1
	2010	7,2
	2009	7,2
Chivas Regal	2011	5,7
	2010	5,5
	2009	5,2
Grant's	2011	5,6
	2010	5,9
	2009	5,8
J&B	2011	5,1
	2010	5,5
	2009	5,9
Dewar's	2011	3,8
	2010	4,0
	2009	4,1
Famous Grouse	2011	3,3
	2010	3,5
	2009	3,4
William Peel	2011	3,1
	2010	3,0
	2009	2,9
Bell's	2011	2,8
	2010	3,0
	2009	2,8
Label 5	2011	2,7
	2010	2,5
	2009	2,5

Source: © The IWSR 2012

Distillery Capacity

Litres of pure alcohol, Scottish, active distilleries only

Roseisle	12 500 000	Jura	2 200 000	Glengoyne	1 100 000
Glenfiddich	12 000 000	Balblair	2 000 000	Glen Garioch	1 000 000
Glenlivet	10 500 000	Bowmore	2 000 000	Tobermory	1 000 000
Macallan	9 400 000	Speyburn	2 000 000	Oban	780 000
Caol Ila	6 500 000	Ben Nevis	1 800 000	Arran	750 000
Ailsa Bay	6 250 000	Glenlossie	1 800 000	Glengyle	750 000
Glen Keith	6 000 000	Pulteney	1 800 000	Glen Scotia	750 000
Glenmorangie	6 000 000	Auchentoshan	1 750 000	Springbank	750 000
Glen Grant	5 900 000	Knockdhu	1 750 000	Speyside	600 000
Dufftown	5 800 000	Bruichladdich	1 500 000	Benromach	500 000
Balvenie	5 600 000	Scapa	1 500 000	Royal Lochnagar	450 000
Glenrothes	5 600 000	Glendronach	1 400 000	Glenturret	340 000
Miltonduff	5 500 000	Glen Spey	1 400 000	Bladnoch	250 000
Ardmore	5 200 000	Knockando	1 400 000	Kilchoman	120 000
Dailuaine	5 200 000	Glencadam	1 300 000	Edradour	90 000
Auchroisk	5 000 000	Ardbeg	1 150 000	Daftmill	65 000
Glen Ord	5 000 000	Glenglassaugh	1 100 000	Abhainn Dearg	20 000
Tomatin	5 000 000				
Tormore	4 900 000				

Summary of Malt Distillery Capacity by Category

Category	Litres of alcohol	% of Industry	Average capacity
Speyside (47)	204 200 000	64,0	4 345 000
Islands (7)	10 570 000	3,3	1 510 000
Highlands (29)	71 950 000	22,5	2 481 000
Islay (8)	19 420 000	6,1	2 428 000
Lowlands (5)	10 815 000	3,4	2 163 000
Campbeltown (3)	2 250 000	0,7	750 000
Total (99)	**319 205 000**	**100**	**3 224 000**

Additional first column entries:

Clynelish	4 800 000
Kininvie	4 800 000
Longmorn	4 400 000
Teaninich	4 400 000
Glenallachie	4 200 000
Glenburgie	4 200 000
Glentauchers	4 200 000
Allt-a-Bhainne	4 000 000
Braeval	4 000 000
Craigellachie	4 000 000
Loch Lomond	4 000 000
Royal Brackla	4 000 000
Tamdhu	4 000 000
Tamnavulin	4 000 000
Mortlach	3 800 000
Linkwood	3 750 000
Aberlour	3 700 000
Dalmore	3 700 000
Glendullan	3 700 000
Aberfeldy	3 500 000
Benrinnes	3 500 000
Mannochmore	3 450 000
Cardhu	3 400 000
Glenfarclas	3 400 000
Macduff	3 340 000
Glen Moray	3 300 000
Laphroaig	3 300 000
Tomintoul	3 300 000
Aultmore	3 000 000
Deanston	3 000 000
Inchgower	2 900 000
Balmenach	2 800 000
Benriach	2 800 000
Tullibardine	2 700 000
Talisker	2 600 000
Blair Athol	2 500 000
Bunnahabhain	2 500 000
Glen Elgin	2 500 000
Glenkinchie	2 500 000
Highland Park	2 500 000
Strathisla	2 400 000
Lagavulin	2 350 000
Fettercairn	2 300 000
Strathmill	2 300 000
Cragganmore	2 200 000
Dalwhinnie	2 200 000

Summary of Malt Distillery Capacity by Owner

Owner (number of distilleries)	Litres of alcohol	% of Industry
Diageo (28)	98 680 000	30,9
Pernod Ricard (13)	59 500 000	18,6
William Grant (4)	28 650 000	9,0
Bacardi (John Dewar & Sons) (5)	17 840 000	5,6
Edrington Group (4)	17 840 000	5,6
Whyte and Mackay (4)	12 200 000	3,8
Pacific Spirits (Inver House) (5)	10 350 000	3,2
Beam Inc (2)	8 500 000	2,7
Moët Hennessy (Glenmorangie) (2)	7 150 000	2,2
C L Financial (Burn Stewart) (3)	6 500 000	2,0
Campari (Glen Grant) (1)	5 900 000	1,8
Ian Macleod Distillers (2)	5 100 000	1,6
Tomatin Distillery Co (1)	5 000 000	1,6
Suntory (Morrison Bowmore) (3)	4 750 000	1,5
Loch Lomond Distillers (2)	4 750 000	1,5
Angus Dundee (2)	4 600 000	1,4
Benriach Distillery Co (2)	4 200 000	1,3
J & G Grant (Glenfarclas) (1)	3 400 000	1,1
La Martiniquaise (Glen Moray) (1)	3 300 000	1,0
Picard (Tullibardine) (1)	2 700 000	0,8
Nikka (Ben Nevis Distillery) (1)	1 800 000	0,6
Rémy Cointreau (Bruichladdich) (1)	1 500 000	0,5
J & A Mitchell (2)	1 500 000	0,5
Scaent Group (Glenglassaugh) (1)	1 100 000	- " -
Isle of Arran Distillers (1)	750 000	- " -
Speyside Distillers Co (1)	600 000	- " -
Gordon & MacPhail (Benromach) (1)	500 000	- " -
Co-ordinated Developm. (Bladnoch) (1)	250 000	- " -
Kilchoman Distillery Co (1)	120 000	- " -
Signatory Vintage (Edradour) (1)	90 000	- " -
Francis Cuthbert (Daftmill) (1)	65 000	- " -
Mark Thayburn (Abhainn Dearg) (1)	20 000	- " -

Do you want to find out more in detail where the different distilleries are situated? We suggest that you pay a visit to www.maltmadness.com/whisky/map/Scotland/ where you will find a very nice, interactive map made by Johannes van den Heuvel. Another favourite is found at bit.ly/daNJMP where Steffen Bräuner has plotted not only all the Scottish and Irish distilleries but there are also maps for the Americas and for distilleries from the rest of the world.

ORKNEY ISLANDS

Wick

Isle of Lewis
129

NORTH HIGHLANDS

132

SKYE

Barra
1

Kyle of Lockalsh

73

Inverness

Loch Ness

SPEYSIDE

Aberdeen

CENTRAL HIGHLANDS

Fort William

EAST HIGHLANDS

WEST HIGHLANDS

MULL

Oban

Pitlochry

Loch Tay

Dundee

Loch Lomond

Perth

St. Andrews

Stirling

JURA

Glasgow

ISLAY

Edinburgh

ARRAN

Campbeltown

Ayr

THE LOWLANDS

Dumfries

Stranraer

131

57

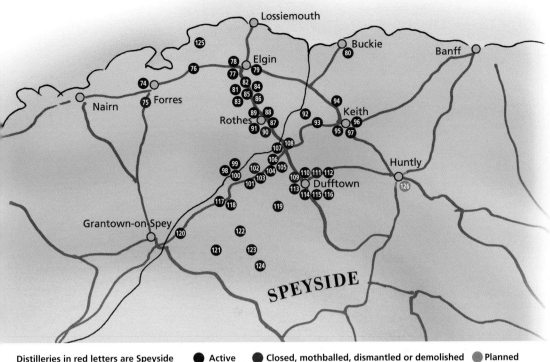

Distilleries in red letters are Speyside ● Active ● Closed, mothballed, dismantled or demolished ◐ Planned

39 Aberfeldy	126 Duncan Taylor	114 Kininvie	1 Barra	45 Deanston	89 Glenrothes
106 Aberlour	38 Edradour	100 Knockando	2 Highland Park	46 Loch Lomond	90 Caperdonich (c)
129 Abhainn Dearg	130 Falkirk	21 Knockdhu	3 Scapa	47 Inverleven (d)	91 Glenspey
127 Ailsa Bay	32 Fettercairn	56 Ladyburn (dm)	4 Pulteney	48 Littlemill (d)	92 Auchroisk
119 Allt-a-Bhainne	13 Glen Albyn (d)	63 Lagavulin	5 Brora (c)	49 Auchentoshan	93 Glentauchers
131 Annandale	105 Glenallachie	64 Laphroaig	6 Clynelish	50 Glengoyne	94 Aultmore
62 Ardbeg	76 Glenburgie	79 Linkwood	7 Balblair	51 Kinclaith (d)	95 Strathmill
25 Ardmore	34 Glencadam	48 Littlemill (d)	8 Glenmorangie	52 Glen Flagler (d)	96 Glen Keith
58 Arran	23 Glendronach	46 Loch Lomond	9 Ben Wyvis (c)	53 Rosebank (c)	97 Strathisla
49 Auchentoshan	116 Glendullan	36 Lochside (d)	10 Teaninich	54 St Magdalene (dm)	98 Tamdhu
92 Auchroisk	85 Glen Elgin	84 Longmorn	11 Dalmore	55 Glenkinchie	99 Cardhu
94 Aultmore	35 Glenesk (dm)	107 Macallan	12 Glen Ord	56 Ladyburn (dm)	100 Knockando
7 Balblair	101 Glenfarclas	20 Macduff	13 Glen Albyn (d)	57 Bladnoch	101 Glenfarclas
120 Balmenach	112 Glenfiddich	81 Mannochmore	14 Glen Mhor (d)	58 Arran	102 Imperial (c)
113 Balvenie	52 Glen Flagler (d)	15 Millburn (dm)	15 Millburn (dm)	59 Springbank	103 Dailuaine
19 Banff (d)	24 Glen Garioch	77 Miltonduff	16 Royal Brackla	60 Glengyle	104 Benrinnes
1 Barra	18 Glenglassaugh	115 Mortlach	17 Tomatin	61 Glen Scotia	105 Glenallachie
30 Ben Nevis	50 Glengoyne	33 North Port (d)	18 Glenglassaugh	62 Ardbeg	106 Aberlour
82 Benriach	87 Glen Grant	40 Oban	19 Banff (d)	63 Lagavulin	107 Macallan
104 Benrinnes	60 Glengyle	111 Pittyvaich (d)	20 Macduff	64 Laphroaig	108 Craigellachie
74 Benromach	96 Glen Keith	128 Port Charlotte	21 Knockdhu	65 Port Ellen (dm)	109 Convalmore (dm)
9 Ben Wyvis (c)	55 Glenkinchie	65 Port Ellen (dm)	22 Glenugie (dm)	66 Bowmore	110 Dufftown
57 Bladnoch	122 Glenlivet	4 Pulteney	23 Glendronach	67 Bruichladdich	111 Pittyvaich (d)
37 Blair Athol	31 Glenlochy (d)	53 Rosebank (c)	24 Glen Garioch	68 Kilchoman	112 Glenfiddich
66 Bowmore	83 Glenlossie	125 Roseisle	25 Ardmore	69 Caol Ila	113 Balvenie
124 Braeval	14 Glen Mhor (d)	16 Royal Brackla	26 Speyside	70 Bunnahabhain	114 Kininvie
5 Brora (c)	8 Glenmorangie	27 Royal Lochnagar	27 Royal Lochnagar	71 Jura	115 Mortlach
67 Bruichladdich	78 Glen Moray	54 St Magdalene (dm)	28 Glenury Royal (d)	72 Tobermory	116 Glendullan
70 Bunnahabhain	12 Glen Ord	3 Scapa	29 Dalwhinnie	73 Talisker	117 Tormore
69 Caol Ila	89 Glenrothes	88 Speyburn	30 Ben Nevis	74 Benromach	118 Cragganmore
90 Caperdonich (c)	61 Glen Scotia	26 Speyside	31 Glenlochy (d)	75 Dallas Dhu (c)	119 Allt-a-Bhainne
99 Cardhu	91 Glenspey	59 Springbank	32 Fettercairn	76 Glenburgie	120 Balmenach
6 Clynelish	93 Glentauchers	97 Strathisla	33 North Port (d)	77 Miltonduff	121 Tomintoul
86 Coleburn (dm)	41 Glenturret	95 Strathmill	34 Glencadam	78 Glen Moray	122 Glenlivet
109 Convalmore (dm)	22 Glenugie (dm)	73 Talisker	35 Glenesk (dm)	79 Linkwood	123 Tamnavulin
118 Cragganmore	28 Glenury Royal (d)	98 Tamdhu	36 Lochside (d)	80 Inchgower	124 Braeval
108 Craigellachie	2 Highland Park	123 Tamnavulin	37 Blair Athol	81 Mannochmore	125 Roseisle
42 Daftmill	102 Imperial (c)	10 Teaninich	38 Edradour	82 Benriach	126 Duncan Taylor
103 Dailuaine	80 Inchgower	72 Tobermory	39 Aberfeldy	83 Glenlossie	127 Ailsa Bay
75 Dallas Dhu (c)	47 Inverleven (d)	17 Tomatin	40 Oban	84 Longmorn	128 Port Charlotte
11 Dalmore	71 Jura	121 Tomintoul	41 Glenturret	85 Glen Elgin	129 Abhainn Dearg
29 Dalwhinnie	68 Kilchoman	117 Tormore	42 Daftmill	86 Coleburn (dm)	130 Falkirk
45 Deanston	51 Kinclaith (d)	44 Tullibardine	43 Kingsbarns	87 Glen Grant	131 Annandale
110 Dufftown	43 Kingsbarns	132 Wolfburn	44 Tullibardine	88 Speyburn	132 Wolfburn

Index

Bold figures refer to the main entry in the distillery directory.

A

Aberfeldy 74-75
Aberlour 76
Abhainn Dearg distillery 206
Adelphi Distillery 269, 278
Ailsa Bay distillery 206
Akashi single malt 226
Akuto, Ichiro 221-224
Alazana Distillery, La 259
Allt-a-Bhainne 77
Amrut Distilleries 45, 256-257
anCnoc 275
Angus Dundee Distillers 121, 201
Annandale distillery 270
Ardbeg 53, 78-79, 264
Ardenstiel 38
Ardmore 80
Armstrong, Raymond 94
Ardnamurchan Distillery 269-270
Arran 81
Asama single malt 225
Auchentoshan 82
Auchroisk 84
Aultmore 85

B

Baker, David 46-47
Bakery Hill Distillery 46-47, 253
Balblair 86-87
Balcones Distillery 229, 250
Ballantine's 120, 177, 266
Ballast Point Brewing & Distilling 249
Ballechin 117
Balmenach 88
Balvenie 83, 89, 274
Banff 212
Barnard, Alfred 194
Barra distillery 271
Barrie, Rachel 96
Barton Brands 185
Batch 206 Distillery 251
Beam Inc 107, 158, 265-268
Belfast Distillery Co, The 272
Bell & Sons, Arthur 20
Bell's 20, 95
Ben Nevis 90
BenRiach 13-14, 91
Benrinnes 92
Benromach 33, 93
Ben Wyvis 219
Bergslagens Destilleri 240-241
Berry Bros & Rudd 276
Bertrand, Distillerie 234
Bignell, Peter 40
Blackadder International 277
Black, John 205
Bladnoch 94
Blair Athol 95
Blaue Maus, Destillerie 235

Bowmore 96-97
BOX Destilleri 40, 240
Braeval 98
Braunstein 231
Bremner, Stephen 10-11
Broger Privatbrennerei, Klaus 230
Brora 211
Bruce, Gordon 162
Bruichladdich 52, 53, 100-101, 268
Buchanan 85, 113
Buckley, Trevor 191
Bulloch, Sandy 169
Bull Run Distillery 248-249
Bunnahabhain 102
Burgdorfer Gasthausbrauerei 242
Burnett, Stephen 175
Bushmills 103, 268-269

C

Cadenhead's 277
Cambus Cooperage 61-62
Campari, Gruppo 264-265, 268, 273
Campbell, Douglas 200
Campbell, John 37-39
Campbeltown 136
Caol Ila 36, 104
Caorunn Gin 88
Caperdonich 212
Cardhu 22, 105
Cedar Ridge Vineyards 251
Chang, Ian 29
Charbay Winery & Distillery 243-244
Chetiyawardana, Ryan 83
Chichibu 221, 222-223
Chivas Brothers 262, 272
Chivas Regal 190, 266
Chokalingam, Ashok 45
Christie, George 186
Clan Campbell 119
Classic Malts 23
Clear Creek Distillery 243
Clynelish 106, 211
Coleburn 212
Colville, Donald 64
Compass Box Whisky Co 278
Convalmore 213
Cooley 107, 267-268
Copper Fox Distillery 248
Corsair Artisan 248
Coull, Graham 9
Coutts, Sandy 196
Cragganmore 108
Craig, Jason 55
Craigellachie 109
Creative Whisky Company 279
Crilly, Bill 34, 37
Cunningham, Alistair 18
Cuthbert, Francis 208
Cutty Sark 55

D

Daftmill 208
Dagnan, Kirsty 147
Dailuaine 110-111
Dallas Dhu 213
Dalmore 83, 112
Dalwhinnie 113
Dandanell, Magnus 43
DCL 20-21, 23, 27, 85
Deanston 114-115
Destilerias Liber 238
Destillatia AG 242
Dewar's 74, 85
Dewar's World of Whiskies 74
Dewar Rattray 279
Diageo 33, 50, 261-262, 268, 272-273
Dingle distillery 271
Douglas Laing & Co 279
DownSlope Distilling 248
Drayman's Distillery 259
Dry Fly Distilling 244
Dufftown 116
Duncan, Tom 61-63
Dundas, Gordon 11-12
Duncan Taylor & Co 277
DYC 238

E

Eades distillery 244-245
Edgefield Distillery 244
Edition Spirits 281
Edradour 117
Edrington 196, 264
Eigashima see White Oak Distillery
English Whisky Co, The see St
George's Distillery
Erenzo, Gable 46
Etter Distillerie 242

F

Falkirk Distillery Co 271
Famous Grouse 153
Famous Grouse Experience, The 153
Fary Lochan Destilleri 232
Fettercairn 9-10, 118
Fitzke, Kleinbrennerei 236
Fuji-Gotemba 222

G

Gammelstilla Whisky 241
Gilbey, W & A 150
Glann ar Mor 233-234
Glaser, John 278
Glen Albyn 213
Glenallachie 119
Glenburgie 120
Glencadam 121
Glen Deveron see Macduff
Glendronach 122

Index

Bold figures refer to the main entry in the distillery directory.

Glendullan **123**
Glen Elgin **124**
Glenesk **214**
Glenfarclas 53, **126-127**
Glenfiddich 54, **128-129**, 266, 275
Glen Flagler **219**
Glen Garioch 11-12, **130**
Glenglassaugh 14-15, **131**
Glengoyne **132**
Glen Grant 22, **134-135**
Glengyle **136**
Glenkeir Treasures 279
Glen Keith **138**
Glenkinchie **139**
Glenlivet 21-22, 36, 50 **140-141**, 266
Glenlochy 90, **214**
Glenlossie **142**
Glen Mhor **214**
Glenmorangie 35, 58, 61, **144-145**, 264
Glen Moray 9, **143**
Glenora Distillery **252**
Glen Ord **146**
Glenrothes **148**
Glen Scotia **149**
Glen Spey **150**
Glentauchers **152**
Glenturret **153**
Glenugie **219**
Glenury Royal **215**
Gold Cock distillery **231**
Gordon & MacPhail 93, 276
Gotland Whisky **241**
Grant & Sons, William 21
Grant's 266
Gray, Alan 23
Great King Street 83
Great Southern Distilling Company **256**
Green Mountain Distillers **249**
Greig, Dr Chris 197
Grythyttan Whisky **239-240**
Guillon, Distillerie **234**
Guinness 20-21
Gwalia Distillery *see* Penderyn

H

Hagen, Brennerei **242**
Hakushu **224**
Hammerschmiede **235**
Hankey Bannister 88
Hanyu **224**
Harris Distillers **272**
Hastie, S H 27
Hazelburn **188-189**
Hazelwood 160
Hellyers Road Distillery **254**
Het Anker distillery **231**
Highland Park 50-51, **154-155**, 274
High Plains Distillery **247**

High West Distillery **251**
Hillman, Terry 121
Hillrock Estate Distillery **251**
Hollen, Whisky Brennerei **242**
House Spirits Distillery **250**
Höhler, Brennerei **235-236**

I

Ian Macleod Distillers 196, 265, 276-277
Immortal Spirits **250**
Imperial **215**
Inchgower **156**
Invergordon Distillers 197
Inver House Distillers 266
Inverleven **219**

J

James Sedgwick Distillery **259**
J&B 161, 192, 266
Jewish Whisky Company **281**
Johnnie Walker 105, 106, 182, 266
Jura **157**

K

Kammer-Kirsch, Destillerie **236-237**
Karuizawa 221, **225**
Kavalan 29, 43-44, **258**
Kilbeggan **158**, 268
Kilchoman **159**
Kilkerran *see* Glengyle
Killyloch **219**
Kinclaith **219**
King Car 44
Kingsbarns distillery **271**
Kininvie **160**
Kinzigbrennerei **236**
Knockando **161**
Knockdhu **162**
Kunze-Conzewitz, Bob 264-265

L

Ladyburn **219**
Lagavulin **164-165**
Laphroaig 37-39, **166-167**
Lark, Bill 29
Lark Distillery **253**
Ledaig *see* Tobermory
Lexington Brewing & Distilling **245**
Liebl, Bayerwald-Bärwurzerei und Spezialitäten-Brennerei **235**
Linkwood **168**
Little, Arthur D 27, 29
Littlemill **215**
Locher, Brauerei **242**
Loch Lomond **169**
Lochside **216**
Logan, Ian 64
Longmorn 53, **170**
Longrow **188-189**

Lost Spirits Distillery **250**
Louis Vuitton Moët Hennessy 9, 263-264
Ludlow, Eddie 65
Lumsden, Dr Bill 35-36, 58, 61, 264
Lüthy, Bauernhofbrennerei **241**

M

Macallan 33-34, **172-173**, 266
Macdonald, John 87
Macdonald, Neil 50, 53, 55
McDougall, John 188
McDowell's **257**
Macduff **174-175**
McGlashan, Duncan 26
McHardy, Frank 34, 188
McHenry and Sons Distillery, William 255
Mackie, Sir Peter 27, 109, 164
Mackillop's Choice **281**
Mackintosh, Ewen 33, 37
Mackmyra 42-43, **238-239**
MacMillan, Ian 199
Maguire, Patrick 44-45
Malt Mill 164
Malts of Scotland **280**
Mannochmore **176**
Markvardsen, Martin 51
Master of Malt **277-278**
Matthews, Charles 24
Meadowside Blending **281**
Millburn **216**
Milne, Jamie 54, 65
Miltonduff **177**
Miquel, Raymond 20
Mitchell, Archibald 188
Miyagikyo **225**
More, Carol 75
Morgan, Dr Nick 33, 36, 39, 50, 52, 54
Morrison Bowmore 263
Mortlach **178**
Mosstowie **177**
Murray, Douglas 39
Murray McDavid **277**
Murree Brewery **257**

N

Nant Distillery **255**
Nashoba Valley Winery **246**
Nettleton, J A 26-27
Nevis Distillery 90
New Holland Brewing **247-248**
New Zealand Malt Whisky Co **256**
Ngoh, Johanna 65
Nickerson, Stuart 14-15, 28-29
Nikka 220
Nikka Taketsuru 220
Norrtelje Brenneri **240**
North Port **216**
Nourney, Julia 65

Index

Bold figures refer to the main entry in the distillery directory.

Number One Drinks Company 221, 225

O

Oban **179**
Octomore 100-101
Oerbaek Brewery **232**
Old Hobart Distillery **254**
Old Raven **230**
Overeem, Casey 228
Owens, Bill 229
Owl Distillery, The **231**

P

Pasteur, Louis 24
Patel, Mahesh 65
Paterson, Richard 36
Pemberton Distillery **253**
Penderyn Distillery **242-243**
Pentlands 27-29
Pepper, Chris 125
Pernod Ricard 170, 262
Picard Vins & Spiritueux 204, 267
Pinckney Bend Distillery **251**
Pittyvaich 218
Port Charlotte 100-101
Port Ellen **217**
Potts, Charlie 17
Preussische Whiskydestillerie **235**
Prichard's Distillery **245**
Publicker Industries 185
Pulteney **180**

R

Rankin, Bill 18
Ransom, Robert 53
Rebecca Creek Distillery **247**
Red River distillery see Abhainn Dearg
Reisetbauer distillery **230**
Rémy Cointreau 100, 268
Reynier, Mark 52-53, 267-268
Ricard, Patrick 262
Richardson, Sir Albert 202
Rieger & Hofmeister **236**
Riffkin, Dr Harry 27, 29
Roberts, Janet Sheed 160
Robertson, David 10
Robertson, Jackie 183
Robertson, James 12-13
Rogue Ales & Spirits **249**
Rosebank 218
Roseisle distillery 39, **207**
Ross, Duncan 65
RoughStock distillery **246**
Rowson's Reserve 262
Royal Brackla **181**
Royal Lochnagar **182-183**

S

St Clair Gray, Dr James 26
St George Distillery (USA) **245-246**
St George's Distillery (UK) **233**
St Magdalene **218**
Santa Fe Spirits **249**
Saunders, Ernest 20
Scapa **184**
Schenley Industries 20
Scotch Malt Whisky Society 280
Scott's Selection 280-281
Sendai see Miyagikyo
Shattock, Matt 265
Shelter Point Distillery **252-253**
Shinshu 221, **226**
Signatory Vintage Scotch Whisky 276
Singh, Sukhinder 280
Sirius 281
Slyrs Destillerie **234**
Smögen Whisky **239**
Solas Distillery, The **249**
Southern Coast Distillers **255-256**
Speciality Drinks 280
Speyburn **185**
Speyside **186**
Speyside Cooperage 59-60
Spirit of Hven **239**
Spreewälder Feinbrand- & Likörfabrik **235**
Springbank 34, **188-189**
Stadelmann, Brennerei **241-242**
Starlaw Distillery 143
Stauning Whisky **232**
Stewart, David 89
Stickum Brennerei **236**
Still Waters Distillery **252**
Stranahans Colorado Whiskey **243**
Strathisla **190-191**
Strathmill **192**
Sullivan's Cove 44-45
Suntory 220-221
SWA 31
Swan, Dr Jim 27, 29-30
SWRI 27-28, 31
Symington, Andrew 117

T

Taketsuru, Masataka 170
Talisker 52, 83, **194-195**
Tamdhu **196**
Tamnavulin **197**
Tasmania Distillery 44-45, **254-255**
Tate, Chip 229
Tayburn, Mark 206
Teacher's 80
Teaninich **198**
Teeling, John 107
Teerenpeli **233**
Telser, Brennerei **237**

Timboon Railway Shed Distillery **256**
Tobermory **199**
Tomatin 10-11, **200**
Tomintoul **201**
Tormore **202**
Tosh, Gerry 50-51
Triple Eight Distillery **245**
Trolden Distillery 233
Tseng, Joanie 43-44
Tullamore Dew 271
Tullamore Dew Distillery 271
Tullibardine 12-13, **204-205**, 267
Tuthilltown Spirits 46, **246-247**

U

Uberach whisky see Bertrand
United Spirits 262-263, 268
Us Heit Distillery **237-238**

V

Vallei Distilleerderij **238**
Victoria Spirits **252**
Victoria Valley distillery **256**
Vintage Malt Whisky Co, The 281

W

Waldviertler Roggenhof **230**
Walker, Billy 13-14
Walker & Co, John 85
Walsh, Paul 261
Warenghem, Distillerie **234**
Wemyss Malts 280
Westland Distillery **251**
Weutz, Destillerie **230**
Whisky Agency, The 280
Whisky Castle **241**
Whisky Tasmania see Hellyers Road Distillery
White Horse 109
White Oak Distillery 221, **226**
Whyte & Mackay 36, 263, 268
William Grant & Sons 271, 273
William Lawson 174
Winchester, Alan 36
Wolfburn Distillery **270-271**
Wolfram Ortner Destillerie **231**
Wolstenholme, Alan 29-31
Woodstone Creek Distillery **247**

Y

Yamazaki 220-221, **227**
Yoichi **227**
Yuanshan distillery **258**

Z

Zuidam Distillers **237**
Zürcher, Spezialitätenbrennerei **241**